Learning Theory,
Instructional Theory,
and
Psychoeducational Design

LEARNING THEORY, INSTRUCTIONAL THEORY, AND PSYCHOEDUCATIONAL DESIGN

Glenn E. Snelbecker

Educational Psychology Department
Temple University

UNIVERSITY
PRESS OF
AMERICA

LANHAM • NEW YORK • LONDON

University Press of America,® Inc.

4720 Boston Way
Lanham, MD 20706

3 Henrietta Street
London WC2E 8LU England

Library of Congress Cataloging in Publication Data

Snelbecker, Glenn E., 1931-
  Learning theory, instructional theory, and
psychoeducational design.

    Originally published: New York : McGraw-Hill, 1974.
    Bibliography: p.
    Includes index.

    1. Educational psychology.   2. Learning , Psychology
of.   I. Title.
LB1051.S635   1985   370.15'2   85-13548
ISBN 0-8191-4836-9 (pbk. : alk. paper)

To Janice, David, Karen, and Laura

Contents

Preface

This book was written primarily for educators, psychologists, and others who are concerned with use of psychological principles in education. But the topics covered should also be relevant to anyone who is interested in using psychological information in other practical situations and for use in psychology courses which teach the practical as well as the heuristic value of psychology learning research.

My major goal was to consider the interface between psychology and education in such a way that better communication would be facilitated. Hopefully, educators will become generally familiar with the activities and findings of psychology learning researchers, psychologists will be more aware of the problems and prospects for educational applications, and the two groups will recognize various ways by which they might exchange information so that both psychological theory and educational practice will be advanced.

The book describes contemporary and historically important psychology learning theories and discusses various attempts to relate this continually growing fund of scientific information to practical education situations. Of the many topical areas studied by psychologists, *learning processes* were chosen because they have been the focus of many theorizing ventures in psychology and because considerable effort has been expended over several decades to relate learning principles and theories to educational practice.

Various *contemporary and historically important* ventures are considered instead of only one position because I believe that students should be exposed to different views. We can learn much from the many different approaches taken to study learning and to relate research findings to practical situations. In this book I describe how such approaches vary in any era (including present times) and how they have changed during the twentieth century. Thus I have tried to provide sufficient historical and contemporary perspective so that students can make informed decisions in choosing a theory or in selecting particular principles from available theories. Similarly, they can make informed decisions about the various ways by which research findings can be related to practical situations. Hopefully, as a result, they will avoid some of the errors of their predecessors (in research and in practice), and they will be able to recognize both the strengths and the weaknesses in extant approaches.

The three major elements of the book title indicate ways in which research information can be organized and related to practical situations. *Learning Theory* reflects my conviction that simply collecting data is not enough, that such findings must be synthesized and organized in some form if they are to have any practical value or if they are to be useful in helping us to understand learning processes. Chapter 3 reviews the various conceptions of learning processes which have been formulated during the twentieth century, including the views of Thorndike, Pavlov, Guthrie, Tolman, the functionalists, the classical gestaltists, etc. Chapter 4 describes today's miniature model emphasis and other contemporary trends and outlines probable future characteristics of learning theories. In Part 2, entire chapters describe selected historically important theories of Thorndike, Pavlov, and Hull and the contemporary views of such groups as operant conditioning, information processing, and mathematical models. Also contained in these chapters are ways by which psychology learning theories can help educators to analyze their practical problems and to find tentative solutions.

Instructional Theory suggests that one contribution of psychology will involve formulation of empirically tested educational theories. Instructional theories are somewhat like psychotherapy theories in that they provide general prescriptive guidelines for practical situations. Though not all instructional theories are closely related to psychology, some are based on certain aspects of psychology learning research. Chapter 5 provides an overview of educational theories and explains how empirically tested instructional theories have been emerging during the past two decades. It is suggested that instructional theories can be evaluated in terms of criteria outlined by the NEA-affiliated Association for Supervision and Curriculum Development. In Part 3, entire chapters describe the contributions of behavior modification, Bruner and other "cognitive construct" theorists, Bugelski and other "principles of learning" theorists, the theories based on task analyses as outlined by Gagne and Briggs, and the generally contrasting proposals of Rogers and other humanistic psychology proponents.

Psychoeducational Design indicates my concern and my enthusiasm about means by which research findings and other kinds of information can be combined to devise educational practice innovations. Scientific information is only one of many sources by which educational practice can be improved: Philosophical positions, common sense, anecdotes about other schools, personal experiences, etc., represent other sources of ideas for changing educational practice. Moreover, there are a number of ways in which research can influence practice. One can gain some ideas from a particular study, from a learning theory or its principles, from instructional theories, etc. In each case, the educator typically has responsibility for integrating such information with other aspects of the practical situation and for evaluating the worth of the resulting innovation. During the past decade it has been more widely recognized that we need to refine, evaluate, and modify *any* innovations before they can reliably be used in a practical situation. Moreover, it has been recognized that "educational development" (or "educational R&D" and "educational technology") strategies and procedures are required for designing and developing educational innovations. *Psychoeducational design* constitutes that aspect of these recently emerging educational development activities whereby psychological facts, principles, concepts, and theories are addressed to educational problems. The Chapter 6 description of psychoeducational design strategies is necessarily limited; however, sufficient information is provided that, at a minimum, psychologists should learn how their findings are used in educational development processes and educators should be better informed consumers and evaluators of educational development innovations.

Recognizing that readers would have diverse backgrounds and expectations—e.g., that some would primarily be interested in doing empirical studies and that others would view themselves mainly as interpreters or users of research findings—I tried to provide a common core of information about psychology learning research and relationships with education. As a result, I kept research and applications details at a minimum while discussing the main concepts and principles of selected learning and instructional theories. I did this on the assumption that readers would then go to journals for details about empirical studies designed to test theories or to accomplish practical applications.

Chapters in Parts 2 and 3 contain lists of suggested readings where students can get more detailed information. In my own courses, students read in areas which are most interesting and useful for them and subsequently provide a report to their colleagues in class. In this way we go beyond the book's common core of information by reviewing such topics as prospects and problems in using a particular learning or instructional theory, contemporary models of attentional processes, current findings about short-term memory, biological and biochemical theories of learning processes, the relevance of individual difference characteristics for basic and applied learning principles, currently available information for evaluating educational development innovations, etc. The particular selections of topics vary each semester, according to interests of students in the course.

Many colleagues and students have assisted me in formulating ideas for this book. Various authors have given me prepublication drafts and other papers which have been very helpful in clarifying respective theories and research and which have enabled me to understand trends in theory construction and utilization. Wherever possible, I have tried to cite appropriate references throughout the book. To all who have shared with me their views and experiences, I express my sincere gratitude and appreciation.

But the contributions of some persons have been so extensive that they merit special mention here. Dr. Joseph DuCette contributed sections and assisted in the preparation of several chapters. The following persons reviewed many chapters and gave extremely valuable suggestions—Dr. Edward Ancello, Dr. Philip Bersh, Dr. Philip Hineline, Dr. Emanuel Mason, and my wife, Janice Snelbecker. In addition to usual editorial suggestions, Robert C. Morgan was especially helpful in planning the final structure and organization of the book.

Glenn E. Snelbecker

Part
I
Focus

This book is divided into three parts. Part One provides an overview of psychological learning research and theory and of relationships between this psychological information and educational practice. Part Two contains six chapters on illustrative learning theories and the kinds of research stimulated by them. Part Three contains five chapters which describe different attempts to formulate instructional theories based on or in reaction to psychological learning research and theory.

Chapter 1 describes several views about research and theory on learning and explains the approach presented by the author. The central role of learning theory is noted with regard to psychology and education, and different definitions of learning are presented. Brief explanations are provided as to how instructional theories have emerged since mid-century, and as to the role which psychoeducational design processes have come to play in relationships between psychology theory and educational practice. It is suggested that education can be viewed as art, science, and technology, and that advantages are accrued when one maintains historical perspective while examining contemporary trends in attempts to improve educational practice.

Chapter 2 presents an introduction to scientific theories and to scientific theory construction. Several functions of theories are presented, and terms relevant to scientific theory construction are defined. "Deductive" and "inductive" approaches to theory construction are compared. Some brief suggestions are presented concerning guidelines for evaluating scientific theories, and special problems are noted for psychological and instructional theories.

Chapters 3 and 4 review trends in psychological theory construction, especially as these trends relate to learning processes, which can be discerned during the twentieth century. It is noted that psychologists had earlier aspired to quite comprehensive theories but that they now more typically prefer to work with "miniature models." Chapter 3 deals with the patterns which emerged prior to mid-century, including some of the theories which influence research activities today. Chapter 4 examines possible explanations for shifts in approaches to theory construction, summarizes characteristics of contemporary approaches to the psychology

1

of learning, and considers possible implications for future theory construction.

Chapter 5 reviews relationships between psychology theory and educational practice, and describes the emergence of new types of theories—instructional theories. Illustrative attempts to formulate learning theories are outlined, and some of these new ventures are considered in terms of instructional theory criteria which have been developed. Several possible ways are identified whereby learning research and theory might influence formulation of instructional theories.

Chapter 6 introduces the concept of *psychoeducational design*, which is presented as an aspect of the contemporary R&D movement whereby psychological information is used to improve educational practice. Both historical influences and contemporary characteristics of the R&D movement are described. Perhaps most importantly, strategies and techniques are presented whereby the reader can use the research and theory on instruction and learning in efforts to improve educational practice.

1
Psychology and Education: Problems of Application

Education has needed a science of man, and a science of man is what it has sought from psychology. In the early days when a new science of man was being created, education adopted the "new psychology." When there were competing psychologies, the profession chose that psychology which seemed to offer a more comprehensive science. When a new or more comprehensive psychological theory appears, education will probably assimilate it. (McDonald, 1964, p. 24)

I recently estimated that in these years I must have interviewed 1,200 psychologists and 1,000 students concerning their training programs, their career objectives, etc. All think of themselves as psychologists, yet they really have quite divergent views about a number of significant issues, and almost to a man each is convinced that his window on the psychological world and society is, if not *the* right one, certainly the most valid one. (Tyler, 1970, p. 219)

"Accountability" and "relevance" are representative of concepts which have emerged in recent years indicating great concern about the adequacy of our contemporary educational system. Despite increased research interest and general concern about our formal educational institutions, there has been growing dissatisfaction during the past decade as to the results of our efforts in education. In this context, psychology and other behavioral sciences have been roundly criticized—and generally quite appropriately so—for their contribution or lack of contribution to educational practice.

Relationships between psychology and education have been discussed on many occasions since the latter part of the nineteenth century when psychology emerged as a science. For example, John Dewey's address as president of the American Psychological Association in 1899 focused on the relation of psychology to education as exemplary of the many ways in which the "new psychology" was to be useful in resolving social problems. William James expressed some reservations about contributions which he and his psychologist colleagues might make, but he displayed sufficient interest in such ventures that his opinions were regularly sought and he subsequently published his famous *Talks to Teachers*. Edward L. Thorndike displayed greater optimism about the potential relevance of psychological research, and he devoted a large portion of his professional career to improving educational practice.

But today even cursory review of relationships between psychology and education reveals that we still have not developed effective means for deriving educational implications from basic psychological research. For example, Hendrik D. Gideonse recently (1969) reviewed the status of educational research and development in the United States in preparation of an official national report to the Organization for Economic Cooperation and Development. Despite over seventy years' effort, we still ask questions such as (1) *Can* science provide the basis for the improvement of instruction in education? and (2) Assuming an affirmative answer to this, what are the elements that must be considered in developing an overall strategy for the support of research and development in education?

Educators have sought a science of man from psychology from which they have hoped to obtain some assistance in improving educational practice. But, perhaps unfortunately, they have found many conflicting positions about psychology instead of the unified science they had expected. Moreover, neither educators nor psychologists have yet found widely accepted procedures for using psychological theories to plan and to improve educational practice. Instead there are several divergent views as to how best to proceed. It is the central theme of this book to show that three general approaches have been used in the past and continue to find favor today. First, *learning theories* have long played a dominant role in basic psychological research. Some psychologists and educators have made concerted attempts to "apply" these learning theories in educational situations. Secondly, within the past two decades *instructional theories* have emerged and have been proposed as more appropriate theories for educators. Many of these instructional theories are derived from psychological learning research or constitute positions at least partially drawn in opposition to learning theories. The third approach is the contemporary research and development movement which the author identifies as a *psychoeducational design* process.

A recurring theme in this book is the contention that theory construction is desirable in psychology and in education and that a psychoeducational design process can foster more constructive relationships between psychology and education in the years ahead than has been characteristic during previous decades of this century.

"APPLICATION" OF PSYCHOLOGICAL PRINCIPLES

It is the author's opinion that the issue of *applicability*, while much discussed, is actually poorly understood by both educators and psychologists. We will attempt throughout this book to clarify this issue and to show how the controversy over "applying the laws of learning" has too often been debated on inappropriate grounds. For now, let us put this in its proper light by saying that this issue is neither new nor unique to education. There has, after all, been a continuing debate for almost a century as to how "applied" any given psychological theory should be. One way in which the issue has been debated is in the controversy over whether psychology should primarily develop a basic science fund of information or whether there should be additional obligations to extend such "knowledge for knowledge's sake" into a set of application principles. This has been true whether the principles were to be applied to industry, to clinical situations, to education, or to any other applied areas. The point being emphasized is that this issue is a general one which has been characteristic of psychology from its start.

Psychology as Science and as Profession

Many educators and even some psychologists are not sufficiently aware of the significance of the fact that "psychology" refers to a science as well as to a profession. In the contemporary concern about social problems in general and in our educational situation in particular, it is all too easy to forget that many psychologists have not made a commitment to *applying* the fruits of their efforts. This may seem strange if the reader does not recognize that many psychologists consider themselves "basic scientists." Just as biologists, physiologists, and physicists are not personally concerned with the applicability of their findings, likewise many psychologists see their contributions to society and their role in life as adding to the fund of knowledge about human and animal behavior. Particularly when we study learning theory we will find that most of the persons who have made major contributions to our understanding of learning processes have had little or no interest in applicability of such information. Of course, that is not to say that they are adamantly against having anyone utilize their growing fund of information in a practical situation. However, it does mean that the nature of their theoretical formulations and general principles more frequently have been determined by basic science considerations rather than by feasibility for utilization in practical situations. Moreover, because psychology is a comparatively new science (having been established less than 100 years ago) and because many psychologists have been quite concerned about protecting their new identity as scientists, there has even been some resistance to having psychology and psychologists prematurely involved in resolution of practical problems lest it endanger psychology's status as a science.

Learning Theories and "Application" as a General Issue in Psychology

For various reasons which are beyond the scope of the present text, the term *psychology* came to be used for designating acquisition of a fund of knowledge as well as application of that fund of knowledge. There has always been a great deal of controversy concerning the means, if any, by which such information might be utilized. Many psychologists who identify themselves primarily as scientists have suggested that it is necessary to have a comprehensive basic science theory of psychology before attempting application of any psychological principles and theories. As a result, applied psychology training programs have been based on the premise that one is a *psychologist* first and an educational or other applied psychologist secondly. The emphasis primarily has been on acquiring basic science principles about human and animal behaviors with little emphasis on developing the procedures by which such a body of information can be utilized in practical situations. For numerous reasons, even after almost a century of existence as a science, we are still trying to find appropriate means for utilizing psychological information in the various aspects of applied psychology, including educational psychology.

In this book we will review some of the major learning theories which have been of value both for stimulating research and for integrating and interpreting the findings of these studies. Contrary to the expectations of educators, we will find that they are primarily "basic science" theories which have been devised almost exclusively to add to the fund of psychological knowledge. But we will also consider the ways in which there has been some attempt to use the resulting implications to plan or to improve educational practice.

Concerning the applicability of *learning theory*, several explanations should be provided at this point. First, the author acknowledges that it has been conventional throughout the twentieth century to raise questions as to *whether any* psychological theories can appropriately be applied in education, and if so *how* such might be accomplished. It should be obvious from the title of the text that the author strongly takes the position that practitioners can benefit from the growing psychological data on learning processes. However, it may be less obvious to the reader at this point as to *how* the author envisions the way in which educators can use psychological learning theory.

First, let us acknowledge and *disclaim* support for a notion that is quite common among psychologists and educators—the rather widely held position that if one is to use psychological principles and theory, the *only possible approach* is to rely primarily on some particular *basic science theory within psychology* as a way of dealing specifically with the educational situation. Thus many debates have been conducted, for example, as to the relative merits of applying Thorndike's connectionistic theory versus the utilization of the gestalt principles; similarly, contemporary debates frequently juxtapose some form of neobehaviorism versus either a cognitively oriented theory or some form of humanistic psychology.

Such an orientation, we might add, has long been popular among academic psychologists as a means for conducting basic research and for interpreting findings. For example, Hall and Lindzley in their classic text on personality theory rather strongly recommended that the psychology student familiarize himself with various personality theories but make an early commitment to *one* of the theories and conduct his research and integrate his findings in the context of the selected theory.

Our general proposal to the student is that he first acquaint himself broadly with the field of personality, and this is precisely what this volume is intended to do. Then let him immerse himself in one theory of personality. Wallow in it, revel in it, absorb it, learn it thoroughly, and think that it is the best possible way to conceive of behavior. Only reserve in one small corner of his mind the reservation that the final crucible for any theory is the world of reality studied under controlled conditions. After the romance is over and the student is seduced by the theory, he may set about the cold hard business of his investigation in order to find out whether his theoretical marriage will withstand the ravages of reality. (Hall & Lindzley, 1957, p. 557)

Their position continues to be a popular one among psychologists as the best way for conducting basic research programs, and among psychologists and educators as ways in which one can use psychological theory and principles in educational practice. But we accept it here as only one of several possible relationships. At least for those who are charged with the obligation of resolving practical educational problems and for designing effective educational experiences, we feel that an individual does not have the *luxury* of restricting himself to only one theoretical position in psychology. Readers are urged to examine each of the basic science theories which have been developed by psychologists in the study of learning and to select those principles and conceptions which seem to be of value for one's particular educational situations. We will also describe the emerging roles of instructional theories and the psychoeducational design process in relating learning theories to educational practice.

We need to dispel another myth about relationships between basic sciences and practical problem resolution. Merely understanding a particular learning theory can in no way guarantee that it will be possible to "apply" the theory in a specific situation. Because of a failure to recognize this, many educators and applied (educational) psychologists have become increasingly disillusioned with psychology in general and with learning theory in particular because they have not been "paying off" in terms of improving educational practice. Part of the reason for writing this book is to show how representative learning theories *can* or *cannot* be expected to result in prescriptions for the educator. Whereas they may not readily provide prescriptions for educational practice, nonetheless practically all learning theories can be of value to educators in that they provide systematic ways for conceptualizing what is happening in both practical situations and theoretical research situations. In part, the discussion of learning theories will focus on the main concepts and principles which have been developed to conceptualize learning processes.

Educators' Applications of Psychological Principles

Scientific methods have been advocated for use in education almost as long as in psychology, but educators traditionally have looked to psychology as a source of information concerning how and why people act as they do. In a sense, educators have viewed psychology as their science of man from which they could draw hypotheses or prescriptions for the practice of education. But they seem to have overlooked the fact that many psychologists have basic rather than applied interests and they have assumed that learning theories will provide educational prescriptions. In this text we will examine some of the different relationships which have existed between psychological theory and educational practice during the past century. We will examine these not only for their historical value but, more importantly, because they help us to understand the range of options and the kinds of patterns and relationships which continue to exist.

Let's consider for a moment a question which has been raised in critiques about relationships between learning theory and educational practice. As you will learn later in this text, various spokesmen have questioned whether psychological learning theory, derived from research involving specially designed laboratory tasks frequently conducted with animal subjects, can have any relevance for practical educational situations. That is, they have raised serious questions as to whether *laboratory* learning research could have *any* practical value for educators. Of course one will always find skeptics no matter what issue might be involved. However, what we are concerned with here is a tendency for educators at different points in history to be quite skeptical about the applicability of *laboratory* learning research conclusions.

Perhaps it would be worthwhile to consider differences between "government laws," which may not be consistently applied, and "laws of nature," which are merely discovered by scientists and which in a sense "apply themselves" whether or not man is aware of their existence. It seems that the question of applying laws of learning carries an implicit expectation that educators decide whether certain laws are to be followed in an educational situation. To some extent, there is the expectation then that the educator can describe those rules which he feels *should apply* in his particular learning situation and can indicate those rules which *should not be made applicable* there.

Even as we discuss such possibilities, it is likely that the reader will begin to wonder whether the educator *has* such a prerogative—a prerogative to decide whether students will follow certain rules in the way they learn—and whether such options actually exist for an educator. One should raise questions as to whether indeed the educator can *declare* how his students will learn, or rather whether it is, in contrast, important for him to recognize how his students most likely *do* learn when the educator plans his students' educational experiences. What is being suggested is that valid laws of learning are not the kinds of laws which the educator may decide to employ or to ignore when describing ways his students learn. The educator does not have the option of declaring what factors do facilitate or impede learning. Rather, the question has to do with whether the educator should heed basic principles or laws of learning when designing his educational experiences. The educator first needs to decide which principles, in his opinion, seem to be *valid* descriptions of nature (that is, valid descriptions of the way his students actually learn) and which seem most relevant to the kind of learning experience which he is planning for his students.

Most dictionaries provide two pertinent definitions of the word "law."

First, law refers to those principles and regulations established by a government and made applicable to a people, either through some form of legislation or through judicial recognition of long established customs and policies. Secondly, "law" in science refers to statements of relationships between two conditions or statements about the occurrence of particular events under specified conditions; these statements are identified as laws if scientific observations have confirmed their validity.

Note that the first definition permits an option, at least in certain segments of the population, to determine whether a particular law will or will not be applied. This is, the law may or may not be enforced. But with regard to the second law, if the specified conditions are present, then it is expected that the "relation or sequence of phenomena" will be *invariable* under these conditions. In the second definition, there is no option as to whether the law will or will not be enforced. The only real question is: Was there provided a *valid* description of the relationship or sequences? If indeed, in the second example, one does have available valid laws for the particular phenomena, then the law *will* be applied in the sense that the particular sequences or relationships will exist.

Given this second kind of law, one which does not permit an option for enforcement or lack of enforcement, there are two general questions that face a practitioner who is trying to resolve a particular practical problem. First, what valid descriptions have been provided which are applicable to the phenomena in the particular situation? Secondly, in the situation where there is controversy about "competing laws" and their *actual* validity, which of the several laws being presented seems most pertinent, most important, to be considered in the particular practical situation? That is, in the absence of some universal or even widespread general agreement that we do indeed know the basic relationships, the ways in which people do in fact learn, one is then faced with a decision or a series of decisions to select from among the competing descriptions of "nature," each of which might have pertinent implications for resolution of the practical problem.

Instead of universally accepted laws or theories of learning, there are a number of competing descriptions as to how students do learn. Until we are at a point where there is adequate empirical evidence accepted by the scientific and professional community, there probably will continue to be laws or theories competing as allegedly valid descriptions of the ways humans learn. Under these circumstances one must then question *which* of the laws we should apply, meaning which of the laws should we consider when analyzing and planning our learning experiences.

One final comment is in order concerning applicability of psychological theory. From time to time reference will be made to educators' use of psychological laws or principles. Thus, it would seem important to clarify what is meant in discussing such utilization. It is recognized that no educator will use any given psychological theory 100 percent of the time. Likewise, it is not likely that all educators in a given era will necessarily use the same psychological theory as a source of ideas. Thus when talking about applications by educators we will primarily be referring to the extent to which some educators some of the time utilize psychological principles in the planning and in the improvement of their educational practice. As you will see shortly, the present text will be primarily concerned with applications to instruction rather than to all aspects of education.

WHY LEARNING THEORY?

We should now concern ourselves with the question: Why does this book focus on utilization of *learning* theory when there are many other aspects of psychological theory which might be utilized by educators? The answer to this question depends to a great extent on whether the spokesman is an educator or a psychologist.

Perusal of any introductory general psychology textbook will reveal a number of areas of academic psychology which potentially may be of interest to educators. The typical introductory psychology textbook includes several basic science areas and selected aspects of applied psychology. Here we will focus on the basic aspects of psychology, which include learning, perception, motivation, development, personality, etc. For psychologists, emphasis on learning theory and research primarily stems from the historical fact that it is learning theory that has occupied center stage in the development of scientific psychology much of the time since the beginning of this century. Indeed, the history of the development of learning theory as a recognizable branch of psychology is almost isomorphic with the history of psychology as a separate discipline.

To know and to understand learning theory and to be able to appreciate the problems that have arisen in the development of these theories is to have a good grasp of the central issues in psychology's theory construction more generally. Any person, therefore, who views himself as a psychologist or anyone who wishes to use psychology for some practical end should understand learning theory. This should not be taken to mean, nor to contend, that such an understanding is *sufficient* for these purposes. Nor is it meant to imply that learning theories *by themselves* are sufficient to solve important problems when viewed in isolation from other psychological theories. What is being contended is that the centrality of learning theories in the history of psychology in the United States makes the understanding of them a necessary condition for appreciation of the development of scientific theories in psychology. One of the purposes of this book is to present the process and the fundamentals of learning theory construction in the hope that the reader will gain an understanding of learning theory as one aspect of basic science psychology theory which is relevant to education.

Rather curiously, one can develop a different reason for selecting learning theory for emphasis if one views the question from the vantage point of education. Stated simply, there is a very long established tradition in education and in educational psychology that students act as they do primarily because of the stage of development which they have reached or because of what they have learned previously as appropriate ways to act in a given situation. For example, some early textbooks (Starch, 1920) identified educational psychology's two major sections as the psychology of learning and genetically determined development. It would be well beyond the scope of this book to consider either the origins or the justifications for such a point of view. However, it is important to note in passing that such an orientation does exist and does greatly influence relationships between psychology and education.

Thus for two fundamentally different reasons—one from psychology and one from education—the author has elected to focus on applications of learning theory in educational practice as a valuable pursuit in and of itself as well as a more general example of relationships between psychology and education. It has been the author's experience that courses on learning theory and education typically include students from psychology as well as from education, and that they have different conceptions as to the basis for taking such a course. Thus it is felt that it is important that the reader recognize the existence of these two different orientations about learning theory and education.

TOWARD A DEFINITION OF LEARNING

Thus far we have been using the term *learning theories* without defining either word. In a sense, everyone has learned and has used the term "learning" thousands of times in their lives. But since we will be reviewing various theories of learning, it seems important here to consider ways in which psychologists and educators have defined the term.

Definitions of Learning: Psychology

Learning is the process by which an activity originates or is changed through reacting to an encountered situation, provided that the characteristics of the change in activity cannot be explained on the basis of native response tendencies, maturation, or temporary states of the organism (e.g., fatigue, drugs, etc.). (Hilgard & Bower, 1966, p. 2)

Learning is a relatively permanent change in a behavioral tendency that occurs as a result of reinforced practice. (Kimble & Garmezy, 1963, p. 133)

Learning is the process by which behavior (in the broad sense) is originated or changed through practice or training. (Garry & Kingsley, 1970, p. 15)

Learning, in contrast with maturation, is a change in a living individual which is not heralded by his genetic inheritance. It may be a change in insights, behavior, perception, or motivation, or a combination of these. (Bigge, 1964, p. 1)

Definitions of Learning: Education
When a man has learned anything he is, for a time at least, changed in his readiness to deal with this or that in his environment. He has become, with respect to certain things, events, meanings, as the case may be, differently sensitive, differently percipient, differently disposed as to the forms of his responsive behavior, whether in action, in understanding, or in feeling. (Eaton, 1938, p. 196)
Learning is active. Learning is a function of the total situation surrounding the child. Learning is guided by purpose and consists in living and doing, in having experiences and seeking to understand the meaning of them. (Yeakam & Simpson, 1934, p. 22)
When we speak of learning, we are talking about how behavior is changed through experience. (Seagoe, 1970, p. 3)

In an initial examination of these definitions—drawn from psychologists and from educators, some of which were presented many years ago—a number of observations can be made. First, there is considerable similarity across the different definitions despite the different time periods from which they were drawn. It is unlikely that this permanence of definition reflects the fact that there has been little argument over the years concerning what learning is. As we will see when we review the various theories of learning, the arguments have at times been violent and are still unresolved. What this similarity of definitions seems to reflect is the fact that arriving at a definition that will include everything that could possible be called learning (which we will call a minimal definition) has been relatively easy. What has not been easy, as we will see, is defining the finer points and specifying the domain over which a learning theory should rule.

Secondly, there is remarkably little difference between the definitions given in these psychological and these educational sources. This is surprising since in practice the two disciplines act as if they are talking about different things. Psychologists typically consider learning to include *any* kind of changes, whether such changes help or hinder the organism in adapting to demands of its environment. Educators usually determine whether learning has occurred in accordance with the general educational objectives of the school and the community. Thus psychologists tend to be rather neutral and educators are more value oriented in more specific definitions of learning. Whereas psychologists might depict students as having learned, educators would hold that they have not learned, even though the students' behavior has changed, if such changes have not been in the direction of the school's educational goals. The fact that these textbook definitions from psychology and from education are so similar in part may indicate the influence of psychology on education. More likely it simply reflects the fact that educational writers and the psychologist authors were providing only a minimal definition of learning.

The third point that becomes apparent in reading the various definitions given in the original sources (and this is probably not obvious from the samples provided) is that most writers spend more time in discussing what learning is not than in reviewing what it is. The Hilgard and Bower definition is a good example of this. This is understandable and in many ways useful since it delimits what the term "learning" has to cover. For example, it is commonly accepted that learning is not meant to include temporary changes resulting from fatigue, effects of drugs, or those changes which are specifically due to maturation.

What do we have, then, as a definition of learning? First of all, it would seem that all definitions of learning include the term *change*. This "change" is usually meant to include the acquisition or modification of some behavior and must be at least permanent enough to be noticeable by some observer. It is clear in some of the definitions that the term *change* refers to an internal event or process, but it is also clear that all the definitions by necessity confound learning with performance. That is to say, "learning" is always inferred by the ability of an organism to "perform" in a manner that is different from the way it previously could. Strictly speaking, learning is not necessarily a "relatively permanent change in a behavioral tendency" (Kimble & Garmezy, 1963) but is instead inferred from such a change. The semantic distinction is not considered crucial in most definitions of learning but is considered crucial in certain theories of learning. In addition, there is agreement that this change must have occurred through practice and must not be due to a temporary state of the organism.

Have we gained anything by this definition? The most that can be said for this definition is that it tells us a few things to exclude. It does not tell us what learning is except in an extremely broad sense. As such, this definition says both too much and too little at the same time—too little because the definition does not really tell us anything about the nature of learning, too much because it includes events that we probably do not want to discuss under the rubric of learning. To take an extreme example of how this definition could be too inclusive, imagine the following example: if you roll a perfectly round clay ball down an inclined plane which at the bottom forms a Y the original probability of the ball taking either the right or the left arm of this Y will be equal. If you perform this act several times, however, each time making sure that the ball is put back in exactly the same position you will find that gradually the ball will begin to go consistently to the right or to the left and that eventually it will always go right or left. By the definition given above, does this not qualify as learning? It is a relatively permanent change that has occurred through practice. If a rat had performed this feat, choosing the right arm each trial to obtain food, there would be no question that the rat had learned. Are we willing to say that the clay ball has learned? Probably not, indicating that our minimal definition of learning is so loosely stated that it has not really given us very much. Rather than attempt to arrive at a definition of learning that would be more satisfactory let us instead simply state what such a definition should and should not include: (1) Any adequate definition of learning must be able to account for the behavior of a wide range of species. There is no doubt that men can learn, and that children can learn, and that monkeys and rats can learn. There is also fairly conclusive evidence that very simple organisms can learn. For example, there are reported studies of paramecia being taught to choose the correct section of simple two-choice mazes. Whatever definition of learning is used will have to include the behavior of this vast variety of organisms. (2) Any definition of learning must be able to encompass a range of behavior from the most simple to the most complex. It will have to cover such diverse changes as learning to turn right in a two-choice maze and the act of learning differential calculus. (3) If the process underlying a piece of behavior is not modifiable or controllable (either by the organism or by an external agent), it will not be considered under the rubric of learning. This would seem to encompass all the separate processes (maturation, drug states, fatigue, etc.) that are usually excluded from a definition of learning. As an example of this, consider the case of imprinting. In certain species (geese, for example), the young of the species will follow a moving object if this movement occurs within a specified range of time after the organism is born. This is an automatic act that is characteristic of all members of the species, thus indicating that it results from heredity rather than from learning. The behavior itself can be modified (as for example, the fact that stimuli different from the natural stimulus can be made to elicit the behavior; a young goose can be imprinted on a man as well as on a mother goose), but an external agent does not and cannot cause an organism to imprint if such a process is not in its genetic makeup. Any such behavior (sometimes called prewired or instinctual) will not be called learning even though it does involve a change in behavior and even though it may seem that experience has played a role.

As we will see in reviewing the various theories of learning that have been formulated, the issue of defining learning has not been a crucial one as long as there is no assumption made in the definitions set forward concerning the essential nature of learning. The behavioral facts of learning are not in question; the theoretical explanation of learning most certainly is. These theories and what they can tell us about learning are a major concern of this book.

WHY INSTRUCTIONAL THEORY?

Although we have focused our attention so far on learning theories, the type of theoretical sophistication needed by an educator has been extended in recent years into a new type of theory. These theories, some of which are derived from learning theory, have come to be called *instructional theories*. They represent an attempt to develop theories which are more directly concerned with application. As such, the emergence of these instructional theories represents a comparatively recent development in the relationship between learning theory and educational practice. While there have been attempts in the past to use learning theories as a base to generate application principles, where such principles were of secondary concern, this new brand of theorist is less concerned with basic principles of behavior and more concerned with principles of instruction bearing on the attainment of educational objectives. Again, to put this in perspective, this type of development is in no sense unique to education since applied science theories have been developed in other areas as well. For example, there are theories of job satisfaction in industrial psychology and theories of psychotherapy in clinical psychology and psychiatry.

All such theories usually relate to one or more of the basic science theories of psychology for their underlying orientation. While this is generally acknowledged, there is still a wide range of opinion as to the most desirable kind of relationship which should exist between such applied theories and the basic science theories—some advocating the development of these applied theories completely independent of the basic theories, and others envisioning some continuous dialogue as being mutually beneficial. Again, this issue is not unique to education and the controversy over whether one type is better or more useful than the other represents more of a pseudoproblem than many realize. We will attempt in this book to show how instructional theories have been developed and where they can be used either alongside of or instead of learning theories.

At this point, students typically raise questions concerning the way in which an instructional theory might differ from an educational method or procedures outlined in a lesson plan. It is important to recognize that we are talking about rather general principles which would not be restricted to a specific learning experience in a classroom or other kind of educational situation. We are concerned with principles for solving practical problems, handling true-to-life practical situations, rather than merely being primarily concerned with the underlying principles which explain *why* instructional methods are successful or unsuccessful.

During the past few decades various educational leaders (Beauchamp, 1961; Getzels, 1952) have been expressing concern about the relatively fragmented and unsystematic manner in which we make decisions about educational practice. Stated in the extreme, educators typically seem to go from one crisis to another, from one instructional plan to the next, almost as though they constitute isolated incidents with no meaningful connection to other events in the educational situation. Much of what we do stems from common sense and previous personal experience rather than from some overall conception or theory as to the prevailing educational objectives and the best means for attaining them. Instructional theories emerged in an attempt to provide for more systematic planning of instruction, based on principles which are tested scientifically.

Others are concerned with differences between learning theories and instructional theories. In brief, the ideal learning theory must be comprehensive as to why learning changes occur, but may be incomplete as to practical implications for educators. The ideal instructional theory must be comprehensive as to practical principles but may be incomplete as to why such procedures are effective.

Perhaps it may be useful if we contrast the way in which an educator would use an instructional theory with ways in which educators and psychologists previously have tried to use learning theories.

Let's consider first how a *learning theory* might be used and then consider how an *instructional theory* might be used. One can, of course, derive some particular ideas about instruction from isolated studies or from single principles. However, the ideal situation would involve drawing from a comprehensive, empirically valid, and logically sound psychological theory of man in planning the general outline and the details of instructional experiences. Any gaps in the theory, any incomplete conceptions of man, force the practitioner to use "common sense" and "intuition" or some *other* theoretical or philosophical source in order to complete the plan for the instructional experiences. In contrast, the utilization of an instructional theory would involve drawing on a rather comprehensive set of principles which are reasonably neutral with regard to educational objectives and are rather extensive as to the range of educational methods and procedures which can be utilized.

The essential emphasis of the instructional theory is *directly* on those procedures which have been proven sound and which are consistent with society's conceptions of educational experiences. The extent to which psychological research and theory in general and that concerning learning processes in particular are of concern to the instructional theorist varies substantially. Some may feel that such "basic science" concerns are of minimal interest, since they are primarily concerned with why a solution works rather than with whether useful solutions for the educational planning can be found. Those who *are* concerned about constructive relationships between instructional theories and psychology theory would primarily attempt to modify the instructional theory so that it is consistent with current thinking in psychology research and theory. With this approach, instead of being concerned whether there existed an empirically valid and logically sound comprehensive psychological theory, the focus would be on utilizing *whatever* research and theory in psychology might bear on the problems of education. In that regard, this author differs with others (for example, Siegel) who contend that instructional theories derived from learning theories "implicitly assume that effective learning implies effective instruction" (Siegel, 1967, p. 33). To the contrary, most modern-day learning researchers recognize that there are a *variety* of ways in which "educational" experiences occur, only some of which may involve formal educational situations.

One final matter which we should consider is the relationship between instructional theories and other educational theories. Gordon's (1968) definition of instructional theory, which is rather widely accepted, is "a set of statements based on sound replicable research, which would permit one to predict how particular changes in the educational environment (classroom setting) would affect pupil learning" (p. 3). Beauchamp (1968) depicts instructional theory as one sub-theory in education, along with curriculum theory, counseling theory, administrative theory, and evaluation theory. Such an organization of these various aspects of educational theory is compatible with the approach taken in the present book.

WHY PSYCHOEDUCATIONAL DESIGN?

The review of learning theories and of instructional theories will indicate that both areas are far from reaching scientifically valid and logically consistent theories at the present time, although considerable progress is being made. In lieu of the availability of appropriate theories, particularly instructional theories, what can educators and educational psychologists do to improve educational practice on the basis of the currently available scientific theories in psychology and in education? How can we develop more constructive relationships between psychology and education, especially between learning theory and instruction?

It will be the contention of the author that there long has been need of a "middle position" between psychology theoretical research and educational practice. We will support the notion that the improvement of educational practice constitutes an interdisciplinary venture which will include the collaboration of professional persons from education, sociology, communications technology, curriculum theory, and various aspects of basic science psychology theory of which learning theory is only one part. We will describe a research and development process which seems to be required for truly sound utilization of learning theory in the improvement of educational practice, and we will designate the role of the psychologist as *psychoeducational design*. We will trace some of the origins of this orientation and we will briefly describe several ventures which have been launched since the middle 1960s which constitute illustrations of implementation of this approach. Finally, we will consider some of the implications of a psychoeducational design approach for psychologists, teachers, and other educators.

A word of explanation seems in order, especially for those educators who are looking for a "cookbook" of instructions as to educational practice. It is the intent here to provide educators with some familiarity with relevant psychological theory and recently emerging educational theory which hopefully will provide a more systematic basis for planning and conducting educational experiences. It is recognized that many students would like to see concrete practical examples illustrating the ways that this author believes one should teach. Quite to the contrary, it is the author's conviction that we need to place greater emphasis on developing a rationale for teaching activities rather than on "indoctrinating" students as to each step they should take in the classroom.

It is the author's belief that we are now developing organization of information in education and educational psychology which will prove quite helpful to educators, and that the contemporary research and development movement—and its related psychoeducational design process—should prove to be a greater value to educators in the long run than would simple "cookbook" prescriptions.

One major objective in this text is to provide educators with some understanding of the range of options which are available for conceptualizing instructional processes and for planning more specific education experiences. It is felt that an educator in the classroom will be able to make wiser choices if he knows something about the range of options which are available than if he is merely indoctrinated with an instructor's or an author's "favorite" position.

SOME OBSERVATIONS ABOUT
EDUCATIONAL CHANGE

It seems important at this point to add some observations about means by which one can foster improvement in educational practice. To some, "improvement" almost automatically means that you discard *all* existing materials and techniques and you choose from one of several scientifically based theories or educational philosophies, with massive, broad-sweeping changes resulting. This would suggest sharp conflicts between education as science versus education as art and would pose a real threat to any prevailing traditions and customs. But this is *not* the *only* way by which one can foster change. It is possible to improve educational practice without destroying the fabric and detail of the many fine features in our present schools. Moreover, change when it does occur can just as well be based on combinations of suggestions from divergent sources if there is some systematic means for integrating and evaluating such information. Karl R. Popper (1957), a noted philosopher of science, has argued that social progress and social science may both be more readily improved if we take a "piecemeal social engineering" approach rather than if we attempt to attain wholesale "Utopian" goals for society. The author would extend Popper's comments to the present discussion and suggest that it may be through some piecemeal approach that we also may be able to improve steadily the quality of our educational experiences. A major facet we would add is the notion that we should judge any innovations in terms of the extent to which they provide demonstrable improvement in educational practice. In this context, instead of seeking evidence that one method is slightly better than another method, the focus will be on the extent to which *any* method is enabling students to attain desirable educational objectives.

It is recognized that some readers may express concern about reliance on an approach to education which places such great emphasis on *outcomes*. Most readers are familiar with the controversies which started in the late 1960s concerning *accountability* in education. In some instances, educational objectives were so narrowly defined that they omitted many of the educational experiences which are considered important to society generally, simply on the basis that some educational objectives are difficult to measure. Other criticisms were raised because some educators were "teaching to the test" instead of trying to provide broadly ranging educational experiences. Finally, others were concerned because the concept of accountability had led many projects to emphasize the *minimal* educational objectives without taking into account the widely ranging ways in which students might differ in achieving their individual human potential.

With regard to such concerns, the author would contend that constructive use of a research and development process, and systematic modifications based on the extent to which educational objectives are being attained, can facilitate educational improvement by building onto the good features of existing practice *or* by creating new systems. We would concur with the observations of a noted educator who played several key roles in the formation of educational research and development agencies. Dr. Francis S. Chase served in various capacities, including chairing the National Advisory Commission for Regional Educational Laboratories during the first critical years of their development. Commenting on directions where educational research and development ventures might lead us "in the remodeling of education," he subsequently depicted them as providing means for *continuous* improvement of education by combining old and new ideas. Although he acknowledged that initial ventures might focus on mastering minimal level skills and knowledge, he expressed the hope and expectation that individual characteristics and creativity could also be fostered as well.

The early emphasis quite properly is on helping all members of society acquire the skills and knowledge essential to effective participation in the opportunities, responsibilities, and benefits of our society; but I anticipate, as we learn how to provide facilitative learning environments, and to manage an array of complementary educational arrangements, attention will shift to the development of human capabilities that lie beyond the skills required for effectiveness and lead into the domains of creativity, spontaneous enjoyment and cultivated sensitivity to values. (Chase, 1970, p. 304)

It is with similar views that we look to psychology learning research and theories, to instructional theories, and to other sources of ideas for improving educational practice.

There are three important components whereby psychological research on learning can be used for improving educational practice. First, various kinds of learning theories are seen as conceptual devices for organizing psychological learning research findings. Second, instructional theories—some of which are based on or related to psychological learning research—constitute means for organizing information and guiding research on scientifically based instructional methods. Third, the psycho-educational design and development process is viewed as a means whereby learning theories, instructional theories, and other sources of ideas can be used to design educational innovations. The title of the book and the nature of the present discussion should indicate that each of these three facets—learning theory, instructional theory, and the psychoeducational design process—can make important contributions to the improvement of educational practice.

EDUCATION AS ART, SCIENCE, AND TECHNOLOGY

It is important to emphasize that the author considers education to involve a very human process which need not be adversely influenced by utilization of scientific knowledge. The comment is made at this point in recognition of the fact that there are different conceptions as to what education is and should be. More specifically, some hold that education is art, others that it is science, and still others that it is a technology. The position taken in this text is that it is all three, and that these three conceptions of education are complementary rather than incompatible. Let's first define these terms, show how they are relevant to education, and then briefly consider their implications for the emergence of psychoeducational design.

Art typically refers to some kind of practice which demands a greal deal of judgment on the part of the practitioner and which is determined more by appropriateness in the practical situation than by direct application of scientific findings. Certainly, there are many instances in which the educator must use "common sense" and "good judgment" in dealing with the humanly complex and almost unpredictable process of education. Certainly, some aspects will never lend themselves readily to rigid application of a set of principles no matter how well established they may be. Similar situations prevail in other professions. In medicine, for example, the good physician must use a great deal of intuition and clinical judgment in deciding what is best for his patient. But just as it is appropriate to talk about medicine as a combination of art, science, and technology, it seems quite appropriate to consider education in these terms as well.

Science, in the sense that we are using it in this text, generally refers to a specific body of knowledge which focuses on certain processes and a rather distinctive set of constructs and principles which depends primarily on some form of empirical test to assess its validity. Thus *the science of education* refers to that body of knowledge about education which is primarily validated by empirical procedures. *Science* is typically used with reference to medicine concerning both the empirically supported body of knowledge about principles and practices of medicine and the related life sciences with which the scientific principles are consistent. Likewise, one can refer to "scientific principles of education" and to the various social sciences with which such practices are compatible.

But the process by which one merges such scientific bodies of information and the artistic skills of the practitioner in the context of the practical requirements of the real life situation is quite complicated.

Technology customarily refers to application of scientific principles in some kind of practical situation. There is no small amount of controversy concerning the best means by which it is possible to utilize social science findings in the resolution of educational and other real life problems (Lanyon, 1971; Singer, 1971). With reference to physical sciences, it is common to refer to the person who actually designed the practical system as either an "engineer" or an "architect." The individual who specifically implements the plan or runs the system is typically referred to as a "technician." But such terms in social sciences and in resolving social problems call forth so many negative connotations that the author has tried to avoid using them in this text lest it sound as though we are promoting some form of a mechanistic or mechanical utilization of social science findings in education.

We use the term *psychoeducational design* to refer to the process by which psychological principles are utilized in the design or improvement of educational systems. Thus, the term refers to the process by which scientific findings from psychology, from education, and from related disciplines are brought to bear in the improvement of educational practice. The choice of terms should indicate to the reader that education is recognized as both an art and a science which is practiced under real-world conditions.

HISTORICAL TRENDS IN PSYCHOLOGY THEORY CONSTRUCTION AND APPLICATION

As in many other human endeavors, in the sciences one finds sharp differences of opinion as to the best approach to a task. Thus, since the emergence of psychology as a science there have been proposed many competing ways for constructing scientific psychology theories and for utilizing the resulting fund of information to resolve educational problems. Moreover, these differences not only are evident from one era to another but also exist simultaneously at any given point in history, including the present time. More specifically relevant to the topic of this book, one can delineate several patterns in the emergence of psychological learning theories and in the prevailing relationships between these theories and educational practice. This book focuses primarily on learning theories in psychology and instructional procedures in education, but both can best be examined with the perspective of general psychology theorizing patterns and changes in relationships between psychology and education.

The next chapter prepares for the presentation of theories of learning by presenting an introduction to theory in general. Subsequent chapters provide an historical overview of the developments in philosophy and psychology that led up to the development of learning theories and instructional theories. It is hoped that with this background the reader will be able to evaluate the theories that are presented and will be able to see how each of them contributed to the ongoing process of the development of psychology as a science and as a source of possible answers to educational problems.

2
An Introduction to Theory and Theory Construction

All theories are trials; they are tentative hypotheses, tried out to see whether they work; and all experimental corroboration is simply the result of tests undertaken in a critical spirit, in an attempt to find out where our theories err. (Popper, 1957, p. 87)

I view science not as a search for imperishable truth but more as a kind of game, a game we play partly for the fun of it, but partly also because it will increase our understanding. (Bolles, 1967, Preface)

A good theory is one that holds together long enough to get you to a better theory. (Hebb, 1969, p. 27)

AN INTRODUCTION TO
SCIENTIFIC THEORIES

This chapter begins with the above quotations in the hope that they will put a number of issues in their proper perspective right from the start. If it is legitimate to say that science is a game rather than a search for imperishable truth, it is equally legitimate to say the same about science in psychology and in education. In the introductory chapter we discussed the science of psychology and the science of education to show the manner in which the two can interrelate. It is undoubtedly true that neither rests upon the solidest of scientific foundations, but both can and do use scientific method to develop their theories. If we can accept that fact as a starting point, we have a basis upon which to begin our discussion. If we then can go further and admit that we are not going to be searching for imperishable truth in our discussion but only for ways to increase our understanding of the problems that psychology and education must face, we have made a very good start indeed.

It is unfortunately the case that raising psychology and education to the level of sciences, which, of course, cannot be done merely by fiat, produces certain problems that we may not be entirely happy we have raised. For one thing, this means that we must be willing to subject beliefs and statements about psychology and education to the same series of tests and to the same kinds of criteria by which statements in other sciences are tested and judged. It means that we must view these disciplines as branches of the philosophy of science rather than merely as help-giving professions, as arts, or even as mere pragmatic technologies. They are, of course, all these and more, but to view them as only this, as only practitioner-oriented disciplines devoid of theory or the need for theory, is to ignore their essence and to relegate them to a level of discourse that is based mainly on intuition and one's personal experience. Many people probably view psychology and education this way, but this book, at least, will not do so. Instead, it will review certain aspects of the attempt that has been made over the years to formulate a science of psychology as well as a science of education.

It is, of course, the case that not all of this attempt can be reviewed in this book. Our discussion will be limited to one part of science that is of special interest. The problems of science can be summarized as falling into four general and overlapping categories: to accumulate accurate data, to utilize correct methodology, to formulate valid theory, and to make proper inferences. As has already been indicated, the topic of this book is *theory*. By emphasizing the particular subset of psychological theory that has been concerned with learning and by broadening this coverage to include those relatively new theories that have come to be called *instructional theories*, we hope to include the majority of the seminal systems in both disciplines as well as give a good overview of the ways in which psychology and education have interacted for more than seventy years.

The theories that we will be presenting, then, represent a sample of the theories that have been generated and developed in psychology, an academic discipline which, if not as yet the best of sciences, at least has aspirations of being one. The term *sample* should also be emphasized. It is obviously impossible to review every theory that has ever been formulated in psychology or education. We have opted for the position of presenting a substantial and representative sample of learning theories, which by themselves represent a good sample of the theories that have been devised in psychology. (Good, but of course not inclusive.) Those theories that will be reviewed that are more strictly educational (that is, the instructional theories) are perhaps not as representative of all educational theory, but instead represent only those theories that are related to psychological learning theories in some way and that concern themselves with general rather than specific problems in the field of education.

Since the topic of this book is *theory*, let us begin by discussing theory as a general topic. The topic is an important one in the philosophy of science and the author will not pretend to present a complete or detailed discussion of it. Instead, the reader will be introduced to a few issues that are salient concerning theory qua theory in order to have a basis on which to discuss and evaluate theories that will be presented in this book.

THE NEED FOR THEORY

Theory Development versus Fact Gathering

Why theory, you might ask, and why not fact? Why waste time on a lot of speculations and hunches when the effort might better be spent on amassing concrete, factual, empirical data on learning and education? Is there a need for theory or could we do better without it? All these are valid questions, and they raise some points which have been debated in psychology and education with increasing vigor in recent years. It is clear from what has been said already that the author does not accept an atheoretical position as being a valid one in psychology or education. As a matter of fact, it will be contended that the formulation of theory is not only important but also vital if either discipline is to progress and to make a contribution toward solving the problems that are considered to be in their domain.

Ceaseless "Corrections" to Theories

As suggested in the quotations by Bolles, by Hebb, and by Popper at the beginning of this chapter, the history of any science can be viewed as a series of failures. If the development of science seems from a distance to be a steady and progressive march toward some ultimate goal, this is probably due to the fact that time tends to make all events seem completely determined. In reality, every science is built slowly and often falteringly by men who are willing to go beyond their data and to speculate about events that either cannot be seen or cannot be understood. More often than not they are wrong, and their theories and speculations are thrown away to be studied as interesting and often amusing historical blunders. Why then, if most theories are completely wrong, and all theories are somewhat wrong, do men continue to invent them and teachers continue to force their students to study them? The answer lies in the fact that the great advances in science have come about because men have been willing to organize their ideas in the form of theories and to let other men evaluate them. Old theories create new theories, and new theories create experiments, and experiments create increased knowledge and understanding. It is difficult to believe that any amount of simple data accumulation could match the importance of a single theoretical breakthrough such as Newton's gravitational theory or Einstein's theory of relativity. Although accomplishments in psychology and education are less dramatic and the theories not always clearly supported by empirical evidence, it is these theoretical statements which have had far greater impact than have the isolated facts no matter how sound the research procedures.

This should in no sense be taken to mean that empirical observation is of less importance than theory or that experimentation must always be performed for purely theoretical considerations. Science progresses when both theory and empirical observation go together in a mutually beneficial manner—the theory indicating the questions that are most meaningful to ask, and the observations showing where the theory is deficient. The two must always be present—theories that are poorly tied to empirical observation are as meaningless and as potentially harmful as facts that are poorly tied to theory. To demonstrate this, consider the following examples.

William James presents the following examples of an interpretation of phenomena that are based on incorrect theorizing:

If some iron filings be sprinkled on a table and a magnet brought near them, they will fly through the air for a certain distance and stick to its surface. A savage seeing the phenomenon explains it as the result of an attraction or love between the magnet and the filings. But let a card cover the poles of the magnet, and the filings will press forever against its surface without its ever occurring to them to pass around its sides and thus come into more direct contact with the object of their love. Blow bubbles through a tube into the bottom of a pail of water, they will rise to the surface and mingle with the air. Their action may again be poetically interpreted as due to a longing to recombine with the mother-atmosphere above the surface. But if you invert a jar full of water over the pail, they will rise and remain lodged beneath its bottom, shut in from the outer air, although a slight deflection from their course at the outset, or a re-descent towards the rim of the jar when they found their upward course impeded, would easily have set them free. (James, 1908, pp. 6–7)

In analyzing either of the examples that James provides it is clear that both represent perfectly reliable and replicable events. Magnets will always attract metal filings and air will always rise to the surface of water. If these "experiments" are performed an endless number of times, these facts will always be "discovered." The theories that were used to account for these facts, however, are obviously wrong. Both examples represent cases of reliable data explained by misconceived theories.

Consider also the recent explorations of the moon. Before the first lunar expeditions, it was felt that the collection of firsthand data from the moon (one form of which would be moon rocks) would settle once and for all the controversy that has been going on for many years concerning the origin of the moon. The history of this scientific endeavor again serves to dramatize the necessity of theory and the essential interplay between theory and observation. First of all, while the collection of moon rocks did settle some issues and did serve to shed some serious doubts on some of the prevailing theories about the moon's origins, it did not turn out to be the case that this direct empirical investigation solved all the problems or relegated the place of theory to one of unimportance. Despite these specimens (at the time of this writing, at any rate), there is still need for theory about the origin of the moon. This should serve as a sobering warning about what expectations we should have concerning the ultimate verification of our theories. Secondly, and probably more importantly, no theory is absolute or so all-inclusive that it can be completely verified by the most extensive of scientific investigations. In fact, some would even argue that we should test for "falsification" rather than "verification." That is, that we should test for the limits within which a theory is valid. In psychology and education we are dealing with phenomena and processes that are at least as nebulous as those involved in the origins of celestial bodies. In such a situation, the development of theories is both understandable and necessary.

Functions of Theories

While it is impossible to list every potential use that a theory could have, there are a few that seem especially critical:

Systematize Findings   A theory can serve to systematize research findings and make sense out of seemingly unrelated phenomena. The amount of research performed in any given year in psychology and education is enormous. Quite often the results from these experiments and studies are apparently contradictory. Even if we are not talking about experimental results but merely casual observations, the same is true. The complexity of the behavior emitted by one individual in one day, let alone the behavior emitted in one classroom, is staggering. On the surface this complexity can be meaningless. A theory can show how to reduce the complexity so that it can be analyzed and also show how the results from various experiments fit together in a unified way.

To make this use of theory more concrete and to demonstrate it by using simpler phenomena, consider the case of color theory. The perception of color in the visual world is characterized by immense surface complexity. In the various theories of color that have been devised (the Young-Helmholtz theory, for example) this complexity is analyzed as resulting from the interaction of a much smaller number (usually three) of basic color receptors located in the eye. Not only does such a theory simplify and, in so doing, aid understanding, but also it can subsume and organize a large range of phenomena into a coherent scheme (for example, negative afterimages, color blindness, etc.). While this example is rather clear-cut, any theory can do the same. Such a use represents one of the primary advantages that a theory has over mere accumulation of data.

Generate Hypotheses A theory is an invaluable generator of research hypotheses. One of the major uses of any theory is to tell scientists where to look for the answers to questions. Far from being a waste of time, a good theory can save a great deal of wasted effort by indicating where it would seem to be most profitable to do research. This heuristic value of theory is extremely important for research at many levels. Returning again to the example of color theory, when it was theorized that it was possible to account for the perception of color with only three receptors, experimenters could progress on a psychological level as if such receptors actually existed, even though their real nature was not known. While the psychological implications of the theory were being worked out, physiologists could begin to search for the physical presence of the three receptors. In this manner, a coordinated attack could be directed at the problem of color vision on many levels, all stemming from one basic theory.

In all fairness, however, it should be pointed out that this advantage can be two-sided, for a poorly constructed theory or a theory which is wrong in its basic essentials can lead to the asking of wrong questions and thereby to the performance of pointless research. While it is difficult to believe that any experimentation could ever be a complete waste of time, it nevertheless is the case that research time is better spent in the pursuit of meaningful goals. While admitting this problem, it is still the case that the vast amount of experimentation in psychology and some research in education have been performed because of some theory.

Make Predictions A theory can be used to predict. This function is similar to the second one presented above, but has stronger implications. Not only can a theory lead a scientist to ask questions that will probably be fruitful, but it can also show him what he might expect to find once he has performed his experimentation or observation. For example, Newtonian theory predicted the existence of planets which had not at that time been seen. By using the theory and by observing the orbits of known planets, it was predicted that there should be planets at certain positions in relation to the sun. In this way the outer planets which had not been discovered were eventually found. Also, genetic theory at a certain time in its development predicted the existence of chromosomes even though they had never been seen in a microscope. In discussing this particular example, Edwin G. Boring notes that the existence of chromosomes was noted in microscopic pictures of genetic material after the theory that postulated their existence came into being and not before. He comments that concepts are not formulated until a theory brings them into being. While this is most certainly not always true, it is interesting that the two examples presented above show that certain "realities" were discovered only after (and probably only because) the theory predicting their existence had been formulated.

Provide Explanations A theory can be used to explain. In essence, this function of theory answers the question *why*. Why do certain events occur and why does the manipulation of one particular variable produce a change in another? Many events in nature are determined or caused by factors which are unknown or only incompletely understood. By definition, the explanation of such events must be theoretical. The explanatory function of theory is widespread and too often misused. Any event can be explained by a theory as long as the explanation is plausible and at least minimally takes into account the observed phenomena. An adequate theory does not simply explain in a post hoc manner but relates several events to each other. Since we will spend some time on this issue in defining theory, we need only say at this time that there is a philosophical distinction that is made between things that are and are not explanations. Speaking precisely, an event is said to be explained when it is shown to be an example of a familiar principle or set of principles. Even this is not complete since such explanations may or may not involve theory depending on the relationship posited between the event or events and the antecedent principles. It is quite possible to explain without strictly using a theory to generate your explanations. Every theory, however, will be a generator of explanations. In this manner, this use of theory comes close to our first reason given.

There are undoubtedly other uses that theory could be or could have been used for in the history of science. Without going any further into these, it should still be clear that theory is an invaluable tool for the scientist. Moreover, this book will hold the view that theory construction is a necessary part of the ongoing process in psychology and education. This is true whether the interest is in a process (such as learning) or in an individual. The fact that organisms learn is clear; what is not clear is how they learn or why they learn. A theory of learning can help us begin to answer such questions. This use of theory is probably little disputed. The fact that a student is not learning may be just as clear to his teacher; how to initiate the process of learning for him or how better to arrange the learning situation so that learning can occur is probably not clear. It is probably not as universally accepted that a theory can be just as helpful in answering this type of question. A theory, no matter how good or inclusive, will not solve every problem. Without theory, however, we often do not know even where to begin.

DEFINITIONS OF TERMS

We have mentioned several terms so far without specifying exactly what is meant by them. Although there is no universal agreement among philosophers of science about the definition of several of the terms that have been mentioned or that will be mentioned later in the book, the following are offered as points from which to begin our review:

Theory

In its most general usage (following the lead of N. R. Campbell), the term *theory* has come to refer to a set of propositions that are syntactically integrated (that is, that follow certain rules by which they can be logically related to one another and to some observable data base) and which serve as a means of predicting and explaining observable phenomena. This is by no means the only way that *theory* can be defined. As Marx (1967) points out, there are at least four different definitions of theory currently used in science ranging from the most general (any aspect of science which is not strictly empirical) to the most restricted (a summary statement which describes and gives order to a series of empirical observations). The one we will be using in this book, however, is probably the most preferred one over a wide range of situations. To demonstrate more exactly this definition, we will quote Spence in discussing the use of theory in physics:

In some areas of knowledge, for example present day physics, theories serve primarily to bring into functional connection with one another empirical laws which prior to their formulation had been isolated realms of knowledge. The physicist is able to isolate, experimentally, elementary situations, i.e., situations in which there are a limited number of variables, and thus finds it possible to infer or discover descriptive, low-order laws. Theory comes into play for the physicist when he attempts to formulate more abstract principles which will bring these low-order laws into relationship with one another. Examples of such comprehensive theories are Newton's principle of gravitation and the kinetic theory of gases. The former provided a theoretical integration of such laws as Kepler's concerning planetary motions, Galileo's law of falling bodies, laws of the tides and so on. The kinetic theory has served to integrate the various laws relating certain properties of gases to other experimental variables. (Spence, 1944, p. 47)

By this definition, a theory is not defined by the range of phenomena it explains so much as by the complexity of the system used for the explanation. A theory can involve predictions or explanations of a unique event as long as this prediction is generated from a system of logically related propositions.

Hypothesis

An *hypothesis* is a statement about a suspected relationship between variables. Unlike a theory, this statement need not involve nor does it necessarily result from an organized system of propositions; it merely states that a future observation will take a particular form. These statements will generally fall into two categories: (1) The relationship may be correlative (a variation in x will be systematically related to a change in y); or, (2) The relationship may be causal (a manipulation of x causes a change in y). There is an obvious and necessary relationship between theory and hypothesis. All theoretical statements are by definition hypotheses in the sense that scientists accept them as tentative statements in the unending search for more accurate explanations of the subject matter. However, not all hypotheses need necessarily be derived from theory.

Model

A *model* is a concretization of a theory which is meant to be analogous to or representative of the processes and variables involved in the theory. A model is said to be correct or adequate by its ability to produce the same data as the object in the real world produces, from which the original theory was generated. Models may be of several types, although the three most used examples in psychology are physical models, computer models, and mathematical models. To make this clearer, consider the following two examples. It is becoming common practice in medical schools to use manikins to teach neophyte doctors about the reactions of a human body under certain conditions. These manikins have certain typical human reactions built into them such as pupil contractions, heartbeat, respiratory responses, etc. Strictly speaking, such manikins are not exactly models but they are close enough to make a point. These manikins are physical analogues to a human body. They are expected to produce a certain sample of responses to specific stimuli just as a human body does. Not all human responses, of course, are produced and the manikin is assuredly not the same thing as a human body; nevertheless, it can act like a human body under specified conditions. Because doctors and physiologists have observed regularities in behavior and have certain ideas about why these regularities occur, they can build a model to duplicate these responses. Another example of a model is the physical representation of atoms commonly found in science expositions. These models are again a representation in the physical domain of what scientists believe an atom looks like in the microscopic domain. All such models have a necessary "as-if" quality about them, and they are usually closely tied to theory. Indeed, some writers contend that a model is a theory and they sometimes use these terms interchangeably. It is probably clearer to make the other assumption and say that a model will almost always represent a theory although it will not, strictly speaking, be one. We will discuss computer models in the chapter on information processing theories and mathematical models in the chapter on mathematical learning theories.

Paradigm

A *paradigm* is a basic pattern or plan in verbal or diagrammatic form which serves to describe recurring basic features of the phenomena being studied and which mainly serves to provide rather specific guidelines for conducting research. Strictly speaking, paradigms are neither models nor theories. They mainly are ways of thinking about research, ways of thinking which prove useful time and again because the paradigm outlines relationships of a general type which applies to many specific instances which must be studied. One can depict a paradigm as a basic building block or basic theme which occurs frequently in articulation of the theory or model. During conducting of research a truly useful paradigm shows little "wear" as the research "plugs in" new variables and new relationships to be studied.

A paradigm may be useful in different situations and even in the development of competing theories but it typically involves implicit or explicit assumptions about the best means for conducting research and for integrating findings. A paradigm more or less signals preference for measuring learning in particular ways and expectation as to the kinds of variables which most likely influence learning. But even more importantly there is some implied assumption as to how at least some types of learning occur. Thus the paradigm serves some of the organizational and integrative functions during planning and conducting of research which theories and models serve during interpretation of the findings.

Some authors either omit use of the term *paradigm* or equate it with model or theory. In this text we will use paradigm mainly in conjunction with the planning of research. As to its conceptual value, we will treat it as being less comprehensive than models and theories in the range of facets with which it can be used.

Later in this text we will discuss Skinner's operant conditioning theory and his approach to the study of learning processes. We will find the recurring theme that "behavior is controlled by its consequences." The theoretical and practical implications of this thesis are not of concern to us at the moment. What is of interest is that virtually all operant research involves a paradigm which stems from this orientation. It can be characterized: $R \rightarrow S^R$, where "R" denotes the response or behavior of the organism, "S^R" denotes the reinforcing stimulus or consequence which follows the response, and the arrow indicates the relationship between the response and its consequences. Readers familiar with this paradigm know that they should especially look for the specific responses and the particular reinforcing stimuli when they read an operant research report.

Law and Principle

A *law* is a statement about a relationship between variables whose probability of occurrence is so high that the relationship can be counted on as being highly dependable. A *principle* is a statement of relationships which has allegedly had some empirical support but which either is not obviously fundamental or is not sufficiently well established to be called a law. Many authors in psychology and education use these terms interchangeably. The "law" of gravity, for example, states an extremely reliable (that is, predictable) fact that the result of certain measurements relating time and the distance an object falls will nearly always be the same. Even this law, of course, is meant to hold only when certain specified conditions prevail. The underlying assumption in the postulation of such laws and principles is that nature is in essence lawful and that it is the job of science to ferret out these regularities and to state them in a manner from which predictions can be generated to new situations. It is possible, of course, to make events lawful or seemingly so when there is no actual regularity involved. Recognizing this fact, several philosophers have serious doubts about the need for the term *law* as it is presently used in science. In psychology the laws that have been formulated are less reliable (oftentimes much less) and may not actually qualify in a strict sense as laws. Many contend that psychology has many principles but few laws. Not surprisingly, these terms are frequently used interchangeably. The fact that such a sliding scale definition exists is less of a problem than the fact that highly unreliable relationships can often masquerade as law in the newer sciences, such as psychology and education. Whether this represents the fact that such sciences are by definition less lawful (because their data base is less regular) is something that will have to be worked out in the future.

Construct

A *construct* is an entity whose existence and properties cannot directly or automatically be empirically deduced and which, therefore, can only be described on the basis of a network of converging operations. In order to make the above formidable-sounding definition clearer, consider the distinction between the concept "chair" and the construct "intelligence." (In most scientific writing, concept and construct are isomorphic terms.) It may seem that the concept "intelligence" is not a reality in the way that "chair" is a reality, and yet, the difference is smaller than it may seem on the surface. While it is true that a particular chair can be adequately and reliably described by any observer (it is brown; it has four legs, etc.), the concept "chair" can only be described in reference to a set of minimally necessary attributes which uniquely differentiate a chair from everything else. These attributes may be physical (a chair has four legs) or functional (a chair is something to sit on), or perhaps something else, but the essential characteristic is that a particular set of attributes is agreed upon by members of a linguistic community to determine uniquely the concept. In other words, in most cases a chair will not be mistaken for something else because people have agreed upon a set of physical attributes that distinguishes a chair from a table.

Compare this now to the construct "intelligence." Just as for the concept "chair," this concept can only be defined by specifying what unique subset of attributes characterize intelligence from any other psychological process. Now, in most cases of an individual sort, there may be fairly good agreement among observers that person X is more intelligent than person Y. What these people are saying is that the people observed differ in the amount of an inferred intermediary which has not and cannot be seen but whose properties are inferred from a series of behaviors. These behaviors are the only thing that can be seen and on the basis of several of them, the one person is said to be more intelligent than the other. The essential characteristic of these behaviors is exactly the same as it was for defining the concept "chair." The set of behaviors that is taken to define "intelligence" must be agreed upon by all observers before anything like an acceptable definition is possible. It should be clear now why psychological constructs, while being of the same essential nature as other constructs, still present more serious problems. It is difficult to believe that there will be in the near future an agreed upon set of characteristics that uniquely define intelligence. (There might be some that get a fair degree of support, such as good grades in school, having a large vocabulary, being able to solve problems quickly, etc., but it is clear that such a list is hardly inclusive or very adequate.) Until such a list is available, the construct "intelligence" will be ill-defined and ambiguous. In general, "intelligence" as a construct is defined by tying it in to a series of behaviors (or more generally, operations) which converge and which are then taken to reflect the amount of an inferred intermediary variable.

This is the general case for most psychological constructs that appear in particular theories. Constructs in psychological theories are most often intermediaries used to name processes posited to account for behavior. "Learning," for example, is a construct; as such, it will always be an inference from behavior. This may strike the reader as a poor way to go about building a science because the question about all such inferred intermediaries would eventually seem to be "what is it really?" What really happens when someone learns? When someone asks such a question about psychological constructs, he usually means "what is the physiological nature of the variable?" To say this indicates that the construct under question may be imperfectly understood, for some constructs used in psychology are never meant to be translatable into physiological terms. While there are many named constructs current in psychology, at any one time most of these exemplify one of two types. Only for one of these types is it meaningful to ask the question about its physiological underpinnings. This distinction has been made by MacCorquodale and Meehl (1948) who termed such variables hypothetical constructs and intervening variables. Since it will come up in our discussion of the various theories, it might be well to spend some time on this distinction now in order to avoid later confusion. In order to make this distinction, we will compare the two examples most commonly used in this regard—gravity and adrenaline.

There is a type of variable (of which gravity is a good example) that is completely and uniquely defined by a logically related system of terms, such as a mathematical formula. Such variables have no meaning beyond the formula or summary statement that is used to define them. It is never meaningful to ask what such a concept looks like or what it "really" is since the construct is nothing more nor less than the statement defining it. In Newtonian physics, gravity (g) is merely a symbol placed in a formula indicating a relationship between other variables. As Newton said, "I have not been able to discover the cause of these properties of gravity, and I make no hypothesis. . . . It is enough that gravity acts according to the laws which we have found" (Bolles, 1967). (In Einsteinian physics, gravity is something more but we will not go into that at this time.) Such an entity is called an intervening variable. On the other hand, there are constructs which do have meaning beyond the measurement processes used to define them. For example, when confronted with a fear-arousing situation, a man will react with a series of behaviors that are characteristic of a human being. These behaviors are measurable and predictable (such things as an increase in heartbeat, certain changes in skin response, constriction of blood vessels, and a series of other physiological responses), is common to all members of the species. There was a time in medicine when it was posited that one substance probably was the causal agent in these varied physiological responses. Even though such a substance had never been synthesized nor seen, it simplified the situation enormously to act as if such a substance existed and to postulate that it (adrenaline) was the cause of the observed behavior. Adrenaline has a real identity, and it is meaningful to ask what it would look like (biochemically, that is). It is not merely a summary statement or merely the name placed upon an intermediary that is inferred from a series of behaviors, even though it, just like gravity, can be inferred from behavior. Constructs such as adrenaline are termed hypothetical constructs.

This distinction is an important one but one which in a practical situation can become cloudy. Intelligence is an excellent example of this. As a construct, intelligence can mean many different things depending on the particular theorist in question. If a man defines intelligence as something like "the total number of neurons in the cortex," or "the more rapid utilization of DNA," he is clearly using the concept as a hypothetical construct. On the other hand, a definition such as "intelligence is what the intelligence test measures" is obviously an example of an intervening variable. While both of the above represent rather extreme and probably unrepresentative cases, the point is the same when discussing other psychological constructs. "Learning" can mean both something physiological (a chemical change in the brain) and behavioral (the ability to perform a new response). In general, whether a theorist uses the intervening variable or the hypothetical construct approach will depend on his own personal preferences in theory construction. There is no universal acceptance of which of these types is better. In general, anyone interested in physiological explanations of behavior will probably be using hypothetical constructs (and almost without exception, physiological variables are hypothetical constructs); anyone interested in behavioral or mathematical relationships in behavior will probably be using intervening variables. Even if the decision is made to use hypothetical constructs, however, inferences will still need to be made from behavior and minimally necessary sets of attributes will still have to be agreed upon in order to use the construct in a psychological theory.

To summarize these various definitions, it would seem that theory is the most inclusive and general term presented, and that the others can be subsumed by or generated from it. A *theory* contains various constructs and generates hypotheses. *Models* are most often intended to translate a theory into some other form from the one in which it was originally invented. *Laws and principles* are often used as the building blocks with which theories are made. At times these distinctions may be forced, and in many cases, the dividing line between the domain of one of these terms and another will be extremely vague. Nevertheless, we will try to maintain these distinctions as we proceed into an exposition of various theories later in the book.

THE CONSTRUCTION OF THEORIES

There is a definite appeal in the assumption that the methods by which theories are constructed follow some carefully devised and universally agreed upon formula. While there are indeed rules about how to create a theory and even a theory about theory (termed *metatheory*), it is still undoubtedly the case that the manner in which theories are constructed is a highly individualized process which will not neatly fit into any single classification. There is also a commonly held belief that a theory is formulated only after some critical point in the development of a science has been reached—when the time and the state of accumulated information in the science are ready for the emergence of a new theoretical breakthrough. While there is undoubtedly an element of truth in this, it seems to be the case that the time for theoretical pursuits is as much determined by the men who perform them as is the way they go about it. The story is told about Einstein that the development of the theory of relativity came about very much as an individual effort, an effort that was little associated with the events that preceded it in experimental physics. It had been thought for many years that Einstein's theory came about as the result of a series of experiments that preceded the publication of his theoretical papers. Most notable of such experiments was the Mikkelson experiment concerning the speed of light. In some letters written in later years, Einstein comments that he barely knew about these experiments and could hardly have based his theory upon them. It still must be the case that Einstein used the accumulated knowledge in his field in order to devise his theory; yet it is too attractive to believe that the pursuit of science and theory building follows a nicely organized path when this is seldom the case. The point in this is that any statement about how theories are made is going to be vastly oversimplified and representative only in a general sense, certainly not characteristic of any actual theorist. Keeping this warning in mind, it is generally agreed that there are two basic modes of theory construction—the deductive and the inductive method.

Deductive Theory Construction

The emphasis in this type of theory is upon building a system of constructs and relational rules which are conceptually and logically consistent but whose empirical verification is open to question. This type of theorist works from the top down, building a theory that seems logical on an a priori basis and then testing the correctness of this theory by performing experiments whose nature is determined by the theory. The clearest example of such a theory in psychology is Hull's hypothetico-deductive theory of learning. In this theory a set of postulates or basic assumptions was first formulated which took into account certain known factors but which was essentially the result of informed guessing. From these postulates, hypotheses (or theorems) were generated. These theorems were then tested and the ones that proved to be correct were retained. In like manner, those postulates that generated correct theorems were retained so that the theory became self-correcting over a period of time. This is characteristic of deductive theories in general, although not typical of all theory building in psychology. Such a theory is always in the process of being corrected, and as such, leads to an enormous body of research (witness the history of Hullian theory). The problem with such a theory is that if the majority of the original postulates are incorrect, the theory will generate a greater amount of more or less needless research. Since a young science is more likely to be wrong than right in hitting upon the correct set of postulates upon which to base its theories, there are many (most notably Skinner) who argue that such a manner of theory construction is not the best one for psychology at this time. At any rate, the incidence of such theory construction is small in psychology and education at present, although quite characteristic of the older sciences and more popular in psychology during Hull's era.

Inductive Theory Construction

In this mode of theory construction, theories become summary statements or generalizations of empirical facts. Such a theorist works from the bottom up, devising systems (or miniature theories) which take several well-verified or replicated research findings into account, then devising higher-level systems which generalize across miniature theories, and eventually formulating a theory which can account for all the statements lower in the schema. The benefit of such an approach is that the theorist is never very far from statements whose "truth" is fairly well verified. In this way he is less likely to go astray in devising his theoretical postulates. The problem in such a method is that it can often lead to a proliferation of very low-level theories, many of which are not unique and which contain considerable overlap in function. Such an approach can become inefficient in that it can lead several theorists to ask basically the same questions in slightly different form and is less likely to produce attempts at integrating different research findings.

Current Practices

As mentioned previously, both these modes of theory construction represent extremes. Any theorist will show preferences for one type over the other, although every theorist will use strategies which contain elements of both approaches. The question is not whether one is inherently better than the other but rather whether one is more productive and efficient at a particular time in the history of a science. A choice between the inductive and the deductive method will probably rest upon the faith a theorist has in the "knowns" in his science. If one can feel that there are some well-established facts in psychology and that there is a pretty good understanding and grasp of the working of basic phychological processes, then the use of the deductive method is warranted. If, on the other hand, one is less secure in his faith about the scientific value of current psychological data, the inductive approach is better. There are those in psychology who deliberately use both methods (the functionalists) in any continuing program of research devised to answer specific questions. Such a functionalistic approach to theory construction is quite characteristic of present psychology and represents a good picture of the state of the science at this time.

THE VERIFICATION OF THEORIES

Unless theory construction is performed as an exercise in mental gymnastics, there eventually will come a time when legitimate questions arise concerning the "truth" of the theory devised. Truth, of course, is not actually the issue—what we really need to know is whether one theory is relatively better than another and whether certain parts of any one theory need to be revised. It is always possible to armchair theorize about any question. Such theories may even turn out to be appealing in a subjective sense since they seem to solve so many problems and seem to fit so well with common sense. One need only review the history of psychology in a cursory manner to demonstrate this point. It was not very long ago, for example, that people were counting the bumps on people's heads to ascertain their personality. Unless there are methods and criteria by which theories can be judged, such theories as the above will retain their place in the list of acceptable scientific systems. In essence, there are three primary tests of a theory: (1) Is it syntactically correct? (2) Is it semantically correct? and (3) Is it parsimonious?

The Syntax

One test of a theory is whether or not it is internally consistent and logical. The science of *syntax* is the study of the relationship of signs to signs. Since all theories are constructed by postulating relationships between constructs, there is a necessary demand placed upon any theorist that his theory include a series of syntactical rules by which the constructs he uses in his theory can be related to each other and eventually to actual data. These rules may be mathematical (as they usually are in the physical sciences) or verbal (as is typically the case in psychology and education).

Syntactical precision is a test that has more salience for the physical sciences than for either psychology or education. This resides partly in the fact that mathematical syntactical rules are by their nature more open to this test since mathematics is a discipline in itself and as such has a definite and clearly stated set of rules. Verbal syntax will probably always be less precise, and psychological theory (except for mathematical learning theory) will probably use verbal rules for a long time to come. It also seems to be the case that syntactical constraints upon a psychological theory are often superfluous since the state of the science is such that some psychological theories stand upon rather shaky ground in their fit with empirical observations of the phenomena they supposedly explain.

The Semantics

Perhaps the primary test of a theory is whether it is experimentally verifiable; that is, whether it makes correct generalizations and valid predictions. This is termed *semantics* since it refers to the meaning of the terms used in the theory in reference to the real world. Philosophically, semantics is the study of the relationship of signs to objects. In essence, a theory will stand or fall upon its ability to meet experimental tests. This automatically implies that a theory must be stated in such a way that it can be tested, a problem that we will find repeatedly in assessing the "truth" of many of the theories we will review. Although it will not be characteristic of the theories reviewed that they can be refuted or upheld on the basis of one crucial experiment (or even a series of experiments), it will be the case that experiments will be extensively used to assess the relative value of one theory over another. One theory is supported over another when the two theories make different predictions and empirical evidence supports predictions from one theory to a greater extent than those from the other theory. This is the semantic test of a theory and it will become obvious in reviewing the theories presented in this book that it has been the crucial test of psychological theories. However, in actuality there are very few instances in which crucial experiments have conclusively demonstrated that one theory is clearly superior to its competitors. More frequently researchers interpret any negative evidence from such semantic tests as an indication that more research is necessary rather than that they should stop using that particular theory. The researchers may decide that the concept which they were studying is quite likely of influence on learning processes but that they may have encountered problems in their "operational definition" (the way they measured the concept). Either a different measure is needed or different amounts of the variable should have been studied. For example, in studies of the influence of feedback on learning they may conclude that the feedback had not been provided clearly enough to the subject or that it had been provided too infrequently. Thus a new study might be designed and conducted.

There is another point along these lines which should be discussed. There are differences of opinion as to how "perfect" predictions should be in an ideal final theory. Granted that we are not now at a point where one can make perfect predictions and produce airtight explanations, what should we expect as our data base grows and our experimental procedures become more refined? Some, following the "classical" conception of science, contend that ultimately we should be able to provide very precise predictions about learning under specified conditions. Others contend that we should adopt the "probabilistic" posture about predictions. We should follow the more recent pattern in science which holds that we should ultimately be able to have a high degree of accuracy in making predictions but that we can never expect to have perfect accuracy in our predictions. Such issues have been debated in many aspects of science and philosophy of science during the past several decades. The former position, the more classical one in science, is sometimes referred to as a "deterministic" position. The latter is typically designated as "probabilistic." We will find that most of the theories we will review in this book, particularly the learning theories which emerged prior to 1950, generally are deterministic in their expectations about theory. For various reasons the mathematical learning theorists and a few other contemporary theories emphasize a probabilistic approach.

Given the present status of our fund of knowledge about psychological processes and educational processes there is no empirical basis by which we can make decisions on this matter. Behavior is so complex and the data base, though rapidly growing, still so limited that even the most deterministic theorists have to settle for substantially less than perfect predictions. But no matter which philosophical position one adopts on this matter, in either case an important test of the theory is the extent to which its predictions are supported by empirical evidence.

Parsimony

Of less importance than the above two tests of theory is the rule of *parsimony* which states that when two theories appear to be equal in terms of value (using the terms we have introduced above, when they appear to be equally syntactically and semantically valid), it is the simplest of the two that should be adopted. In the real world of psychology and education, it is somewhat doubtful if we are in a position to be much concerned with this test since there are still so many questions left unanswered about the semantic validity of most of our theories.

Nonetheless, a theory which is overburdened with theoretical constructs should be open immediately to question since it will probably in the long run violate the rule of parsimony. There are certain theories in psychology which have so much superstructure that they practically fall of their own weight. Since we are not really in a position to reject any theory that might be correct, such theories are still discussed. It is still true, though, that simpler theories are desirable and should be emphasized.

There are undoubtedly other tests of theories than the three we have mentioned. If we keep the above criteria in mind in reviewing the theories presented, however, we will have some method by which to judge them. The point, again, is not to find the one theory that is correct or truthful or perfect, but rather to find the one theory that is better. A better theory will be one that meets the tests more adequately than any other.

SPECIAL PROBLEMS OF PSYCHOLOGICAL
THEORIES AND INSTRUCTIONAL THEORIES

We have been discussing psychological theory so far in reference to a set of criteria that are applicable to any scientific theory. There is no doubt that this must be the case and that psychological theory, if it is to be scientifically reputable, must meet these criteria. It is also the case, however, that psychology has problems which are unique to it and which immensely complicate the job of a theoretician in either psychology or education. To finish this chapter, let us review these problems as framework in which to place the theories we will present later in the book. As Scriven (1964) points out, psychology as a science has three problems that limit its development:

1) *Psychology must compete with common sense for its subject matter.* As we have noted earlier in this text, in a sense every person is a theoretical psychologist and an applied psychologist: All of us have our "common-sense" theories about people and how to get along with them. Fortunately, some of our informal principles are correct in the sense that scientific studies confirm them. Of course there are many instances in which our "common-sense" formulations are in error, but even here we find the general population modifying its views in light of new findings although it sometimes takes several decades for such changes to occur. However, this is also somewhat unfortunate for the scientist-psychologist in that *psychology as science* must go beyond the common-sense level and must typically deal with problems for which there are no easily obtained answers. Scriven suggests that such a task was not faced by Galileo, Newton, and early scientists in other fields.

2) *Psychological problems are constantly being annexed by other disciplines,* such as biochemistry, physiology, genetics, etc., leaving

psychology with fewer problems that are uniquely its own. Here we find a disadvantage in being, comparatively, one of the newer sciences.

3) *The basic questions with which psychology* (and education, too, we might add) *must concern itself are in essence more complicated than those which other sciences must deal with.* Behavior is influenced by such diverse factors as genetic constitution, previous or current damage to the nervous system, previous learning and maturational patterns, and the many variable characteristics of everyday situations. Like the weather forecaster, the applied psychologist and the educator must attempt predictions without knowing precisely what conditions will prevail in the real-life situation of concern. More often than not, such conditions are not under the control of the psychologist and educator despite their relevance for the behavior under study.

Scriven's arguments are worth considering since they bring into focus issues that we will be meeting throughout the rest of this book. Psychology and education have been forced to devise solutions for real problems long before they were quite capable of doing so, and long before another science of the same age or state of sophistication would have been asked to do so—that is, would have been asked to "pay off" in terms of solutions to practical problems. There is an essential difference between predicting and explaining the movements of the planets and predicting who will do well in a classroom. It is different not only because the realms of discourse are different, but also because the second question is more crucial in a practical sense. Society may find the answer to the first question interesting and perhaps eventually useful, but it finds the answer to the second one an *immediate* necessity. This forces a science to answer questions which are very difficult and which are at the same time strongly demanded. Eventually this will mean that society will become angry and disenchanted at such a science because it will not be producing acceptable answers soon enough. The cry will then go out to begin to do practical things and to give up what seems to be a needless and wasteful search for correct theory. It is, of course, just such an attitude that will produce a slowdown in the science and not an advancement. With its unique problems and its important subject, psychology must still use and develop theory. Education must do the same, or at least be willing to modify theory from other disciplines. The need for theory in both disciplines is great not only to provide organization for our accumulating, and somewhat scattered, facts and principles, but also to provide a more systematic basis for dealing with practical problems.

3
Psychology Theories and Learning: Part 1

Science does not advance by piling up information—it organizes information and compresses it. (Simon, 1968, p. 623)

A science-in-the-making is not, in practice, an abstract, impersonal affair. It comprises a not-entirely cooperative group of human beings, each of whom has his own background of knowledge and research, his own peculiar capacity, his own prejudices and preferences—in a word, his own individuality. Disagreement and controversy are, therefore, almost inevitable, even with respect to very fundamental questions. (Keller, 1937, p. 101)

PHILOSOPHICAL ORIGINS

The roots of any science can be traced back into philosophy, in most cases at least as far back as the Greeks. In the writings of such men as Aristotle, Plato, and other Greek philosophers it is often possible to find the beginnings of ideas which, in the hands of later generations of thinkers, were to become the central ideas of Western philosophy and science. While such searching for philosophical roots can take on the nature of a rather pointless academic game, and while it is often the case that such procedures are used to legitimize rather poorly thought-out ideas, it is nevertheless true that it is very difficult to understand why a particular scientific theory was formulated without understanding its philosophical origins. Since our immediate concern will be with psychological learning theory, it will be necessary to present the prevailing thought concerning the nature of psychology that immediately preceded the formulation of these theories. In addition, at least a rapid overview of a few reoccurring issues will be necessary in order to understand the background of theories we will be presenting.

The history of psychology as an experimental science is usually said to have begun in 1879, the date that Wilhelm Wundt founded at Leipzig the first laboratory explicitly designated for psychological experimentation. This date can serve as a useful bench mark, but it would be incorrect to imagine that *all* the trends and issues that have occurred in the history of academic psychology can be traced solely back to Wundt. Wundt himself is the product of several intersecting lines of thought and there are other issues that are currently important in psychology that were not considered crucial in Wundtian thinking. In order to understand the philosophical underpinnings of the theories we will be reviewing, it will be necessary to go back before Wundt and other early psychologists such as James and Titchner to set the stage for these men in terms of the historical origins of issues which they considered important and which are still represented in modern thought. Since the history of modern learning theory is usually considered to start with Thorndike, we will prepare for the presentation of this theory by tracing the origins of two separate trends in philosophical thinking which are brought together in Thorndike's conceptualizations. Philosophically, these two lines of thought have been termed *hedonism* and *associationism,* or in more psychological jargon, those aspects of behavior that are *motivational* and those that concern *learning.* After briefly reviewing these two lines of thought, we will then present the ideas that were current just previous to the turn of this century when Thorndike and other psychologists became interested in the problem of learning.

Hedonism

It is obvious from even a cursory observation of animal or human activity that behavior is directed toward the goal of increasing pleasure and avoiding pain. Such "hedonistic" causation of behavior has customarily been acknowledged in much of Western philosophy. But it should not be assumed that such hedonistic influences were considered the only determinants of the behavior of man. Man, after all, was considered to be rational (unlike animals) and, through the power of his reason, he could overcome hedonistic considerations for intellectual ones.

Such ideas go back at least to the Greeks where we find Plato contrasting the behavior of men to the behavior of animals. For Plato, animals must always pursue the sensual aspects of life and are dominated solely by the pleasure derived from them. Man, however, possessing the faculty of reason and free will, could overcome the sensual aspects of existence. Human behavior, then, can be determined by pleasure but need not be. Animal behavior, however, will always be so determined. It is clear in such a system that a sharp distinction is made between animals and man in at least one regard—that human behavior is free and at least partially rational. The same essential point of view can be discovered in the writings of Democritus, Epicurus, and other Greek philosophers. Democritus, in discussing the influence of the animal passions in human behavior, contended that such influences should be divorced from moral considera-tion; animal passions (or, hedonistic causes) were not necessarily inferior to intellectual or rational considerations, only less useful in the long run. For Epicurus, the point of life was happiness or pleasure—the pleasure of the here and now as opposed to the happiness of the hereafter, this latter alternative being the one fostered by the Christian philosophers who came five centuries later.

It is not our intention to present an extensive review of this issue as it was developed throughout the following centuries. Such a review would have to contain at least some treatment of several overlapping issues, such as dualism and determinism. The point of this review would be to show how succeeding generations of scholars tried in various ways to solve the issues that the Greeks had raised. How, for example, could the obvious discrepancy between the two aspects of man (the sensual and the rational) be resolved? For Descartes, the answer was a type of dualism of mind and matter with the two interacting in a specified manner. The basic premise, however, that the future course of an organism's behavior is at least partially determined by the consequences of such behavior can be traced through the history of Western philosophy in the writings of such men as Bentham, Mill, Hobbes, and others. For our purposes, we will review only the position of Herbert Spencer since it represents one of the immediate historical antecedents of modern learning theory.

Spencer's theory can be seen as an extension of Darwin's theory of evolution into the hedonistic realm. One aspect of Darwin's history is the contention that one crucial aspect of any behavior or characteristic of a species is its survival value. Those things that foster the ability of a species to adapt and to change, those behaviors that help the species to survive, will in the long run persist and be carried on from generation to generation. One does not have to assume that there is any great plan or purpose in such a scheme, only that through time and natural selection the fittest will survive. To this basic contention, Spencer added the dimension of pleasure and pain. It would seem logical, he argued, that natural selection would tend in the long run to foster a relationship between those things that aid survival and those things that create pleasure. It is pleasurable to eat, for example, and it is also necessary to eat if one is to survive. Not only is this true, but it is also clear that certain kinds of food are perceived as more pleasurable than others (sweet things over bitter things, for example). An analysis of the types of food that are available for an organism to eat (mammals, at least) would indicate that more often than not, sweet foods are better for the organism than are bitter ones, "better" in this case meaning more nutritional or less likely to injure the organism. What has happened through natural selection, then, is that a member of a species will seek pleasure and will avoid pain by eating sweet foods and by not eating bitter ones (the hedonistic principle), but in so doing, it will be performing behaviors which are beneficial to its survival. It will act because of the pleasure that had been obtained from such activity previously (sometimes called a "hedonism of the past") but it will be fostering its own survival (and that of its species) by so doing. In a later chapter we will see how an almost identical idea is used by Thorndike as the basis for his theory of learning.

To seek pleasure and to avoid pain are obvious aspects of behavior. Any theory attempting to account for behavior must take such considerations into account and we will see how the hedonistic principle is incorporated into theories that we review later in the book. Just as it is clear that this type of activity represents one aspect of behavior, it is also clear that it does not account for all behavior that must be explained by a theory of learning. Hedonism can explain why an act was originated and to what goal it is tending; it cannot explain how the effects of the act are retained through time. For this we must turn to another philosophical position—associationism.

Associationism

When a person is asked to provide a response to the word "table," he will most likely say "chair." This response will be quite automatic, as if the two words were in some sense linked together by some cerebral mechanism. Such behavior is extremely common—elements are linked or associated in such a way that the occurrence of one will produce or result in the other. The inculcation of this fact into philosophy again can be traced through the writings of several men back to the Greeks. For Aristotle, memory was explained by the association of mental elements. Through similarity, contrast, or contiguity one idea will be produced by another. The reason that a person will respond with the word "chair" to the word "table" is that the two have been presented contiguously together in the past. The reason that the response to "white" is "black" is that the two are associated as opposites, and so on. The primary development of this school of thought came at the hands of a group of British philosophers, usually called *British associationists.*

At the center of British associationism is the basic contention that the workings of the mind follow rules and laws which are similar in nature to the mechanistic laws that underlie physical phenomena. Physical laws such as Newton's gravitational laws or Boyle's law are descriptive of what happens under specified conditions. Such laws do not commit one to any particular philosophical or theological position but merely describe a series of events. By observing the workings of the mind, argue the associationists, its laws can be deduced in a similar fashion.

The founder of associationism is usually considered to be Thomas Hobbes, although the major developments were carried out by other men, most notably John Locke, David Hume, David Hartley, James Mill, and John Stuart Mill. It was Locke who coined the phrase "the association of ideas."

For Locke, the mind at birth is a tabula rasa, or blank slate, upon which experience writes. All knowledge is given to the mind by way of experience, through sensation. By forming simple ideas from sensations and by combining simple ideas into complex ones, the mind performs the complex activities demanded of it. In essence, this is a type of mental chemistry where the basic building blocks are simple sensations which, through association, are linked or bonded together to form immense complexity. For example, the nineteenth-century philosopher and economist John Stuart Mill theorized that some kind of "mental chemistry" process may occur in the formation of ideas. He conjectured that simple ideas are derived from one's sensations and memories, and that complex ideas are formed by various combinations of simple ideas. Mill recognized that the complex idea formations may sometimes consist of simple ideas summed together, but that more often than not they probably are "generated" by the simple ideas.

There is little doubt that associationism of the type devised by Mill or some variant of it represents one of the major building blocks of modern psychology. For example, associationism played a major role in psychology textbooks written in the late ninteenth and early twentieth century. William James, a philosopher and psychologist, was one of the best-known authors of this era. His text, which served for many years as the primary reference and textbook for American psychology, had one entire chapter devoted to the topic of associationism. James discussed associationism much as Aristotle had, by means of the three laws of contiguity, similarity, and contrast. With the addition of some physiological speculations (which is characteristic of most of James's psychological writing) and with a few relatively minor changes in emphases (for example, switching from the association of ideas to the association of objects), James establishes association as a major philosophical force for the new psychology. We will observe how its ideas permeated the theories that came early in the history of this psychology and how its basic contentions are still represented in psychological thinking.

Associationism and hedonism, then, represent two (but certainly not all) of the philosophical origins of learning theory. In many ways, these origins may not always be explicitly recognized by the theorists who used them, but as general orientations, they are in some form represented in their theories.

EMERGENCE OF PSYCHOLOGY AS A SCIENCE

As we have mentioned previously, the beginning of psychology as a science is taken to be the date (1879) when Wundt founded his psychological laboratory at Leipzig. Through this institute were to pass many of the men who were to be instrumental in founding and developing the new psychology from which learning theories ultimately were to originate. We cannot present the history of this movement without presenting some of the ideas of this remarkable philosopher, physiologist, and psychologist. For Wundt the essence of psychology was to be experimentation, an experimentation that was to solve the problems of the *mind* that philosophers before had raised but could not adequately answer. It was to be the "science of experience" and was to have as its subject matter the following three problems: (1) the analysis of conscious processes into the most fundamental, irreducible elements; (2) the determination of the manner of connections among these elements; and (3) the determination of the laws of these connections. Thus, following the lead of the apparently very successful atomic theory in chemistry, Wundt and his students and colleagues conceived psychology's goal as involving study of the fundamental elements, or "atoms," of mental experience.

It is relevant to consider briefly one of the main research procedures employed by Wundt and his colleagues—*introspection*. Psychologists, frequently serving as subjects themselves, were primarily concerned with subjects' sensations and perceptions, their mental experiences, of stimuli. Subjects were carefully trained to identify the "elements" of such experiences. For example, instead of reporting that they see a pencil presented to them they would be expected to report such basic experiences as longness, thinness, yellowness, flatness, pointedness, etc., those basic elements of experience, those sensations which lead one to report the total experience "pencil." The extent of importance attributed to this particular research method and the general theoretical orientation associated with it is indicated by two writers of that period:

A psychological experiment consists of an introspection or a series of introspections made under standard conditions. (Titchener, 1901, p. xiii)

Nevertheless, all our knowledge of mind derived from its objective study must come back to consciousness, either for its meaning or for its verification. No language concerning mental facts is intelligible unless we have had experience of the facts for ourselves. No theory of them is verified until we have composed it with the facts in our own consciousness and have found them to agree. Psychology, then, is finally based on introspection. It is a subjective rather than an objective science. (Bowne, 1887, p. 3)

In the years that Wundt headed the laboratory at Leipzig, a continuing stream of studies issued from him and from his students. Many of the early psychology leaders were directly or indirectly influenced by his work. Thus it is noteworthy that his research did *not* focus on learning but instead was mainly concerned with such diverse topics as sensation, perception, emotion, reaction time, and general relationships between the physical world and our conscious experiences of them—all devoted to analyzing the workings of the mind. It was Wundt's eminent student, Edward Titchener, who was primarily responsible for carrying this brand of psychology to America and who quite indirectly stimulated psychological studies of learning. It is important to understand that psychology started out as a science with a methodology mainly built upon the conscious analysis of mental contents. Though there were other important figures in the early development of the new science of psychology, most of them were likewise concerned with the workings of the mind and were especially concerned with how we sense and experience our world. But soon there developed competing ideas as to the nature of psychology, its subject matter, and the problems to which studies should be devoted.

SCIENTIFIC THEORY CONSTRUCTION
IN PSYCHOLOGY

Thus far, we have been describing the emergence of psychology as a science as though there were some relatively unanimous agreement as to how psychology might be established as a science. Nothing could be further from the truth. As a matter of fact, there has been a continuing series of debates as to how best to develop scientific theories in psychology generally, and especially as regards scientific theory about learning processes. Several different patterns have emerged, with some orientation more popular among psychologists at certain periods of history than at other times.

In Chapter 2 we noticed that psychologists have disagreed as to whether a deductive or an inductive approach is best in theory construction. In addition, there have been substantial disagreements as to the range which a theory should cover. It is this latter aspect which is of primary concern throughout the present chapter. In the present section, we will identify six different ways in which one might proceed once a finding has been obtained in a scientific study of learning processes. Then we will briefly explain that four of these approaches have been particularly popular among psychologists at certain points in history, although all six patterns can be identified among *some* researchers at any given point in history.

Throughout this text we will maintain the position that it is rare anywhere in science for isolated findings to be of more than passing interest, and that most research results prove to be of value mainly as they are related to other findings and organized into some form of theory. The reader well might raise questions as to how wide a range of phenomena should be incorporated in such a theory or synthesis of findings. Psychologists long have disagreed as to what constitutes the most desirable approach.

First, one might prefer only to relate the findings from a given study to those obtained with similar procedures in related studies. For example, in reading the research reports in most experimental psychology journals one typically finds the author referring to ten to fifteen other studies in the interpretation of his findings. If the research has been concerned with learning of verbal material, it is quite likely that the studies cited by the author will have been conducted with subjects of a similar age group who completed verbal learning tasks quite similar in nature to those of the particular study being reported. Thus, one degree or level of integrating findings from the study is to integrate them with *related* studies.

A second level of synthesis involves relating the findings of a given study to some *miniature model* which focuses on the particular process or sub-process of psychology studied. For example, there have been developed theories of verbal learning and theories of attention, as well as theories of short-term memory. If an author were reporting a study on short-term memory, he might choose to relate his findings—and even indicate that he proved his hypotheses—in accordance with a particular theory as to how humans store and retain verbal material for short periods up to thirty seconds in duration. Or the author of a verbal learning study might relate his findings to a theory which encompasses (only?) how humans learn nonsense syllables, meaningful words, and other verbal material. Although it is possible that the miniature model ultimately may be related to other miniature models or other more comprehensive theories, in fact there is a tendency simply to work at the level of the miniature model.

Third, other researchers have preferred to relate their findings to more comprehensive theories. The learning theories on which this book focuses are examples of some of the comprehensive learning theories which have been developed within psychology. Although there are differences in the range of coverage, there is some tendency to encompass all learning processes by humans and animals within one theoretical framework.

But psychologists are concerned with more than learning processes. A truly comprehensive theory of psychology at a minimum must account for the way that organisms perceive situations, how they learn to cope with demands of the situation, what motivation processes are involved, how they differ at developmental levels from infancy through old age, etc. There are two basic ways (number 4 and number 5 in our types of theory construction) in which psychologists have attempted to integrate all psychological processes within one theoretical framework. The fourth approach to theory construction was based on an initial expectation that there would be a single science of psychology. But different people had different ideas about how to develop a comprehensive science of psychology. Fifth, we will find that "schools" of psychology emerged, with each emphasizing a particular orientation in developing a competing comprehensive scientific theory of psychology. Thus, both approaches attempted to develop a single theoretical framework for all psychology. At one point in time, it was assumed that all were working toward the development of one psychology theory. At another point historically, there were *competing* efforts with each group attempting to formulate a comprehensive psychology theory.

Finally, a sixth approach to theoretical integration of research findings assumes that one should take into account all the behavioral or social sciences. That is, some have argued that we should develop "behavioral science theories" which encompass all of psychology plus sociology, anthropology, economics, etc.— for example, Talcott Parsons has outlined his recommendations for a general social science theory, and James G. Miller has proposed the development of a general system theory for the social sciences.

One can readily find evidence of all six approaches at almost any given point in history, starting in the late nineteenth century. But there are periods in which one of these approaches has been rather dominant in psychology theorizing. It is the general thesis of the present chapter that four basic periods can be identified. First, in the latter nineteenth century it was generally expected that there would emerge a single science of psychology. Second, in the first few decades of the twentieth century, "schools" of psychology emerged as competing comprehensive systems. Third, from 1930 to 1950, comprehensive learning theories had a dominant role in research and theory construction in psychology. Fourth, at mid-century psychology entered a fact-gathering phase and many psychologists adopted a miniature-model approach to theory construction.

We have already discussed the philosophical origins and the early emergence of psychology as a science. We will now consider the latter three eras of theory construction in psychology. But, it should again be emphasized that at any given point in time one can find instances of all six approaches to theory construction in the psychology of learning.

THE ERA OF "SCHOOLS" OF PSYCHOLOGY—
1900 TO 1930

Shortly after psychology emerged and developed an identity as a science in the latter part of the nineteenth century, different groups of early psychologists set forth *their* views as to the substance and methodology of this new science. It soon became evident that instead of *one* "new science of psychology" there were several competing conceptions. Partly following the nineteenth-century pattern in philosophy from which it had recently emerged, there developed a group of "systems" or "schools" of psychology like the then existing schools of philosophy.

Heidbreder (1933) describes the nature and scope of theorizing which was characteristic of these early psychologists in their formulation of their "systems of psychology":

Ideally and in its finished form a system of psychology is an envisagement of the total field of psychology as a consistent and unified whole. It assumes that the apparently chaotic particulars which lie within its domain can, if properly understood, be brought into order and clarity: that the subject-matter can be defined, a central problem stated, the methods of investigation agreed upon, the relations to other bodies of knowledge determined, the elements or basic processes identified, the distinctive features brought into relief, the general outline or characteristic movement indicated. To know a system is to know how it stands on all these matters, and especially to know the point of view from which it regards them. For the essential fact about a system of psychology is the position from which it surveys its field, the vantage-point from which it examines the concrete data of the science and from which it discerns a coherent pattern running through them and giving them unity. (Heidbreder, 1933, pp. 18-19)

Thus, we'll briefly consider major characteristics of five representative schools which are especially relevant to our study of learning theories and which essentially described American psychology in the first several decades of this century. We will consider the conceptions of psychology as advanced through structuralists, functionalists, behaviorists, gestalt psychology, and psychoanalysis.

Structuralism

Edward Titchener, an eminent student of Wundt, brought the Leipzig brand of psychology to America. At Cornell University he founded one of the first psychological laboratories in the United States. His brand of psychology came to be called *structuralism*, since he, like Wundt, was concerned with the analysis of consciousness into its elements, its "structure."

Titchener championed the cause of structuralism with such zeal that he personally and his brand of psychology dominated American psychology around the turn of the century. His positions on the nature, substance, and methodology were so strongly asserted that they both served to guide much of American psychology of that era and served as a "standard" against which many of the subsequent schools asserted themselves. One legend at Cornell University holds that Titchener gave his lectures in his Oxford Master's gown because he contended that it conferred the right to be dogmatic.

He identified psychology as a pure science, rather than an applied science, whose domain was the normal, adult human. As with Wundt, the main objective was to analyze and identify the contents of consciousness. The main means and standard of all methods of research was that of introspection, with great emphasis placed on training subjects to be keen and objective observers and reporters of their experiences. One fundamental assumption held that even complex states of consciousness are made up of elementary processes, and that different combinations of such basic elements ("mental atoms") go together to form such cognitive experiences as perception, imagination, emotion, and thought.

It was to be through the use of introspection as a scientific method of observation that the structuralists would be able to find and classify these mental atoms. To any naïve observer, a given situation would take the form of conscious experiences which include various interpretations as well as the fundamental mental atoms. At the core of any experience can be found some combination of three elements—sensations, images, and affections. Only through rigorous training and intensive concentration could the highly skilled experimental introspectionist identify these elements. For example, sensations would consist of the sounds, sights, and touch of objects we perceive in toto. Images, though perhaps related to sensations, are the elements of which ideas are composed; they would include the fleeting images of the changing present scene and the memories of previous experiences. Affections are those elements of which emotions are composed and are illustrated by the fragmented experiences of pain, pleasure, boredom, and curiosity which float through our consciousness in practically all situations. The job of the trained introspectionist was to catalog these fundamental elements of consciousness so systematically that they could be related to respective objectively identified situations and events.

Strongly held positions are highly prone to attack; structuralism, by being a strongly held position (almost a religion to its adherents), began to develop a group of critics. By being almost solely based on introspective analyses of mental contents, structuralism was readily subject to certain inherent shortcomings. The data from such analysis were supposedly objective and reliable observations, if the observer was trained correctly. In practice, this turned out to be as much of a hope as it was a reality and arguments inevitably broke out among laboratories.

Functionalism

One of the schools which emerged in reaction to structuralism came to be known as functionalism. Although the original intent was to broaden the conception of psychology as science, it was practically forced into existence as a competing school by Titchener when he attempted to "excommunicate" functionalism's founders from psychology. John Dewey is generally acknowledged as the "founder" of functionalism, although James Angell, Harvey Carr, and other contemporaries were also active influential leaders in this movement.

As the name implies, the functionalists were primarily interested in the activities of humans not merely in terms of the elements of mental experience but mainly in the functions they serve in aiding the individual to adapt to and cope with its environment. The functionalists broadened psychology's domain to include all human and animal activities. They accepted introspection as one method of research but they also emphasized the need for controlled objective observations as well. They were greatly influenced by Darwin's notions that members of a species survive and produce offspring because of their success in coping with changing demands of their environment. Thus it was easy to lay the groundwork for the notion in psychology that changes in behavior (that is, learning) might also be understood in terms of their degree of success in the organism's various attempts to cope with its environment. Thus those activities which remain might be interpreted as having served a useful function in coping with the changing characteristics of the environment.

Two other aspects of functionalism are especially relevant to our present concern, both of which derive from the conception of an organism in dynamic interaction with its environment. First, common-sense notions were not rejected categorically but instead were considered in light of emerging scientific information. Thus the growing fund of scientific information was depicted as closely related to the world outside the psychologist's laboratory. Second, there was no sharp distinction between pure psychology and applied psychology. This also follows from the notion that behaviors and experiences of an individual cannot be completely separated from the purposes and consequences of such activities. The distinction between pure and applied research would depend mainly on the reasons one had for conducting such studies, rather than on their being somehow inherently different.

The latter interest in applied problems, including educational issues, probably developed partly because functionalism emerged as a school at a time when psychologists in this country were being asked to assist in resolution of social problems. But Dewey's personal influence should not be underestimated. Primarily a philosopher, with some earlier training as a psychologist, Dewey subsequently was to become one of the leading educators of his time. It is of interest to note in passing that for some unknown reason Dewey subsequently influenced educators to adopt gestalt learning theories rather than the principles which came from functionalism. We will consider this matter later when we examine the various relationships between learning theories and educational practice.

Behaviorism

Another important reaction against structuralism led to the formation of *behaviorism*, a school largely under the initial influence of John B. Watson. Watson approved of the reactions of the functionalists, but he felt that they had not departed sufficiently from the structuralists either in the substance or in the methods of psychology. Behavior, not consciousness or mind, should be the subject matter of the new psychology. Psychology should be broad enough to cover the behaviors of all living organisms, not just normal adult humans as suggested by the structuralists. Moreover, the introspective method was denounced as being so subjective that it could have *no* place in the objective science of psychology. Relying heavily on the *reflex* concept from neurology, Watson advocated development of a science of psychology which studied the organism's responses to stimuli. Hence, the "S-R" (stimulus-response) formula came to be used as the main paradigm, the cornerstone and main building block for the new science of psychology. All complex events, including so-called "mental experiences" and (in today's terms) cognitive activities, would be understood by identifying the basic elements of behavior. Thus, parallel to the structuralists' "mental atoms" which make up conscious experience, Watson advocated identification of the reflex-like stimulus-response units which make up simple and complex behaviors.

One point is especially important with regard to our study of learning processes. The functionalists had advocated a concern with the organism's adaptation to its environment. They laid a basis for studying learning processes since it was theorized that largely *through learning* an organism would develop more and more effective means for coping with the changing characteristics of its environment. Watson took this conception one step further by arguing that, though some of the basis for our behavior might be inherited, most animal and human behavior could be accounted for as a result of learning. One of Watson's boasts with which many educators are familiar is his contention that learning is so important that he could take virtually any infant and provide the kind of experiences which would enable that child to grow into whatever kind of adult was desired—lawyer, mechanic, criminal, etc.

There are several aspects of these reactions by the functionalists and the behaviorists against the structuralists which relate to the psychology of learning. First, learning became a more central issue and soon dominated experimental psychology as an area of study. Secondly, greater rigor and objectivity was demanded in psychological experimentation as the direct result of this new interest in objective studies of behavior. Third, drawing heavily from the then acceptable reflex concept in neurology, the stimulus response (S-R) unit was adopted as the basic unit to study both simple and complex behavior and as the orientation to be adopted in developing large-scale psychology theories. Moreover, psychology adopted a pattern which had already been accepted by other sciences in assigning greatest credibility to that kind of research which involves careful observation under highly controlled laboratory conditions. By this time, all the groundwork was laid to study both practical and theoretical problems in the confines of the controlled experimental laboratory situation. Although the debate would continue for years concerning the relative importance of heredity versus environment, the focus had shifted from the study of "the mind" to the study of behavior with special emphasis on learning processes.

Gestalt Psychology

But even while these schools and these trends were becoming established in the United States, developing in Europe was a reaction against the "reductionism" in science. Philosophers and scientists in various areas were raising great objections to the undue emphasis, in their opinion, on the study of complex phenomena by *reducing* them to their smallest common element. With regard to psychology, leadership came from three German psychologists—Max Wertheimer, Wolfgang Kohler, and Kurt Koffka. Kurt Lewin was a fourth influential leader associated with the gestalt school.

Gestalt psychology, as the school was to become known, got its start in research on perception. Wertheimer conducted a series of studies such as the following: (1) When a subject is presented two straight lines, not too far apart, and the lines are alternately exposed, the subject reports seeing not two lines but one line moving back and forth (named the "phi phenomenon"). (2) Subjects routinely describe windows as being rectangular in shape when viewed from various angles, despite the fact that the image actually striking the retina (that is, the physical basis for the sensation) takes many forms of quadrilateral shapes, only on rare occasions actually conforming to the shape of a rectangle. (3) A scattering of dots on a surface are perceived not as individual isolated spots but as parts of patterns or configurations, depending upon (among other things) their proximity and the shape which the combinations of dots can form.

The essential point made by the gestalt psychologists was *that the whole is not merely the sum of the parts*. Thus, they held that psychology and other sciences were wrong in emphasizing "basic, fundamental elements" as the central problem for study. Rather, they contended that it was the organization, or patterning, which should be the central emphasis for psychology. As most readers are aware, the word "gestalt" was brought from the German language into the English language because there is no direct translation possible in English words. The term roughly refers to patterning, shape, configuration, or forms which are involved in the totality of one's experiences of a situation.

The gestalt psychologists took issue with the behaviorists and the structuralists because both were attempting to reduce the complex activities to common, simple elements. They agreed with the structuralists that psychology should be the study of experience. However, instead of using "trained introspectionists," they advocated the use of relatively "naïve" observers who could report their perceptions in toto rather than in terms of some "atoms of consciousness."

In the heredity-environment debate which continued for many years during this era, the gestalt psychologists took the position that most of what one can do is a function of heredity. The behaviorists, as we have already noted, took the position that what one does is a function of learning. Whereas the behaviorists contended that learning could be studied in stimulus-response units, the gestalt psychologists held that complex cognitive activities must be studied in toto. Thus most of their subsequent studies on learning consisted of problem solving, and they contended that learning should be considered as a form of problem solving and thinking rather than vice versa. The last point is particularly interesting today because, as we will see in a later chapter, certain contemporary psychologists ("information processing theorists") also contend that learning can best be understood as part of problem-solving processes.

Psychoanalysis

The final school which we will consider is different in several ways from the others and, according to some psychologists, has never been incorporated clearly as a part of academic general psychology. Most of the schools which developed during this era, including all those enumerated above, were developed in conjunction with laboratory research with a major or even total commitment to "pure science" findings. Sigmund Freud founded his position in conjunction with his medical practice. Although psychoanalysis has had indirect rather than direct contact with the psychology of learning and the practice of education, it has had sufficient impact on psychology as science and as profession that our review of systems during this era would be incomplete without at least acknowledging its existence and many contributions.

First, it should be recognized that *psychoanalysis* is a term which refers both to a body of theory and to a method of treatment. Freud, a very creative physician-psychiatrist-neurologist, originally established psychoanalysis as a method of treatment for certain psychiatric disorders. Because of the nature of his medical training, he was much more familiar with case-study methods (a research procedure in which hypotheses are generated and tested primarily by following the progress of individual patients) than with the more usual experimental methods of scientific psychology. He developed a set of procedures for treating patients, but he also developed a theory because he was interested in understanding the underlying problems and the explanations as to why his methods work. The theory is typically considered to be primarily concerned with psychiatry and abnormal psychology, but it is also acknowledged as being the first truly comprehensive personality theory and as constituting one of the earliest theories of motivation in psychology.

Although Freud's conception of psychoanalysis was not directly concerned with learning processes or with education per se, there are a number of direct and indirect ways in which psychoanalysis has influenced the evolving learning theory and instructional theory. For example, he called attention to the fact that many of our adult personality characteristics have their origins in childhood experiences. He observed that changes of all kinds, including informal learning and education, may provoke considerable anxiety and generally may constitute a more difficult experience than may be obvious to the casual observer. Freud also called the attention of psychologists, and the general population as well, to the fact that despite man's rational behavior, man does many things for reasons of which he is not fully aware. Freud popularized the concept of the "the unconscious" as a major determinant of man's behaviors. He also developed the thesis that change of any kind—including learning—tends to precipitate some anxiety for the individual. Thus it follows that a person may not react to learning situations passively but, instead, may even resist such changes. We will consider some of these implications when we deal with comprehensive learning theories later in this chapter. For now it is sufficient to recognize that this was one of the positions of influence which developed during the era of schools in psychology.

The Schools in Retrospect

It is now apparent that the schools of psychology were influential in guiding and stimulating research during the first few decades of this century. Many call attention to the debates which raged during this time and they contend that much of the ensuing research was not productive in building a scientific fund of knowledge in psychology. But others take a more positive point of view; they note that many of the facts of psychology which have been supported even down to the present time have been accumulated largely as a result of the existence of these schools.

But whatever their contributions, it is apparent that schools were losing their dominant influence in psychology by the 1930s. In their place developed programs of research focused around central processes of psychology—such as learning, motivation, and perception—and the theorizing processes were likewise developed around these basic processes of psychology. Thus it was in this context that theories of learning emerged as dominant influences on research and on theoretical integration. Of course in our necessarily simplified coverage of the history of theorizing in psychology it is important that readers recognize that there was no neat and clear change of patterns in theorizing. Actually some of the seminal studies for these emerging comprehensive learning theories had been conducted and principles developed in the late nineteenth and early twentieth centuries. But it was especially in the 1930s and 1940s that the comprehensive learning theories were dominant forces in psychology.

As a result of developments during the schools of psychology era, several patterns were established: (1) There was fairly universal agreement that psychology should be based on experimentation; (2) The tide was beginning to turn away from introspection as a method and the mind as the main focus, with new trends emphasizing objective experimentation and observations of behavior as the main focus of psychology; (3) Partly as a function of the influence of behaviorism and functionalism, learning processes took a central role in experimental psychology; (4) Although some maintained their interest in studies of complex cognitive processes (for example, the gestalt group), the stage was set for a stimulus-response analysis of behavior. The expectation was that, if psychologists could understand the more fundamental and simpler forms of learning, they would then be able to construct valid explanations of complex learning processes as well; and (5) Perhaps because of the considerable controversy about the nature of psychology as science, most of the ensuing research on learning processes was conducted as "basic science" ventures rather than as applied studies with a direct intention to deal with practical patterns in education and elsewhere in psychology.

We will now consider the next phase of theorizing in psychology, the comprehensive learning theories which were especially important in psychology in the 1930s and 1940s, with some continuing their influence up to the present time.

THE ERA OF COMPREHENSIVE LEARNING
THEORIES: 1930 TO 1950

As we have already noted, the groundwork for learning theories was established within the first two decades of the twentieth century. However, you will recall that it was also during this era that the dominating theme in psychology theory construction was that one should develop a total psychology system or school. It was around the early 1930s that psychology theorists accepted a somewhat more circumscribed area for consideration in their theory construction, and that learning processes came to have a dominant influence in psychology theory construction more generally.

A paper presented by Clark L. Hull to the American Association for the Advancement of Science in 1934 is especially appropriate for our consideration here. Hull's (1935) paper was entitled "The Conflicting Psychologies of Learning—A Way Out." Hull's ideas about science and about how psychologists might best develop comprehensive learning theories dominated much of the research and theoretical activity in the era from 1930 to 1950.

He first acknowledged the existence of the many competing systems or schools of psychology, some of which we discussed in the previous section of this chapter. He then went on to point out that he was pessimistic as to whether sheer argument and debate would enable clarification as to which orientation or orientations would produce the most valid descriptions of psychological processes. Moreover, he referred to the emergence of interest in theories about learning processes and he made few distinctions between psychology theories in toto versus psychology learning theories. It seems that he recognized that psychology was in the midst of moving from the wider, more comprehensive theories to somewhat narrower learning theories. But he did not feel that narrowing the focus of psychology's theoretical efforts would result in development of sound, scientific learning theories. He proposed that psychology must embark on a more systematic approach to data collection and theory construction if the then current debates about competing psychologies were to be resolved. In brief, his approach—which is usually depicted as a "hypothetical-deductive approach"—is one form of the deductive theory construction which we discussed earlier in this text. It consists mainly of developing postulates and assumptions about the general framework of the theory and the further logical development of more specific aspects of the theory. Then one conducts critical experiments to determine whether the resulting deduced principles fit with empirical data.

Hull had two main influences on subsequent theorizing about learning processes. First, many of the comprehensive learning theories were greatly influenced by his notions about theory construction despite the fact that they did not follow his recommendations to the letter. During this era, most psychologists felt that they should first develop theory-oriented hypotheses and then test them empirically. Secondly, Hull's adaptations of Thorndike's and Pavlov's positions were of considerable influence on the kinds of studies which were conducted by psychologists during this period.

The period from 1930 to 1950 has been designated as the "era of comprehensive learning theories" because competition among the comprehensive learning theories of this period greatly influenced the kinds of research which were conducted on learning processes and to a great extent dominated theory construction in psychology more generally. In this section we will consider some of the research paradigms and main emphases of these comprehensive learning theories. The main purpose of this section is to provide an overview of the theories as they emerged and of some of the debates which influenced research activities and theory construction during this period.

Some General Types of Theories

At some risk of oversimplification, one can divide learning theories into two major groups—namely, stimulus-response or conditioning theories, and cognitive theories. Of course, it is important to recognize that these are quite gross categories in that at times there have been greater differences within these two general groups than there have been between some pairs of theories across these two groups. Nonetheless, it would be useful for our purposes here to recognize some of the main characteristics of these two general orientations about learning processes.

Stimulus-Response or Conditioning Theories   The stimulus-response or conditioning theories typically have emphasized objective analyses of behavior as a means for deriving learning theories, and they usually have accepted the assumption that one can understand complex learning processes best after one has gained at least a fundamental understanding of the simpler learning processes. This assumption carries with it the expectation that understanding such simple processes can be accomplished more readily and that the findings and theories which result will have implications for explanations about more complex learning processes. There is a distinct tendency for conditioning theorists to characterize psychology as a natural science and to emphasize that psychology's task is to search for lawfulness of the organism's behavior in the context of a specified situation. This has led some critics to contend (erroneously, in the author's opinion) that the resulting theory must characterize man's learning as excessively mechanistic and automatic. It is beyond the scope of the present book to discuss this issue in great detail, but it is noteworthy that stimulus-response theorists have objected to such criticism and have contended that there is nothing "mechanistic" implied in a search for order in nature.

Conditioning theories of learning have dominated much of the research and theory construction about learning processes and have attained such visibility within academic psychology that many would equate the term *learning theory* with some form of conditioning conceptualization. There are two main traditions from which most conditioning learning theories have been derived. One is generally referred to as *instrumental conditioning* and is derived from the work of Edward L. Thorndike. In brief, the central assertion is that behavior is controlled by its consequences and that we learn to do that which produces pleasant effects and to avoid that which has unpleasant effects. The other major conditioning tradition is generally called *classical conditioning* and is derived primarily from the work of Ivan P. Pavlov. Briefly, this theory depicts the stimuli in the situation as prodding the organism into action. Previously "neutral" stimuli acquire their ability to control behavior and thus cause learning as a result of being paired with a stimulus which already has the capability of eliciting such a response. Most conditioning learning theories emphasize classical or instrumental conditioning, modify one of these two approaches, or provide some combination of these two orientations in developing a hybrid theory.

Cognitive Theories Cognitive theories of learning primarily emphasize complex intellectual processes such as thinking, language, and problem solving as major aspects of the learning process. It has often been said that one can more readily identify what cognitive theories are *against* than what they are for. They are especially critical of learning theories which primarily emphasize simple learning processes as the basis from which one can derive explanations of more complex learning processes. In many respects, they attempt to describe learning as experienced by the learner himself and thus they set for themselves the objective of understanding "experience." Instead of looking for some kind of basic element—such as the reflex in behaviorism and the "mental atom" of the structuralists—they contend that primary emphasis should be placed on how one organizes one's experiences of a situation and the ways in which one learns alternative or more appropriate kinds of organizing experiences. In brief, cognitive theorists contend that humans learn cognitive structures or understanding rather than movements and that the behaviorists are merely looking at the results of learning (rather than the process of learning) when they focus on behavior per se.

Throughout most of the first half of this century the cognitive learning theories served mainly as a corrective factor and as constructive critics of the stimulus-response and conditioning theory formulations. However, there were some attempts to develop comprehensive theories of learning within the cognitive tradition. One of the earliest was the result of work by Wertheimer, Koffka, and Kohler, who are routinely identified as the "classical gestalt group." But one of the more visible ventures in the cognitive tradition was launched by Tolman, especially with *Purposive Behavior in Animals and Men* (1932). It is especially relevant for the present book for two reasons. First, it was a cognitive theory which was avowedly behavioristic and was developed alongside the stimulus-response formulations enumerated above. Secondly, it was at the center of the debates which were conducted in the 1930s and 1940s as to the best way for constructing comprehensive theories of learning.

Illustrative Emphases of Comprehensive Learning Theories

Thus it was especially in the 1930s and 1940s that several major learning theories became prominent in psychology, each of whose proponents had explicit or implicit expectations for that position as the one most likely to provide a comprehensive learning theory. Much of the learning research and many of the debates about theory centered around these theories and stemmed from debates among them. We will briefly consider some examples of the comprehensive learning theories which dominated data collection and theory construction during the 1930s and 1940s. The selection of theories is merely to illustrate representative positions rather than to provide an exhaustive account.

Thorndike's Connectionism

Edward L. Thorndike (1874-1949) was perhaps the most influential of all psychologists on learning research and theory construction during the first several decades of this century. Given the nature of this textbook, it is also noteworthy that Thorndike simultaneously was of tremendous influence in the newly developing field of educational psychology. He wrote over 500 books, papers, and monographs on a variety of basic and applied psychology topics. Although he frequently was concerned with practical classroom learning problems, he typically dealt with each matter on its own terms rather than systematically applying his learning principles per se.

His doctoral dissertation research, which was published as a monograph (1898) entitled *Animal Intelligence: An Experimental Study of the Associative Processes in Animals,* and his subsequent studies are widely credited with launching psychology research on learning processes. But one cannot appreciate the significance of his contributions unless one considers the context in which his work was initiated.

Thorndike began his work at a time when psychology was defined in more mentalistic terms as compared with the behaviorally oriented definitions of today. His teachers and his contemporaries were in the midst of evolving appropriate research procedures. His observations about then current conceptions of psychology are illustrated by some of his comments in a paper describing Darwin's contributions to psychology: "Psychology, as you all know, means the science of mental, as opposed to physical, facts—the study of thoughts and feelings, as opposed to physical objects" (Thorndike, 1909, p. 65). Thorndike believed that it should be possible to conduct research in rigorous fashion, and he contended that psychology must be more empirical than speculative. His biographer, Joncich (1962), has summarized Thorndike's views: "Psychology no longer needed to be a branch of philosophy; it could become a rigorous science, adopting the appropriate methods of the physical sciences and worthy of the credentials of objectivity and verifiability" (p. 2).

Thorndike was particularly interested in studying how man and animals learn, by which he referred to the changes in behavior which enable them to adapt to and to cope with their environment. It had been customary during the nineteenth century to believe that not only human behavior but animal behavior as well was mediated by ideas. For example, it was assumed that both man and animals act purposefully in situations after having considered each of their alternative activities. But these beliefs were almost entirely based on quite casual observations and general anecdotal reports.

Thorndike believed that it must be possible to develop more rigorous research procedures for studying learning processes more systematically. Largely as a result of practical considerations, his doctoral dissertation research and many early studies used animal subjects. These studies produced the data from which he evolved most of his initial learning principles. Typically he placed his subjects individually in problem situations from which they could escape and he observed their behavior under different experimental arrangements. He concluded from his data that his subjects had not "thought through" their problem solutions but that they had engaged in a series of "trial and error" attempts until they chanced upon successful solutions. Thereafter they gradually refined their solutions in light of previous successes and failures.

He theorized that successful acts were strengthened by virtue of their having been followed by pleasurable effects. He later referred to learning as the strengthening and weakening of "bonds" or "connections" between situations and how one acts there. The cornerstone principle in his theory, the *law of effect*, holds that behavior is primarily influenced by its effects, so that those acts which are followed by satisfaction are increased (the connection between that situation and that act is strengthened). Thus Thorndike drew from the hedonistic and associationistic traditions described earlier. He theorized that "satisfying" *effects strengthen connections* between a situation and how one acts there. Early formulations of his theory held that "annoyers" or unsatisfactory effects weaken such connections, although he later theorized that annoyers do not have important influences on connections.

In various papers he professed some interest in developing a comprehensive theory of learning. However, what he ultimately produced was more a collection of principles than a formalized theory. Instead of having a neatly organized set of syntactically sound statements, the particular principles he formulated more often than not arose because of the specific practical or theoretical questions which he had encountered and which had stimulated research on the matter.

But the impact of Thorndike's initial work and subsequent revisions of the connectionism learning theory was so great that for decades thereafter psychologists routinely indicated ways in which they agreed or disagreed with Thornike whenever they presented papers on learning. It is a curious fact of history that Thorndike was subjected to criticism both by the more globally oriented, cognitive theorists who felt that he was reducing man to a mechanistic form and by the budding behaviorism supporters who contended that he was too subjective and mentalistic in his conceptions.

Nonetheless, Thorndike did start experimental psychologists in the systematic study of animal and human learning. Moreover, the kinds of learning research which subsequently were conducted to a great extent stemmed from or were drawn in reaction to his initial conceptions of learning processes.

Pavlov's Classical Conditioning

Around the same time in the latter nineteenth century that Thorndike was conducting his learning studies in the United States, a Russian physiologist by the name of Ivan P. Pavlov (1849-1936) made a serendipitous finding which caused him to make a major change in his career even after having won the Nobel Prize for his work in physiology. He had been conducting work on the digestive system. His work essentially consisted of "sham feeding," in which food is placed on the tongue of an animal to stimulate salivary flow while various physiological processes are observed. The discovery, stated simply, consisted of the observation that animals frequently started salivating when the experimenter came into the room, but before any food was placed on the tongue. Pavlov initially dubbed these "psychic reflexes," following the pattern in which he had been studying physiological reflex activity when the food was actually placed on the tongue of the animal. He became so enthused about the prospects of this serendipitous finding that he changed his laboratory focus to explore the phenomena and he even discussed this new work in the speech which he gave at the acceptance of the Nobel Prize. He characterized his work as "the first sure steps along the path of a new investigation," in which he contended that he would use the method of the conditioned reflex (or, conditional reflex) to study the functions of the cerebral cortex.

Not at all surprisingly, Pavlov contended that he was actually studying an aspect of physiology rather than some form of the newly emerging science of psychology. But the nature of his work and his impact on psychology is such that most historians consider it as a new venture in psychology and a major focus of research on learning processes. This is consistent with Pavlov's aims if we recognize that he expected to study and to understand the nature of behavior of an animal in rather precise physiological terms, and that he felt that even very complex activities of animals and man should be understood within the context of his paradigm.

Pavlov's theory and research plan focused around a simple theme, which can be described as *stimulus substitution* and which is at the core of all his research procedures and theoretical principles. In brief, this principle holds that if one stimulus can elicit a given response, the mere pairing of it with a neutral stimulus results in the neutral stimulus also becoming capable of eliciting that response. It was Pavlov's fundamental assumption that all nervous activity and brain-behavior relationships could be understood in terms of *reflex activity*.

Stated simply, a reflex consists of a stimulus applied to an organism which evokes or elicits, involuntarily, a specific response. Most readers are familiar with the notion of a reflex, which frequently is illustrated by a tap to the forepart of the knee, the patellar tendon, which immediately results in a contraction of the leg throwing the foot forward abruptly. Though he recognized that the reflex does not exist in isolation from the rest of the workings of the nervous system, Pavlov considered this a useful concept with which to build a theory of physiology and of psychology.

He distinguished between two types of reflexes—unconditioned and conditioned. By an unconditioned reflex, Pavlov referred to a definite inborn capacity of the organism to respond in a specific way to an internal or external stimulus. Such unconditioned reflexes occur with appropriate physiological maturation of the organism with virtually no influence of experiences (that is, no need for learning) although, of course, it is recognized that the conditions of the organism and the various experiences of the organism might influence how the unconditioned reflex occurs under various circumstances. In contrast, the conditioned reflex comes about during life as a result of some kind of experience of the organism. More specifically, Pavlov proposed that his dogs were "learning" to respond to the presence of the experimenter in the room because of the association which was established between "sight of the experimenter" and "food on the tongue."

Pavlov was particularly critical of any kind of subjective psychology which would suggest something less than rigorous scientific pursuit. He did not deny the right of psychologists to be concerned with "mental activity," but he did strongly feel that such study should be conducted with rigorous experimental control and with adequate provisions to assure objective observations. Following the tradition of many scientists in various areas, he felt that complex phenomena could best be understood if they were identified in terms of their most fundamental, their most elementary processes. His fundamental process in learning was that of conditioned and unconditioned reflexes. If one were able to understand the conditions under which such simple forms of learning occur, one could then go on to grasp the workings of the mind in all its complicated activities. It is important to recognize that he saw this paradigm of classical conditioning as applicable not only to the salivation of dogs (to food and to sight of the experimenter), nor even to simple processes alone; rather, he saw it as a fundamental conceptual device by which one could understand *all* forms of complex learning and behavior by humans.

Readers who are primarily concerned with complex intellectual changes involved in classroom learning quite appropriately may raise questions as to how Pavlov's studies with dogs producing saliva might have any relevance. Three aspects should be considered. First, Pavlov strongly felt that one should not lose sight of the fact that the investigator in natural sciences merely exposes nature to his view, and that he does not declare how natural (in this case, psychological) processes *should* operate. Secondly, it was his contention that one can best discover the nature of complex learning processes by understanding first the most elementary forms of such processes. He considered the conditioned reflex to be a fundamental cortical reaction, and he viewed it as the most basic learning process. Third, he visualized at least two ways in which the simple conditioned reflex could be extended to complex learning processes. A number of simple conditioned reflexes could be arranged sequentially in "chains" of stimulus-response associations to form more complex learning processes. Or, the concept of a conditioned reflex could be used with words or speech (which Pavlov called the "second signal system") as well as with physical stimuli (the "primary signal system"). In this second extension, words are associated with other words through recognition of their meanings and the appropriate responses for them, similar to the ways that Pavlov's dogs associated the salivating response with auditory and visual stimuli.

Guthrie's One-Trial Contiguity Conditioning

One of the several positions advanced in the 1930s which drew at least partly from the work of Thorndike and Pavlov was the approach to learning formulated by Edwin R. Guthrie (1886-1959). Guthrie's work is especially relevant and important in our review of learning theories because it proposed the "nonreinforcement" conception of learning, because it provided some of the initial notions from which later theorists were to derive a "stimulus-sampling" conception of learning processes, and because it was one of the first theories which raised questions as to whether learning occurred gradually or whether it involved some "all at once" phenomenon.

Guthrie was coauthor of one of the first general practice books which made extensive use of Pavlov's conditioning concept (Smith & Guthrie, 1921), although he and Smith broadened Pavlov's concept to be a stimulus-response relationship rather than the more narrowly defined reflex referred to by Pavlov. It is reasonably accurate to say that Guthrie's theory used much of the terminology and some of the fundamental thinking of Pavlov, but that Guthrie did not feel obligated to utilize many of Pavlov's basic conceptions in formulating his own learning principles.

Like both Thorndike and Pavlov, Guthrie enthusiastically endorsed the notion that psychology should be an objective science. But he was far less interested than either Thorndike or Pavlov in describing the physiological detail of psychological processes. He acknowledged the fact that psychological phenomena do have physical and physiological correlates but he argued that psychology should stand on its own as a science and that the terms thus should be psychological in nature. He held that the psychologist should be primarily concerned about how learning occurs (the process of learning) rather than merely what it accomplishes (the products of learning). In that regard, he was especially critical of Thorndike's law of effect in that he contended that it focuses on the product rather than on the process of learning. In a similar vein, he noted that more abstract principles of learning must be derived explicitly from observations of what an individual does under specified conditions. Thus, throughout his learning principles, one finds references to the *movement* of the organism as an essential focus for the study of learning processes.

In place of a reinforcement explanation, Guthrie asserted that the occurrence of a response in a stimulus context would be adequate for that stimulus to gain control over the response which occurred there. "A combination of stimuli which has accompanied a movement will, on its recurrence, tend to be followed by that movement" (Guthrie, 1935, p. 26).

As a result of his concern with process, Guthrie concluded that learning involves an all-or-none status, in which learning occurs full-strength on a trial, rather than involving some kind of strengthening as a result of practice. Thus, the stimulus pattern, or at least some aspects of the stimulus pattern, gains full associative control over the particular responses at full strength on the first occasion that the response occurs in the presence of those stimuli. "A stimulus pattern gains its full associative strength on the occasion of its first pairing with a response" (Guthrie, 1942, p. 30). In brief, Guthrie criticized other psychologists as having ignored the process of learning. He suggested that instead of one simple stimulus and one simple response there were actually many sub-stimuli and many sub-responses which could be associated. Thus, what really happens, as a result of "practice," is that more aspects of the stimulus situation are noted by the organism and are associated with more aspects of the response involved. He asserted that the notion that practice leads to the strengthening of a connection simply stems from too gross an observation of the process. More microscopic analyses, he contended, would lead to the conclusion that there are many associations being formed and that these occur full strength when responses are made in the presence of stimuli which are noted by the subject.

It is this latter aspect of Guthrie's one-trial conditioning which has been picked up by contemporary learning theorists. In a sense, Guthrie laid the groundwork for conceptualizing learning processes as involving a variety of stimuli and a variety of responses. More recent theorists (for example, Estes and other mathematical learning theorists) have expanded on Guthrie's notion and have conceptualized learning process in a given situation as associations between samples of stimuli and samples of responses.

Hull's Hypothetico-Deductive Drive-Stimulus-Reduction Theory

Clark L. Hull (1884-1952) is the learning theorist whose ideas were of greatest influence on learning research and theorizing in the 1930s and 1940s. One of his most important theoretical books was presented in

1943, *Principles of Behavior.* Here Hull emphasized that science has two equally important and generally inseparable components—the empirical or fact-gathering phase and the theoretical or synthesizing phase. He held that the most appropriate and effective way for building a science is to formulate a set of basic assumptions which are adequate to account for the fundamental aspects of behavior and to derive logically any principles from these fundamental assumptions for continuing empirical testing and modification of the theory. The logical derivations must be sound. The validity of the theory ultimately can be determined directly or indirectly as one deduces the researchable questions based on the assumptions and principles. Hull contended that the theory could be "self-corrective" since the theorist presumably would modify his fundamental assumptions and derive principles in light of the empirical evidence. He argued that one must avoid "pussyfooting" statements and should not hide behind "weasel" words; instead, one's theoretical statements should be presented precisely and in a form which would permit testing and correcting.

Hull was concerned with formulating a total system or theory of behavior, and thus resembles some of the proponents of the earlier "schools" of psychology. But he saw learning processes as being so central and fundamental that he used his conceptions of learning as a major point of departure in formulating his more general theory of behavior. He characterized heredity as responsible for initial stimulus-response relationships, but he held that the individual organism's ability to adapt to its environment depends on the modification of such stimulus-response associations in light of its successes in coping with its environment. Thus learning was visualized as one of the most fundamental processes in psychology.

At least by 1930 Hull was convinced that psychology should clearly be considered to be a true natural science in that it was ready for a form of hypothetico-deductive theory construction. He took the position that psychology would best proceed if a minimum number of assumptions were first set forth outlining the range of phenomena to be dealt with by psychology as a science; that primary laws could be developed with a moderate number of mathematical equations; and that explanations of even complex phenomena could be derived from these primary laws. Like most other stimulus-response and conditioning theorists, Hull took the position that complex forms of learning could *best* be understood in light of the fundamental stimulus-response relationships of which they are composed.

He initially considered Pavlov's theory to be of primary importance as a fundamental basis for learning, but he later adopted the Thorndikian position to the extent that he characterized Pavlov's classical conditioning as a special case of Thorndike's law of effect. One of Hull's major contributions in his theory was that he tried to show how this law operates. He theorized that effects of responses influence subsequent behavior when attainment of the goal objects cause gratification and reduction in the motivating drives of that organism. These motivating drives were depicted as stemming from unmet tissue needs (need for food, water, air, etc.), from need to avoid or escape uncomfortable conditions (pain, excessive pressure, etc.), or from effects of stimuli somehow associated with these deprivation or aversive conditions. Because he subsequently focused on the internal experiences associated with such drives, his theory frequently is identified as a "drive-stimulus-reduction" theory.

He depicted learning as occurring practically automatically when an organism interacts with its environment. "Just as the inherited equipment of reaction tendencies consists of receptor-effector connections, so the process of learning consists in the strengthening of certain of these connections as contrasted with others, or in the setting up of quite new connections" (Hull, 1943, pp. 68-69). One need refer only to the stimuli present in the situation, the internal motivating drives and other internal states, previously learned "habits" or associations, and the organism's "equipment of action tendencies at that moment." He deplored any reference to a "mind" which might be described as monitoring the process; instead, he contended that a true science must be objective rather than subjective in nature, and that even internal states of the organism must be related to observable stimuli and responses. How one acts in any subsequent situation depends upon one's response capabilities, stimulus sensitivities, habits or associations previously established, and the stimuli prevailing in that situation.

But despite his consistent emphasis on observable phenomena, it is pertinent to note his great concern with the internal states of the organism. As a result, some authors have identified his theory as "S-O-R" rather than merely "S-R." The additional "O" refers to "organism" and indicates that an individual's behavior cannot be predicted simply on the basis of the prevailing stimulus conditions. Actually, much of Hull's theory consisted of attempts to describe these different kinds of internal states of the organism and to relate the states to overtly observable stimulus and response characteristics.

He depicted learning as essentially involving "habit formation," although he used habit in a broad sense. He theorized that some minimal amount of reinforcement is necessary to increase habit strength; that is, for an association to be formed between stimuli and responses. Additional amounts of reinforcement would affect the performance of the individual but would not necessarily cause greater habit strength (that is, would affect behavior but not learning).

Skinner's Operant Conditioning

Like Hull, B. F. Skinner (1904-   ) was greatly influenced by Pavlov's and Thorndike's work. However, Skinner differed from Hull both on his preferred approach to theory construction and on a number of substantive issues. These similarities and differences are noteworthy not only because of their relevance to the era of comprehensive learning theories but also because of their implications for contemporary learning research and theory. Whereas Hull's influence seems to have diminished by 1950, Skinner's impact on basic and applied psychology has been increasing.

Skinner has long and enthusiastically endorsed an inductive approach to theory construction. Even many otherwise knowledgeable psychologists have misunderstood his orientation and have depicted him as a "Grand Anti-Theorist" (Skinner, 1969). This misunderstanding largely has resulted from his many criticisms of a hypothetico-deductive approach because, he contends, it frequently leads to *premature* and *misleading* theorizing. To avoid the wasted time and effort which can result from premature erroneous theorizing, Skinner argues that one should stay close to one's data (that is, avoid prolonged interpretations) and follow an inductive approach to theory construction. Although he acknowledges that one must start with some ideas to investigate a problem, he argues that best results will be obtained if one's research efforts are guided primarily by the empirical evidence obtained rather than by preconceived conceptions and expectations.

In addition, he is quite critical of reliance on *statistical* summaries of a group of subjects. Noting that there is no "average" person or animal, he contends that the only sound approach is through experimental manipulation of conditions and observations of changes in *each* subject's behavior. Thus he has pioneered in the development of basic and applied research procedures whereby *single* subjects are studied under carefully controlled conditions with selected variables manipulated experimentally. He credits Pavlov with having shown the way whereby one can find *orderliness* or *lawfulness* in nature if one controls conditions and carefully observes the behavior of the subject. He has expressed reservations about many theoretical statements because they have been based on the statistical averages of a number of subjects. Instead of such short periods of observations of *many* subjects, Skinner favors prolonged and careful study of *each* organism until the experimenter can reliably identify lawful relationships between the experimental conditions and the subject's behavior.

Skinner has acknowledged the existence of the classical conditioning learning process studied by Pavlov, but he has contended that it is Thorndike's law of effect which typifies the kinds of learning which are of greatest importance in real-life situations. Thus, unlike Hull who considered Pavlovian classical conditioning to be a special case of the law of effect, Skinner acknowledges two types of learning. Each of the two types has its own set of controlling conditions—classical or "respondent" conditioning controlled by eliciting stimuli, and operant or "instrumental" conditioning controlled by the effects of behavior on the environment. But practically all his own research and theory has been concerned with operant conditioning—in many ways an elaboration and extension of Thorndike's law of effect.

Both Skinner and Hull thus have used Thorndike's law of effect as a main starting point, but their approaches from there on are quite divergent. While Hull was emphasizing the internal states which mediate between stimulus and response, Skinner was contending that psychology's main concern should be with systematic relationships between behavior and its consequences without any reference to physiological correlates or other internal states. Skinner has also avoided any teleological or mentalistic references, contending that psychology as a science must be concerned with observable phenomena. One of his reasons for choosing "operant conditioning" rather than "instrumental conditioning" (preferred by some psychologists) is that "instrumental" is too suggestive of purposiveness on the part of the organism under study. Similarly, he prefers "reinforcement" over "reward" because the latter term may imply the existence of some contractual relationship, a relationship which Skinner views as too mentalistic and unscientific.

For Skinner, the main focus of psychology should be on "contingencies of reinforcement"—that is, the various relationships which can exist between behavior and its consequences. Characterizing Thorndike's law of effect as specifying merely "a simple temporal order of response and consequence" (Skinner, 1963, p. 514), Skinner and his operant colleagues have attempted to identify the various kinds of contingencies which might prevail and to indicate their respective influences on behavior. Skinner has consistently objected to being classified as an "S-R" theorist because he contends that he has given no special place for antecedent stimuli (those stimuli which precede the response) as an independent variable. Instead, his focus has been on the relationships between behavior and its consequences, with antecedent stimuli allegedly gaining their influence on behavior primarily because they are present when responses are reinforced.

Skinner's research and theory approach was established in his doctoral dissertation at Harvard University in 1931. Although he subsequently published many research and theoretical papers, his first major statement of his position was contained in *The Behavior of Organisms* (1938). Most authors consider Skinner's position to be one of the comprehensive learning theories which were so influential during the 1930s and 1940s, but which diminished in their influence by mid-century. But for some reason(s), it appears that Skinner's influence has been even greater since mid-century than it was before. Of course, an easy explanation could be that most of the other theorists either were no longer living or were not active professionally, while Skinner continued to provide active and dynamic leadership. But another distinct possibility is that Skinner's approach to research and to theory construction, which was of moderate influence during the 1930s and 1940s, was quite consistent with the orientation which became more popular in basic and applied psychology at mid-century.

The Classical Gestalt Conception of Learning

We have already indicated in our discussion of "schools" that the gestalt psychologists objected strongly to any form of reductionism in psychology. Luchins, acknowledging that there was no common learning theory among the classical gestalt psychologists, has pointed out that they did have a common approach to research which influenced their theoretical formulations. In contrast with the reductionistic analysis of the S-R theorists, which Wertheimer names the method "from below," the gestalt group favored research which deals with the *structure* of psychological phenomena, the method "from above." From the latter point of view, psychological analyses of any process, including learning processes, "should be preceded by attempts to grasp its structural features, and that analysis should deal with the natural structural and functional units of the phenomenon in attempts to understand their role and function in the structure" (Luchins, 1961, p. 7).

The gestalt psychologists objected to the behaviorists' excessive (in their opinion) concern with rigorous research methodology; in contrast, they emphasized the centrality of one's philosophical conception of man in selecting theoretical models and research procedures. They preferred characterizing man as capable of seeing meaning and structure in the world around him. They acknowledged that man's behavior sometimes is determined by his emotional feelings and pressing needs or drives, while at other times it is shaped by the stimuli in his environment. But the gestalt psychologists contended that greater concern in the psychology of learning should be diverted to understanding man's ability to see meaningful relationships and structure rather than to "merely" identifying how man acts "blindly" under the influence of such compelling emotional states and environmental conditions. Thus instead of focusing on stimuli which elicit behavior or which reinforce responses, according to the gestalt psychologists, one should find ways for measuring how subjects *experience* situations and should find those factors which facilitate structuring experiences so that one can best cope with one's environment.

A phenomenon which illustrates some of the characteristics of the gestalt approach is that of "insightful learning." When faced with problems, subjects frequently have been observed to try many solutions in vain when suddenly, typically after brief periods of inactivity and reflectivity, they rapidly identify the critical acts and move to solution of the problem. This is the "Aha!" experience which we all have had at one time or another. Consistent with their general reliance on perception as the most central process in psychology, the gestalt psychologists adapted perception principles as their main means for describing learning processes. Thus the insightful learning was depicted as *perceptual reorganization*, in which the subject initially fails and later succeeds in problem solution as he develops different ways of perceiving the problem situation. Although the insightful learning experience is not the sole type of learning considered by these psychologists, it is representative because of its primary emphasis on perceptual reorganization and the relationships among critical aspects of the situation.

Most authors credit Max Wertheimer as founder of gestalt psychology in 1912 as a result of his research on the *phi phenomenon* in perception (that is, the apparent movement we "see" in motion pictures). His views were extended subsequently by Kurt Koffka, Wolfgang Kohler, Kurt Lewin, and others. But despite their individual variations, they all maintained a conception of learning as change through perceptual reorganization. Thus in place of associations between stimuli and responses, the gestalt psychologists conceptualized learning as changes in the way one views his situation. Behavior merely reflects the learning which has already occurred, rather than constitutes the learning per se.

One other emphasis merits mention. The gestalt psychologists, like other cognitive theorists, contend that some central ideational process is involved in learning, probably even in very simple forms of motor-skill learning. Conceptualizations of this ideational process have been modified over the years. For example, during the nineteenth century it was rather commonly assumed that human and animal behavior were routinely mediated by ideas, whereas in the twentieth century most cognitive theorists acknowledge that even some human learning may take place without thinking or conscious awareness. They do raise questions as to how much learning is of this kind, and they particularly emphasize that all complex forms of learning involve some form of ideation or information processing.

Throughout this era of comprehensive learning theories the gestalt position most frequently was cast in the role of critic and corrective agent for the dominating behaviorally oriented learning theories. Some applied psychologists, notably those in educational and clinical psychology, were attracted by the gestalt views about learning. But within academic psychology the gestalt learning conceptions have never constituted a major influence on learning research or theory. Their main impact was to raise questions about certain aspects of other theories and thus to produce changes in the most dominant theories. By mid-century their conceptions of learning were largely being supplanted by the newly emerging information processing theories (which we consider in a later chapter). But even in the 1930s there was available a learning theory which incorporated many of the gestalt concepts along with many behavioristic emphases. This was the position advanced by Tolman, to whom we now turn.

Tolman's Cognitive Behaviorism

Edward Chance Tolman (1886-1959) proposed a "purposive behaviorism" theory which embodied many of the positive features of cognitive and behavioristic conceptions. He had the unusual opportunity of having studied each of the several competing camps before he began formulating his own position. For example, while a graduate student he learned about structuralism from Langfeld and Munsterberg and about behaviorism and comparative psychology from Yerkes, and he spent a month during the summer of 1912 with Koffka at the University of Giessen where he learned about gestalt psychology even before the school was known in this country. Later in 1923 he went back for further study about the gestalt group at Giessen while continuing to develop his interests in rigorous behavioristic psychology.

In 1932 Tolman published *Purposive Behavior in Animals and Men*, in which he presented a point of view about behaviorism which in many ways was decades ahead of its time. Tolman's views were presented in a context in which Watson, Lashley, and others were emphasizing that psychology should be an objective science like the other physical and biological sciences. But unlike many of his contemporaries of that era, Tolman presented a point of view which emphasized the unique characteristics of psychology as science and which maintained an even balance between the physiological and metaphysical extremes which were frequently promoted at that time. Although he contended that any true psychology as science must deal with *purpose* and *goal*, he held that such concepts must be strongly and richly rooted in observations of situations and how one acts there. Probably in response to the dominant orientation in theory construction while he was writing his book, he portrayed his position as constituting a new "system" of psychology. However, he carefully pointed out that he considered learning processes to be the fundamental keystone of his system. Moreover, despite his recognition of physiological correlates and of some physiological states as determinants of action, he identified *internal cognitive processes* as the main determinants of behavior and the central focus for psychology as a natural science. "Learning" was characterized as a "matter of the refinement, integration and invention of sign-Gestalt-readiness and -expectations" (Tolman, 1932, p. 319).

Tolman acknowledged the existence of three main competitive theories of learning—conditioned reflex theory, trial-and-error theory, and gestalt theory—along with various combinations of these three. He depicted his own theory as a subvariety of the gestalt approach but he rejected introspection as a research method and he stressed the need for relating these mental processes to situations and to behavior. Throughout *Purposive Behavior* and his many subsequent writings he consistently emphasized that learning involves more than the overtly observable movements in a situation, and that the *real* process of learning consists of a central, cognitive operation.

Thus he rejected the Pavlovian notion that learning consists of a stamping in of reflexes or that it only involves connections between a stimulus and a response. He held that learning actually involves building up "sign-gestalt-expectations," or conceptions of what happens when one acts in different ways in a given situation. Instead of accepting Thorndike's law of effect, he contended that the cognitive change occurs *before* overt responses are made. Thus he suggested that a punishment might be just as effective as a reward in learning, since both the punishment and the reward could serve to confirm or to refute the subject's expectations about relationships between respective responses and their consequences. In brief, behavior in any given situation reflects the individual's selection of responses based on their expected outcomes.

One curious thing about Tolman's theory is the way that it was regarded in the 1930s and 1940s compared with contemporary reactions in the 1970s. During the 1930s and 1940s Tolman's theory was sometimes criticized because of its philosophical "flavor." Reservations were particularly expressed about his cognitive constructs because some felt that they would not lend themselves to concrete representation or to direct observation. Nonetheless, as we shall see in a later section, psychologists eventually did obtain rather rigorous means for researching and theorizing about cognitive processes.

Throughout his professional life Tolman was recognized as an astute critic of other theories and a source for stimulating research on a number of theoretical issues. But his own *theory* never attracted continuing interest among a large enough group of psychologists so that it could be further elaborated and extended. Even today, when information processing conceptions *could* be closely identified with Tolman's conceptions, they frequently are associated with other influences. Perhaps Tolman's main contribution lies in his influence on other theories rather than in the continuation of his own theory.

Functionalism and Learning Theory

One final position on learning theory needs to be acknowledged at this point even though it has not resulted in the kind of learning theory to which we have been referring throughout most of our discussion thus far. That position, functionalism, derives from the earlier school of psychology to which we referred previously. What is particularly noteworthy for our purposes here is the general orientation to research and to theory construction which is evident in the functionalistic approach. Briefly stated, it simply involves accepting each theoretical problem and each practical problem very much on its own merits, and then trying to draw from any and all theories which might help to resolve the theoretical issue or the particular practical problem. As the name implies, it takes a pragmatic functional orientation to the delineation of a problem and to attempts to solving the problem. It is characterized less by any particular theoretical bias in conceptualizing learning processes and more by its open attitude for both the method of research which might be used and the kind of data and theory which might be brought to bear on the theoretical or practical problem. It is an orientation which was not particularly valued by most psychologists who were involved with theory construction during the first half of the century, but it is more compatible with the inductive approach to theory construction which we will find emerging after mid-century.

COMPREHENSIVE LEARNING THEORIES
IN RETROSPECT

Many characterized the 1930s and 1940s as being an era in which debates were conducted primarily between the learning theories of Hull and Tolman. Of course, the other comprehensive learning theories enumerated above were also involved in this discussion and were subsequently influenced in their formulation as a result of the data which were collected and the interpretations which were generated in the context of these debates. Perhaps it would be instructive for the student to be aware of some of the issues which were raised around this time.

One issue at once involved psychological phenomena and the presumed physiological underpinnings of learning. Questions were raised as to whether an organism learned *movements* or whether, instead, some kind of cognitive map or conception of a situation was learned, on the basis of which the organism therefore moved. Those who held that learning actually consisted of making responses were characterized as believing that the neurophysiological changes during learning were peripheral rather than central. In contrast, those who contended that some form of cognitive structure was the essence of learning contended that even sensory motor learning involved changes in the individual's conception of the situation and that the process was occurring centrally in the nervous system.

Secondly, Tolman was especially responsible for pointing out the importance of distinguishing between an organism's *performance* and its *learning*. He held that one might not necessarily observe learning at the point that it occurs simply because there may have been no reason for the organism to have demonstrated the learning at that time. This led to a whole series of experiments which focused on "latent learning" in which Tolman and his colleagues showed that subjects might have learned a particular task and that it might lie "latent" until there was some occasion which made it worthwhile for the subject to respond in accordance with that learning.

Another example of the kinds of issues which were debated in the 1930s and 1940s is the one having to do with "continuity" versus "noncontinuity" in learning. Goldstein, Krantz, and Rains (1965) describe the issue: "Basically, the problem can be stated as follows: is the learning process a gradual, continuous one, or does it begin to occur suddenly, and does it reach full strength in a single experience or trial?" (p. 345) The continuity position was more compatible with the reinforcement tradition followed by Hull and Skinner, whereas the more cognitively oriented theories and the position developed by Guthrie held that learning actually occurs in a stepwise, noncontinuous fashion.

In retrospect, many have even debated whether these issues were worth debating in the first place. On the negative side, it can be accurately stated that many of the issues which held attention in the 1930s and 1940s were never conclusively resolved by any definitive or critical experiments. Instead, many of the issues merely seemed to die out after they had been phrased countless times. On the positive side, it is quite evident that the theories were greatly influenced by the questions which were raised and the kinds of data generated in attempts to find answers. It appears that the learning theories were modified, sometimes quite substantially, as a result of the research and debates. Of course, one cannot know whether there may have been some more efficient and effective manner for evolving learning theories.

But by mid-century, there was ample evidence that the comprehensive learning theories which had dominated research and theorizing for a few decades were no longer maintaining their influence in the psychology of learning. Moreover, serious questions were being raised not only as to the adequacy of the theories which had been developed but even as to the kinds of theory construction which had been followed for several decades. It is to this controversy and reassessment at mid-century that we shall turn in the next section.

4
Psychology Theories and Learning: Part 2

We appear to be in a period of intensive data collection and, theoretically, of the development of "miniature systems" based on relatively limited types of experimental phenomena. (Spence & Spence, 1967, p. vii)

(W)hether particular experimental psychologists like it or not, experimental psychology is properly and inevitably committed to the construction of a theory of behavior. (Skinner, 1969, pp. vii-viii)

(S)election of any theoretical model, be it physiological or phenomenological, or for that matter, physical, mechanical or statistical, is in the last analysis a decision having no *truth character.* (Kendler, 1952, p. 276)

THEORETICAL CRISIS AT MID-CENTURY?

The previous section listed some of the major comprehensive learning theories which were developed and which dominated psychology learning research during much of the first half of the twentieth century. In each case, there was explicit or implicit suggestion that the particular theory would be the best candidate for an eventual *comprehensive* learning theory. By the 1950s it was evident that these comprehensive learning theories were no longer influencing learning research and theorizing to the extent that they had in previous decades.

The actual date that such change occurred cannot be precisely identified, though apparently the transitional period had started sometime during the Second World War and subsequently continued at least up into the middle 1950s. Furthermore, the reader should recognize that there was no "official decision" per se to make such a change nor even widespread agreement that such a change should or did occur. But examination of a few papers and books written around mid-twentieth century will provide the reader with some understanding of the nature and importance of these changes.

Emergence of a Fact-gathering Emphasis

Even by 1949 it was apparent that psychologists were no longer following as closely along the lines of the comprehensive theorizing that had been prevalent prior to World War II, and that indeed an antitheoretical or atheoretical attitude had developed. Hebb took note of this change and expressed concern as to what it might mean for the advancement of theory within psychology. Though he had acknowledged that perhaps earlier psychologists had been premature and overly enthusiastic in their development of grand, theoretical systems, he felt that his contemporaries of the late 1940s had gone to "another extreme, scientifically just as sinful" (Hebb, 1949, p. 162). He seemed to feel that psychologists had so overreacted to these earlier "excesses" in theorizing that they now were inappropriately denying *any* role for theory in their research. But time would show that this atheoretical or antitheoretical trend had only begun. Other spokesmen would make their own recommendations for alternatives to the previous comprehensive theories.

Sigmund Koch (1951) described psychology in the two decades prior to World War II as having been organized primarily around the three systems of psychoanalysis, gestalt theory, and stimulus-response conceptions, with respective spokesmen promoting different points of view for psychology. He was particularly critical of these theorists' apparent universal expectations for applicability of their theories, and for their implied contention that *aspiration to develop* a factual-based theory was equivalent to *having in existence* such a theory. Koch's statement was forceful and dramatic. He characterized psychology at mid-century as having entered a "theoretical crisis" period, and he contended that he would have to be quite pessimistic about the future of theory in psychology if we were to pursue the grand, comprehensive theories which were popular in previous decades. Essentially depicting psychology as being in a "pretheoretical" status, he nonetheless recognized the need for speculation and conjecture both in planning research and in interpreting findings. But in contrast with the mainly logically derived, wide-scope theories popular previously, Koch proposed that valid psychological theory would more likely result if psychologists would restrict themselves to more limited coverage in interpreting their findings and in formulating their theories. He also urged that psychologists needed better training in development of scientific theory.

In a paper written in 1950 Skinner provoked considerable and continuing controversy when he provided a generally negative answer to his question, "Are theories of learning necessary?" He took the position that psychology was not ready for hypothetico-deductive theories. He expressed the opinion that psychology needed more facts in order to develop postulates and a general theory which would subsequently be supported empirically. He objected to interpretations which make extensive reference to presumed physiological correlates or to internal mental events, or which make extensive use of constructs to represent behavior. In contrast, he recommended that psychologists would be better advised to focus on collecting more empirical data concerning behavior and at least temporarily to constrain their drawing of inferences beyond the data collected. Though many subsequently misinterpreted his position as being totally antitheoretical, he did advocate that theory does have an important role in organizing the facts which would be accumulated; he thus encouraged an inductive rather than a deductive approach in theory construction. Moreover, he did have a distinct preference for the use of operant techniques and he preferred to interpret data in line with reinforcement principles. Thus this 1950 paper and the contentions about theories of learning are compatible with the picture of Skinner as one of the traditional comprehensive learning theorists, but one with preferences for inductive theory construction.

Howard H. Kendler suggested that learning theorists had too frequently become involved in questions for which there was no real empirical answer, and that these questions had served to impede the progress of learning theorizing in psychology. As a major example, he contended that learning theorists had spent considerable time and effort in debating whether cognitive maps or stimulus-response associations were the result or product of learning, whereas, in Kendler's opinion, the validity of such an answer could not really be established by empirical evidence per se. He contended that "selection of any theoretical model, be it physiological or phenomenological, or for that matter, physical, mechanical or statistical, is in the last analysis a decision having no *truth character*. . . . That is, in spite of the fact that the choice of a model may, and usually does influence both experimentation and theorizing, *the choice itself* cannot be evaluated as being right or wrong. It is a matter purely of personal taste" (Kendler, 1952, p. 276). Kendler recommended that psychologists become more concerned about the data with which they are working, and he seemed to imply that one should be tolerant of the diverse conceptual schemes by which experimenters might attempt to integrate and to interpret their findings. While acknowledging the importance of "personal taste" in selecting a theory, he did stress the need for evaluating one's choice in terms of the explanatory capacities of such formulations.

A similar acknowledgment of change was recorded subsequently by Kenneth W. Spence and his colleagues (Spence & Spence, 1967). Considering the fact that it was Spence whom most psychologists expected would carry on the Hullian tradition, it is noteworthy that he merely acknowledged the change in theorizing in psychology without providing even a brief explanation as to why such changes may have occurred. He merely reported: "We appear to be in a period of intensive data collection and, theoretically, of the development of 'miniature systems' based on relatively limited types of experimental phenomena" (p. vii). This mere acknowledgment of change is also interesting because seventeen years previously he had ventured the opinion that elimination of theorizing would really not be in the best interests of building a scientific body of knowledge about learning (Spence, 1950, p. 171).

A point of view which one might mistake as being in opposition to the above comments was advanced by Joseph R. Royce (1957). He contended that by 1956 there was an increase rather than a decrease in theorizing within psychology. While acknowledging that others might differ with him in his perception of trends within psychology, he suggested that there had been an antitheoretical attitude prevailing in psychology since the early 1930s and that by 1956 it was becoming somewhat more acceptable to theorize in psychology. But Royce's own comments provide clarification on this and actually indicate that he is quite in agreement with the other authors cited above. He acknowledged that theorizing had been popular in psychology even as much as a century previously, but that such theorizing was primarily speculative and generally little supported by fact. In contrast, he characterized psychology in the 1950s as involving "much fact and little [experimentally anchored] theory" (p. 402). While emphasizing that facts really are of limited value until they are integrated or synthesized within some greater system, he recommended that the contemporary psychologist-theorist should be neutral with regard to the earlier grand systems. He accepted Koch's description of psychology as being in a "pretheoretical" stage; rather than depend on a premature hypothetico-deductive system which might be overly speculative, he suggested that "theoretical psychology will be most fruitful at this time if it is inductive rather than deductive, qualitative rather than quantitative, relatively loose rather than rigorous, closely anchored to empiricism rather than sophisticated from the point of view of philosophy of science, and both circumscribed and all-inclusive in the direction of its effort" (p. 409). As the reader should recognize by this time, Royce's suggestions were generally in opposition to the approach advocated by Hull and in most respects were compatible with the descriptions of psychology theorizing in the 1950s as described by the authors cited above.

Why Changes in Theory Construction at This Time?

At this point many readers probably will wonder: Why did psychologists decide at mid-twentieth century that not enough facts were available to formulate sound theory if in previous decades many had been promoting the value of such grand schemes to develop a science of psychology? What implications might there be for the value of learning theory qua theory, as well as for the merits of the "learning theories" which had emerged? How widespread is such sentiment concerning the futility or inadvisability of developing comprehensive systems? What alternative synthesizing or integrating mechanism might be proposed? It is important that the reader recognize that each of the above commentators did see the value of theory and did feel that facts or findings of studies would be of only limited and temporary value unless they were related to some more general and abstract theoretical framework.

Even an intensive search of the literature leaves one less than certain as to why in the 1950s psychologists entered this fact-gathering phase. Many historians and reviewers of the literature currently seem merely to note the change in passing without being concerned as to *why* such a state has developed. Nor do they show much concern about the implications of the emergence of this intensive fact-gathering phase in contemporary psychology. But it would seem very important for students of learning theory and of instructional theory to consider the causes that led to such a change at this particular point and to ascertain possible implications for future development of theories. Moreover, the problem is perhaps even more acute for the practitioner who wishes to make application of the basic science findings. Since it is unlikely that one can take findings from an isolated experiment and apply them to any practical situation, it is reasonable that the practitioner would need to know something about contemporary synthesizing of such findings and the changes in patterns of synthesis. Finally it would seem important to consider the bases for these changes in theorizing patterns particularly—for both the basic scientist and the practitioner – if the cause mainly indicates that the previous theorizing was invalid or generally not as sound as it should have been.

In considering the current status of affairs, many different explanations could be proposed. It will not be possible to state definitely which is "the correct explanation" for this development. However, we can present some possible explanations, note the extent to which there is evidence that these explanations are at least partially sound, and, further, delineate some possible implications if indeed such explanations are valid.

Insufficient Facts Are Available to Construct Theories   It's quite easy to build a case for showing that psychology is in a pretheoretical stage in that it simply has not yet acquired sufficient data about learning processes in order to integrate them into some comprehensive theory. Despite the fact that learning process has held a central position in research among psychologists for many decades, there are still many unresolved questions and areas of controversy. Therefore, it is quite clear that more data are available about the kinds of processes involved in learning and the factors which seem most influential with these processes. But this has been known since the beginning of the century. Early psychologists were quite aware of the lack of available facts and yet they chose to proceed in system building. Why? Quite obviously, they felt that systems would guide them in planning their research and in obtaining the facts about learning processes. Heidbreder suggested that system building was considered to be "all but inevitable" (Heidbreder, 1933, p. 8) as a step to obtain more empirical evidence concerning learning process: "Why does psychology not turn from its systems and devote itself to collecting the facts it so sorely needs? The answer to this question is the justification of systems: that without the systems few facts would be forthcoming. For scientific knowledge does not merely accumulate; it is far more likely to grow about hypotheses that put definite questions and which act as centers of organization in the quest of knowledge" (Heidbreder, 1933, p. 15). Since many *more* facts had been accumulated by mid-century than had been the case a few decades earlier, we are in the strange position of having to acknowledge that psychologists early in the century decided to theorize with fewer facts than did psychologists at mid-twentieth century. Obviously, we cannot *merely* say that psychologists at mid-century decided to postpone theorizing *because* insufficient facts were available on which to base a theory.

There is a strong indication that mid-century psychologists did not consider system building as "all but inevitable"; at a minimum, they changed from a deductive to an inductive approach in theory construction. It seems that it was more a difference in philosophy about how one develops a scientific theory of learning, rather than the sheer number of facts available, which led to this mid-twentieth century de-emphasis on system building. Thus we will need to consider other possible explanations as to why such a change occurred at mid-century.

Empirical Evidence Did Not Support the Comprehensive Learning Theories Since early psychologists had built their theories on a minimum of empirical facts, perhaps subsequent research simply did not produce data in support of the theories. Comprehensive learning theories may have been rejected or ignored at the middle of the twentieth century mainly because they were not consistent with empirical evidence and therefore were not valid theories.

Certainly there was a tremendous amount of controversy concerning the validity of each of the comprehensive learning theories proposed. Debate was frequently emotionally charged, and allegations were made from time to time that opponents were attempting to distort propositions of each of the theories. There were indeed marked substantive changes in theories as a result of the issues which were raised and in the research which was stimulated by the ongoing debates. But it would be less than accurate to contend that the research evidence actually was so devastating as to indicate that *any* of the proposed comprehensive learning theories were actually grossly in error. From the start, there were differences in philosophical assumptions and general interpretations concerning the process by which one should build a theory of learning. However, it was because of these nonempirical bases, rather than from facts which were gathered by research, that various conclusions were drawn about the merits of each of the theorizing ventures. Most contemporary psychologists probably would accept the conclusions on the matter presented by Goldstein et al: "Finally, and perhaps most important, although most of the issues are considered 'dead,' it becomes clear in reexamining them that many of them are by no means settled. Research in these fields seems to have petered out without actually clearly resolving the issues" (Goldstein, Krantz, and Rains, 1965, p. vi).

Let's entertain the possibility that facts actually *had* proven the available comprehensive learning theories to be invalid. It's quite possible, if such had conclusively occurred, that *new* comprehensive learning theories would have been proposed which would have been corrective for the errors of the earlier theories. Thus, mere invalidation of one set of theories would not necessarily dictate that psychologists should drop the whole objective of developing comprehensive learning theories. Again, though it is quite clear that empirical evidence did not consistently support the proposed comprehensive learning theories, one cannot really say that it was on the basis of the accumulating evidence that one could find basis for changing from a system-building to a fact-gathering phase in the psychology of learning. That is, empirical evidence at times supported the theories and at other times indicated that some revision was necessary. However, empirical evidence per se was not so substantially at odds with the various theories to the extent that such data might indicate that the theory was totally invalid. Of course, some psychologists quite possibly may have felt that the theories were sufficiently inadequate that some substantially different approach would be necessary. Moreover, it is quite possible that some psychologists moved into the data-gathering phase because they felt that such additional evidence would be necessary before a more appropriate theoretical system might be devised. However, since the amount of empirical evidence accumulated by mid-century certainly was greater than that available in the early 1920s, it seems reasonable to conclude that such a data-oriented approach probably comes from philosophical and theorizing preferences rather than from merely the conclusions based on available evidence. Nonetheless, one should entertain the possibility that the trend at least in part stems from the fact that accumulating evidence was not sufficiently in support of the theories to make psychologists confident that it was appropriate to continue building the available comprehensive learning theories.

The Complexity of a Single Comprehensive Learning Theory   Too many facts have been accumulated to be integrated within one comprehensive learning theory. One could argue that the problem was that *too many* facts had accumulated by mid-twentieth century so that it was no longer possible to integrate such facts within the currently available comprehensive learning theories. One could then suggest that as a result many psychologists simply became uninterested in the theoretical integrating process beyond the scope of their particular area of research.

The reader is aware of the tremendous amount of empirical data which have been collected in studies on learning processes. Students frequently are concerned about their ability to master even those facts which are contained in a textbook such as the present one. Thus it would not be surprising to find that many researchers feel that they have enough problems trying to integrate the data within their own particular though somewhat narrowly defined research area, and that they do not express an interest in relating their theoretical models to other areas of research in learning process.

Of course such an approach would have some short-term value in enabling us to build a fund of knowledge about *some* of the aspects of learning process. However, in the long run it would seem that someone, sometime, will need to integrate these findings from the various subareas of learning research. In addition, it would seem that such a short-range approach would even have some limitations in that models in short-term memory, for example, might substantially be improved if the short-term memory theorist was aware of and was able to relate his findings to those of other learning processes.

Traditional Comprehensive Learning Theories Adequate for Animal Learning, but not for Human Learning New students of learning theory and psychology research frequently complain about the great deal of emphasis that some researchers place on the use of animal subjects rather than human subjects. Certainly, such a criticism can and has been leveled at learning research. Therefore, one might propose the explanation for a shift away from traditional learning theory as stemming from the fact that most of the principles in the traditional learning theories are based on studies in which animal subjects rather than human subjects were used. The principal problem here lies in the fact that researchers in *animal behavior* have been almost as concerned as human researchers in their criticism of the adequacy of traditional comprehensive learning theories.

Computers May Be Used to Integrate Findings from Various Studies As the reader should be aware by this point, one major function of a theory is to integrate findings from individual studies. But some critics have suggested that, with the advent of the "computer age," it may no longer be necessary to use theories as a mechanism for interpreting and integrating findings from a variety of studies (Wrigley, 1960). The argument follows along these lines: It is acknowledged that in the pre-World War II era theories were necessary as language devices for integrating and synthesizing findings from various areas. However, it is suggested that such "indirect" integration may no longer be necessary. Instead, some propose that replicated findings from research can be incorporated in computer programs and that the synthesizing process is accomplished more directly than would be possible by means of theory. Thus, advocates of such computer usage contend that theories are not obsolete, and that new synthesizing procedures are available in the form of computer programs. Consequently, it is suggested, a major reason for the decline of interest in and use of traditional learning theory is that learning researchers discovered the availability of this more direct means for integrating significant findings from their research.

It does seem reasonable that the mid-twentieth century development of computer technology quite likely has had considerable impact on psychology learning theorizing. There is also some basis for suggesting that computers and their related programs have had an impact on the kinds of theorizing which have been attempted for learning research. In a later chapter we will consider some of the information processing theories which have emerged at mid-twentieth century, and in considering their development we will comment on the impact that computers and their programs have had on stimulating the development of this particular type of theorizing about learning processes. However, instead of diminishing the interest in theoretical integration, it seems more likely that the "program analogy" (cf. Neisser, 1967; Miller, Galanter & Pribram, 1960) has been primarily responsible for mid-century renewed interest in cognitive processes and in the formulation of certain types of rather comprehensive learning theories. In that respect, computer technology probably is responsible for rejection of *certain* traditional comprehensive learning theories but *not* for rejection of *theorizing* on a large scale. Moreover, it seems more accurate to state that the computer program itself can quite accurately be depicted as a type of learning theory rather than as a replacement for theory per se. For example, one formulation of Feigenbaum's verbal learning theory (1959) actually consists of a set of computer programs. Thus it appears that computer technology has substantially influenced the nature of learning theorizing, but it does not seem correct to state that computers have provided any viable alternatives to *theory* per se.

Popularity of Humanistic Psychology: The Effect on the Behavioristic Learning Theories   One could argue that a major reason for diminution of comprehensive learning theorizing is that these theories were based on an outmoded conception of psychology. That is, it could be suggested that the reason that comprehensive learning theories no longer were popular by mid-twentieth century is that many psychologists were no longer defining "psychology" in the same say as they had been defining it during the first half of the century.

In some respects, we can find at mid-twentieth century a reemergence of interest in how a man "feels" as well as how he "behaves." There was considerable interest at the turn of the century in introspectionism and in other means by which psychology might study the experiences of an individual. However, one major development in psychology was the insistence on more rigorous research methods and more quantifiable forms of data to be studied by "scientific method." Along with this insistence for rigorous research methodology, many early twentieth century psychologists advocated the position that we can understand complex meaningful human experiences best if we reduce them to their simplest form. Thus most of the research on which the comprehensive learning theories were based consisted of studies involving comparatively simple learning processes, frequently with animal subjects under highly controlled experimental conditions.

Many psychologists individually and collectively took exception to this point of view throughout the first half of the twentieth century. Though they have variously been identified as "humanists," "phenomenologists," "existentialists," etc., we will refer to any of these various overlapping groups simply as "humanists" in our present discussions. At mid-century there was a substantial increase in interest in such a point of view so that a national association subsequently was formed (cf. Bugental, 1967). The humanists contended that research and theory should take into account the fact that "psychology" involved subjective experience as well as overt behavior, quite complex psychological processes as well as more simple forms of activity, and individual as well as group principles of behavior. It is quite clear that there did evolve at mid-century a point of view which was not really compatible with the position out of which the comprehensive learning theories were developed. Thus it is evident that there did develop a reformulation of "psychology" in a manner which was not consistent with the definition of psychology around which the traditional learning theories were developed. However, we need to consider two further questions: (1) Were learning researchers involved in the humanistic psychology movement? and (2) Would a redefinition of "psychology" necessarily dictate that one should not continue with comprehensive theorizing?

Some spokesmen for humanistic psychology have done learning research and in some ways may be classified as leaders in learning theory; however, most of the support for humanistic psychology has come from clinical psychology, personality theory, social psychology, and other groups which ordinarily do not focus primarily on studies of learning process. Thus it is conceivable that such a position could have developed *alongside* the traditional comprehensive learning theories, rather than necessarily displacing them. Later we will consider such a possibility. Thus, though some learning researchers have become involved in the movement for a more humanistic psychology, it does not appear that the loss of interest in traditional comprehensive learning theories really came from this redefinition of psychology per se.

Let's consider for a moment those learning researchers who were concerned and are concerned about a more humanistic definition of psychology, and the implications that it might have for theory about learning processes. It would not seem surprising that such individuals would have been critical of the traditional learning theories formulated during the 1930s and 1940s but it would seem reasonable to expect that they would propose a more appropriate type of comprehensive learning theory—more appropriate in that it would be more compatible with the redefinition of psychology advocated by the humanists. Thus, instead of diminishing interest in theorizing, it seems more reasonable to expect that there might have been an increase in theoretical development about learning but that such kinds of theorizing would have been more compatible with the philosophical assumptions and general orientation of the humanistic psychology movement. Nonetheless, there does not appear to have developed during the third quarter of this century a really concerted attempt to reformulate learning theory along the lines of humanistic psychology conceptions of learning.

The Development of Other Aspects of Psychology Theory   Perhaps learning theory was diminished in importance because other aspects of psychology theory were beginning to be developed at a greater pace at around mid-century. From our discussions earlier in this text, it is evident that learning theory has had a central role in theorizing generally within psychology throughout most of the first half of the twentieth century. Of course in making such a statement, one must keep in mind the fact that there were other areas of theoretical interest, and that, for example, sensation and perception were processes considered to be of primary importance at the beginning of the twentieth century. But during much of the first half of this century, such great emphasis was placed on learning processes that many have come to equate learning theory with general behavior theory. One explanation of a decrease in interest in traditional comprehensive learning theory might stem from "competition" with theorizing in other areas of psychology. This could occur either because the learning theory was no longer so "visible" in comparison with the emergence of theorizing in other areas, or because the nature of the earlier learning theory was such that it did not compare favorably with the kind of theory newly emerging in these other areas.

Perusal of the psychology literature will reveal the fact that indeed there were a number of theories which began to emerge or which gained new importance at mid-century. But one does not get a simple, clear picture as to the nature of their influence on learning theory development. For example, McClelland's 1955 book on motivation research seems to be emphasizing the importance of a "fact-gathering" phase for motivation, with an explicit acknowledgment that knowledge at least at that point in time was "too imperfect to allow for any elaborate theorizing" (p. v). In contrast, Hall and Lindzey (1957) quite clearly were taking a position for "theory building" rather than "fact gathering" in their book on personality theory. For example, they recommended "strongly that the student should, once he has surveyed the available theories of personality, adopt an intolerant and affectionate acceptance of a particular theoretical position without reservation" (p. 556). The approach they took was substantially similar to that of the comprehensive learning theories of the 1930s and 1940s, and even, in part, was similar to the "schools of psychology" orientation extant just after the beginning of this century. They acknowledged that some theorizing in psychology is quite limited in scope, and they cited examples such as research and theorizing on "perception, audition, rote memory, motor learning, discrimination." However, they depicted personality theory as being "ready to deal with any behavioral event that can be shown to be of significance in the adjustment of the human organism" and thus that personality theories can be characterized as general theories of behavior (Hall & Lindzey, 1957, p. 18).

Other examples could be cited of theorizing processes in psychology in which some psychologists at mid-century were rather comprehensive in their concern whereas most psychologists were more limited in the range of phenomena with which they tried to deal. It is apparent that there was some increase in theorizing in other areas of psychology, but it does not seem clear that the increased theorizing necessarily dictated a de-emphasis on comprehensive learning theorizing. Furthermore, the kinds of theorizing elsewhere in psychology were sufficiently diverse that one could hardly build a case that any particular approach there had necessarily dictated the form of theorizing that should go on with regard to research on learning processes. Of course, if any of these theoretical ventures were to attain sufficient stature among psychologists, it would be conceivable that learning process might be subsumed within that theoretical framework and thus theorizing about learning processes might have a subordinate rather than a dominant role for theorizing in psychology. However, no such dominant theoretical venture can be identified at mid-century. (Note: "interdisciplinary theories," "general theories," etc. are discussed below.) In later sections of this text, we will consider information theory and other information processing conceptions and some of the mathematical models, all of which emerged at the middle of the twentieth century.

Traditional Learning Theory Lost Its Appeal When It Proved Unsatisfactory for Practical Application   In the following chapter on the emergence of instructional theories we will consider some of the relationships which have existed between learning theory and educational practice during the twentieth century, as well as some of the apparent causes for the changes in such relationships and the implications of these changes. However, it is pertinent here to consider the possibility that traditional learning theories lost their appeal because applied psychologists did not find them of value in dealing with practical problems.

Whether mere coincidence or cause-effect relationships, it is of interest to note that applied psychology expanded extensively during that same post-World War II period when traditional learning theory seems to have been diminishing in popularity. Many authors have attributed this "loss" in prestige by learning theory to its *irrelevance* for practical application. Of course, review of our earlier chapters will quickly indicate that all has not been smooth in the relationship between learning theory and educational practice at any point in this century. Thus it is unlikely that one could really claim any "new" development at mid-century. However, the number of applied psychologists in the United States increased considerably in the post-World War II era, and substantially larger amounts of money, particularly from federal government sources, became available for support of applied research. Some experimental psychologists who had worked entirely in the laboratory previously became interested and involved in application of the principles derived from laboratory research. For these and other reasons, the opinion of applied psychologists concerning the relevance of learning theory was given new weight, new importance in its implication for the course of development of learning theory. Whereas applied psychology training programs had traditionally been conducted in liberal arts college psychology departments primarily under the direction of academic psychologists, there now developed a welter of critical opinion that the "basic science" theory in psychology, including especially learning theory, was not proving to be satisfactory in practical situations. Moreover, many began to question the adequacy of theory qua theory because of its failure in applied situations.

Given such critical opinion, and given the fact that this applied psychology opinion was receiving the attention of academic psychologists more than had ever previously been the case, it does seem reasonable that academic psychologists may quite likely have been influenced by such critical comments about the adequacy of traditional learning theory.

But even assuming some role of applied psychologists in the "demise" of traditional comprehensive learning theory, one still is left with the question: Why did not the academic learning researchers merely attempt to correct the inadequacies of their theories, or to propose substitute comprehensive learning theories, instead of embarking on this data-gathering phase? Some (for example, Koch, 1951) suggest that this failure of theory in application was sufficiently devastating that it resulted in a "theoretical crisis." In various papers Koch takes the position that the problem was in trying to make psychology more unified than it ever could possibly be. Therefore, in some respects, he seems to feel that the failure of applicability for traditional learning theory served primarily to indicate that too broadly encompassing an area had been attempted by the learning theorists. But what if the practitioner is "denied" the synthesizing accomplishments which result from comprehensive theories? As is indicated at various points in this text, the author takes the position that relationships between basic research and application will be accomplished through some theory or integrating mechanism, and that it is unlikely that there will be direct application to practice from the findings of any isolated single study. If such is the case, then it would seem that the criticism of the practitioner and applied psychologist should have been in the direction of correcting comprehensive learning theories rather than in pushing basic sciences learning researchers from a theory-building to a fact-gathering phase.

Learning Theories and Social Science Theories Traditional learning theories could not be incorporated in the general social science theories which developed about the middle of the twentieth century. About the middle of the twentieth century several persons (Miller, 1965; Parsons, 1950; Thorne, 1967) proposed that what was really needed in the behavioral sciences was a comprehensive interdisciplinary theory which would encompass all aspects of human activity. Perhaps the demise of traditional learning theory can be traced to the fact that it cannot be incorporated in these more comprehensive social science theories—actually even more comprehensive than the systems found in psychology prior to the 1930s.

Perusal of the literature on these various views leads one quickly to conclude that learning theory per se did not have that dominant a role in any of these theories, and that it did not seem to be substantively influenced by them. If anything, there seems to be even recognition of a need for comprehensive learning theories rather than the rejection of their utility. Again, one gets the distinct impression that there should have been "pressure" for rather than against comprehensive theorizing from these broader-scope interdisciplinary ventures.

A Loss of Leadership Comprehensive learning theories lost their forward thrust and development when they each lost their respective leaders. Careful review of science history will quickly reveal the fact that individual theorists provide emotional as well as intellectual leadership. Perhaps the reason that traditional learning theories lost their central position in psychology at the middle of the twentieth century may stem from the fact that many of the leaders were lost around this time. For example, Hull, one of the most important figures for hypothetico-deductive theorizing in psychology, died in 1952; likewise Tolman and Guthrie died in 1959. Though Skinner continues to be quite active as a leader in psychology, one should recall that he was never one to promote the kind of grand comprehensive learning theorizing more characteristic of his colleagues and "competitors." Also, Spence, who was apparently considered the leading figure to carry on the Hullian tradition, never seemed to be particularly interested in as wide scope a theory as that advocated by Hull.

Mid-century also marked the end of an era when European-trained psychologists were the outstanding leaders in American psychology. By that time, United States trained psychologists had acquired enough seniority and prestige to have considerable influence on the shaping of ideas generally and of theories in particular. Thus the customary European combination of philosophy and psychology was missing in the training and orientation of many of the replacements. Moreover, those men who assumed leadership positions in American psychology came more frequently from departments which had been established as independent entities; in contract, readers will remember from the biographical information on each of the learning theorists here that many earlier American-trained psychologists received their graduate education in sections of psychology which were part of philosophy departments. Thus loss of leadership may have been a rather important factor in the demise of importance of comprehensive theorizing generally, including learning theory in particular.

Psychologists Have Received Rigorous Training in Research Methodology but Have Poor Backgrounds in Theory Development Aside from the serious leadership gap created by the lack of training in the elements of theory development, one can also raise questions about the relevance of training programs in theorizing for the "working" psychologists who operate today's laboratories. Perusal of any university catalog or observation of many graduate psychology programs will easily reveal the fact that psychology departments routinely provide courses in research methodology but only infrequently list courses in constructing theory. These courses often treat theory construction at a very elementary level. Perhaps the problem is that inadequate training is provided in the procedures required for psychologists to integrate findings from various studies and to develop theories. One could even say that some departments are so concerned about having scientifically based principles that they look with suspicion at anyone who wishes to get beyond more than a very modest inference from the data. That is, it is felt by some that contemporary American psychologists should have substantial training in research methodology and should be able to relate their particular studies to one or several other studies. However, many other psychologists feel that students are receiving inadequate training in the significant procedures involved in integrating findings from several studies into miniature models, and from these miniature models into more widely encompassing theoretical syntheses. If this is a valid description of contemporary psychology training programs, it is conceivable that the lack of emphases on training in theory development may have contributed to the demise of traditional comprehensive learning theory. As we trace the course of development of research-oriented psychology journals, we find an increase in the number of journals devoted to specific research areas or to applied problems, but relatively few journals concerned with the integration of findings.

The Demise of Learning Theory May Be a Passing Phase   One could attribute the demise of comprehensive learning theory to its being merely a phase in the historical cycle, with a particular zeitgeist that is more oriented toward fact gathering than the system building. One could dismiss all the above "causes" as being merely coincidental, and one could take the position that psychology and human history generally follow cyclical patterns. Pursuing this line of reasoning, one could then suggest that at different times we will be gathering facts and that at other times we will be integrating these facts into more and more comprehensive theories. With such a line of reasoning, then one might depict the so-called "demise" of traditional learning theory as having been just one more phase of a recycling process between gathering facts and building them into explanatory systems or theories.

These are some of the explanations for the shift away from comprehensive theorizing in psychology generally, and away from the comprehensive learning theories which we have considered in other chapters, in favor of greater interest in "fact gathering" and miniature model building. Perhaps only with some lapse of time—several decades at a minimum—will we be able to see more definitively what changes actually occurred at mid-century and for what reasons. However, we have outlined above some of the causes which we feel have played a role in this change in the theorizing process about learning.

THEORIZING PATTERNS SINCE MID-CENTURY

From the previous discussion it is obvious that some major changes occurred in theory construction at mid-century. Of course, it is important to keep in mind the fact that there is no "official" statement or pronouncement that learning researchers *should* interpret their data in a given way, nor even is there usually a general awareness on the part of individual learning researchers as to how other individuals in the field are interpreting and integrating their findings. Thus, it is not unusual to find a variety of approaches in the synthesizing of findings and in the interpretation of results at any given point in history, with proponents of respective approaches being somewhat oblivious to the efforts of their contemporaries. This was amply illustrated by Tyler's comments which were quoted at the beginning of Chapter 1, in which he suggested that one may get as many different views about current developments in psychology as one has respondents to such a question. But some patterns can be discerned. What kinds of theorizing ventures can be identified in the third quarter of this century? Three patterns will be described in this section—continuation of some comprehensive learning theories from previous decades, emergence of a few new approaches to large-scale theory construction, and a new emphasis on "fact gathering" and construction of "miniature models."

Status of Previous Comprehensive Learning Theories

We have already noted in the previous section that there was great controversy as to the adequacy of the comprehensive learning theories which were established primarily in the 1930s and 1940s. It is quite obvious that they were no longer maintaining their dominant position after mid-century as they had for the previous few decades. Nonetheless, some of these learning theories did maintain a band of followers who were sufficiently productive in their research activities and synthesizing efforts that at least some semblance of the earlier comprehensive learning theory was maintained throughout the third quarter of this century, even up to the writing of the present book. Let us consider each of the theories to which we have referred as illustrations of the comprehensive learning theories from previous decades. We'll first consider the stimulus-response theories and then we will evaluate the status of the cognitive learning theories.

Theories in the Thorndikian tradition have maintained a highly visible position in learning research up to the present time. Most of Thorndike's personal contributions had been completed by the 1930s, but there are some scattered efforts to conduct sets of studies within his tradition today. However, the more recent theorizing in the law of effect tradition was carried out under the guidance of Clark Hull and B. F. Skinner. Hull's theory per se did not maintain the strong leadership position which it had established in the 1930s and 1940s after Hull's death in 1952. We have already noted that Spence, Hull's "heir apparent," did not seem to have great interest in large-scale theory construction. For this or other reasons the Hullian tradition has been carried on in a somewhat fragmented way with many different groups of researchers pursuing various aspects of learning and behavior which were stimulated by Hull's earlier efforts. However, there is practically no concerted attempt to integrate the findings from these somewhat disparate subject areas back into the general Hullian theoretical framework.

Somewhat in contrast, Skinner's position seems even to have gained strength in the third quarter of this century. It is difficult to say whether this is due to the personal leadership which Skinner has so artfully maintained—making him one of the most "visible" psychologists today—or to the merit of the theory as judged by contemporary psychologists. Certainly it is a fact that his conceptions of applied psychology, generally referred to as *behavior modification*, have partly been responsible for an increase in conducting operant research with human subjects and it is possible that some similar impact has resulted in animal operant research as well.

Guthrie's theory has maintained some scattered support, but its main impact in present times seems to be most evident in some formulations of mathematical learning theories. More specifically, the notion that Guthrie advanced concerning "stimulus sampling" and his notions that learning occurs on one trial instead of gradually have been adopted by some mathematical learning theorists.

Most historians seem to agree that gestalt theory is either dormant, dying, or sufficiently incorporated in other theories that it no longer is visible as a position in and of itself. The main place where one hears about gestalt theory seems to be in rather scattered attempts to show how it has practical implications. This does not mean that there is no contemporary gestalt research on learning processes. Rather, we are merely suggesting that it is not a highly visible force in *learning* research. Actually, the greater emphasis throughout gestalt tradition has been on perceptual processes; but even here one does not find a very active group pursuing the principles advanced by the classical gestalt psychologists. Instead, one finds newer versions of cognitive learning research, some of which we discuss under the chapter on Information Processing Theories of Learning.

Tolman's learning theory presents a somewhat puzzling situation. There has been a resurgence of interest in cognitive learning research since mid-century which had no parallel in the earlier decades of this century. Moreover, the kind of cognitive research which is being conducted now bears many striking similarities to some of the positions advocated by Tolman even in the early 1930s in that there is an emphasis on rigorous research closely related to the behavior which Tolman traditionally emphasized. Nonetheless, one finds only occasional references to his theory, suggesting that the cognitive research of present time is derived from a variety of theories, of which Tolman's is only one. Thus, it seems safe to say that most of Tolman's ideas are evidenced in contemporary research on cognitive processes but there has been comparatively little effort in present time to continue development of his theory per se.

Finally, the functionalism approach to learning theory presents us with another curious state of affairs. Whereas there is little that one can point to as a unique functionalistic theory of learning, there is ample evidence in present times of the somewhat pragmatic and generally eclectic approach to research on learning processes which one associates with the functionalistic traditions. As a matter of fact, one can accurately say that the emphasis in the third quarter of the century on miniature models and the general fact-gathering process is entirely in keeping with the predominantly inductive approach to theory construction which has long been associated with the functionalistic traditions.

Emergence of "New Learning Theories"

Several ventures in theorizing emerged at mid-century even though the traditional comprehensive learning theories were no longer maintaining their dominant positions and despite the fact that psychology learning researchers had begun to emphasize data collection more than theory construction. We will briefly consider the two most prominent ones in contemporary learning theory construction—information-processing theories and mathematical learning theories.

In some ways one could say that information-processing learning theories are as old as recorded history, in that they deal with "how the mind works." But they differ even from the positions of the classical gestalt theorists and of Tolman's purposive behaviorism. Three major trends emerged in the third quarter of this century which cast the concern with cognitive processes in a different framework than had been used before. The first development, which is called *information theory*, is not so much a *theory* as it is a means for *measuring* the amount of information transmitted from a sender to a receiver. Of particular interest is the fact that the previously nebulous concepts of "understanding" and "information processed" were being defined in operational terms which could be quantified. Information theory provided means for measuring the extent of correspondence between a message as sent and as received, a means which allegedly could be used without regard to the meaning of the message contents. In addition, unlike the traditional comprehensive learning theorists, the information theorists studied events which actually occurred in terms of the various stimuli and responses which *could* have occurred. Procedures for improving efficiency in information transmission typically are examined for their relevance to an understanding of learning processes in humans. A second development within the information processing approach is that of computer simulation. Whereas the information theorist focuses particularly on *efficiency* in transmitting information, computer simulation researchers are primarily concerned with the details of information *processing*—that is, with the steps and procedures which go on within the person (inside the "black box"). Some computer simulation proponents additionally contend that writing a theory in the form of a computer program provides a more precise, a more rigorous and synthesized, statement of the important learning processes. Thus they contend that there is a *formal* advantage in writing a learning theory in the form of a computer program rather than in sentences. The third development involves information theory and computer simulation concepts and strategies to formulate a model and theory of learning. While rejecting the necessity of using the information theory measures and the computer simulation programs, these theorists contend that a new conception of man has been spawned—that is, a processor of information. This conceptual model of the learner as an active processor of information is alleged to have special advantages in understanding both simple and complex human learning processes.

The second "new" learning theorizing venture is that of mathematical models or mathematical theories of learning. There is some overlap in the nature of the approaches and in the researchers involved in mathematical learning theory and information processing. However, there are certain features of the mathematical learning theory approach which warrant separate designation as a theorizing venture. The first characteristic is the particular *formal* approach to theorizing. Though all researchers use numbers and try to get objective operational definitions, mathematical learning theorists advocate defining all terms numerically and presenting theoretical statements in the form of mathematical equations. The objective is to use such mathematical equations to describe various learning processes (that is, with different kinds of subjects, different tasks, different experimental conditions, etc.) so that they can be compared and contrasted. If the *same* mathematical equation fits different sets of data, then it is held that those learning processes are similar and that important influences on learning have been identified. It is further believed that the theory in mathematical form can be more readily integrated for basic research purposes and, ultimately, should be more useful in practical situations. Aside from these dominating formal qualities, most contemporary mathematical learning theories share certain substantive characteristics. These characteristics, incidentally, arise more from basic assumptions than from empirical findings. Most mathematical learning theorists are interested in *sequential effects* and hold that learning at a given point will reflect both the amount and the kinds of learning which have preceded and the amount of learning which can still be attained. Also, as do the information processing theorists, mathematical learning theorists typically evaluate behaviors which occur in terms of their probable occurrence, given the kinds of stimuli and responses which *could* have occurred.

Dominance of Miniature Models

The most dominant characteristic of learning research during the third quarter of this century can be depicted as a fact-gathering phase with little interest in synthesizing findings beyond the particular problem under investigation. One could generate a lengthy list of topical areas which have been studied, some problems coming from the traditional comprehensive learning theories but investigated with more limiting boundaries, other questions being derived from the newly emerged information processing and mathematical model ventures, and some research questions simply being studied because of a methodological or substantive detail from a previous study. When some synthesis of findings has been attempted, the scope of the conceptual device has typically been so narrowly defined that the term *miniature model* has been used to refer to these ventures. Without any suggestion of priorities or importance, these topical areas and miniature models would include but not be restricted to the following: attention, perceptual learning, imitation learning, short-term memory, long-term memory, concept learning, paired associates learning, discrimination learning, problem solving, etc.

If one takes an extreme inductive approach to theory construction, the emphasis on fact gathering *can* be considered a healthy development in psychology. According to such a point of view, the researcher is more likely to have empirically sound principles generated when the theory construction is kept close to the data. Earlier in this chapter we cited some psychologists who seem to approve of inductive approaches to theory construction.

However, we also pointed out the fact that others have expressed concern if antitheorizing attitudes are taken to an extreme (for example, Hebb, 1949). Moreover, even ardent supporters of a sound, inductive approach to theory have emphasized that theory construction, rather than mere accumulation of facts, is the necessary and appropriate goal of research efforts (for example, Skinner, 1969).

There are at least three matters which concern this present emphasis on fact gathering. First, at some point the researcher will be faced with decisions concerning satisfactory conceptual schema and strategies whereby he can relate the findings of his own narrowly defined area to the findings and principles of researchers in other areas. At the moment, many of these researchers seem to have difficulties in coming to agreement as to which of several models are best designated as *the* miniature model for their respective area. For example, there are now extant a number of models or miniature theories of attention, each one of which has certain merits and flaws. In some respects, the battles among the comprehensive learning theories have partly been replaced by disagreements among competing miniature models. Similar problems will be encountered when theorists try to select the means for integrating several miniature models.

Second, there is a considerable problem in communicating information about the current status of findings and principles within the respective miniature models, and in assessing—at a basic science level—how these miniature models relate to each other. For example, how does one assess the ways that attention principles, discrimination learning principles, perceptual learning principles, and problem-solving principles relate to each other? What does one do when incompatible findings are delineated among two or more of these content areas? And even more distressing, how does any one psychologist keep abreast of current findings in these and the many other areas of learning under investigation by unaffiliated researchers? We carefully specified "at a basic science level" above when we posed some of these questions. Actually, it is possible simply to identify oneself as a specialist in one (or a few) of these miniature-model research areas and to dismiss the question as being personally irrelevant. But this cannot be done so easily by the poor student who is trying (desperately?) to learn about these different areas.

Third, even more importantly for the readers of this book, the practitioner or applications-oriented psychologist has serious problems indeed! In a sense, the miniature models and other isolated findings force those who know least about the details of the research areas—the students and the practitioners—to carry out the synthesizing processes whereby principles from these various areas can be compared and integrated. Even granted the possibility that miniature-model builders will someday continue the inductive theory construction process to a higher level of integration, what should the practitioner and the student do in the meantime? Do they merely ignore potentially relevant findings and principles simply because they have been collected by researchers who choose a miniature model instead of a more comprehensive theory? Do they try to use intuition and common-sense ideas in synthesizing such information, or what can they do? In Chapter 6 we will suggest ways in which such rather isolated principles and findings can be used by practitioners, although it will also be contended that the practitioner's and student's job is much easier when the basic learning theorist has explored and empirically tested such syntheses.

One feature of the miniature-model research which is particularly relevant to our discussion in this book is that there has emerged considerable interest in human learning processes. In the long run, this will obviously have desirable benefits for the educator and educational psychologist who wish to use a psychological data base when designing instructional procedures. However, the problem at the present time, as suggested above, is that there are relatively few attempts to integrate these findings into a more comprehensive theory or to interpret them in such a way that they would be useful in practical situations. As an illustration of what could and should be done, let us briefly consider the work on memory.

Most earlier comprehensive learning theorists seem to have assumed that there is only one kind of memory storage or location. In contrast, contemporary miniature models and research approaches are based on the assumption that there are at least two or three memory processes. (It is still an open question as to whether the different types constitute different kinds of processing and/or whether the storage is accomplished in different locations in the nervous system.) Many contemporary researchers theorize that there is a sensory storage register which is capable not only of receiving relevant stimulation (for example, visual stimuli at the eye's field) but also of holding some impression of the stimulus for an extremely brief time even after the stimulus is no longer physically present. Next, there is a short-term memory storage which has quite limited capacity but which can handle and retain incoming stimuli for a time span on the order of ten seconds to a few minutes. Finally, there is a long-term memory storage which has extensive capacity but which requires a number of coding steps before an item can be stored there.

There are two ways in which this information about miniature-model memory research has been handled which make the findings and principles more readily usable by practitioners than ordinarily is the case with miniature-model research results. First, some information-processing theorists have incorporated these findings and principles in their theories. We will consider this aspect in some detail in Chapter 11. Secondly, Kumar (1971) summarized relevant aspects of the contemporary research results and identified some educational implications. The practical suggestions can be summarized as follows: These findings suggest that retention is not as much an automatic process as has been indicated by those earlier theories which primarily focused on reinforced repetitions. Instead, the student not only has a considerable amount of "veto power" so as to negate learning effects, but in addition can take a number of steps which will positively influence retention and later transfer. Teachers should help students to develop coding and organizing strategies which both facilitate retention and make later use easier. Teachers should also recognize that students are more selective when confronted with a large amount or difficult kinds of information, and that they tend to reject (correctly or incorrectly) a considerable portion of the available information in order to focus on the selected items. Students and teachers should try to identify those characteristics of stimuli and features of the learning situation which facilitate coding and processing of the information presented to them.

Our discussion of the contemporary research on memory, above, mainly focused on information-processing types of concepts. Some researchers prefer one of a variety of other theoretical orientations. But practically all researchers in the miniature-model tradition insist on clear conceptual and operational definitions, and they typically search for the controlling variables of which the behaviors (of their particular research area) are a function. This pattern is sufficiently evident in contemporary research that many authors have depicted the third quarter of this century as an era "behavioristic functionalism" or "functionalistic behaviorism." The dominant mode of theory construction, to the extent that one can say that it truly exists, is that of an extreme form of inductive theory construction, with rather limited attempts to synthesize findings beyond narrowly delimited problems. Most researchers with this orientation seem to be focusing so intently on the specific research problems which they have delineated that they have virtually ignored theorizing processes at least for the moment.

There are different views as to what ultimately will come of these miniature models. Some simply contend that one cannot have a comprehensive learning theory or general psychology theory, and they comment critically about the earlier "futile and misguided" comprehensive learning theory ventures. A second group holds that theoretical integration eventually will occur but that psychologists should now continue to collect data without worrying about this later integration; most of such spokesmen do not indicate what form such larger-scale theorizing may take. A third group rather confidently predicts that the miniature-model findings from the various research areas will be incorporated in an information-processing theory. A smaller, fourth group (which includes the author) expects that several different comprehensive theories will incorporate the miniature models, and that these comprehensive theories will respectively resemble the several examples which have existed previously and which have been described in this book. Moreover, since theorizing patterns seem to have changed on the average every twenty years and because there are a number of indicators that some learning research psychologists are showing renewed interest in theory construction (Gagne, 1970a; Kintsch, 1970; Newell & Simon, 1972; Razran, 1971; Saltz, 1971; Schoenfeld, 1970; Skinner, 1969; etc.), it is conceivable that we have already entered the beginning phase of a new era in theory construction in the psychology of learning.

PRESENT AND FUTURE LEARNING THEORIES?

In closing our review of trends in theory construction in psychology, let us now consider some of the current developments and probable future trends. It is noteworthy that during this third quarter of the century when psychologists have been more involved in fact gathering than theory construction some psychologists have continued to point out the need not only for comprehensive learning theories but also for larger-scale theories which would encompass the social sciences more generally. For example, Pfaffmann (1970) has called for the "development of a unified conceptual framework for the study of behavior at all levels" (p. 438). Similarly, Dollard (1970) characterizes psychology as "urgently in need of a theory of learning" (p. 417). Wolman (1968) and J. G. Miller (1955) have independently presented their version of such a comprehensive theory for psychology and other sciences. But readers familiar with these particular authors and their work may recognize that these individuals are especially concerned with the practical applicability of such theories. Thus, one may legitimately inquire as to whether such concern with theory construction in the present era is merely a manifestation of the practitioner's need for pulling all kinds of relevant information together.

Actually, many experimental psychologists likewise recognize the need for theory construction in psychology. A noteworthy comment has been made on a number of occasions by B. F. Skinner:

"In a paper published in 1950 I asked the question 'Are theories of learning necessary?' and suggested that the answer was 'No.' I soon found myself representing a position which has been described as a Grand Anti-Theory. Fortunately, I had defined my terms. . . . whether particular experimental psychologists like it or not, experimental psychology is properly and inevitably committed to the construction of a theory of behavior. A theory is essential to the scientific understanding of behavior as a subject matter." (Skinner, 1969, pp. vii-viii)

Granted that there is some press for theory construction for learning processes and about psychology more generally, what types of theory construction might we anticipate for the future? First of all, it should be recognized that many psychologists feel quite strongly that there are highly desirable advantages accrued by tightly knit, narrowly circumscribed areas of theory. Thus, any large-scale theory construction should attempt to incorporate these models. But what kind of framework can we anticipate for future large-scale integration? Three different emphases are apparent today which are especially relevant to learning research. First is some form of neobehaviorism, which would involve a stimulus-response theory much like some of the earlier versions but with the advantage of the more recent rigorous research in cognitive psychology. A second possibility is a cognitive theory, probably along the lines of the human information-processing theory which has emerged since mid-century. Third, certain positions, which some would not separate from the cognitive position, collectively are referred to here as *phenomenological psychology*. Simply stated, it emphasizes the experience of the individual as being of foremost importance in psychology, and it contends that behavior is important only so much as it enables the psychologist to draw inferences about how the individual experiences a given situation. Some recent papers illustrate the relationships and characteristics of these three orientations in theory construction in psychology today.

A few years ago invited speakers participated in a symposium in which they discussed the advantages and disadvantages of behaviorism and the advantages and disadvantages of phenomenology as theorizing ventures in psychology. Though the various arguments are too extensive to be considered in any depth here (see Wann, 1964, and Hitt, 1969), it would be useful to consider some of the main points emphasized. First, as we have already noted, behaviorism emphasizes objectivity in research and considers psychology to be a natural science which deals with human behavior largely like any other natural phenomena which might be studied by scientific method. The advantage, of course, lies mainly in the relatively objective and consistent statements which can be made about human activity. However, some feel that such a "cold," "impersonal" approach to man destroys the very essence of psychology. These persons, many of whom are proponents of the phenomenological approach, contend that psychology's real commission is to understand the experience of the individual. For them, behavior is a mere manifestation which may or may not reflect how the individual is experiencing a given situation at a particular time. Though admittedly less precise, proponents of the phenomenological approach contend that they are dealing with more meaningful aspects of psychology than had been possible with the "research-oriented" natural-science conception of psychology.

Can these positions be reconciled, or are they inherently incompatible? Many debates have been raised as to which, if any, of these orientations should dominate theorizing in psychology. Frequently, it is held that it is impossible to reconcile these positions, and that one must choose from one or the other in developing psychological theories. However, it is the author's contention that these two positions can and must be reconciled. Moreover, the author accepts the point of view that such can be accomplished by viewing the phenomenological approach as a "first person" view of learning, whereas the behavioristic or neobehavioristic orientation provides a view of learning process largely like that gained by a "third person" observer of the situation.

Others have juxtaposed some form of cognitive learning theory against a behavioristic representative. It is frequently contended that one must choose from one rather than the other, and it is argued that these two positions are incompatible. Moreover, many view the first part of this century as having been the province of stimulus-response psychology and they contend that since mid-century we have moved into an era that will be completely dominated by some form of cognitive psychology, most likely under the information-processing orientation. Segal and Lachman (1972) provide a discussion of such an orientation. They contend that stimulus-response theory has been found to be so inadequate that not only can it not cope with complex human learning processes, but also the modifications which had been required have left neobehaviorism with only rudimentary fragments of its earlier coherent system. Thus, they contend that the neobehavioristic approach is so diluted that it is no longer recognizable. Sharply in contrast are opinions which are provided by proponents of the neobehavioristic orientation. Kantor (1970), for example, presents a much more optimistic view of neobehaviorism particularly as it is represented by the operant experimental analysis of behavior. In contrast with the criticisms of Segal and Lachman (1972), Kantor suggests that the operant approach had been eminently successful in dealing with certain aspects of behavior and that the time has now arrived for addressing other, previously ignored topics. Moreover, one recent review of contemporary operant research (Hendry, 1969) suggests that the operant orientation is now ready to deal with at least some aspects of information processing in animals and in human learning. Again, proponents of each approach contend at times that theirs is the one and only orientation which one can accept. We might again remind you of the quotation from Tyler at the beginning of the first chapter, in which he pointed out that there is a tremendous range of opinion as to what is the best vantage point to view psychology and hence to construct psychological theories of learning. With regard to the present controversy as to the behavioristic versus the cognitive formulation, the author again recommends that some form of reconciliation is possible and, indeed, absolutely necessary. Stated simply, it is the point of view taken here that the operant orientation provides a pertinent system for describing the overt activities of the individual, whereas the cognitive orientation provides for a psychological conception of those events which occur within the organism. As with the behavioristic versus phenomenological debates, we argue for compatibility and complementarity rather than incompatibility with regard to these debates about cognitive versus behavioristic formulations of learning processes.

Two basic themes are prominent not only within university departments but throughout society as a whole in the early 1970s—*ecological validity* and *relevance*. Ecological validity refers to the extent to which a laboratory finding may constitute a meaningful statement about the world outside the laboratory as well as within the somewhat artificial, highly controlled conditions of the laboratory. Relevant, in the sense in which we are using it here, refers to the extent to which some bit of knowledge has practical implications either for an individual person or for society at large. Though the first term more obviously relates to basic research, whereas the second deals with practical applicability, both terms imply a concern with the real value of any knowledge which man might gain. The implications for the present area of study are simple and direct. In a sense, much of society is asking whether the results of learning research simply constitute evidence of "games scientists play," or whether such information might help us to understand how man and the rest of the world acts as it does, with the further possibility of dealing with man's social and other problems.

It is likely that these two basic concerns in society will influence psychology learning theorists to be more concerned in the future, as compared with the past, with the ecological validity and social relevance of their theoretical formulations. Such pressures are being brought to bear not only by the funding agencies and other institutions which support psychological learning research but also by both students and experienced psychologists who have been conducting rather intensive self-examinations of the past ventures in psychological theorizing. In some respects, one could consider these concerns as mere extensions of the semantic and syntactical tests which we indicated earlier should be used with any scientific theory. But they go beyond previous concerns of this kind. Psychologists, educators, and the general public have shown such interest in ecological validity and social relevance for science generally that it is likely that future learning theories will need to meet these tests in addition to the previous criteria for judging scientific theories. Hopefully, this may foster renewed attempts to assess the validity of laboratory-based findings in naturalistic settings outside the laboratory and in attempts to resolve practical educational problems.

One final "problem" needs to be reexamined by learning theorists—namely the issue of "individual differences" in learning ability and in learning style. Throughout most of the first half of the twentieth century, there has been a division between two major research groups within psychology. The first group, with whom we are primarily concerned in this text, is one which has been particularly concerned with learning processes and which has consistently placed highest priority for *experimental* laboratory research as the preferred research method for practically all problems of concern to them. The second group, for various historical reasons which cannot concern us here, has traditionally been separate from the first group; they have not been as concerned with learning processes per se, although they indirectly have had them as a major focus too. Their primary substantive concern has been *individual differences*, which usually refers to both the ability (especially as related to intelligence) and the habitual behavior or customary ways of acting (usually referred to as personality characteristics). Their preferred and sometimes exclusive research methods are the correlational methods. Closely aligned with this group is the developmental psychology tradition which has been particularly concerned with the way that individuals differ at various ages and stages of development; their preferred method of research most frequently has been that of naturalistic observation or some other form of observation in a more controlled or contrived situation. The failure to communicate between these two groups—experimental psychologists and correlational psychologists—has been so extensive and so widely recognized that some (for example, Cronbach, 1957) referred to them as the two sciences or the two research orientations of psychology.

But by now the reader may be wondering: How does this relate to our present concern with learning processes and learning theories? One of the major trends in recent years is for a rapprochement between these two scientific disciplines of psychology. Although the efforts have not met with overwhelming success even by the time of this writing, there is some basis for optimism for better relationships in the future.

Unfortunately, in the author's opinion, there has been too little concern among learning theorists—at least in the traditional theories—to consider the possibility that there may be "individual differences" which should be considered in the formulation of learning theories. Workers in this particular area of psychology have typically been so concerned with formulating general laws of behavior that would cut across species as well as across individuals within a species that they have generally been unconcerned with variations in the extent to which individuals have "followed" such general laws of behavior. In some cases, such variations among subjects have been considered "annoying error" which learning theorists at least must tolerate and at best can ignore. But there has been substantial evidence in recent years that at least some learning theorists and researchers are interested in reversing this well-established trend of the past. One concrete bit of evidence on this is a report of a symposium on learning processes and individual differences which was held in April 1965 at the University of Pittsburgh (Gagne, 1967).

This report is of interest in several ways. First, it is of note that it was only around 1965 that there was some concerted attempt to try to bridge the gap between these two disciplines of scientific psychology. Secondly, this particular symposium discussed the historical relationships between individual difference research and the research on learning processes. Third, the participants in the symposium examined the extant relationships and made recommendations about the future course of psychological learning theory. In brief, it seems fair to state that the participants—who constitute some of the major figures in contemporary psychology learning research—seem to be unanimous in their opinion that psychology's learning theory must take into account individual differences. Moreover, there was some implied expectation that individual differences of concern should include not only the demographic characteristics of the individual—such as age, intelligence, sex, socioeconomic status—but also the kind of characteristics which one finds inherent in the learning process per se. The latter attributes would include the extent to which the individuals are susceptible to distraction, the extent to which they can maintain constructive attentiveness to a task, their general level of arousal or activity, and the degree of consistency/variability in their performance on specific learning tasks. Moreover, it was recognized that the laboratory learning researcher must examine the pertinence of the kinds of laboratory learning tasks being studied for the learning activities of the individual outside the artificial conditions of the laboratory.

It does not seem appropriate to try to provide a mystical projection of the "learning theory of the future." However, it does seem necessary for us to make some kind of statement about the course of development which we should expect in current and future psychological learning theories.

At a minimum, it seems likely that syntactically sound and semantically valid theories of the future will be scrutinized for their ecological validity and for their potential relevance for resolution of social problems. Psychologists and others quite frequently can be expected to ask the psychology learning researcher "So what do your findings really mean?" The answer will need to go beyond the characteristics of the task and conditions of the laboratory situation. Moreover, it seems quite likely that many will be examining the fruits of the research for their potential relevance to social problems.

Hopefully, learning theorists will build on the research of the past instead of ignoring it. Berlyne (1966) has pointed out that frequently in psychology we have been too quick to reject theories of the past whenever new ventures have been launched. Moreover, he points out that many of the explanations for adoption of the new position are based on "strawmen" accusations which are not really pertinent to the most recent developments of the previously established theories. Thus, it is our expectation, and hope, that future learning theories will build on many of the historical theories considered in this book. This would be desirable not merely because of the knowledge that one gains from something that has happened in the past but because of the value it has in helping us to avoid recommitting some of the errors of past theorists.

There is some suggestion that the behavioristic or neobehavioristic theories may provide some interesting facets for integration in new theories along with the information-processing conception which has become more and more popular in recent years. But there are two aspects of the miniature-model movement which should offer a more sophisticated expectation for learning theories. You may recall that we noted that some miniature models have been restricted to specific types of learning, whereas others have focused on particular aspects of the learning or retention process. One potential implication here is that the "monolithic" traditional comprehensive learning theories may not have been quite so incompatible as their respective proponents have suggested. Perhaps the various theories have been dealing either with different types of learning or with different aspects of the learning process. The implication for future learning theories is that they probably will have to be much more complex than one might have expected from the focus of traditional comprehensive learning theories. At a minimum, they will need to incorporate the many disparate findings of the currently popular miniature models of learning processes.

Finally, it seems mandatory that contemporary psychology learning researchers and builders of the future must take into account the quite compelling individual difference findings. As a result, it is likely that psychological learning theories will need to specify what kinds of prerequisite skills are involved and what kinds of learning styles are involved. If the current research relating students' individual differences to various instructional methods can be used as an indicator, it is conceivable that new ways of describing individual differences will also result. In later chapters we will consider the relevance of "learning to learn" and some skills or knowledge specifically related to a given learning task at hand as new types of individual differences.

5
Emergence of Instructional Theories

Not everything in psychology or education that is of interest or even of conceivable usefulness to the prospective teacher can be included in educational psychology.... Selection and restriction of content must be made, and this can best be done in terms of some unifying conceptual scheme or focus. (Getzels, 1952, p. 382)

... [F]ormal education is relatively long on practice and short on theory. Current practices often reflect, on the one hand, considerable inertia, and, on the other, an almost frantic search for innovation to alleviate currently pressing problems. (Siegel, 1967, p. viii)

Theory is in the end, as has been well said, the most practical of all things, because this widening of the range of attention beyond nearby purpose and desire eventually results in the creation of wider and farther-reaching purposes, and enables us to use a much wider and deeper range of conditions and means than were expressed in the observation of primitive practical purposes. (Dewey, 1929, p. 17)

In the 1950s there began to emerge a group of positions in educational psychology and in education which came to be named *instructional theories*. Of course, it would be naïve and inaccurate to contend that *no education* theories existed previously, or even to imply that educators went about their work without understanding what they were trying to do and why. What we do find emerging at mid-twentieth century are several positions which *systematically* try to identify those educational objectives which are considered important, to provide a detailed description of ways one arranges learning experiences to attain those objectives, and to use *scientific* methods to assess merits and to plan modifications of educational methods.

This chapter will be divided into five major parts. In the first section we will consider definitions of instructional theory and several closely related terms. Secondly, we will describe various ways in which psychological research and theory have been related to educational practice and we will consider expressions of dissatisfaction concerning attempts to "apply learning theories," leading to proposals for formulating instructional theories. Third, a rather antitheoretical and generally pragmatic approach to education will be depicted as the context in which instructional theories have been emerging. The fourth section illustrates the range of opinions as to how one should develop instructional theories. In a context of rather loosely formulated educational theories, identified are five different conceptions as to how one could use psychological learning research and principles to formulate instructional theories. Finally, these varied attempts at instructional theory construction are evaluated with regard to both their present status and their future prospects. Of interest are not only the instructional theories but also the impact they may have in stimulating more constructive relationships between basic psychological research and educational practice.

INSTRUCTIONAL THEORIES, TECHNOLOGY, SCIENCE, PSYCHOLOGY

What is meant by "instructional theory," and by the alternative designations, "instructional technology," "instructional science," and "instructional psychology"? As you will recall from our earlier discussions, we use the term *theory* in basic sciences to refer to a set of propositions which are systematically integrated and which can serve as a means for predicting and explaining phenomena. Additional considerations are involved for applied sciences and in practical situations, where it is not sufficient to "explain" phenomena. The educator, for example, is obligated to assist students in attaining educational objectives in *some* way. Whether or not the educator understands fully *why* the methods work is generally less important than is the task of finding some methods which consistently *will* work. Of course, ideally it would be desirable to know which methods are successful and to understand the principles underlying the methods.

Instructional Theory

We define *instructional theory* as an integrated set of principles which prescribe guidelines for arranging conditions to achieve educational objectives. It is assumed that these principles will be applicable to educational situations in which a teacher is present as well as to the various contemporary educational methods implemented primarily through the *design* of the educational *materials*. These contemporary methods include computer-assisted instruction, programmed instruction, inquiry learning methods, discovery learning techniques, various forms of individualized instruction, etc. It is also assumed that instructional theories in general must be neutral with regard to selecting educational objectives, although it is expected that some instructional theories may be especially oriented toward certain objectives. Consistent with the emphasis throughout this text on theories, we assume that instructional theories ideally should be both empirically valid and logically consistent— that is, that they meet semantic and syntactic tests described in Chapter 2. Various authors have proposed that some form of *teaching theory* should be developed. We will use the term *instructional theory* rather than teaching theory on the basis that the former is more inclusive about the process of instruction.

Instructional Technology

Some authors have preferred to talk about a "technology" of instruction instead of a "theory" of instruction. Apparently there are several reasons why this has occurred. First, there is a rather distinct skepticism expressed by practitioners about *theory*. Theory is frequently used to refer to ideal but impractical principles. Second, some prefer the term *technology* because of its more pragmatic connotations and its implied relevance to practical situations. There has been a trend in recent years for persons from various disciplines to use *instructional technology* not only with reference to "hardware" and "software" (for example, audiovisual aids, general educational media, and computer-assisted or computer-managed instruction), but also with reference to principles providing guidelines for the use of these devices (McMurrin, 1970). Thus there is considerable overlap in contemporary definitions of *instructional technology* and *instructional theory*, with the choice of the terms frequently being based on the background of the spokesman rather than on distinct differences in meaning.

But some authors consciously choose one term rather than the other because, in their opinion, each constitutes a different approach to developing logically and empirically sound educational principles. You will recall that there were different strategies adopted by various individuals in their attempts to formulate *learning* theory, some emphasizing a deductive approach, with others preferring an inductive approach and even expressing reservations about formulating theories prematurely. Likewise you will find differences of opinion about instructional research and theory. One difference relates to whether one should start with broad, encompassing instructional principles and later evaluate empirically the validity of these principles or whether it is better at first to accumulate a set of facts out of which some broader principles are eventually expected to emerge. As we noted in Chapter 2, the former is generally called a deductive approach to theory construction; the latter, an inductive approach.

We will find that those who prefer the deductive approach or some combination of inductive and deductive theory construction typically use the term *instructional theory*; those who are somewhat more pragmatic and who prefer initially to focus on collecting a body of facts will tend to prefer the term *instructional technology*. Part of the problem for you, the reader, is that some people will use the word "technology" to refer *only* to equipment, whereas others will intend the broader definition of technology, including the set of principles involving all aspects of the educational experiences. In this text we use the broader definition unless otherwise specified.

Instructional Science and
Instructional Psychology

The 1970s have also produced some popularity for the terms *instructional science* and *instructional psychology*. The first term has come to indicate the various social sciences and communication sciences which relate to instruction as well as those interdisciplinary ventures in education which utilize scientific methods for developing fundamental principles of instruction. *Instructional psychology* generally refers to the theory and the principles derived from the application of psychological principles in the improvement of instruction or which result when psychologists conduct research in practical instruction-learning situations. As with the distinctions above, the author uses *instructional theory* or *instructional science principles* to refer to the fruits of instructional science and instructional psychology.

Educational Objectives versus
Instructional Methods

Many students seem to have difficulty in distinguishing between selection of educational objectives and selection of the means by which one can attain these objectives. Perhaps this should not be surprising since papers obliterating such a distinction frequently can also be found in the professional literature in education and educational psychology. For example, many educators seem to have chosen gestalt theory over Thorndike's formulation to a great extent because they believed that these two theories dictated instructional methods which would *necessarily* lead to different educational objectives. They did not distinguish between educational objectives and instructional methods. As a result, it has been contended by Thorndike's critics that utilization of connectionism principles will necessarily result in having students who are mere repositories of facts and who are incapable of "thinking."

Let's consider an analogy. Students in graduate classes have frequently been asked the question: "If you are taking a trip, would you go through Dover, Delaware?" As puzzled expressions are evident throughout the group, they are asked an additional question: "Would you take an expressway?" This question seems to add to the confusion. The students seem to be thinking, and often verbalize such questions as: "How can the instructor possibly be expecting us to answer questions with the information he has given us?" "How can I decide what *route* I would take, or whether I'd use an expressway, when I don't know where I'm starting from and what destination I hope to reach?" "How can these questions possibly be relevant to education or to educational psychology?"

Students are then asked: "When preparing materials and lesson plans for a new course, is your choice of textbooks one of the first decisions which you ordinarily make?" "Do you usually use films in teaching your course?" At this point, students seemed to feel more comfortable with the questions and they proceed to answer the questions. With little hesitation they quickly outline the kinds of textbooks they would use if they were asked to start a new course, and they frequently discuss the kinds of audiovisual materials which they would like to incorporate in such courses.

At this time, the instructor asks them: "Why were you so concerned about having additional information to answer the questions about taking a trip, whereas somewhat parallel questions were answered with ease with regard to taking an educational trip?" Certainly, it *does* seem reasonable to know where one is going, and what starting point is involved when we decide whether we will go through a particular city, and whether we decide to use an expressway or another travel route. Each of these decisions primarily will depend on where we are going to and where we are starting from. But, similarly, we should also (at least in the author's opinion) take into account our starting point (students' status at start of the course) and destination (educational objectives) when we make decisions about the "route" we will take and the kinds of "experiences" which will be provided when we plan our methods of instruction.

Just as the "destination" is typically distinguished from the mode of transportation and the route to be taken when we plan a trip, likewise it seems reasonable that we should be able to distinguish between the educational *objectives* which we hope to attain and the *means* by which we expect to attain them. Such a distinction is generally accepted in our discussion about traveling, but is customarily ignored with regard to educational procedures. The instructional theories which we will examine ideally should be neutral with regard to selection of educational objectives or should be designated as such if they are only designed for certain types of educational objectives. In any case, the selection of educational methods involves decisions which are separate from those decisions in choosing educational objectives.

Instructional Theories in This Text

Now that we have alerted you to the range of opinion and to the variations in the use of such terms as *instructional theory, instructional technology, instructional science,* and *instructional psychology,* we will use *instructional theory* in a broad sense in this chapter and throughout the rest of the book, as was done with the parallel controversy about "learning theory." The author believes that all the individuals involved are primarily concerned with getting some systematically organized set of principles, and that they differ primarily in terms of the way by which they try to achieve such an objective.

As noted earlier, our main interest here is in instructional theories which are either based on psychology learning research and theory, or developed in reaction to learning theory. In the next two sections we will examine some reasons for developing instructional theories as well as or in place of learning theories, and we will consider the status of theories in education.

APPLYING PSYCHOLOGICAL THEORIES?

One of the themes in this book is that different types of relationships have existed between psychology and education since the late nineteenth century when both were first being identified as sciences. Moreover, the kind of relationship which exists in any particular situation depends partly on the status of available psychological theory and partly on the attitudes and expectations held by both psychologists and educators concerning the use of psychological theory in education.

Previous chapters have pointed out that there are many "competing" theories or conceptions of learning in psychology, and that the organization of psychological research findings ranges from practically isolated findings from single studies to relatively comprehensive models and theories. We have identified ways in which psychologists in some historical periods have emphasized gathering data while at other periods they have focused on theory construction. In addition we have noted that the various approaches to theory construction can be observed at almost any historical point, since there is no "official" pronouncement as to how psychologists should conduct research or how they should interpret their findings.

In the present section we will review representative observations by psychologists and educators concerning actual and/or desirable ways for relating psychological research and educational practice. A major result of these deliberations about ways for improving educational practice is the relatively recent emergence of instructional theories. We will try to show how these instructional theories can be complementary to learning theories and that there can be mutually beneficial exchanges between them. Our discussion in this section will be organized historically in terms of the dominant approaches to theory construction in psychology learning research, discussed in Chapters 3 and 4.

The "New Sciences" of Psychology and Education

As you will recall from earlier discussions in this text, psychology was delineated as a new area of science late in the nineteenth century. Early psychologists were exceedingly protective of their new designation as "scientists" and they tried almost desperately to protect their new venture from any criticism that they were being "unscientific."

In what sense might their concern with identification as a science be relevant to our present discussion of relationships between psychological theories and educational practice? For one thing, some early psychologists felt strongly that their efforts should be restricted to the accumulation of a fund of knowledge, rather than be committed primarily to solving social problems. For example, Titchener, a dominant force in the shaping of psychology in the United States at the turn of the century, was dogmatic in his contention that psychology should be restricted to the scientific study of the normal, adult human and that it should be a basic or pure science with no real concern about practical problem resolution.

Though others—for example the functionalists—considered psychology to be an applied as well as a basic science, many psychologists around the turn of the century had obvious reservations both as to whether psychologists should become involved in resolving practical problems and as to whether psychology as science per se would have any real contributions to make in the resolution of such problems.

William James (1899), for example, in some respects seemed to conceive psychology and education as developing in parallel. He characterized psychology as a science and education as an art, and he contended that arts are never dictated directly from sciences relevant to them. James took the position that educational practice must *agree* with the psychology *but* that psychology per se could *not dictate* pedagogy since different methods actually could be consistent with sound psychological principles. Despite the numerous occasions on which James was asked by educators to provide suggestions for pedagogy, he seemed to maintain his position that psychology should be a pure science and that it would not dictate directly what teachers should do in the classroom.

H. H. Schroeder (1913), a "normal school" psychology instructor whose job involved training teachers to use psychological principles, depicted educators as being urgently in need of help from psychologists and criticized the position of James, Muensterberg, and others who (according to Schroeder) felt "that psychology can render no real service to pedagogy" (p. 470). Since Schroeder seemed to feel that Thorndike *did* conceive of psychology as having more direct relevance for educational practice, it may be useful to consider what Thorndike's announced position was during this period.

In 1910, Thorndike characterized psychology's contributions to education under the four topics: "aims, materials, means and methods" (Thorndike, 1910, p. 5). Thorndike, too, acknowledged psychology's role as a pure science in which there would be an accumulating fund of information about human activity, but he called for research on the utilization of these psychological principles in education and in other areas of society. Without proclaiming that psychology had indeed achieved such a state, he held that a truly complete science of psychology would enable us to understand the kinds of individual characteristics which we had inherited as well as those which we had learned, and would help us to understand the causes of our various activities. Thus workers in the science of education would be better able to identify and to measure their educational aims, would be able to derive from psychological principles some direction for devising educational methods, would be able to determine which of various educational methods were successful, and would be able to use knowledge of psychological principles to understand why educational methods may not be working. He maintained that this relationship between the science of psychology and the science of education could be mutually beneficial in that, in educational application, psychologists would find a new means for testing their theories and a new source of hypotheses to be explored. Finally, he maintained that an understanding of the underlying psychological principles would enable educators to make their plans for education most likely successful ones if they made them compatible with these scientifically derived "truths" about the ways we learn.

William James and E. L. Thorndike seemed to be in agreement that psychology would continue as a basic science and that application of such a fund of knowledge would largely come as a result of workers in the newly established science of education. While Dewey took a generally similar position, he at least did make reference to "a special linking science" which would exist *between* theory and practical work (Dewey, 1900). But Dewey was rather vague as to his conceptions of this special linking science; to some extent he seemed to place the burden for application on a select group of educators who would be identified as the general educational theorists or scientists, but there is some possibility that psychologists or new professional persons would do this work.

The positions of these three prominent spokesmen seem to be representative of the expected relationships between psychology theory and educational practice around the turn of the century. The division of labor would be rather simple and straightforward although there was lack of clarity as to means for using psychological principles. Psychologists would conduct basic research and accumulate a fund of knowledge about human learning and other activities. Someone, perhaps educators, would take this fund of knowledge and apply it in developing their educational programs. But a host of additional problems develop when there is not *one* psychology, but several; when there is not *one* theory of learning, but many, particularly when the "many" have somewhat contradictory implications for educational practice.

Applications from "Schools" of Psychology

Relationships between psychology and education had to undergo changes when different systems, or "schools," emerged as contenders for designation as the real science of psychology. The problem no longer merely consisted of checking for compatibility between *the* extant psychology and educational practices; instead, one was faced with questions concerning selection of the most appropriate conception of this new science. Before the psychologist or educator could determine whether particular educational practices fit with psychology principles, he had to decide which of the several available schools should be considered the most authoritative, the most valid. Recall that each of the respective schools was depicted—explicitly or implicitly—as *the* most appropriate and valid scientific explanation of human activity. With this competition among schools there also developed tendencies to encourage practitioners, including especially educators, to accept particular positions. Thus there developed a more active role for psychologists as to application of their principles, at least more active in "promoting them," than was evident at the turn of the century.

With the emergence of several schools and the resulting competition among them, spokesmen seemed to lose their reservations about the *tentative* nature of their practical suggestions. More and more recommendations were made as "scientific facts" rather than as tentative descriptions for the real world outside the laboratory. Moreover, since the contentions were drawn from total conceptions of psychology as science, this meant that a particular spokesman was advocating that his system should be accepted and that other systems in total should be disregarded. Since only relatively few educational principles had been empirically validated this meant that the educator was mainly accepting a point of view and the basic assumptions of the psychology system. During subsequent decades in which the comprehensive learning theories became more clearly delineated, there developed an expectation among psychologists and educators that it should be possible to derive quite explicit prescriptions for educational practice from the comprehensive learning theories.

Applications from Comprehensive
Learning Theories

As we noted earlier, this was an era in which comprehensive learning theories were coming into existence and were competing with each other for the attention primarily of psychologists involved in basic research. It was an era in which learning was a dominant area of interest for psychology researchers, and thus the theories of learning which developed also tended to dominate theory generally in psychology.

If an educator is going to select a learning theory, it would seem reasonable to expect that he would want to pick the theory which provides the most complete and valid description of learning as it occurs in the classroom. Many educators would add that it should not only describe but should also *prescribe* what educators should do in order to facilitate learning of their students. But you should recognize by this point that neither description fits learning theory as it emerged during the first half of this century. First, from the standpoint of validity and accuracy in describing learning process, *no* single theory had been identified by learning researchers in toto as being clearly the most valid and comprehensive theory of learning extant. Instead, proponents of each of the major theoretical positions we have considered thus far in our text have believed that *their position* constitutes the best candidate for eventually developing a valid, comprehensive theory of learning. Secondly, it should be quite clear to the reader by this point that virtually none of the learning researchers specifically selected their experimental arrangements on the basis that they would be directly representative or even generally similar to the kinds of learning which go on in the classroom. Instead, though some of the initial questions which prompted learning studies were practical problems, learning researchers typically selected experimental arrangements and problems on the basis of their relevance to their previous research or theory, rather than on the basis of their value for immediate classroom application.

On what basis, in retrospect, have educators apparently selected a comprehensive learning theory for practical applications? McDonald advances the interesting thesis that at least during the first half of this century, educators were only minimally influenced by a theory's validity, prescriptiveness, and practicality. Instead, apparently the *main* reason that a given theory was selected was "its consistency with the thinking of influential educational and social theorists, and more subtly on the Zeitgeist" (McDonald, 1964, p. 3). Moreover, he suggests that it is necessary for *educators* to perceive such compatibility, that it is not sufficient that the theory's proponents recognize that their approach is compatible with current educational thinking. McDonald acknowledges Thorndike's initial influence in education, but he designates gestalt theory as having been of greatest influence on educators during most of the first half of the century. He contends that Dewey and the "progressive educators" particularly were influential in selecting gestalt theory because it was considered philosophically compatible with their position.

Many authors contend that educators prior to this century had accepted new ideas mainly because a given spokesman was identified as an authoritative source, rather than because the particular ideas had been shown to improve educational practice in helping students to learn. In many respects, it would appear that educators mainly viewed psychologists as new authoritative sources who would be accepted or ignored largely on the basis of their credentials as authorities and on the extent to which their proposals about education seemed reasonable as compared with existing educational practice. Educators and educational psychologists during this period were not in a strong position to determine whether the learning theory-based educational prescriptions were improving students' learning since educational objectives were not usually defined operationally.

If one has difficulties demonstrating whether basic science findings are improving educational practice, there are many questions which can be leveled about the credentials of the theorists and the merits of their findings—questions which may be only indirectly related to the potential value of educational prescriptions in the classroom. For example, many of the criticisms had to do with the fact that the wrong *conception of man* had been promoted by various learning theorists. Some suggested that Thorndike's *connectionism* was based on a conception of man which was "mechanistic." As a result, some rejected Thorndike's ideas about education because they stemmed from a mechanistic conception without checking whether such ideas would help the classroom teacher to do a better job. Other theorists were criticized because their paradigm focused on relatively simple processes, because they had used animal subjects for their research, because their studies were conducted under controlled laboratory conditions, etc. On the basis of criticisms such as these, some theorists were discredited as potential authoritative sources.

Let us not completely reject these criticisms; one should examine any basic research results to determine whether they can be directly applied in practical situations. In most cases basic findings should be submitted to a series of tests in practical situations before their practical value can be determined. What is being pointed out is that acceptance-rejection decisions typically were made on the basis of the theorist's credentials as an authority and his compatibility with contemporary educational philosophy rather than as a result of empirical evidence as to whether his educational suggestions were worthwhile.

Lynch provides an example of one of the countless papers, symposia, and books which were devoted to relationships between psychology and education. He observed: "Whether the results of laboratory experimentation are applicable to the larger activities of everyday life seem to be a matter of controversy more often in psychology than any of the other sciences" (Lynch, 1945, p. 289). Citing criticisms like those outlined above, Lynch presented support for his view that by 1945 there had developed a trend "toward the establishment of a sharp line of division between general theoretical psychology and psychology employed for primarily practical ends" (Lynch, 1945, p. 290).

But unlike many of his contemporaries, Lynch went much further in considering the nature of the relationship between this general theoretical psychology and applied psychology, notably educational psychology. He described quite well the cleavage which had developed between the basic researcher and the psychologist who was more applied in his orientation, and he acknowledged that many saw the two as being so substantially polarized as to prohibit their having any meaningful dialogue or mutual constructive exchange. Moreover, he also advanced the thesis that the "application" of learning theory really may *not* involve applications of the theory per se. He observed: "The educational psychologist, who recommends an educational plan or a curriculum organization based on the psychologist's results, does not adapt the theory; he tests it" (Lynch, 1945, p. 292).

Lynch's paper captures much of the controversy which had been developing during the 1930s to the 1950s, anticipated some of the proposals which would be made at mid-century, and advanced a solution which really did not emerge with any substantial impact until the late 1960s to early 1970s. He acknowledged that some would consider theory and psychological laboratory learning research as having *nothing* of relevance for the practical classroom situation. But he also criticized the typical academic psychologist's position that one can readily deduce from academic psychology learning theory prescriptions for activities in the classroom situation. He noted that some would propose to develop theories of school learning, theories which some would then hold to be independent of the animal and human learning laboratory-based theories. He contended that the laboratory learning psychologist, the applied educational psychologist, and the educational practitioner were *not* involved with mutually exclusive theories but that there must be underlying principles which have implications in common across all three types of situations.

In many respects, Lynch anticipated a three-level model for relating academic psychology learning research to the concerns of the practical situation in somewhat the same way that Dewey had suggested earlier (1900), but in ways which educational psychologists and other applied psychologists would not move until a decade or more later. In Lynch's paper we find evidence of a trend away from the kinds of applications which seemed to be more characteristic in this comprehensive learning theory era—that of "applying" a point of view, of using the theory to check out the soundness of educational practice, and/or to deduce specific educational practice from some principle embodied in a particular learning theory.

Lynch's recommendation, which would not be followed in any great extent until at least a decade later, involved an alternative position to that which had been promoted in social science, but one which had been widely used in the attempts to utilize physical and biological science information in other practical situations. That is, he called for an "engineering" level which would be juxtaposed between the basic science and the practical situation, so that some would have the responsibility for bringing to bear the data which had been accumulated in a form which could be utilized in the practical situation. He concluded: "Instead, then, of wishing to seize upon some psychological theory or principle which may be put to immediate use, it will treat the theories of psychology as generalizations to be tried out—to be tested by ascertaining whether their operation in specific, concrete cases will produce results agreeing with their demands. It will serve as the agency through which psychological theory guides and directs educational practices toward improvement" (Lynch, 1945, p. 295).

Lynch clearly specifies ways by which psychology learning theory is to be translated into educational practice. Recall for a moment the positions of various spokesmen at the turn of the century, at which time it was indicated that there should be some kind of relationship between psychology (as science) and education (as science and practice). But the nature of this relationship and the designation of individuals who would bridge the gap between the basic science theory and educational practice were not spelled out as precisely as was done in 1945. Of course, more careful search of the literature will show that there were other individuals at various points during this century who made similar kinds of suggestions. However, as we near mid-century, we find that there are more individuals who expressed such an opinion; as we move into the 1960s, we will find fruition of the idea at least as an initial venture.

Mid-Century: Growth of
Applied Psychology

By mid-century, the gap between academic learning theory and educational practice seems to have grown substantially larger than it had been in previous decades. To complicate matters further, post-World War II society had become more interested in the applicability of behavior research findings, and support was mustered for research which might facilitate resolution of society's problems. Prior to World War II applied psychologists in various areas were so closely identified with measurement processes and with their function as assessment experts that they were routinely identified in clinical psychology and in educational psychology by the briefcases containing their intelligence test kits, and in industrial psychology by the various kinds of personnel testing procedures with which they routinely worked. But during and following World War II there developed a concept of applied psychology going far beyond measurement expertise per se and involving applicability of psychology learning research and other academic findings to an extent not apparently envisioned by most psychologists in previous decades. It may be easier to grasp the extent of this change if one realizes that not only learning theory, or even psychology generally, but a wide range of social sciences and life sciences were involved in this attempt to cope with society's problems. It has been pointed out (David, 1969) that the label *behavioral sciences* came into common usage during the late 1940s as these representatives from different disciplines attempted to cope with society's problems. Another development in applied psychology during this period of time was the emergence of engineering psychology or human factors approaches in the utilization of psychology findings in work with man-machine systems. Human engineering is primarily relevant to our present discussion because it constitutes one of several areas of applied psychology which developed during this period, and because engineering psychologists also encounter difficulties in relating the academic psychology theory to resolution of practical problems (see Chapanis, 1967).

This was an era in which applied psychology began its greatest rate of development. It was an era in which both newly graduated psychologists and those with years of experience found the challenges in resolving society's problems more appealing than the more traditional pursuit of experimental laboratory research. Some have even said that the late 1940s represented a period in which experimental psychology reached the nadir of its popularity.

It was also in this same period when clinical psychology emerged from essentially a testing function to one in which it had major concern with planning and implementing of treatment programs with patients. Previously clinical psychologists had customarily served as diagnosticians and measurement specialists in medically dominated situations. However, during this era, both practical circumstances and the interest of leaders in clinical psychology facilitated a much more extensive and active role for clinical psychologists. The Veterans Administration was faced with such large-scale problems in caring for emotionally disabled veterans and for the general emotional needs of returning veterans that they sought help from several disciplines, including clinical psychology, in carrying out their mission. Though it is beyond the scope of the present discussion to provide details, it is worthwhile noting here that extensive training programs were developed in collaboration with the Veterans Administration and a number of university psychology departments around the country. Of special relevance to our present discussion is the fact that *very large numbers* of graduate students and faculty members became involved in these clinical psychology training programs, and they began to create an identity of the applied psychologist as being one who utilized psychological principles in resolution of real-life problems to an extent which had not really been characteristic of applied psychology in previous decades.

Around this same period of time, there developed an interest in application of social psychology by people who had varying ranges of interest in academic research. Though these individuals came from various segments within social psychology and psychology more generally, many of them were particularly closely identified with the Lewinian tradition. In a sense, we find these individuals trying to cope with a number of community problems by drawing on the theory and research findings which focus primarily on intergroup relations and other social psychology processes. Very quickly it became evident that there would be some criticism and extensive controversy as to whether these allegedly research-based principles were being correctly articulated and appropriately addressed to the specific practical problems. Furthermore, there developed a range of controversy as to whether one could use the traditional research methodology in evaluating the applicability of these principles. Terms such as *action research*, or sometimes *operations research*, were used to identify the efforts of these social psychologists' ventures into resolution of community problems (Chein, Cook, & Harding, 1948; Sanford, 1970). Without going into detail concerning the various facets and aspects of this particular approach we can get some quick understanding of the general orientation by reviewing Chein, Cook, and Harding's description of the field of action research: "It is a field which developed to satisfy the needs of the socio-political individual who recognizes that, in science, he can find the most reliable guide to effective action, and the needs of the scientist who wants his labors to be of maximal social utility as well as of theoretical significance" (Chein, Cook & Harding, 1948, p. 44).

It is very important for the reader to recognize, however, that the theoretical base from which the action researcher was drawing was quite different from that of the traditional learning theory which we have reviewed in the present text. Indeed, it drew from philosophical assumptions and a theoretical rationale which many find quite different from or even incompatible with the traditional comprehensive learning theories which we have examined. However, it is quite significant and relevant to the discussion on relations between learning theory and educational practice to recognize that this "action research" movement did develop during the late 1940s and early 1950s. It is, as we have noted in other cases above, another example of the growing body of psychologists who were actively proclaiming their interest in *applying* the findings of psychological knowledge rather than merely in adding to that fund of knowledge.

It was in this context, then, that educational psychologists and educators were beginning to raise more and more questions as to the actual or potential applicability of traditional comprehensive learning theory for educational practice. The questions were raised during an era in which there was even greater expectation and hope for the practical utilization of such findings, and at a time when more psychologists were actively involved in concerted attempts to use such information.

And yet, it was an era in which these applied psychologists were guided in their training program with the dictum "a basic psychologist first, an educational, a clinical or an applied social psychologist secondly." Despite the growing ranks of applied psychologists, the academic psychology departments maintained their dominant influence on the training of applied psychologists and on the equally important matter of designating those kinds of research which are to be considered more prestigious.

In an introduction to a set of papers—"A symposium: Can the laws of learning be applied in the classroom?"—the editors of the *Harvard Educational Review* made these comments in the spring of 1959: "Psychological experimentation was once closer to education than it is now. The juxtaposition here of papers by three eminent experimental psychologists may be a modest contribution to the revival of an old partnership" (p. 83). The papers which followed by Kenneth W. Spence, Arthur W. Melton, and Benton J. Underwood were very much "psychology oriented" in that they were specifically concerned with the extent to which psychological research, especially that on learning process, might enable educators to derive implications for educational practice.

This is much in keeping with the approach advocated by proponents of the traditional learning theories which we have studied earlier in this text. But in many ways, the *Harvard Educational Review* set of papers *closed* an era instead of opening a new one. They were published at a time when renewed close relationships were established between psychological research and educational practice. But the nature of these relationships came under scrutiny and severe criticism in the ensuing decade, with the result that a new orientation, different from that advocated in these particular *Harvard Educational Review* papers, evolved for relating psychological theory to educational practice. Instead of taking the position that *psychology* could offer something *to education*, there evolved a greater emphasis on considering the *educational* situation *first* and then trying to see if implications could be *drawn from psychology and other disciplines*. In the decades of the 1960s and 1970s educators were assigned a more active role in assessing and in delineating implications for improving educational practice. This is somewhat reminiscent of expectations at the turn of the century for the "new science of psychology" and the "new science of education." One major difference lies in the fact that the more recent pattern involves interdisciplinary collaboration with, for example, psychologists expressing more interest in educational applications of their theories than had been true earlier. In this context more persons began to call for problem-oriented educational theories which would exist between the concrete practical teaching-learning situations and the more abstract formulations of the basic scientist-psychologist's laboratory research. Many psychologists who were primarily or concurrently involved in learning research became involved in the new emphasis on instruction.

Problems in Psychology-
oriented Principles

A common criticism has been that heretofore educators had been given incomplete psychological theories and fragmented findings from research from which the educators were expected to draw implications for educational practice. It is primarily this criticism of forcing teachers to make inferences from psychological research and theories to practical educational situations that has been the most consistent criticism across all spokesmen advocating the development of instructional theories. Of course, such authors acknowledge that the educators should not expect cookbook instructions detailing, for example, what they should do each day with their students. However, the argument is presented that previous educational psychology principles have been so oriented to psychology laboratory learning situations that they provide insufficient guidelines for educational practice or they have not been comprehensive enough for characteristics of practical educational situations. In brief, the contention is that psychology theory has focused on underlying principles of behavior but that educators need scientifically tested general prescriptions for educational practice.

Nathaniel L. Gage has taken the position that one should not expect learning theory to dictate to education, and that historically there has been little evidence of prescriptions derived simply from learning theory. He contends that theories of teaching should be developed which would be compatible with learning theory and other fundamental theories. He argues that one does not necessarily know how to teach even if one has a reasonably comprehensive theory of learning. He uses an agricultural analogy, in which he points out that farmers need to know something about how plants grow, the way they depend on soil, water, and sunlight, but that farmers must also know something about the process of farming. Similarly, teachers need to know how children learn and what relevance motivation, readiness, reinforcement, and other psychological processes have for learning; but they especially need to know more about the teaching-learning process in practical situations. "Too much of educational psychology makes the teacher *infer* what he needs to do from what he is told about learners and learning. Theories of teaching would make *explicit* how teachers behave, why they behave as they do, and with what effects. Hence, theories of teaching need to develop alongside, on a more equal basis with, rather than by inference from, theories of learning" (Gage, 1963, p. 133).

In various papers, B. O. Smith (for example, 1960) has also articulated the position that understanding a phenomenon does not necessarily lead to helping one deal with that phenomenon in practical situations. "The point is that knowledge of the causes and mechanisms of learning is not a necessary condition for developing a practical science of teaching. Such knowledge may be a step toward the development of instructional operations, and it may help us to understand better the teaching operations used already; but it is not the case that we can derive teaching strategies and tactics from learning theory" (Smith, 1960, p. 88). By his comments Smith was not denying the relevance of psychological research for education nor was he questioning the value of psychological research per se. He did assert that it is not appropriate to expect the classroom teacher to draw inferences from the learning theory and research and to conjecture about possible classroom implications.

But the most important point which Smith makes germane to our present discussion is the notion that knowing the cause of a phenomenon does not *necessarily* enable one to control it for practical ends. He cites various examples, including those in medicine, in which *knowledge of cause* is separate from *knowledge of what to do* in treating a disease. For instance, he observed that in some cases we have medical solutions which control or cure diseases despite our actual ignorance as to why the method works; in other cases we may know the causes of a disease without having been able to develop a method of treatment. "The history of practical science is replete with examples of this disjunctive relation between knowledge of causes and means of control" (Smith, 1960, p. 87). Although he implies acceptance of the notion that it's desirable to know *both* the cause and the method of treatment, he does emphasize that the two are disjunctive.

In the first review of instructional psychology in the *Annual Review of Psychology*, Robert Gagne and William Rohwer (1969) acknowledged, with some regrets, that even studies of *human* learning, retention, and transfer are typically only remotely applicable to instructional designs, despite the fact that naïve common sense would dictate the probability of such applicability. They noted that one, of course, does derive some improved understanding of learning process as a result of the theory and research reviewed earlier in this text. However, like many other authors, they contended that isolated findings and even basic science theories are relatively useless as regards practical application unless someone has integrated such findings into a theoretical scheme which takes account of additional variables found in the practical situations.

Educators Need Instructional Theories

Paul Saettler (1968), writing from the vantage point of educational media, conducted an extensive review of theory, research, and practice in education. He concluded that, at least as of 1968, education essentially lacked any widely accepted theories of instruction despite a need for them. On the basis of his review of the literature, Saettler concluded that there is need both for delineating instructional technology concepts and principles and for developing instructional theories to integrate and to synthesize those principles. Advocating more direct concern with instruction, he suggested that instructional theories could fulfill a mediating role between basic science learning theory, curriculum issues, and the communication theory currently emerging in instructional hardware technology.

Siegel has also proclaimed the need for theories of instruction. He points out that there are countless questions about practices, curriculum, administration, and learning which require answers in order to have sound educational programs. He characterizes current information as being quite fragmented and somewhat voluminous. In the absence of some systematic organization of such questions and findings, he depicts formal education as being "relatively long on practice and short on theory. Current practices often reflect, on the one hand, considerable inertia and, on the other, an almost frantic search for innovations to alleviate currently pressing problems" (Siegel, 1967, p. viii). Proclaiming his commitment to the notion that it *does* make a difference as to how students are taught, he attributes the confusion and the significant influences as having been obscured by a relative lack of adequate theory. "A sound theoretical base can (1) suggest better educational practices than are now prevalent; (2) permit predictions about the likely effectiveness or ineffectiveness of contemplated innovations, thereby offering educational administrators a highly practical basis for making judgments; and (3) guide future research efforts in systematic rather than fragmented directions" (Siegel, 1967, p. ix).

One of the most vocal advocates of a theory of instruction is Jerome Bruner. In a series of papers and books, he has taken the position that learning theories and developmental theories make their contributions but that in addition there must exist a theory of instruction as a "guide to pedagogy." For example, in *Toward a Theory of Instruction* (1966) Bruner characterized educators' usual sets of guidelines as merely involving a set of "maxims" or general truths, in contrast with the more systematically organized scientific educational theory which he feels is necessary for educators if they wish to improve their practice. He depicts developmental theories and learning theories as being "descriptive" in that they describe processes which are fundamental to practical aspects of the educational situations. He contends that educators need theories which "prescribe" educational practice.

B. F. Skinner has consistently argued for directly studying the activities of individual learners to develop a *technology* of teaching. Although he does not routinely explicitly emphasize *theory* in his writings, he does hold that we need direct study of the teaching-learning process in order to develop principles concerning *teaching*, rather than merely being satisfied with an understanding of the underlying psychological processes involved in *learning*. But as with learning processes he prefers an inductive rather than a deductive approach to instructional theory construction. The essence of his position is that we need to develop a set of principles stemming from a direct analysis of teaching methods. Starting with various papers which he wrote in the middle 1950s, he has contended that there is adequate basis for formulating such principles and testing them in practical situations.

Robert Glaser has also presented many papers in which he has argued for development of principles of instruction based on direct investigations of training and education situations. He takes the position that psychological research can provide a basis for developing principles but that the modification and refinement of these principles will depend upon empirical results derivable directly from the training and education situations. Like Skinner, Glaser is more pragmatic and inductive in his approach to theory but there is implied in his work the expectation that some kind of integrated set of principles will emerge. The role of psychology research is reasonably evident in one of his comments in a 1966 paper: "If it can be agreed that the science of psychology must supply the knowledge for the precepts of instruction, then it follows that the translation of scientific knowledge into practice requires technological developments" (Glaser, 1966, p. 433).

Ausubel (1968) has primarily used cognitive theory as a point of departure in declaring that we need to develop theories of instruction which take as their central concern *meaningful school learning.* He is critical of past conceptions of educational psychology in which one typically samples the various areas of general academic psychology and then suggests that inferences can be drawn for teaching practice. He advocates a focus on meaningful school learning as being the legitimate area of educational psychology as an applied science. He has contended that learning theories and instructional theories are interdependent and that both are needed for a complete science of pedagogy since neither can adequately serve as a substitute for the other.

This is but a brief sampling of the countless papers which have been written in recent years concerning the *need* for theories of instruction and their potential relationships to educators and to psychology learning theory. Granted that there is a need for instructional theories, what kind of theories might be developed? By what means can they be developed? Given the focus of the present book, how might instructional theories relate to psychological learning research and theories? These questions can best be understood by first considering the status of theories in education.

PRAGMATIC VERSUS THEORETICAL
EMPHASIS IN EDUCATION

Educational practice in the United States has largely been developed on the basis of pragmatic, common-sense, intuitive attempts to help children to become good citizens, rather than on the basis of principles systematically derived from scientific theories. Moreover, because of the decentralized political organization of our public schools—with state and local governing bodies having primary authority and responsibility for schools—there have emerged many differences in the objectives and methods found in schools today despite their obvious common function in society. Of course the resulting diversity could prove to be desirable *if* existent educational practices are enabling our schools to attain the educational objectives set by their respective communities. But given the quite fragmented way in which our educational systems have developed, there is little basis by which we can even determine how effective schools have been. Some guidelines have been provided through various state and regional certification agencies but the resulting information typically has been both subjective and quite general, with qualitative indices mainly concerned with such matters as the number of course credits provided in selected subject areas. One comparatively recent attempt has been designed to provide censuslike data concerning national eduational progress (Womer, 1970). However, at least at the present time, there is little systematic basis for determining how satisfactory contemporary educational practice has been in attaining a community's educational objectives.

Perhaps it should not be so surprising that this somewhat fragmented state of affairs has been permitted to exist in education for such a long period of time. Part of the problem may stem from the lack of clarity in stating educational goals. Long has there been accepted the general notion that society should provide schools to foster the development of "good citizens," but there have been sharp differences of opinion as to what leads to good citizenship. There also have been many debates as to what constitutes other appropriate educational objectives. Each decade has produced new functions for schools, most of which have simply been added to the seemingly ever-increasing curriculum. In addition to the "three R's" of an earlier era ("reading, 'riting, and 'rithmetic"), modern educational programs are expected to include such diverse curricular areas as civics courses, driver education, knowledge and appreciation of science, sex education, ecology, etc. At times educators have contended that vocational training should be given highest priority, while in other periods the focus has been on general intellectual development. In recent years many have raised questions as to whether we have placed too much stress on cognitive academic areas at the expense of students' personal-social-emotional development. Thus both the educational objectives and the instructional procedures selected to attain the objectives have been modified mainly as a result of societal pressure rather than as a function of new scientific findings or theory development.

Educational Theorizing Before
Mid-twentieth Century

"Theory" in education has typically had a negative connotation, with the implication that the speaker is talking in abstract terms which may have little or no productive results when someone actually tries to apply his suggestions in a practical situation (Sizer, 1972). This attitude, coupled with the tradition among educational researchers that use of scientific method should primarily consist of a "fact-finding enterprise" (Cellura, 1969; Travers, 1962) makes it less than surprising to find that for most of the first half of this century there was little interest in formulating a *scientifically based* educational theory.

Nonetheless, the notion that educators could benefit from *theories* is really not a new idea. Practically throughout recorded history one can find numerous examples of various "theories" which have been devised for "educators" however they may be designated in the particular eras considered. But of more recent origin is the notion that such theories should be tested in terms of their actual success in helping someone to learn; also a recent development is the anticipation that such theories would somehow relate to underlying psychological principles of learning which are more or less independently being developed.

Saettler (1968) provides an extensive review of the various kinds of theories which were developed during the past several centuries. For example, he concludes that a group of elder sophists in the fifth century B.C. could perhaps be designated as early instructional theorists. It is of some interest that they apparently developed and made extensive use of expository lectures, group discussion techniques, and other procedures commonly associated with modern educational practice. Moreover, most education textbooks contain descriptions of various more modern "theories," practically all of which were developed from philosophical positions or were generated as a result of the author's personal experiences.

But it is rather widely acknowledged that none of these prescientific theories has had a consistent major impact on educators at large. Most educational practitioners probably would be hard pressed to articulate a theory or to delineate the rationale underlying procedures they routinely use in the classroom. Various authors have acknowledged the numerous problems in developing sound and useful theories for educators and have deplored a state of affairs in which the educational practitioner has virtually been forced to operate atheoretically in a general piecemeal fashion. Many would concur with Siegel's (1967) observation that education is long on practice and short on theory.

Of course, there have been a number of significant figures in education who have developed points of view and who have influenced a certain portion of teachers to adopt their theories in their educational practice. For example, one can cite the earlier efforts of such individuals as Froebel, Dewey, Montessori, Pestalozzi, and others who developed fairly comprehensive theories of teaching and instruction. But for the most part, these theories were based on philosophical positions or rather casual observations. Moreover, it seems that most educators primarily derived a "point of view" rather than any particular details or even general principles for planning and conducting educational programs. Thus Getzels (1952) was led to conclude that even by mid-century there remained a serious gap between theory and practice at least for the majority of educators in the United States. There seems to be the suggestion in his and others' critical analyses (for example, Chapman, 1972; Gideonse, 1968; Mackie & Christensen, 1967; Travers, 1962) that we have never really been able to utilize scientific methods in formulating and improving educational theory to the extent that has been suggested by leaders in psychology and in education at the turn of the century (for example, see Dewey, 1900).

Educational Theorizing Since Mid-century

Since mid-century there has been increasing interest, among educators and professional persons outside of education, in using scientific methods to improve educational practice. Of course it is difficult to say what precipitated this interest, though world events and other professional educational developments quite likely played major roles. Certainly the whole country suddenly seemed to be talking about the quality of our educational program when the Russians gained worldwide recognition for their launching of Sputnik in 1957. All at once it became fashionable to make pronouncements about the strengths and weaknesses of our educational systems and to propose new means for improving educational practice. Whereas society had been prone to ignore activities in our schools, suddenly many different professional groups "discovered" schools. Around the same time—probably in some form of cause-effect relationship—private and governmental funds became available for research, innovations, and training in education.

In this context, four general developments occurred which not only made feasible the utilization of scientific educational theories but even can be depicted as having almost demanded that such theoretical principles come into existence. Although there was some overlap, each of these general developments involved both an aspect of the educational process and a group of professional persons typically associated with that process.

Programmed Instruction, Educational Objectives, and Systematic Instructional Principles   The first development to which we refer (though the four could be considered in any order) is that of programmed instruction and its impact on the specification of educational objectives in measurable terms. This development was primarily stimulated by B. F. Skinner and his associates, who attempted to use operant theory and techniques in the improvement of instructional procedures. It is noteworthy that the programmed instruction movement placed such great emphasis on delineating educational objectives as a major first step in planning instruction that it forced the educational community to reevaluate its stand against specifying educational objectives.

Controversy continues as to whether the behavior-modification approach can deal with all the educational objectives considered to be important in society today. For example, some contend that this approach is conducive to attaining factual-oriented objectives but that neither the affective nor more complex cognitive educational objectives can be attained by this means. Moreover, some continue to resist even stating educational objectives in any explicit form, contending that the objectives of educators are so complex that they do not lend themselves readily to articulation. Others contend that it is impossible to identify the most important results of successful educational experiences in measurable terms since they may become evident throughout the life-span of those who benefit from good educational programs. The present research and professional literature is replete with statements pro and con concerning the current status and probable future course of delineating educational objectives in any kind of measurable form. But one of the culminating effects apparently partly attributable to this general concern with stating educational objectives was the application of the concept of *accountability* to educational practice.

In the late 1960s and early 1970s there emerged such a great interest in having educators *accountable* for the results of their effects that it is unlikely that educators will ever completely drop this interest in knowing the outcomes of their efforts as well as the details of their educational process per se. The focus on *outcomes* of instructional experiences made feasible the specifications of educative objectives and methods, and provided self-corrective evaluation for the instructional methods. Also, the programmed instruction technology required such explicit descriptions of instructional procedures that it became essential to describe rules or principles for organizing and sequencing the educational materials. It rapidly became evident that much *research* and *theory* was needed concerning *instruction*. Out of this awareness emerged instructional theories as separate entities rather than as mere extensions of operant theory.

Classroom Interaction Analysis Systems and Instructional Principles Secondly, the decade of the 1960s witnessed a tremendous development and growth in systems specifically designed to describe what teachers and students do in classroom situations. Under the title "teacher behavior," "classroom interaction," "classroom behavior," or similar titles a whole series for objectively recording and classifying classroom activities emerged. It is beyond the scope of this book to provide an evaluation of the various observational systems developed within this movement or to consider the respective systems' influences, if any, on educational practice.

It is noteworthy that approximately seventy such systems were developed within a decade (Simon & Boyer, 1969; Medley & Mitzel, 1963). Germane to our present discussion is the fact that for the first time in education there became available many different systems which could provide objective reports of teacher and student activities in a classroom situation. For the first time, therefore, it became possible to describe the extent to which teachers and students were carrying out prescribed instructional activities, thus enabling researchers to validate that a particular instructional system or principle had been utilized and to determine its utility and efficiency in attaining delineated educational objectives (for example, see Soar, 1972-NSSE).

Although some authors attribute specific theoretical preferences to various classroom analysis procedures, it would seem to your present author that their major import lies in the reasonably objective means which became available to examine what was happening in the classroom and that they made more apparent the need for having instructional theories.

Educational Media and Instructional Technology Principles Third, support for developing theories of instruction also came from the persons who are concerned with various forms of audiovisual and other devices for instructional purposes. The group has been identified by a series of different names throughout the past several decades which in part indicates the changing concern leading up to the contemporary interest in instructional theories. Earlier in this century, *visual aids* was used to refer to the supplementary materials and devices which could be utilized in the classrooms. Later, various forms of audio devices became available, and the group—after some considerable debate—became identified as concerned with *audiovisual* aids. An even broader concern was attempted in the name *educational media*, but even that label gave way to newer terms. *Educational technology* and *instructional technology* are terms which have been used during the past two decades. At first, these terms referred almost exclusively to the *hardware* technology. This included television, films, overhead projectors, and computers, as well as the earlier-used blackboard, slide projector, etc.

But it became more and more evident as the hardware became more complicated that instructional principles were needed as guidelines for judicious use of the hardware technology. Thus it became necessary to redefine the term *instructional technology* so that it would refer to more than any particular set of media or devices. For example, one federal commission (McMurrin, 1970), which actually started out to study the impact of public broadcasting on education, redefined its role so as to consider instructional principles and to encompass the more general purpose "to improve learning." In this context, instructional technology was defined as a "systematic way of designing, carrying out, and evaluating the total process of learning and teaching in terms of specific objectives, based on research in human learning and communications and employing a combination of human and non-human resources to bring about more effective instruction" (McMurrin, 1970, p. 5). Educational media instructional technologists expressed interest in formulating instructional theory in collaboration with curriculum specialists, psychologists, educational philosophers, and other educators.

Curriculum Reform Movement, Curriculum Theory, and Instructional Theory   The fourth and final group which was instrumental in stimulating educational theorizing is composed of various persons who are concerned with the theory, design, and improvement of curriculum. Though there are numerous smaller groups and individuals who are concerned with this general area, one national organization which has been especially concerned is that of the Association for Supervision and Curriculum Development (ASCD). The interest in theory construction emerged during the curriculum reform movement of the 1960s. There have been various curriculum reform movements at different points throughout the past century. However, in the late 1950s and early 1960s there developed a great interest in having some more systematic basis for planning a curriculum. Eminent scientists and other scholars collaborated with educators to update science and mathematics curricula. In the course of these interactions it became obvious that there was a need for formulating curriculum theory and instructional theory. It became obvious that the rather loose and generally speculative theory which had been characteristic of education throughout most of its history in the United States would no longer be adequate. In this context there emerged an interest in using scientific means for testing principles of curriculum construction and instructional design. Later we will examine some of the ASCD recommendations concerning instructional theory. For now it is noteworthy that interest among curriculum specialists was partly responsible for the emergence of instructional theories.

This leads us to questions concerning relationships between instructional theories and curriculum theories. It is often observed that there are many terms in education which are so ambiguously defined that confusion results with their use. Such is the case with regard to *curriculum* and *instruction* (for example, Macdonald, 1965). Nonetheless, some distinctions must be made. We accept Alpren's (1967 and personal communication) definition of curriculum as the planned substance for intended learnings. This definition is complementary to our earlier description of instruction as the means by which one attains educational objectives, although there is some overlap in the terms. Thus despite this overlap, curriculum theory is especially concerned with the substance and objectives of education, whereas instructional theories primarily focus on the means by which educational objectives are attained.

ILLUSTRATIVE EFFORTS TO PRODUCE INSTRUCTIONAL THEORIES

Thus there were at least four different groups in the late 1950s and the 1960s who recognized the need for instructional theories and who took what they considered to be initial steps to develop such theories. Before considering instructional theories which are based on or drawn in reaction to learning theories, we will consider some activities of ASCD members and other educators as illustrations of the range of theories which have been developed.

The ASCD Commission on Instructional Theory

Many point to Tyler's work in the 1930s (for example, Tyler, 1934) as having anticipated much of the current concern with scientific theories of curriculum and instruction. But Beauchamp (1968) suggests that the first concerted attempt to bring together ideas about curriculum theory was held in 1947. However, it was only around the time of the launching of Sputnik in the late 1950s that theory construction efforts really became evident. Interest among ASCD members in theory construction apparently was especially stimulated by the work of Jerome Bruner, whom we have already identified as one of the proponents of instructional theories. Largely as a result of his earlier papers and books on the topic, Bruner was invited to address the 1963 ASCD convention and various other meetings of educators where the concern focused on theories of curriculum and instruction.

An ASCD commission on instructional theory was formed in 1964 and was active through 1967. The commission was chaired by Ira J. Gordon, and included as members Nicholas Fattu, Marie M. Hughes, Grace Lund, E. Brooks Smith, and Robert M. W. Travers. A major objective of the commission was to delineate scientifically based instructional theories from the more intuitively based and somewhat speculative "theorizing" which had been so characteristic of education previously. Robert M. W. Travers seems to be representative of commission members in his emphasis on the need for a systematic, empirical approach to instructional theory construction.

I pointed out that such a theory would have to be derived from empirical statements that represented the end products of research and that the statements of the theory would have to have clearcut relationships to the empirically derived statements on which the theory was based. Undocumented statements representing personal views on the nature of good teaching would not fall within this definition of a theory of instruction, however attractive and inspirational such statements might be. The development of a theory of instruction, thus conceived, would cease to be the happy, carefree, do-it-yourself activity it has been in the past, and would become a painstaking, meticulous, and empirically oriented activity that would have to enlist the efforts of high-level scientists. What was proposed is not likely to be particularly popular, partly because talent for scientific theorizing has always been rare, and partly because it shows up, in proper perspective, the happy breed of educational reformer who can concoct a brand-new, rabble-rousing theory of educational reform while waiting for the water to fill the bathtub. (Travers, 1971, p. 23)

It was the suggestion of the ASCD commission that nonscientific or prescientific theories should be designated as *philosophical positions*, or as *social reform positions*. They also recognized the probable development of *models* of instruction as well as *theories* of instruction. Although there were some inconsistencies in various members' statements on the topic, they seemed to agree that models would consist of more concrete representations or more specific examples of instructional procedures and that theories would involve more abstract formulations.

One of their culminating and concluding activities was the delineation and publication of a booklet, *Criteria for Evaluating Theories of Instruction* (Gordon, 1968). Although the criteria were mainly prepared for an anticipated audience of supervisors and teachers, the commission hoped that their proposals would be useful for persons formulating theories as well as for those who might wish to review and to choose from among the emerging instructional theories. The criteria were presented as necessary (but not sufficient) conditions whereby satisfactory instructional theories could be formulated.

ASCD Criteria for Instructional Theories The following criteria were developed by the ASCD commission. Although some of the statements are applicable to scientific theories in general, the commission primarily tries to orient criteria to theories specifically designed for instruction. The following brief descriptions indicate the nature of the criteria developed by the commission; however, the reader is advised to consult the original publication (Gordon, 1968) for more details about these criteria, the basis for their selection, and their use with emerging instructional theories.

"I. A statement of an instructional theory should include a set of postulates and definition of terms involved in these postulates." At a minimum, the commission recommended that pupil, goal, and instructional situational characteristics should be defined. They also pointed out that scientific theories include a minimum number of "primitive terms"—those terms which are not easily defined operationally. The commission recommended that the pupil characteristics and the situational characteristics should be specified together with the relationship they are expected to have to educational goals. Although they do not use the term, there is an implied expectation that the educational goals will be in *measurable* terms.

"II. The statement of an instructional theory or sub-theory should make explicit the boundaries of its concern and the limitations under which it is proposed." On this point, the commission seemed to be somewhat ambivalent, but they were quite concerned that the instructional theory should have realistic boundaries for instructional processes to which it might be applicable. It is also noteworthy that the commission anticipated that some instructional procedures will be more appropriate at one age level rather than others.

"III. A theoretical construction must have internal consistency—a logical set of interrelationships."

"IV. An instructional theory should be congruent with empirical data." On this point, the commission was concerned that the theoretical statement be derived from data and/or be compatible with empirical data. Wherever possible, some documentation should be evident—so that one can check the validity of the extrapolation from empirical data to the theoretical statements. The commission expressed great reservation about using "personal experience" or "single case histories" as being sufficient for documenting the empirical validity of the theory. Also, they point out the importance of determining whether the empirical data were collected from subjects and under conditions which are actually analogous to the instructional principle and situation to which they are being applied.

"V. An instructional theory must be capable of generating hypotheses." Here the commission criticized theories which are so broadly presented and poorly defined that it is almost impossible to derive hypotheses which can be tested empirically.

"VI. An instructional theory must contain generalizations which go beyond the data."

"VII. An instructional theory must be verifiable."

"VIII. An instructional theory must be stated in such a way that it is possible to collect data to disprove it."

"IX. An instructional theory must not only explain past events, but also must be capable of predicting future events." Here the commission was primarily concerned that the theory should not only explain data but that it should also be possible to derive predictions about students' performance and learning under stated conditions.

"X. At the present time, instructional theories may be expected to represent qualitative synthesis." The commission expressed the hope that future developments would permit quantitative relationships among variables in a theory.

These criteria have been used on a number of occasions to evaluate various educational models and theories. In light of our earlier comments about the status of educational theorizing, it is not too surprising to find that very few, if any, theories have met the criteria set by this commission. As some of the commission members have pointed out, this probably is more a reflection of the rudimentary status of scientific theory construction in education rather than an indication that the commission's criteria are unrealistic. Gordon's evaluation of selected follow-through models will at once illustrate this point and will provide some indication of the range of conceptions which have been advanced in educational theory construction.

Follow Through Models as Indices of Instructional Theories   One aspect of education in which there has been some concerted attempt to develop models and theories of instruction is that of early childhood education. As most readers are aware, the 1960s witnessed major advances in early childhood education when federal funds became available to establish preschool programs for children of families who would otherwise not be financially able to send their children to such programs. The Head Start programs which resulted have been commended for their attempts to help children but have been criticized for the somewhat inconsistent results which frequently have been obtained.

Constructive criticisms were made that there should be specific provision to follow up the Head Start program so as to prepare children for more successful entry into the public school program, and that these Follow Through programs should be more systematically planned and theoretically based than was true of the Head Start programs. As a result, the U.S. Office of Education invited various universities and other educational agencies to draw up tentative plans for training early childhood teachers and, later, to develop programs for early childhood education which would be theoretically based. Detailed descriptions of these resulting programs are available in various publications elsewhere (for example, Maccoby & Zellner, 1970; Weber, 1970).

Gordon (1972) has examined the most widely used Follow Through models and evaluated them in terms of the ASCD criteria. He acknowledged that the Follow Through programs had involved models rather than instructional theories, in that they are more concrete and specific in their statements and that they essentially represent plans for achieving *particular* goals. But he assumed that these models had been derived from reasonably precise theoretical points of view and that they should thus be capable of meeting the ASCD criteria. Observations by Travers lend support to Gordon's assumption: "A reputable model of instruction should certainly be documented so that the theory of instruction, together with the research on which such a theory has been based, can be properly identified" (Travers, 1971, p. 25). Following are brief descriptions of each of the six childhood education models examined by Gordon.

The model developed by the Arizona Research and Development Center is sometimes referred to as the Tucson Early Childhood Education Program. This model was originated from a bilingual program for financially disadvantaged Spanish-speaking children. It is thus basically an *educational model* which places great emphasis on the special educational needs of such children. The Bank Street College of Education model likewise is now used with disadvantaged children but it was derived primarily from the long-standing Bank Street College conception of early childhood education. It, too, is primarily an educational model. The Education and Development Corporation model was devised to help schools to adopt the approach of the British Infant School. Though it has been used with Follow Through children, its characteristics are allegedly appropriate not only for all children but for students of various ages.

The Engelmann-Becker model draws extensively from operant conditioning principles. Of the six Follow Through models, this is the one which is most closely related to psychological learning principles. The Far West Laboratory for Educational Research and Development model is also somewhat based on certain aspects of learning research, primarily those which emphasize learning how to learn and some aspects of discovery learning. It emphasizes use of environments which are responsive to the exploratory activities of children and those activities which facilitate attainment of affective educational objectives. The Florida Parent Education program is primarily a home-oriented educational model which was devised for assisting parents in stimulating their children's affective and intellectual development. Initially emphasizing home activities, it was expanded by University of Florida Education faculty members to include recommendations for classroom activities as well.

Thus, of the six models studied by Gordon, only two have an explicit connection with psychological learning research and theory. Most of the models are entirely or heavily weighted in the direction of educational theory, although the proponents of all the models have made some concerted effort to relate their procedures and materials to available psychological research and theory. The programs differ considerably in the extent to which they provide detailed information about instructional procedures and materials to be used. Whether by chance or through inherent characteristics, the program which provides the most explicit recommendations also has more narrowly defined goals. This is the Engelmann-Becker program, which is so closely related to the operant learning principles. Perhaps for this reason, Gordon depicted the providing of explicit recommendations for instructional procedures and materials in a negative way, suggesting that this results in low-level activities for the educator. For example, he seemed to be favorably disposed toward providing fewer explicit instructions to the educator and was quite critical of instructional models which provide such explicit instructions that there were very few decisions which would be made by the teacher. This seems somewhat curious, but probably is typical of the way that educators generally will respond to instructional theorists who tell them how they might carry out their tasks.

Gordon characterizes the six models as differing substantially in their overall structures, despite many common elements, and points out that rather unique features are distinguishable for each of the models. He also felt that there were reasonably close connections between the articulated educational goals and the instructional procedures designed to attain those goals.

His comments concerning the support of empirical data are quite interesting. He characterized many of the major assumptions and basic principles of each of the theories as constituting "beliefs" rather than being clearly established by empirical evidence. Though he did not detect any cases in which the instructional models were *inconsistent* with available empirical data, he noted that there were many instances in which relevant empirical data simply had not been obtained.

Gordon characterized these models as a start toward developing scientific instructional theories, but he acknowledged that a great deal of work remains to be done. All the theories do provide interesting hypotheses which can be submitted to empirical test. There are some problems in that critical statements do not lend themselves readily to empirical test mainly because variables are stated somewhat ambiguously. Also, according to Gordon's analysis, there are elements of tautology in all the theories. Finally, Gordon urged that these models could each be considered as viable alternatives and that they should be assessed in terms of the educational objectives delineated by their performance, rather than be pitted against each other in some kind of meaningless "horse-race" comparison.

Learning Theory-related
Instructional Theories

The Follow Through models constitute examples of the range of instructional theories or rudimentary ventures which are expected to produce instructional theories which exist today. As you can see, not all the theories are based on learning research nor are they necessarily closely affiliated with the learning theories which we have been examining in this text.

There is a wide range of opinion as to the most appropriate relationships between learning theory and instructional theory. Some contend that psychological learning research is so substantively different and methodologically unrelated that there can be little of relevance from learning theories for instructional theories. Others take the position that learning theories and instructional theories are interdependent, with each developing somewhat independently and involving ongoing exchanges with the other. Many take the position that psychological theories may constitute the best basis for evolving instructional theories, and they frequently cite learning theories as being the primary source from which instructional theories can be derived.

Among such advocates for the influence of learning theory, there are differences of opinion as to whether instructional theories should be derived from some particular learning theory or from a distillation of findings from the various learning theories, or whether there are features of learning research and theory which may contain other direct implications for the formulation of instructional theory. Five different approaches can be identified, each of whose proponents consider theirs to be the best way to use psychology learning research and theory in the formulation of instructional theory. We will briefly consider major characteristics of these five approaches in this section. Later chapters provide more detailed descriptions of these respective learning theory-related instructional theories. They are identified here as behavior modification, cognitive construct instructional theory, principles of learning instructional theory, task analysis systems theory, and humanistic psychology's freedom to learn.

Behavior Modification Approaches Behavior modification has typically been defined as the educational and clinical application of modern learning principles derived from laboratory studies on learning processes. Actually behavior modification approaches typically draw from certain learning theories, especially those of Skinner, Pavlov, and Hull. We are primarily interested here in the Skinnerian-oriented behavior modification approach.

The Skinnerian behavior modification position emerged in the middle 1950s when B. F. Skinner attempted to use some of his laboratory-based operant principles in the teaching of mathematics and other academic subjects. It was his original notion that if his laboratory animals could learn rather complex tasks, perhaps school children also might benefit from the principles he had found to be valuable in working with his laboratory animals. Two major themes characterize much of his work.

First, he encouraged educators to utilize his reinforcement principles both to identify the most important aspect of the educational situation and to arrange conditions so that students would receive some kind of recognition for other rewards as they progressed gradually toward their educational objectives. Second, he contended that *nothing* could be substituted for direct experimental research on the educational processes of concern. Thus, following procedures in his own laboratory learning studies, he urged that educators identify the students' individual characteristics and the characteristics of the learning situation so that it would be possible to determine what kind of progress students are making toward their educational objectives. Although a tremendous range of behavior modification programs have emerged in the operant tradition during these ensuing decades, they contain one or both of these two basic themes. But in addition to the initial emphasis on reinforcement principles, contemporary behavior modifiers tend to be considerably more eclectic, drawing from other kinds of psychological research in an effort to find the best possible solution to the practical problems with which they work. As was true of the operant approach to learning theories, there is a distinct preference for utilizing an inductive approach to instructional theory construction.

One of the frequent criticisms of the behavior modification approach is that the objectives are usually rather precisely dictated, but that they tend to be narrow and even somewhat simplistic in nature. Moreover, many critics feel that there is too great reliance on instructional procedures which encourage students to believe that there is always a "correct" answer to a problem rather than encourage them to recognize that many of life's problems have no clear right or wrong answers.

Cognitive Construct Instructional Theories   Many psychologists and educators have been quite critical of the traditional learning theories and they have emphasized their contention that instructional theories can best be formulated from *cognitive* psychology learning research and principles. We refer to them as "cognitive construct instructional theories" because they contend that instructional principles must take account of the *internal*, cognitive changes which occur during meaningful classroom learning. One of the most prominent spokesman for this orientation is Jerome Bruner.

In his emphasis on conceptual changes as the major characteristic of meaningful educational learning, Bruner contends that the best instructional theories will be those which provide "discovery learning" experiences for the students and which enable them to incorporate new information and skills in ways which take into account the previously learned information and skills. For example, instead of emphasizing the actual behaviors of the student as an indication of his learning processes,

Bruner contends that the teacher should be concerned with the kinds of conceptual tools and skills which the student is mastering, which presumably underlie the behaviors which are more readily observable. He acknowledges that other types of more structured learning experiences are important, but he places great emphasis on his "discovery learning" or "inquiry training" educational principles.

Bruner's instructional theory is to have at least four major principles. First, he recognizes that the theory must deal with the motivation of the learner, and that it must identify principles which will encourage the student to be willing as well as able to learn when he enters an educational situation. Second, he focuses on the organization or structure of the content to be learned. Generally he emphasizes the need for conceptualizing instruction and information in such a way that it can be understood and used by the student, as well as for taking into account the structure which might be inherent in the particular body of knowledge. Third, he expresses concern with the sequence of instructional experiences. He takes into account the developmental finding that children initially deal with their environment at a concrete level and that they later are capable of more abstract conceptions. Thus he suggests that instruction, likewise, should proceed from concrete examples to more abstract formulations. Fourth, he concerns himself with the nature and spacing of rewards and punishments. It is of note that he does recognize this aspect of learning processes, despite its frequent association with the behavior modification approach. But somewhat like Tolman, Bruner emphasizes the kind of *information* which one derives from reinforcement rather than the drive reduction or motivational value of the reinforcement.

Most reviews of the research literature on this approach suggest that greater emphasis is placed on finding out how to get students to use these discovery learning approaches than on evaluating whether discovery learning approaches are necessarily the best kind of instructional principles to be used. However, the cognitive construct instructional approach complements the behavior modification orientation in the delineation of educational objectives and in the identification of potentially useful instructional methods. The educational objectives tend to be broader though, unfortunately, frequently ambiguously formulated; they especially are concerned with procedures for helping students to formulate questions and to look for answers.

Principles of Learning Instructional Theories   Some have suggested that one should not rely on any one learning theory but that instructional theories can best be formulated if the theorist is free to draw from any and all learning research which might bear on the particular educational problem. Thus a number of authors have tried to identify learning principles which have been based on laboratory research and which might be useful for practical educational situations. Some have contended that the most appropriate thing would be to see which learning principles draw almost universal support from extant learning theories. Bugelski has contended that a more appropriate approach would be to find various principles that have had a reasonable amount of empirical support, regardless of whether *all* learning theorists would agree with the particular principle. Once having identified these rather broadly drawn and satisfactorily supported learning principles, Bugelski contends that one would then be able to formulate instructional theories.

Bugelski (1971) identified fifty-nine suggestions which he believes have had reasonable support in psychology learning research and which constitute principles of some relevance for educators. But he further condensed this information to four basic principles in his instructional theory. Bugelski acknowledges that only the first two of his principles are actually *learning* principles; he somewhat apologetically notes that his theory contains only a few few principles and that it is somewhat incomplete. However, he also suggests that teachers may see this as an advantage rather than a disadvantage because it means that they have fewer principles to keep in mind in planning instruction.

In his first principle he emphasizes the fact that in order for a student to learn he must be *attentive* or responsive to the material involved. Thus if properly arranged, the situation can command the attention of the student whether the student wishes to be stimulated or not. The second principle acknowledges that all learning takes some amount of time and that there are limitations in the quantity of learning that can take place at a given time. If the capacity of the individual is "overloaded," the student may learn less than if an appropriate amount of material has been presented. This results in limitations on the number of activities in which we can engage in a given time. The third principle contains speculation about the internal regulator which controls the motivation of the individual and which determines to what extent and in what ways that individual will behave in a given situation. Incorporated under this principle is the notion that how we respond to stimuli in a given situation depends to a great extent on the previous capabilities we have developed for comprehending and coping with such stimuli. The fourth principle focuses on knowledge of result as a response control. Here Bugelski emphasizes the informational value of reward as a means for guiding attention and the general behaviors of the students.

Throughout his theory, Bugelski emphasizes the need for continuity between the learning situation and the real-life experiences for which the learning constitutes preparation. He contends that the degree of correspondence between the two will determine the extent to which subsequent performance is satisfactory. He recognizes that his principles are rather "common sense" in character, but he points out that successful implementation of them is not an easy task. For this he depends extensively on the fifty-nine learning principles which he feels are pertinent to the educational situation.

Task-analysis Instructional Theories   Each of the three positions enumerated above has assumed that certain principles derived from laboratory learning research can be useful in practical educational situations. The position which we will consider in this section emerged because its proponents were very dissatisfied with the results they got when they tried to apply laboratory-based learning principles in military and industrial training situations. As a result, they have contended that some other approach is necessary to use the results of learning research and theory in practical training and education situations. In brief, they suggest that the real way psychology learning research can be useful is in its providing a systematic way for analyzing the kinds of tasks which are involved in practical training and educational situations. The work of Robert Gagne and Leslie Briggs illustrates the approach of those who advocate conducting task analysis as a major means for formulating instructional theories.

Gagne (1962) provides a brief history of the unsuccessful results obtained when experimental psychologists were called into military situations and were asked to use their laboratory learning research principles to help in the training of military personnel. He addressed himself to the task: "[H]ow can what you know about learning *as an event* or *as a process*, be put to use in designing training so that it will be maximally effective?" (p. 84) Gagne proceeded to identify some of the principles which are most widely acclaimed among laboratory learning researchers, and he recounted several experiences illustrating the fact that these principles frequently do *not* work out in the real world quite as one might expect based on laboratory experiences.

His response to such unsatisfactory results was not to discredit the value of psychological learning research but to suggest that a different tack was necessary. The cornerstone of his approach is the notion that instructional principles and instructional theory can best be evolved after conducting an intensive task analysis of the educational objectives. Moreover, he contends that psychology learning research and theories can be useful for identifying the different types of learning which are involved and for organizing the different types into hierarchical relationships. Thus he identifies eight different types of learning, allegedly arranged hierarchically, and he describes the kinds of conditions in educational situations which supposedly are necessary for facilitating each of these types of learning (Gagne, 1970). Thus his instructional principles include such concepts as task analysis, intratask transfer, component task achievement, and sequencing (Gagne, 1962, p. 88). Briggs (1970) has taken Gagne's types of learning and the conditions which facilitate each type as a basis for formulating further instructional principles and for outlining the procedures to be followed in designing instructional theories.

The task-analysis approach to instructional theory has seemed most appealing to those educators who are concerned with educational objectives which more readily lend themselves to precise definition. Others who have either long-term objectives or who have rather ambiguously described educational objectives have been somewhat critical of the task-analysis approach. Some have suggested that a more appropriate system for identifying educational objectives is the taxonomy of educational objectives advocated by Bloom in various publications (for example, see Bloom, Hastings, & Madeus, 1971). Others have raised questions as to whether indeed the components of the task and the different types of learning *necessarily* have hierarchical relationships, or whether the different types of learning are parallel rather than subordinate in relationship. Nonetheless, despite such criticisms, the task-analysis approach has drawn support from many educators and training specialists.

Humanistic Psychology and Instructional Theory   During the past few decades there emerged a movement and a school in psychology which has come to be known as *humanistic psychology*. Some contend (Buhler, 1971; Maslow, 1962) that it should be considered as an alternative both to neobehaviorism and to contemporary psychoanalytic theory. This position should be considered in conjunction with the other instructional theory positions we have enumerated above *not* so much because it is *based on* contemporary learning research and theory as because it is to a great extent a *reaction against* such academic psychology learning research and theory. For the most part, the humanistic psychology movement can more accurately be depicted as coming from personality theory and psychotherapy theory rather than from learning theory.

In brief, most humanistic psychologists contend that learning theories involve a conception of psychology modeled on physical sciences, that this is an error, and that man's emotional experiences and other *unique* attributes must be considered in formulating a theory of psychology. There are certain other characteristics which are dominant in the humanistic psychology tradition, although the reader should realize that there are considerable differences of opinion among these persons who advocate the humanistic psychology position. They especially emphasize that psychology should deal with the *whole person* rather than with some kind of "fragmented," "reductionistic" analysis of all the sub-aspects of man. In a sense, they are also concerned with describing one's activities from the viewpoint of the person rather than from that of an observer. That is, the humanistic psychologist feels that most other psychologists take a "third person" point of view in looking at man, whereas they feel that the real way for studying psychology is through the "eye" of the person himself, that is, from a "first person" point of view. They also emphasize the role of one's emotional experiences as ends themselves and as influences on how we act. They are especially concerned about "self-actualization," "self-fulfillment," or "self-realization." There is a concern with the growth of the person in whatever direction that person chooses or values. "The common denominator of these concepts is that all humanistic psychologists see the goal of life as using your life to accomplish something you believe in, be it self-development or other values. From this they expect a fulfillment towards which people determine themselves" (Buhler, 1971, p. 381). Thus, self-understanding to make better choices about one's own directions for growth and *creativity* as a means of fulfillment are central concepts in the humanistic psychology position.

One set of instructional principles which illustrate the humanistic psychology approach is presented under the title *Freedom to Learn*, by Carl Rogers (1969). Rogers divides learning into two broad, general types along a continuum of meaning. The first type is very low in meaningfulness for the student because the educational objectives are selected by others; the conditions of the classroom are chosen and arranged by the teacher or others; and the learning experiences are presented in such a way that they may be meaningful to the teacher or to experts in the particular field of study but have little meaningfulness and relevance for the student. The second type is that of significant, meaningful, experiential learning. The second type has a quality of personal involvement, is self-initiated, tends to be pervasive in its impact on the student, and is evaluated by the student as well as by the teacher.

Rogers criticizes many learning theory-related instructional theories as fostering the first type of learning. He contends that such school learning has little, if any, value for students in modern society. He also contends that most educational practices likewise encourage the first type rather than the second. Central to Rogers's position is the notion that the second type of learning is more appropriate and that conditions can be identified which foster this more meaningful, significant, and experiential learning. Most of his writing elaborates on the conditions which "free" students to learn rather than "force" them to do so.

As readers will recognize from these few brief comments, the humanistic psychologists have taken exception to many of the principles advocated by instructional theorists who have some direct affiliation with psychology learning research and theory. Not only have they raised questions about the *methods* of instruction advocated by these instructional theorists, but they have also raised questions as to who should set goals for the individual and who should determine educational objectives. They have also emphasized the need for examining value systems of individuals and of society as a whole.

The approach advocated by humanistic psychology has been warmly received by many persons who have felt alienated, perhaps even isolated, in our society which in many respects has come to emphasize *technological* development. This is particularly true about technology which emphasizes utilization of machines, sometimes to the detriment of human values. Similar concern has also been expressed about the utilization of behavioral science principles in the planning and modification of instructional procedures. But even more than the position previously described, the humanistic psychology "instructional theory" is incomplete and requires much more empirical testing.

INSTRUCTIONAL THEORIES: CURRENT STATUS AND FUTURE PROSPECTS

We have just enumerated several examples of instructional theories which have been emerging during the third quarter of this century. The need for instructional theories has been proclaimed by many spokesmen who typically contend that one cannot derive instructional theories simply from learning theories. Many also suggest that the time has come when educational theories can no longer be presented on the basis of personal experience or good intentions alone, that we have finally reached the point where scientific data will be expected as demonstration of the value of any admonitions about instruction. Given that this interest has been expressed for at least a decade, what can be said about the current status of, and future prospects for, instructional theories?

Conceptions as to how one can best develop instructional theories have ranged widely. Some contend that the main or only source should be extant educational practice and improvements on it. Others advocate the use of various social science theories, including psychology theories. As with learning theories, some advocate an inductive approach based on growing mounds of empirical data; others contend that, at a minimum, basic assumptions and a few general principles should be formulated so that more specific principles can be deduced from these basic general statements. As evident in the follow-through models, not all instructional theories draw explicitly from learning theories and research. There are even disagreements as to the best approach to follow among those who do contend that instructional theories should be closely related to psychology learning theory and research. Some draw from particular theories; some look for widely supported principles; and others use learning research in various ways to evaluate educational goals and to plan instruction.

But practically all agree that their instructional theories are incomplete and that much work remains to be done before we can legitimately claim to have scientifically sound and practically relevant instructional theories. It seems that Bruner's 1966 book title, *Toward A Theory of Instruction*, is descriptive of the current status in that we still seem to be going *toward* instructional theories. Moreover, though there is a considerable amount of evangelistic fervor evident among proponents of each emerging instructional theory, there seems to be widespread acceptance of the notion that more than one theory may ultimately find empirical support and practitioner acceptance. For example, Bruner, Rogers, and various behavior modifiers independently have expressed favorable recognition of the merits of principles in theories competitive with their own. It would appear that the emergence and acceptance of diverse instructional theories may provide options to educators and to students so that it may become feasible to attempt individualization of instruction through matching instructional procedures with a student's needs and preferences.

But to what extent do we *now* have instructional theories which are logically sound and scientifically valid? At the present time there really are no candidates which meet the criteria set by the ASCD commission nor those outlined earlier in this book. Although there is considerable variation in the delineation of goals and in the identification of instructional principles, many aspects of the theories in their present form involve beliefs and aspirations of their proponents rather than independently established facts. While there are comparatively few instances in which the instructional principles actually conflict with empirical data, there are many for which no appropriate data have been collected.

One might also consider future prospects for further development of existing theories and emergence of new instructional theories. Many of the present positions began emerging in the 1950s, with few new ideas becoming evident in the 1960s. In fact, for some time it even looked as though instructional theories may have been just one more "fad" in education and that the vigorous efforts to produce instructional theories would not be made. But interest in scientifically tested and systematically developed theories has continued into the 1970s and even is increasing at the time of this writing. For example, many key papers during the 1972 American Educational Research Association (AERA) Convention were devoted to instructional theory construction and to the use of theories in the design of instruction. The 1972 AERA president-elect, Patrick Suppes, chose the topic, "Relevance of Research to Facts and Fantasies of Education." He first sharply attacked uncritical acceptance of widely ranging theories from Piaget to Skinner because many of the instructional admonitions advanced in their names simply have not been submitted to empirical test in educational situations. He then proclaimed: "We do not need ill-worked-out theories from other disciplines. We do not need fantasies of abstractions and platitudes unsupported by serious and rigorous development. What we need for relevance in education are theories of intellectual power and rigor, and we should not rest until we get them." (*Report on Preschool Education*, 1972) Another indication of growing interest was the establishment in 1972 of an international journal, *Instructional Science*. But the rate of progress in developing instructional theories will require funding as well as professional interest. Given the past influence of federal funding on educational progress, it is quite likely that the National Institute of Education's administrative and funding policies will directly determine the extent to which instructional theories are further developed, tested, and used.

Many readers are probably wondering about the practical value of instructional theories in their present form. It is quite generally acknowledged that common-sense, intuitively guided educational practice may be as effective as scientifically tested instructional theories at this stage of progress. In fact, many acknowledge that it may take more years of work before efforts required for systematically developing and testing theories may begin to show encouraging results.

In the meantime, while we await more extensively developed instructional theories, just what can practicing educators turn to as a means for using psychological information in the improvement of educational practice? In the next chapter we will suggest that *psycho-educational design*, and the educational research and development (R&D) movement more generally, can provide a means for using instructional theories, learning theories, and other information in the improvement of educational practice.

6
Psychoeducational Design

"It is something that we are only now beginning to understand. Innovation, by whatever theoretical derivation, involves vast development and engineering." (Bruner, 1971, p. 101)

"It may be true, it is true, we are told, that some should take hold of psychological methods and conclusions, and organize them with reference to the assistance which they may give to the cause of education." (Dewey, 1900, p. 109)

"In this process of making a continual checkup on the fundamental concepts of learning theory, the educational psychologist bears somewhat the same relationship to psychology and to education that the mechanical engineer bears to chemistry and to the medical profession. His function is that of providing material for further testing in the field; of making the findings of the laboratory available to the educational practitioner for trial in the classroom." (Lynch, 1945, p. 295)

"When the biologist, social scientist, and indeed natural scientist collaborate with the engineer on these large new systems' problems, their classical roles as *analyzers* of existing systems in contrast to the engineer's role as the *synthesizer* of previously nonexisting 'hardware' systems need reappraisal." (Milsum, 1966, p. vii. Italics added)

In previous chapters we have considered the utility of learning theories for organizing psychology's information about learning processes, and we have reviewed the various attempts made to apply this fund of information to educational practice. We have also considered the extent to which instructional theories have emerged as a means for organizing information about that aspect of education commonly called "instruction." We have considered the extent to which instructional theories have been useful in designing and improving educational practice. It is evident that considerable progress has been made in organizing this information in the form of learning theories and instructional theories, as well as in applying them to educational practice. But it seems quite clear that we have not yet reached that point—if indeed such a point can ever be reached—where one can go *directly from* learning or instructional *theories to* educational *practice*.

The present chapter will advance the notion that a design-development process is necessary for relating this scientific information to educational practice and that some kind of middle position is desirable between the theoretician-researcher and the educational practitioner. We will acknowledge that such a middle position had been anticipated since the turn of the century but that it did not emerge until around the middle 1960s. Moreover, we will note that the middle-position manifestation occurs today not only in education and educational psychology but in other areas of applied psychology as well. Such a design-development position has emerged during an era in which society has increasingly looked to psychology and other social sciences for assistance with social problems. As we noted above, this middle position emerged after many decades of psychological research effort and after an almost equally long period of attempts to use the resulting fund of knowledge in the resolution of social problems. But even today the actual processes of relating theory to practice are so inadequately defined that we still are asking such questions as: *Can* science contribute to the improvement of educational practice? If so, by what means or procedures might this be accomplished?

We will consider briefly some examples of R&D activities elsewhere in applied psychology generally but will mainly focus on the movement as it emerged in educational situations. We will consider some of the barriers which have obstructed the emergence of this R&D movement and the accompanying middle-position emphasis, and we will enumerate some of the major features of this kind of orientation. Finally, we will explore possible implications for psychologists and educators who may wish to use such an approach but who may not be in a position to do so on a large scale. Thus, we will outline some of the steps an educator or a psychologist might follow in using a psychoeducational design orientation in the design of new instructional experiences or in the improvement of existing educational practice.

PSYCHOEDUCATIONAL DESIGN

Psychoeducational design is simply that aspect of the design-development process whereby one utilizes *psychological* facts, principles, and theories when making plans for improving educational practice. Educational design and development routinely involve interdisciplinary collaboration, with the practical problem solution ultimately being based on some combination of ideas derived from practical considerations, educational philosophy, curriculum theories, instructional theories, educational sociology, psychological theories, etc. In this context, it is less important that one rely exclusively on *one* psychological theory (as sometimes seems to be suggested by proponents of psychological theories) than it is that the ideas—no matter what their origin—*demonstrably* facilitate attainment of the desired educational objectives.

As a result of the educational R&D movement, there has been emerging a new set of "middle positions" in various aspects of the educational profession and related professions, including psychology. In each instance the professional position lies midway between theoretical research activities and educational practice. It is generally expected that these newly emerging professional persons are somewhat knowledgeable about both theory and practice but that their unique function lies in relating these two activities. Of direct concern in this book is the person who serves as a psychoeducational designer, especially with regard to applications of learning theories and principles.

In some respects educational psychologists can be depicted as always having been in a "middle position" in that they have tried to keep educators informed about current developments in psychological research and theory. However, their translation of the psychological information has frequently been conducted on an intuitive basis with the organization of the information stemming from the psychological theory rather than from the practical problem.

When "empirical" tests have been used to assess the value of the psychology theory-based educational suggestion, the innovative approach has typically been pitted against some rather vaguely defined "traditional practice" or against some competing educational method. Various authors have characterized this as "horse-race research." The unfortunate part is that this kind of approach doesn't really tell the ways in which either method was good or bad. It merely tells, at some level of statistical significance, that one method was "better" than the others.

We routinely accept many educational methods which have merely been shown to be better than some other poorly defined method of instruction, frequently at a .05 level of significance, which simply says that chances are nineteen out of twenty that the one method is better than the other method. In contrast, in educational development, psychological theories and other sources of information are evaluated for their relevance in terms of the extent to which they demonstrably facilitate students' attainment of delineated educational objectives.

Although the practical problems and the theoretical base are far from identical, the psychoeducational designer plans and tries out learning theory-based ideas about educational practice somewhat as the engineer does in the industrial utilization of physical science knowledge, and as the medical researcher does when he designs solutions for medical problems. Thus the psychoeducational design process provides procedures for using psychological information in the resolution of specific educational problems. Such information can be drawn from theories, including learning theories and instructional theories, as well as from more or less isolated facts and principles. We will consider some of the changes in the organization of information that are required when one attempts to resolve specific educational problems. But the one main continuing theme which we will emphasize is that the *utility* of any facts or theories will be determined primarily by the extent to which these facts demonstrably facilitate developing effective, efficient, and humanistic educational procedures and materials.

NEED FOR INTERMEDIARY POSITION BETWEEN THEORY AND PRACTICE IN EDUCATION

You will recall from earlier comments that many psychologists and educators at the turn of the century anticipated that there would be some kind of middle position between psychological research and educational practice. Dewey (1900), for example, suggested that the middle position might be filled by "an educational theorist." Many leaders in psychology and education at that time contended that education should draw on the findings of psychology, but it was not obvious as to what steps might be involved in relating psychological research findings and theory to educational practice.

In the ensuing decades various persons continued to express support for some kind of middle position between scientific psychology and educational practice, but they either found themselves in a minority or found their recommendations somewhat misinterpreted. For example, some seem to have considered the middle position as merely involving suggestions made by educational psychologists who would be "well read" in psychological theory and who would make thoughtful pronouncements about applications in education. Travers (1966) has characterized these attempts as constituting metaphorical extensions rather than scientific generalizations partly because they involve intuitive and logical extensions and because they typically involve very great differences between the research and practical situations.

But more systematic notions also were advanced. For example, some (such as Lynch, 1945) were quite explicit in recommending that the educational psychologist should develop a role more like that of an engineer than like that of either a technician or a scientist. It was suggested that the educational psychologist would not really be mechanistic or mechanical in his utilization of psychology and other social science findings, and that he should treat them with at least the degree of reservation that the typical design engineer has when he looks at physical science data and theory. It was suggested, for example, that the educational psychologist would treat the basic science theory as containing *hypotheses* of potential relevance for educational practice but that they should not be fully accepted until their value had been demonstrated in tryout tests during development of education procedures based on them. But at least until the early 1960s such an orientation in educational psychology received little support.

The problem partly resulted from the fact that many psychologists who were conducting the basic research were not really familiar with conditions in the practical educational situation and educators were not sufficiently informed about the psychological literature. But the problem did not stop there by any means! There simply had not been developed, anywhere in applied psychology, a systematic procedure for utilizing psychological information in the resolution of practical problems. Chapanis (1967) points out that research methodology textbooks in psychology uniformly provide all kinds of interesting suggestions and rules for conducting *laboratory research* but that they routinely *ignore* the steps which are involved in taking the findings *from laboratory* situations and *utilizing* them in the *practical situations* in the real world outside the laboratory. Mackie and Christensen (1967) conducted an extensive review of the translation of psychological research into a form which is useful for resolving educational and training problems. They concluded that no research-to-application process had ever been properly developed for the psychology of learning at least up to the 1960s. Moreover, one of their major recommendations was that society needs "learning engineers" who are specially trained for relating research findings to practical training and educational situations. Five years later an interagency panel explored some of the gaps and needs in early childhood research and development. One of their major conclusions was that society needs specialists who can synthesize the findings from widely ranging studies and address them to designs for solutions to educational and other social problems. Though their study followed the Chapanis and the Mackie and Christensen publications by about five years, the Chapman report's conclusions about the need for design and development specialists were strikingly similar.

It is noteworthy that other educators also became aware of the need for evolving a middle position juxtaposed between theory and educational practice. For example, although Goodlad (1969), like Beauchamp (1961,

1968), had acknowledged the need for emergence of curriculum theory, he also pointed out that there is need for "curriculum engineers" who would be aware of the developing curriculum theory and who would be familiar with practical aspects of the educational situation. Similar suggestions have been made by those persons in education who are particularly concerned with the development of audio devices, visual displays, and other media, including computers, to facilitate instruction (cf. McMurrin, 1970). They, too, have expressed the need for emergence in education of a middle position which would draw from various sources and integrate them in the process of designing effective, efficient, and humanistic instructional experiences.

Implications for Applied Psychology

At this point it should be noted that the emergence of an R&D movement and a design function has not been restricted to educational psychology but has also been evolving in other aspects of applied psychology. Of course, it would be beyond the scope of this book to explore this in great detail. However, this is called to the reader's attention not only to maintain some perspective about the change in educational psychology but also to point out the considerable importance of its development in applied psychology. It is the author's opinion that this may turn out to be one of the most important developments in applied psychology since its establishment.

Earlier chapters have made some reference to the great gap which has persisted in psychology between the basic scientist types and the professional types of psychologists. It is worth noting that such differences in the conception of psychology's nature were so great earlier in the century that two separate psychology organizations were established. The two groups (the American Psychological Association and the American Association of Applied Psychologists) merged in the mid-1940s to form the present American Psychological Association. However, there has been almost continuous controversy about basic science versus applied science emphasis in psychology, resulting in such heated debates that there have been several threats to split the organization again into a basic science group and an applied group.

The internal professional problems among psychologists would not be relevant to this book except that the debate frequently has centered on the extent to which psychology should be concerned with practical problems (including educational practice) and the manner by which psychological data can be used in resolution of social problems. In this context, it is worth noting here that the emergence of a middle position, that of psychoeducational design in educational psychology, has counterparts in other aspects of applied psychology, and that it has considerable potential implications for relating psychology's fund of information to the resolution of social problems.

These debates have been especially lively concerning the nature and characteristics of clinical psychology. Some emphasize that psychologists should primarily focus on research concerning abnormal or pathological processes, while others have advocated a more active role for psychologists in the intervention and resolution of social clinical problems. Something of a compromise arrangement has taken the form of an R&D proposal.

Lanyon and Broskowski (for example, Broskowski, 1971; Lanyon & Broskowski, 1969) have been some of the more vocal proponents of a research and development model for clinical psychology. They have been particularly enthusiastic in their support for the emergence of a clinical psychologist as a "middleman" similar in purpose to the psychoeducational designers described earlier. Broskowski and Lanyon have depicted the clinical psychologist in the role as being somewhat sophisticated about basic research and knowledgeable about the delivery of services to clients, but with the *unique* function of *designing* procedures and techniques to help solve or prevent various clinical problems.

Of course, both Lanyon and Broskowski have acknowledged that other clinical psychologists may continue with the more traditional roles of the basic researcher in abnormal psychology or of the therapist who provides direct services to clients/patients. However they have suggested that there is need for training at least *some* clinical psychologists as design specialists. "The R&D model will train Ph.D.-level psychologists to systematically *conduct* and *utilize* relevant research for the *development* of procedures and techniques to help solve or prevent various clinical problems in individuals, groups, and institutions" (Broskowski, 1971, p. 236).

Similar examples of an interest in an R&D emphasis can be found in other aspects of applied psychology, but consideration of them takes us beyond the scope of the present book. Moreover, we would find that patterns evident in educational situations are representative of the characteristics of the design-development process in other aspects of applied psychology.

Barriers to Translation of Psychological
Theory into Educational Practice

Without conducting an extensive review of the problems, we can identify here three barriers to the development of an adequate system for translating psychology learning theory into educational practice. This is not an exhaustive list, nor does the order with which we consider the barriers have any significance for their degree of importance. These barriers provide cues as to some characteristics required for the emergence of middle positions. The first barrier concerns the *nature of psychological research and the organization of potentially relevant information.* It should be obvious to the reader that much psychological research has been *analytic* rather than *synthetic* in character. Many psychological studies involve identifying one or a few factors which individually influence various learning processes, but they too infrequently explore the manner in which various factors *interact* in influencing learning processes. Of course, there are some studies which consider two, three, four, or five factors, but rarely do laboratory studies take into account the *multitude* of factors which are routinely encountered in practical situations. Moreover, the training of the scientist is such that he is more disposed to analytical types of research than synthetic research. Apparently the problem is not unique to the social sciences, since – as indicated in the quotation in the beginning of the chapter – Milsum (1956) has observed that similar problems long have been encountered when biological scientists and physical scientists collaborate in the resolution of practical problems in industry.

Moreover, as we have tried to emphasize with regard to learning theories, the resulting findings are organized along disciplinary lines around theoretical topics, rather than around particular practical problems. Some transformation in the organization of information is required when one goes from scientific pursuits to practical concerns. Geutzkow (1959) identifies several different roles and functions of persons who are involved in the accumulation of scientific knowledge and in the utilization of this information to resolve society's problems. Although social science has not adequately distinguished among the functions of scientist, engineer, technician, practitioner, and policy maker, even more troublesome is the little recognized problem concerning the structure of the knowledge and information involved. Whereas the basic scientist organizes his information in terms of some issue within his particular discipline, the practitioner finds value in such information only to the extent that it enables him to attain specific concrete purposes in the practical situation. In many respects, Geutzkow's comments apply not only to the learning theories but also to the instructional theories which we have been considering in this text. He suggests that there is definite need for a broad-gauged "middleman" social engineer who is able to transform basic knowledge *from* its *disciplinary structure into* forms which are usable for *solving practical problems.* The middleman must have a means whereby he can draw from the various theories which are *potentially* applicable to the practical problem and can systematically check out the extent to which such theories actually prove their utility in attaining the desired educational objectives. Thus though the social engineer may find facts organized into learning theories and instructional theories useful as a starting point, he must restructure the information in ways which make it more readily applicable to the particular educational problem on which he is working at that time.

The second barrier concerns the lack—until the middle 1960s—of *institutionalized support* for identification of such middlemen, and the lack of substantial *financial support* available for their activities. In contrast, for example, states routinely have established certification requirements for school psychologists; other certification programs outline the training and the functions of guidance counselors. Even educational researchers, for whom no formal certification programs routinely exist, have had sufficient visibility that their roles and functions are traditionally defined (for example, research design, statistical analysis, computer analysis, etc.) and their training programs are very well established.

By contrast, most authors seem to agree with Glaser's (1966) observation that at least until the mid-1960s an entity relating research and theory to practice, with professional persons known as educational technologists or as instructional designers, practically was nonexistent in our society (p. 433).

Third, there does not seem to have been any *model for relating psychological theory to educational practice* which took into account the synthesizing middle positions which are routinely found in the utilization of the physical and biological sciences such as that of engineers, architects, medical researchers, etc. Prior to the mid-1960s—and even today—many psychologists and educators assumed that some form of linear model was appropriate for relating psychological theory to educational practice, with the flow of information going from the laboratory to the classroom. This is evident, for example, in the various attempts which were made to "apply learning theories." It has long been recognized that some kind of transformation is necessary when taking a psychology learning principle and trying to use it in a practical educational situation. For example, Ernest R. Hilgard (for example, see Hilgard & Bower, 1966), one of the most widely respected authorities on learning theories, suggests that there are six steps or stages from the pure basic research on learning to the most applied application in educational situations. The first three levels are basic science or pure science activities, in which there are gradations in the degree to which the theoretical problem itself is at all relevant to educational situations. Under *technological research and development* he classifies three stages, with the laboratory classroom and special educational arrangements constituting the level closest to basic science research, with an intermediary tryout phase in a normal classroom, and with final widespread adoption in classrooms as the sixth step. The problem with this kind of model is that it does not provide *adequately* for inputs from the practical situation or from other basic science theories, philosophical positions, educational theories, etc. Of course it is possible that persons who use linear models for relating psychology theory to educational practice may actually recognize the importance of considering these other contributions to the design of instructional sequences. However, the point here is that there is no specific provision for such relationships in the linear models which were available up to the 1960s. Later we will discuss a nonlinear model which does make formal provision for two-way communication and for various kinds of inputs.

EDUCATIONAL R&D AND
PSYCHOEDUCATIONAL DESIGN

It is quite widely acknowledged that educators traditionally have depended on appeal to authority as a basis for selecting ideas for the improvement of educational practice. In earlier chapters we pointed out that some reactions both for and against applications of learning theories stem primarily from the status of the particular learning theorist's "credentials" to comment on educational practice. In part, instructional theories emerged as an attempt to provide for more systematic and scientifically tested approaches to instruction. However, as competing instructional theories have emerged, again we have seen controversy as to which theory should be used, with the conclusions frequently being based on the extent to which the given spokesman has credentials to speak on educational matters.

Readers may also recall that in our discussion of instructional theories it was suggested that it is quite possible that "common-sense" or intuitive approaches to educational problems sometimes may come up with appropriate answers even more readily than will instructional theories at their current stage of development. In the development process, one takes into account practical implications as well as any other kinds of interdisciplinary suggestions. As a result, at times not only will the instructional designer gain additional implications for the improvement of educational practice, but the instructional theorist and the learning theorist will also derive implications for reevaluating and modifying their theories.

Not too long ago, one of the directors of a regional educational laboratory observed: "Writing on the nature of educational development at the present time is as speculative as writing on the nature of industrial development would have been in the seventeenth century" (Schutz, 1970, p. 39). Nonetheless, we will try to indicate pertinent characteristics of this emergent process by defining research, development, and practice; showing how these interdependent activities relate to each other; and then outlining some strategies and techniques of psychoeducational design processes.

Definitions of Development, Research, and Practice

Development has been defined as the "systematic use of scientific knowledge directed toward the production of useful materials, devices, systems or methods, including design and development of prototypes and processes" (National Science Foundation, 1965). Schutz (1970) points out that the domain of development lies midway between the acquisition of a fund of scientific knowledge (*research* activities) and the actual application of this fund of information in the day-to-day *operations* of *educational practice*. The development process is that aspect of technology in which one attempts to bridge the gap between the forces which are acquiring the fund of knowledge (the *researchers*) and the practitioners who are desperately seeking help in coping with daily educational matters. It may be helpful to understand the role of development in technology if we briefly consider the role of research in science. By comparison, *research* is usually defined as consisting of "systematic, detailed, and relatively prolonged attempts to discover or to confirm the facts that bear upon a certain problem or problems and the laws or principles that govern them" (English & English, 1958). Thus in many respects, the process of development has the same kind of function in technology that research has in science. Whereas one uses systematic and empirical procedures to produce principles and theories in science (basic and applied), in technology the systematic and empirical *development* efforts are focused on the resolution of some practical problem. Parallel to the principles and theories in science, the end result of development efforts may consist of educational materials, instructional procedures and techniques, and other rather concrete and practical aspects of the teaching-learning process. In a sense, research efforts help us to draw logically consistent and empirically sound *conclusions*, while development efforts enable us to have logically consistent and empirically sound bases for *making decisions* about the planning and management of instruction.

A Model for Relating Research, Development, and Practice

This is an appropriate point at which to consider some of the ways in which research, development, and practice activities relate to each other and to examine how various psychological theories, principles, and facts are utilized in the educational development process. We use the term *psychoeducational design* to refer to that aspect of the development process in which psychological information is used to design educational innovations or to improve existing educational practice. Though we will focus on the activities of the psychoeducational designer especially in his use of learning research and theories, we assume that he would collaborate with other "middle position professionals," such as the curriculum engineers and educational media engineers recognized in the previous section.

Gideonse (1968) took exception to the popular linear model concept that information flows from theoretical research to educational practice. It was in the context of the contemporary R&D movement in education that his alternative model for relationships among research, development, and practice activities was formulated. Three basic notions underlie the model which he proposed (see Figure 6-1). First, he contended that research, development, and educational practice constitute substantially different kinds of activities especially in that each has a unique set of objectives or outputs, with each satisfying different kinds of internal and external needs.

Second, he suggested that activities routinely occur simultaneously on all three levels, and that interactions between any two of these levels of activities can be initiated by any one of the three. Third, he proposed that more constructive relationships among the three levels of activities can be attained more readily if we emphasize the desired *outcomes* of each of

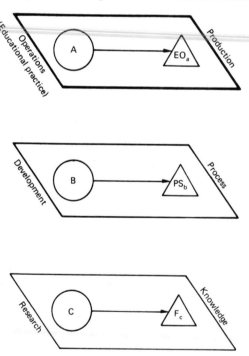

Figure 6-1 A three-level, outcome-oriented model for relationships among research, development, and educational practice activities. (Adapted from Gideonse, 1968, p. 159, with permission of the publisher)

these three activities (research, development, practice) and if we recognize the different expectations and decisions stemming from the different outcomes. This third idea is especially important for understanding the nature of educational development and psychoeducational design.

Three levels of activities are represented by the three planes. The top level depicts school operations and general educational practice. Gideonse takes a conventional position that the objective of educational practice is to work with human beings so that they can develop the various skills, attitudes, beliefs, and knowledge which are identified for a given educational institution. He characterizes the outcome at this level as *production*, by which he refers to the activities which indicate that students have been able to obtain those educational objectives identified by society. Operations which are initiated and which occur *within* this plane specifically are selected because they are believed to be consistent with society's conception of educational experiences and because they are considered to be means by which students are helped to obtain the educational objectives.

The middle plane symbolizes the educational development activity. The objective of educational development is to produce the procedures, techniques, materials, hardware, processes, and organizational formats which presumably would be useful as operations in educational practice. The outcome of the developmental activity is thus some educational process. The educational process is identified at the time that one institutes a given developmental activity. Of course, that does not mean that one would not modify the outcomes of the development activity. However, it does mean that the "targeted" outcome provides guidance to the developer as to what theories and other sources of ideas should be considered in designing his educational program. It also provides criteria whereby he can evaluate which kinds of input are enabling him to attain those development objectives. In this context, *performance specifications* are designated as the output characteristics of the development activity.

The lower plane represents research activity, with the ultimate objective of adding to our fund of knowledge about a particular area, with such knowledge consisting of facts, principles, and theories. In contrast with the *developmental* level, where the end *outcome* is known from the start, at the *research* phase, it is the *inputs* which are known and the outcomes (facts, principles, theories) which remain to be determined through research.

Gideonse points out that many activities occur in parallel within each of the three levels of activities delineated in his model. For example, we have already noted that many research activities are conducted entirely at that level, with practically no interest in involving either a developmental phase or the operations typically found in educational practice. Similarly many professional educational activities are conducted strictly within the operations plane—for example, various educational institutions attempt to help their students attain the educational objective delineated by society for that particular institution—without any major reference to research or to development.

It is also conceivable, but presumably less frequent, that activities would be carried on entirely within the developmental plane without involving either the operations or the research levels. For example, simply on the basis of their previous developmental activities, an R&D organization might decide that it would be appropriate to develop a particular educational procedure or product. This developmental activity conceivably could be conducted strictly with the context of the information available within that developmental activity, without relying on additional information either from research or from educational practice. Thus it is conceivable that activities at all three levels may occur in parallel without contact with activities at either of the other two levels.

Given the focus of this book, it is also relevant to note that activities in any one of the three levels can result in activities in either one or both of the other two levels. Problems encountered in educational practice may result in initiation of developmental projects; in the course of planning designs of educational procedures and techniques certain information may be needed which requires conducting basic or applied research. Occasionally, a research finding or principle may be viewed as so reliable and potentially useful that educators may adopt it in practice without any formal developmental efforts. More frequently, the research findings and principles will produce change in educational practice only after some kind of developmental process has been carried out so that both the positive and negative effects of the ideas can be assessed before they are widely adopted. Though research activities will more frequently be initiated as a result of previous research or developmental questions, in some cases research activities may also be initiated directly because of questions posed at an educational practice level. Only a few possible relations between the different levels are outlined here, but they illustrate how activities at any given level can be independent and yet can influence what happens at other levels.

Now that we have used Gideonse's model to locate the design-development process at a middle position between research and educational practice, let us consider how learning theories and instructional theories can facilitate the improvement of educational practice. Hopefully the reader will also see how each type of theory has a legitimate and important existence as an independent entity as well as a contribution to make in improving practice. Throughout our discussion, please remember that solutions for educational problems and designs for educational innovations are based on a *combination* of ideas drawn from many diverse sources—traditions in the community, educational philosophy, educational theories and sub-theories, subject-matter characteristics, curricular aspects and theories, personal experiences—as well as from psychological learning theories and other psychological and social science theories. The frequent reference here to learning theories and instructional theories mainly results from the focus set for this book rather than from the belief that the other ideas are less important. Actually, at present sound ideas may come quite readily from "common sense" and traditional ways of doing things, while it may take some time before we have refined such educational prescriptions so that we know which ones are most supported by empirical evidence.

As should be obvious, learning theories are conceptual devices for organizing information primarily at the research level, and at least in some cases, only certain kinds of information at that level. Other psychological theories, for example, focus on motivational processes, on perceptual processes, etc. Of course, we have already noted that the learning theories have been used by some educators and psychologists—appropriately or inappropriately—as means for organizing more practically oriented ideas at the practice and development levels as well. Information at the practice level more frequently has been organized as educational methods or techniques. With the relatively more recent formulation of instructional theories, we now have available means for organizing information at the development level and for relating information from research activities to ways for changing educational practice.

There are several ways in which learning research and theory influence educational development projects and, ultimately, educational practice. Most developmental activities are initiated when someone either recognizes an educational problem or decides that certain aspects of educational practice should be improved. Thus the objectives of the developmental efforts frequently are determined on the basis of these *educational* needs. However, in some cases the developmental efforts have been initiated as a result of findings from research or through potential suggestions deduced from theory. Not too surprisingly, when this occurs the developmental outcome is characterized in terms which are more compatible with the *research* and *theory* from which the ideas were derived, so that they may or may not be consistent with *educational* needs as conceived by practitioners. Finally, occasionally developmental efforts are proved to be sufficiently successful in one project that they are used to plan developmental efforts in other projects. Obviously, the conception of the second developmental effort tends to be greatly influenced by the conceptions of the first *developmental* efforts. Thus the way that the outcomes for the developmental activities are characterized depends in part on the influences which led to launching that particular developmental venture.

PSYCHOEDUCATIONAL DESIGN
STRATEGIES AND TECHNIQUES

Design strategies and techniques differ somewhat among the various development ventures existent today, but there are certain characteristics which can be identified. The comments here will focus on these characteristics with particular concern with ways in which psychological learning research and theory as well as instructional research and theory are used to prepare initial designs and to modify the merging educational innovation. But the reader is well advised to realize that these comments are observations of the design-development process while it is still undergoing many changes. For example, Baker and Schutz similarly observed: "Most instruction is dispensed, not developed. In contrast to the writing and publishing of text materials and the producing of audio-visual materials, the programmatic development of instruction is a recent concept, the how-to, or technology, of which is still primitive. Programmatic instructional development efforts conducted during the last few years are only just beginning to produce generalizable procedures and strategies" (Baker & Schutz, 1971, p. xv). The reader should also recognize that the strategies and techniques summarized in these few pages actually take teams of professional persons anywhere from several months to several years to carry out. Thus the following comments only highlight some of the major features and outline illustrative steps involved.

It has long been recognized (for example, Thorndike, 1910) that there are at least three major ways in which psychological research and theories can influence educational practice. Briefly, they are (1) clarifying educational objectives; (2) delineating instructional methods; and (3) troubleshooting. Our discussion will be organized under these three topical areas.

Clarifying Educational Objectives

One major characteristic of development activities is that they are oriented toward delineated outcomes in the form of educational objectives. Thus, one strategy is to state educational objectives in some form which will enable the instructional designer to determine whether the materials and methods are enabling students to attain the desired objectives and, if not attained, to provide information which will indicate where improvement is needed. Later, these objectives are used by the student and the instructor as a basis for selecting appropriate educational sequences and as a reference against which the student's progress can be compared.

But unfortunately, the widely ranging objectives which society sets for our schools are not easily conceptualized in measurable form! In fact, some educators and other interested persons have challenged the idea that objectives can be determined in advance of a given learning experience and have contended that predetermined objectives somehow may even hinder the educational growth of the student. On the various issues which have been discussed over the past several years concerning delineation of educational objectives, two relatively extreme positions can be identified. Some would argue that educational objectives *must* be stated as behaviors of students which can be objectively observed and quantitatively recorded under specified conditions at the conclusion of a given learning experience. Opposing spokesmen contend that activities in which students engage may have no specifiable immediate results, may be so personal as to be discernible only to the individual student, and yet may be some of the most important aspects of ways in which educational institutions help students to become healthy, happy, self-fulfilled, and self-sustaining citizens. Steps for identifying educational objectives which embody these widely ranging views follow.

We have identified six steps by which one can assess community-determined educational needs and translate them into a form which can be used to develop appropriate and effective educational methods and materials (see Figure 6-2). In practice, it would not be unusual to have work occurring concurrently for two or more of these steps, or to have changes made in step 1 results (that is, determination of general community expectations) after subsequent steps had been completed. But there is some logical basis for the order noted: It is more likely that one would start and complete step 1, 2, etc., before later steps.

You should also note that there is a "knowledge base" which is consulted for each step. By "knowledge base," we are referring to any sources—for example, empirical research results, theories, philosophical positions, community traditions, and existing practices, etc.—from which one can derive information about education. The kinds of sources used will vary, depending upon the background of the instructional designer, the educational goals involved, and the particular steps in the development process. But in each case the instructional designer would search the relevant sources for information pertinent to that particular situation. As indicated in our discussion of learning theories, frequently such information is not organized in ways pertinent to the practical problem. In some cases, empirical studies must be conducted. Practical considerations typically determine how much time, energy, and money can be devoted to these reviews. As a result, it is considered good practice to record the sources searched for a given decision and to "document" or record the bases for decisions made. We'll comment briefly about knowledge bases which might be used for these decisions.

Determining General Community Needs For Education   One of the first steps is to find out what expectations and requirements community members hold for their schools. For example, although all schools, hopefully, help to produce "good citizens," there are many ways in which

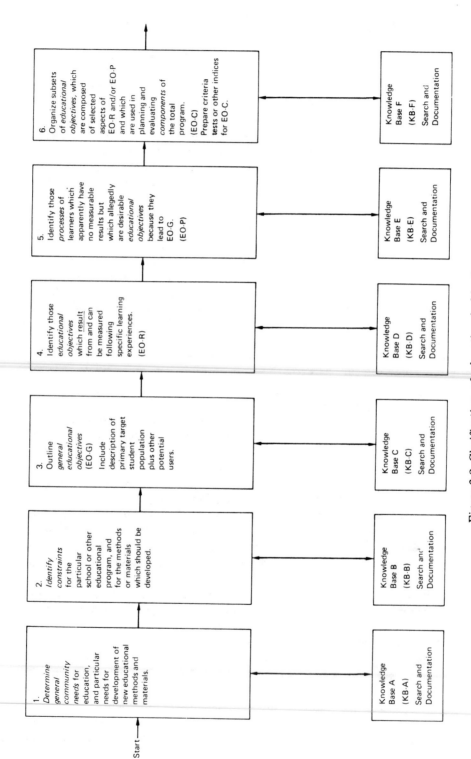

Figure 6-2 Clarification of educational objectives.

174

communities may differ in their expectations as to what constitutes "good citizenship" and how schools can contribute to society. In addition, the role that schools will have in any given situation will be influenced partly by the other kinds of institutions for learning and the kinds of circumstances or opportunities which exist in that community. At one time schools were charged with teaching the "three Rs"—reading, 'riting, and 'rithmetic. Today some schools are expected to teach such diverse topics as science, sex education, ecology, consumer guidance, career education, etc. There are quite substantial differences between a rural school whose graduates would primarily work on farms and schools whose graduates primarily enter college or work in industry; of course, there are many common features, as well.

The knowledge base consulted would primarily include the community and school leaders, sources describing current and previous programs, sources outlining the educational philosophy and views about education which are valued by that community, curriculum theorists, and other experts on educational matters, etc. Some psychological theories and instructional theories would have indirect influence especially in the ways that they have influenced professional educators' and general community members' views about education.

Identifying Constraints It would not be too difficult to enumerate a Utopianlike set of educational objectives based on community expectations. After all, wouldn't it be nice if schools could eliminate poverty, crime, unhappiness, and malice as well as all forms of ignorance? But there are realistic limitations on the amounts of time, manpower, money, and other resources which will be available for educational programs. Knowledge base B (KB-B) would include many of the same kinds of sources which one would consult in KB-A, although the kinds of questions asked and the information sought would be different. For KB-B, we would be trying to set priority levels for the various general objectives emerging during step 1. It is also quite likely that different members of the development team would have the expertise required for step 1, since in step 2 we would be trying to understand how the community uses its various resources in satisfying its individual and collective needs. In addition, throughout this process we would be gaining some information about constraints on the kinds of educational methods and materials which would be permitted and/or encouraged.

Outlining General Educational Objectives (EO-G) With this step we would be in a position to describe the general goals that can be assigned to a total school program as well as the different kinds of educational experiences which might be valued. For example, we would have some idea as to what balance is to be arranged for career education versus general education and "liberal arts" types of courses, and we would be able to determine what age ranges and ability levels will be represented in the school population. More specific kinds of information could also be obtained. For example, what kinds of objectives can be identified for specific courses, how do courses relate to each other, how much flexibility is possible and/or desirable for sequencing courses, how much emphasis is to be placed on independent studies and what objectives would be set for them, etc.?

Although there would be some overlap in sources consulted under KB-C as compared with KB-A and KB-B, professional educators and allied professional persons would have important funds of knowledge to contribute to KB-C. For example, curriculum theorists and educational philosophers would have important roles both in making decisions about EO-G and in identifying scholarly and practical sources of information. Overlapping their contributions would be suggestions provided by instructional theorists, learning theorists, and other psychologists who are concerned with analyses of hierarchical relationships among learning objectives and among prerequisite skills.

We would have identified *general* statements about educational experiences as they relate to objectives, and we would have some indication of the various courses, independent learning experiences, and other educational experiences which would compose at least some major part of the school program. In past approaches to planning instruction, it is typically at this point that one would decide to "apply" some particular educational philosophy or theory, or a psychological theory (for example, Thorndike's connectionism, Bruner's discovery learning, Piaget's developmental psychology theory, Skinner's operant theory, etc.—at least as conceived by some educator or educational psychologist). One would typically apply this theory to the entire school program. But a different approach is more usually found in contemporary R&D strategies and techniques.

A major concept of educational R&D is that one actually can combine a number of different orientations in planning methods and materials. Instead of using *one* position or theory to plan *all* aspects of the educational program, the instructional designer tries to identify rather specific objectives and to select any relevant ideas which will be useful in planning effective, efficient, and humanistic methods and materials. Thus, we include three more steps in clarifying educational objectives before we are ready to design instructional methods and materials. In step 4 we identify those educational objectives which can be observed and measured following completion of a given instructional sequence. Step 5 focuses on those processes which can be observed *during* the learning experience and which are known or believed to be related to general educational objectives, but which apparently do not produce measurable results at the time the learning sequence is completed. Step 6 involves taking an "inventory" of "results" types of educational objectives (EO-R) and "process" types (EO-P), and organizing them in meaningful arrangements and sequences so that educational objectives can be identified for modules or components (EO-C).

Identifying Educational Objectives as Measurable Results (EO-R) Many instructional designers contend that, to be useful, educational objectives must be stated in an observable (or behavioral) and quantifiable form. For example, instead of merely stating that a student is "to learn English composition" in one course, or "to learn to understand and appreciate music" in another, the educational objectives would include statements as to what behaviors can be observed, under what kinds of conditions, and with what degree or level of accuracy or appropriateness. Thus the English composition course might include such specific objectives as "can state and explain correctly, without any references, twenty pronoun and verb forms, with at least 80 percent accuracy"; and "can write a 600-word essay about a personal experience with no more than ten grammatical and/or punctuation errors." But such measurable objectives need not be confined to factual rote memorization or to rigidly defined verbal activities. At least some instructional designers would also accept as useful educational objectives those statements of results which may depend upon judgments by the instructor or even by the student. For example, the music teacher would be expected to define what is meant by "understand" and "appreciate"; this could be done by stating what activities of the student would indicate that he can "understand" and "appreciate" music. This might consist of the student's listening to an unlabeled music passage and being able to state what composition style is represented, or from what era the music was most likely drawn. Or, it might involve the teacher's and the student's judgments as to whether the student has become sufficiently sophisticated and interested in music that he can not only tell whether he likes a given record, but can also explain what aspects are particularly pleasing and why he likes certain sections and not others, noting composition styles, artistic form, etc.

The knowledge base (KB-D) would include the information collected for step 3 plus any instructional theories and learning theories which would be useful in specifying educational objectives. Of particular help would be those theories which provide some systematic means for analyzing and classifying tasks in hierarchical relationships.

Identifying Educational Objectives as Processes (EO-P) Certain instructional designers and instructional theorists contend that human learning, especially meaningful school learning, involves many processes which do not readily lend themselves to measurement nor even to observation following learning experiences. Instead, they contend that some very important *processes* occur *during* a learning sequence, and that it is such "learning-to-learn" and other processes which will be most useful after the student completes a course or graduates. For example, they contend that students will be better able to conceptualize problems and solve them in later life if they learn by "discovery" in school, particularly if they learn how to ask questions and to formulate problems on their own with little or no direct guidance by the instructor. Others contend that real learning takes place only when something is personally relevant; thus, they would encourage students to participate actively in selecting educational objectives and in deciding about sequences of courses and independent learning projects. Although such spokesmen would not completely disregard factual learning, skills, and techniques which students can demonstrate following learning experiences, they contend that educational experiences should also be judged in terms of the extent to which students are encouraged to take responsibility in decision making, exploration, and problem solving throughout the learning experiences. Such processes are more complicated and more difficult to measure than are the end results of EO-R but it is possible to have some systematic procedures for determining whether or not students engage in the desired activities. Moreover, though some critics might contest the relationship between such processes and long-term educational objectives (EO-G), similar questions can be raised about EO-R statements. Actually it is incumbent upon educators to show that there are valid relationships between indices of both EO-R and EO-P *and* the long-term EO-G.

The knowledge base (KB-E) would include information collected for step 3 plus those instructional theories and learning theories which particularly emphasize processes which occur during learning. For example, cognitive construct theorists would provide means for describing and measuring discovery learning processes and would provide some research and theory about relationships between discovery processes and long-term educational objectives.

Organizing Educational Objectives for Instruction Components (EO-C) We have already noted that it is generally good design practice to delineate separate components within a course rather than to design one whole unit. The resulting learning "modules" permit greater flexibility in using different theories during the design-development process, and they also are sufficiently independent that they can be assembled in different sequences and combinations by students. During step 6 the designer would take an inventory of the EO-R and EO-P objectives, reevaluate their relationships with each other and with the long-term objectives, decide how the EO-R and/or EO-P objectives can independently or collectively serve in planning modules, and determine how many different modules will be used for that particular course or independent learning sequence.

The knowledge base (KB-F) would include information collected during the previous three steps about the various educational objectives and their relationships with each other. Also useful would be any educational and psychological theories about hierarchical relationships among objectives and about any learning which should be completed as prerequisite to the particular modules.

Delineating Instructional Methods

Once the educational objectives have been formulated as results or processes (EO-R or EO-P) and have been organized for a specific number of learning modules (as EO-Cs), it would be possible to design and develop the educational methods and materials which could enable students to attain the respective objectives. There are several phases in the design and development of instruction. Apparently there are some differences in terminology, but at least three phases can be delineated. At the first phase, initial plans for an instructional module are made, a *prototype* is constructed, and it is tested and revised several times on the basis of use with a few representative students. At the second phase, the module is *field tested* with larger groups of representative students under conditions which are typically controlled by the development personnel. For example, the developers may have an ongoing relationship with a local school whereby students on a volunteer basis would be presented newly developed modules. In some cases related modules would be presented to larger groups of students as part of an appropriate existing course. Thus the field tests could be limited to single modules initially but at some point would include the combination of all modules prepared for a given course or larger educational program. At the third phase, the group of modules would be tested in *operational form*—that is, organized as the total course or program which would later be used by students in regular classrooms. During the operational test phase, the developers would be interested in determining how the instructional methods and materials work in regular classroom usage and in identifying any special problems which might be encountered by students and instructors. The initial operational tests would be conducted with one or a few schools, followed by testing in diverse conditions with a wider range of students.

Several characteristics can be found during these three phases of testing and development. First, the designer typically starts with a particular instructional theory or other theory (educational, psychological, etc.) to guide his initial planning. Second, he typically would feel free to draw from any other sources which might provide supplementary or contradictory implications. Third, it is generally good practice to use available methods and materials which seem appropriate rather than to create *entirely new* approaches; criteria for selection usually are primarily derived from the main instructional theory. Fourth, the designer orients most of his efforts toward the educational objectives which have been delineated for the respective components (the EO-C referred to in the previous section). Fifth, the development process is especially known for a continual test-and-revision cycle which can be found throughout the three phases. We will consider this test-and-revision cycle generally and will comment briefly on features mainly associated with the prototype, field test, and operational test phases.

Planning, Testing, and Revising Instruction   Figure 6-3 outlines illustrative steps involved in the planning, preparation, evaluation, and modification of methods and materials until they demonstrably enable students to attain desired educational objectives. We'll discuss these steps with reference to a single module, although it should be noted that some developers would prefer to work with larger units of instruction.

One would first select an educational objective for a given module (EO-C). On the basis of the EO-C and information about the kinds of students for whom the instruction is to be developed (KB-G) (all part of step 7), the designer would prepare initial plans for the educational methods and materials which, hopefully, will enable such students to attain the objectives. At step 8, the designer would use any research and theory (KB-H) which might indicate the types of specifications which should be prepared for the methods and materials. It would be assumed that more than one approach would satisfactorily fit with the EO-C; the strategy would simply be to design some methods and materials which would enable students to attain the objectives effectively, efficiently, and in a way which would foster their general educational growth.

Typically, the instructional designer would rely primarily on one instructional theory, but he would also note ways in which the theory may be incomplete or deficient with regard to the particular instructional task. Obviously, the more complete and empirically sound the instructional theory is, the easier it will be to outline the specifications. Unfortunately, some developers seem content to work strictly at the educational-methods level without determining how sound the empirical support is, and they simply use intuitive means and "common-sense" bases for filling in any gaps left by the theory. Ideally, the developer should make extensive use of the knowledge base (KB-H) to identify alternative methods and materials and to select those which are likely to be appropriate for the instructional problem at hand.

Let's briefly consider how the psychoeducational designer could derive implications from learning and instructional research and theories. He could identify different instructional approaches, drawn from different

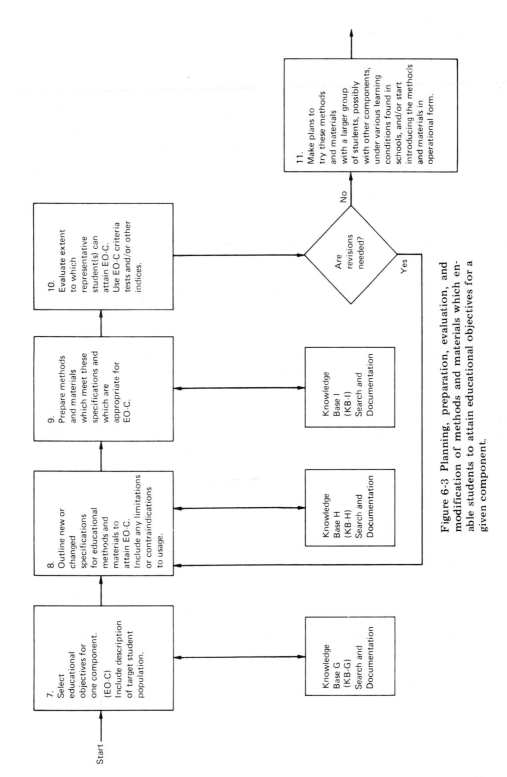

Start →

7. Select educational objectives for one component. (EO-C) Include description of target student population.

8. Outline new or changed specifications for educational methods and materials to attain EO-C. Include any limitations or contraindications to usage.

9. Prepare methods and materials which meet these specifications and which are appropriate for EO-C.

10. Evaluate extent to which representative student(s) can attain EO-C. Use EO-C criteria tests and/or other indices.

Knowledge Base G (KB-G) Search and Documentation

Knowledge Base H (KB-H) Search and Documentation

Knowledge Base I (KB-I) Search and Documentation

Are revisions needed?

Yes

No

11. Make plans to try these methods and materials with a larger group of students, possibly with other components, under various learning conditions found in schools, and/or start introducing the methods and materials in operational form.

Figure 6-3 Planning, preparation, evaluation, and modification of methods and materials which enable students to attain educational objectives for a given component.

181

theories, and he could review the empirical evidence concerning them. Not only would he be interested in knowing their characteristic uses and ways in which supporting empirical evidence had been obtained, he would also be interested in knowing their limitations and any contraindications to their use. Given the present status of instructional theories, it is necessary to rely on underlying psychological research and theory to get ideas and to evaluate tentative specifications. But even in future times when empirically supported instructional theories exist, it probably will be desirable to identify and document research and theory which supports instructional principles. This would parallel current procedures in medical research where manufacturers of new drugs not only are required to provide information about experimental and clinical results with the drugs (main effects and positive or negative side effects), but also are required to describe and document the underlying biochemical processes. Thus, the instructional designer ideally describes the instructional theory rationale on which the specifications are prepared, and also describes and documents the underlying psychological learning principles as supported by human and animal studies.

In step 9 tentative drafts of the methods and materials are prepared in accordance with the specifications from step 8. As with the relationships between the EO-C and the specifications, it is assumed that not only one but several types of instructional procedures could be consistent with the specifications. Again, the strategy is to find some set of methods and materials which will effectively and efficiently foster constructive educational progress. The knowledge base (KB-I) would include pertinent information drawn from the previous knowledge base (KB-H) plus any information about existent methods and materials and tactics for constructing new approaches. It is not appropriate to "reinvent the wheel"—that is, to develop new methods and materials where existent ones could be used or modified. Of course, whether one selects existent items or develops new ones, it is important that they are compatible with the specifications. Again, it is important to search potentially relevant resources and to document bases by which the methods and materials are selected and prepared. Both strengths and weaknesses of the respective items should be noted; it is even helpful to point out limitations or contraindications for use as well as to summarize research supporting the theoretical rationale and previous uses of similar methods and materials. This information will be useful when problems are encountered during tryout periods—some problems are almost always encountered—and can be helpful when planning future instructional methods and materials. Also, such documentation information and empirical results sometimes are used by instructional theorists and learning theorists who view practical applications as tests of their principles and theory.

Step 10 is very important but can be quite complex. It is at this point that the developer tests the methods and materials which are being developed. At the time of this writing, authorities are still debating the merits of different strategies by which one can evaluate instructional methods and materials. Much of the discussion has centered around the problems which occur when one tries to use rigorous research procedures to evaluate methods and materials under the widely ranging and relatively uncontrolled (compared with laboratories) conditions in classrooms. We will briefly note two main issues, one concerning *formative evaluations* and one concerning *criterion-referenced measures*.

It is only since the early 1960s that educators have generally recognized the importance of evaluating educational procedures during the time that they are being developed (called *formative evaluations*) as well as after their final form has been cast (called *summative evaluations*). We have commented about some of these changes in evaluation strategies in the previous chapter. Of particular relevance to step 10 is the concept that one should use empirical evidence to evaluate the quality of the instructional approach being developed and to make decisions about where and in what ways they might be improved. Typically one or more sets of criteria are delineated for each educational objective, and students' progress is evaluated in terms of their performance on different types of tests (for example, essay or multiple-choice written tests, oral examinations, performance on selected tasks, etc.) prepared from these criteria. This brings us to the next issue.

Authorities currently are debating the merits of *criterion-referenced* versus *normative-referenced* measures. Simply stated, in criterion-referenced measures a given student's performance is judged in terms of his accomplishment of specific tasks which presumably sample the population of activities summarized by the particular educational objective. In contrast, in normative-referenced measures, the student's performance is compared with other similar students who take the same test or with normative data concerning how a large number of students performed on that test.

Obviously these two issues will not be resolved in a few paragraphs. But it is important that the reader recognize the importance of evaluating instructional methods and materials during the process of their development, and that the reader is aware of such problems (as noted above) in carrying out this step. It is highly desirable that the developer record the procedures followed in obtaining the evaluation data as well as the results obtained. At some point the developer must make a decision as to whether there are revisions required. If revisions are required, the characteristics and the bases for the specifications are reexamined, and the developer repeats steps 8, 9, and 10.

It is fairly common that one can move to step 11 after having gone through the test-and-revision cycle several times. What happens during step 11 depends primarily on whether one is dealing with prototype materials and methods, field tests, or operational tests. At the end of tests and revisions of prototypes, the developer makes plans for further tests under relatively controlled classroom conditions, frequently called field-test conditions. Although the students are representative of the population for whom the instruction is being developed, the development personnel typically have such an active role that one does not have usual classroom conditions for these tests. The steps outlined in Figure 6-3 are generally followed except that one is now evaluating the specifications and procedures rather than creating them. Once the developer feels satisfied with data obtained under field-test conditions, plans are made for using the methods and materials with students under usual classroom conditions, though on a limited and selective basis. The development personnel are primarily available as resource persons, and the classroom teacher and other educators are mainly in charge of trying the experimental forms of the methods and materials. Again, steps outlined in Figure 6-3 illustrate the questions which are answered from these operational test results. Following sufficient test-and-revision cycles in operational form, the methods and procedures are finally ready for widespread classroom usage.

Disseminating/Adopting Developed Methods and Materials One might (mistakenly) think that methods and materials which have gone through the design and development process would be automatically and quickly adopted. But R&D personnel have found that more work must be completed even after operational testing has been completed. In fact, enough problems have been found during the utilization step that some R&D projects and institutions have focused on delineating strategies and techniques to facilitate appropriate utilization of development-validated educational methods and materials. Figure 6-4 outlines illustrative steps which would be taken by educators—teachers, coordinators, administrators, etc.—who are looking for new educational methods and materials or for ways to improve existent educational practice. Our enumeration of these steps does not continue from Figure 6-3 because we wish to emphasize the fact that the potential users have a different frame of reference from which they view these results of the educational design and development process, as compared with the viewpoint of the R&D personnel.

In step 1 the educators (*potential* users) have some reason for reviewing their current educational practice and come to the conclusion that there are certain aspects which need to be improved or new educational offerings which should be added. The review could have been prompted

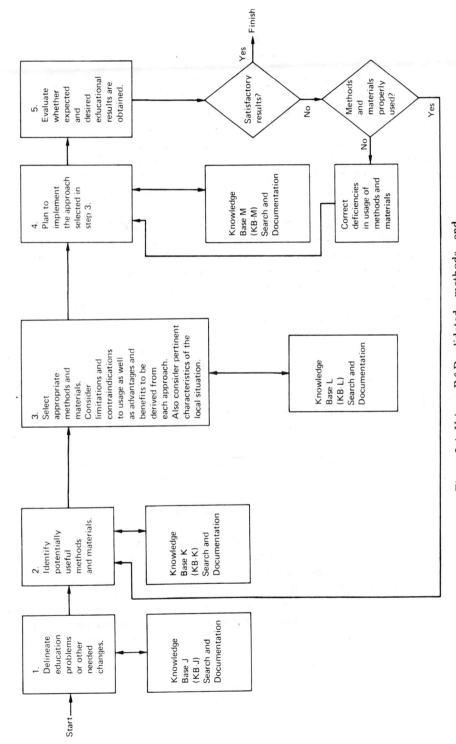

Figure 6-4 Using R&D-validated methods and materials.

185

by a variety of reasons—periodic reappraisal of the school programs, annual consideration of programs being offered or search for methods and materials for particular courses, recognition of the fact that certain new approaches have been developed, being contacted by someone who would like the school to consider particular methods and materials, etc. To some extent, the educators would be involved in the same kinds of processes which we outlined for clarifying educational objectives at the beginning of the design-development process. Thus their first step would involve identifying those problems and needs which most merit review and changing in the context of the school's general function in the community and its major educational objectives.

The knowledge base consulted (KB-J) would vary substantially depending upon the reasons which prompted the consideration of change and depending upon what problems and needs had been identified. In some respects KB-J would resemble resources consulted as part of KB-A, KB-B, KB-C, KB-D, KB-E, and KB-F of Figure 6-2, though the search process would not be as extensive. Some educators would restrict themselves to consulting descriptions of existing school programs and suggestions about possible changes.

In step 2 the educators would identify the various available educational materials and methods, including those which had been validated during a design-development process and those which, more conventionally, have been created without benefit of empirical data about their effectiveness. The knowledge base (KB-K) could thus be restricted to descriptions of the materials and methods, or it could include empirical data concerning previous tests conducted during design-development processes; KB-K could be restricted to details concerning the positive benefits which allegedly will result through using the respective approaches, or it could include statements concerning limitations and contraindications for using the respective methods and materials.

In step 3 the educators would evaluate these methods and materials identified in step 2 and would consider whether they would be appropriate for their particular educational institution. They would also consider ways in which students and/or teachers might object to the proposed methods and materials and would try to identify any special training programs which might be necessary to show teachers and students how to use the new approach to instruction. Thus the knowledge base (KB-L) would include information about methods and materials identified in the previous step plus any "local" information which would indicate the feasibility and desirability of using the respective approaches at that particular school. Information on the theoretical rationale and on empirical tests would be combined with descriptions of the practical situation.

In step 4 the educators would make plans for implementing the methods and materials. It may *seem* a minor point, but it is very important that provision is made for determining that both students and instructors understand how to use the new approaches properly and that they implement the methods and materials in accordance with the ways in which they were designed. In no way does this imply that one *must rigidly* follow directions for usage; in some cases, there will be highly structured procedures for usage, while in others considerable latitude will be given to instructors and students. Another point is that it is generally desirable to implement new methods and materials on a comparatively small scale until one can determine whether expected educational results are being obtained. If successful, then a larger number of students and a wider range of courses might be involved in the new approach. The knowledge base (KB-M) would primarily be drawn from the descriptions of the educational methods and materials, their instructional and learning theory support, and any relevant empirical evidence.

In step 5 the new approach would be implemented and evaluated. If successful results are obtained, one could either consider expanding the usage of that approach—if such is appropriate—or one could move to the next educational problem or need which merits attention. But if expected and desirable results are not being attained, one has several steps which can be taken to clarify the problem and to decide how to handle it. First, it is commonly found that many problems simply stem from the fact that students or teachers have not used the new methods and materials properly. If such a problem is found in a given situation, one should make plans for helping instructors and students to use the methods and materials properly. Then steps 4 and 5 would be repeated and further evaluations would be conducted. However, if the methods and materials are being used properly, then one should repeat steps 2, 3, 4, and 5 with modifications in the approach or with new materials and methods until expected and desirable educational results are obtained.

Troubleshooting

We have labeled the third way in which psychological research and theories can influence educational practice as *troubleshooting*. By this term we propose that instructional theories and learning theories can be useful in diagnosing the nature of problems when existent instructional procedures do not satisfactorily help students to reach educational objectives, and that these theories can help in identifying possible ways by which educational practice can be improved. Figure 6-5 outlines steps which might be followed as one systematically tries to determine where corrective action or changes in objectives is indicated. Several assumptions about relationships between educational objectives and instructional methods were indicated earlier but should be restated here. It is held that one should articulate the comprehensive general educational objectives which one has for a particular program or course, and that more specific results (EO-R) and process objectives (EO-P) should be derived from them. One should then derive specifications for instructional methods and materials from meaningful organizations of these specific objectives so as to plan and develop modules or components of the larger educational program. It is assumed that these strategies and techniques will lead to the development of instructional procedures which demonstrably enable students to attain the kinds of educational growth which they and society set for their particular learning situation.

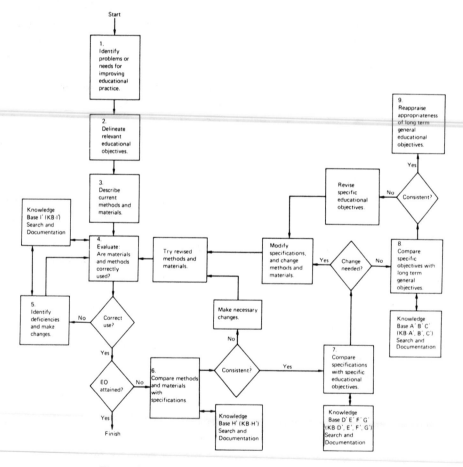

Figure 6-5 Troubleshooting procedures when existing methods and materials do not produce desired and expected results.

A few more assumptions are relevant to the troubleshooting process. First, it is assumed that one should find the most effective trouble-shooting procedures while keeping effort expended at a minimum. Second, it is assumed that one should first examine the manner in which instruction is being conducted and that one should critique such educational practice in light of extant theory and research on instruction and learning. As a result, the procedures followed in troubleshooting are similar to the strategies and techniques involved in developing the new educational methods and materials, but some of the sequences are reversed.

The troubleshooter in our example will be designated as an educator, but it is quite conceivable that a number of persons could have such a role, including psychologists and other interested persons. The educator would start by identifying the particular problems or other indications that educational practice should be improved. Once having located the trouble, he would then delineate the relevant educational objectives (step 2) and would describe the methods and materials currently being used to attain these educational objectives (step 3).

At this point the educator would make the first attempt to determine why the educational objectives are not being attained (step 4). The knowledge base (KB-I') would consist of information describing how the methods and materials are to be used, particularly based on the information used to develop them (KB-I in Figure 6-3), and any details which indicate how students and instructors currently use them. Of course the amount and validity of such information would vary substantially, depending upon the particular methods and materials and the means by which they were produced. A rather common problem is that students and/or instructors have misunderstood some of the procedures or that they have simply ignored some directions because they considered the directions to be unimportant. If this has caused the trouble, the educator would take steps to help correct the misunderstanding about the directions or procedures and, having corrected these deficiencies, would again check whether satisfactory results are being obtained. If so, the trouble would be resolved. If not, the next troubleshooting step would be followed.

Another common problem (step 6) is that the particular methods and procedures do not fit with the specifications outlined; this may occur and not be noticed even after the methods and materials have been in use and producing marginal results for some time. One would typically consult a knowledge base (KB-H') quite similar to the information which was used during the design-development process by which the methods and materials were produced (KB-H in Figure 6-3). If inconsistencies are detected, they would be corrected by selecting or developing methods and materials which fit the specifications, following which they would be tried out with students. If there are no inconsistencies between the specifications and the methods or materials, the next step (step 7) would be followed.

But before describing step 7, we should consider how one handles situations when insufficient information is available for step 6. This would most frequently occur with methods or materials which had been produced with little or no empirical validation, and would be found with most educational procedures in use today. Given such circumstances, one probably would not have information about the underlying theoretical rationale on which they were based. Under these circumstances we would recommend that the educator try to find an instructional theory, learning theory, educational philosophy, or other systematically organized body of information with which the methods and materials are most nearly compatible. Then, one would use this adapted theoretical rationale as a frame of reference against which one might find deficiencies which could be corrected. The more complete the particular theory is, the easier it would be to see how various kinds of methods and materials are or are not compatible with the prescriptions derived from that theory. The more systematically organized empirical evidence which is available, the more readily one could determine whether the problems being encountered are usual or unusual for the particular methods and materials. Thus these more informal troubleshooting steps would mainly consist of systematic checks to determine whether the particular methods and materials conflict with extant theory and research on learning and instruction.

In step 7 the educator would compare the specifications for the methods and materials with the results and process objectives (EO-R and EO-P) delineated for that learning experience. This would require consulting (KB-D',E',F',G') sources which describe the formulation of educational objectives for the respective modules and for the overall learning experience (similar to KB-D,E,F,G in Figures 6-3 and 6-4). Again instructional and learning theories could be useful, especially if they indicate relationships between particular kinds of objectives and instructional methods or materials. If inconsistencies are detected, more appropriate instructional methods would be selected or devised and would be evaluated. If no inconsistencies are detected between the objectives and the specifications for methods and materials, the next step would be followed.

The final step would require reappraisal of the long-term educational objectives and would raise questions as to whether there is a reasonable basis for expecting that the delineated educational objectives can be attained *within the constraints set* for these particular learning experiences.

We have already noted above that educators and society more generally sometimes set goals for schools which cannot realistically be attained. As this book is being written, there are various issues being debated which concern the concepts of "accountability" and of "relevance." Although it would be highly desirable for educational institutions to help students become happy, productive, and self-actualizing individuals, there are limits on what can be accomplished by our educational system as it is currently conceived. Moreover, there will always be limits no matter how much we change our approaches to instruction and our views of model schools. These facts become more forcefully obvious as we apply the concept of accountability and try to determine how much educational practice facilitates the educational growth of the individual. Perhaps, if we reach this point in our troubleshooting process, we may find ourselves reappraising our views of educational institutions and the kinds of educational experiences we should create there (cf. Shane, 1973).

EMERGENCE OF FORMALIZED
EDUCATIONAL R&D ACTIVITIES

The quotations at the beginning of this chapter included a rather remarkable observation by Bruner: "It is something that we are only now beginning to understand. Innovation, by whatever theoretical derivation, involves vast development and engineering" (1971, p. 101). The observation is "remarkable" in that it can accurately be made after huge amounts of time, money, and energy had been devoted to use of the scientific method to improve educational practice. It is remarkable not because an inordinate amount of resources had been wasted; any numerical comparisons would quickly show that our investment in educational research and development has been very modest at best. Rather, it is remarkable because since the beginning of this century we seem to have been trying to use scientific findings in a way that never really could be expected to work from the start, and it has taken us so many decades to recognize the problem.

But before the reader concludes that we are being excessively critical of previous efforts in educational research and development, we would like to add that we recognize that the task we set for ourselves—namely, improving educational practice—is enormously complex with few sound precedents from which we might draw guidelines. Simon and Newell (1971) depicted psychology's contributions to education as "meager," but acknowledged that difficulties generally exist in establishing sound relationships between professions and basic sciences which might nourish them. They note that only in the twentieth century could medicine "be said to rest solidly on the foundation of deep knowledge in the biological sciences, or the practice of engineering on modern physics and chemistry" (p. 158).

Perhaps the reader can better understand the magnitude of the problems and the massive size of efforts required to cope with them if we describe some of the formalized educational R&D activities which were initiated in the mid-1960s. Since these activities were mainly supported by federal government funds, we'll consider the educational R&D centers and regional educational laboratories which were created by the U.S. Office of Education and which are now partly continued by the National Institute of Education.

It is widely acknowledged that the first concerted systematic attempt to employ research and development strategies in education started in 1964 when USOE established four R&D *centers* as a result of amendments to existing educational legislation. The intent was to identify high-priority educational problems which could benefit either from newly initiated research or from systematic accumulation and synthesis of information available from already completed studies. The R&D centers were to review relevant research literature and to plan and conduct basic research on remaining pertinent unanswered questions. Within a few years, companion regional educational *laboratories* were planned and established whose function was to field test and to modify further educational procedures and materials which had been started by the R&D centers or by other emergent R&D efforts. The laboratories were also charged with providing for dissemination and diffusion of those resulting innovations, initially through a network of selected experimental schools and later to all interested schools.

Many of the programs were initiated and supervised through the National Center for Educational Research and Development (NCERD) in USOE. NCERD was created to identify crucial problems in education and to support research and development activities which would have good prospects for resolving the problems. A policy was established for focusing on a few critical areas and for mounting quite sizable R&D efforts to maximize the likelihood of achieving major breakthroughs. Although some activities were carried on directly by NCERD personnel, most of the efforts were to be conducted through grants or awards to the centers, laboratories, universities, and other agencies. In 1972 NCERD was largely absorbed by the newly established National Institute of Education, which carried on some of these R&D activities. Although additional changes have been and will be made in the amounts and methods of federal funding, it will be helpful to consider some of the characteristics of the centers and laboratories and the R&D activities in which they have been engaged.

Characteristics of R&D Centers

The educational R&D centers were established after an educational problem area had been identified and arrangements had been made with a university which had the necessary professional persons available who were capable of working on that particular problem area. In some cases the federal funds were supplemented by private foundations or by other governmental agencies, but the main support was the federal source. Although there was some variation in administrative arrangements for the centers, there was a conscious attempt to relate the center R&D activities to other ongoing research at the university involved with that center.

The number of centers has varied over the years, mainly because of increases and decreases in federal funds. There were about ten main centers in the middle 1960s, whereas six years later there were eight general centers, two vocational R&D centers, two policy research centers, and a group of institutions collectively known as the National Program on Early Childhood Education.

A few examples will illustrate that a rather wide range of areas were covered although each center focused on some particular area of education or kind of problem. The University of Wisconsin center chose to focus on cognitive learning processes and related educational efforts which would foster that type of learning in schools. One specialization of the Learning Research and Development Center (LRDC) at the University of Pittsburgh was the study of techniques used to design, develop, and test educational innovations. Two centers focused on effectiveness of selected teaching procedures. One, at the University of Texas, specialized on teacher education; the Stanford University center chose classroom learning interactions for special study. A center for the study of evaluation was established at the University of California at Los Angeles, with the objective of developing evaluation systems which could be used to evaluate educational practice at various levels. Other centers focused on administrative decision-making processes, social psychological processes and school organization, career education, etc. As noted above, an attempt was made to cover the major issues in educational practice but to have individual centers focus on selected aspects, on the assumption that the focused ventures would more rapidly produce changes in educational practice.

Characteristics of (Regional) Educational Laboratories

A network of Regional Educational Laboratories (REL) was established as a result of 1965 amendments to the previously passed Cooperative Research Act. Initially, in 1966, the country was divided into twenty regions and a laboratory was established in each region. Subsequently the regional division was de-emphasized, the number of laboratories was reduced by one-half, and greater emphasis was placed on development efforts centered around a particular educational problem or issue. As with the centers, the laboratories have been greatly dependent on federal support, so that their number and extent of activities have varied with the size of federal appropriations.

The original idea for the REL was to relate to schools and other educational agencies within respective regions and to the research organizations so as to help bridge the gap between research and educational practice. It was recognized that extensive testing and modification would be required for innovations produced by the laboratories, and that schools would need assistance once the innovations were ready for adoption. Thus the laboratories not only would be concerned with needed modifications in the educational innovations, but also would have to identify problems and solutions which might be encountered when a school tried to implement a given innovation.

Some examples of the laboratory missions will illustrate the breadth and scope of these developmental efforts. One laboratory (Appalachia Educational Laboratory) focused on problems especially important in rural and isolated schools, while another laboratory (Center for Urban Education) developed programs to improve the quality and relevance of urban education. Particular grade levels were selected by some laboratories (for example, Southwest Educational Laboratory, preschool and primary levels), while certain academic subject areas were chosen by others (for example, Central Midwestern Regional Educational Laboratory, mathematics and aesthetic education). Of course, there would be changes made in the laboratories and the specializations they chose, but these illustrate the kinds of problems and issues covered.

Although most laboratory efforts tend to be rather eclectic, some projects do reflect preferences for certain theories in designing instruction. For example, the Individually Prescribed Instruction project, which was initiated by the Pittsburgh Learning Research and Development Center and was further developed by Philadelphia's Research for Better Schools, was greatly influenced by Gagne's task hierarchies and by programmed instruction principles. However, it should be noted that both the laboratories and centers deviate substantially from any initial theoretical position when it is evident that this is necessary to attain the educational objectives which have been selected for the particular project.

Some Characteristics of
Center and Laboratory Activities

As we have noted above, the laboratories and centers are still in the process of finding desirable ways for improving educational practice even at the time of this writing. Perhaps this should not be too surprising since most of the centers and laboratories have been in existence for no more than a decade and there were no institutions previously in existence which had as their primary concern the creation and refinement of educational materials and procedures based on research and validated in practice (Schmidtlein, 1970). But despite this somewhat transitional process, certain observations can be made about these centers and laboratories, and about their modes of operation.

First, there has always been some controversy as to the kinds of problems which should be chosen. While it is practically universally acknowledged that some delimitation is necessary, many have been concerned that the educational problems selected might be so narrowly conceived that they might be meaningless when the innovation would subsequently be introduced in the classroom. Concern on this matter has diminished over the years as more and more projects have been tried out in growing networks of cooperating schools. Experience has supported an early observation by Dr. Francis Chase, the first chairman of the National Advisory Committee on Educational Laboratories and an authority on the laboratories and centers. He predicted that successful laboratories would be those which focused on some identifiable and testable research product or a well-formulated hypothesis about education (Schmidtlein, 1970).

Second, questions were raised as to what theories and research findings should guide developmental efforts, and the extent to which one should ignore such "theoretical underpinnings" in favor of the more pragmatic "try-anything-which-might-work" philosophy expressed by many educators. Here there have been great differences across the laboratories and centers and even within any given institution, but two features do stand out. It is a routine principle that all pertinent research literature should be considered at least during the early formulations of projects and even during at least the first modifications. An attempt is made to take into account quite pragmatic considerations, including such mundane matters as established traditions in the ways educators currently cope with the particular educational problem. Moreover, there typically is a concerted effort to receive inputs from all professional persons and disciplines which might be pertinent to the task at hand. But there is also widespread acceptance, among educational R&D personnel, of the principle that the real test of any idea is the demonstration that it actually facilitates students' learning. It is accepted that there should be continuous tryout and revisions of the particular educational procedures or materials until there is sufficient evidence that they actually work in practice.

Third, especially early in their existence there was some question as to how closely and in what ways the laboratories and centers should establish relationships with schools, universities, governmental agencies, and other institutions. Both the laboratories and the centers have maintained some autonomy and independence, although the latter typically were established with at least some connection with a university. Not too surprisingly, the centers developed closer affiliations with universities and other research agencies, whereas the laboratories have tended to develop stronger ties with schools and those agencies which are more directly concerned with using the innovations. However, it should be noted that the nature of such relationships varies from one institution to another and that both the laboratories and the centers typically have some contacts with "consumer-type" agencies, such as schools, as well as with those agencies which are more explicitly involved with research activities. The nature of these contacts depends more on the kinds of ongoing projects than on the fact that the institution was established as a laboratory or a center.

Fourth, some comments should be made about the relationships between the centers and the laboratories. Initially it was assumed that the typical R&D center would identify a particular educational problem area and either review relevant research findings or conduct necessary research. Then preliminary plans for the educational materials or procedures would be developed, and they would be modified by the center on the basis of tryouts with a few carefully selected schools. It was expected that some regional educational laboratory would become involved around the time that the innovation was ready for field testing, and that the laboratory would essentially be responsible for the subsequent modifications, dissemination, and diffusion. In practice this division of labor and responsibilities has been maintained generally but there are many exceptions to strict adherence to these respective roles. For example, there are instances in which centers become greatly involved in field testing and dissemination, while laboratories sometimes have carried either a major role or entire responsibility from inception to diffusion of an innovation.

Fifth, it is hoped that the reader has recognized that the R&D movement has overcome the barriers referred to earlier in this chapter. With federal funds supporting establishment of the centers and the laboratories, there became available institutional and financial support for design-development activities, resources for translating theoretical information so that it can be made applicable to educational practice, and models for systematically relating psychological information to educational practice. The importance of such federal support was dramatically demonstrated in the 1970s when the federal government, through the National Institute of Education, changed funding primarily to projects evaluated annually rather than providing funds on a continuing basis to the institutions.

Finally, one clear pattern which has emerged in the various R&D ventures in applied psychology is a shift from comparing some newly proposed innovation, for example, "Method A," against either "traditional methods," or "Method B"; that is, some other approach to the problem. Implied in this earlier orientation is the notion that the best method of evaluating some innovation is by comparing it with some other approaches to the problem. What emerged in the context of the R&D movement was an assessment of a proposed innovation in terms of the extent to which it facilitates attainment of delineated educational objectives. Thus, instead of merely determining how well the newly proposed method compares with alternative approaches, the focus is shifted to the extent to which any given method is effective and efficient in attaining delineated objectives.

The implications of this pattern in the educational R&D activities are illustrated by parallel developments in clinical psychology. A panel discussion held during the 1972 meeting of the Society for Psychotherapy Research was entitled "All Have Won, So All Shall Have Prizes: Comparative Results of Psychotherapies." The essence of this discussion was that instead of determining whether one method is "somewhat" better than another method, the real focus should be on the extent to which *each* of the methods satisfactorily leads to delineated objectives. Instead of having *one* right approach, it is acknowledged that there may be several approaches. In that kind of context, one is able to start identifying favorable characteristics of each method and to determine whether each method may be better with certain individuals than with others.

It would seem that similar comments can be made about competing instructional methods. If we can use demonstrable educational progress as our main basis for evaluating instructional methods, it is conceivable that more than one method will be found effective. As a result, educators may be able to choose among alternative methods for the one or more methods most appropriate for a given student, teacher, practical situation, etc.

Perhaps it would help the reader to understand the design-development process if we consider one educational project—Individually Prescribed Instruction (IPI)—as it was initiated by an R&D center— Pittsburgh's Learning Research & Development Center (LRDC)—and was field tested and improved by a regional educational laboratory— Philadelphia's Research for Better Schools (RBS)—which had accepted development and diffusion responsibility for IPI. This particular project was chosen as an illustration here because it is representative of good collaboration between centers and laboratories, because it was one of the first projects in the educational R&D movement, and because it has been tried out by an increasingly expanding network of field-test schools.

It is not our purpose here to comment on IPI as an educational program or to evaluate its qualities as a *finished* educational development project. Readers who are particularly interested in using IPI are advised to go to the many other sources now available which critically examine the educational quality of IPI and other ventures to individualize instruction. Additional relevant information should also be available from LRDC and RBS concerning evaluations data which were obtained during development and modifications of IPI. The main purpose in choosing IPI here is that it illustrates steps taken by centers and laboratories collaborating in the educational R&D process.

IPI constitutes one of several modern-day attempts to adapt instructional procedures to the needs of individual students. Any reliable history of American education will reveal that various predecessors have expressed concern and sometimes launched projects to provide such individualization since at least the first few decades of this century. However, the post-World War II developments in computer technology, programmed instruction, and curriculum theory stimulated renewed efforts to provide some degree of individualization of instruction with results which have surpassed the earlier efforts.

Three major aspects can be delineated, each of which sets some pertinent variables for consideration—educational goals, individual capabilities, and means of instruction. Several features of IPI should be called to your attention with regard to each major aspect. Educational goals are defined in some measurable form with regard to both the long-range objectives and the various subgoals throughout the IPI program which lead up to the final goal. Individual students are routinely evaluated and their progress is monitored, mainly in terms of their attainment of the delineated educational goals. The instructional means are varied primarily in that students are advanced or are referred to remedial work depending upon their progress. There is also some attempt to individualize instructional means in terms of what is taught and how it is taught. Though the developers of IPI aspired to provide alternative forms of instruction, comparatively few options currently exist to accommodate to learners' cognitive style and their "preferred" mode of learning. IPI can be implemented in a nonautomated fashion, with computer monitoring and management for selection of instructional sequences, or with actual computer-assisted instruction.

Before describing the nature of the collaboration between LRDC and RBS on IPI, let us first briefly consider the range of activity conducted at these representatives of educational R&D centers and regional educational laboratories.

An Example of an
Educational R&D Center

LRDC was established in 1964 as one of the first educational research and development centers. From its inception it has had a major commitment to both research and development activities. It has been characterized as having a key role in enhancing development of instructional theories and technology as well as in conducting basic learning research and promoting the relevance of learning theory for educational practice. It is, perhaps, in the concerted combination of research and development activities within the same institution that LRDC's greatest strength may lie. As readers will recall from earlier chapters, many visualized learning applications only as going from theory into practice. In the course of development activities at LRDC many different relationships prevail. There are numerous occasions on which development issues either raise problems for learning research or cast doubt and show need for revision of principles based on previous laboratory research. Any one of the LRDC projects will have both the task-oriented objectives associated with a delineated educational problem and the discipline-oriented objectives typically found in conjunction with basic research and theory. Of course, such research and development activities may not be occurring concurrently. But over the course of time, a given project will have involved both research activities and developmental activities.

Although the actual research activities vary from one year to the next, it would be useful to consider examples of research conducted by LRDC. The intent is to have staff members who are expert in particular fields of learning research so that they can keep LRDC personnel aware of current developments. As a result, there is some attempt to have a rather wide range of contemporary learning research areas represented in the LRDC staff and program activities. One series of verbal learning studies was planned in accordance with contemporary verbal learning theories but also provided practical information for the planning of computer-based instruction by showing predictable relationships between the amount of time it takes a student to respond to a question and the amount of practice required to provide the student with optimal retention of the material. Another series of studies attempted to identify some of the basic mechanisms of attention and the findings were related to contemporary theoretical models of attention. Other basic research focused on hierarchical relationships among different types of learning, and on the different types of styles of learning displayed by students. LRDC staff members routinely draw from the work of such widely ranging theorists as Piaget, Skinner, mathematical learning theorists, Gagne, etc. In addition to these and other areas of research conducted at LRDC, project personnel routinely review the literature of psychological learning research and educational research to determine what other investigators may have found which might be pertinent to the educational design of the particular project.

LRDC has been engaged in development activities since its establishment in 1964. Most of their development activities have been centered around two main center projects—the Individually Prescribed Instruction (IPI) project and the Primary Education Project (PEP). LRDC has also been engaged in projects which are more specifically related to particular subject areas, such as mathematics, science, and reading. LRDC has been interested not only in completing their particular development projects, but also in developing models for the design and evaluation of instructional systems, and in the training of personnel who could work in educational research and development activities. In the realm of instructional theory, they have expressed a major commitment to exploring ways in which expository teaching techniques and exploratory or discovery learning procedures each may have a role in contemporary educational practice.

An Example of a
Regional Educational Laboratory

Research for Better Schools (RBS) was chartered and funded in 1966 as the regional learning laboratory for eastern Pennsylvania, New Jersey, and Delaware, with the main mission to individualize and to humanize education. In its first year of existence it became involved with LRDC's IPI program. LRDC had conducted relevant research and had completed the beginning developmental stages of IPI to the point that IPI was being tested on a limited basis in a suburban Pittsburgh school. Later we'll discuss the collaboration of RBS and LRDC on the development of IPI. For now, it should be pointed out that IPI was one of the major programs developed and disseminated by RBS. IPI is part of a larger program at RBS which is concerned with individualizing learning. The Individualizing Learning Program (ILP) formulates, tests, and disseminates educational programs which individualize instruction based on applications of learning theories and technology. ILP includes three major components—IPI, Automated Learning Management Systems (ALMS), which is a type of computer managed instruction, and Computer Assisted Instruction (CAI). The Humanizing Learning Program (HLP), a second major area of concern, primarily focuses on those skills required for social, emotional, as well as intellectual growth. HLP is based on the premise that educational programs should include considerable emphasis on human values and personal-social-emotional growth. In terms of Bloom's Taxonomy of Educational Objectives (1956), HLP primarily emphasizes the affective domain. The third and smallest RBS development program is the Administering for Change Program (ACP). ACP is concerned with the study of change in educational programs and the processes by which innovations can be introduced into existing schools. ACP is concerned with how to encourage, nurture, effect, measure, and maintain such innovation processes.

It is noteworthy that almost thirty educational programs were considered before these particular three were chosen for emphasis by RBS. The choices were made on the basis that the innovation would be likely to produce significant improvement in educational thought and practice, that the innovation was validated as being potentially effective and feasible, and that it had reached a stage in its development where some additional modifications would be possible but that it had already undergone some initial field testing.

Collaboration on Educational Development—IPI

IPI constitutes a good example of center and laboratory collaboration. IPI was started almost simultaneously with the establishment of LRDC in 1964. LRDC personnel reviewed literature and assessed practical needs before initial plans for IPI were drawn up. Once a commitment had been made to *individualization of instruction*, LRDC staff identified specific curricular needs and decided to emphasize mathematics and reading in the initial programs.

Drawing on both educational and psychological research literature, and deriving many of its ideas from programmed instruction, particular educational objectives were identified and tentative instructional sequences and units were prepared. The initial instructional materials were tried out with representative students and were modified wherever students were experiencing difficulties in reaching the educational objectives. By the fall of 1964, preliminary versions were tried out in a suburban Pittsburgh school. In subsequent years, IPI was expanded to such curricular areas as science and spelling. Evaluation plays a major role in development activities. Thus, the initial results of this tryout with students were carefully evaluated by LRDC personnel and modifications were introduced into the IPI materials and procedures. Then a new version of IPI was tried out, evaluated, and modified. This process went on until 1966, at which time RBS expressed interest in collaborating with LRDC in the further development and eventual wide-scale diffusion of IPI.

It is noteworthy that despite the numerous changes which had been incorporated by LRDC during initial evaluations and modifications of the design, changes were introduced almost annually for the first five years after RBS became involved with IPI. In subsequent years, further expansion occurred in several ways. First, the number of curricular areas was increased. Second, the tryout areas increased from the initial one suburban school to a national network of over 375 schools in more than forty states involving over 130,000 students and over 5,300 teachers. Moreover, the ensuing publicity about IPI stimulated other groups to launch their own versions of individualized instruction.

It is important for the reader to recognize that throughout the development process, IPI materials and procedures were evaluated in terms of the extent to which they were enabling students to attain delineated educational objectives. Space here will not permit us to describe the various educational and psychological theories and research on which IPI was based. However, it is important to recognize that many diverse ideas were considered and incorporated in plans for IPI. Moreover, the standard by which these ideas were judged was the extent to which they enabled students to attain educational objectives. The revisions to the IPI materials and procedures were not based on the simple dictates of a particular theory but were introduced and continued because empirical evidence indicated the merits of the ideas during the various tryout periods.

SUGGESTIONS FOR USING A
PSYCHOEDUCATIONAL DESIGN APPROACH

Most of the comments in the present chapter have been concerned with ways in which teams of persons drawn from different disciplines may collaborate in the design and development of improvements for educational practice. A considerably large number of man hours is required for each of the steps involved in the design-development process. For example, several persons working full time typically are required to review the literature on research and theories which might be relevant to a particular development project. It is quite likely that readers of this text may be wondering whether an individual educator, educational psychologist, or other person can benefit from understanding the psychoeducational design approach. Two affirmative answers seem in order. First, it is expected that readers of this book may be better informed "consumers" or users of the educational processes and products which are being developed by the centers, laboratories, and various educational R&D groups. Second, psychoeducational design strategies and techniques may also prove useful in deriving practical implications from the various learning theories and instructional theories which we examine in this book. This second matter requires more elaboration.

This book has attempted to present the positive and negative aspects of the respective learning and instructional theories. The position is taken that the practitioner can ill afford to ignore any theories which might provide useful implications, and that one should not rely unduly on any given theory until its actual merits have been established with regard to *practical* situations. This poses no small number of problems, especially with regard to psychological learning theories, because traditionally there has been considerable pressure toward accepting *one* theory and *rejecting* its competitors. This occurs, in part, because the information is typically organized along psychology's disciplinary lines and the particular sub-aspects of interest to the respective theorists. By contrast, the educator is interested in any theories and research which bear on the *educational problems*. Various authors have commented on the desirability of drawing from different theories, but they do not generally provide guidelines as to how one can organize information drawn from diverse sources. For example, Drucker contends that the schools of the future will be neither "behavioristic" nor "cognitive" nor "child-centered" nor "discipline-centered," but that they will be all these and more.

"These old controversies have been phonies all along. We need the behaviorist's triad of practice/reinforcement/feed-back to enlarge learning and memory. We need purpose, decision, values, understanding—the cognitive categories—lest learning be mere behavior activities rather than action." (Drucker, 1972, p. 86)

He goes on to describe the need for schools of the future to draw from *any* theories which might provide implications for improving educational practice. Moreover, the present author agrees with his further contention that most educational applications which *allegedly* have been drawn from *one* psychological theory *actually* have involved components of *many* theories instead.

We will conclude this chapter by making a few brief suggestions as to how an individual educator or psychologist can use other information in this book, drawn from diverse sources, to improve educational practice. We will suggest that the instructional theories and learning theories reviewed here can serve as an initial or abbreviated knowledge base for making decisions about clarifying educational objectives, delineating instructional methods, and troubleshooting. We recommend that the reader use one instructional theory or learning theory as the main means for organizing information and that additional theories and research be utilized to supplement or to correct the main theory used. To facilitate such use, we provide illustrative R&D implications at the end of chapters on learning theories in Part Two, and we point out strengths and weaknesses of instructional theories discussed in Part Three chapters. Earlier chapters in Part One have enumerated additional theories and research on learning and instruction, some of which you may wish to explore in greater detail. We recommend that you use Figures 6-2, 6-3, 6-4, and 6-5 and the associated commentary at least as tentative ways for organizing your efforts.

Because the psychoeducational design strategies and techniques place such great emphasis on outcomes (either as results or processes, EO-R or EO-P), one of the most important steps to take for any practical problem is to find some means for organizing and clarifying educational objectives. They should be stated in forms which permit use as judgment standards, so that one can determine whether methods and materials are enabling students to reach desired objectives; but they should not be so narrowly conceived that important but difficult to measure goals are overlooked. In most cases the goals will be primarily based on educational theories and philosophies along with practices and traditions established in the respective communities. But instructional theories and learning theories can be of use in organizing the educational objectives.

Ideally, one should organize educational objectives so that different categories are indicated and their interrelationships described. One widely recognized system, developed by Bloom and colleagues (see description in Bloom, Hastings, & Madaus, 1971), classifies educational objectives in terms of three domains—cognitive, affective, and psychomotor. Some of the learning theories and instructional theories which we discuss also provide guidance in classifying types of learning processes. For example, one might wish to consider Gagne's task analyses (Chapter 16) or Razran's more recent hierarchical arrangement of learning types within the general Pavlovian tradition (Chapter 8). The humanistic psychology group (Chapter 17) recommends that students participate in delineation of educational objectives, and that personal-social-emotional needs should be considered extensively. The behavior modifiers (Chapter 13) and most learning theorists stress the importance of formulating objectives in some measurable form.

As with the educational *objectives*, the main characteristics of the instructional *methods* would most likely be based on contemporary educational theory and practice. However, the instructional theories and learning theories could be quite helpful in analyzing the bases for specific methods and materials and in assessing ways in which they can be improved. As noted above, we would recommend that you choose some instructional theory as a main means for organizing information and that you supplement those designs by drawing from other instructional theories and learning theories. We would strongly recommend that you separate larger educational programs into components so that the most appropriate methods and materials can be planned for specific objectives or problems.

A few comments about relative emphases will illustrate ways in which different learning theories and instructional theories can actually be complementary rather than competitive, once one has analyzed components of the objectives rather than trying to use one theory for the entire educational program. Both the humanists and the cognitive construct groups would place great emphasis on relatively unstructured learning experiences in which the student can "discover" problems and problem solutions in such a way that the knowledge and skills gained can be readily conceptualized. Guidelines derived from behavior modification and from the various learning theorists would enable you to predict how students will react to different kinds of stimulus and reinforcement/feedback arrangements. The fact that the behavior modifiers and many learning theorists would stress *explicit* descriptions of instructional objectives and methods can actually facilitate rather than hinder the creation of learning experiences which foster discovery learning.

You probably will have greatest likelihood of success in using research and theory on learning and instruction if you understand the intentions of the respective theorists and researchers. Though we only provide a survey-type introduction, one major objective of our comments is to help you to understand *why* these various persons approached their tasks the way they did as well as *what* principles seem to be emerging from their efforts. Thus we essentially view instructional psychologists as focusing on principles for prescribing educational practice and learning psychologists as being more concerned with the underpinnings of such principles. Viewed in this way, the accumulating body of information about learning and instruction should help us to discover why instructional methods and materials will or will not be appropriate with different students under various conditions and for various kinds of educational objectives.

Perhaps it will be in troubleshooting that the real value of research and theory will be most evident. In a sense, when one is confronted with a problem one needs help most in clarifying the nature of the problem and in identifying various possible explanations. Viewed in this way, when we try to cope with problems of instruction we would look to the existent theories and bodies of research results to get cues as to why expected and desired results are not being obtained.

This book is organized so that some guidance about available theories and research is provided through the general overview chapters in Part One. Additional information about selected learning theories is provided in Part Two, along with suggested readings where interested students can obtain additional information. Similarly, chapters in Part Three provide illustrations of ways in which learning theories and research can be used to formulate instructional theories; suggested readings indicate where more information is available.

Part

II

Focus

Part Two contains six chapters describing illustrative approaches to the construction of learning theories. The Thorndike, Pavlov, and Hull chapters (Chapters 7, 8, and 9) are primarily included because of their historical importance; however, it will be shown that they continue to have considerable influence on learning research today. The Skinner chapter (Chapter 10) describes an approach of historical importance (especially during the era of comprehensive learning theories) which has gained even more support from basic researchers during the past two decades and even greater visibility as a result of its involvement with practical educational matters through behavior modification activities. Both the chapter on information-processing theories and that on mathematical learning theories (Chapters 11 and 12) constitute ventures which have emerged since mid-century. Both approaches involve collections of researchers who share common interests but who also have differing views as to optimal ways for evolving sound learning principles and theory.

There are some general topics around which these chapters are organized, although the specific outlines of the chapters reflect a number of differences relevant to each approach. Each chapter includes but is not limited to these topics—introductory description; background; the main concepts, principles and focus of the theory; extent and nature of practical applications; and educational R&D implications.

The major purpose of the R&D implications section is to provide a few illustrative suggestions as to ways in which one may find these theories and the related research findings useful in improving educational practice. To some extent these comments summarize points which were made about the respective theories in the chapter. But they also lead to questions which the reader may wish to pursue either through relevant chapters in Part Three or through suggested readings listed at the end of each chapter.

The main intent in this part is to provide the reader with information about these six approaches to learning theory, including the main concepts, principles, and the general focus of the theory. On the basis of this information readers should be able to decide whether they want to learn more about a particular theory's basic research activities and/or its potential usefulness in improving educational practice.

7
Edward L. Thorndike and Connectionism

The experimental analysis of learning did not begin with Thorndike, but it can be said without too much controversy that his theory of learning represents one of the first recognizable and influential systems that dealt with this topic. "Influential" is hardly adequate in describing Thorndike's effect on psychology and on education. His works represent dominant positions in both disciplines for the first several decades of this century. His influence in the psychological studies of learning was so great that for half a century it was almost mandatory for other theorists to indicate ways in which they agreed and disagreed with his position. As we have already noted, of the theories that historically followed Thorndike's, all (with the exception of Pavlov's) somehow took cognizance of his theory, either by accepting its basic premises or by rejecting them. In addition, Thorndike is the only example of a theorist whose work we review who dominated both psychology and education at the same time.

BACKGROUND

Edward Thorndike was born in Williamsburg, Massachusetts, in 1874. His father, a Methodist clergyman, moved the family several times as his ministry was changed, forcing Thorndike to study in several different preparatory schools before entering Wesleyan University in 1891. It was at Wesleyan and later at Harvard that the majority of Thorndike's ideas on psychology were formed. After graduating from Wesleyan with honors, Thorndike entered Harvard where he came under the influence of William James.

Early in his graduate career he began to conduct some experiments under the direction of one of his professors. It is of interest to note that his first choice was to do research with children but practical circumstances led him to initiate animal learning studies instead. The studies with the children were apparently quite harmless—they mainly involved recording children's reactions to various facial expressions while Thorndike and his colleagues played guessing games with them. The children seemed to enjoy the experience. But school authorities of that era were not accustomed to having research conducted with children, and it was decided that Thorndike could not continue his studies. Searching for research prospects which would involve fewer administrative complications, Thorndike decided that it might be easier to work with animal subjects. Thus he proposed to his professor that he might study the instinctive and intelligent behavior of chickens. Though he did not have to contend with regulations of the school authorities, he did encounter problems in housing his new subjects. However, through the hospitality and good humor of William James, Thorndike at last was able to make housing arrangements for his subjects and was able to begin his studies.

It is more than a historical curiosity that Thorndike was actually interested in studying human learning but that practical circumstances virtually forced him to study animals instead. His primary interest was (and remained through most of his life) the study of humans. But partly as a result of his problems first at Harvard and later at Columbia, animal experimentation was used to form the data base for his learning theory. Many later psychologists would likewise choose to conduct animal studies rather than human research for practical convenience. And to the present day, critics raise questions about the applicability of the animal findings in psychology even though researchers in other sciences (for example, biology, medicine) do fundamental research with animals before conducting human studies.

Thorndike decided to continue his graduate work in psychology at Columbia University. Apparently he had some problems in arranging housing for his animal subjects, but again he found it easier to do animal research than studies with humans. His new advisor at Columbia, James McKeen Cattell—generally considered to be the founder of applied psychology in this country—aided him in setting up his animal studies but also subsequently encouraged him to consider practical problems as well.

Thorndike's earlier graduate research subsequently served as the basis for his doctoral dissertation, entitled: "Animal Intelligence: An Experimental Study of the Associative Processes in Animals." Based on a series of studies with chickens and cats, Thorndike conceptualized animal problem-solving activities in associationistic terms.

Following graduation from Columbia University, Thorndike taught pedagogy (educational psychology) for a year at Western Reserve University. However, he soon returned to Columbia University where he stayed throughout most of his professional life. At Columbia he continued his basic psychology research but he also became the dominant figure in the newly emerging area of educational psychology. Many of the persons who later established educational psychology programs throughout the country got their start under the guidance of Thorndike. Through his students and his numerous (over 500) papers and books, Thorndike simultaneously had considerable influence on basic psychology learning research and practical applications in educational psychology.

A few observations about Thorndike's professional life style will provide some cues as to what kind of theory we can expect from him. In his various autobiographical notes and papers, Thorndike gives a curious picture of himself. He warns his readers that, instead of carrying out some preplanned career, he has typically responded to job demands and opportunities. Thus some of his books were carefully reworked and extended lecture notes which he had had to prepare for various classes. He reported that many of his studies were conducted because particular research questions emerged and he had some opportunity to try to answer them.

One gets the distinct impression that Thorndike has characteristically been thorough and careful in his work but that he has not followed some systematic master plan. It should not be too surprising to find that his "theory" is more or less a collection of "major" and relatively "minor" principles; Thorndike has not adhered to a general framework to guide his research or to integrate his various principles.

In the section which follows we will examine some of the laws which were generated by Thorndike's research. Three laws can be considered of major importance, while the other five are of some lesser order of importance. Though each involves systematic studies, one should not expect a close-knit interrelationship among the laws which Thorndike formulated.

THE THEORY

Since the main experimental techniques and the foundations of Thorndike's theory were outlined in his thesis (Thorndike, 1898), those studies will be used as the basis for some of our discussion. Compared with today's complicated apparatus and sophisticated research designs, Thorndike's procedures seem primitive and even simplistic. But one must realize that he began conducting his studies at a time when casual observation and anecdotal reports were widely accepted as the basis for conclusions about human and animal learning. For that era, Thorndike's experimental arrangements were creatively and cleverly designed.

Many of his studies were conducted with chickens and cats as subjects. Experimentally, a study consisted of careful observation of a subject which had to solve some problem in order to get a reward, usually a food known to be preferred by the subject; the experimental manipulations usually included different kinds of tasks which were presented to the subject, but the escape process and food reward were a usual feature. One example of a simple arrangement is the task presented to chickens: They were individually placed in one box which was part of a maze; the box had two exits, one which led to another enclosed box and one which led to the food. Given different kinds of mazes, the experimenter observed the processes and the rapidity with which the subject got to the food over the course of many trials.

The experimental arrangements for the cats illustrate a more complex task. Typically the cats were placed in a box approximately twenty by fifteen by twelve inches in size. The top had a removable cover so that the experimenter could place or remove subjects as required by each experiment. One wall contained a door which would open and provide access to food when a button or some portion of the wall was pushed; some escape procedures required that the subject claw, bite, or rub against a wire or string which, in turn, would open the door. In some cases the door opened inward and the escape "solution" required both that a particular movement was made and that the door was free to open.

For example, a three- to six-month-old kitten might be placed in the box when hungry, with some fish placed outside the door. In its various wanderings and explorations of the box, sooner or later the kitten would chance upon the escape mechanism and the door would open, providing access to the food. When placed back in the box shortly thereafter, the kitten's movements would not be so random but would tend to involve the activities in which it was engaged just prior to its previous escape.

Thorndike was, among other things, interested in knowing whether such activities were influenced by "ideas" or whether one could identify some lawful process whereby associations would be formed between the situation and certain activities as a result of the food rewards. He recognized that a naïve observer, watching a kitten which had escaped many times, would probably say that the cat was quite clever in "knowing" how to escape and to get the food. But Thorndike conjectured that some more parsimonious explanation might be applicable. He suggested that the repeated trials were resulting in associations, or connections, between the features of the problem situation and the particular responses the subject made there.

Let us assume that we had timed each of these kittens in their attempts at getting out of the box, averaged these times, and then plotted these averages against trials. Typically, these data would appear somewhat like the hypothetical data summarized below.

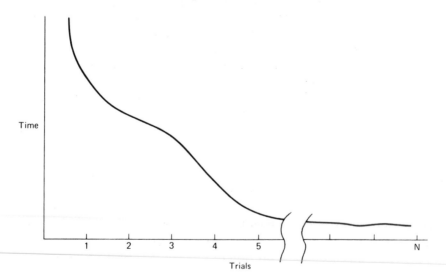

Do these data, Thorndike asked, indicate that the cats have "thought out" or "reasoned" a solution to the problem? No, Thorndike concluded, for if this were the case the data would appear quite different, showing discrete jumps and step-wise improvements. Instead of theorizing that the kittens had planned or reasoned how to get out of the puzzle box, one need only theorize that a certain response had been "selected" by the kitten in that situation (initially, perhaps, on a chance basis) and that a connection was gradually strengthened between the response and particular features of the situation. That is, a bond was formed between features of the situation (for example, the characteristics of the box's walls, the door, etc.) and certain acts by the kitten in that situation (such as walking to the wall, pushing the escape mechanism handle, etc.) because those acts in that situation led to satisfying results (getting out and eating the food). This description of selecting responses and strengthening connections is all that is needed to explain the gradual improvement of the kittens as they were given a series of trials in getting out of the box. Diagrammatically, this can be shown in a very simplified fashion. In the illustration below several responses to the situation in a puzzle box are possible. From Thorndike's viewpoint, these responses include some which have been modified through previous experiences along with other acts which could be identified as part of the organism's innate response tendencies. (It is interesting to note that in Thorndike's three-volume series, *Educational Psychology*, the first volume, *The Original Nature of Man*, is essentially a listing of the possible responses and connections that exist at birth and that can be strengthened in man.) In the situation involving a kitten in a box, the possible responses include clawing, purring, jumping, etc. Only response E (manipulation of the apparatus that opens

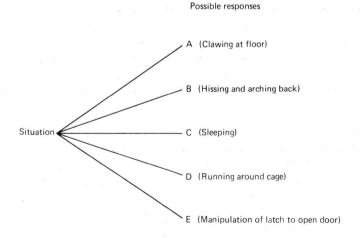

Possible responses

Situation
A (Clawing at floor)
B (Hissing and arching back)
C (Sleeping)
D (Running around cage)
E (Manipulation of latch to open door)

the box), however, will result in the kitten's being freed from his confinement and being allowed to eat some food that is available outside the box. Gradually, the connection or bond for this response will be strengthened and the cat will perform response E over all the others. Using these terms and several principles, one could explain how the kitten has learned to escape from the box.

Major Laws

On the basis of his doctoral dissertation research and a continuing stream of studies, Thorndike decided that several principles or laws could summarize most learning processes. He presented these laws in many papers and several books, periodically making changes in light of new data, interpretations, and constructive criticisms. One of the most complete statements of his general position was presented in a three-volume series, published in 1913 and 1914; it was entitled *Educational Psychology, Volume I, The Original Nature of Man* (Thorndike, 1913a); *Volume II, The Psychology of Learning* (Thorndike, 1913b); and *Volume III, Mental Work and Fatigue and Individual Differences and Their Causes* (Thorndike, 1914). We will refer to the above described hypothetical experiment while we present the three major laws and five comparatively minor laws which outline Thorndike's theory as it was presented around 1913. In a later section we will describe some of the changes which he made in his theory. Despite such changes, the 1913-1914 statement provides an indication of Thorndike's theory throughout several decades when it was having considerable influence on learning research and educational practice.

Thorndike identified his three major laws as the law of effect, the law of exercise, and the law of readiness. Many psychologists subsequently concluded that there was only one real law, with the other major and minor "laws" essentially elaborating on the law of effect. Partly in deference to the pre-Thorndikian era in which "practice makes perfect" was a generally accepted maxim, we will describe the law of exercise before considering the law of effect, followed by the law of readiness.

Law of Exercise Many psychologists and people more generally during the nineteenth century accepted the old maxim that "practice makes perfect" without many questions. In a sense, Thorndike's *law of exercise* mainly formalized this belief and related it to the empirical data he collected. In brief, this law holds that, other things being equal, learning occurs to the extent that the particular acts are practiced. In Thorndike's connectionism theory, one can state that practice strengthens bonds or connections. Thorndike identified two aspects, a *law of use* and a *law of disuse*.

Law of Use "When a modifiable connection is made between a situation and a response, that connection's strength is, other things being equal, increased" (Thorndike, 1913*b*, p. 2). Such is the *law of use.* Given the fact that an individual starts life with certain actions of which he is capable and situations in which they are most likely to occur, the more that an individual practices that act—or, makes that response—in a given situation, the more likely that the particular response will be made the next time that individual is in the same situation. The reader should note that this law does not indicate any relevance for the appropriateness of the response or the correctness of the act in a given situation; however, it was acknowledged by Thorndike that how much strengthening occurs would be affected by such matters as the vigor and duration of the practice periods. Moreover, the reader should note that Thorndike's apparent dependent measure of learning was the *probability* or likelihood that the particular response would be made the next time that same (or, similar) situation occurred again.

Law of Disuse The *law of disuse* follows from the law of use: Without practice, the connection weakens. Or, in Thorndike's terms, when such modifiable connections between a situation and a response do *not* occur during a period of time, other things being equal, the connection will weaken.

Given the fact that Thorndike later diminished the role of the law of exercise in his theory—a matter which we consider later in this chapter— one should note here that he long had contended that one should consider the law of exercise in conjunction with the law of effect.

Law of Effect Thorndike's *law of effect* can be stated: "When a modifiable connection between a situation and a response is made and is accompanied or followed by a satisfying state of affairs, that connection's strength is increased: When made and accompanied or followed by an annoying state of affairs, its strength is decreased" (Thorndike, 1913*b*, p. 4).

At a simple descriptive level, this law is not hard to accept and, in many ways, is difficult to reject. Stated simply, it suggests that we tend to do that which is pleasant and to avoid doing that which is unpleasant. But critics were quick to point out that many questions are raised when one examines the law more closely. For example, what constitutes a "satisfying state of affairs" or an "annoying state of affairs"? For some critics, such terms seemed too subjective at a time when psychologists were becoming more concerned about having objective, measurable definitions for their concepts. But other critics saw in Thorndike's work a threat to the concept of "free will" and "individual autonomy." Was he not suggesting that such increases or decreases in bond strength would occur almost automatically? And where do such "connections" exist anyway? In considering such questions, one must take into account the historical and contemporary context in which Thorndike was formulating his theory. This brings us to the *law of readiness*.

Law of Readiness In essence, the two major laws described above represent restatements of the associationistic and hedonistic positions described earlier in this book, but in a slightly different format. No longer are we speaking about laws or principles which govern the operation of the *mind*; instead, Thorndike's laws are generalizations about *behavior*. The method of approach is behavioristic, although not behaviorism, since this term had yet to be popularized. The major function of the law of readiness is that it ties these observations about behavior to physiology. Thorndike's attempt to relate behavioral observations to physiology was not so much prompted by the fact that such relationships could easily be made; rather, it apparently resulted from the influence of William James and others in the early twentieth century who considered that psychology's laws should be rather closely related to the known or assumed physiological correlates. Given the connectionism focus, Thorndike's obvious charge in this context would be to comment on the neurophysiological characteristics of "connections."

Thorndike theorized that somewhere in the nervous system there must be "conduction units" which provide connections between sensory stimulation and response activation. He suggested the term *conduction unit* be used to refer to those aspects of the nervous system which mediate between the time that a stimulus is detected and a response is finally made. Moreover, he theorized that the "readiness" of these conduction units to transmit neural impulses would vary from time to time, and that their readiness to conduct would partly determine whether an act was experienced as "satisfying" or "annoying." "Successful operation can in fact be satisfactorily defined, and what will originally satisfy and annoy can be safely predicted, only as a characteristic of the internal behavior of the neurones" (Thorndike, 1913a, p. 125). Thus, Thorndike suggested that "satisfying" experiences would occur when a "ready" conduction unit activated a response; "annoying" experiences would occur when a "ready" conduction unit was *not* activated *or* when a "not ready" conduction unit was forced to activate a response. He also entertained the possibility that not firing a "not ready" conduction unit could lead to satisfying experiences, but he expressed the belief that it would be hard to collect data supporting this idea.

The law of readiness thus deals with the momentary readiness of the conduction units to conduct neural impulses, and the effects that this readiness can have on determining whether acts are experienced as satisfying or annoying. In retrospect, some psychologists and neurologists challenge the soundness of Thorndike's conjecture about neuro-physiological correlates of learning. In light of today's knowledge about brain-behavior relationships, they seem rather simplistic. But these questions about neurophysiological details of learning processes need not necessarily invalidate Thorndike's learning theory in toto, not even if his most severe critics should prove to be accurate.

These "conduction units" can remain unspecified while still recognizing what Thorndike intended—that the laws he was establishing were to be grounded solidly in the physiological apparatus of the organism. The "conduction units" or "connections" or "bonds" that were to form the backbone of his theory were clearly intended as hypothetical constructs, the exact physiological nature of which was not completely known but which could nevertheless be discussed as if one were indeed talking about physiology. We will observe this tendency in almost all of Thorndike's writing. For example, in later years, in attempting to specify more clearly what is meant by the law of effect, Thorndike would discuss a "confirming reaction" that occurred somehow and somewhere within the nervous system when an act was followed by a satisfying or dissatisfying state of affairs. Thorndike was not essentially a physiologist and his speculations along these lines always had a decided "as if" quality about them. Given the prevailing notions about psychology, however, it is clear that he had little choice but to make such speculations just as James had done before him.

Minor Laws

To turn from physiology to behavior, there were other aspects of the kittens' behavior which seemed so regular as to represent general characteristics of learning. Thorndike was sufficiently intrigued with these characteristics that he identified them as minor laws, and he depicted them as secondary in scope and importance only in comparison with the three major laws described above. He identified these minor laws as multiple response or varied reaction; set or attitude; partial activity; assimilation or analogy; and associative shifting.

Law of Multiple Response or Varied Reaction   When an individual enters a new situation, many different responses are made, at least initially. For example, when the kittens were first put into the experimental box, they each displayed a wide range of behaviors, such as walking around the box, purring, scratching their ears, rubbing against the walls, etc. Because such a wide range of responses was evident with most of his subjects, Thorndike conceived the *law of multiple response or varied reaction*. This law holds that, instead of persisting in only one response in a new situation, most subjects display multiple (numerous) responses or varied reactions.

The significance for learning lies in the possibility that each response can be one which is to be learned and which can lead to satisfiers (depending upon prevailing conditions); thus there is the possibility that a variety of different connections can be strengthened in that situation.

Law of Set or Attitude   Thorndike observed that one cannot make general statements about how an organism will act in any given situation without considering the dispositions and characteristics of that organism. Its energy level, motivations, and general determination to make given responses will influence what responses are made at least initially. For example, if a kitten is tired or not particularly bothered by confinement in the box, it may not work very hard at getting out. The *law of set or attitude*, as should now be evident, holds that the organism will act in any given situation in accordance with its "set" or "attitude" or "adjustment" or "determination" to make given responses, other things being equal.

Law of Partial Activity   It was noted that the kittens do not pay attention to every part of the box when they are put into it, and that after a time certain aspects of the situation (that is, certain stimlui) seem to be more crucial in influencing the subjects' behavior. The prepotent stimuli may differ from subject to subject at similar points in experimental boxes, or for the same subject at different times. This law holds that a part of the situation may come to have special impact on all or part of the subject's behavior there, becoming so prepotent that some responses may become practically bound to those stimuli no matter what else is happening in the situation.

Law of Assimilation or Analogy   Thorndike noted that no two situations are identical with those one has encountered in the past, and yet somehow one uses past experiences when confronted with new situations. His *law of assimilation or analogy* holds that, when confronted with a novel situation, an organism will respond as it would to situations which are most similar to those which it had encountered in the past. Thus our kitten subjects would respond to the experimental box in ways by which they responded to "box-like" environments in the past.

Law of Associative Shifting   Thorndike theorized that even rather complicated acts can be "shifted" from one stimulus to another without having the response disintegrate into its several parts. This law holds that "*any response of which a learner is capable* [can become] associated with *any situation to which he is sensitive*" (Thorndike, 1913*b*, p. 15). Thus our kitten subjects could learn to respond in time to a completely new situation if the original situation is only partly changed on each successive trial in a series, replacing a few prepotent parts of the first situation with a few aspects of the new situation. Assuming that the situation in which the kitten is originally taught actually consists of a combination of several stimuli, all of which have been connected to the correct response, these stimuli can be faded out one at a time and replaced with new stimuli while maintaining the correct response throughout. Through such a procedure, an entirely new situation in which no actual training had occurred can now bring forth the learned response. Because of the gradual change, the subject apparently simultaneously responds to the influence of the old stimuli and builds connections with each of the new stimuli being presented.

Some Changes in Thorndike's Laws

There are a number of things that strike one about these laws, the major portion of Thorndike's original theory. For one thing, there are several undefined or loosely defined terms. We have already mentioned the unspecified nature of the physiological meaning in such terms as *conduction unit, modifiable connection,* and even *strength.* Strength certainly means something like "probability of response" in behavioral terms but it also probably was meant to indicate a physiological increase of some sort, again unspecified. There are attempts in the three primary laws to make them more than mere tautologies (defining satisfying as something that the animal does nothing to avoid, for example) but it is still the case that the laws fall far short of the type of specificity required of a physical law.

It is also clear that the laws are uneven in terms of promising prediction and control. Several of the secondary laws are little more than empty descriptions of relatively regular occurrences. It could be argued that the same is true of all these laws, including the three primary ones, and yet there does seem to be an essential difference between the type of statement included in the law of varied reaction and the law of effect. The first merely describes a situation; the second does this also but then leads further into a statement such as, "and therefore the following procedures are recommended." The law of effect, the law of exercise, and the law of associative shifting all have this "and-therefore" quality about them and with time came to play increasingly important roles in Thorndike's theory.

A final point about the three basic laws in the theory is that they are not unique and probably represent restatements of one general theme. Certainly the law of readiness can be subsumed under the law of effect since it could be seen as a statement concerning why the law of effect works. Also, it is difficult to imagine very many situations where exercise without reward would occur. In any situation when a learner has the opportunity of observing his own progress, merely the fact that he is making progress will act as some type of reward. The law of exercise then could be viewed as a weak form of the law of effect. Thorndike obviously did not originally intend this, but in further revisions of his theory the law of effect came to take on more significance; eventually Thorndike identified the law of effect as the fundamental law of teaching and learning. Since understanding this law is so crucial in understanding Thorndike's theory, we should be clear in assessing what it says.

In essence, the law of effect is a restatement of Spencer's hedonism tied to objective data and to some limited extent buttressed with physiological speculation. Just like Spencer, Thorndike describes a hedonism of the past—that which has occurred in the past will affect future courses of action. In modern learning parlance, when an S-R connection has been followed by a reward, this connection will be strengthened. Stated thusly as an empirical fact rather than a theoretical law, the statement is relatively vacuous—there are at least two terms that are unspecified: "S-R connection" and "reward." We will observe later how various theorists have tried to specify more closely what these mean, just as Thorndike did. As an empirical statement, of course, the law of effect is difficult to attack. Since it is so obvious and so pervasive, it has come to represent the essence of Thorndike's theory.

These laws formed the core of Thorndike's original theory. He was to change certain aspects of it later as further experimentation showed that some parts of the theory were in error. For example, the original law of effect was stated in such a way that punishment was opposite but equal to reward as a modifier of behavior. Several experiments by Thorndike and others led him to the conclusion that punishment was not as effective as reward with the result that he shortened the law of effect to emphasize positive satisfiers over negative ones. One demonstration of this that we will discuss later in the chapter used a Spanish word translation as the task. Certain of the responses were called "right" and others "wrong." In looking at the change in response probability over time, Thorndike found very little weakening as a result of "wrong" but noticeable improvement in response to "right." It is not clear if this represents quite the crucial test that Thorndike seemed to think but on the basis of the experiment and several others (including some case-study data on the ineffectiveness of punishment in school practice and childrearing), he came to de-emphasize (but not totally to disregard) the negative half of the law of effect. The least that can be said for punishment is that if it is not opposite to reward, it is different from reward in its effect upon behavior.

It also became clear that mere repetition of an activity without knowledge of results will not necessarily result in improvement in the activity or learning. In a classic experiment, Trowbridge and Cason had subjects attempt to draw a three-inch line blindfolded without knowing how close they were coming to the correct criterion. The subjects did not show improvement over time, indicating to Thorndike that mere use (or disuse) would not produce learning. This again is probably too strong a conclusion to be drawn from this experiment, but it did lead Thorndike to de-emphasize another part of his original theory—the law of exercise. As before, stress must be placed upon "de-emphasize" for the law of exercise was not totally removed. When mere practice does produce learning, Thorndike would speak of "belongingness"—the fact that certain responses are biologically (or socially) appropriate for certain stimuli. Mere repetition of such S-R situations will produce learning even though no reward seems to be involved. These changes in his theory obviously represent meaningful attempts on Thorndike's part to modify his thinking on the basis of experimental data and to meet criticisms of his theory from opponents—especially the gestaltists. Such changes should be viewed, however, more as shifts in emphasis than as radical departures. The mechanical strengthening and weakening of bonds was throughout the crucial element in Thorndike's thinking, a position he did not ever basically change. Such things as "belongingness" were meant to take into account the wholistic approach to behavior that was becoming popular in Thorndike's later years (1935 and on). These changes were more in the nature of acknowledgments than retreats, however. For example, he conceptualized "organization" as the simple belonging of situation and response, rather than some mystical and unanalyzable gestalt. Despite his humanistic leaning in his social writings, his theory remains throughout stamped with his own particular brand of mechanism.

Human Learning

Even though the primary data base in the theory was derived from animal experimentation, Thorndike was still vitally concerned with human learning. He distinguishes four types:

(1) connection-forming of the common animal type, as when a ten-months-old baby learns to beat a drum, (2) connection-forming involving ideas, as when a two-year-old learns to think of his mother upon hearing the word, or to say candy when he thinks of the thing, (3) analysis or abstraction, as when the student of music learns to respond to an overtone in a given sound, and (4) selective thinking or reasoning, as when the school pupil learns the meaning of a Latin sentence by using his knowledge of the rules of syntax and meanings of the word-roots. (Thorndike, 1913b, p. 17)

These four types of human learning should *not* be viewed as differing in quality from animal learning since the same three major and five minor laws still apply. Human learning still consists of the selecting and strengthening of connections; any differences that might exist reside in such factors as a lesser degree of specificity and increased responsiveness in human behavior. Human beings, for example, can respond to a wider variety of cues in a situation, making learning more general than it is for animals. A dog who has learned to respond to the sound of his master's voice may not respond to another voice giving the identical command. A man, on the other hand, will produce a learned response to a wide variety of cues as long as there is some similarity to the original stimulus. Consider the type of behavior required in driving a car. It is obvious that an experienced human driver can perform those learned responses necessary in a wide variety of different automobiles. His behavior is still habitual but not so dominated by the original training situation as would be the case with an animal.

Another distinction between human and animal learning is that human beings are not as likely as animals to blindly absorb a situation but are more likely to actively participate in learning in the manner of choosing those elements of a situation that are most crucial and important (the type of activity described by the law of partial activity). These differences, however, do not represent radical departures in moving from animals to humans, but again represent shifts in emphasis. Essentially, Thorndike took the position that his three major laws and five minor laws based on animal studies could, at a minimum, outline the fundamental characteristics of human learning, too. Thorndike did recognize that learning processes are more complicated in at least some human activities, but he held that it would not be possible to understand such complex processes if we did not have some understanding of simpler learning processes. He even expressed the possibility that such simple learning laws might be all that may be needed to describe many complex human learning activities.

Thorndike actually did less animal experimentation after he accepted the faculty position at Columbia University, apparently, in part, because human subjects were easier to come by for a professor than for a graduate student. Nonetheless, his willingness to extend the principles derived from animal research to human learning indicated his belief that the essential nature of the two was not substantially different. When Thorndike did perform animal experimentation later in life, including some primate studies, the purpose was usually to trace the evolution of man's intelligence back through more primitive species, very much in the Darwinian tradition.

THE THEORY APPLIED TO SPECIFIC TOPICS

To demonstrate how the basic idea of the strengthening of bonds could be used to account for a variety of phenomena, we will look at three separate topics that Thorndike studied in his academic career. These in no sense exhaust the topics that he considered important or capable of being discussed within the confines of connectionism. They merely represent a sample of topics that Thorndike considered capable of verifying certain aspects of his theory.

A Theory of Transfer
and a Theory of Intelligence

There can be little doubt that learning one thing can have an effect on learning something else. The ice skater more rapidly learns to roller skate, for example, and the typist more rapidly learns to play the piano than does someone who has not been trained in either original activity. Why is this the case? In general, the answer to this question throughout much of the nineteenth century would have been mental or formal discipline, the underlying assumption of which was that the faculties of the mind could be strengthened, just as any muscle could be strengthened, by exercise. To use an analogy, a man can lift weights to strengthen the muscles in his arm. This strengthening of muscles is applicable not only to weight lifting, but also to any physical activity that involves roughly similar movement. In the theory of mental discipline, the mind is considered to be analogous to such a muscle. If it were strengthened by appropriately difficult mental activity (such as learning Latin or Greek), it should be able to perform better in other intellectual pursuits. At the time that Thorndike was writing his early theoretical papers, this idea was already beginning to fade, although it was still a widely accepted pedagogical theory. The reason given for learning material such as geometry or classical languages was that such intellectual gymnastics would facilitate the ability to reason and think. In an attack on this idea William James had performed what at the time was considered a classic experiment on learning poetry and had not reported any generalized effects of this activity on other pursuits. Thorndike himself, along with Woodward, reported a similar although more extensive experiment which validated James's data and again supported the contention that the formal discipline theory was not adequate. If this theory would not stand, then what could replace it? Connectionism could be extended to account for the phenomenon of transfer without the use of formal discipline, or so Thorndike thought.

Consider three activities, A, B, and C (as below).

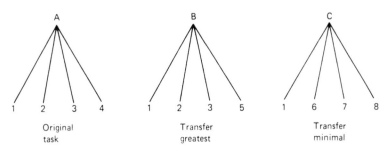

Activity A is the task that is originally learned and it is composed of elements 1, 2, 3, and 4. Having learned this task, the question becomes: To which new task will transfer be the greatest? According to Thorndike, transfer will be greatest to task B since there are more common or identical elements (or bonds) between it and A than there are between A and C. The effect of a previous activity is now no longer viewed as being general in nature but rather specific to tasks which share common elements. Those bonds that were strengthened in one situation will retain this strength in the next, thereby producing transfer. This identical elements interpretation of various sets of empirical data seemed compatible with Thorndike's beliefs about the underlying neurophysiological processes and with his observations of practical situations.

With regard to presumed neurophysiological details, it seemed reasonable to expect that transfer of training would occur more readily when the same conduction units and cell actions in the brain were required for the training situation and the new situation. For example, if certain acts required that particular connections in the brain be formed during learning, then it would make sense that acts in a new situation would come more easily if such new acts also required the same or similar connections in the brain.

Thorndike contended that results in practical situations are also compatible with his identical elements transfer theory. For example, a student who studies Latin and does well in that course may also be expected to do well in certain studies of the English language (specifically, those which are based on or closely related to Latin characteristics); but while this student might also do well in other Romance languages, there may be no difference or even some negative effects apparent in other languages (for example, German, Russian) which have fewer elements in common with Latin. Thorndike's main point was that transfer occurs because of similar elements (or to an even greater extent with *identical* elements) in the training situation and the new situation.

In very much a similar vein, Thorndike proposed a theory of intelligence based on the basic notion of bonds termed the multiple-factor theory of intelligence. It set forward the idea that intelligence consisted of a large number of highly specific abilities. In testing, these abilities would not all appear for they would share certain elements in common. A person who could be considered to be more intelligent would be one who possessed a greater number of possible connections.

The correctness of either of these theories need concern us less than what they show—that the idea of bonds as the basis of behavior was almost infinitely expandable in its ability to account for the totality of human as well as animal behavior.

The Spread of Effect

The "spread of effect" is the name given by Thorndike to a phenomenon that he discovered somewhat late in his experimental work and that he eventually came to believe demonstrated rather forcefully the correctness of his theory. In particular, it was discovered that if a subject was presented with a task that included a series of events (such as supplying a missing word in a long sequence of statements) and if only a few of these were rewarded while the others were punished, there would result a gradient of strength around the rewarded responses. For example, if a subject was given ten pairs of nonsense syllables and was reinforced for getting number 5 correct, not only would he remember the rewarded pair (number 5) more than chance but he would also remember numbers 4 and 6. It is as if the effect of the reward has worked not only on the correct connection but also on surrounding ones, even if these connections had previously not been rewarded and had even been punished. Whatever the effect of reward is (and this for Thorndike would be explained by some mechanical and physical reaction in the nervous system, probably central), it has the capacity of spreading throughout the nervous system, this strength being roughly proportional to the distance from the rewarded connection. The gradient of strength would ideally appear as below:

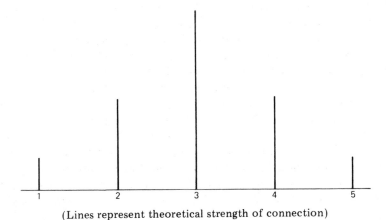

(Lines represent theoretical strength of connection)

In this diagram, item 3 has been rewarded. If a measure of learning is taken (such as asking the subject the response he made when the list was presented), he would most probably remember the response to 3 and, to a lesser extent, the responses to 2 and to 4.

Thorndike was convinced that this spread-of-effect phenomenon was an important contribution to the psychology of learning and an important verification of his theory. Since it was somewhat surprising, it aroused considerable controversy and attempts at replication by both Thorndike's supporters and critics (cf. Hilgard Bower, 1966). Whether this is a true phenomenon or not is probably not as important as the fact that Thorndike could explain it by using the basic constructs of his theory.

Learning without Awareness

This is an area of research that is similar to that involved with the spread of effect in that it has aroused considerable controversy and research. We will present one of Thorndike's experiments from which this research sprung which again demonstrates the kind of experiment that could be involved with his theory. Thorndike performed an experiment using Spanish words followed by five English words as the task to be performed.

The subjects were told to guess which of the five English words provided was the correct translation of the Spanish word. In reality, Thorndike was not concerned with the correct translation of the words but was instead trying to get the subjects to perform a response that they were not aware was being reinforced. Thorndike reinforced more of the responses on the right side of the page and discovered that with time, the subjects began to choose these alternatives over those on the left. There was little indication that the subjects were aware they were performing this way, indicating to Thorndike that learning without awareness was a demonstrable phenomenon. This experiment was followed by several others with similar results, both by Thorndike and by researchers who came after him. For example, Greenspoon performed what is now a classic experiment using verbal reinforcement. In this experiment subjects were interviewed individually and reinforced (by having the experimenter smile or say "um-hum") whenever they pronounced a plural noun. As in the Thorndike experiment, Greenspoon discovered that the subjects began to emit increasing amounts of plural nouns over the course of the experiment, again without apparently being aware of having done it. This experiment is representative of a large amount of literature on this subject which is more or less related to the original Thorndike experiment and which clearly owes its lineage to Thorndike's theory. If learning is due (in part, at least) to the mechanical strengthening of connections, then awareness is not a necessary condition for it to occur.

The phenomenon of learning without awareness, just like the spread of effect, is open to question on several points. Without going into detail about the arguments, the point is clear that this is another area that demonstrated to Thorndike that his theory could account for a variety of phenomena. Awareness must certainly be considered sufficient for learning and it is clear that Thorndike perceived this fact. Nonetheless, it was to attack a similar type of idea that he originally published *Animal Intelligence*. Animals do not learn by cognitively restructuring a situation or by "figuring out" what to do. Since man represents a continuation of this, why should it not also be possible for him to learn by similar processes? By such reasoning, it is evident that learning without awareness fits nicely into the Thorndikian scheme. The finding is not crucial, but it is certainly comfortable.

It should be emphasized that the above examples of work derived from Thorndike's theory are not necessarily crucial in verifying the theory in either a positive or negative sense. The theory does not automatically predict the spread-of-effect phenomenon nor would it be shown to be false if this phenomenon could not be verified under tightly controlled conditions. As such, this is not a significant semantic test of the theory. The same is true of learning without awareness. As we indicated in discussing human learning, Thorndike was ready to admit that there were several types of human learning and that ideation certainly played a role in most examples of human information acquisition. It really would not harm the theory to any great extent if it was discovered that human beings could not learn without awareness since all Thorndike would have to do is assume that awareness was a necessary condition in human learning. The fact that he found both the spread of effect and learning without awareness did fit nicely into his conceptions of what his theory could do. If learning is the mechanical strengthening of connections, and if reward produced some type of change in the nervous system by modifying or changing the probability that a conduction unit would act in a certain manner rather than another, these effects and others like them could be comfortably explained. They are not so much crucial as they are convenient; they are interesting phenomena that the theory could explain without serious wear and tear on its essential fabric.

OBSERVATIONS ABOUT THORNDIKE'S INFLUENCE ON LEARNING THEORY

In Thorndike we can see the first systematic attempt to develop a unified theory of learning. In discussing this theory we have not stressed its semantic or syntactic validity because the theory is too loosely stated to warrant these tests. In reality, the theory's value resides far less in its scientific soundness than in what it meant for psychology in general; it has made its mark because of what it produced in terms of criticisms and reformulations. Some of these can be foreseen by looking again at the basic Thorndikian experiment—the cat in the puzzle box. Thorndike concludes from looking at these data that learning is characterized by the following factors: it is gradual; it is practically automatic; it is affected by consequent events (rewards); it is accomplished somewhere in the nervous system by a change in the strength of an S-R bond. As we noted in Chapter 3, in the theories that followed Thorndike's, all these points were brought into question. Thorndike thus raised the issues even if he did not solve them.

There is one further aspect of Thorndike's work that again will serve as a preview of future difficulty. There is always a danger in using one type of data base to generate predictions about another realm of discourse. Thorndike's original work was with animals, and although he de-emphasized this type of work later in life, it might be the case that his theory would have been different if he had started with human experimentation rather than animal. There is an easy and obvious way out of this difficulty; all that need be done is to assume that there are several types of learning—one for animals, one for human beings, one for children, etc. Most of the theories that we review did not take this option but tried to simplify as much as possible. (It should be remembered that one criterion of a good theory is parsimony.) Should there be more than one type of learning or should there be only one? If there is only one type, what is it like and what kind of subject should be used to study it? Thorndike does not provide answers but others did. It is this type of controversy that became characteristic of learning theories after Thorndike.

This theory serves as a useful starting point, not only because of what it tried to do in psychology and accomplished in education, but because of what it led others to do in response. The issues Thorndike raised were debated by others, but he perceived them clearly and found a way to answer some of them.

ATTEMPTS TO APPLY THE
LEARNING THEORY IN EDUCATION

It is not clear whether Thorndike perceived any clear or sharp distinction between his theory as a theory of learning and a theory of educational practice. But almost from the start, and increasingly so as he became older, his concern was with educational problems. We have already mentioned his criticism of formal discipline as one of these concerns and there were several others. For Thorndike, the prescriptions to be derived from his theory were fairly straightforward; the essence of teaching is creating an atmosphere where the correct connections could be strengthened. As he comments in *Educational Psychology*: "Learning is connecting, and teaching is the arrangement of situations which will lead to desirable bonds and make them satisfying. A volume could well be written showing in detail just what bonds certain exercises in arithmetic, spelling, German, philosophy, and the like, certain customs and laws, certain moral and religious teachings, and certain occupations and amusements, tend to form in men of given original natures; or how certain desired bonds could economically be formed" (Thorndike, 1913b, p. 55).

While we cannot adequately describe his many contributions to the field of education, there are a few points that stand out in sharp detail:

1.   Thorndike's work and writings concerning the inadequacy of formal discipline undoubtedly had a noticeable effect on the changing of curriculum throughout every level of education. While it cannot be said with certainty that these curricular changes would not have occurred sooner or later without Thorndike, it is clear that he gave impetus to a movement that was under way when he began to write. If Thorndike's ideas about the effects of curriculum were true, then the entire focus of education should change. No longer should subjects be taught in order to strengthen the mind; instead they should be designed to further those specific goals that the educational system wished to foster. Increasingly, for Thorndike as well as for American education in general, this came to mean social utility. In his later years Thorndike turned from strictly psychological matters to a concern for social engineering. It is clear throughout his writings that he always perceived this to be psychology's function and role in society, and the curricular changes he fostered came to reflect this more and more through the years. To reiterate, the changes in the curriculum that have occurred during the last fifty years cannot be traced solely to Thorndike. Part of the movement, however, is most certainly due to his writings and his theory.

2.   Thorndike also gave impetus to the measurement movement that has become so characteristic of American psychology and education. As he commented in 1903, "We conquer the facts of nature when we observe and experiment upon them. When we measure them, we have made them our servants." For Thorndike, if something truly existed, then it could be measured. Such an attitude was a necessary but not sufficient condition in making education a science, a goal that Thorndike must have kept constantly in mind. With this attitude several programs of research were created in his laboratory, including a categorization of the frequency of word usage in the English language. This was a measurable quantity and led to educational objectives; if your intention was to teach English words, social utility could best be served by knowing what the most frequent words were. If it is not necessarily true that you conquer nature by measuring her, it is true that you will not conquer nature unless measurement is attempted. This is largely the way that the physical sciences advanced and it is the only way that psychology and education could advance. It is difficult to appreciate the value of this now since measurement has become so characteristic of social science, but in large part this orientation can be credited to Thorndike.

3.   Through his supervision of dissertations and other research efforts, Thorndike began the movement of using school settings as places for doing research. For example, the classic experiment on moral develop-

ment by Hartshorne and May was performed with Thorndike's supervision in a school setting, not necessarily because the data derived from this experiment was directly relevant to the educational setting, but merely because the type of subjects found there were a valuable source of data.

4.   Thorndike is one of the few theorists we will meet who spent most of his life in a teachers' college. As such, he had a direct and substantial effect on several generations of teachers. In addition, his own personal doctoral students carried his ideas to other schools so that his effect on education was great.

Throughout much of the twentieth century one can find many papers in most years in which someone has attempted to "apply" Thorndike's connectionism learning theory in education. The basic theme is almost always the same: no matter what learning is involved, whether academic or motor skill learning, it is assumed that one should break down complex acts into simpler ones and that systematically rewarded practice will build up bonds or connections between the situation and the appropriate behavior there.

Fitch (1961) provides one of the countless papers which have been written advocating use of connectionism in education. He suggests utilization of Thorndike's learning principles in teaching typewriting. A few main themes stand out. First, he characterizes the role of the teacher of breaking large units of work into their fundamental elements. Thus, the teacher would help the student to identify what it is that is to be learned in that section in the typing lesson. Next, the teacher sets up practice sessions where the student has opportunity to type correctly and to get knowledge of results which serve to reward his efforts. A third and important function of the teacher is to arrange the practice sessions so that the student naturally goes from the very simple, elementary aspects of the task to more complex and integrated completion of the task.

Like many educators who have attempted to apply Thorndike's learning theory, Fitch tends to focus on the more specific and more readily measured aspects, and he de-emphasizes or totally ignores more complex and "intangible" educational objectives. It is such an approach which has been severely criticized by contemporaries of Thorndike and educators down to the present time. But it is noteworthy that such an "application" does not derive inherently from Thorndike's approach. Rather, it constitutes a somewhat narrow interpretation of Thorndike's general orientation to education.

Thorndike was interested in complex activity as well as the simpler and more readily measurable aspects. But he thought that this could be accomplished by building up to such complex activities from utilization of the simpler elements of which such complex activities are supposedly composed.

In part, the reader must judge for himself whether Thorndike's theory is adequate to account for complex cognitive activities and other more "human" types of learning, or whether it must be restricted to only simple, straightforward elementary activities. One can readily find many papers taking either point of view. It is the author's belief, however, that it was Thorndike's intention that his theory would account for all aspects of learning rather than simple rote memorization and elementary motor skill learning. But Thorndike's critics have taken the position that such an extension *cannot* be accomplished.

EDUCATIONAL R&D IMPLICATIONS

Thorndike was an energetic researcher and a prolific writer whose numerous papers and books dealt with practical educational problems as well as with theoretical issues. Examination of his writings on practical matters reveals that he frequently found it useful to draw from his basic research and theory in seeking practical problem solutions, but that he also acted pragmatically. He used his "connectionistic" concepts and principles as a main framework to conceptualize classroom learning situations, but when the need arose he also drew potentially useful ideas from competing theories, from existing educational practices, or from wherever they might be found.

Many years and much research has been completed since Thorndike formulated his ideas, but many of his views about educational matters still merit consideration. For example, his description of psychology's contributions as involving "aims, materials, means and methods" (which we considered in Chapter 5) are strikingly similar to some of the contemporary discussions about measurable objectives and accountability in educational practice. His notions that classroom learning consists of "selecting and connecting" may sound overly simplistic or mechanistic to some readers; but these notions can serve as guides to questions which need to be answered about practical situations in education. A useful approach in improving educational practice is to identify relevant learning acts, the stimuli with which they should become connected, and the rewards which might strengthen the connections. If one additionally compares the classroom situation with characteristics of the outside world for which we are preparing students, we can begin to outline educational objectives and methods in greater detail than if we merely indicate that we are trying to help students become "good citizens."

Obviously, one should check for contemporary evidence which might contradict some of the principles or raise questions about concepts which resulted from Thorndike's work. But because he outlined many of the problems which continue to concern both theoreticians and practitioners today, both his basic research reports and his practically oriented papers can provide implications for improving educational practice today.

SUGGESTED READINGS

Joncich, G. M. (Ed.) Psychology and the science of education: *Selected writings of E. L. Thorndike.* New York: Columbia University, 1962.

Joncich, G. M. *The sane positivist: A biography of Edward L. Thorndike.* Middletown, Conn.: Wesleyan University Press, 1968.

Thorndike, E. L. The contributions of psychology to education. *Journal of Educational Psychology,* 1910, 1, 5-12.

Thorndike, E. L. *Education: A first book.* New York: Macmillan, 1912.

Thorndike, E. L. *Educational psychology.* Vol. 1. *The original nature of man.* New York: Teachers College, Columbia University, *1913*a.

Thorndike, E. L. *Educational psychology.* Vol. 2. *The psychology of learning.* New York: Teachers College, Columbia University, 1913b.

Thorndike, E. L. Educational diagnosis. *Science,* 1913c, 37, 133-142.

Thorndike, E. L. *Educational psychology.* Vol. 3. *Mental work and fatigue and individual differences and their causes.* New York: Teachers College, Columbia University, 1914.

Thorndike, E. L. *Human learning.* New York: The Century Co., 1931.

Thorndike, E. L. *Selected writings from a connectionist's psychology.* New York: Appleton-Century-Crofts, 1949.

Thorndike, E. L. *Educational psychology.* New York: Arno Press, 1969.

8

Ivan P. Pavlov and Classical Conditioning

By any measure, Thorndike's connectionism represents one of the major seminal positions in the history of learning theory and in psychology in general. Indeed, if one were to divide learning theories into two groups, one group would include those researchers who followed Thorndike into the analysis of events which follow a response and the effect these events have on the strength of that response. In general, these would be the men who have concentrated on the detailed analysis of reinforcement and the way such reinforcements affect behavior and would include men such as Skinner and Hull. The other group would include those men who have followed the work of Ivan P. Pavlov (1849-1936) into an analysis of the conditioned response. This dichotomy is so well established that the two trends in learning theory are often termed instrumental (or Thorndikian) versus classical (or Pavlovian) conditioning. Since we will discuss this distinction in detail later, it will be sufficient here merely to comment that Pavlov's influence in psychology is at least equal to that of Thorndike and that his theory is still widely discussed and utilized.

BACKGROUND

Ivan Pavlov was born in 1849 in the town of Rayazan, Russia. His father was a parish priest in a poor district and most of Pavlov's early years were spent in trying to help his father maintain a large and growing family. But despite such hardships in the family situation, circumstances did allow Pavlov to begin his education in an ecclesiastical seminary, an opportunity which at that time provided a far superior education than that available in the normal Russian school. Rather early in his life Pavlov became interested in the natural sciences and eventually entered the University of St. Petersburg where he took his degree in physiology. Through a series of postgraduate positions Pavlov eventually became director of the physiological division of the Institute for Experimental Medicine at St. Petersburg, a position he maintained throughout his life. In large part his early years at the Institute (1901-1912) were devoted to the study of digestion and the effects gastric secretions have on the utilization of food, as well as the mechanisms that underlie these secretions. Through this work, Pavlov was granted the Nobel prize in physiology in 1904.

The picture that emerges of Pavlov from his contemporaries is one of a completely dedicated scientist and hard worker who devoted most of his life to research. Despite the influence of his father, it would seem that Pavlov's devotion (if we can use that term) was not to religious issues but to science, almost as if this word should be spelled with a capital "S." To quote Babkin, one of Pavlov's students and fellow workers, Pavlov envisioned science as a means for learning all about our world, even about people. "In his speeches and articles Pavlov very often likened the living organism to a machine. 'Indeed,' he remarked, 'in all stages mentioned in

our discussion, the living organism showed itself to be merely a machine—
a very complicated one, of course, but just as submissive and obedient as
any other machine' " (Babkin, 1949, p. 86). But by the same token it
must also be added that Pavlov considered humility rather than arrogance
to constitute the key mark of the scientist. No matter how brilliant a
scientist might be, he could *not* decide how nature *should* act. Instead, the
scientist's role is to use his skills to the fullest to expose nature to his
view, so that he can understand lawfulness inherent in nature. With regard
to psychological processes, the scientist merely tries to understand how
humans learn; the scientist does *not* decide how they *should* learn. His
principles and theories are valid descriptions of human learning only to
the extent that they are supported (or at least not contradicted) by
empirical data.

THE THEORY

Perhaps the most remarkable aspect of Pavlov's contribution to the
psychology of learning is that his main research in this area came about
largely by chance. His discovery of the conditioned reflex was the result
of serendipity, an offshoot of work in a totally different area. The
brilliance of any scientist, of course, is reflected far more in what he
actually accomplishes than in what he originally set out to do; Pavlov was
able to follow up a line of investigation that others might have overlooked. To show how he came into this area, we will describe the type of
research that Pavlov was engaged in before his discovery of the conditioned reflex.

The major emphasis in Pavlov's early physiological research was the
study of the function of the nervous system in digestion. An integral part
of this work involved collecting secretions from the mouth of the organisms studied, in most cases these organisms being dogs. As a way of
accomplishing this economically and without harm to the animal, Pavlov
used a technique that involved sham feeding the dog, who had been
operated on in such a manner that the food never reached the stomach. (It
is interesting to note that Pavlov was also one of the founders of the use
of antiseptic surgery with animals. By performing such surgery an animal
would be used for many years as an experimental subject without serious
discomfort to the animal.) When the dogs were fed in this manner they
would eat frequently over long periods of time since their hunger was
never satiated. Sham feeding produced large quantities of saliva which was
collected in bottles from a small fistula inserted in the underside of the
dog's mouth. (This technique became so workable that Pavlov was able to
collect enough secretions to sell and earn money for his laboratory.)

Now, in itself, there was nothing especially important or new in this
technique; it was simply an efficient method of performing research. This

procedure became important in the study of learning when Pavlov noticed, apparently by chance, that the dogs in such experiments would often begin to salivate *before* the food was actually put in their mouths to begin the sham eating. The dogs were acting as if the food were there even though it was not. They were reacting to a stimulus that was not physically present, or, as Pavlov came to call it, a "psychic stimulus."

The process of responding to such a psychic stimulus did not of course happen immediately but was produced only after the dog had been subjected a number of times to the sight of the laboratory assistant coming into the room, followed by the sensation of food in the mouth. To Pavlov, this represented the key to unraveling the mysteries of the higher cerebral centers. As such, he presented his original formulations to his colleagues with the intention of using his newly discovered psychic reflex as a means for studying, in today's terms, relationships between the nervous system and the behavior of organisms. Pavlov was so enthused about this research that he made it the topic of his Nobel speech. Some of Pavlov's colleagues did not consider this to be the wisest choice at that time since it represented a considerable departure from Pavlov's primary research. Despite these warnings from his fellow scientists, Pavlov decided to investigate these processes more fully and spent the remaining years of his life doing so. The importance of this chance finding for us is that it represents a type of learning that is highly predictable and suggestive of answers to questions about the *basic nature* of learning.

The Pavlovian Classical Conditioning Paradigm

To simplify the situation somewhat we will present the basic Pavlovian experiment in a more controlled and restricted form than that involved in the sham feeding of laboratory dogs. To do this we will use Pavlov's terminology and present his thinking on how this particular kind of learning occurs.

In all but the most primitive organisms, there are several naturally occurring reflexes that are produced by rather simple stimuli. For example, a blow on the patellar tendon will result in a jerk of the lower leg; the shining of a light in the eye will result in pupil contraction; putting food in an organism's mouth will result in salivation, etc. In the specific case of Pavlov's experiment with the dogs it can be seen that the reflex utilized was salivation resulting from food placed in the dog's mouth. All these reflexes and many more are naturally occurring and unlearned, a part of the innate response tendencies of the species. Pavlov called them *unconditional reflexes*, using the adjective "unconditional" the way we employ the word in casual conversation—that is not conditional upon anything. But somehow the word was initially translated from Russian to English as "unconditioned" rather than "unconditional"; thus we will talk about "unconditioned" and "conditioned" reflexes, stimuli, and responses in this book.

Let's suppose that we start with such an unconditioned reflex and its eliciting stimulus. Then, we might arrange the situation in such a way that another stimulus, one that will not originally elicit the reflex, occurs temporally just previous to the unconditioned stimulus (within approximately one to four seconds). We will find that, in time, the neutral stimulus has taken on the properties of the unconditioned stimulus.

To put this in Pavlov's terms, the originally neutral stimulus has become conditioned. The classic example of this process involves the ringing of a bell just before putting food in a dog's mouth. Diagrammatically, this is presented below. The essential features of any such experiment involving Pavlovian techniques will always be the same: there will be a stimulus (UCS) that will produce some observable response without prior learning (UR); an additional stimulus ("CS") will be placed in some temporal relation to the original stimulus and be paired with it several times; this new stimulus will eventually be tested alone (CS) (that is, presented without the unconditioned stimulus following it), with the result that this originally neutral stimulus will at some time produce the original response (or a response very similar to it) (CR). This is the basic Pavlovian experiment and most of Pavlov's work until the end of his life was spent collecting data from such experiments under a multiplicity of conditions.

Just as in the typical Thorndikian experiment, the results from Pavlovian experiments as described above are highly predictable and lawful in that the same conditions will always produce the same results. For

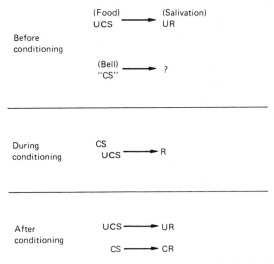

Figure 8-1 Stimulus-response relationships and the classical conditioning paradigm.

example, there are certain time relations that can be applied within the Pavlovian experiments which will produce highly reliable results. By varying the time interval between the conditioned and unconditioned stimulus an experimenter can produce some lawful relationships in terms of "ease" or rapidity of conditioning and persistence of responding until extinction.

To demonstrate this, consider the following three modifications of the basic Pavlovian experiment. In the first case the time between the onset of the CS and the UCS is lengthened beyond five seconds (up to as much as four or five minutes). This has the effect of increasing the number of trials that are required to produce conditioning and will eventually result in the elicitation of the CR at a time proportional to the length of time between the CS and the UCS. In the second case, an interval of time is allowed to intervene between the offset of the CS and the onset of the UCS (termed "trace conditioning"). This will produce a conditioned response that will occur after the time when the CS ceases, but before the UCS begins, this time depending on the length of the CS-UCS interval. In the final case, the reverse of the ordinary conditioning process is used in that the UCS occurs before the CS (termed "backward conditioning"). This procedure results in conditioning that is very similar to regular conditioning, although such conditioning takes far longer than normal to produce and the resulting conditioned response tends to be very weak (to such an extent that there is some question whether this phenomenon actually exists).

The important fact about these modifications (and these are only a few of the many possible ones that Pavlov tested in the course of his experimentation) is that they are lawful and predictable and lie within the rubric of the basic experiment. Just as in the case of Thorndike, this lawfulness could serve as the basis of a theory that would eventually be used to explain a multiplicity of phenomena.

Let us now extend the Pavlovian experiment beyond the acquisition phase of learning and note that the lawfulness mentioned above can be demonstrated also in extinction. If the CS is presented alone a number of times without the UCS, the conditioned response will gradually fade in strength until it is no longer noticeable and can no longer be elicited by the CS. This extinction effect is systematically related to a number of conditions such as the strength of original conditioning, the conditions under which the extinction takes place, and several others.

Pavlov made an additional discovery concerning the dynamics of the extinction process. If an animal is placed in the conditioning apparatus and repeatedly presented with the CS without the UCS until the CR is extinguished and is then removed, when he is placed back in the apparatus and again presented with the CS the response will have returned. However, this regenerated response will be smaller and slower than before extinction procedures were begun.

This "spontaneous recovery" of the response can be demonstrated in most experimental animals and follows a lawful course. If the animal were put back in the apparatus several times under the conditions described above, the spontaneous recovery phenomenon would reappear for several occasions until the response would eventually no longer appear, or until total extinction took place. This entire process including acquisition, extinction, and spontaneous recovery is presented in the following diagram:

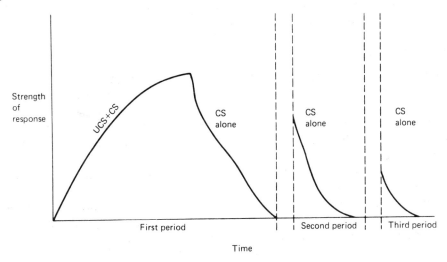

Figure 8-2 Changes in response strength during acquisition, extinction, and spontaneous recovery (hypothetical data).

The feature of this graph that deserves special emphasis is the fact that it is a "theoretical" graph rather than a directly measured empirical one. The facts of acquisition, extinction, and spontaneous recovery are essentially as depicted. However, it should be clear that the exact nature of the curves representing these phenomena cannot be directly known, but can only be inferred from observations of behavior and stimuli.

In an actual example of a Pavlovian experiment it is often impossible to know exactly what the strength of the learned response is at any particular moment. In most cases the procedure calls for the continual pairing of the CS and the UCS until the experimenter feels fairly certain the conditioning has taken place. The ability to make such judgments, of course, would come from many experiments and would depend on such factors as the nature of the conditioning experiment being performed, the nature of the organism being conditioned, etc.

When the experimenter feels that the animal has been conditioned, the CS would be presented alone to ascertain whether or not conditioning has taken place. While it is possible to measure drops of saliva, for example, to attempt to measure the actual strength of conditioning, it is clear that even this will not always serve as a true measure of strength since learning (or conditioning) must be above some threshold level before the organism will salivate to the CS. It is apparent, then, that a curve such as the one presented in Figure 8-2 will most certainly be only an estimation for the lower levels of the acquisition phase. This is essentially true for both extinction and spontaneous recovery.

Measures of Learning

This classical conditioning paradigm served as a plan not only for Pavlov's own research but for many other conditioning and learning researchers. Moreover, Pavlov's research called attention to three measures of learning which have been used singly or in combination by many learning researchers, including many who do not care to use the classical conditioning paradigm.

One measure of conditioning is *amplitude.* In Pavlov's research, this rather obviously referred, for example, to the amount of saliva produced with the conditioned response. This amount could be compared with the amount of saliva produced by the unconditioned response, and the experimenter could determine whether the eliciting power of the conditioned stimulus matched that of the unconditioned stimulus. When adopted by other learning researchers, amplitude came to be defined in a number of different ways, including the amount of force exerted by an organism on a lever or the extent of movement produced with a learned response.

Latency constitutes another measure of learning which emerged with Pavlov's studies but which has been incorporated in a variety of other studies as well. For Pavlov, latency could be measured as the lapse of time between the presentation of the conditioned stimulus and the occurrence of the conditioned response. Again, the conditioned reflex latency could be compared with the unconditioned reflex latency. Some researchers, using other research paradigms, have found latency to be a sensitive index of learning. For example, in some studies where correct responses can be scored as well as latencies measured, it is often found that the latency measures provide indications of differences in test item difficulties even when such differences are not easily seen in the correct/incorrect response data per se. Typically, one can find positive relationships between correctness of answers and response latencies, with greater proportions of correct answers on an item (for groups of subjects) being associated with shorter latencies for responses to that item than to items on which fewer correct responses are provided by the group.

Resistance to extinction is another learning measure which emerged as an interesting dependent variable from Pavlov's conditioning studies. For

Pavlov, this involved taking the organism through a series of conditioning trials and then presenting the conditioned stimulus alone until it no longer elicited the conditioned response. This resistance to extinction could be measured in time units but it more frequently has been defined in numbers of trials on which the conditioned response is elicited until no more responses occur or until a very low number of responses is made for a series of trials. For example, using the latter operational definition, the experimenter might continue providing the conditioned stimulus until the organism makes no more than one response in a series of seven successive presentations; once that point is reached, the experimenter would record the number of stimulus presentations from the beginning of the test series until the low occurrence rate was reached.

Some Other Phenomena Which Occur during Conditioning

Up to this point we have merely described the main behavioral effects of conditioning in their simplest form. In an extensive series of experiments, Pavlov was able to demonstrate many other effects. A sample of these will be provided to illustrate the complexity of the Pavlovian theoretical scheme.

External Inhibition Pavlov recognized that stimuli can both inhibit responses as well as elicit them, and that the inhibiting processes may indeed take a variety of forms. One rather obvious form is *external inhibition*, in which some external stimulus, extraneous to the conditioning process, can inhibit a response. A necessary condition is that this "random" stimulus is present just before or during presentation of the conditioned stimulus. We will comment more on external inhibition after we introduce and define the concept of internal inhibition.

Internal Inhibition *Internal inhibition* is that aspect of inhibition in which conditioning has taken place and has resulted in stimuli which inhibit the response. In a sense, such effects are internalized and consequently do *not* depend upon the physical presence of a random stimulus prior to or during presentation of the eliciting conditioned stimulus. The internal inhibition concept is interesting and important because it partly accounts for situations in which a given response is not elicited even when no opposing or inhibiting stimulus is apparent. External inhibition is viewed as a passive form due, according to Pavlov, to the diversion of energy from the excitation center (within the nervous system) of the conditioned stimulus which would otherwise flow to the appropriate excitation center and produce the response. Internal inhibition is an active form of inhibition in that it involves an actual blocking of the conditioned response by means of previously established conditioned inhibiting stimuli.

Disinhibition   *Disinhibition* can simply be described as an inhibition of an inhibition. In brief, one can envision a hypothetical situation where stimulus "A" is the conditioned stimulus which can normally elicit response "A." But either through a random stimulus and the external inhibition process or through some internal inhibition process, another stimulus "B" has come to inhibit response "A," thus reducing the signaling power of the conditioned stimulus "A." Now a third stimulus "C" occurs and at least temporarily blocks the effects of the inhibiting stimulus "B," thus increasing or restoring the eliciting power of stimulus "A."

Stimulus Generalization   When a CR has been created to a specific stimulus, similar stimuli will frequently have the power of eliciting the response. For example, if a tone of 254 cycles per second were used as the CS, tones which are similar in pitch to this tone will also produce the response, with the strength of this effect diminishing as the tones become increasingly different.

Response Generalization   After a specific response has been conditioned to a specific stimulus, it can be demonstrated that the same stimulus will also produce similar responses. For example, if a dog has been trained to flex his right leg when a light comes on, he may also produce the response of flexing one of his other legs if the original response is in some way inhibited.

Summation   A combination of stimuli will often have a stronger effect than any of the components taken separately. For example, both the sight and smell of food can act on the dog to produce a conditioned response. These two sets of stimuli will summate to produce a heightened effect.

Discrimination   Since an animal will often respond to stimuli other than the one originally used in conditioning (stimulus generalization) it is often important to have the organism respond to only a limited set of stimuli rather than to the entire complex. This can be done by pairing only the specific stimulus with the UCS and not pairing any of the alternative stimuli. For example, 254 cps could be followed by food while 275 would not be. With time the animal would come to discriminate between the two stimuli by salivating to 254 but not to 275.

This list is in no sense complete but includes only a sample of the lawful phenomena that Pavlov discovered in his laboratory. The power of the theory lay in its ability to subsume so many phenomena under a common and fairly simple fabric.

Classical Conditioning and Complex Behavior

The picture presented above of the basic Pavlovian experiment can now be extended to include more complex forms of behavior. We will do this through a description of an experiment and then show how Pavlov used the basic idea of the conditioned reflex as a building block for highly complex behavior.

In performing a typical Pavlovian experiment, it becomes evident that stimuli other than the original CS can also come to elicit the CR. For example, if a light is flashed just previous to the sound of the bell (which has been paired enough times with the UCS to have been conditioned) the light itself may acquire the power to elicit the conditioned response. In other words, a different neutral stimulus may become the CS by being associated with the primary CS.

This phenomenon, termed by Pavlov *higher-order conditioning*, can serve as the mechanism for building complex "chains" of stimuli that control the behavior of organisms. If any stimulus can become associated with the response of a primary reflex with the proper pairing and sequencing, it should be evident that highly complex behaviors, which on the surface might appear to be of a different nature than simple conditioned responses, are in fact not any different.

The rules and principles that govern such behavior may well be the same as those that Pavlov had delineated for the conditioned response. This assertion must remain essentially theoretical (for one thing because long chains of higher-order conditioned reflexes are extremely difficult to produce in the laboratory). However, it represents what Pavlov intended his theory to do—to explain the many varieties of behavior by a parsimonious principle.

It is a common experience for certain tastes or smells to elicit the memory of events that have happened long ago. The power of such stimuli to arouse memories can be viewed as a long-term effect of classical conditioning. Such stimuli, having occurred in temporal contiguity with some environmental event (such as hearing a song while on a date), have become conditioned stimuli capable of producing a complex series of responses that bring forth the memory of the event.

The strength of this effect (both in that it probably has occurred as the result of one pairing, and in that it has lasted so long) can indicate how the basic conditioned response can serve as the foundation of molar behavior. The following will serve as an example: Imagine that a child on his first day of school is given some chocolate milk that is spoiled. By drinking this milk the child subsequently becomes ill.

The fact that this event happened in school is, of course, not causally related to the event of getting ill, but those stimuli that occur in the schoolroom can become conditioned to the events leading to the illness. The effect of this, through stimulus generalization and higher-order conditioning, could be to produce illness whenever the child enters any classroom. If the events leading up to this had not been known it could be assumed that this behavior is complexly determined. In reality, it is merely an example of classical conditioning. While the above is probably too simplified to be anything close to reality, its point should be clear. Any behavior, if its developmental course could be traced, could be found to originate in some original reflex which has been associated with originally neutral stimuli. Such is the character of Pavlovian psychology.

In much the same way, Pavlov attempted to explain the acquisition and function of language. It is generally agreed that man, unlike animals, has the ability to use speech and writing as means of communication. Pavlov theorized that, for animals and humans, reflexes could account for ways in which we respond to many physical stimuli in our environment. But man can also respond to words, sentences, phrases, and other parts of language. What is particularly significant is that we can respond to the *meanings* of sounds (sounds such as words, sentences, etc.) as well as to the physical qualities of the sounds.

Pavlov theorized that language might be treated as a complex form of higher-order conditioning which not only follows many principles which are relevant to simple conditioning processes but which also involves special additional principles as well. He called physical objects *primary signals*, and used the term *secondary signals* to refer to language. He viewed words, for example, as *secondary* signals because they are signals of signals: a chair would thus be a primary signal while the *word* "chair" would constitute a secondary signal, since it can be used in place of the physical object through language.

As a simplified example, take the response to the word "apple." Originally, this word will elicit no response from a preverbal child. However, with time the *sight* of the apple will come to elicit many of the same responses as does the actual taste of the apple. In other words, the sight of the apple has become a conditioned stimulus. Now, if the sound of the word "apple" is paired with the sight of the apple, this sound will come—through the process of higher-order conditioning—to produce the same response (or similar response) as does sight and taste of the apple. The word has come to have "meaning" because it produces the same set of responses as the original environmental stimulus. When the word "meal" is pronounced in the presence of a hungry man, his mouth will water. In essence he is responding just as he would if the meal were actually in his mouth. By processes such as this (and these processes would of course become more complex when units of language were analyzed) the phenomenon of language could be explained.

It should be recognized that a dog could just as well be conditioned to respond to the word "food" as could a human being. In a dog, however, something quite different is happening since he is responding to the specific *sound* of the word and *not* to its *conceptual meaning*. Only in the human organisms, possessing the capacity to utilize the second signal system, can speech be developed. Pavlov theorized that it was the human nervous system which enables us to respond to the symbolic meaning of the sounds we call speech. He held that the principles which he had delineated for primary signals should also apply to secondary signals since the same nervous system was used for both. Thus it was the capacity of the nervous system and not the fundamental laws of behavior which would distinguish between primary signal system activities and secondary signal system activities. As Pavlov has been reported to say, "Speech is a real conditional stimulus to human beings, as real as the others, which are common to animals as well; but this one stimulus is far more inclusive than any other. In this respect there is no comparison, qualitative or quantitative, between speech and the conditional stimuli of animals" (Cuny, 1965, p. 86).

Can classical conditioning principles, in regard to the paradigm which we have considered here, adequately account for complex animal and human behavior? For some, an enthusiastic, positive answer was proposed when Pavlov's ideas first became known in this country. For many others, a more cautious answer is indicated. But few seem to deny the likelihood that at least some concepts and principles from classical conditioning can serve to provide useful guidelines for studying complex animal and human learning. We will consider this matter again in the next section.

BASIC RESEARCH IN
THE PAVLOVIAN TRADITION

It has been estimated that over 6,000 experiments have been conducted using the Pavlovian classical conditioning paradigm (Razran, 1965). They have ranged all the way from conditioning of organisms with extremely simple nervous systems to attempts to condition quite complex human language and other symbolic processes. Researchers have differed in their interpretations of the meaning of the Pavlovian paradigm, with some suggesting that it constitutes an externalization of fundamental learning processes and others regarding it merely as a convenient and highly useful set of experimental procedures to study various theoretical questions. Thus some essentially accept the paradigm as a tentative *model* of internal, physiologically based learning changes, while others use the experimental procedures but draw on other theoretical systems to conceptualize their data.

Focusing on *those* psychologists and other researchers *who accept some form* of a classical conditioning *model*, there are at least three different views which can be identified as to the kinds of learning processes which can be conceptualized within this model. First, a vocal and not insignificant minority contend that there is only one type of learning process and that classical conditioning constitutes the basic form by which learning processes occur. Others, probably the majority by far,

hold that there are two fundamental types of learning, classical conditioning and some form of instrumental conditioning in the Thorndikian
tradition. Actually a substantial number of the classical conditioning
studies had at least a minor objective of determining ways in which the
classical and instrumental conditioning processes are similar or different.
For example, Bindra (1972) suggests that the two are the same fundamental "contingency learning" process and that the apparent differences stem
from the particular controlling stimuli in each type. In the classical
conditioning experimental arrangement, the environmental correlate is an
antecedent stimulus with eliciting influences on behavior, whereas a consequent stimulus is the environmental correlate and controlling influence in
the instrumental conditioning paradigm. Other researchers theorize that
the differences between classical and instrumental conditioning constitute
such characteristics that different aspects of the nervous system are
involved. As an oversimplified but brief characterization, classical conditioning is theoretically involved with involuntary behavior while instrumental conditioning involves voluntary behavior.

The third group—one which seems to have grown steadily over the
past two decades—accepts classical conditioning as one fundamental type
or aspect of learning but contends that there are a number of other types
as well. Moreover, these researchers frequently consider classical conditioning to be one of the simplest forms of learning. For example, Razran
(1971)—a long-time authority on classical conditioning—has proposed
eleven neurophysiologically oriented and evolution-based types of learning. This hierarchical arrangement is sufficiently outlined and related to
experimental data that it almost certainly will influence future conceptions. There are four levels within which the eleven types are organized.
The simplest form is "a primitive category of nonassociative, precondi-
tioned learning [which includes] two types" (p. 17). "Habituation"
primarily seems to involve decreases in reacting to stimuli. "Sensitization"
is the increase in responsiveness as a result of stimulation. At the next
level, "simple-associative, or conditioned, learning," are three types—
"inhibitory conditioning," which involves decreases in associations
through incompatible or inhibiting associations; classical conditioning; and
instrumental conditioning which Razran calls "reinforcement conditioning." There are three types at the perceptual learning level—"sensory
preconditioning" is a conditioning to signs or symbols; "configuring" is a
higher order conditioning process somewhat like gestalt patterning;
"eductive learning" is a higher level of the configuring process which
involves anticipation or apprehension of things and events. The highest
level is that of "symboling" or thinking, which also has three types—"(1) a
specific-symbolic level, in which neurocognitive meanings are not yet
separated from effector units of language and for which the term symbo-
semic will be coined, (2) a sememic level, when ultimate units of identical

as well as related meaning are served by different linguistic units, and (3) a *logicemic* level, with general logical propositions dominating particular language" (Razran, 1971, p. 279).

It is noteworthy that Razran depicts his book as "a ramified outgrowth of my long interest in what is termed, in Pavlovian tradition, 'evolution of higher nervous activity' " (Razran, 1971, p. vii). He illustrates the fact that the Pavlovian conditioning *paradigm* discussed earlier in this chapter is an important component of classical conditioning but that at least some proponents of the Pavlovian approach do not confine themselves to a narrow conception of this paradigm.

Many other researchers in the Pavlovian tradition have focused more on the particular set of experimental operations than on classical conditioning as a theoretical framework. The papers published in *Classical Conditioning II: Current Theory and Research*, edited by Black and Prokasy (1972) illustrate this view. These editors selected papers and organized them under four topics—"models and theory; the conditioned stimulus; multiple response measurement; and the relationship of classical conditioning to operant conditioning" (p. xi). They depicted the unifying theme of classical conditioning "as a set of operations from both speculations about the kinds of effects that CS and UCS events may have on S, and theories or hypotheses intended to account for behavior changes contingent upon the pairing of CS and UCS" (p. xi). In brief, they and many other researchers view classical conditioning procedures as viable means by which one can externalize and unravel some of the simple and complex associative processes which are believed to go on in conjunction with learning processes. In part the Black and Prokasy volume reflects the atheoretical or antitheoretical orientation which emerged in the psychology of learning since mid-century. But perhaps more importantly, it also illustrates that many contemporary psychologists continue to see merits in using long-established approaches to the study of learning despite or in conjunction with some of the more recently emerging approaches.

EXTENT OF PRACTICAL APPLICATIONS

Though the Pavlovian classical conditioning paradigm has had such great impact on *basic* psychology learning research, the matter of practical applications poses a puzzling situation. It is alleged that much Soviet educational practice is or was based on Pavlovian learning theory, but our extensive search of the literature reveals comparatively few details about these applications at least in English-language journals. Those reports which have been available seem to indicate that the "Pavlovian theory" has been very broadly interpreted so as to include many different psychology theories rather than the more delimited experimental arrangements and theoretical concepts which we have considered in this chapter. With regard to the United States, there have been comparatively few direct applications of Pavlovian theory in education but, interestingly enough, rather extensive uses in clinical psychology and psychiatry. Moreover, the applications typically have been attempted by practitioners who have been taught or have read about the theory, with little apparent interest on the part of most basic researchers, with a few notable exceptions.

One of the earliest applications of Pavlovian theory was attempted in the 1930s by O. H. Mowrer (1938), a researcher and practitioner. In brief, he treated an enuresis problem by direct application of the classical conditioning paradigm. The plan requires that the child sleep on a special mat containing two metal grids. If urine hits the pad, an electric circuit is completed and a loud bell or buzzer is sounded. Within a short series of such events in which the child is awakened by the sound, he soon begins to awaken in time to go to the bathroom. The loud sound serves as an unconditioned stimulus whose control over the waking process (response to be conditioned) is transferred to the internal bladder pressure and other sensations (conditioned stimuli).

But despite rather widespread recognition that Mowrer's technique was effective, classical conditioning procedures were not generally used in clinical or educational situations for the next decade. However, at mid-century a number of such applications emerged. For example, Salter (1949; 1961) published a therapy book based on Pavlovian classical conditioning theory. His choice of a featured quotation indicates his orientation: ". . . 'all the highest nervous activity, as it manifests itself in the conditioned reflex, consists of a continual change of these three fundamental processes—*excitation, inhibition,* and *disinhibition*'—Ivan P. Pavlov" (Salter, 1949, p. iii).

Salter criticized the psychoanalysis-dominated psychotherapy methods which emphasize "depth" explanations of neurotic behaviors. For example, it was customary then—and now, for many therapists—to theorize that maladaptive behavioral patterns such as anxiety, phobias, and asocial behavior represent some underlying emotional experience, and that the overt behavior will really change only after the underlying conflicts or other problems are resolved. Salter argued that these ideas had been formulated by Freud and others before we had adequate understanding of learning processes, and that many symptoms actually could be relieved directly without explicit concern with such alleged, and possibly no longer existent, underlying problems. He proposed that both the initial maladjustment and the attempted psychotherapeutic ventures can most effectively and economically be conceptualized as *learning* processes. Moreover, he advocated using Pavlov's classical conditioning model as the basis for understanding the maladaptive behavior and for planning psychotherapeutic interventions.

To Salter, one of Pavlov's key concepts relevant to psychotherapy (at least as interpreted by Salter) is that the psychologically healthy individual has some optimal balance between excitation and inhibition. That is, we maintain a certain degree of spontaneity while having our behavior elicited by some stimuli and inhibited by others. Maladjustment—especially in neuroses—frequently involves an excessive extent of inhibited behaviors so that the person feels too constrained. This excessive inhibition in turn leads to pent-up feelings which are handled through hostile expressions, some of which may be destructive or cause harm for the person or others. Classifying persons as "excitatory," "inhibitory," etc. in terms of their responsiveness to stimuli, Salter claimed: "We know that the inhibitory are more prone than the excitatory to be filled with hatreds. We know that though the characters of people may vary under different societies, disinhibition is the same thing organically and chemically in any culture, and individuals in a state of excitatory-inhibitory balance will get along quite well with each other" (1961, p. 318). While acknowledging that some patients need to build up appropriate excitations and inhibitions—that is, they need to learn, through classical conditioning, to respond to some stimuli and to be inhibited by others—he suggested that many of his patients need to break the influence of inhibiting stimuli. In brief, he adapted the classical conditioning paradigm to teach his patients how to react spontaneously to stimuli without being concerned about the consequences of their acts. Wherever possible, the change was facilitated by pairing words and visual images of the currently inhibiting stimuli with stimuli which elicited quick responses.

During therapy sessions and throughout their daily activities, Salter had his patients practice responding spontaneously to situations without thinking excessively as to whether their particular acts would be socially proper. He recommended that they state how they feel and that they express their feelings by facial expressions and body movements. Particularly inhibited patients are encouraged to use "I" frequently in their conversations and to agree and provide an appropriate return compliment when someone comments favorably about them. Salter contended that he was adapting Pavlov's disinhibition techniques by these procedures.

For whatever reasons, Salter's approach was not widely accepted when he presented it in 1949, although he did continue to publish papers about it. Some critics questioned the accuracy and sophistication of his use of Pavlovian concepts, but the main reactions at that time seemed to center around the contention that he was merely(?) changing symptoms without resolving the problems underlying and allegedly producing the symptoms. In part, this reflected the considerable influence that psychoanalysis had on psychotherapy procedures during the 1940s and 1950s.

Another psychotherapy position which also drew some of its concepts from Pavlovian theory was that of Wolpe (for example, 1958). Wolpe presented a position called psychotherapy by reciprocal inhibition which seems at once to be more systematically related to learning theory and to be oriented to practical human learning processes in psychotherapy. It is noteworthy that other therapists were rather slow in adopting Wolpe's concepts and techniques in the late 1950s but that the popularity of learning theory–based psychotherapy theories increased substantially by the middle 1960s. As we will discuss in later chapters on Skinner's operant conditioning and on behavior modification, this interest grew to such an extent in the 1960s that the Association for the Advancement of Behavior Therapy was formed and began to have a dominating influence on psychotherapy training and practice.

Wolpe had read about Pavlovian and Hullian theories and had conducted some experiments applying Pavlovian procedures with animals before formulating his views about psychotherapy. He showed, at least to his own satisfaction, that animals can develop neurotic symptoms as a result of classical conditioning processes. For example, he replicated some earlier classical conditioning studies in which one shape, a circle, is paired with electrical shock and another stimulus, an oval, is paired with food. As the oval is made more and more round, so that it becomes difficult to distinguish it from the circle, animals begin to urinate and otherwise act as though they are quite anxious. Wolpe theorized that if anxiety and other neurotic symptoms seem to be produced by classical conditioning processes, then it may be possible to eliminate neurotic symptoms by psychotherapy techniques which also follow the classical conditioning paradigm.

One type of symptom widely treated by the procedures Wolpe and colleagues developed is a phobia, or abnormal (excessive) fear of particular objects, places, or conditions. One aspect of Wolpe's approach is to identify the stimuli which elicit phobic anxiety and general discomfort and to arrange the stimuli in terms of the degree of anxiety elicited. These stimuli are subsequently treated as conditioned stimuli. He then selects other stimuli, which will serve as unconditioned stimuli, which elicit an incompatible pleasant response.

The task set for the therapist and patient is to transfer the control of the unconditioned stimuli to the conditioned stimuli so that they will elicit pleasant experiences and inhibit anxiety responses. With a patient who has an intensive fear of snakes, the therapist would try to find the kinds of snake-related stimuli which elicit a great deal of anxiety and those which cause only slight discomfort. For example, touching a live snake would be rated very high, whereas looking at a picture of a snake at a distance of six feet (from the patient to the picture) would be rated low. The therapist and patient would also choose stimuli which elicit feelings of relaxation and pleasure, such as soft music and a very comfortable chair. After having learned how to relax in the absence of any words or other stimuli related to snakes, the patient would be presented a stimulus (such as the picture at a distance) related to snakes. Gradually higher and higher rated stimuli would be presented, with periodic rest and uninterrupted relaxation. Subsequently, the patient would learn to remain relaxed and to have pleasant experiences even when confronted with the live snakes which had previously produced great anxiety.

In order that the patient would also gain greater comfort outside the therapy situation, he would be conditioned to objects, words, and visual imagery which would assist him in attaining feelings of relaxation and pleasure. With the combination of systematic practice periods during the therapy sessions and techniques for extending the stimulus control outside, the patient would learn (be conditioned) to relax and feel pleasant even under conditions which previously had produced considerable anxiety and discomfort.

These brief descriptions illustrate a few of the many psychotherapeutic applications of classical conditioning found in clinical psychology and psychiatry today. In recent years, these and other learning theory-based techniques have been adopted not only by therapists who primarily identify themselves as "behavior therapists" but also by therapists of various other theoretical persuasions. The current trend seems to be toward using techniques based on many different theories rather than toward relying exclusively on only one theory. In this context, many therapists view classical conditioning as an acceptable model for conceptualizing some problems and for planning certain therapeutic interventions.

It is conceivable that similar changes may be occurring in educational applications as well. As we indicated earlier in this chapter, some have suggested that classical conditioning might account for ways in which children sometimes develop bad feelings about going to school. Other educators have also suggested that paired presentation of object pictures and words can be a useful means for teaching English vocabulary, and that pairing of English words and foreign language words (such as French, German, etc.) might help students to build their vocabulary in a foreign language. Whereas the earlier and rather limited attempts to use classical conditioning frequently included the contention that *all* aspects should be considered as part of this paradigm, future applications will probably be made on a more limited and carefully defined set of educational tasks.

EDUCATIONAL R&D IMPLICATIONS

Pavlov's papers and books on psychological topics include a large number of basic studies, mainly published in the first few decades of this century, and various essays about practical problems, which were mainly published in the 1930s and 1940s. Though classical conditioning continues to be an active area of interest in psychology today, some authors seem ready to dismiss this theory as of limited historical interest or, even worse, as an example of an unproductive blind-alley venture in psychology. Such a view is partly supported by the fact that many contemporary classical conditioning papers do focus on narrowly circumscribed problems of little interest except to other researchers engaged in similar studies.

But it would seem unfortunate totally to dismiss this theory's potential contributions to education. No matter what theoretical preference one might have, one cannot easily ignore the wide range of phenomena which lend themselves to conceptualization within the classical conditioning framework. Moreover, the extensive popularity of certain behavior modification procedures which are primarily based on Pavlovian theory argues for the possibility that more extensive use could be made of similar concepts and principles in educational situations.

We have already commented on the differences of opinion among classical conditioning proponents as to the range of phenomena which can be handled by this theory. But we have also summarized some suggestions (by Razran) that the Pavlovian theory can serve as a basis for organizing a hierarchy of learning processes ranging from simple to very complex phenomena. Even at a minimum, it would seem that the classical conditioning literature can serve as a rich source of ideas, concepts, and principles about ways in which stimuli elicit behavior.

SUGGESTED READINGS

Black, A. H., & Prokasy, W. F. (Eds.) *Classical conditioning II: Current theory and research.* New York: Appleton-Century-Crofts, 1972.

Kimble, G. A. *Hilgard and Marquis' conditioning and learning.* New York: Appleton-Century-Crofts, 1961.

Korolev, F. F. Main trends of methodological research in the field of pedagogy. *Soviet Education,* 1969, 11(12), 7-24.

Paul, G. L., & Berstein, D. A. *Anxiety and clinical problems: Systematic desensitization and related techniques.* Morristown, New Jersey: General Learning Press, 1973.

Pavlov, I. P. *Conditioned reflexes.* London: Oxford University Press, 1927.

Pavlov, I. P. *Lectures on conditioned reflexes.* New York: International, 1928.

Pavlov, I. P. *Conditioned reflexes and psychiatry.* New York: International, 1941.

Prokasy, W. F. (Ed.) *Classical conditioning: A symposium.* New York: Appleton-Century-Crofts, 1965.

Razran, G. *Mind in evolution: An east-west synthesis of learned behavior and cognition.* Boston: Houghton-Mifflin, 1971.

Wolpe, J. *The practice of behavior therapy.* Elmsford, New York: Pergamon, 1969a.

Wolpe, J. Psychotherapeutic efficacy and objective research. In Strupp, H. H., & Bergin, A. E. (Eds.), Critical evaluation of some empirical and conceptual bases for coordinated research in psychotherapy. *International Journal of Psychiatry,* 1969b, 7, 157-159.

9
Clark L. Hull and Hypothetico-Deductive Behavior Theory

If any psychologist were asked to name the individual whose research and ideas were most influential in the psychology of learning during the 1930s, 1940s, and into the 1950s, it is highly probable that Clark L. Hull (1884-1952) would be the person designated. Hull drew many concepts strategies, and ideas from Pavlov and Thorndike, but for more than two decades it was largely Hull's personal views which dominated psychology's theorizing ventures, not only about learning but also about behavior more generally. His endorsement and vigorous advocacy of a hypothetico-deductive approach to theory construction almost dictated the ways in which both students and more experienced psychologists prepared their research plans and interpreted their data during this time. His drive reduction (later, drive-stimulus reduction) conception of reinforcement as a fundamental process in learning served as a rich and fruitful source of research questions for several decades.

In the 1970s some say in retrospect that Hull's original theory no longer has any major impact on contemporary theorizing about learning; others contend that his ideas continue to influence contemporary research, though even his most loyal supporters have reservations as to whether Hull's grand theory is still being followed or developed. But all would agree that students of the psychology of learning should have at least a basic understanding of the approach and the nature of learning theory which Hull envisioned and to which he devoted practically all his professional life.

Earlier (Chapter 3) we described some of the contributions Hull made to psychology theory construction. It is the main purpose of the present chapter to provide more details about the major concepts and principles incorporated in his theory. But it is neither feasible nor necessarily desirable to get involved in the more intricate aspects of his theory—some aspects of which even his most ardent "neobehavioristic" heirs no longer endorse. Thus we will review Hull's background and general orientation to the psychology of learning, his fundamental assumptions or postulates and the major concepts of his theory, illustrations of his quantitative statements, his own modifications and other psychologists' contributions to contemporary neobehaviorism theory, and Hullian-neobehaviorism views about practical applications.

BACKGROUND

Hull was born in 1884 in a log house near Akron, New York, but he spent most of his youth under "pioneer conditions," by his own account (Hull, 1952a), on a farm in Michigan. In many respects the first thirty years of his life seemed quite common, with no clear indication that he subsequently would command such widespread respect in psychology. But early in his career he did demonstrate capacity for developing his intellectual abilities despite adversity. For example typhoid fever resulted in partial memory impairment, and a year's setback with poliomyelitis (at age twenty-four) disrupted his plans to become a mining engineer. Instead of being deterred from useful activities, he decided to become a psychologist. He wanted some contact with philosophy, in that he was interested in theory, but he did not want to get involved with the metaphysical questions posed by philosophers of that era. He apparently chose psychology partly because he felt that there was room for advancement and that he would have opportunity to combine his interest in theory with his interest in working with automatic apparatus.

Hull had at least a fair share of difficulties as he tried to pursue his academic career. In addition to the medical problems mentioned above, he also lacked financial support. Thus he had to alternate between going to school and teaching in rural schools, on one occasion for a year, and on another for two years. His graduate fellowship application was rejected by Cornell and Yale. But through the intervention of one of his professors he was appointed as a graduate student teaching assistant at the University of Wisconsin, from which he received his Ph.D. in psychology in 1918. It is of some interest that during this time, because of fears about memory problems, he began writing his reactions to ideas he read and heard, recording them in a series of notebooks. These notebooks served an even more important purpose later because they stimulated him to think critically and systematically about psychology and they aided him in a number of ways in formulating his learning theory. His first 13 years as a psychologist (two of them while a graduate student) were spent as a faculty member at the University of Wisconsin. In 1929 he became professor of psychology at Yale University's Institute of Human Relations, where he became the key architect in evolving a comprehensive learning theory, a theory which influenced Yale psychology research for the next several decades.

At least by 1930 Hull was convinced that psychology could be a true natural science, that quantitative laws could be delineated and quite rigorous research procedures and sound empirical theory could be developed. Possibly drawing from his earlier training in the physical sciences, he contended that even the complex behavior of an individual organism could be measured and reliably predicted if psychology embarked on a systematic program to develop logically derived and empirically tested theory.

The main thrust would be to delineate a small set of primary laws from which additional secondary laws could be derived. The complex phenomena of learning processes, and behavior more generally, would most readily and rapidly be understood once the primary laws of simple processes were outlined. "With these and similar views as a background, the task of psychologists obviously is that of laying bare these laws as quickly and accurately as possible, particularly the primary laws" (Hull, 1952a, p. 155).

From various accounts, it seems clear that Hull examined most of the theories extant at that time before formulating his own ideas. As a result, it is not easy to indicate the one or more psychologists most influential on Hull's thinking. He obviously was greatly influenced by Pavlov and Thorndike. He initially chose classical conditioning as the most fundamental learning process but then decided that it was only one special case of the law of effect. He considered many of Watson's ideas about behaviorism, but he concluded that Watson and his supporters were too dogmatic and evangelistic to be taken literally in establishing psychology as a science. Hull arranged for Koffka to spend a year at the University of Wisconsin and he tried to see ways in which gestalt theory might be valuable in studying fundamental learning processes. He concluded that the gestalt psychologists were serving as reasonably well-informed critics of behaviorism but that they were mainly acting as a corrective influence rather than offering a viable alternative.

Hull obviously was quite aware of the debates which raged among proponents of the various competing "schools" of psychology during the first few decades of this century. Even though his own position was compatible with some of the views being promoted, he was quite critical of the process of *debating* about psychological theory. The title of a paper he published in 1935 indicates his concern about the state of psychology theory at that time; it was titled *The Conflicting Psychologies of Learning—A Way Out*. Criticizing the speculation which he felt was characteristic of most debates, he argued that psychologists would be better advised to spend their energies conducting research rather than debating. More specifically, psychologists should follow the example of Newton's *Principia* as a model of how scientific theories could and should be developed. He pointed to Newton's reliance on logic to outline the topic to be studied and to identify basic assumptions from which a first outline of fundamental principles could be derived, with the results from extensive experimentation serving to test out and to modify the theory.

Hull was such a prolific writer and great influence on other researchers and theorists that we can present only a sample of his major theoretical contributions. In addition to a continuing stream of research papers and countless informal papers circulated among Hullian proponents, several key theoretical books can be identified. *Principles of Behavior* (1943) was the first in a series of three books (only two of which were ever completed) in which he had planned "to cover in an elementary manner the range of ordinary mammalian behavior" (Hull, 1952b, p. vii).

In the first volume he gave a tentative systematic description of the fundamental principles of behavior as viewed from a molar behavioristic view rather than from a molecular physiological view. He revised these principles in a supplementary book, *Essentials of Behavior*, in 1951 and shortly thereafter—just before his death—presented the second of his planned three major theoretical books. The third book in the planned series, which would have dealt with social behavior and some practical implications of his work, was never completed.

We will primarily focus on Hull's theory as outlined in *Principles of Behavior* (1943) because it is recognized as the "most influential, true reinforcement theory of learning" (Logan, 1971, p. 45) and because many contemporary neobehaviorists refer to this theoretical book when comparing their interpretations with Hull's views (cf. Kimble, 1961).

ESSENTIALS OF THE THEORY

Hull viewed psychology as a true natural science capable of having quantitative laws of behavior much as have been evolved over a period of many years in other sciences. He contended that every science involves a continuous interaction between tentatively formulated principles based on logically derived assumptions and interpretations of data and ongoing laboratory studies which are designed to test and to modify the theory. We will first describe Hull's conception of an adaptive organism and then will describe examples of the three major classes of variables (independent, intervening, and dependent) which he used to conceptualize learning processes, and the original sixteen postulates from which his principles were derived with some of the major concepts in his theory.

Hull's Adaptive Organism

To Hull, both humans and lower animals are characterized as "self-maintaining mechanisms." By this he meant that one can view an organism as a dynamic system whose behaviors occur and are modified (*learned*) in accordance with the extent to which the organism's most pressing needs are satisfied and a more or less general state of equilibrium is maintained. Hull considered it conceptually useful to view the organism's behavior as being controlled by environmental stimuli (internal and external) which guide it to need gratification. Although he acknowledged that organisms have a large number of complex acts in which they engage for protracted survival and need gratification, he felt that all behaviors (simple as well as complex learning processes) have as a core certain fundamental principles. Since these fundamental principles can be more easily observed in simple processes, one major task for psychologists is to identify simple behavioral processes and to search for basic laws which describe these simple processes.

Independent, Intervening,
and Dependent Variables

One way to proceed would be to agree on ways by which one can measure learning—that is, to select *dependent* variables—and then to identify those variables which influence learning. But Hull recognized quite early that the identification of variables which influence learning would not be an easy task. For example, he observed that what an organism does in any given situation "...depends jointly (1) upon the state of disequilibrium or need of the organism and (2) upon the characteristics of the environment, external and internal" (Hull, 1943, p. 384). Thus learning would be viewed as being influenced not only by *independent* variables which can be more or less directly measured but also by *intervening* variables which are functionally connected to both independent and dependent variables. Instead of direct measurement, these variables must be estimated or inferred from stimulus and response conditions. We'll comment briefly about each of these three classes of variables—dependent, independent, and intervening—as incorporated in Hull's theory.

Dependent Variables   Like many other learning researchers, Hull used three dependent variables delineated by Pavlov. These are practically self-explanatory: *amplitude* refers to the amount or strength of the response; *latency* involves the lapse of time from the occurrence of the stimulus until the response occurs; and *resistance to extinction* can be measured in number of responses or time until the last response is made after reinforcement is discontinued. Hull also sometimes used probability statements concerning the likelihood that certain behaviors would occur.

Independent Variables   Given his general behavioristic orientation and his views about an adaptive organism, it is not too difficult to identify some of the independent variables which he believed to influence behavior. For example, one would include all the measurable external and internal stimuli impinging on the organism, those stimuli of which the organism is deprived which are relevant to pressing needs, and the kinds and amounts of rewards which might strengthen behavior. One could rather easily measure external stimuli in terms of physical properties of the environment. For example, one could quantify the amount of noise in a room, the colors and sizes of visual stimuli which might evoke responses, and the foods and liquids which might satisfy respective hunger and thirst needs. One could even quantify such internal stimuli as muscular tensions and glandular secretions. Though not explicitly included as an independent variable in his earlier formulations, Hull also subsequently considered measurable descriptions of response requirements as independent variables; for example, one could measure the amount of force and distance of movement required in order to operate a lever or to make some particular response. But despite many varied attempts to quantify such independent variables as incluences on behavior, Hull was convinced by the work of a number of other psychologists (for example, Woodworth, Tolman, Spence) that he would also have to consider summary variables which intervene between stimuli and responses and which are important influences on behavior.

Intervening Variables In comparison with Hull's dependent and independent variables, his intervening variables are less obvious and, for some students, more difficult to understand. Whereas one can observe the actual occurrence of behaviors and can describe characteristics of the external and internal stimuli, additional *intervening* variables may be useful in summarizing the residual effects of past experiences and/or the interacting effects of current circumstances.

Wherever an attempt is made to penetrate the invisible world of the molecular, scientists frequently and usefully employ logical constructs, intervening variables, or symbols to facilitate their thinking. These symbols or X's represent entities or processes which, if existent, would account for certain events in the observable molar world. Examples of such postulated entities in the field of the physical sciences are electrons, protons, positrons, etc. A closely parallel concept in the field of behavior familiar to everyone is that of *habit* as distinguished from habitual action. The habit presumably exists as an invisible condition of the nervous system quite as much when it is not mediating action as when habitual action is occurring; the habits upon which swimming is based are just as truly existent when a person is on the dance floor as when he is in the water. (Hull, 1943, p. 21)

It is important to emphasize that Hull considered it essential to "securely anchor" (Hull's terms) *all* intervening variables to *observable* independent and dependent variables. Accordingly, most of his intervening variables may be viewed as formal constructs (that is, without any mystical connotations) which have been introduced to summarize and replace many empirical generalizations with a few explanatory concepts. While Hull apparently thought of these intervening variables as representing physiological processes and events, it is possible to ignore or to eliminate all the alleged physiological properties of most intervening variables without damage to the theory.

As examples of intervening variables, let us briefly consider five which were of central importance in Hull's 1943 system and which were included in similar or revised forms in his final theory (Hull, 1952): *habit* or *habit strength* $(_SH_R)$, *drive* (D), *excitatory potential* $(_SE_R)$, *effective reaction potential* $(_S\bar{E}_R)$, and *momentary effective reaction potential* $(_S\dot{\bar{E}}_R)$.

Hull depicted learning as involving formation of connections between responses and evoking stimuli; he called these connections *habits*. He proposed that extent of learning, or *habit strength*, be measured or estimated on a 100-point scale with 0 representing no connection (that is, the response would not be evoked by a stimulus other than on a chance basis) and 100 representing the maximum learning possible. Habit strength is calculated for the training situation, while generalized habit strength must then be calculated for new situations.

Hull conceptualized the motivational status of the organism as involving a number of needs or *drives* (D). He proposed that, since such drives would vary in strength, each drive strength should be stated on a 100-point scale with 0 constituting no motivation of that kind and 100 representing the strongest possible drive strength.

He took the general language idea of reaction tendency or potential for making a given response to a particular stimulus and suggested that it be given more precise meaning. He proposed that the term *excitatory potential* ($_S E_R$) be used to describe the evoking power of a stimulus. (He sometimes used the terms *reaction potential* or *reaction-evocation potentiality* instead of *excitatory potential*.) Though he later modified his views, in his 1943 system Hull generally characterized an organism's excitatory potential as being based on habit strength multiplied by drive. However, a number of other variables must be considered in predicting whether a given stimulus will evoke a particular response.

Effective reaction potential ($_S \bar{E}_R$) is generally defined as excitatory potential less the total inhibiting influences which can diminish the likelihood that the stimulus will evoke the response. But Hull also recognized that the organism's responsiveness to a stimulus might vary over time as a result of possible undesignated influences or "chance." Thus he proposed the concept of *momentary effective reaction potential* ($_S \dot{\bar{E}}_R$) to represent the organism's *momentary* potential for responsiveness to a stimulus. Operationally, $_S \dot{\bar{E}}_R$ is calculated by considering the range through which $_S \bar{E}_R$ *can* vary and identifying the actual or estimated reactiveness at that particular moment.

Before considering Hull's 1943 postulates, we would again remind the reader that the foregoing intervening variables are illustrative of Hull's approach but that some changes were made in the role these variables were assigned in the 1952 statement of Hull's theory. The purpose in introducing these five intervening variables was mainly to provide the reader with examples of concepts describing processes within the organism which might account for or help explain otherwise somewhat isolated phenomena. Each intervening variable was anchored to observable stimulus and/or response conditions.

Postulates and Related
Concepts in the 1943 Theory

Most of Hull's system was derived from or somehow related to a set of postulates or basic assumptions which he outlined for human and mammalian behavior. In part, he viewed these postulates as rules by which to manipulate and relate the various independent, intervening, and dependent variables so as to account for learning and behavior processes. Though the 1952 theory involved extensions and modifications, his 1943 postulates illustrate the scope and general characteristics of his theory. Our discussion will be organized around the sixteen postulates in *Principles of Behavior* (Hull, 1943). It is consistent with Hull's approach to science that one should view any set of theoretical statements as nothing more nor less than a progress report. This was evident in Hull's own writing as he reworked the order of the postulates, added on and modified his subsequent 130-plus corollaries, and periodically made changes in the equations which he routinely tried to formulate for each major verbal statement.

Stimulus Effects The first postulate was concerned with events which occur when a stimulus impinges on and activates a receptor organ. He assumed that the stimulus would not only affect the sensory organ while it is physically present, but that some kind of trace or memory of the stimulus would persist for a measurable time span (probably for a maximum of a few seconds) before it would essentially disappear. Postulate 2 recognizes that stimuli differ in their effects on receptors, that they interact with each other in a variety of competitive and facilitative ways, and that the organism's responses are also influenced by such conjoint effects rather than solely by isolated stimuli.

Motivation and Learning The third and fourth postulates are particularly relevant to learning and are in many ways especially concerned with explaining why the law of effect works as it does. Hull accepted the proposition that strengthening of stimulus-response (or receptor-effector) connections occurs automatically when such connections provide need gratification. This would include strengthening of innately available connections as well as the establishment and strengthening of new connections. The third postulate acknowledged that some behavioral adaption patterns may result from innate stimulus-response patterns, where there also exists some kind of process whereby the organism acquires or learns new connections and modifies (increases or decreases) the strength of the innate connections. Hull used the term *habit* to refer to an organism's connection between a stimulus and a response and he roughly depicted learning as a change in habit strength. He acknowledged that temporal or spatial contiguity between a given stimulus and response might account for some changes in habit strength, but he felt that such changes primarily occur because of gratification of the organism's needs. Moreover, he offered some tentative estimates of the relationships between numbers of reinforcements (singly and in combination) and the resultant changes in habit strength. In addition to identifying the reinforcement conditions under which learning occurs, Hull was trying to evolve quantitative statements relating increases in habit strength to the occurrence of reinforcements. He theorized that habit strength would increase with number of reinforcements, rapidly at first and then more and more gradually until a limit is reached. Both amount and quality of reinforcement would limit the maximal habit strength, as would any delay in presentation of the reinforcing stimulus.

Characteristics of Stimuli   The fifth postulate was concerned with ways in which an organism distinguishes among stimuli in a situation and the subsequent effects on both habit strength and behavior. (Note that whether or not a particular response occurs depends on habit strength as well as on the status of a number of other intervening and independent variables.) In brief, habit strength is more likely to increase in the presence of stimuli which previously were present when that response was reinforced; habit strength for other stimuli depends upon the degree of similarity between a given stimulus and the stimulus actually associated with reinforcement. Moreover, there are interacting effects of the various stimuli present in a situation, with the probability of a response depending in part on their summated habit strengths.

Hull acknowledged that it is all too easy to underestimate the complexity of real-life situations when one tries to formulate principles of fundamental learning processes under highly controlled laboratory conditions. Thus he devised a series of corollaries which would at least tentatively encompass the many facets of these complex stimuli. He pointed out that even in a supposedly controlled laboratory situation there are a number of other stimuli (in addition to the stimulus manipulated by the experimenter) which impinge on the organism. Although for practical convenience the experimenter uses the narrower specification of the manipulated stimulus, even in classical conditioning the "conditioned stimulus" is associated with extraneous sounds, lights, kinesthetic stimuli, etc. Hull suggested that an experimenter must anticipate that the "extra" stimuli may tend to facilitate or to inhibit a given response (depending primarily upon their inherent characteristics and the organism's reinforcement history) and that behavior laws ultimately must deal with stimulus *compounds* rather than *isolated* stimuli. Thus though for pedagogical purposes or for conceptual clarification one may refer to simple stimulus control, in fact, any given "stimulus 'object' represents a very complex aggregate of more or less alternative potential stimulations, often extending into numerous receptor modes" (Hull, 1943, p. 221).

Drives, Drive Stimuli, and Excitatory Potential   Postulates 6 and 7 describe ways in which drives and "drive stimuli" (internal stimuli produced by and associated with drive states) are important determinants of an organism's behavior. It should be noted, first, that Hull acknowledged the importance of both primary and secondary motivation as influences on behavior. By *primary motivation* he referred to those needs (and associated stimuli) which require gratification to optimize survival of the organism and/or of the species. By *secondary motivation* he designated those needs (and associated stimuli) which are learned by some association with gratification of the primary needs.

Hull recognized that a primary reinforcer could only *directly* affect responses which had occurred within close temporal proximity (probably no more than twenty or thirty seconds between the response and reinforcement). But somehow the reinforcements could influence a whole series of stimuli and responses which had occurred in a sequence leading up to the response which is followed by primary reinforcement. Drawing ideas from Pavlovian research on higher-order conditioning, Hull proposed that these more remote (that is, at a distance from primary reinforcement) receptor-effector processes can be explained in this way:

(T)he power of reinforcement may be transmitted to any stimulus situation by the consistent and repeated association of such stimulus situation with the primary reinforcement which is characteristic of need reduction. Moreover, after the reinforcement power has been transmitted to one hitherto neutral stimulus, it may be transferred from this to another neutral stimulus, and so on in a chain or series whose length is limited only by the conditions which bring about the consistent and repeated associations in question. (Hull, 1943, p. 97)

Hull used the term *secondary reinforcement* to refer to this process, and emphasized that a stimulus's reinforcing and evoking power will be determined by how close it is to the primary reinforcer: The closer a stimulus is to the primary reinforcement, the greater its strengthening effect.

According to postulate 6: "Associated with every drive (D) is a characteristic drive stimulus (S_D) whose intensity is an increasing monotonic function of the drive in question" (Hull, 1943, p. 253). Hull theorized that these drive stimuli exist within the organism at an intensity level directly proportional to the drive level, and that the drive stimuli could have some selective role in guiding behavior. The "guidance" capacity would occur because they are part of the (internal and external) stimulus complex present at the time of reinforcement. Like external stimuli, these internal stimuli become conditioned stimuli which can evoke responses because they lead to reinforcement. Moreover, whether habit strength results in behavior depends partly upon prevailing drive states. According to postulate 7: "Any effective habit strength ($_S\bar{H}_R$) is sensitized into reaction potentiality ($_S E_R$) by all primary drives active within an organism at a given time, the magnitude of this potentiality being a product obtained by multiplying an increasing function of $_S H_R$ by an increasing function of D" (Hull, 1943, p. 253).

Some students have difficulties understanding these abstract descriptions of internal stimuli and the ways in which they are believed to evoke behaviors. Perhaps a personal example will aid in clarification. All of us have at one time or another experienced the pressure sensations and heard the "gurgling" sounds from our stomachs when we are very hungry. These internal stimuli prompt us at the earliest opportunity—that is, when other competing stimuli and responses permit—to obtain food or to take other steps which will subsequently satisfy this prevailing drive condition. In a sense, these postulates hold that the organism will have somewhat parallel internal stimuli as correlates of any given drive. The organism will respond to stimuli from the strongest drives and act in accordance with existing habit strengths and general response capabilities if permitted by external environmental conditions. Within some constraints—for example, limitations in the environment, or other strong competing stimulus-response associations—the organism will emit those behaviors which satisfy the most pressing needs.

Inhibition and Oscillation   In our discussion of intervening variables we introduced the concept of excitatory potential ($_SE_R$). Generally, $_SE_R$ summarizes the organism's maximal potential for making a given response. Most psychologists consider excitatory potential to be a central, pivotal concept in Hullian theory since the independent and intervening variables determine it—in fact, are summarized by it as to their net effects—and the dependent variables are derived in one way or another from it. Excitatory potential is especially influenced by prevailing drives and habit strengths. But other factors are also important in determining whether a particular response is evoked by a stimulus.

Postulates 8 and 9 try to account for the fact that responses may not occur because of some active *inhibiting* processes rather than simply because of the organism's passivity. Hull theorized that one effect of having made a particular response is that the organism is less likely to repeat that response immediately thereafter. This is partly due to the effort required and the resulting fatigue caused by making the response. Though this inhibition would tend to disappear rather quickly, stimuli which are present would acquire the power to inhibit the occurrence of those responses. Thus it would be possible for stimuli to acquire the power to inhibit responses in a manner quite similar to the ways whereby other stimuli acquire the power to evoke those responses. In calculating effective reaction potential ($_S\bar{E}_R$), one would have to consider the summated effects of inhibition generated by making the responses plus the effects of the inhibiting stimuli, and subtract these combined inhibitions from excitatory potential ($_SE_R$).

In the tenth postulate, Hull recognized that the prediction of individual behavior is very difficult: "It is an everyday observation that organisms vary in their performance even of well-established, habitual acts from occasion to occasion and from instant to instant on the same occasion. We are able to recall a name at one time but not at another; in shooting at a target we ring the bell at one shot, but not at the next; and so on" (Hull, 1943, p. 304). Of course, others have long been concerned with such variability, and some have even contended that it is impossible to have a science of behavior. Hull's answer was to include this variability as a part of his theory under the name "behavioral oscillation," on the basis that even the variability could be estimated and predicted.

Hull depicted this variability, or *oscillation*, in behavior as stemming from fundamental characteristics of the nervous system. "It is at once evident that the spontaneous firing of nerve cells, if general throughout the nervous systems of normal adult organisms, must when taken in conjunction with the neural-interaction hypothesis imply an incessantly varying modification of both afferent and efferent impulses" (Hull, 1943, p. 45). As a result, in each of his many equations for quantitatively predicting behavior, Hull typically incorporated one component which had a mean value but which was understood to vary above and below that point within a specified range. Thus, this organismic variability could be recognized and yet a set of scientific statements could be made. Momentary effective reaction potential ($_S\dot{\bar{E}}_R$) was to be calculated from effective reaction potential ($_S\bar{E}_R$) as modified by this oscillation.

Other Determinants of Response Evocation   For most of these first ten postulates, Hull anchored the concepts to observations about the antecedent stimulus conditions. Logan (1959) calls them "input intervening variables." Thus Hull tried to describe the nature of major factors of influence on habit strength, the ways in which deprivation and aversive conditions could produce drives and drive stimuli, the fact that organisms have various influences which serve as barriers to making respective responses, and that these plus momentary oscillations in neural states would culminate in a theorized momentary potential for action.

The last six postulates were more concerned with the likelihood that a response would occur, once the organism had attained certain levels of habit strength and motivational conditions. Most students are familiar with the concept of "threshold" with regard to our detection of stimuli: For example, a sound must be loud enough and a light must be bright enough in order for us to detect them; the stimuli must be at or above our threshold level for the respective sensory organs to detect such stimuli. Similarly, Hull theorized that there is some minimal point which must be reached before the potential for making a response will actually result in the particular behavior. He used the concept of "reaction threshold" to identify this minimal level. The eleventh postulate holds that the momentary potential for making a response must reach some minimal level before the response will occur. According to the twelfth postulate, once that threshold is reached any additional amount of reaction potential increases tne pr⌣ ɩbility that the response will be made, with an ogival functional relationsʰip between such "excessive" reaction potential and the response probability levels.

Somewhat similarly, postulate 13 holds that there is a negatively accelerated decreasing relationship between above-threshold reaction potential and response latency. Thus when momentary reaction potential is high, the response would almost immediately follow the stimulus; when momentary reaction potential is low, the response would occur more slowly. Postulate 14 holds that resistance to extinction (the number of responses made after reinforcement is withdrawn) is greater with high effective reaction potential, and that there is a simple linear relationship between reaction potential and number of responses made. Postulates 12, 13, and 14 were primarily concerned with striated-muscle responses and so-called "voluntary" behavior. Postulate 15 theorizes that the amplitude or amount of autonomic nervous system mediated responses will have a simple, direct linear relationship with momentary effective reaction potential.

The 16th and last postulate deals with incompatible responses. Hull cited this as a major explanation of why a response might not occur even though the momentary reaction potential exceeds the reaction threshold. In one of the ways in which Hull acknowledged the great complexity of the natural environment in which an organism lives, he pointed out that there are many instances in which the general stimulus complex impinging on an organism may simultaneously bring forth two or more competing responses. He theorized that the only response made would be that one whose momentary excitatory potential is greatest. In some situations, this could mean that it would be the oscillation value which would determine which response was made.

Learning, Reinforcement, and the 1943 Theory

At some risk of oversimplification we can now summarize Hull's 1943 views about learning processes and their role in his general behavior theory. A key notion is that organisms can best be conceptualized as self-maintaining mechanisms which adapt their behaviors so as to maximize the likelihood that most pressing needs will be gratified. We can outline the theory and concepts described above in two steps—first, by summarizing means by which learning (habit-strength change) occurs; second, by summarizing ways in which habit strength and other variables determine whether stimuli will evoke responses.

Figure 9-1 outlines major determinants of learning, defined as changes in habit strength. Hull recognized that stimuli could evoke responses through unlearned receptor-effector connections which stem from organic

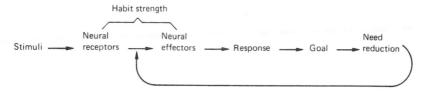

Figure 9-1 Hull's (1943) explanation of strengthening of connections between receptors and effectors as a result of need reduction—a reinforcement theory of learning.

evolution, through learned connections, or by chance occurrences. For whatever reason, when stimuli singly or in combination evoke responses which result in satisfaction (reduction) of a dominant need, connections between receptors and effectors are strengthened. The strengthening effect is *not* limited to the particular receptor-effector connection(s) which mediated the reaction, but may also affect other receptor discharges which occur at about the same time so that they, too, acquire or strengthen connections with the effectors mediating the response (cf. Hull, 1943, p. 386).

Hull suggests that these strengthened receptor-effector connections will increase the likelihood that such stimuli will evoke the same responses in future situations where that (those) drive(s) might prevail.

As a result, when the same need again arises in this or a similar situation, the stimuli will activate the same effectors more certainly, more promptly, and more vigorously than on the first occasion. Such action, while by no means adaptively infallible, in the long run will reduce the need more surely than would a chance sampling of the unlearned response tendencies ... at the command of other need and stimulating situations, and more quickly and completely than did that particular need and stimulating situation on the first occasion. (Hull, 1943, p. 387)

Such changes will facilitate the organism's adaptability, and hence its survival chances are improved. In this way learning is intimately related to adaptation and survival.

Figure 9-2 summarizes ways in which habit strength and other variables determine whether stimuli will evoke responses. With regard to any given stimulus and the response it *may* evoke, one must consider a number of other variables which can facilitate or impede the occurrence of that particular reaction. We have already considered ways in which habit strength can emerge and increase for connections between a receptor and an effector for that reaction (see Figure 9-1 and related discussions). In determining *effective* habit strength, which is the generalized habit strength available for evocation of a response, one must consider differences between the training situation and the new situation. The greater the similarities between the training environment and the new environ-

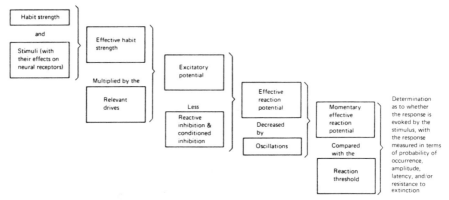

Figure 9-2 Outline of habit strength and other variables as they influence the extent to which a stimulus evokes a response.

ment, the greater will the effective habit strength be, thus the more likely that the response will be evoked in the new environment. Excitatory potential is then derived from effective habit strength multiplied by prevailing drive conditions—taking into account those drives which relate to the particular stimulus-response connections as well as those which may involve other stimuli and responses. The inhibiting influences stemming from the amount of energy required to make the response plus other conditioned inhibiting influences are subtracted from excitatory potential to calculate effective reaction potential. Recognition of spontaneous or chance variability in behavioral characteristics provides a basis for calculating *momentary* effective reaction potential. If the momentary effective reaction potential is equal to or greater than the threshold for the particular reaction, the response will occur and can be measured in terms of probability of occurrence, amplitude, latency, or resistance to extinction.

Complex Behavior

We again remind the reader that Hull's basic conception of the organism centered around its attempts to satisfy pressing needs and to adapt to changing environmental demands. Many fundamental characteristics are believed to exist in complex as well as simpler forms of behavior. By now it should be rather easy to envision how stimuli might elicit a particular response by an organism. But how can these concepts be related to more complex acts, any one of which may consist of many stimulus-response units? It is to answer such questions that we now consider the Hullian concepts of cue-producing responses, chains, pure-stimulus acts, fractional antedating goal reactions, and habit family hierarchy. Some of these concepts were noted in the 1943 system but received greater emphasis in the 1952 theory.

Cue-producing Responses, and Chains Hull theorized that behavior consists of a multitude of concurrent streams of stimulus-response units. Rather simple behavior might be conceptualized as two stimulus-response units, each with an excitatory potential level, with one response being made because its greater momentary effective reaction potential resulted from some combination of compelling environmental conditions. But not all behavior is this simple. Hull suggested that the response units might be arranged in temporal sequence, much like two or more links form a chain. He had consistently suggested that not only are responses produced by stimuli, but that the responses, in turn, produce other stimuli which serve as cues for other responses. It was a simple extension to suggest that one response might produce stimuli which evoke another response, thus forming chains of stimulus-response links. Moreover, this would also make conceptually feasible the idea that a given stimulus could gain its control over behavior not only if the response it evoked was reinforced but also if the chain of which it is a part would ultimately lead to reinforcement. One key idea in Hull's conception of chains was the notion that the stimuli within the organism as well as external stimuli might have a guiding as well as evoking influence on behavior. This leads to our next concepts.

Pure-stimulus Acts In an early paper, Hull (1930) proposed that such processes as "knowing" and "purposefulness" can be explained by means of stimulus-response habit analyses. This conceptual move from observable behavior to such internal "cognitive" processes would be rather simple. Hull contended that one merely need theorize that there are internal sequences of stimulus-response connections for which there is no observable behavior, but which culminate in an observable response. One of the key concepts used to analyze cognitive processes is the *pure-stimulus act*, an act which has no instrumental value in obtaining reinforcers and whose sole function is to provide cues (stimuli) for instrumental acts.

Hull (1930) cited anticipatory defense reactions as examples of acts which are chiefly valuable in serving as stimuli for instrumental acts. He first noted that many of our internal stimuli originate in or are stimulated by our own movements and overt responses. As a result, the organism carries about a series of internal representations of overt stimulus-response connections. Some of these internal stimulus-response connections are linked into chains. As a result, an organism need not necessarily wait until the last link of the chain is completed before recognizing the particular consequence of that goal act. If, for example, some noxious stimulus or other aversive consequence will occur, the organism need not wait until the last link of the chain "to know" that undesirable consequences will follow. Rather, because of the associations transmitted to the first link in the chain, the organism can be said to have some "foreknowledge" of probable consequences. But it is important to note that Hull used a behavioristic framework rather than mentalistic or phenomenological concepts to account for this "foreknowledge": Within the Hullian framework, the stored stimulus-response associations in various combinations constitute the "knowledge"; "knowing" involves nothing beyond them.

Fractional Antedating Goal Reactions The fractional antedating goal reaction provides a more formalized illustration of a pure-stimulus act. Fractional antedating goal reactions constitute an attempt by Hull to show that subgoal activities occurring within the organism, which are part of a chain, can be reinforced by association with the goal response and can have a guidance and evoking influence on behavior. "Fractional" merely means that the subgoal reaction is part of the sequence of events leading up to the goal reaction. It is "antedating" in that it precedes the response of consuming the reinforcer. Hull explained that not only the final response, but also the preceding stimulus-response connections are affected by reinforcement for the last response in a chain. As with external stimuli, the fractional antedating goal stimuli vary in strength depending upon their proximity to the primary reinforcer. Thus the fractional antedating goal stimuli which are closest to the goal will have the greatest influence on behavior and thus can be depicted as having a guidance as well as an evoking function. Some would characterize the fractional antedating goal reactions and the proprioceptive stimuli as internal contributors to the observable stimulus-response links in chains of behavior.

Hull suggested that the fractional antedating goal reaction concept could be used to account for the organism's "cognition" that its acts were leading up to a goal. "The fact that the fractional goal reaction (r_G) occurs in an antedating manner at the beginning of the behavior chain or sequence *constitutes on the part of the organism a molar foresight or foreknowledge of the not-here and not-now.* It is probably roughly equivalent to what Tolman has called 'recognition' " (Hull, 1952*b*, p. 151).

To some extent, Hull is using a concept not unlike the chain of objectively observable behaviors to account for processes going on inside the organism. Just as each link in a chain is strengthened because of the association with subsequent reinforcement of the goal response, likewise these internal associations of fractional antedating goal reactions might be characterized as internal chains. Given the fact or the assumption that stimuli vary in strength in accordance with their proximity to goal stimuli, we are now ready to consider the possibility of two or more chains leading to the same goal.

Habit Family Hierarchy   Given the background of these concepts, we are now ready to examine a way in which one could use Hull's stimulus-response reinforcement theory to describe how an organism "makes a choice." *Habit family hierarchy* refers to a group of chains which are of different lengths (more or fewer stimulus-response links) and which may include different stimuli and responses, with all chains leading to the same goal; the chains are organized in a hierarchy in terms of effort (number of links) needed to reach the goal. In a hypothetical situation, an organism which is confronted with the first stimulus of each chain would predictably be most likely influenced by the stimulus which is highest in the hierarchy—namely the one with the fewest links. While some observers might conclude that the organism had "chosen" the shortest route to the goal, the Hullian psychologist would propose a behavioristic explanation: Because it was closer to the goal stimulus, the shorter-chain stimulus simply had more evoking power. Other things being equal, the chain of the fewest links will be the one which is "chosen" by the organism.

Explanations of Complex Behavior   Hull assumed that classical and instrumental conditioning research would provide bases for theorizing about more complex behavior, although he acknowledged that additional concepts may have to be devised. In the foregoing paragraphs we have tried to sketch ways in which available Hullian concepts sometimes have been used to conceptualize cognitive and other complex processes. Unfortunately, according to the views of some critics, the additional research and theoretical constructions were not provided by the time of Hull's death in 1952. Some therefore question the wisdom of Hull's assertions about extensions of his theory.

Let us discuss two aspects of such criticisms. First, one could argue that the Hullian reinforcement theory on which we have focused thus far in this chapter—or even the incentive theory which we will briefly consider in a later section—can *never* be expected to account for complex human learning and other processes. Advocates of such views may find a more appropriate theoretical position in the chapter on information processing theories (Chapter 11). Second, others may criticize Hullian theory for its failure to fulfill promises concerning descriptions of cognitive processes; while these critics may be optimistic about the potential of a Hullian-type theory as a general theory in psychology, they may criticize the current status of the theory. In particular, they may seize on statements which Hull, quite confidently, made in each of the several presentations of his theory.

In many ways, this positive assertion of concepts that were in fact tentative and principles which had little supporting data, along with broadly encompassing sketches of his theory, is characteristic of Hull's approach to psychology and to theory construction. (Of course, we have only provided a few representative samples of his theory in the present chapter; interested readers would have to go to original works and more extensive commentaries, some of which are suggested at the end of this chapter, to learn about the full range and complexity of Hullian theory.) Perhaps unfortunately, Hull sometimes made unqualified positive statements which may lead readers to believe (incorrectly) that Hull considered his theory to be a finished product. Nothing could be further from the truth.

Hull simply believed that it would be better to sketch the broad outlines to provide perspective and guidance in developing his theory. He knowingly took the risk of making errors in his verbal statements and in numerical values he identified for his concepts (sometimes as a result of only one or a few experiments) on the basis that it would be easier to identify strengths and weaknesses of the theory and to plan the additional research and theorizing required to improve the theory. His views on this matter were quite clearly noted in one of his last books: "Psychology as a systematic science is relatively young. As a consequence it is to be expected that as time goes on marked changes will continue to be made in the fundamental assumptions underlying the systematizations" (Hull, 1951, p. 2). By continuing to present synthesized interpretations of data and conducting crucial experiments to test them, Hull was confident that someday the psychology of learning would be accepted as a valid quantitative science.

Illustration of Hull's
Quantitative Statements

In the previous sections we have presented the essentials of the postulates and major concepts on which Hull's theory was based. It is very important for readers to realize that his theory is much more complex than we have described here—we have provided only samples of the theory—and that Hull spent much of his time devising and testing quantitative statements about learning processes. We have not attempted to present the mass of quantitative detail which has accumulated over the years partly because, even today, the actual formulations (equations as well as quantitative values for concepts) are still the subject of experimentation and modification. However, we'll provide an example of the mathematical formulations here merely to illustrate the extent to which he attempted to introduce quantitative precision in his theory. We are not concerned with the contemporary accuracy of the particular equations and quantitative indices since our sole purpose in using this example is to illustrate Hull's attempts at mathematical formulations.

In *A Behavior System* (1952), Hull presented a corollary (number *xvi*) on simple trial-and-error learning (following experimental procedures somewhat like those associated with Thorndike's law of effect research). In this corollary he tried to quantify the relationships between reactive potentials for a reinforced and an unreinforced response as the reinforced response was learned over a series of trials. He theorized that learning of one response (which we'll designate response "A") can also increase the reaction potential for another response which involves some of the same muscles (which we'll call response "B"). Moreover, the partial or complete extinction of response B will also cause a decrease in the reaction potential for response A.

Drawing both from the general structure of his theory and from supporting experimental data, Hull outlined theoretical projections of the changes in reaction potential for the two responses. He estimated that the generalizing effect for response B would be approximately 20 percent of the increase in reaction potential for response A; similarly, the inhibition of response A would be approximately 20 percent of the decrease in reaction potential for response B. Hull calculated changes in reaction potential and reaction probability over a series of fifteen trials for the two responses and for the probability that response A would be more likely to occur than response B. His calculations showed that it would take approximately ten trials for response A to dominate response B, given these particular starting values for reaction potentials. Of course, the curves would be different for responses which have different initial reaction potentials.

Hull then deduced a theorem which both summarized the foregoing theory and pointed directions for needed research. For example, one could generate statements about changes in response A domination with different starting reaction potentials for two responses, A and B. One could examine the extent to which the characteristics of reaction potential curves differ as a function of various starting values. Ultimately he would attempt to formulate a series of theorems and equations from which it would be possible to predict how an organism would respond in a two-choice situation.

HULL'S MODIFICATIONS AND
CONTEMPORARY NEOBEHAVIORISM

This chapter primarily focuses on Hull's 1943 formulation of his theory. This particular Hullian statement was chosen because it is recognized as the major description of a true reinforcement theory of learning, and as the general outline of the most comprehensive behavior theory which focuses on learning processes. But it is important that the reader recognizes that many changes subsequently were made in Hullian theory despite the fact that the 1943 general outline continues to be useful in understanding contemporary neobehaviorism in the Hullian tradition. Obviously we cannot even begin to describe here *all* the changes in the quantitative relationships; what we can do is to provide brief descriptions which illustrate the formal and substantive changes which have been proposed at various times by Hull, his colleagues, and his successors.

Hull's Modifications

In his 1943 theory, Hull had proposed to develop a comprehensive behavior theory which would focus on·learning processes and which would encompass human and other mammalian behavior. He chose to study simpler learning processes first on the basis that principles so derived would be applicable to more complex behavior, although he recognized that additional principles *might* be required for complex human behavior.

Hull made comparatively few *formal* changes from 1943 until his last theoretical papers published in 1952, but he made several *substantive* changes which we should consider here. Formally, he maintained his preference for a hypothetico-deductive approach to theory construction, along with assumptions that fundamental laws could be derived from intensive study of classical and instrumental conditioning processes. He made a number of changes in the description and organization of postulates and corollaries, but these reflected data-influenced substantive differences rather than dissatisfaction with his hypothetico-deductive approach to theory construction.

Substantively, several interesting shifts can be noted. In his 1943 theory, Hull essentially postulated not only that reinforcement is a major ingredient and necessary condition for learning, but that the amount of learning would depend directly on the amount of reinforcement. In addition, reinforcement was explained almost solely as reducing prevailing drive states.

By 1952, Hull depicted reinforcement's major influence as involving performance, with less emphasis on its contribution to increases in habit strength (learning, in the earlier theory). Instead of emphasizing drives, he assigned greater importance to the stimuli produced by and associated with drives. In his last theoretical papers he seemed to view reduction of drive-stimuli as the major mechanism underlying the concept of reinforcement, although he continued to entertain the possibility that drive reduction was equally important. In conjunction with this greater concern with stimuli associated with reinforcement and drives, goals (or incentives) were viewed differently in the 1943 theory. Quantity or amount of reinforcement no longer was viewed as a direct influence on increasing habit strength (learning)—except in that some unspecified minimum amount would be necessary for a stimulus to be considered a reinforcement. The main determinant of habit-strength increase was number of reinforced trials. Amounts of reinforcement as well as delays in reinforcement were now viewed as influencing whether a stimulus would evoke a response (that is, as an influence on performance rather than on learning). Some would interpret Hull's changes as indicating practically only nominal importance for reinforcement influences on learning, although others would contend that Hull never completely abandoned his earlier belief that reinforcement is an important and a necessary condition for learning (cf. Logan, 1971).

K. W. Spence's Influence

When Hull died in 1952, his theory was far from complete and was being critically examined by both supporters and critics. Kenneth W. Spence (1907-1967) had been one of Hull's students at Yale University and a close collaborator with Hull for many years. Although Spence developed a theoretical position worthy of recognition on its own merit (for example, Spence, 1936 & 1956), he was generally regarded by most psychologists as the one most likely to carry on the Hullian tradition in theory construction. But Spence's views about theory and theory construction always had been somewhat at variance with those of Hull, and those differences grew even greater during the fifteen years which Spence survived Hull.

Whereas Hull was committed to a hypothetico-deductive approach to theory construction, with emphasis on stating the broad expanses of theory at least in tentative terms, Spence leaned more toward an inductive approach which kept interpretations close to the data. Whether a part of the zeitgeist in psychology or simply due to his own preferences, Spence did not continue to develop the grand theory to which Hull had devoted his professional life.

Spence did not ascribe as central a position for the influence of motivation on learning in a rather automatic way as had Hull. Instead, Spence long had emphasized perceptual processes and had over a period of time become more interested in cognitive facets of behavior than had Hull. Spence placed less emphasis on drive, and generally linked incentive motivation more closely with the cognitively oriented fractional antedating goal reaction. It should be emphasized, however, that Spence utilized behavioral explanations of cognitive processes.

Spence eliminated the role of reinforcement as a necessary condition for the acquisition and strengthening of S-R connections in the case of appetitively motivated instrumental conditioning. Instead, Spence theorized that habit strength is a function only of the number of stimulus-response pairings. However, Spence did theorize that drives, along with incentive motivation, are important determinants of excitatory potential. Thus, drive in a Hullian sense was still a significant variable for Spence.

It is worth emphasizing that there were many similarities between Hull's theory and the approach Spence took. For example, both contended that the fundamental laws of conditioning processes are also applicable to more complex processes, including language, although both acknowledged that new concepts and procedures would have to be devised. In a sense, one could depict Spence as having carried on Hull's tradition of critically examining the various details of the theory but as not having been overly concerned as to how changes in these details would or would not require modifications in Hull's more comprehensive theoretical structure.

More Recent Developments

Judging from work accomplished since Spence's death in 1967, it appears that many followers of the Hullian neobehavioristic position have gone even further than Spence in focusing on data collection rather than comprehensive theory construction. One volume (1971), edited by Howard H. Kendler and Janet Taylor Spence (K. W. Spence's widow as well as former colleague) and published as a memorial to K. W. Spence, contains a sample of neobehaviorism papers in the Hullian-Spence tradition. None of these papers was primarily concerned with general synthesis of principles; all were concerned with one facet or another of learning and general behavioral processes. Each contained the traditional emphasis on classical and instrumental conditioning principles, although there were examples of greater interest in cognitive processes than one finds in papers published prior to the 1960s. A few comments by the editors of this volume reveal some of the major contemporary trends.

Neobehaviorists have largely abandoned their attempts to erect a theoretical structure with broad implications, and along with others with whom they share the behavioristic tradition, including most of the builders of mathematical models, attack limited problem areas about which they develop "miniature systems." Emboldened perhaps by the successes of neobehaviorism as well as by its failures, and often guided by theoretical models of quite different origins, many contemporary psychologists have redirected their interests to cognitive-perceptual problems which neobehaviorism historically has tended to slight, either because of its preoccupation with learning or of its tactical decision to concentrate on the investigation of relatively simple phenomena. (Kendler & Spence, 1971, p. 37)

Thus two main patterns can be discerned for many but not all neobehavioristic psychologists in the Hullian tradition. First, there is an emphasis on an inductive rather than a hypothetico-deductive approach to theory construction. This constitutes a formal change from Hull's approach—at least for some psychologists, for the past several years. Secondly, there is greater emphasis on cognitive-perceptual processes than was evident in Hull's work. Along with this, a substantive pattern can be discerned: Hull had relied on conditioning processes as a main source of learning principles, with some expectation that additional principles might be needed for complex human learning. Spence seemed more certain that such additional principles would be required, although he, too, was intrigued with the contributions from conditioning research. But present-day neobehaviorists have greater reservations about the adequacy of conditioning principles; some even suggest that one may have to interpret conditioning principles in the context of cognitive processes, rather than utilizing conditioning principles to explain cognitive processes. In this context, some suggest (cf. Estes, 1971) that even some neobehaviorists have revised their stance about the extent to which drive-reduction or drive-stimulus-reduction produces automatic strengthening of S-R connections, as suggested earlier by Thorndike and by Hull. Instead, it is suggested that some neobehaviorists would theorize that such may be true for motor learning in animals, young children, and retardates, but that for mature adult humans rewards and punishments are primarily of value in the kinds of information they convey about an organism's transactions with its environment.

Despite the general atheoretical attitude or emphasis on miniature models which one finds with many neobehaviorists, there are some who continue in their attempts to formulate more comprehensive theories. One active researcher and theorist is Frank A. Logan. In various papers he has suggested that these new views and the earlier contributions can be accommodated within a general theoretical structure which he refers to as "incentive theory," distinguishing it from Hull's "reinforcement theory." Logan suggests that, in traditional Hullian reinforcement theory, there was only one learning process, "the strength of which depends not only on the number of times the response has occurred in the presence of the stimulus but also on the consequences of that response" (Logan, 1971, p. 46). In contrast, there are two types of learning process in incentive theory, the learning of habits and the learning about incentives. Habit formation is "the association of a response with a stimulus so that subsequent occurrences of the stimulus are likely to evoke the response" (p. 47). To some extent, Logan is closer to Guthrie's conditioning by contiguity than he is to Hull's conceptions of reinforced stimulus-response repetitions, although Logan uses Hull's (1952) terminology and he does acknowledge that rewards can heighten or strengthen habit formation. Incentive learning involves an "association of a stimulus with a response, so that subsequent opportunities to make the response lead to an expectation of the consequent stimulus" (Logan, 1971, p. 48). In many ways this is reminiscent of Tolman's views about "expectancies" and cognitive processes, but Logan seems to rely extensively on such concepts as the Spence-Hullian fractional antedating goal reaction and its value in giving an organism "foreknowledge" (cf. Hull, 1930, etc.) about relationships between acts and consequences. Although it is not possible at present to determine the long-term acceptability of views such as Logan's concerning incentive theory, it is conceivable that these views may provide a useful mechanism for integrating emerging data and interpretations with some of the earlier data and the general theory of the Hullian tradition.

EXTENT OF EMPHASIS
ON PRACTICAL APPLICATIONS

It is of interest that Hull had some experience with applied aspects of psychology and education early in his professional career. We already have noted that he taught in rural schools when he ran out of funds to continue his graduate studies. He also became involved with applied psychology problems at least on two occasions—he did some early research on aptitude testing and on hypnosis—both of which resulted in major publications. But he dropped these areas apparently because he felt that greater gains in psychology could be attained by establishing sound *basic* research and theory. His general preferences are rather obvious in a comment he made concerning people who wrote to him for help when they found that he had been conducting studies on hypnosis: "Many such letters are very pathetic, but my commitments to pure, as contrasted with applied, science have prevented me from considering them" (Hull, 1952, p. 153).

Hull's general approach to practical problems is well illustrated by his chapter in a book on the contributions of learning research to educational practice (Hull, 1942). The title chosen for his paper indicates his approach to the subject—"Conditioning: Outline of a Systematic Theory of Learning." After acknowledging that educators are primarily concerned with *practical* learning problems, he thereupon began a long discourse on his theory of learning, covering many of the topics which have been covered in the present chapter. Over thirty-two pages later, and just two paragraphs before the end of the paper, he finally got around to the topic of practical educational applications. Aside from pleadings that there were severe space limitations for discussing practical applications, and that his recommendations would probably sound like those of some other learning theorist (Guthrie), Hull's practical recommendations were covered in two sentences: "On the basis of the preceding principles it seems reasonable to suppose that if children from an early age were systematically trained to find the solution of genuine individual problems by means of their own symbolic processes, intellectual education might be far more effective then it is at present. However, the situations would need to be such as would not be readily solved by manual or other instrumental trial-and-error behavior" (Hull, 1942, p. 93).

Somewhat similarly, Spence (1959) also alluded to the possibility that fundamental neobehavioristic research *somehow* should be relevant to education, and he commented on the many problems in relating theory to practice. But he declined to become involved personally because, he claimed, he had to hasten back to his waiting animal and human research subjects.

Such lack of interest concerning practical applications is quite characteristic of Hullian-oriented researchers throughout the past several decades. A search of the literature reveals that some educational psychologists and educators have taken the liberty of converting or interpreting Hullian theory (or its contemporary modifications) for practical applications—sometimes using the concepts and principles correctly, while at other times not appreciating the many problems in translating this quite complex theory into practical implications. Unfortunately, those who are most knowledgeable about Hullian theory typically have not become involved in such attempted practical applications, with a few notable exceptions.

One example of a knowledgeable Hullian researcher and theorist attempting to delineate practical implications is a paper published by Logan (1971), entitled "Incentive Theory, Reinforcement and Education." Logan's general orientation is indicated by the proportion of pages allocated to theory versus those allocated to applications, and by his comments about education. The paper is divided approximately equally between theoretical discussions and practical implications, and he suggests that Hullian theory can most likely be useful if one considers it a source of ideas as to how one can make decisions about arranging conditions which will help students to learn. In many respects, Logan's orientation is quite compatible with the views expressed in the present book that Hullian theory (and other learning theories) can help one to evolve instructional theories and to arrange optimal conditions for facilitating classroom learning.

Logan suggests that classroom learning can be classified under three types—"stimulus discriminations, response differentiations, and reward/punishment consequences" (Logan, 1971, p. 53)—and that both temporal sequences and motivational conditions affect learning processes. By stimulus discriminations, Logan refers to ways in which the learner distinguishes among stimuli as well as ways in which stimuli are grouped or associated. A major determinant of stimulus discriminations is temporal contiguity: One learns to associate those stimuli which occur almost simultaneously or in close temporal sequence. Thus, as you read these pages, you tend to associate the information derived from them with the characteristics of the room in which you are reading. A teacher should consider those stimuli which are present during classroom learning and should decide whether they represent conditions which can facilitate classroom learning. The stimuli which are most important are those which are spatially and temporally most closely associated with the learning acts. The teacher should recognize that both internal and external stimuli influence learning, and that students vary in the particular stimuli to which they attend, with changes occurring particularly after prolonged exposure to the same stimuli. The teacher and student should try to use those stimuli which can facilitate attentiveness and foster learning.

With regard to learning to differentiate responses, Logan points out that one tends to learn those particular responses which we actually make in the learning situation. Unless other provisions are made, we tend to use the same rates and styles of solving problems as we did during the actual learning process. Logan, of course, recognizes that some changes in our actions will occur later, but he suggests that the most direct effect of learning is that we tend to act almost exactly as we did during the learning process. Thus the student may continue to pronounce words very slowly and carefully or to continue using the exact procedures in calculating mathematical problems, both approaches which may have been necessary during early stages of learning but which may constitute handicaps in coping with situations outside the classroom. Such characteristics are frequently found with students who are learning foreign languages and with university students who have just had their first course in statistics. One can avoid such deleterious effects by teaching fundamentals and then helping students to differentiate different ways of handling real-life problems.

Although Logan shows some preference for conceptualizing some aspects of learning as conditioning by contiguity, he also recognizes the Hullian emphasis on motivational factors. He suggests that, at a minimum, rewards and punishments heighten emotional involvement in the learning process and that they can actually influence learning in a variety of ways. He seems to prefer an interpretation of their effects as being partly influenced by the individual's recognition of relationships between behaviors and their consequences, and partly influenced by the more or less automatic effects which are believed to occur when drives or drive-stimuli are reduced in conjunction with stimulus-response connections. This is consistent with our earlier observations that his "incentive theory" involves two kinds of processes—the learning of habits and the learning about incentives. Logan observes that questions about students' motivations for classroom learning involve two parts—the drives or needs that the student has with respect to the learning situation in particular or to learning in general, and the expectations the student has as to probable consequences which would result from different study activities. Logan's position about motivational influences on learning emerges more clearly in his discussions of intrinsic versus extrinsic motivation effects.

We'll consider Logan's distinctions between intrinsic and extrinsic motivation, and their relevance for conceptualizing an individual's needs and the incentives in a learning situation, and we'll note some practical implications. Consistent with Hullian theory, Logan depicts *intrinsic motivation* as drive reduction which results inherently from making certain responses. *Extrinsic motivation* involves need reduction which does not *directly* come from the response or which occurs in addition to any intrinsic motivation effects.

With regard to classroom learning, Logan proposes the generally untested hypothesis that there is a "primary drive to learn" (Logan, 1971, p. 58) which can be intrinsically satisfied through learning activities in general and/or through particular learning activities. Though not necessary for organism survival, this learning drive may be somewhat like sex in that it facilitates survival of the species and it has identifiable physiological correlates. The main practical implication, if Logan's conjecture is valid, is that teachers and administrators should plan learning activities in accordance with observations about students' drive to learn. "In the presence of a prevailing learning drive, learning is inherently reinforcing; the greater the learning, the greater the reinforcement and hence the greater the incentive motivation to practice those responses that led to learning. In turn, the learning drive increases asymptotically with deprivation of an opportunity to learn" (Logan, 1971, p. 58).

Logan contends that it is erroneous to assume that one must "motivate" students to learn; rather, they have a natural motivation to learn. What is needed is to channel incentives in such a way that classroom learning will be facilitated, since the learning drive can be satisfied by nonacademic as well as academic learning activities. Moreover, Logan suggests that the learning drive, like other motivational conditions, can become reduced to the point where the student will not have a pressing need to learn. Thus he suggests that teachers and administrators should try to schedule classroom activities so as to make optimum use of students' natural push to learn.

At this point, some readers may have reservations about the practical value of Logan's observations. Unfortunately, many teachers find only small numbers of their students with apparently strong needs for learning, or at least for school learning. Logan apparently would suggest that some students are finding other outlets for their learning drive and/or that students simply have not found in the past that they can learn from school programs. Under these circumstances, some form of incentives, quite likely involving extrinsic learning, may be indicated.

While advocating that best *long-term* results accrue from intrinsic motivation, Logan acknowledges that many school activities do and, perhaps, must involve extrinsic motivation. While indicating that there are two aspects to extrinsic motivation with which the educator should be concerned—drives and incentives—Logan acknowledges that it is much easier to identify effective incentives than to delineate prevailing drives. Thus most of his comments are directed at ways in which educators can arrange incentives so as to satisfy extrinsic motives and, hopefully, to stimulate gratification of intrinsic needs as well through the learning experiences.

One of his key ideas is that of "correlated reinforcement." Drawing from the position that "maximal incentive motivation results from maximal reward," Logan (1971, p. 57) advocates arranging conditions so that some aspect of the reward (such as amount, delay, quality, or probability) should be correlated with some characteristic of the response to be learned (such as its accuracy, promptness, vigor, rate, etc.). He contends that we can be reasonably certain that more rewards should be given as students' performance gets better, but he acknowledges that we presently do not have adequate data which indicate how such rewards should be provided. For example, we don't know if we should give smaller, equal, or larger rewards at first, as compared with later learning segments. "We do not yet have general principles, much less specific guidelines to advise the teacher" (Logan, 1971, p. 57).

These few comments give illustrations of ways in which Logan suggests that one can use Hullian and other neobehavioristic concepts and principles to conceptualize practical situations and to plan possible ways for improving educational practice. While balancing his comments with cautions that practical situation data are required to validate his suggestions, he tries to show that an understanding of fundamental characteristics of learning processes may enable an educator or psychologist to plan tentative educational methods and procedures. Other neobehaviorists might select other aspects of the theory, but Logan's comments illustrate some tentative guidelines which might be derived.

EDUCATIONAL R&D IMPLICATIONS

Researchers in the Hullian tradition have generally depicted themselves as basic scientists whose practical contributions, whenever they might be derived, would most likely come from their data-based conceptions of learners and the learning process. Consequently, research papers tend to focus on rather narrowly circumscribed theoretical issues. Integrative papers most frequently are concerned with interpretations of data which might clarify some basic research question or with the implications for some particular miniature model or some aspect of a Hullian-neobehavioristic theoretical system. The delineation of practical implications is not typically considered a high-priority topic for discussion, though some papers provide cryptic, tentative suggestions about ways in which one might view the learning process or try to arrange conditions which would facilitate learning. Nonetheless, some suggestions can be derived from the very extensive body of literature provided by Hullian-neobehaviorism researchers and theorists.

A key notion in the Hullian-neobehaviorism theory is that organisms can best be conceptualized as self-maintaining mechanisms which adapt their behaviors so as to maximize the likelihood that most pressing needs will be gratified. Thus, learning is viewed as being intimately related to adaptation and survival. Whereas earlier workers in this tradition emphasized the automatic strengthening of stimulus-response connections through drive reduction, at least some contemporary neobehaviorists now also consider as equally important the ways in which the individual recognizes relationships between behaviors and their consequent (or probably consequent) rewards or punishments.

Thus this theory stimulates such questions about education as: How do stimuli in the classroom guide students' learning activities toward intermediary goals and long-term educational objectives? What needs are most important for each student? What incentives may be relevant to such needs? How may classroom activities be planned so as to take into account these needs and incentives? In addition, the possibility of a generalized learning drive and/or several more specialized learning drives raises other questions as to how one can heighten such needs and make classroom activities more appropriate for them. Given the current concern in education about "motivating students" and making education "more relevant" to students' needs, the Hullian-neobehaviorism literature can serve as a source of ideas about formulating instructional theories and preparing educational plans.

SUGGESTED READINGS

Hull, C. L. Conditioning: Outline of a systematic theory of learning. In *Psychology of Learning*, 41st Yearbook, NSSE, 1942, Part 2, Chapter 2.

Hull, C. L. *Principles of behavior*. New York: Appleton-Century-Crofts, 1943.

Hull, C. L. Behavior postulates and corollaries - 1949. *Psychological Review*, 1950, 57, 173-180.

Hull, C. L. *Essentials of behavior*. New Haven, Conn.: Yale University Press, 1951.

Hull, C. L. A behavior system: An introduction to behavior theory concerning the individual organism. New Haven, Conn.: Yale University Press, 1952b.

Kendler, H. H., & Spencer, J. T. *Essays in Neobehaviorism*. New York: Appleton-Century-Crofts, 1971.

Logan, F. A. Incentive theory, reinforcement and education. In R. Glaser (Ed.), *The nature of reinforcement.* New York: Academic, 1971. Pp. 45-61.

Logan, F. A. Experimental psychology of animal learning and now. *American Psychologist,* 1972, **27**, 1055-1062.

Spence, K. W. *Behavior theory and conditioning.* New Haven, Conn.: Yale University Press, 1956.

Spence, K. W. *Behavior theory and learning.* Englewood Cliffs: Prentice-Hall, 1960.

10
B. F. Skinner and Operant Conditioning

As with Hull, the experimental strategies and theoretical conceptions evolved by B. F. Skinner (1904-   ) were greatly influenced by both Pavlov and Thorndike—especially by Thorndike's law of effect. But there are also numerous ways in which Skinner differs from Hull's views as to how one might formulate a psychology of learning. Skinner has emphasized experimental study of single subjects rather than compilation of averaged group data. He also has advocated an empirical-inductive approach to theory construction and has insisted that psychologists should rely on observable behavior and avoid using internal concepts—rejecting reliance on physiological as well as mentalistic concepts. Moreover, though Skinner was a contemporary of the other key figures during the comprehensive theories of learning era, he and his theory have survived the mid-century disillusionment with contemporary theories and subsequent reliance on miniature models.

In many respects, Skinner's operant conditioning approach can be depicted accurately as an elaboration and extension of Thorndike's law of effect. Skinner acknowledges the existence of Pavlovian classical conditioning phenomena in human and animal behavior, but he relegates it to a position of lesser significance. He contends that his main, perhaps even sole, interest is in the behavior of an organism as it is controlled by its effect on the environment.

In this chapter we will describe Skinner's background and the origins of his theory; the basic concepts used to account for fundamental behavioral processes; their relevance for basic human behavioral processes; the means by which operant conditioners conceptualize complex behavior; and the practical implications of the operant approach.

BACKGROUND

Burrhus Frederic Skinner was born in 1904 in the northeastern Pennsylvania community of Susquehanna. By his own accounts, Skinner's home environment was warm and stable with strict standards but little use of physical punishment. He had numerous opportunities to develop a budding scientific curiosity and to learn manual skills while building cages for his pets and inventing a wide array of machines and gadgets. Even at this early stage he seemed interested in the behavior of animals and men and was curious as to why they act as they do. But he also had interests in art, music, and writing. Apparently greatly influenced by one public school teacher and family friend, he majored in English literature at Hamilton College. It was while at Hamilton that Skinner decided to become a writer. But after a few years of unsuccessful attempts—including some time spent in Greenwich Village and in Europe—he decided that he didn't really have anything to say at that time. At this point he decided to enroll in graduate school at Harvard to become a psychologist. He had had no courses in psychology as an undergraduate, although he had some background in biology and, in the process, had become aware of Pavlov's then newly ·published *Conditioned Reflexes*. Apparently he was greatly influenced by an article by Bertrand Russell in the popular magazine *Dial* in which Russell discussed Watson's behaviorism. Despite the fact that it was Russell's intent to criticize Watson's behavioristic position, the effect on Skinner was to make him more interested in learning about behaviorism. He subsequently decided that Watson was wrong, not for his behavioristic emphasis, but because he had not developed a sufficiently strong case for such a scientific pursuit.

We've already noted that Skinner did not have any formal background in psychology before entering graduate school. Actually that was not uncommon for new graduate students at that time. However, Skinner seemed particularly sensitive about this lack and he embarked on a vigorous campaign to learn about his newly adopted science doing extensive reading and experimentation. Apparently the ideas about a behavior psychology which he subsequently developed were shaped more by his reading and research and by contacts with certain fellow graduate students—notably Fred S. Keller and Charles K. Trueblood—than by any particular Harvard faculty member. In fact, he even had the temerity to challenge openly many of his instructors' ideas, suggesting that a more rigorous approach to psychology as science was in order. Of course, this is not meant to imply that he did not benefit from the distinguished Harvard faculty members or from the continuing stream of eminent persons who visited Cambridge. Rather, we are suggesting that they were not the primary influences on Skinner's initial and subsequent formulation of operant conditioning.

Skinner's Harvard graduate student days occurred in the late 1920s and early 1930s during an era in which the more mentalistic conceptions of the nineteenth century were still widely respected and Titchener's structuralism was still dominant in American psychology. Though the Harvard psychology faculty was very interested in developing research psychologists, there were widely ranging views of psychological research, with only a few faculty members endorsing any version of the emerging behaviorism. And, consistent with the emphasis on schools of psychology during this era, it was routinely assumed that one should draw from extant theory to formulate research hypotheses before engaging in research. In this context of an emphasis on hypothetico-deductive theory-dominated research, Skinner began to develop his ideas that a true science of behavior should be based on solid empirical facts and that these facts would be most readily obtained by primary or even sole reliance on empirical methods. In his view, what were needed were tools and techniques by which one could control experimental conditions so as to observe the orderly patterns of and influence on behavior. Rather than "theories" and "laws," he was content to search for *lawfulness* in behavior. "Russell and Watson had given me no glimpse of experimental method, but Pavlov had: control the environment and you will see order in behavior" (Skinner, 1970, p. 10).

Emphasizing that psychology is a natural science, Skinner viewed learning as the change in behavior which is observed under properly controlled conditions. Thus he endorsed "the investigation of behavior as a scientific datum in its own right" (Skinner, 1938, p. 4). Moreover, he contended that it would be through the methods and strategies of behaviorism that a true science of psychology could emerge.

To me behaviorism is a special case of philosophy of science which first took shape in the writing of Ernst Mach, Henri Poincare, and Percy Bridgman. . . . Behaviorism is a formulation which makes possible an effective experimental approach to human behavior. It is a working hypothesis about the nature of a subject matter. It may need to be clarified, but it does not need to be argued. I have no doubt of the eventual triumph of the position—not that it will eventually be proved right, but that it will provide the most direct route to a successful science of man. (Skinner, 1970, p. 18)

Moreover, he argued that psychologists should not rely on either mentalistic or physiological conjecture about the underpinnings of behavior. From his doctoral research to more recent projects, he has always insisted that psychological principles must be based on sufficiently sound observations about behavior, and that they would be little influenced by whether or not they fit with currently available neurophysiological detail or subjects' verbal reports of their experience. Because he used the concept of reflex extensively in his early writings, some may question whether Skinner may have been as concerned with neurophysiological detail as was Pavlov, with whom the concept of reflex is even more closely associated. This can be clarified by a few comments by Skinner about his own doctoral dissertation research and other studies conducted during the additional years in which he conducted research before leaving Cambridge.

It had been said of Loeb, and might have been said of Crozier, that he 'resented the nervous system.' Whether this was true or not, the fact was that both these men talked about animal behavior without mentioning the nervous system and with surprising success. So far as I was concerned, they canceled out the physiological theorizing of Pavlov and Sherrington and thus clarified what remained of the work of these men as the beginnings of an independent science of behavior. My doctoral thesis was in part an operational analysis of Sherrington's synapse, in which behavioral laws were substituted for supposed states of the central nervous system. (Skinner, 1959, p. 362)

Consistent with the above, another Skinnerian emphasis is that a science can best be evolved by conducting research on simpler and fundamental processes, and then using such principles to study more complex processes. In all cases, a three-term contingency arrangement is the basic paradigm. "An adequate formulation of the interaction between an organism and its environment must always specify three things: (1) the occasion upon which a response occurs, (2) the response itself, and (3) the reinforcing consequences. The interrelationships among them are the 'contingencies of reinforcement' " (Skinner, 1969, p. 7).

Skinner further contends that while observations of simpler processes are, of course, interesting in their own right, they also enable the researcher to "see" contingencies of reinforcement in much more complex laboratory studies and under the many uncontrolled conditions prevailing outside the laboratory. It is assumed that studies with animal subjects and human research involving simpler processes will reveal relevant principles but that they must stand unproven as hypotheses subject to direct analyses of the more complex processes.

Granted that Skinner was interested in establishing or continuing to develop psychology as an independent science, and that the focus should be on lawfulness of behavior of organisms, where might one look for factors which might be most important in influencing behavior? Skinner gives great credit to Thorndike for having shown psychologists an important source of influences on behavior. Before Thorndike's work, psychologists had relied exclusively on stimuli which precede responses (antecedent stimuli) as the main influence on behavior. Thorndike's research in conjunction with the law of effect had shown that stimuli which follow the response could also have a very great influence on subsequent occurrences of the behavior. Skinner (1963) suggests that this recognition by Thorndike of the importance of consequences of behavior in controlling behavior may have been suggested by Darwin's theories of evolution. For example, instead of stating that the well-developed eye helps the organism to see better, Darwin's principles of natural selection hold that if good sight is necessary for survival, organisms with well-developed eyes will survive and will produce similar offspring. In a similar vein, one can depict behavior as having been molded by its environment, in that those behaviors which are necessary for survival and for coping with situations will tend to be retained in future activities of the organism.

Many students inquire whether Skinner considers his own behavior to be shaped and influenced like that of his research subjects. Perhaps some of the best illustrations that he does view his own behavior this way can be gleaned from the various comments that he has made about scientific research. Throughout these comments there runs the notion that the researcher's behavior is influenced by its consequences, and that the most effective scientists' strategies are planned in recognition of such processes. Several years ago (1959) he presented five "unformalized principles of scientific practice." Though it is not feasible to present them individually here, their essence can be briefly noted: The successful researcher is not one who rigidly sticks to preconceived elegant research designs with large numbers of subjects; rather, it is he who is persistent in arranging experimental conditions until the behavior of interest is modified. The successful researcher is he who sometimes is lucky or finds one thing when looking for another, but who *always* is more attentive to the data obtained from his subjects than to any preconceived notions he may have had about the behavior under study, so that he ultimately understands the learning process so well that even an individual's behavior can be predicted under specified conditions.

With this viewpoint, Skinner has consistently held that nothing can be substituted for modification of behavior via experimentally manipulated conditions. He holds that this is especially important for any practitioner who is faced with real problems to be solved. Contrasting some researchers' preferences for abstract principles and using statistics instead of experimental research he observed:

When you have the responsibility of making absolutely sure that a given organism will engage in a given sort of behavior at a given time, you quickly grow impatient with theories of learning. Principles, hypotheses, theorems, satisfactory proof at the .05 level of significance that behavior at a choice point shows the effect of secondary reinforcement—nothing could be more irrelevant. No one goes to the circus to see the average dog jump through a hoop significantly oftener than untrained dogs raised under the same circumstance, or to see an elephant demonstrate a principle of behavior. (Skinner, 1959, p. 370)

Skinner's objection to the use of statistics is almost legendary among psychologists, but it is sometimes overlooked that operant researchers sometimes do conduct statistical analyses. Later we will examine some examples in conjunction with our discussions of complex behavior.

Let us conclude this section by describing briefly some major highlights of Skinner's career which are relevant to the present topic of learning. After he left Harvard in 1936, he began teaching and doing research at the University of Minnesota, remaining there until 1945. From 1945 to 1948 he served as professor and chairman of the psychology department at Indiana University; by this time a growing number of students and faculty had begun adopting some of Skinner's research strategies. In 1948 he became a permanent member of the Harvard University faculty, where he continued to teach, to do some research, and to write. One of the monumental projects in the operant tradition was completed at Harvard with Charles Ferster. The resulting book, *Schedules of Reinforcement*, described many of the contingency relationships which can exist between responses and their consequences and provided empirical data concerning the kinds of behaviors found with each schedule. This source has been the basis for classifying relationships between responses and their consequences in most research conducted since that time, although occasionally some other systems have been presented (such as Schoenfeld, 1970).

Several other major developments occurred around mid-century. The number of psychologists conducting research in the operant tradition had grown sufficiently that a journal devoted to operant conditioning, *Journal of the Experimental Analysis of Behavior*, was started quite successfully. This is particularly noteworthy in view of the fact that most other traditional comprehensive learning theories were losing support around this time. Second, laboratory and field studies were initiated with human subjects, although there continued to be an emphasis on animal research. Third, Skinner and his colleagues began to explore ways in which their findings might be relevant to educational and other social problems. Fourth, Skinner began writing a series of essay-type papers and books (for example, *Walden Two, Beyond Freedom and Dignity*) in which he expounded social-political implications which can be drawn from his research and theory. As a result of his various activities, especially those related to practical applications, Skinner has frequently been designated one of the most visible—and controversial—figures in psychology during this third quarter of the century.

ESSENTIALS OF THE THEORY

There are two important points to remember when searching for the essentials of operant learning theory. First, there is a conviction held by proponents of this approach that data rather than preconceived ideas should primarily influence the evolution of theoretical formulations; this results in a gradually but constantly changing set of principles which are elaborated and modified as new data are collected. Second, there is a preference for organizing and interpreting data in terms of the fundamental notion that consequences of one's actions have great influence on one's subsequent behavior. This notion initially was greatly influenced by the work of Thorndike and Pavlov but in recent years can be more accurately depicted as involving a *contingency* statement—an "if-then" statement about relationships among situations, actions, and consequences.

Many students and even some psychologists have misconceptions about the nature and emphasis on theory construction within the operant tradition. These misconceptions arose in part because of Skinner's advocacy of an inductive approach to theory construction, with an emphasis on data collection for the present; however, these misconceptions were especially facilitated by a paper Skinner published in 1950. This often-cited paper was entitled "Are Theories of Learning Necessary?" In it, Skinner essentially answered his own question, "No," that at least certain kinds of theories are not necessary. He criticized the then-popular emphasis on hypothetico-deductive theory formulations and he contended that existing theories had been prepared without adequate data formulations and that theories prepared without adequate data could even interfere with the eventual emergence of sound, empirically based theoretical formulations. Many misunderstood his stance as being against *all* forms of theory construction and some even depicted him as a "Grand Anti-Theorist" (Skinner, 1969, p. vii).

In contrast, Skinner actually holds that theory construction is the ultimate goal of experimental research. He recognizes that facts can be of only limited value if they are not integrated with other information. However, he has always preferred theoretical formulations which are stated in terms of the data collected, rather than in terms of physiological or mentalistic concepts which are inferred from such data. This is sometimes called a "black box" approach because Skinner is interested in predicting the behavior of the organism on the basis of external events without dependence upon knowing what is going on *inside* the organism.

Moreover, he has held that frequency of occurrence of a particular behavior, plotted as changes in frequency of occurrence over a period of time, constitutes a major advance in organizing our observations about behavior. Thus, instead of conjecture about some kind of physiological or mentalistic process, the researcher can identify the conditions under which certain behavioral events will occur or will change in their likelihood of occurrence. Expressing his confidence in such an approach, Skinner observed: ". . . Unlike hypotheses, theories and models, together with the statistical manipulations of data which support them, a smooth curve showing a change in the probability of a response as a function of a controlled variable is a fact in the bag, and there is no need to worry about it as one goes in search of others" (Skinner, 1969, p. 84).

As a result of such views, operant conditioning has become noted as much for its techniques and strategies of research as for the empirical findings produced by them. The operant approach has not been identified with large-scale theory construction ventures nor even with a closely integrated set of learning principles, though one could cite some attempts to organize general psychology principles within a predominantly operant framework (such as Keller & Schoenfeld, 1950). Instead, its theoretical and practical contributions primarily are derived from a general research paradigm and way of conceptualizing learning processes, a collection of basic concepts and a few general principles, and mounds of empirical data more frequently collected from animals than from human subjects.

Operant (R-Type) versus Classical Conditioning (S-Type) Paradigms

Skinner is generally credited with popularizing distinctions between Pavlov's classical conditioning and learning processes outlined by Thorndike's law of effect. These distinctions emerged naturally in the course of Skinner's attempt to describe learning processes. Unlike Hull, who was quite concerned with physiological or motivational explanations about *why* learning occurs, Skinner's efforts have largely been devoted to obtaining reliable descriptions of behavior and its controlling influences. Without detracting from the *independent* value of physiological theorizing, Skinner holds that psychology's role as a science is to consider behavior as a datum in its own right.

With that fundamental guiding assumption, one of Skinner's first tasks was to decide how many types of learning there are and to delineate the appropriate paradigm(s) for studying the type(s). Apparently it was in a series of papers around 1937 (Skinner, 1937) that Skinner publicly broke with traditional S-R theory and began to emphasize the concept of "operant" conditioning. In his first major theoretico-experimental work, *The Behavior of Organisms* (1938), Skinner outlined two types of learning. He defined these two types in terms of the environmental stimuli which influence or change behavior. Pavlov's classical conditioning paradigm serves as one of Skinner's types of learning. There is an identifiable eliciting stimulus for Type-S behavior; the S-Type or classical conditioning process is "distinguished by what is done to the organism to induce the change; in other words, it is defined by the operation of the simultaneous presentation of the reinforcing stimulus and another stimulus. The type is called Type S to distinguish it from Conditioning of Type R . . . in which the reinforcing stimulus is contingent upon a response" (Skinner, 1938, p. 19). Type-R conditioning is primarily characterized by the fact that there are no eliciting stimuli and that the behavior is controlled by its effects or its influences on the environment; though there may be stimuli identified in whose presence the behaviors are more likely to occur, these stimuli gain their control over that behavior because they previously have been present when that behavior was reinforced. We will discuss this matter again later under the topics of "discriminative stimuli," "stimulus generalization," and "stimulus control." Skinner makes this distinction: "The conditioning of an operant differs from that of a respondent by involving the correlation of a reinforcing stimulus with a *response*" (Skinner, 1938, p. 19).

Traditionally S-Type conditioning has been described in terms of an eliciting stimulus and a response, with the learning change consisting of a transfer of stimulus control for a response from one stimulus to another stimulus. Many have held that these changes are applicable to so-called "involuntary responses" which usually have been believed to be mainly under the control of the autonomic nervous system. In contrast, R-Type or operant conditioning is described in terms of a response for which there is no identifiable eliciting stimulus but whose probability of occurrence is controlled by stimuli which follow or are produced by it. In contrast with

S-Type conditioning, R-Type conditioning involves presentations of rein-forcing stimuli after certain responses are emitted; thus the stimulus remains the same but there are changes in the responses. Many theorize that R-Type conditioning and operant responses correspond to so-called "voluntary" responses of the central nervous system. In recent years there have been a number of instances in which classical conditioning has been demonstrated with behaviors previously believed to be voluntary, and operant conditioning has been conducted with such involuntary responses as heart rate and electrical activity in the brain. Thus some currently are raising questions about the relationships and possible overlap between S-Type and R-Type conditioning. But so long as one stays at Skinner's descriptive level in which behavior is considered in terms of identifiable controlling stimuli—that is, either antecedent eliciting stimuli or conse-quent reinforcing stimuli—Skinner's earlier distinctions still have merit.

But despite Skinner's occasional reference to Type-S or classical condi-tioning, most of his professional life has been devoted to the study of Type-R or operant behavior. A hint as to how he came to be interested primarily in operant behavior comes with a comment in his paper in the important series *Psychology: A Study of a Science*: "So far as I can see, I began simply by looking for lawful processes in the behavior of the intact organism. Pavlov had shown the way: but I could not then, as I cannot now, move without a jolt from salivary reflexes to the important business of the organism in everyday life" (Skinner, 1959, p. 362). Skinner has acknowledged that he introduced the term "operant" because he wanted "to distinguish between reflexes and responses operating directly on the environment" (Skinner, 1963, pp. 504-505).

Skinner did not come to make the Type-R versus Type-S conditioning distinction on the basis of idle speculation; rather, as with most of his research contributions, it emerged on the basis of his interpretations of data as tested by follow-up experiments. He had been studying the postural reflexes of young rats and had been giving the rats food when they came down a laboratory runway as part of his research procedures. At first annoyed because the rats paused after receiving their food, Skinner soon recognized that there were certain patterns in their pauses which seemed to be associated with the manner in which they received the food. He had long been dissatisfied with the notion that all behavior could be accounted for by the classical conditioning paradigm and was not surprised to hear that other researchers had been unsuccessful in identify-ing eliciting stimuli for a rather wide range of responses. Contending that much behavior might remain unaccounted for by classical conditioning, he was particularly pleased when he observed these lawful relationships between the rat's responses and provision of the food. Most of his professional life has been devoted to the concepts and procedures which have been used to outline the relationships between responses and their consequences.

Concepts and Principles

In one of his more recent theoretical books Skinner (1969) has outlined some questions which have been addressed by operant researchers: "(W)hat aspects of behavior are significant? Of what variables are changes in these aspects a function? How are the relations among behavior and its controlling variables brought together in characterizing an organism as a system? What methods are appropriate in studying such a system experimentally?" (p. xii). (He also raised the matter of practical applications, but we will consider this aspect in a later section.) The reader may find it useful to consider these questions as we describe some concepts and principles which illustrate how operant researchers study and conceptualize both basic and applied learning questions.

Stimulus and Response Descriptions   Operant researchers typically emphasize that behavior is the natural datum for psychology. They study both theoretical and practical problems by experimental laboratory procedures which are selected to identify functional relationships among situations, responses, and consequences.

Stimuli are described in terms of their physical properties, rather than in terms of subjects' experiences or reported perceptions of them, but their relationship with the organism's behavior is of concern. These relationships, and thus the significance of given stimuli, can best be delineated when one manipulates the stimuli and observes systematic changes in the organism's behavior. Although operant researchers are interested in complex processes as well as simple stimulus changes, they prefer to use external rather than internal descriptions.

The experimental analyst does not manipulate inner states as such. He manipulates not hunger, but the intake of food; not fear as an acquired drive, but aversive stimuli; not anxiety, but preaversive stimuli. He administers a drug, not the physiological effects of a drug. He takes the age of an organism, not a level of maturation, as a variable. (Skinner, 1969, p. 79)

Later, we will outline characteristics of antecedent stimuli (those which precede the response) and consequent stimuli (those which follow or are produced by the response).

In both laboratory and field studies, with practical problems as well as with theoretical issues, one of the first steps to be taken is to determine what behaviors are important and how they are to be measured. Typically in laboratory situations the subject's behavior is measured continuously, directly, and automatically by electronic switches and recorders. Thus it is possible not only to specify that a certain lever press or panel press constitutes the measured response, but it is possible to indicate (or to manipulate) how much force and what range of movement is required to activate the lever or panel switch. In basic field studies or practical situations, such measures of responses are more typically recorded by human observers who, similarly, try to establish objective criteria as to what constitutes the behavior being studied. For example, the observer might record the number of times (or the duration) that a student looks at (attends to) a book during a study period, or the number of constructive comments a student makes during a class period. To demonstrate the importance of teacher approval, observers might measure the incidence of students' comments, using two different groups of common nouns during class discussion until the two frequencies of usage are apparent. The more frequently occurring nouns could arbitrarily be called group "A," the less frequently occurring nouns called group "B." Then, additional measures would be taken while the teacher gives various expressions of her approval (such as smiling, saying "Fine!," etc.) each time the student mentioned one of the group B common nouns. Almost invariably there would be a substantial increase in the usage of group B nouns with little increase and possibly a decrease in group A nouns.

Free-operant and Discrete-trial Studies   Most readers are familiar with psychological research in which a situation is presented to a subject, the subject responds, and the experimenter records the subject's response; then, another stimulus is presented and the subject's response is noted, etc. Such procedures frequently are called *discrete-trial* studies to distinguish them from the *free-operant* experimental arrangements which Skinner devised and which are typically used by operant researchers. The name of these particular experimental arrangements is derived from the fact that the subject is *free* to make or not make an operant response and is free to respond rapidly or slowly.

In this experimental arrangement, Skinner observed that there seemed to be systematic relationships between presentations of food and other reinforcers he gave to his subjects for responding and their subsequent rates and patterns of responses. Thus he began to focus on the number or rate of responses as a major dependent variable in his free-operant studies. When conducting discrete-trial studies some operant researchers also use Pavlovian-type dependent variable measures such as latency or amplitude of the response.

Shaping and the Method of Successive Approximation   From our discussions so far, it is not difficult to see how operant researchers would deal with the way an organism presently acts. One could merely reinforce those behaviors which one wishes to maintain or to increase, and would withhold reinforcement for those behaviors which one wishes to diminish. Moreover, operant researchers tend to use immediate, positive reinforcement for every appropriate response although, as we shall consider later, one can best *maintain* behavior by providing reinforcement on an intermittent basis rather than for every response.

But how does the operant researcher use reinforcement principles to bring about behaviors which currently are not in the organism's repertoire? Such new behaviors are "shaped" by a "method of successive approximations." Though a demonstration of the process is highly desirable, the process can be described rather simply. The terms are virtually self-explanatory. The researcher first identifies behaviors which the organism now displays which are at least grossly similar to the desired behaviors. Then drawing from his information about which reinforcers are effective with that organism, he differentially reinforces those behaviors which most closely approximate the desired behaviors. He gradually sets more stringent criteria so that the organism must more closely approximate the desired behaviors before reinforcement is provided. Gradually the behaviors more and more closely resemble the desired behaviors, with the changes being shaped by the differential reinforcement.

One characteristic of this shaping process is especially important because it embodies an emphasis of the operant approach more generally. The main focus is on "improvements" being made, rather than on "mistakes" or "inappropriate" characteristics which occur. For both theoretical research and practical purposes, the operant researcher uses positive reinforcement to bring out desired characteristics while essentially ignoring "flaws" in the organism's behavior. Although *negative reinforcement*—aversive stimuli which reinforce responses when such stimuli are removed—is used in some practical and research situations, greater emphasis is placed on the presenting and withholding of positive reinforcement to shape behavior.

The Importance of Response Rate and the Cumulative Recorder There are a number of ways in which major breakthroughs can occur in science. They sometimes occur with the presentation of data or new interpretations which answer critical research questions. However, they can also occur when scientists obtain new tools or devices, such as occurred with the invention of the microscope. Skinner (1963) suggests that such methodological and technological advances occurred in psychology when he invented the *cumulative recorder* and discovered the importance of *response rate* (in real time) as a major dependent variable.

As has already been noted in a previous chapter, Thorndike's law of effect had pointed out the relationship between behavior and its consequences. But it remained for Skinner to classify the nature of these relationships. Up to the time of Skinner's studies in the 1930s, researchers had typically used one or more kinds of discrete-trial arrangements in their experiments and they simply summed the number or latencies of subjects' responses across the trials presented. But, partly by chance, Skinner began to record his subjects' responses as events in real time—that is, as they actually occurred over the course of several minutes, rather than with reference merely to the presentation of some stimulus. This enabled him to examine changes and stability in the patterns of responses. As a result he began to notice that there were quite subtle changes in his subjects' response patterns and he subsequently invented a device (the "cumulative recorder") which made these otherwise subtle patterns more obvious.

Figure 10-1 shows a cumulative graph of data which are directly, continuously, and automatically indicated on a cumulative recorder while the subject is in the experimental room. A cylinder (G) revolving and feeding paper at a constant rate of speed provides a time measure during which responses can be made. A pen (F), which is linked to the response device in the subject's room, "steps" across the sheet of paper each time a subject makes a response. Each time the pen reaches the top edge of the paper it resets to the bottom automatically (E). Most cumulative recorders also have provision for marking the presentation of reinforcements and the occurrence of other experimental events, although none is shown on the present illustration. The slope of the line indicates the rate at which the subject is responding. At points B and D the horizontal line indicates that no responses were emitted. The lesser slope at A as compared with C indicates that the subject was responding rapidly at point C.

Response Rate, Operant Level, and Steady State   Until Skinner noted their utility in detecting lawfulness in behavior and its controlling consequences, describing arrangements for presenting reinforcements and patterns of responses during real time would have been regarded merely as arbitrary actions by the researcher. "Rate of responding is one of those

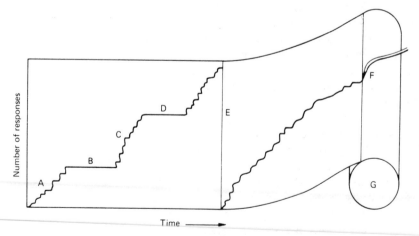

Figure 10-1 Illustration of a cumulative graph being drawn "on-line" by a cumulative recorder.

aspects of a subject matter which do not attract attention for their own sake and which undergo intensive study only when their usefulness as a dependent variable has been discovered" (Skinner, 1963, p. 505). But Skinner did note that there were lawful relationships between reinforcements and behavior, and he initiated a program of research which greatly elaborated on Thorndike's law-of-effect contention that behavior which is reinforced will be repeated. Later we'll consider some "reinforcement schedules" and their effects on behavior. But two concepts should be introduced at this point: *operant level* and *steady state*. Operant level refers to the response patterns and frequency of occurrence for specifiable operant behaviors before any interventions by the experimenter. In both laboratory and field situations, for theoretical as well as practical questions, the operant level serves as a frame of reference against which effects of subsequent interventions can be compared. Some authors also use the term *baseline* to refer to this natural pattern of behavior. *Steady state* (or, for some authors, *stable state*) came into usage to refer to terminal regularities in operant behavior because it was observed that schedule effects seem to level off and remain steady after some period of time or number of reinforcements.

Antecedent and Consequent Stimuli   Earlier we noted that operant researchers are concerned with environmental stimuli which precede as well as those which follow responses. This contrasts with Pavlov's classical conditioning, which traditionally has essentially ignored consequences of responses and has focused on the "goading" (Skinner's term, following the etymology of "stimulus") power of the antecedent stimulus. The operant emphasis is on the consequent stimulus to the extent that it is theorized that most antecedent stimuli come to influence behavior because they are present when responses are reinforced. In the next sections we will consider different types of consequent stimuli and antecedent stimuli which control operant behavior.

Reinforcement   The stimulus which follows a response and which strengthens or increases the probability of that response is called a *reinforcer* in operant terminology. Reinforcers can consist of food and liquids which increase behavior frequency without prior training (*primary reinforcers*), or such items as money and praise or pictures of primary reinforcers which are capable of increasing behaviors because they have frequently been associated with primary reinforcers in the past (*secondary reinforcers*). Typically these secondary reinforcers tend to be somewhat less potent, compared with primary reinforcers, if they are associated with particular needs. They also tend to vary in their strengthening action in accordance with the drive which underlies the primary reinforcer with which they are associated in the acquisition of their secondary reinforcing power. However, generalized secondary reinforcers may vary considerably in their strengthening power, depending upon local circumstances as well as the organism's specific drives. It is also noteworthy that responses themselves may serve as reinforcers for other responses (Premack, 1959). For example, if in a free-choice situation a student is more likely to work on mathematics problems than on English compositions, mathematics activities can be used as a reinforcer to increase the probability of work on English compositions. This could be done by making the mathematics activities permissible only after a given amount of English work has been completed.

Reinforcers can also be classified as "positive" or "negative." Positive reinforcers are those stimuli which *strengthen* the *responses* which *produce* them; negative reinforcers *strengthen responses* which *remove* them. In a laboratory experiment, an example of a positive reinforcer could be food provided after an animal operates a lever a certain number of times; or, it could be points added on a counter whenever a human subject has a series of correct answers to problems presented. Again, in a laboratory experiment, an example of a negative reinforcer could be cessation of shock when an animal presses a lever; or, it could be a temporary pause in the continuous subtraction of points from an initial 500 points on a counter, with the pause in point losses lasting ten seconds each time a human subject gets a correct answer. Although there is little question as to the strengthening effect of negative reinforcers for responses which *remove* them, there is some controversy among operant researchers as to their effects on responses which produce them. This is somewhat similar to the controversy about punishment effects in Thorndike's theory. Hence, we will next consider the roles of extinction and punishment in the weakening or lessening of a response's probability of occurrence.

Extinction and Punishment Effects   Most of our comments thus far have focused on the *strengthening* of response probability. But there are a number of situations in which one may wish to *diminish* or to *eliminate* certain behaviors. There are two operant concepts and procedures which are relevant—extinction and punishment. First we'll define these two terms and then consider their known or assumed effects.

Extinction is an operant term which is used somewhat like the Pavlovian concept of extinction. It can refer to certain experimental arrangements or to a state of behavior. It refers to those experimental arrangements in which one withholds reinforcement for previously reinforced responses. It can also refer to the subsequent effects on those behaviors in that they no longer occur (that is, are completely extinguished) or that they diminish to their preconditioning operant level.

Punishment is both a general language term as well as a term which has been assigned more precise technical meaning during the past ten years. In casual language, punishment typically refers to some "bad" experience (such as spanking, limitation of privileges, public censure, etc.) which one individual or group administers to another when certain "undesirable" actions are taken. But both "bad" and "undesirable" are typically defined within the frame of reference of the person(s) administering the alleged "punishment," without adequate concern as to whether the recipient views them similarly. Moreover, when the undesired behaviors persist—or even increase, as frequently happens—one does not know whether "punishment" simply does not "work" in reducing or weakening behaviors, or whether the recipient simply did not view the "punishment" as a bad experience.

For these reasons and others, some operant researchers have contended that punishment should be more precisely defined if we are to learn what effects punishment has on behavior. Azrin and Holz (1966) have contended that punishment, like reinforcement, must be defined with respect to its effect on behavior. In a sense, they would rely on the reactions of the recipient rather than on the beliefs of the administrator of so-called "punishment" in order to determine whether the term (punishment) had been correctly used. For them—and many other operant researchers—one can properly use the term *punishment* with a stimulus which is "a consequence of behavior that reduces the future probability of that behavior" (p. 381). Actually, this definition avoids the questions as to how the administrator and the recipient *perceive* the particular stimulus; instead they look to changes in behavior as bases for concluding that a punishing stimulus has been correctly identified.

But there are differences of opinion among operant researchers as to theoretical and practical questions about procedures for reducing or weakening response probabilities. Throughout most of his writing, Skinner has contended that the best controlled results come from arranging and rearranging schedules or contingencies for *positive* reinforcement. For example, if one wishes to weaken a response, one should change the contingencies so that the behavior is no longer being reinforced, thus implementing procedures which should bring about extinction of that response. To facilitate this process, he would recommend positive reinforcement of competing responses which may further preclude the occurrence of the undesired response. While he has periodically acknowledged that some mild form of punishment may also facilitate weakening the undesired response, he has consistently argued that the effects of punishment not only may be unpredictable but even may result in increases of undesired behaviors.

Other operant researchers have contended that new information has been and can be obtained concerning the effects of punishment as a means for weakening behaviors. As with reinforcement, they have contended that a key means for unraveling these effects may lie in a more careful analysis of *contingencies* between behaviors and their punishing stimuli, as well as in the more precise definition of punishment noted above (see discussion in Rachlin, 1970). Johnston (1972) has reviewed the research on punishment and has acknowledged that many of the studies, not too surprisingly, have been conducted with animal subjects; however, many human studies have been conducted, and interest in this area seems to be increasing. From his review, Johnston suggests that mild punishment of undesired behaviors and simultaneous positive reinforcement of an incompatible, appropriate behavior can constitute an effective approach to modifying behavior. As a result, one can find a number of authors advocating restrained and judicious use of punishment, despite Skinner's personal cautions against reliance on punishment and his advocacy of the combined use of positive reinforcement and extinction procedures.

Stimulus Control Stimulus control refers to the effect of antecedent stimuli on operant behavior. Such stimuli are believed to gain their control primarily as a result of being present when responses are reinforced, although at least some operant researchers also recognize the possibility that inherent stimulus features (such as a loud noise or a bright color) or classical conditioning processes could also be involved. Operant researchers traditionally distinguish between "discrimination" and "differentiation" processes. Differentiation refers to an organism's making one response rather than another and acquiring the capability to control the characteristics of the response. Discrimination involves distinguishing among stimuli and the process whereby an organism recognizes different stimulus features. An organism might act inappropriately in a situation because of either differentiation or discrimination deficits. In some of the early studies with human subjects, Lindsley and Barrett (Lindsley, 1960; Barrett & Lindsley, 1962) devised laboratory operant procedures for conducting clinically relevant assessments of schizophrenics' and retardates' behavior. They tried to determine whether individuals were having difficulties in recognizing cues as to what constitutes appropriate behavior or whether they recognized the cues but were having difficulties in differentiating and making appropriate responses.

Operant researchers define stimulus control as the extent to which antecedent stimuli influence the probability of occurrences of responses under specified conditions (cf. Terrace, 1966). The most frequently studied case is that of "discriminative stimulus" control of single operant behavior. Typically, responses are reinforced in the presence of (or following) one class of stimuli (such as green objects), which are designated "discriminative stimuli," and are noted S^D (pronounced "ess-dee"). Contrasting stimuli are noted $S^\triangle$ (pronounced "ess-delta"). Typically these are stimuli which generally are similar but which differ in some critical respect (for example, same objects but colored red); they are not associated with reinforcement. Under test conditions or transfer situations, the S^D stimuli are much more likely to be followed by the particular responses than are other stimuli. "Stimulus generalization" is the term which labels those instances in which other stimuli also produce the conditioned responses. In a sense, stimulus generalization constitutes an example of an organism's failure to discriminate among certain stimuli.

Although it is commonly held that some errors *must* occur during learning, it has been shown (Terrace, 1966) that subjects may produce the responses only to the S^D stimuli if an "error-free" training program has been followed. In brief, error-free learning comes about when the experimenter (or teacher) initially presents S^Δ stimuli which are substantially different from the S^D, generally introducing stimuli which are more and more similar while differentially reinforcing responses only in the process of S^D stimuli.

Research has supported the conclusion that differential reinforcement is important for establishing stimulus control (cf. Terrace, 1966), although there are other theoretical positions which have raised questions about the generality of currently available findings (cf. Gibson, 1969). The status of stimulus control of single operant behavior seems less open to question than is that of *concurrent* operant behavior, which we will discuss briefly later. In general most operant researchers advocate providing immediate, positive reinforcement for each appropriate response. Because it is difficult to carry out such contingencies in many practical situations (for example, a teacher with thirty students in a classroom), Skinner (1961) suggested that electronic or mechanical devices could be used to schedule and to provide reinforcement. In education these devices have been called "teaching machines." But provision of immediate positive reinforcement for each appropriate response has not consistently produced the expected results: some data indicating that other reinforcement arrangements may be more effective. This matter is still under investigation as the present chapter is being written. Part of the problem may stem from the fact that certain operant principles were based on studies of single operant behavior, whereas situations outside the laboratory typically involve many responses and various cues which indicate when respective responses are appropriate.

Complex Behavior: Chains, Concurrent Operants, and Other Contingency Statements

Skinner has rather consistently taken the position that sciences can best proceed by studying simple phenomena at first, with later analyses of more complex processes benefiting from the findings and techniques of the simpler processes.

"As the techniques of an experimental analysis of behavior become more powerful, more and more complex behavior is analyzed under more and more complex circumstances. We ignore some things for the sake of studying others, but we do not ignore them permanently. They will be studied in their turn" (Skinner, 1971, p. 103).

He argues that other sciences have gone through similar stages and have undergone the criticism which frequently is leveled at the experimental analysis of behavior: It does not deal adequately with complex phenomena. But, like these other sciences, according to Skinner's views, operant psychology will likewise subsequently weather the storm of criticism. Granted the position taken by Skinner and his optimism that analyses of more complex phenomena will come later, what form might such analyses and principles take? Judging from trends in recent years and contemporary emphases, it seems certain that they will consist of complex contingency statements, the nature of which has not yet been formulated. But two concepts which have been used for many years may provide some guidelines—*chains* and *concurrent operants*.

Skinner seemed to be greatly influenced by Pavlov when he wrote his initial theoretico-experimental book, *The Behavior of Organisms* (1938). In it, he presented "The Law of Chaining": "The response of one reflex may constitute or produce the eliciting or discriminative stimulus of another" (p. 32). In many respects, Skinner's ensuing theoretical statements de-emphasized the classical conditioning aspects and focused on operant behavior, but he always has provided descriptions of chains or other sequential relationships in his discussions of complex behavior. In the more recent theoretical book (Skinner, 1969), he provided an illustration of the contingency of reinforcement for "chained operants": "Pecking a green disk changes the color to red, and pecking the red disk is followed by food. (The frequency of occurrence of the chain of responses increases)" (p. 23). Perhaps future analyses of complex behavior will incorporate some aspects of this concept.

Another concept seems to have some promise for complex behavioral analyses, namely, stimulus control of concurrent operant behavior. We have already noted that a number of studies have attempted to delineate characteristics of stimulus control of the single, isolated operant, usually under the topic of discrimination or stimulus generalization. Comparatively little work has been done until recent years on stimulus control of concurrent operant behavior. Ferster and Skinner (1957) have defined concurrent operants as "two or more responses, of different topography at least with respect to locus, capable of being executed with little mutual interference at the same time or in rapid alternation, under the control of separate programming devices" (p. 724). Subsequently, Catania (1966) has suggested that analyses of concurrent operants may be substantially more complex than one might anticipate from single operant findings: "In the case of concurrent operants, the organism's alternatives are not simply to respond or not to respond, but, given that it responds, to emit one or another of the available operants" (p. 213). Even the behaviors of changing from one response to another pose additional contingency arrangements to be studied. Similarly, Cumming and Berryman (1965) commented that concurrent operants are much more complex than the mere sum of several single operant behaviors. Catania (1966) observed:

Thus, the analysis of concurrent operants must consider not only the absolute rates of the separate operants, but also their relative frequencies and the frequencies of changeovers from one to another. It is for this reason that it is generally agreed that the dynamics of two concurrent operants are more than twice as complicated as the dynamics of the single operant . . . Concurrent operants behave differently together from the ways in which each operant behaves in isolation. (pp. 213-214)

The possibility that concurrent and sequential arrangements may play a major role in Skinner's future complex contingency statements is supported by one of Skinner's comments about the progress attained by operant researchers: "Concurrent and sequential arrangements of contingencies permit the study of aspects of behavior which were once attributed to higher mental processes, among them many which bear upon decision-making" (Skinner, 1969, p. 95).

Two reviewers of Skinner's relatively recent theoretical statements (1969) agree that he envisions using the contingency statements for complex behavior, but they could not envision how this might be accomplished (Kendler, 1970; Terrace, 1970). It was suggested that Skinner may have to resort to the kinds of theoretical constructs which he has so vigorously opposed for simpler phenomena. Only with time will we know the form of the theory, for even Skinner acknowledges that his experimental analysis of behavior is still evolving.

You will recall that one of the questions which Skinner posed for himself was: "How are the relations among behavior and its controlling variables to be brought together in characterizing an organism as a system?" (Skinner, 1969, p. xii) He has consistently emphasized the basic fact (to him) that most behavior is controlled by its consequences; he contends that this fact should serve as the main building block for learning theory. Skinner's more detailed answers to his own question have changed over the years—not a surprising observation about a theorist who has contended that data rather than preconceived notions should shape his theory.

One encounters major difficulties in trying to describe the status of operant theory at any point in time because of the concerted attempts to conduct direct analyses of diverse behaviors so as to accumulate a constantly growing and gradually changing fund of empirical data, and the quite limited efforts to synthesize the information into theoretical principles. Given the inductive theory construction emphasis, there simply is no existing high priority for formalizing theoretical principles. We have given a few examples of findings in some research areas when we discussed operant concepts in the previous sections, but we have not provided many details concerning the topical areas covered by operant theory.

In some respects, operant researchers are very much like other contemporary, atheoretical experimental psychologists who typically choose to relate their research findings to those of around a dozen other studies. Perusal of any current journal will provide countless examples in practically all substantive areas of psychology today. But there is one difference: operant researchers at one time or another all come back to reinforcement contingency statements as their main, or even sole, guiding principles for interpreting their findings and for synthesizing them with other operant data.

From S-R to Type-R Laws to
Three-term Contingency Statements

Throughout most of his professional life, Skinner has taken issue with turn-of-the-century S-R theory and has formulated an alternative model. Nonetheless, he frequently is incorrectly identified with the less sophisticated S-R paradigm.

In *The Behavior of Organisms* (1938), Skinner's initial theoretico-experimental book, he presented a set of static and dynamic laws for S-Type conditioning, dynamic laws for R-Type conditioning, and other laws which were concerned with interactions among the examples of the two learning types. But these laws are now primarily of historical rather than current theoretical interest because of the great amount of data which have been collected by operant researchers since that time and because attention has been focused almost exclusively on operant rather than classical conditioning processes.

Of course, vestiges of these earlier laws remain in the research strategies and in the data interpretations. But the key notion which pervades most of Skinner's more recent writing is an invigorated three-term contingency statement. Terrace has depicted contingency of reinforcement as "the basic variable in Skinner's *theory* of behavior" (Terrace, 1970, p. 532). While one may question whether this constitutes a "variable," there is no question of its preeminent importance in Skinner's contemporary theorizing. Kendler (1970) has concluded that Skinner uses a rather simple model for characterizing an organism as a system:

"Pigeons pecking a disk, humans solving a problem, social behavior, private behavioral events can all be represented by the simple descriptive formula: Responses (R) are made to discriminative stimuli (S^D) as a function of contingencies of reinforcement (S^{reinf})" (Kendler, 1970, p. 529).

Although many operant researchers would question Kendler's apparently critical comment that it is such a "simple" formula, this three-term contingency statement serves as an integrating conceptual device in practically all areas investigated by operant researchers. In lieu of more formal theoretical books, one can find attempts to integrate principles in a number of books primarily designed for teaching undergraduate and graduate students (for example, Bijou & Baer, 1961 and 1967; Ferster & Perrot, 1968; Honig, 1966; Keller & Schoenfeld, 1950; Millenson, 1967; Reese, 1966; Reynolds, 1968; Skinner, 1953; etc.). Typical topics indicate the range of behaviors covered by operant research: acquisition, maintenance, and extinction of single operant behavior; characteristics which become apparent when two or more operants are studied—that is, concurrent operant behavior; stimulus control of operant behavior; development of secondary reinforcers; classification and characteristic effects of reinforcement schedules; response patterns when organisms try to avoid or to escape from negative reinforcers; extrapolation and/or use of operant techniques with social interactions and other forms of more complex behavior.

Throughout all topics covered there runs the basic theme that behavior is primarily controlled by its consequences, with various facets of the environment coming to influence single responses, concurrent responses, and chains, all to the extent that they are associated with reinforcement. Given either basic research questions or practical problems, one's operant strategies to change behavior are quite similar. One first identifies both appropriate and inappropriate behaviors in measurable terms and delineates the reinforcers which naturally are operating in the observed situation. Questions are resolved as to whether new forms of behavior are to be shaped, whether some extrinsic reinforcers are needed in addition to the natural reinforcers, and what alternative sequences of action might be taken. Actual and potentially useful discriminative stimuli are identified. Modifications in the behavior (for theoretical or for practical purposes) are then attempted through a combination of changing reinforcement contingencies so that only the appropriate behaviors are now being reinforced and making maximum use of discriminative stimuli to cue the organism to make the appropriate responses so that reinforcement will follow.

Schedules of Reinforcement

The most systematically organized aspect of operant research and theory is the set of various possible ways in which reinforcements can be provided for responses. One obvious schedule consists of reinforcing every response, which has conventionally been designated "continuous reinforcement" (crf). Another is to provide *no* reinforcements, for which

Pavlov's term of "extinction" (ext) is used. And then there are a large number of schedules, some of them quite complicated and all of which provide reinforcement on an intermittent basis. Some are based on the passage of time and are called "interval schedules"; others are based on the number or rate of responses emitted, which are called "ratio schedules." Some interval and ratio schedules provide reinforcement on a regular or "fixed" basis—for example, fixed interval, reinforcement every nth second; fixed ratio, reinforcement every nth response—while others provide reinforcement on an irregular or "variable" basis—for example, variable interval, the periodicity of reinforcement varies but reinforcement occurs on the average every nth second; variable ratio, the number of responses varies but reinforcement is provided on the average every nth response. In addition, reinforcement can be made contingent on a particular range of response rates—either a high rate or a low rate. A number of reinforcement schedules can be arranged in sequential order, with the particular schedule being determined either by the subject's behavior or by external rules, with antecedent stimuli which signal which schedule is in effect or with no such cue stimuli. Finally, quite complicated schedules can be set when two or more operants are being studied, with components drawn in various combinations from the above arrangements.

In a chapter such as the present one it is not possible to describe the kinds of effects which have been obtained with each of these schedules. One major volume (Ferster & Skinner, 1957) is practically exclusively devoted to such information about schedules and their empirically determined effects; hundreds of papers have added huge volumes of additional data. Each schedule is, in essence, a rule or strategy for determining which occurrences of a response will be reinforced.

Practical-minded readers particularly may become disenchanted with the prospects of examining the detailed accounts of reinforcement schedule effects because the data sometimes merely provide rather esoteric details which are primarily of interest to the basic researcher. But at a minimum, all readers should realize that the consistency of the findings which are reported about schedules lends strong support to Skinner's contention that contingency statements are powerful summaries of behavior influences. Moreover, all readers should be aware that operant researchers have gone far beyond Thorndike's important but rather simple law of effect. Not only can it be said that behavior which is reinforced will have a higher probability of being repeated but also the reinforcement schedule data indicate that response patterns are so highly sensitive to the particular arrangements by which reinforcements are provided that quite precise predictions (some in the form of mathematical equations) can be made about an organism's probable behavior with a specified schedule—during acquisition, maintenance, and extinction phases—with each schedule producing particular features. The data have been sufficiently consistent across a number of animal species that operant researchers can confidently talk about essentially universal lawfulness in behavior. Moreover, similar patterns have been obtained with human subjects, although certain features of their pre-experimental reinforcement histories apparently result in somewhat unique response patterns, too. For example, Weiner (1969) has commented:

We are, of course, a long way from complete mastery over inter-subject variability under FI (fixed-interval) schedules with humans. But it has been shown that such inter-subject variability may be evaluated and controlled by experimental operant conditioning procedures rather than statistical manipulations. In doing so, we have demonstrated that inter-subject variability is not intrinsic to human operant behavior but is, rather, a lawful orderly function of manipulable variables such as response cost and conditioning history. (p. 372)

Weiner's comments are not only relevant to fixed-interval schedule effects, but are reasonably descriptive of other response-reinforcer relationships as well. But there is rather considerable controversy as to the extent to which operant principles account for other complex human processes, especially those relating to stimulus control in general and to language in particular.

ANIMAL DATA AND HUMAN OPERANT PRINCIPLES

The initial operant principles were based on research with animal subjects on tasks which were admittedly quite simple and primarily involved psychomotor activities rather than explicit concern with cognitive processes. Of course, one should recall that the law of effect, from which some operant concepts originated, did result from Thorndike's concern with problem solving, and that many basic and applied operant studies have been conducted with human subjects in recent years. Nonetheless because of the use of animal subjects and the emphasis on psychomotor processes, many critics of the operant approach long have questioned its relevance for human behavior. At least three issues can be identified: relevance of animal findings for formulating human operant principles; extrapolations from simpler processes to more complex processes and creative activities; and the extent to which externally described stimulus control can account for more abstract human processes such as those involved in language.

In various papers, Skinner has explained his use of animal subjects as being primarily a matter of convenience. It simply is possible to do research with animal subjects which would either not be economically feasible or, in some cases, not be ethically permissible with humans. For example, many studies go on for several hundred hours, during which the research subject is studied throughout the twenty-four-hour day. Although there are some exceptions, this ordinarily would not be possible with human subjects. In addition, some of the studies which need to be conducted involve completely naive subjects; animals, raised from birth in special conditions, can provide data which would not be ethically available from human subjects. But if one grants such practical considerations, is it logically and empirically sound to try to extrapolate such findings to human subjects? Skinner answers in the affirmative and points to physiology and other sciences where it is common practice to do initial studies with animal subjects before testing the findings as to their relevance for humans. On the basis that there are bound to be some commonalities, Skinner argues that only by doing such research will it be possible to use scientific procedures to identify any uniquely human characteristics. The operant literature varies considerably on this point, but there is acknowledged the further need to determine experimentally to what extent a given principle based on animal data may have to be modified for humans. Moreover, readers may be interested in noting that some authors have also raised the point concerning cross-species comparisons among animal groups and have urged that comparative studies be conducted to assess the validity of generalizing principles across species (cf. Breland & Breland, 1961 and 1966). But pending disproof, operant researchers are inclined to assume that animal principles at least qualitatively apply to human behavior as well.

This matter has particularly been raised with regard to findings which are based on relatively simple experimental tasks. On this point, we simply should point out the logical and philosophical orientation endorsed by Skinner. He contends that it is difficult, indeed, to make sense of the many complicated processes which occur in the real world outside the laboratory. Moreover, he argues, progress will more likely occur (and may not even occur otherwise) if we first simplify matters under the highly controlled conditions of the laboratory. There, according to Skinner, one can identify lawful relationships which, subsequently, will be seen in the real world and will serve as sound bases for describing more complex processes in the comparatively uncontrolled and multifaceted real-world situation. "An experimental analysis of behavior is necessarily a science in progress. The assertion that it cannot explain some aspect of behavior must be qualified with the phrase 'as of this date.' The analysis has grown steadily more rigorous and more powerful, and it is constantly reaching into new areas, but it no doubt has a long way to go" (Skinner, 1969, p. 100).

In the meantime, operant researchers almost unanimously are willing to place their confidence in the fundamental principles they have delineated in simpler studies as they try to study more complex processes. They contend that they are always open to new data, but that they have more confidence in laboratory-tested principles than they do in common-sense speculation or hypothetico-deductive principles derived more by logic than by data.

Some of the most heated discussions have centered on symbolic processes and language. Over a decade ago, Skinner wrote a book on *Verbal Behavior* (1957) in which he suggested that his $S^D - R - S^{reinf}$ model could account for language as well as for psychomotor activities. In brief, he suggested that words could serve as discriminative stimuli and reinforcers for such language activities as reading, writing, speaking, and listening. In a widely cited paper, Chomsky (1959) severely criticized the approach and essentially categorically dismissed the operant approach as inadequate to handle psycholinguistic processes. Although Skinner has never formally rebutted Chomsky's criticisms, MacCorquodale (1970a and 1970b) has defended this extension of operant theory.

MacCorquodale contends that many of Chomsky's criticisms are more pertinent to the long-outdated Watson behaviorism and some earlier form of S-R theory, but they do not accurately refer to Skinner's operant conditioning. However, Chomsky identifies three issues which, in Mac-Corquodale's opinion, are relevant to operant theory. The first acknowledged criticism is that Skinner has advanced an untested hypothesis that his contingency statements would be applicable to verbal behavior. Mac-Corquodale asserts that this is a reasonable possibility, since both verbal and motor behaviors are emitted by human organisms, and that it is a hypothesis worth exploring, rather than dismissing it out of hand. "The hypothesis may prove to be wrong, but our antecedent confidence in its correctness is at least enhanced by the fact that the basic laws which it invokes have become very sophisticated and impressively well researched" (see Honig, 1966) (p. 85). Chomsky also cites a number of ways in which the hypothesis may not work. Whereas Chomsky contends that the operant system *may* not work with verbal behavior, MacCorquodale argues that it would be worth trying.

Second, Chomsky contends that Skinner has merely paraphrased and renamed concepts which were already adequately designated by other experimental psychologists. He includes such terms as stimulus, deprivation, reinforcement, probability, etc. MacCorquodale counters: "Skinner's analysis is no more a paraphrase of linguistic-philosophical mentalisms than modern physics is a paraphrase of pantheism. . . . Every term in Skinner's account names some real thing which must be physically involved and locatable in any verbal event for which it is invoked. *That* is objectivity" (MacCorquodale, 1970b, p. 89).

Third, Chomsky contends that language is so complex as to require a complex theory with mediating concepts and neurological-genetic components. MacCorquodale explains that Skinner's functional analyses may, indeed, subsequently require mediational processes with neurological underpinnings, but that the task before psychology primarily is to identify behavior's controlling influences rather than to restrict itself to relationships between behavioral and neurophysiological levels of analysis. He characterizes Skinner (as we have earlier in this chapter) as cautioning against premature concern with such concepts lest they lead to nonproductive research. He suggests that "they may generate research whose only usefulness is to disconfirm the mediating entity or redefine it without higher organisms such as may may deal with stimuli in a more abstract way become the absorbing focus of an inquiry and so deflect attention from behavior itself; and they can become a 'refuge from the data,' as motivation has tended to be in psychology" (MacCorquodale, 1970b, p. 91).

MacCorquodale (1970a) depicts Skinner's *Verbal Behavior* as "a *great* book" which elucidates the power of operant theory addressed to such complex human activities as language. He holds that Chomsky and other critics primarily react negatively to the book not because it is not sound but because it embodies a conception of man which is foreign to the long-established notion of "autonomous man." Although MacCorquodale's comments were written prior to publication of Skinner's more recent book, *Beyond Freedom and Dignity* (1971), both professional and general public reactions would seem to bear out MacCorquodale's conjecture that it is the philosophical rather than the scientific issue which most raises critics' objections. Skinner essentially has taken the position that man is not so free as popular opinion might hold, that instead man's behavior is subject to lawful relationships like those which can be observed about other natural phenomena. Critics take the position that Skinner's reinforcement principles might enable some individuals to manipulate other people to their detriment. Skinner and his colleagues contend that, as things now are, people influence and control other people, often in unfortunate ways; man can only be "free" if he understands the lawfulness of his own behavior.

But other producers or supporters of operant theory also have raised questions about the applicability to human behavior, at least given the present status of operant research on simpler processes, especially with animal subjects, but they have called for new and bolder ventures in the experimental analysis of complex human behavior (cf. Kantor, 1970). Some have suggested that contemporary revisions in our conceptions of reinforcement—in the direction of an information interpretation rather than the Hullian-dominated drive-reduction conception—may dictate radical revisions in human operant principles (cf. Glaser, 1971). Others (cf. Hendry, 1969) are optimistic that only minor revisions are necessary to incorporate an information interpretation of reinforcement. Finally, some have been particularly concerned about discriminative stimulus control principles as they apply to humans; they have expressed the view that higher organisms such as man may deal with stimuli in a more abstract way than do lower animals, and that it may be necessary to incorporate the very kinds of mediating constructs which Skinner has so vigorously avoided (cf. Day, 1972; Kendler, 1970; Mowrer, 1972; Terrace, 1970). Given the great commitment to inductive theory construction, with modifications to be made in light of new data, it seems less likely that such changes will prove devastating for operant theory as some suggest (cf. Koch, 1964) than that operant theory will incorporate such new findings and interpretations in its ongoing self-correcting evolution.

PRACTICAL APPLICATIONS

It is an understatement to note that Skinner is optimistic about and interested in practical applications of his theory. No other psychologist in this third quarter of the century has captured the attention of both professional colleagues and the general public alike in considering his views about resolving society's problems. One might agree or disagree with his views, be optimistic or pessimistic about the results of their application; but it is unlikely that many well-read persons in these times are unaware of the existence of Skinner's ideas. His impact has been sufficiently great that we will devote a later chapter to behavior modification as an instructional theory which has been evolving an identity of its own. In this section we will be more concerned with the means by which the basic operant research procedures and principles have been oriented toward practical application.

Skinner has contended that the experimental analysis of behavior and operant theory may be on the verge of providing society with a set of workable procedures for dealing with our most pressing problems and for improving our general quality of life. "The scientific method which has made it successful in the laboratory makes it almost immediately available for practical problems. It is not concerned with testing theories but with directly modifying behavior. Its procedures are therefore relevant whenever a change in behavior is a consideration" (Skinner, 1969, p. 97).

Skinner recognizes that there are limitations in applications drawn from operant theory in its present state of development, but he feels that some practical implications can be directly derived. Two broad steps can be identified—namely, contingency management and stimulus control—both of which emphasize positive rather than aversive forms of control.

In a variety of papers started in the middle 1950s, Skinner has decried the extensive use of aversive control in our traditional school programs. He has contended that positive control would not only be more pleasant, thus fostering a more favorable attitude toward education, but that it would also be more effective. Using his three-term contingency model (discriminative stimuli, responses, reinforcers), he contends that the major role of educators is to arrange that only appropriate (educationally oriented) behaviors are reinforced and that discriminative stimuli be used to maximize the likelihood that such appropriate behaviors will be emitted.

He advocates the direct functional analysis of activities in practical situations so as to identify pertinent appropriate and inappropriate behaviors and to delineate effective reinforcers. Further, the educator should keep objective records of the students' progress so that changes can be made in the students' programs when they are needed and so that the general information can be used for subsequent improvement of the educational materials and techniques.

In a much-cited paper on characteristics of such *applied* behavior analyses, Baer, Wolf, and Risley (1968) have pointed out that behavioristic applications and pragmatic attempts go "hand in hand." The key emphasis here is on describing what tasks are being attempted, what solutions are being tried, and what results are obtained.

Bijou provides an outline of educational programming which is based on operant research and theory:

(1) state in objective terms the desired terminal or goal behavior, (2) assess the child's behavioral repertory relevant to the task, (3) arrange in sequence the stimulus material or behavioral criteria for reinforcement, (4) start the child on that unit in the sequence to which he can respond correctly about 90% of the time, (5) manage the contingencies of reinforcement with the aid of teaching machines and other devices to strengthen successive approximations to the terminal behavior and to build conditioned reinforcers that are intrinsic to the task, and (6) keep records of the child's responses as a basis for modifying the materials and teaching procedures. (Bijou, 1970, p. 404)

A main feature of these procedures is that they emphasize immediate, positive reinforcement for each appropriate behavior or set of behaviors. There is some controversy as to whether it is best to provide immediate continuous reinforcement; research currently in progress may provide indications of optional schedules though data are not clear at the time this chapter is being written. But the general importance of reinforcement arrangements is widely endorsed among operant researchers. One frequently used technique is called "cueing and fading." This essentially consists of introducing discriminative stimuli which have a very high probability of triggering the appropriate behaviors. But because these special cues will not typically be available in natural situations, the student is gradually "weaned" from them as they are faded out. Pitts, for example, uses the concept of fading and defines it as the "shaping process where terminal or desired behavior is presented in model form for the student to duplicate. In successive trials the model is presented in increasing abstraction as the student practices duplication of the model" (Pitts, 1971, p. 226). For example, a teacher might provide the outline of letters for kindergarten students to copy, later expecting them to write the letters with fewer and fewer cues. Or, another teacher might provide a structured laboratory exercise in biology, gradually fading the cues so that the student-scientist becomes more and more independent of such cues in planning and carrying out experiments. We have already pointed out the fact that one of the major features of operant conditioning applications is that evaluation is considered to be a built-in part of the intervention process. But how is this accomplished? There are two techniques which have been used by applied behavior analysts in practical situations—the reversal technique and the multiple baseline technique. As in basic operant research, both techniques involve identification of particular classes of behaviors, some of which are considered desirable and which are to be strengthened by differential reinforcement, and others which are considered undesirable for which reinforcement is withheld. Also in both techniques, data are first collected concerning the natural rate of occurrence or operant level for each of the classes of behaviors, both desirable and undesirable ones.

In the reversal technique, at least one set of desirable behaviors is reinforced for a period of time and data are collected concerning changes in their frequency of occurrence. Once it is evident that substantial change in rate has occurred, the reinforcement is discontinued and the educator observes whether these same behaviors return to approximately the pre-conditioning operant level. Observation of such a diminution in rate would confirm the educator's belief that an effective reinforcer had been identified, and appropriate educational interventions could then be planned and implemented.

In some cases it is not feasible or desirable to use a reversal technique, in which case the multiple baseline technique could be used. When at least two classes of appropriate behaviors can be identified, the educator can first provide reinforcement for the one class and later add reinforcement for the other class of behaviors as well. An increase above the operant level for each of the behavior classes at points corresponding to their differential reinforcement would confirm the effectiveness of the reinforcements and the educational program could then be planned and implemented. Such a decision would be made on the basis that changes due to irrelevant other events would be unlikely to coincide consistently with these manipulations of reinforcement; hence it would be concluded that the changes were due to the reinforcements rather than to such irrelevant other factors.

These are a few examples of ways in which applied behavior analysts have implemented practical suggestions drawn from operant research and theory. But there have been so many people and ideas involved in the application of Skinnerian and other learning theories that a "behavior modification" group could be identified for the past several years. Because their activities bear directly on the emergence of instructional theories, a later chapter will be devoted to behavior modification.

The operant group, both basic and applied, has constituted a small but highly visible group of psychologists. Both proponents and critics have noted the extent of this visibility and the enthusiasm frequently found associated with their basic and applied ventures. Critics have dismissed such enthusiasm as being unscientific, evangelistic fervor, or that it may result from "release from the anxiety of theory construction." Skinner has a different explanation: "There is a more obvious explanation: the analysis works" (Skinner, 1969, p. 86).

EDUCATIONAL R&D IMPLICATIONS

Of the various theorists we consider in this book, none except possibly Thorndike has been more outspoken and more influential in articulating practical educational applications than has B. F. Skinner. Many other operant researchers share Skinner's enthusiasm but there is also a sizable number who view themselves almost exclusively as basic scientists. Consequently, the operant literature ranges widely, with some papers focusing almost exclusively on theoretical interpretations and other papers being considered exclusively applied in nature. Since Chapter 13 deals more explicitly with operant theory-oriented instructional principles and behavior modification theory, our comments here will focus on educational R&D implications which can be derived from the more basic operant papers and books.

There are two major ways in which this basic operant literature can provide implications for educational design and development—methods for evaluating students' progress and substantive information concerning different reinforcement contingency arrangements. The operant approach is almost unique in its emphasis on intensive study of individual subjects. As a result, operant researchers have had to devise strategies for delineating pertinent variables and for obtaining objective indications that the individual subject's behavior was actually being influenced by manipulated variables. Since educators are similarly concerned with individual students' progress, the operant literature can provide suggestions whereby their progress can be measured and evaluated. In this regard, even a number of laboratory techniques can be adopted or adapted for use in classrooms.

Substantively, the operant literature poses a curious situation. It contains a wealth of information concerning relationships among discriminative stimuli, responses, and reinforcements. But most of these data have been derived from animal research. For some unclear reason a pattern has been established over the years whereby basic studies have been conducted with animal subjects but funding agencies and operant research psychologists have appeared somewhat reluctant to promote basic research studies with human subjects. As a result, many behavior modification procedures have been extrapolated from animal studies without determining whether the respective principles are empirically sound with human subjects. Concurrently there seems to be an increase in fundamental research with human subjects but it is too early to determine the extent, if any, of interspecies differences. There seems to be considerable research activity with "atypical" populations (for example, retarded, emotionally disturbed, or brain-damaged persons) but there is also increasing interest in conducting basic operant studies with normal populations ranging from children through adults. Thus the educational development specialist can, with some caution, derive implications from the extensive animal research literature and can find more directly relevant ideas in the growing fund of basic human operant research findings. It is also worth noting that these methods and substantive implications quite likely will be relevant to the arrangement of reinforcements no matter whether one prefers to interpret reinforcers as drive-reducers, as incentives, or as information-feedback.

SUGGESTED READINGS

Bijou, S. W., & Baer, D. M. *Child development.* Vol. 1. *A systematic and empirical theory.* New York: Appleton-Century-Crofts, 1961.

Bijou, S. W., & Baer, D. M. *Child development: Readings in experimental analysis.* New York: Appleton-Century-Crofts, 1967.

Chomsky, N. Review of B. F. Skinner, *Verbal behavior and language,* 1959.

Hendry, D. P. *Conditioned reinforcement.* Homewood, Ill.: Dorsey, 1969.

Honig, W. K. (Ed.) *Operant behavior: Areas of research and application.* New York: Appleton-Century-Crofts, 1966. Pp. 305-308.

MacCorquodale, K. On Chomsky's review of Skinner's *Verbal behavior. Journal of the Experimental Analysis of Behavior,* 1970, 13, 83-99.

Schoenfeld, W. N. (Ed.) *The theory of reinforcement schedules.* New York: Appleton-Century-Crofts, 1970.

Skinner, B. F. *Verbal behavior.* New York: Appleton-Century-Crofts, 1957.

Skinner, B. F. An operant analysis of problem solving. In B. Kleinmuntz (Ed.), *Problem solving: Research, method and theory.* New York: Wiley, 1965. Pp. 225-257.

Skinner, B. F. *The technology of teaching.* New York: Appleton-Century-Crofts, 1968.

Skinner, B. F. *Contingencies of reinforcement: A theoretical analysis.* New York: Appleton-Century-Crofts, 1969.

Skinner, B. F. *Beyond freedom and dignity.* New York: Alfred A. Knopf, 1971.

11
Information Processing Theories

Thinking, language, decision making, problem solving, and other complex cognitive processes have always had some interest for psychologists. Advocates of the traditional, comprehensive learning theories either explicitly or implicitly noted that their basic models would be adequate to handle such complex human cognitive processes even though their primary experimental research was with simpler phenomena. But despite such optimistic aspirations among learning theorists, critics throughout this century have contended that no such extension from simple processes to complex cognitive ones can be made successfully. Nonetheless, the primary emphasis of experimental psychology generally and learning research in particular throughout most of the first half of the century was on processes which would lend themselves more readily to direct observation and measurement.

As a result, cognitive processes were of interest to a comparatively small group of psychologists. You already know from earlier chapters that Tolman attempted a reconciliation between cognitive and behavioral processes, with rather modest success at best. The gestalt theorists, primarily extending their principles of perception, gave rather general outlines of cognitive processes and their relevance for learning theory. One could cite a number of other investigators who did continue work in the area of thinking and cognition—Bartlett, Brunswick, de Groot, Duncker, Luchins, Maier, Piaget, Selz, etc.—but their contemporaries who were doing more "objective" research tended to dominate research and theory construction for several decades.

In the 1950s and 1960s, there was a substantial revival of interest in cognitive processes. This was reflected in new ventures in research and new conceptions in theorizing. Since many of these investigators take the position that learning *really* consists of acquiring and using "rules" and "information," the results of their efforts are relevant to our concern about contemporary theorizing on learning processes. Moreover, since many educators and some educational psychologists prefer direct rather than indirect study of complex cognitive processes, it would seem particularly important to recognize the series of events involved in this new concern with "information processing" and to have some understanding of the research and theorizing involved.

Although one could try to point out deficiencies in the previous learning theories and could question their primary concern with comparatively simple learning processes, we feel that it would be more appropriate to look at other, more positive influences on this revival of interest in cognitive processes. There is a wide-ranging, heterogeneous group of researchers who can be identified as information processing theory proponents. Some (for example, Piaget) have been more vitally concerned with developmental changes in the individual's ability to handle information and have, to some extent, subsumed learning as part of development.

Others, who are more directly relevant to our consideration of learning theorists, have depicted learning processes as constituting the acquisition and use of information. Of this latter group, we have selected three aspects for consideration.

First, we will review and evaluate the emergence of psychological *information theory*. We will find that this "theory" is more of a set of measurement procedures and that the "information" is more technically defined than the ways that the term is used in our general language. Moreover, the focus of information theory is on quantifying the similarities between the message as sent and as received, with no real provision for conceptualizing how the information is processed or what it means and how it is used.

Secondly, another group claims that the *real* precipitating factor in fostering renewed interest in cognitive processes was the impact of the newly emerged computer technology. Most importantly, they point to the computer program as having provided a "program analogy" of human information processing, and they advocate the use of computer programs as conceptual devices for formulating psychological theory. We will examine some ventures which emphasize writing their theory as instructions in a computer program and using a computer somewhat as an imitating subject to test the accuracy of the theory.

One of the striking things one notes is that this *computer simulation* approach, though in some ways related to that of *information theory*, usually involves a set of investigators and theorists who have little overlapping interest with members of the information theory group. For example, a major bibliography on information theory (Johnson, 1967) omits names of Simon, Newell, Shaw, Feigenbaum, Selfridge, and others who are major figures in the information process-computer simulation group. Conversely, computer simulation proponents contend that they see no advantage in using information theory measures and procedures. Whereas the information theory focus was on measurement of information, the computer simulation group particularly is concerned with steps involved in storing and using information, with the program serving as a major conceptual tool for organizing such details.

The third group constitutes a somewhat more recent trend, although proponents of all three views continue to do research and construct theory today. The members of this third group readily acknowledge the influence of information theory and computer simulation, but they routinely disregard the informational analyses of information theory and they display little interest in computer simulation. But they use the language and concepts derived from information theory and computer simulation in developing their theories of human cognitive processes. To some extent, they acknowledge that there is a greater degree of acceptance for the study of cognitive processes which resulted from the information theory measures and the computer simulation programs. Now, given this aura of "respectability" among other experimental psychologists, they devise theories of learning which depict man as a processor of information.

Writing in 1960, Newell and Simon made several comments which are pertinent to the various contemporary information processing formulations. They acknowledge that the previous attempts of the gestalt group, of William James, and of other cognition researchers frequently resulted in rather vague and ambiguous formulations of learning and cognition. Moreover, they acknowledge that the behaviorists and other operationalists in psychology are right in demanding objective and rigorous research methodology. "The task is not simply to restore thinking to the center of the psychological stage; it is to study thinking with as much methodological sophistication as we demand for simpler phenomena" (Newell & Simon, 1961, p. 153). They expressed some reservations as to whether sufficiently objective methods and research techniques had been developed at the initial phase of popularity in this approach around 1950. However, they contended that by 1960 the necessary technology had been developed so as to permit rigorous formulation and testing of theories of thinking and other cognitive processes.

As in our other chapters in Part Two, we conclude this chapter with a section on practical applications and one on educational R&D implications.

INFORMATION THEORY
AND LEARNING THEORIES

Kintsch (1970) described his conception of human learning as involving how people "acquire information, how information is retained, and how what a person already knows guides and determines what and how he will learn" (1970, p. vii). He went on to note that with some authors this would carry him into the areas of perception, thinking, and problem solving, as well as with the more usual processes studied by traditional learning researchers. Nonetheless, he depicted this as *his* conception of learning within the context of man conceptualized as a processor of information. In a similar way, other psychologists in the late 1940s and early 1950s drew ideas from communications technology to aid them in their study of learning and other psychological processes.

Background of Psychological
Information Theory

Psychological information theory emerged as a derivative and modification of mathematical theories which were devised by engineers to measure and to improve sending of messages across noisy communications channels. To understand the relevance of information theory in the contemporary study of cognitive processes, it will be helpful to consider briefly how psychologists typically have reacted to such concepts as "information" and "cognition," and to review briefly the nature of the practical problems faced by the communications engineers.

"Information" and Learning Theories   By this time you should be quite aware of the importance attributed to reinforcement by many of the traditional learning theorists. There typically has been an implicit or explicit assumption that reinforcement "works" because of drive reduction or motivational incentive qualities of the reinforcer. Some have long questioned whether it is indeed the motivational qualities which produce learning effects and performance changes, or whether it is the *knowledge about* the existence of the reinforcer and its relationship to behavior which is mainly of influence with humans and, perhaps, with animals. Aside from those researchers who have been content to work with a purely descriptive conception, most learning researchers have opted for some kind of motivational rather than informational explanation.

But in recent years more researchers have reexamined this matter and have taken the position that it is the informative value of reinforcers which is important and that the relevance of information for learning processes had been underestimated by earlier researchers. Some have even suggested that there has been a "paradigm shift" in the direction of emphasizing information in psychological processes as a major determinant of action. Some operant researchers (cf. Hendry, 1969) have suggested that the "information hypothesis" (that is, that uncertainty-reducing stimuli are reinforcing) must be considered by behaviorists as well as by more cognitively oriented psychologists. Given this contemporary interest in information and cognitive processes, it is likely that you will wonder why these concepts were not accorded greater importance previously.

One of the major reasons that cognitive processes were not considered extensively by earlier theorists is that psychologists simply lacked means for quantifying such a concept as "information," and there was a generally "mentalistic" or "mystical" aura associated when one spoke about the "informative" value of a satisfier or reinforcer. One had to be talking about "something" going on inside the organism without being able to point to any concrete representation of this "something" and without being able to measure how much information was being communicated.

It was in a context where rigorous research methods and objective measurements were being emphasized in psychology that certain researchers became aware of the fact that communications engineers had devised means for quantifying information in messages sent across communications channels. Even more enticing was the fact that the measures were related to a statistical model and that they had been considered so universal in application that similar techniques had been used with machine-machine and man-machine exchanges as well as with man-man communications.

Electronic Communications Systems and Psychology   Given our present concern with the educational use of psychological theory, it is of interest that information theory was developed in a practical situation rather than in some basic research laboratory. Various equipment problems during World War II—such as improving accuracy of anti-aircraft control systems, developing guidance systems for missiles and for aircraft—had presented problems not previously experienced by engineers. As a result, psychologists started to work more closely with engineers than had been typical previously. These psychologists not only made some practical contributions but also gained new ways for studying psychological problems and constructing theories. In contrast with the more popular approach in psychology where one uses a theory to describe and predict activities in a situation, the engineers taught psychologists to examine an existing, working system and to search for ways by which that system might be improved in carrying out its mission. With an approach which focuses on improving current operating standards, one can characterize improved changes as reductions in errors. Moreover, if one can depict ineffective or inaccurate system performance as resulting from inadequate information, then any improved performance can also be said to result from a *reduction in uncertainty* as to what appropriate actions are required.

Some psychologists were working with communications engineers. In that situation, the engineers needed to know how effectively messages were being transmitted across particular communication channels as well as whether different types of equipment or ways of coding messages would improve the quality of the information transmission. In addition, engineers had to contend with various amounts of "noise" from extraneous sources which could get mixed in with the signal being sent and with time constraints concerning how quickly the message had to be sent, either of which could produce additional distortions in the information transmitted. But prior to 1948 no widely used system for quantitatively evaluating messages was available despite the fact that many recognized the desirability of being able to measure information.

Informational Analyses

Claude Shannon (1948, 1951) is generally acknowledged as the "father" of information theory by electronics communication engineers (Pierce, 1965; Gilbert, 1966). Shannon's major contribution was his formulation of a set of measures and a general experimental design for measuring information under various conditions (Shannon, 1948; Shannon & Weaver, 1949). Since we do not plan to use these mathematical procedures to any great extent here—for reasons which will become obvious in a later section—we will consider only the general nature of Shannon's measures with reference to the simplest case to which they are applied.

Simply stated, Shannon's measures primarily focused on the similarity between the message as sent and as received, while calculating how much information *could* have been available both at the sender and at the receiver. Shannon characterized communication as an exchange of messages between two or more selection processes. The sender has a finite potential ensemble or vocabulary from which a message can be drawn and sent. The receiver identifies the message sent as also being drawn from some finite ensemble or vocabulary of potential messages. The larger the vocabulary, the more information which could be sent and be received; or, stated another way, the larger the vocabulary the greater the uncertainty as to which message will be sent and, for the receiver, the greater the uncertainty as to how to identify a message which has been received. (For the moment we will ignore the fact that different amounts of noise and variations in efficiency of coding may influence the information transmission.) In contrast with the other learning theories which we consider in this book, information theory thus considers the influence of messages which *might* have been sent as well as the signals which were actually transmitted.

Let's consider a hypothetical example which illustrates ways in which psychologists (cf. Attneave, 1959) adapted Shannon's informational measures and theory. Stimuli presented to a subject correspond to the *source* and *transmitter* in a communications system. The human subject is characterized as a communications *channel*, and the maximal accuracy by which the subject decodes and responds correctly to the signals is called his *channel capacity*. The responses of the subject correspond to the *receiver* and *terminal* point of the communications system.

At least one more concept is necessary for our illustration, the unit of measurement of information. The term *bit* was devised as the informational unit. The source of the name gives some idea as to its meaning—*bi*nary dig*it*, a contraction of these two words. Within a context where information is equated with reduction in uncertainty, a bit is defined as that amount of information which enables one to reduce the possible alternative answers by one-half. Thus in a children's game where the participant is trying to identify a number from 1 through 8, one bit of information would indicate that the answer is 4 or lower, another bit would reveal that the answer is 2 or lower, and a third bit would indicate that the correct answer is 2. Thus, by now you may have guessed that there are four bits of information in an ensemble of sixteen items, five bits in an ensemble of thirty-two items, etc. As we noted above, we are considering only the simplest possible case. Our calculation of bits here is based on the assumption that there is no noise involved and that each item in a set has an equal likelihood of occurrence. Violation of either of these assumptions requires that we use a more complicated formula to calculate the available information, with the total number of bits available being less than when items are equally probable.

The informational analysis primarily focuses on consistency with which the subject responds to stimuli being presented over a large number of trials. For example, we could present pure tones which vary in pitch but which are identical in all other respects (such as loudness, duration) and ask a subject to associate response 1 with the lowest tone, response 2 with the next, etc., so that response 4 is associated with the highest tone. We could then assess the subject's consistency in responding to tones presented in random order after the subject had had enough practice with the tones that his degree of accuracy was consistent across a series of trials. We could then plot a matrix and count the number of times he gave responses 1, 2, 3, and 4 for *each* of the lowest to highest tones. Without going into the details of the mathematical calculations, we can report that it is possible to determine whether subjects were processing all of the information available in that situation (which, in this case, would be two bits), or whether a subject was so uncertain about some of the tones (probably the middle two) that he sometimes gave correct responses and other times gave a variety of incorrect answers.

In the simplest kind of arrangement, the number of stimuli in a set equals the number of possible responses, and each item in the stimulus and the response sets has an equal probability of occurrence. Thus there would be an equal number of presentations over a given series of trials, and there would be no "response bias" whereby a subject might be more likely to make one response than another.

When unidimensional stimuli (stimuli of a class which are identical in all other respects but which differ along one stimulus dimension) are presented to adult humans, some interesting patterns appear. Once subjects have had enough practice so that they know reasonably well which response goes with each stimulus, their accuracy reaches an asymptote and they maintain that accuracy in performance (plus or minus some error variation). Moreover, the number of items which can be identified correctly vary comparatively little even though different sensory modalities and arrangements of stimuli have been used. There have been a number of studies published with controversial findings, but a paper published in 1956 by George Miller indicates the stability of such findings. It was entitled "The Magical Number Seven, Plus or Minus Two: Some Limits on Our Capacity for Processing Information." As the title indicates, Miller's review of almost twenty studies had shown that there apparently is a structural limit on how much unassimilated (that is, relatively isolated and unlearned) information can be handled by human subjects. This limit seems to hold even under circumstances where greater amounts of information could be processed; for example, when a subject is presented stimulus and response sets which include more than five to nine items, they typically make so many errors that their performance parallels *accurate* processing of approximately five to nine items. Miller's paper was published almost two decades ago. In the intervening years hundreds of information theory studies have been conducted by psychologists. Although many have questioned procedures for calculating some *absolute* kind of human channel capacity (cf. MacRae, 1970), many psychologists have come to accept the findings Miller reported as having some interesting implications for psychological studies on learning and retention. Some have more or less accepted such findings as indicating that man has a very limited capacity for short-term memory storage. Others, responding to another point that Miller made concerning the fact that we can organize information into "chunks," have suggested that we should place greater emphasis in research on ways that man organizes information. But before considering further how psychologists currently regard information theory, we should briefly review their previous reactions.

Psychological Information Theory?

In communications technology, response to Shannon's measures and techniques was quick and favorable. In fact, his ideas received such warm and widespread acceptance that many have characterized information theory in the 1950s as constituting a "glamor science" (Gilbert, 1966). Somewhat similarly, psychologists were so enthusiastic in their response that some seemed to suggest that information theory might provide answers "to one's problems whatever these problems may be" (Quastler, 1955, p. 2). But during the first half-dozen years of its existence, more rational appraisals were made, and many focused on the contributions which might be derived from information theory and from the particular information measures.

Psychologists had been attracted to information theory not only because it could (hopefully) provide some quantitative measure of information—and, thus, perhaps provide long-sought secrets as to how the mind deals with its vast experiences—but that the informational measures might serve as some kind of universal measure of task difficulty and task performance which could be compared across sensory modalities under various experimental conditions. But their hopes were not to be fulfilled. Instead of the stable findings which they had expected, studies provided results which suggested that one cannot ignore how human subjects organize and process the stimuli which are presented to them. Whereas the communications engineers could depend on little variation in their equipment's responses to signals, psychologists found considerable variability in the performance of their human subjects. Other theories and systems were proposed as alternatives to information theory, but since they primarily involve sensory-perceptual processes rather than learning processes (cf. Corso, 1967), we will not consider them here.

In retrospect, one can ask: Is there or was there ever an "information theory" in the sense that we have been using the term *theory* in this book? Our review of the literature has produced three kinds of answers. First, some suggest that information theory is basically a theory of measurement and that, for most psychologists, it merely constitutes another kind of statistic—something like the analysis of variance in that it can be used to analyze data. Second, some regard information theory as a *formal* theory rather than a substantive theory (cf. Frick, 1959). They contend that there are techniques for organizing data as well as certain measures of information which can be useful. Third, some (see discussion in Garner, 1962) acknowledge that substantive emphases in information theory may play a minor role but they contend that psychologically relevant substantive characteristics can be identified. This third group contends that information theory has helped to produce a model of man as a processor of information; they contend that this model is probabilistic rather than deterministic, and that it portrays man in the role of an active selector among stimuli and responses rather than in the more "passive" role which they allege is found in S-R and conditioning theories.

Impact of Information Theory on
Information Processing Learning Theories

Many conflicting opinions have been written as to the extent to which psychological information theory has proven to be of value in learning theorizing in particular and psychology theory in general. It almost seems to depend upon the individual and the research area or theoretical persuasion he represents as to whether information theory is depicted as having had a favorable impact or even any kind of impact on psychology theorizing and research. We'll sample a few comments—drawn from papers which span over a decade, but which also reflect the range of contemporary opinion—and then we will add our own impressions.

We already have noted the initial unrestrained enthusiasm among some psychologists and the later, more judicious, uses made in applying the information theory measures and techniques to various psychological processes (Garner, 1962; Pierce, 1961; Quastler, 1955). We have also implied that interest in information theory has diminished sharply since the mid-1960s. Norman (1969) seems ready to give merely historical importance to information theory: "The information concept ran into one serious problem in studies of memory: it didn't work. This is not to say that the basic concepts of information theory were not valuable, but they did provide useful new interpretations of psychological phenomena. The problem was that the way the communications engineer measured information just did not apply to the human" (p. 72). Of course, Norman is referring to the fact that information theory provides the engineer with ways of quantifying how much information has been transmitted but it does not indicate the numerous ways in which humans can "chunk" or organize information. It focuses on the effectiveness and efficiency of information transmissions but it does not take into account how such information has been coded.

A somewhat more favorable comment was provided by Postman (1964), although he, too, had reservations about information theory's contemporary import. Postman acknowledged the analytical tools provided by the informational analyses and he noted the theory's particular ways for organizing research findings. But he gave a rather mixed reaction concerning information theory results on human immediate memory. "Interestingly enough, it was not the goodness of fit of the theoretical model but rather the organism's failure to behave like a communication channel with a fixed capacity for the transmission of information which constituted the finding of greatest psychological significance . . . The fact that the span is limited by the number rather than the type of item led Miller (1956) to the suggestion that the functional unit in immediate memory is a 'chunk' of information" (Postman, 1964, p. 149). Postman pointed out that such findings suggest that a key idea is to group many items within each chunk if one wishes to increase one's capacity for short-term retention. For example, instead of remembering isolated numbers one could chunk them in familiar patterns such as one's age, address, phone number.

These coding or organizing processes were also of concern in Cherry's (1964) opinion as to the contribution of information theory to telecommunications. He, too, referred to the various studies which had been conducted on human channel capacity, and he emphasized the positive contributions of Shannon's measurement procedures. He especially liked the fact that one could determine amount of information transmitted even when there were "noises" or extraneous stimuli distorting the messages.

Scheerer (1954) reviewed research and theories on cognition up to the early 1950s. He acknowledged that some psychologists, especially those most directly related to communications engineering, had suggested that information theory might be useful in studying cognitive processes. However, he seemed to reject or minimize such a possibility, apparently because he considered information theory to be too similar to S-R theory and to have (in his opinion) the limitations of S-R theory. He seemed especially concerned about information theory's ineffectiveness in dealing with the coding processes which are of such great interest to cognitive psychologists. He contended that information theory was overly concerned with the overt stimulus and response aspects, and was not sufficiently concerned with the cognitive representation of the symbols or with the internal processing which would be involved in dealing with such symbols. In contrast, by 1967 Moray (1967) was maintaining that information theory *could* be useful in studying such central processing and in identifying those kinds of internal self-programming changes or learning which would enable the individual to function more effectively.

As a result of reviewing these and many other papers on information theory, the author has concluded that information theory has not been widely accepted as a learning theory but has influenced the ways that psychologists view learning processes. Partly as a result of information theory, many psychologists now opt for a probabilistic rather than a deterministic view of human learning. Secondly, many psychologists now recognize the importance of those stimuli in a set which *might* have occurred as well as the stimulus which actually was presented to a subject as having considerable influence on learning and behavior. In Chapter 12 we will consider both these features and their effects on the emergence of mathematical learning models. Third, despite the problems in obtaining stable estimates of short-term memory capacity for *all* situations—thus nullifying the earlier aspiration to get definitive measures of man's channel capacity—researchers now are more alert to the fact that there are stringent limitations on the amount of unassimilated information which the learner can hold in short-term memory. Moreover, Miller's 7± 2 "dictum" is taken as a rough rule-of-thumb estimate of the "gateway" limitation on how much new information can get into long-term storage and be learned. Fourth, the problems encountered in trying to measure channel capacity have served somewhat as an additional incentive to renew research on internal coding and processing. Fifth, and perhaps most importantly, even though the particular measures did not work out as expected, information theory gave some support and respectability to the notion that researchers could study cognitive processes in more rigorous fashion than had been typical of many studies earlier in psychology.

But other procedures became available for describing human cognitive processes. We're referring to the computer simulation research which started around the same time (mid-century) as the early work on information theory. It is this orientation in information processing theories which we will now consider.

INFORMATION PROCESSING
AND COMPUTER SIMULATION

"Computer" as part of the title of this section may very well cause many readers to expect an impersonal and generally mechanistic conception of man. Such expectations could not be further from the actual theory which has been developed within the computer simulation orientation. Instead, most researchers within this rather recently emerging tradition tend to be quite concerned with cognitive processes and other forms of complex human activity. We will find rather extensive use of introspective reports by the subjects as they experience the various kinds of tasks presented, and as they try to inform the experimenter of the ways in which they thought about the problem and attempted to find solutions to it. It is very important for the reader to recognize that this conception of man as a processor of information developed somewhat accidentally in association with computer technology, that this theoretical formulation *could* have originated in some other context. Some would even view the computer simulation approach as a revival of Titchener's structuralism, since introspective self-analysis is such an integral part of the methodology and substantive conceptions of learning processes in the contemporary computer simulation research.

"Simulation" in the Classroom

Computer simulation may sound very complicated, or otherwise may make readers apprehensive as to the nature of the discussion which follows. Perhaps you might feel more comfortable if we first describe a kind of "simulation" which occurs in most classrooms. All teachers at one time or another have encountered some students who do particularly well and who seem to grasp the subject matter in any particular course; at the same time, there are those individuals who experience great difficulty even with the most elementary aspects of a course. Frequently, either the student will ask the instructor for assistance or an instructor may take the initiative in contacting a student who has difficulties in his course. A usual question involves something like: "What should I do in order to learn better in this course?" At that point, either the instructor or the student may raise questions as to how some hypothetical "good student" studies. Of course, it's quite possible that the same approach may not be appropriate for both persons. But let's ignore this potential problem for a moment. For illustration, let's say that Jack needs help, and that Frank does quite well in the course. The primary reason for considering Frank's study habits is that Jack may benefit by following similar procedures. But therein lies a problem. How can the teacher describe, or even how can Frank describe the ways in which he studies? When it is possible to specify the detailed steps followed by a good student, one might be able to help a poor student to do better by imitating, or by "simulating" the study habits and general learning activities of the better student. But this sounds much easier than it actually is to accomplish. For one thing, the good student may not know all the steps that he follows in working on a given course. Also, even if he were able to describe the steps that he goes through, the instructor could not be certain that the poor student would be able to follow precisely all the steps outlined by the good student in describing his study habits. This might occur either because insufficient details were provided, or because the poor student simply was unable to monitor himself so as to determine that he is in fact following all the procedures outlined.

Computer Simulation

Similar problems are faced by a group of researchers who use computers to simulate human problem solving and learning processes. They contend that the very detailed manner in which one must write computer programs will enable us to develop valid theories about how man thinks and learns. Whereas psychological information theory, discussed in the previous section, did provide quantitative measures of information processed, it closely resembled traditional learning theory in its primary emphasis on stimuli and responses with comparatively little attention paid to what happens *inside* the organism (the information processing per se). In this section, we'll examine the nature of the computer simulation approach and its implications for theorizing about complex cognitive processes and learning. These theorists especially emphasize the various aspects of information processing rather than merely the end results. We will review the development of this approach, consider some examples of theoretical statements which have been written and tested in the form of computer programs, and evaluate the extent to which the "computer program analogy" has contributed to our theorizing and understanding about learning processes.

Background Factors

It should be of considerable interest to educators to know that *practical* requirements were instrumental in fostering the development of computer technology. We'll briefly consider some of those developments in computer technology which stimulated the use of computer programs for describing psychological processes.

Computer technology primarily grew out of military data-processing requirements during the Second World War. High-speed aircraft and complex weapons systems presented problems to communications engineers which were unlike those previously experienced. The sheer volume of details which needed to be considered and the rapid rate at which decisions had to be made surpassed demands which had existed prior to the Second World War. But more than mere "hardware" changes were required in order to handle these data-processing tasks. It was also necessary to devise efficient and effective procedures for using computers in processing information to perform the tasks.

Development of Computer Technology   The emerging computer technology produced innovations in equipment and in the procedures by which information is coded, stored, retrieved, manipulated, and used in making decisions. By 1948, a computer had been devised which had a capability for storing internally the set of instructions for analyzing data, with the result that more complicated processing could be accomplished in a shorter period of time than had been possible when each segment of instructions was separately fed to the computer. Electronic components became available which enabled processing at a rate one thousand times as fast as had been possible with earlier components, and storage capabilities were greatly modified and improved.

Later advances made it possible for the computer instructions to be modified in light of the operations conducted on data submitted for analysis. Thus the computers were no longer restricted to the programmed instructions exactly as they had been entered; instead, it became possible to have the computer generate new instructions or to modify the instructions originally entered. For the communications specialists and computer technologists, this meant that there would be less tedious work required by the operator of the computer. But psychologists saw other interesting implications: perhaps the computer *program* might serve as a description of ways in which man thinks and learns.

The fact that the computer programs could be arranged to be self-modifying led to the notion that perhaps the rules or procedures that were followed both in the initial formulation of the program and in its various changes might constitute a means for describing human information processing. Miller, Galanter, and Pribram (1960) described the enthusiasm with which many psychologists recognized the potential importance of this "program analogue" of man's thinking and learning. "It is impressive to see, and to experience, the increase in confidence that comes from the concrete actualization of an abstract idea—the kind of confidence a reflex theorist must have felt in the 1930s when he saw a machine that could be conditioned like a dog" (pp. 56-57). No longer need psychologists merely conjecture as to what was going on inside the "black box"; perhaps by writing the details of their theory in a computer program might they have concrete examples of the thinking and learning processes which they had long hoped to describe. Within a decade after the existence of the first computer with a self-storing and self-modifying program (1948), a large number of studies and many theories had been developed in the form of computer programs.

Computer Information Processing Let's consider some of the basic operations which are involved in computer processing. Most of you are probably familiar with such terms as "input," "processing," and "output." These, respectively, involve means by which the computer receives (as man "senses") information, analyzes or evaluates or makes decisions about such information (processes information), and reports the outcomes of such processing (responds and acts). In our discussion here, we will have comparatively little concern with the means by which information is fed into the computer and the various means by which one can obtain reports of the results of such computer processing. Instead, our main concern will be with the processing which goes on within the computer.

Most of you probably are aware that *program* refers to the total set of instructions which are required for processing a given set of data. There are certain features of these processing steps which need to be clearly detailed in the program in order for the computer to process the data appropriately. For example, some temporary or comparatively long-term storage must be arranged for each item or set of data submitted to the computer. In most cases, there is not one but many operations which must be conducted in the course of analyzing the data.

The program instructions must include specification of the point at which a given operation is to be performed, the extent to which the computer should continue performing such an operation, when such processing is to stop, and the procedure for storing or reporting the results of each of these operations. In most contemporary computers, such operations are done serially rather than in a parallel fashion. That is, the computer rapidly goes through one sequence or routine before starting another routine. As a result, the computer program must indicate a sequence in which each of the operations is to be performed. There is some debate as to whether humans act the same way in proceeding through one particular logical operation or whether humans conduct several "parallel" operations at the same time. At any rate, the computer simulation approach which we will examine here assumes that both computers and humans process information serially rather than in parallel fashion. We will restrict our discussion to serial processing, but you should recognize that there could be ways for conducting parallel processing and that it is merely a matter of economy of space which prohibits us from considering such alternative approaches here.

In most cases, both with humans and with computers, there are many different steps which need to be followed rather than one simple operation. As a result, there are many "decisions" which must be made as to whether one should proceed with a given operation, or whether some subsidiary or alternative logical operation would be more appropriate at that point in time, perhaps even interrupting an operation before it is completed. Thus we are suggesting that options may be provided for modifying the sequence in which a computer follows its instructions.

Computers as Symbol Manipulators   From these brief comments about computer technology developments, it should be obvious that the computer and the instructions of the computer, referred to as *the program*, involve much more complex activities and greater varieties of activities than are possible, for example, with a typical desk calculator. But, more importantly, the computer and the programmed instructions involve manipulations of *symbols*, only some of which may happen to be numbers. Moreover, it is important for you to recognize that these symbols may *not only* be single symbols such as letters in an alphabet, but may involve *words* or *strings of words* (sometimes called "list structures"). We can even accurately depict some of these manipulations as involving *transformation of patterns*. Thus, it is the contention of many that advances during the past decade in computer technology essentially enable a programmer to manipulate symbols much the way that humans use language in solving problems.

"Artificial Intelligence" and "Simulation"   Two major developments should be delineated concerning computer versus human information processing. First, many of the information science specialists have minimal interest in human cognitive processes but do have great practical interest in improving the manner in which computers process information. It was early suggested that they might be able to use man's thinking processes as a guide for improving the procedures by which computers process data. Though there is some controversy as to the actual origin of the term *artificial intelligence*, it is frequently used to refer to the information processing steps followed by computers, whether or not they simulate the actual ways in which humans process information (Simon, 1969). A primary practical objective in artificial intelligence is to find the optimal ways that computers can store, retrieve, operate on, and generally use information. There is no great concern with determining whether humans follow similar procedures in processing information except in the extent to which they may provide implications for improving the effectiveness and efficiency of computer processing. As a result, some computer programs combine human problem-solving techniques with the "perfect memory" and the rather unique ability of computers for conducting rapid, repetitive symbol manipulation.

Other persons interested in computer processing have focused on the simulation of human problem solving. "Simulation" or "computer simulation" generally refers to an approach in the development of information processing theories which makes use of computers and computer programming language to describe human information processing. It is important to recognize that this is a *process* simulation, rather than a hardware simulation. That is, there is no intent among computer simulation proponents to contend that man's nervous system in any sense necessarily resembles the characteristics of the computer hardware. Rather, just as was the intent of the essentially *verbal* comprehensive learning theories studied earlier in this text, the computer simulation theorists are concerned with describing human thinking, problem solving, and learning. Certain characteristics are generally associated with this approach to thinking and learning. First, concepts for describing human learning characteristically are the same as those used in computer technology—for example, "input," "buffer," "memory storage," "sub-routines," "output." Second, the theory itself is written in the form of a computer program. Third, the theory is characteristically tested by having a computer operate under that program and by comparing its results with those of human subjects confronted with similar tasks and apparently following similar steps. The intent is to write the psychological theory in the form of a computer program so that a computer, operating under the instructions of the program, will produce the same kinds of successes and failures as those evident in the problem-solving activities of a human working on the same task.

Some contemporary researchers in the computer sciences suggest that at some point computer simulation and artificial intelligence principles may be subsumed under a more general theory of problem solving encompassing both man and machine systems (cf. Hunt, 1968). Thus, some authors contend that the distinction between computer information processing and human information processing is really a result of the current state of affairs, and that we may wish to reconsider our distinction between man and computer at that point in the future when we have a better understanding of the various kinds of information processing possible.

Approaches in Computer Simulation   Space will not permit us to consider the many ways in which computer simulation researchers have attempted to derive problem-solving and learning theories. We will focus primarily on the work of Newell and Simon who have developed a theory of human problem solving primarily in conjunction with their "General Problem Solver" program. We will also make some reference to research and theorizing by Feigenbaum, formerly a student and colleague of Simon and Newell, who has developed a program on verbal learning, primarily that of rote verbal learning. We will spend most of our time considering Newell and Simon's General Problem Solver program because the Feigenbaum Elementary Perceiver and Memorizer (EPAM) has many features in common. However, you should note that there are differences in the way these two programs have been developed and in the way that empirical data for the programs are evaluated. In brief, Newell and Simon typically study the problem-solving activities of *individual* subjects and try to generate a computer program-theory of *general* human problem-solving characteristics. They typically *test* the adequacy of their program-theory by comparing the "trace" of a computer following the program-theory with observations of human subjects on similar tasks. In contrast, Feigenbaum has worked more directly with the principles of rote verbal learning and essentially compares statistics from computer runs with statistics on human subjects' performance on similar tasks.

But before reviewing their work it will be helpful if you are familiar with one characteristic of their approach. Most authors agree that one of their most important contributions involves a distinction between *algorithm* and *heuristic* approaches to solving problems—a distinction which actually resulted from their early findings and which has been adopted in both artificial intelligence and computer simulation studies since that time.

Let's briefly consider the distinction between these two approaches in searching for problem solutions. An algorithm approach essentially consists of specifying steps required for every possible solution to a problem, and is sometimes referred to as a "brute force" approach because it so directly depends on exhaustive use of the system's power for searching for problem solutions. If all possibilities have been exhausted, any given problem would virtually be guaranteed a solution. In contrast, a heuristic approach consists of using various shortcut methods, or rather sophisticated ways of guessing answers to problems presented. Whereas it is recognized that these heuristic procedures or "rules of thumb" may not guarantee a solution to every *possible* situation, there is implied the assumption that solutions to most problems will come with considerably less searching than would be required with the algorithm approach. The significance of the heuristic approach lies mainly in the fact that the early work indicated that human beings seemed to use such rules of thumb in solving problems and in processing information, and in the implication that *machine* information processing might actually be more effective and efficient if similar kinds of rules were written into computer programs.

Development of Human
Information Processing Theories

Let's first consider in general terms the steps followed by researchers in computer simulation studies. First of all, they take the position that an individual's behavior is governed by elementary information processes, arranged in hierarchical relationships. They try to determine how an individual has internally represented the problem situation, the various possible alternative solutions or partial solutions to that problem, and the sequence in which he takes various steps to solve that problem. Newell and Simon's group induces or generates their theory on the basis of intensive observations of single subjects as they attempt to solve problems. For example, a subject is presented with a task and is instructed to "think aloud" and to describe all steps which he takes or considers taking in the course of solving a problem. A tape recording is made of his comments and of any comments which the experimenter makes; typed scripts of these comments plus any materials the subject produces are taken as the "protocol" of his problem-solving behavior. On the basis of this fund of information, along with the specifics of the particular task, the investigator then attempts to write a detailed description of all steps taken by the subject in trying to solve the problem.

It is important for us to emphasize that computer simulation researchers focus on an individual subject's behavior on a particular task, and from this information try to generate a theory about human problem solving in general. There are obvious strengths and weaknesses in this approach. If indeed one is able to derive and subsequently to predict human behavior, of course one would have a more powerful theory than one which merely talks about a general set of laws with rather gross errors in predicting individual behavior. However, in generating theories on the basis of an individual subject's behavior, or even on the basis of several subjects who have served under the same past conditions, one never knows for certain how many of the features of the process being observed are idiosyncratic characteristics of that subject or subjects. Moreover, the process by which they derive the computer program for simulating human thinking involves a considerable number of subjective judgments by the subject and by the researcher. But given the ways in which the resulting principles are tested, one can conclude that the computer simulation research methodology rivals the methodology of studies on simpler learning processes, a feat which could not have been or at least was not accomplished prior to mid-century.

Essentials of the Theory

One can accurately state that whereas Simon and Newell have not *explicitly* formulated a learning theory, the impact of their computer simulation theory of human information processing is such that it demands a different conception of learning processes than was held in traditional learning theories. It is worth noting in passing that Thorndike's research, at least in its earlier problems, had a similar mixed concern with learning and problem-solving activities. We will first describe ways in which the learner and the learning process are conceptualized and then we will briefly review some common characteristics, capabilities, and constraints in human problem solving.

They conceptualize the human as a processor of information whose learning and behavior reflect conjoint effects of the information processed in a given situation and the kinds of retrievable and usable information stored internally in the organism. They assume that man has an internal representation or set of images for his current and previous external and internal environments. These representations are not necessarily exact copies of the external and internal experiences but may (and frequently do) involve various kinds of transformations and coding of the individual's sensations. The information consists of characterizations of such experiences plus problems or tasks with which an individual is confronted, the current status or lack of solutions to problems, goals to which one may aspire, and various rules and means by which problems may be solved and goals attained.

In a given situation, an individual considers what problem is being presented, examines the current status of trying to solve the problem, and considers the various means by which he might progress in solving the problem. Since some errors are inevitable, there will be occasions on which the person attempts a solution to a problem but finds that he is even further from the solution after trying than before he had tried to use that particular means. One has available a finite number of rules, any one of which *might* bring one closer to the solution. The individual is faced with a series of decisions as to which move to make next, how long to persist in any given attempted solution, when to change tactics, etc. But throughout the process, one is periodically making comparisons with the present state of knowledge (problem unsolved), with the desired state (problem solved), and is identifying ways of characterizing differences between unsolved and solved states and delineating various means by which one might improve upon one's current status in the direction of solving the problem.

A special comment should be made about the kinds and ways that information is believed to be stored. Earlier in our description of computers as symbol manipulators, we noted that computers can deal with symbols in a variety of ways. In addition to manipulating single numbers or letters, whole words or multidigit numbers can be processed. Less obvious is the fact that computers can handle structures of words in the form of sentences or other kinds of organization (words which are synonyms, are frequently used together, are alternative labels, are sequentially arranged in terms of some qualitative dimension, etc.). Similarly, the theorists whom we are now considering also assume that man, as a processor of information, can store and manipulate information in a variety of forms. Thus they theorize that human memory consists of an organization of list structures, and that the components of any given list structure may also consist of lists (Simon, 1969). Moreover, these list structures can include information drawn from various sensory modalities, at different times, and produced by a variety of coding strategies.

One basic idea that runs throughout Newell and Simon's theory is that man is an adaptive organism who constantly is processing information in various ways, limited by the characteristics and constraints of the information processing system as well as by the environmental features, so that he can seek goals and gratify needs under changing environmental demands. At times the limits of the information processing system *may* be evident in the ways that the organism copes with problems, but usually the problem-solving activities do not test the system that much because man is a flexible and highly adaptive organism. Newell and Simon have developed four propositions which summarize the major features of their human problem solving theory:

1. A few, and only a few, group characteristics of the human IPS (information processing system) are invariant over task and problem-solver.
2. These characteristics are sufficient to determine that a task environment is repre-sented (in the IPS) as a problem space, and that problem solving takes place in a problem space.
3. The structure of the task environment determines the possible structures of the problem space.
4. The structure of the problem space determines possible programs that can be used for problem solving. (Newell & Simon, 1972, pp. 788–789)

Newell and Simon contend that the human information processing system has only a few basic characteristics which are invariant from one task to another, and from one person to another. That is, they contend that there are only a very few fundamental characteristics which one can find in people, with regard to the way they solve problems. Although they acknowledge that sensory processes obviously involve parallel inputs, at a cognitive level information processing apparently occurs in serial rather than parallel fashion. The fundamental information processing steps are so rapid that they take only tens or hundreds of milliseconds. Both the inputs and the results or the outputs of such processes are retained in a short-term memory which has a capacity of only a few symbols but which accomplishes storage very rapidly. There is also a longer-term memory which has a much greater capacity for storage, but which requires a storage process of seconds or tenths of seconds in duration. Thus, they summarize their primary properties "serial processing, small short-term memory, infinite long-term memory with fast retrieval but slow storage" (Simon & Newell, 1971, p. 149) and indicate that these characteristics greatly influence the kind of problem solving and learning which is possible for humans. Although they acknowledge structural capabilities as having some influence on the way one processes information, they also attribute a great deal of influence to the kinds of tasks to which subjects are exposed. Thus, for example, for some time they have emphasized that human information processing involves utilization of "heuristics" ("rules of thumb") but they contend that the *kinds of heuristics* which are possible depends to a great extent on the kinds of tasks presented and the rules which are given to subjects for dealing with those tasks. Thus they contend that little actual trial and error problem-solving efforts are evident in data. Rather, they feel that the kind of attempts to solve problems which become evident depend to a great extent on the nature of the task presented and its subsequent influence on the *internal* representations which subjects can formulate under those task conditions.

In a number of papers Simon and Newell have reported studies on human problem solving with a variety of experimental tasks which have revealed ways in which particular limitations of the human information processing system influence how man solves problems and learns. He summarized some of these findings:

> The evidence is overwhelming that the system is basically serial in its operation; that it can process only a few symbols at a time and that the symbols being processed must be held in special, limited-memory structures whose content can be changed rapidly. The most striking limits on subjects' capacity to employ efficient strategies arise from the very small capacity of the short-term memory structure (7 chunks) and from the relatively long time (5 seconds) required to transfer a chunk of information from short-term to long-term memory. (Simon, 1969, p. 46)

Simon also has concluded that memory is organized in associated words and groups of words (similarly, associated numbers and groups of numbers, etc.) which technically are called "list structures." We have mentioned earlier that computer processing technology also stores information this way instead of as isolated letters or words.

Partly in response to these limitations and characteristics of memory, the human information processor apparently seeks ways by which he can adapt and cope with situations in the most efficient way possible. By this we are only making a general observation rather than implying that man is *always* "efficient" in coping with his environment. For example, Simon and Newell have found that subjects in their experimental problem-solving tasks typically make best use of short-term memory capacity by first searching for those aspects of the problem which can quickly be resolved so that such findings can be then utilized in identifying other more difficult aspects. This parallels the common-sense approach of solving problems through the "process of elimination" of less likely solutions.

In this internal representation, Newell and Simon theorize that a major feature consists of the presently attained state of knowledge and the few most likely next steps which can be attained as well as the means (operators) by which one can move to each of these potential steps toward solution. Again, they contend that the search process is quite selective, with little or no randomness and trial and error searching evident.

To a great extent, they suggest that the selectivity in search is based on the kind of structure which the problem spaces possess as well as the actual size or number of potential states of knowledge in this problem space. To some extent such structure is determined internally by the extent of redundancy or repetitiveness which the subject can discern in the details of the task presented to him. No matter which kind of tasks were presented to subjects, they usually developed some general rules which were used by various subjects which had the main characteristic of having high probability of attaining solutions.

Simon and Newell contend that their characterization of such internal representation is involved not only in finding solutions to problems but also in the defining of the nature of the problem which has to be resolved. Moreover, their entire emphasis on internal representation leaves them sufficiently disenchanted with traditional S-R concepts that they feel some radically new formulation of learning process is demanded by the data which they have obtained about human problem solving.

Comparison with S-R Learning Theory

This text primarily focuses on psychology learning theory, and the changes in theorizing about learning processes during the twentieth century. There are two major ways in which the computer simulation approach differs from that of the traditional comprehensive learning theories which we've examined thus far. First, the *mechanics* of theorizing involve a reliance on a computer *program* as the format in which the theory is cast, rather than the verbal form found with the traditional comprehensive learning theory. Secondly, there are *substantive* differences between the traditional comprehensive learning theory and the position advocated by the computer simulation group. Let's consider each of these.

From our discussion above, you should know that the computer *program* actually consists of a set of instructions under which the computer operates. But you should also recognize that the computer is not the only agent which can operate under these instructions; actually, a human subject could test out and follow the instructions just as well. Of course, with some programs, it turns out that the computer is the most economical and even perhaps the only feasible means of following the instructions in the program if the program consists of many subroutines and rather complicated options. But it is *critical* that you recognize that it is the *program* rather than the *computer* which is the primary conceptual device. In accordance with the definitions earlier in our text, the computer program serves both as a *model* and as a developing *theory* of cognitive processes. Advocates of the computer simulation approach contend that there are four advantages accrued by testing the theory in the form of a computer program: (1) The theorist is compelled to be quite specific and greatly detailed in describing the processes about which he is theorizing. *Every step* must be spelled out in order for a computer to run under a given program. (2) Some suggest (Shepard, 1964) that computer simulation provides an experimental *synthesis* of factors influencing cognitive processing, rather than merely enabling an experimenter to conduct an experimental *analysis* and thus to conclude that a given factor does have some influence on cognitive processes. That is, such proponents contend that the organization of these various factors in the computer program permits one to determine what happens when various factors are operating in a given situation, rather than merely to study the effects when *one* or a *few* factors are manipulated in the conventional experimental designs. (3) Since it is possible to get a print-out of the sequences followed by the computer operating under this program, this computer "trace" can be compared with the recorded activities of human subjects attempting to solve the same problems under similar conditions. Thus, it is contended that one power of the computer simulation approach is its enabling the theorist to see behavioral results of an application of a model to a representative task (Langhery & Gregg, 1962). This, of course, is particularly important whenever quite complex processes are being studied since it would take a considerable amount of time to go through the various branches or possible problem-solving attempts except that the computer can do so rapidly if the theory is written in the form of a computer program. (4) Some (Feigenbaum & Feldman, 1963; Shepard, 1964) contend that a major advantage of the computer simulation approach is that one can handle much more complicated models via the programs, and yet they can be described in instructions quite close to the actual activities of the human subjects. Thus, not only is it possible to have a greater degree of complexity in the program, but the descriptions are not transformed to the extent that mathematical theoretical formulations would involve.

There also are substantive differences between the information processing theories and the more traditional comprehensive learning theories which we have examined earlier. Green (1966) made these comments concerning a comparison of behavioral learning theories and the information processing approach advocated by Newell, Shaw, Simon, and their colleagues. The traditional behavioral learning theorists have conceptualized problem solving as an extension of learning; the computer simulation group "believes that learning is often problem solving in disguise" (Green, 1966, p. 6). Characterizing problem-solving research prior to 1955 as "sporadic," he gave credit to Newell, Shaw, and Simon (1958) for having provided a new theory of problem solving which was not only important in its own right but which had spawned a whole new wave of interest in research and theory on problem solving. Given the comparatively recent publication of an even more extensive presentation and documentation of their theory, Newell and Simon (1972) probably will continue to have considerable influence on those theories of learning and problem solving which are based on information processing and computer programming concepts. Though written several years previously, Green's (1966) comments comparing this kind of theory with behavioristic theory are still valid and pertinent.

The behaviorists press for simplicity, wanting clear relationships and unencumbered theories. They view the organism as an inaccessible black box, and they seek the relationships between the inputs and the outputs of that box by choosing appropriate stimuli and recording appropriate responses, so that the contingencies are manifest and clear. The information processors prefer complex, or as they say, "rich," experimental situations so that the complex structure of man's behavior can be displayed. Evidence for the processes intervening between input and output are sought usually by obtaining "thinking aloud" protocols from the subjects. (Green, 1966, pp. 5-6)

Whereas the gestalt psychologists and some of their contemporaries were convinced that some form of hierarchical organization does exist in complex human behavior, most of their efforts were concerned with establishing the phenomena of insight and general perceptual organization rather than with detailing the cognitive organizations per se. In contrast, the computer simulation theorists have diverted most of their efforts to identifying the structures of information and the strategies and procedures which are found in human information processing systems. Moreover, these contemporary theorists have insisted on a degree of rigor in research methodology and theory construction which far surpasses parallel activities of their gestalt and other predecessors. Some would even argue that the computer simulation theorists have accomplished a degree of rigor and sophistication which rivals or even surpasses contemporary behavioristic theory—although, of course, critics and behavioristic theory proponents would not agree. But even within this loosely structured group which can be identified as information processing enthusiasts one can find many who have been dissatisfied with both information theory and computer simulation. It is this group to which we turn next.

OTHER INFORMATION PROCESSING THEORIES

A number of individuals in recent years have taken the position that information theory and computer simulation research have made contributions in psychology but are no longer necessary for the development of conceptual systems or for the derivation of practical applications. One such individual is Ulrich Neisser, who conducted some of the early work on artificial intelligence and computer simulation. He has long taken the position (for example, Neisser, 1963) that computers cannot *really* simulate cognitive processes. He contends that they typically are programmed to be single-minded in carrying out their tasks, are relatively undisturbed by "emotional" factors such as is true of the human, and that the perfect memory and other "cognitive resources" characteristically included in the program are too perfect to be representative of human information processing. Moreover, he contends that there are limitations in the complexity and the possible modifications of the program analogy of human information processing, limitations which will not permit one to have an adequate description or test of human learning and information processing.

If one has any questions as to the scope of the change brought about by the contemporary interest in cognitive processes, one would be well advised to review some of his comments (Neisser, 1967) as to the origin, scope, and significance of these contemporary ventures. His observations are applicable not only to his particular theory of cognitive processes, but also to other contemporary information processing theories as well. He acknowledges the influences of computer simulation and information theory on contemporary theory and research on cognitive processes. But he also calls attention to the contributions of other researchers and theorists who maintained their interest in cognitive processes throughout the first half of the century even when such psychological research was relegated to lesser degrees of importance than some of the other areas under study in experimental psychology. He defines "cognition" as "all the processes by which the sensory input is transformed, reduced, elaborated, stored, recovered, and used. It is concerned with the processes even when they operate in the absence of relevant stimulation, as in images and hallucinations. Such terms as *sensation, perception, imagery, retention, recall, problem solving,* and *thinking,* among many others, referred to hypothetical stages or aspects of cognition" (Neisser, 1967, p. 4). Moreover, he points out that cognitive psychology not only is concerned with all aspects of human activity including learning, but that such concern is articulated and studied from a particular point of view. Thus there are cognitive processes to be studied, and there is also a particular theoretical orientation in psychology, the cognitive theory or information processing theory.

There are a number of ways in which Neisser and other theorists borrow from information theory and computer simulation approaches and yet maintain a definite degree of independence from these two approaches. Neisser does acknowledge, for example, that the respectability of studying "mental images" and other psychological processes in cognitive psychology to a great extent has been attained once it was acknowledged that it was "information" which was being taken in, transformed, stored, examined, and reexamined, and generally used as a basis for behaving. Thus he feels free to partake quite freely of the concepts and the terminology of these two early approaches but he does not feel constrained to use them unless it can be shown that they are of value in developing the cognitive theory as a *psychological* theory.

In summary, Neisser makes two important points concerning *cognitive psychology*. First, he emphasizes that this does constitute a point of view, a way of looking at *all* psychological processes. Secondly, he points out that cognitive psychologists—including Neisser—typically study certain processes, and that this constitutes only one aspect of psychology. He acknowledges the importance of the study of such areas as motivation, personality, and social interaction, and suggests that the findings from psychological processes must be incorporated along with the findings from these other areas in order to have a truly complete psychology.

Neisser's Constructive Cognitive Processes

As for Neisser's theoretical position per se, the single most important term is that of *construction*. "The central assertion is that seeing, hearing, and remembering are all acts of *construction*, which may make more or less of stimulus information depending on circumstances. The constructive processes are assumed to have two stages, of which the first is fast, crude, wholistic, and parallel while the second is deliberate, attentive, detailed, and sequential" (Neisser, 1967, p. 10). While describing them at least at the present time as hypotheses which are speculative and which must undergo empirical tests, he outlines six statements which might serve as future principles of cognitive processes. First, continuing his emphasis on the *constructive* nature of cognitive processes, he holds that stored information involves the residue or traces of various previous mental and overt actions. Secondly, he identifies the primary process and a secondary process. The primary process, which occurs just after stimulation by external events or internal experiences, involves various aspects, with parallel processing involving relatively crude or minimal transformation of the input so as to form thoughts or ideas on the basis of stored information. The primary process seems to be relatively automatic and is controlled by stored information. Third, the secondary process involves more direct conscious control, with more sophisticated transformation and constructions of ideas and images. These are only partly determined automatically by the stored information and more influenced by the momentary wishes and intentions and expectations of the individual. These processes are assumed to be serial in character, in contrast with the parallel processing in the primary level. Fourth, he posits an executive control of thinking much like the executive routine that one finds in contemporary computer programming. Thus, he avoids the behaviorists' long-time criticisms of cognitive psychology that it *demands* some kind of "little man within a man," or homunculus. Fifth, he theorizes that the cognitive operations of the secondary process are learned, though they are partly determined through structural and genetic factors. Thus, both the content of memory and the strategies for transforming and reconstructing the content are considered to be learned. Sixth, he uses the analogy of visual perception to describe and to explain remembering and forgetting. Just as an observer may scan and momentarily miss a visual stimulus, the "attention" of the executive routine may be directed elsewhere either deliberately or as a result of an inappropriate or misguided search strategy.

Hunt's Conception of Man as a Computer

Hunt (1971) provides one of the few general integrative theoretical papers available which focuses on computer simulation. However, we include discussion of his theory in this section because he also incorporates in his theory data and principles from research conducted outside the computer simulation groups. For example, he derives implications from several areas of research on retention and on verbal learning processes.

The question to which Hunt addresses himself is "What kind of computer is man?" His theory can accurately be described as a distributive memory theory. But it is important to recognize that he not only deals with the different storage structures, their capabilities, and the content of such memories, but also is concerned with the kinds of processing strategies which are involved in the operating system. He utilizes our current understanding of computer technology to integrate findings from a wide range of comparatively limited models and principles for various subprocesses of learning and retention. In characterizing his model as a "distributive memory model," he uses the designations of memory storage areas primarily as a frame of reference to describe the cognitive operations which he feels are involved in human learning and retention.

It is interesting to compare his conceptions of learning processes and forgetting-retention with treatments of the same topic by the traditional comprehensive learning theorists. For example, in comparison with Thorndike's comparatively simple bond between stimuli and responses, Hunt theorizes that the connections are very complex. He assumes that there is both a central system and a series of parallel peripheral channels connecting out to the various sensory organs which are capable of receiving stimuli. Three different levels of memory are hypothesized, a short-term store, an intermediary level, and a long-term memory. Both the central system and the various parallel peripheral systems have a short-term memory which is capable of storing events of the preceding several seconds, and an intermediate-term memory which is capable of recalling what transpired during the past few minutes. In addition, there is a long-term memory store with an extensive capacity for storing but with a very slow retrieval process. Whereas both the peripheral and the central systems can draw on the long-term storage, for example, to interpret stimuli of the preceding few seconds or few minutes, it is only through the central system that information can be transformed into long-term storage.

It is beyond the scope of the present book to consider Hunt's theory in detail, but it is relevant to review briefly his comments concerning learning processes. First, he suggests that the systems can be modified as a function of experience in some aspects but not in others. For example, the rather rudimentary storage which is characteristic of the short-term memory storage process is sufficiently primitive that it is relatively unaffected by learning, except, possibly, after very long periods of time. Of course, what is stored is obviously influenced greatly by the experiences of the organism. However, both the contents and the coding processes for subsequent storage processing are changed as a result of experience in the intermediate-term memory and in the long-term memory. Likewise, the short-term memory is relatively little influenced by conscious thought, whereas both intermediate and long-term memory storage processes can be influenced or controlled by thinking processes.

In our usual meaning of the term "learning," we imply some relatively long-term storage. Therefore, this book is more concerned with long-term storage than it is with the short-term or intermediate-term storage except in the role that they play in permitting events to be recorded in long-term storage. In this sense, Hunt holds that long-term memory storage, thus learning, is controlled by conscious memory and some type of pattern detection and pattern recognition procedures. "What is learned" mainly consists of the contents of long-term storage and the sentence problem-solving strategies or information processing procedures which have been evolved. In terms of our discussion earlier of computer technology terms, learning therefore includes both the "data" which are stored and the various "programs" which are available to process such data, including strategies for shifting from one data processing stage to another.

Hunt takes an intermediate position on the issues concerning whether learning is gradual or whether it occurs all at once. In many respects, he seems to be favoring a position held earlier by Guthrie by suggesting that, at a microscopic level at least for simple processes, learning occurs in an all-or-none status. But with regard to more complex cognitive processes, particularly as seen from the vantage point of the external observer, he acknowledges that problem-solving progress and learning of complex activities appears to occur gradually. However, he seems to be reserving judgment at least for the present time, and he avoids taking any extreme positions on this issue.

One of the points that he emphasizes is that one cannot neatly separate conceptions of the structure of man as a computer from the information processing operations in which he engages in learning and problem-solving situations. Thus despite the fact that he frequently makes reference to his theory as a distributive memory model, he also recommends consideration of the cognitive strategies involved in processing of information. For example, characterizing problem solving as a set of strategies which can be depicted as going from a starting point through several intermediate points to an ultimate goal, he points out that one must take account of the kinds of storage systems and the retrieval operations which are necessary in order for such information processing to be accomplished. He recommends that concept learning theorists, for example, try to understand where human subjects slow down or encounter difficulties in problem solving. He proposes that the distributive memory model might facilitate designating where such bottlenecks in processing exist. Both the range of capacities and the rapidity of retrieval would be important considerations.

Finally, Hunt's theory is especially relevant to our present topic for two main reasons. He uses the terms, the concepts, and the general framework of computer technology with which to organize his principles and his assumptions. He even suggests that it would be possible, though expensive, to test out through computer simulation the validity of the model which he proposes. Secondly, he draws extensively from other bodies of research and quite limited models and attempts to integrate some of these principles to an extent which is not, unfortunately, characteristic of many contemporary researchers.

Comparison of Neisser's
and Hunt's Theories

Thus there are many striking similarities between the model proposed by Hunt and that described above by Neisser. Of course, it would be well beyond the scope of this book to do an in-depth analysis, but a few observations are appropriate here. First, both use the concepts and the terminology of computer simulation and information theory. Both are interested specifically in cognitive processes, but they also adopt a "cognitive" point of view in looking at psychological processes more generally. A major difference between the two lies in the emphasis which Hunt places on the different kinds of storage or memory, in contrast with the greater emphasis by Neisser on the transformation processes or operations on information; that is, his primary concern with *construction* as a major aspect of cognitive processes. There are additional differences in the kinds of memory posited in the two models, at least at this stage. And there is some difference of opinion, though no major divergence, as to the nature of the processing involved. It seems likely, however, that there will be a continuing exchange between theorists such as these in the cognitive tradition, and that these individual ventures in the long run will tend to be complementary rather than competitive.

Whereas Hunt thus suggests that his theory *could* be submitted for computer simulation, Neisser (1967) has presented a position which uses many of the concepts and some of the hypotheses from computer simulation and information theory but which essentially stands independent of these two approaches. Neisser does acknowledge the "philosophical reassurance" provided by computer simulation, but he long has insisted (cf. Neisser, 1963) that computers are not adequate to simulate human cognitive processes, and he contends that the "transmission wire" analogue of information theory is equally inadequate as a basic conceptual device. Assuming his characterization of cognition is even roughly accurate, Neisser argues that it will, at best, be a long time before a computer programmed computer will be able to simulate human cognitive processes.

Neisser places primary emphasis on "cognitive structures" and he contends that they are of central importance in determining, learning, and remembering. Thus, it is important not only that the organism "constructs" representations of his experiences, but the very nature of these cognitive structures is considered of utmost importance. "Cognitive structures play a particularly interesting role in learning and remembering. In this connection, they are most frequently called 'schemata,' after Bartlett (1932). It is easy to see why the schemata controlled the state of stored information: they are themselves information of a similar sort. The hypothesis of the present chapter is that cognition is constructive, in that the process of construction leaves traces behind. The schemata themselves are such constructions, elaborate at every moment in the course of extensive activity. Recall is organized in terms of these structures because the original experience will elaborate in the same terms. It probably is unwise to think of them as filing systems into which specific memories can be put; they are integral parts of the (p. 287) memories themselves" (Neisser, 1967, pp. 287-288).

Thus in contrast with Hunt's *distributed memory* concept of cognitive processes, Neisser places much greater importance on the content and the structure of content in memory. Of course, Neisser does acknowledge that memory is a central process. It is important in learning. However, he places more emphasis on what is remembered and how it is organized than is implied in the model presented by Hunt.

Kintsch's and Saltz's Observations

Two other recent reviews of information processing ventures merit consideration here—Kintsch's (1970) *Learning, Memory, and Conceptual Processes* and Saltz's (1971) *The Cognitive Bases of Human Learning.* Though they do not actually constitute theories per se, they do have important comments about contemporary human learning theory construction.

Walter Kintsch (1970) provides another example of the cognitive psychology approach to learning. From the start he declares that he is concerned with how people learn. Moreover, he clearly indicates that his chosen theoretical framework is that of the new cognitive psychology of human information processing. He depicts human learning as involving the acquisition of information, its transformation and retention. The subsequent utilization of what one knows and what rules one has developed for dealing with information reflect what really has been learned, which then determines how one acts in a situation. He makes no apologies for talking about perception, problem solving, and thinking, since he feels that these are integral to any sound contemporary theoretical formulations of human learning. He depicts his book as eclectic, in that he draws from a variety of research and theoretical areas, but he does profess a great interest in theoretical formulation. Apparently one of the reasons which prompted him to prepare the text was that experimental psychologists too frequently tend to be concerned with methodology and general treatment of experimental research results; they too infrequently are concerned with interpretation and synthesis into some kind of theoretical formulation. Thus in many respects Kintsch provides an attempt to interrelate or integrate the findings from somewhat disparate groups of researchers and theorists; but at least to the present time, he has not presented his model or theory of learning. Perhaps an apt title might be *Toward a Theory of Human Learning*. His work is mentioned here both because it reflects the fact that some experimental psychologists are becoming increasingly concerned about synthesis of their findings and because the framework which many are adopting is that of the cognitive psychology which really only became popular in experimental psychology since mid-century.

Kintsch (1970) expresses great reservations about the contemporary appropriateness of the global theories of earlier decades but does attempt to integrate the findings from a variety of research and theoretical efforts on human learning. He primarily organizes his synthesis along the lines of selective problem areas which have been studied by experimental psychologists in the psychology of learning. For example one section is on verbal learning, another on mathematical models, another on memory, another on decision processes, discrimination, concept formation, and rule learning and language. It is relevant that he depicts "school learning" as being closely related to or having laboratory analogues in the form of verbal learning procedures, including paired associates learning and serial learning.

Another quasitheoretical venture in the contemporary information processing orientation is that of Saltz (1971). Whereas Kintsch (1970) seemed to attempt to contrast the theoretical conceptions of S-R theory with the newer cognitive information processing theories, Saltz chose instead to depict S-R theory as dealing with one aspect and the information processing conceptions as dealing with other aspects of psychology. For example, Kintsch provided an extensive review of the cognitive information processing conceptions of memory and decision making and other processes. He sometimes uses mathematical formulations, but always deals with the theoretical issues in the context of information acquisition, transformation, retention, and utilization. Somewhat in contrast, Saltz contends that one should distinguish between "learning for retention" and "problem solving." Saltz, like Kintsch, expresses reservations about the global, all-encompassing learning theories which were popular in the 1930s and 1940s. He contends that there is no singular process of learning but that it involves many aspects, with each aspect possibly having different factors of influence. "That is, we may anticipate seeing a number of different *learning* variables, in addition to the association. Eventually, behavior may be predicted on the basis of a formulation which involves a complex of performance variables interacting with a complex of learning variables" (Saltz, 1971, p. 10). He characterizes his own position as involving a multifactor approach to learning as a multifaceted process. With regard to the present topic, that of information processing theories, Saltz therefore tends to suggest that these involve different aspects of psychological processes rather than that they involve different theoretical conceptions of the same process.

Implications for Future Learning Theories

It is appropriate at this point to note that we will not have an answer for some time to come as to whether indeed the human information processing conceptions are dealing with different aspects of learning psychology or whether they constitute a new way of looking at learning processes. "Cognitive psychology" can refer to the study of certain aspects of psychological processes or to the particular point of view which one chooses to use to integrate findings from the various aspects of academic psychology. Neisser (1967) has used the term with both meanings. But with regard to the latter, which is what Kintsch and Saltz seem to be dealing with, perhaps only time will enable us to provide appropriate answers. Bourne, Ekstrand, and Dominowski (1971) suggest that some quite complicated theory or theoretical formulations probably will be necessary in order to encompass the various findings about thinking. It would seem to follow that a very complex theory will be needed to incorporate the many aspects of psychology theorizing and research. Certainly it is unlikely that the simple global hypotheses of the traditional learning theorists can be considered adequate. It seems reasonable to expect that results from information processing theory will be incorporated with findings from more traditional academic psychology in any eventual comprehensive theories of learning.

PRACTICAL IMPLICATIONS DERIVED FROM INFORMATION PROCESSING THEORIES

There is no great effort among the various computer simulation groups to develop and apply their theory to education. However, Simon and Newell

(1971) do take the position that their work on human problem solving has implications both for theories of learning and for educational practice.

The theory of problem solving described here gives us a new basis for attacking the psychology of education and the learning process. It allows us to describe in detail the information and programs that the skilled performer possesses, and to show how they permit him to perform successfully. But the greatest opportunities for bringing the theory to bear upon the practice of education will come as we move from a theory that explains the structure of human problem solving programs to a theory that explains how these programs develop in the face of task requirements—the kind of theory we have been discussing in the previous sections of this article.

It does not seem premature at the present stage of our knowledge of human problem solving to undertake large-scale development work that will seek to bring that theory to bear upon education. (Newell & Simon, 1971, p. 158)

Thus, Newell and Simon do suggest that their theory might be applied to education, and they build a case, though briefly, that their approach to learning process is quite appropriate for the kinds of learning which go on in the classroom. However, there are others who are more explicit in their derivation of implications for education. As an example of such advocates, let's consider the position taken by John B. Biggs (1968).

In contrast with Neisser, who sees little current applicability of the approach, and with Newell and Simon, who provide only cryptic suggestions, Biggs takes the position that the information processing framework provides a relatively new way for conceptualizing school learning. He outlines what he feels are direct implications for educational practice. Biggs is a psychologist in the Higher Education Research Unit, Monash University, Victoria, Australia. He is obviously quite concerned about improving educational practice, and he feels that even though psychology is incomplete as a science, the current findings can be made useful for educators. "The present book is an attempt to provide an information processing framework for many matters that are of direct educational concern and cover such familiar psychological topics as learning, forgetting, concept attainment, concept development, motivation and, in passing, cognitive styles and mental measurement" (vii). He comments on the various positions which have been taken in considering the advisability of trying to apply psychological findings, and acknowledges that some would prefer to wait the 100 or more years found in other sciences between establishment of a "fact" and the applicability of that fact to some practical problem. However, he takes the position that one need not wait so long, and that one can apply psychological findings in educational practice. He points out the gap between the simple learning processes traditionally studied by learning theorists and the more complex processes with which the educator is concerned in the classroom. He also notes that the extent to which an educator is "child-centered," placing emphasis on emotional needs and personality development, versus "subject-centered," in which one is more knowledge oriented, determines in part the psychology which an educator may try to apply. He takes the position that the information processing approach can cope with *both* child-centered and subject-centered educational objectives, and that there is a means for relating the tentative body of knowledge in psychology to educational practice. His approach has been characterized as "a cybernetically inspired model" which "attempts a 'sneak preview' of the activities going on in The Black Box (the title of the second chapter) by drawing analogies with computer operations. So, the black box is revisited and yesterday's telephone switchboard models with its relays have a counterpart in today's computer model with its programs, memory storage, and the like" (Di-Vesta, 1969, p. 467).

Like most workers in the information processing approach, he is quite careful to distinguish between the simulation or articulation about information processing in humans versus the structural characteristics or "hardware." Thus, he is in agreement with the previous theorists who are trying to develop a psychological theory of human learning and cognitive processes.

He is also quite careful to point out that the theory is incomplete and that some caution must be exercised in generalizing to the practical situation. However, he suggests that the utility of this theory for the teacher may lie in enabling the teachers to conceptualize what they do and what their students do in the classroom. Of course, by now you should recognize that this is similar to other recommendations, which have been made with increasing frequency in recent years, that learning theories are most useful to the educator as conceptual devices. Let's try to identify some characteristics which seem different from the traditional comprehensive learning theories.

Biggs's model includes three basic elements: "the complexity programme," "the immediate memory span (IMS)," and "the economy programme." The complexity programme is in charge of the general activities of the organism, especially assimilation of information. It is noteworthy that this aspect seems to be concerned not only with input information, but also with the general state of the organism and the consequences (effects) of activities of the individual as well. Immediate memory span refers to a structural property of the organism in that there are limitations, spatial or temporal, on amounts of information that an individual can deal with at any given time. As you will recall from some of our earlier discussions on information theory, most persons can handle about seven independent units or chunks of unassimilated information, with the range for the general population going from five to nine depending on the particular circumstances involved. The larger amounts of information which we handle in daily activities are processed in conjunction with some kind of coding process. The economy program governs this coding process and attempts to achieve maximum economy so that messages are received and processed efficiently while noise (distortions) are kept to a minimum.

Thus, Biggs's model characterizes the individual as a processor of information. Both the strategies of the complexity program and of the economy program are considered, along with the structural limitations of IMS, in the ways that the individual attempts to deal with input information. If there is sufficient redundancy or repetitiveness in incoming messages, then the "learning" merely consists of the additional information which is stored within the context of the existing code. If, on the other hand, the input message is sufficiently discrepant with previous information or does not fit with the existing coding procedures, then changes in the coding process are required in order for the message to be processed and stored. In this case "learning" involves both the new message or new information to be stored as well as the new coding strategies which are to be developed.

On these matters as well as other aspects of his practical suggestions, Biggs draws not only from the information processing theorists whom we have considered earlier in this chapter but also from developmental psychology theorists. For example, readers familiar with Piaget's concepts of assimilation and accommodation will recognize that they underlie Biggs's foregoing comments about storing information versus developing new coding strategies. In brief, assimilation roughly involves storing information within existing structures, whereas with accommodation incoming information may result in changes to the coding strategies.

Biggs uses his model to account for the fact that when the student is under stress he is capable of learning less than his coding strategies and IMS would ordinarily permit. According to Biggs, this comes about because the complexity program speeds up usual processing rates, therefore losing some parts of a message, and because the emotional experiences themselves consume part of the very limited capacity IMS space. Thus processing of complex information deteriorates under stressful conditions. The teacher should be alert to the emotional state of the student, so that input information can be adjusted accordingly.

Consistent with the emphasis of most information processing theorists, Biggs points out that education involves not only the storage of new information but, perhaps more importantly, the modification and improvement of coding strategies. In common-sense, general language, Biggs is referring to the way that we think about and generally deal with new information. He points out that there are also individual differences in the way that we process information. Biggs points out that we are neurologically capable of different kinds of processing, depending upon the particular developmental stage which we have achieved from infancy through late adulthood. In part, this stems from the fact that our IMS increases up to the normal adult level of 7±2 independent elements which we can handle in our immediate memory span (cf. Miller, 1956). With maturity, the individual develops coding procedures which are less and less reliant on the gross physical properties of the stimulus (are less "stimulus bound") and thus permit the more abstract formulations which are necessary for complex logical thinking. Such considerations are particularly important with preschool and elementary school children because they are going through the process of developing cognitive structures and coding strategies which later enable them to deal with stimuli at an abstract level. But there are also more implications for adolescents and adults in that, for example, under stressful conditions one tends to be less proficient in dealing with the abstract characteristics and one tends to deal with stimuli on a more concrete level.

Biggs primarily presents the educator with a means for conceptualizing practical learning situations. Within the context of his theoretical model he makes a number of suggestions concerning the kinds of activities of the teacher and the student which are associated with specified learning results. He depicts the teachers as controlling such learning and code construction through the teacher's structuring of the environment for the child, and he does make some practical suggestions as to what teachers might do to attain various kinds of coding and subsequent learning results by their students. But it is noteworthy that he acknowledges that the practical suggestions he makes are not particularly new in educational practice; rather, he suggests that the "unique" aspects of his suggestions lie primarily in the total theoretical scheme which he provides. He asserts that the teacher's adoption of the information processing model will enable the teacher to deduce practical implications which would not be so readily apparent with either scattered consideration of the findings or by means of some other theoretical framework.

EDUCATIONAL R&D IMPLICATIONS

The information processing theorists constitute the fastest-growing group of learning researchers today. For the most part, the theorists whom we have considered in this chapter are primarily concerned with establishing a sound empirical basis and with formulating basic theory; comparatively little importance has been given thus far to delineation of educational implications. An exception is that group of researchers, theorists, and practitioners whom we have designated as "cognitive construct instructional theory" proponents and whom we consider at some length in Chapter 14. At the moment we are mainly concerned with ways in which this basic information processing research may have educational R&D implications.

As with the other theories we consider in Part Two, the information processing theory provides a fund of information about processes which are relevant to education. Even better than some other theories, much of the data has been collected with human subjects, though more frequently with adults than with children or adolescents. These data should stimulate questions, and provide some answers, about such matters as: What capabilities does the student have for receiving and organizing potentially useful information? With the question there is implied the suggestion that such capabilities may differ as a function of age, intellectual ability, brain damage, emotional disturbance, temporary stress, etc. How does the learner presently organize his information about the subject matter or skills to be learned? How can new information best be incorporated into the learner's existing store of information? What ways for displaying information will best fit with the learner's sensory modality(ies) preference, rate of processing, style of organization? Moreover, though it may not be desirable or even feasible to depict all educational activities as involving information processing, this orientation provides a different conceptual model of learning as compared with most other theories.

SUGGESTED READINGS

Attneave, F. *Applications of information theory to psychology.* New York: Holt, Rinehart & Winston, 1959.

Berlyne, D. E. Uncertainty and conflict: A point of contact between information-theory and behavior-theory concepts. *Psychological Review*, 1957, **64**, 329–339.

Biggs, J. B. *Information and human learning.* North Melbourne, Victoria: Cassell Australia, Ltd., 1968.

Frick, S. C. Information theory. In Sigmund Koch, *Psychology: A study of a science.* Vol. 2. New York: McGraw-Hill, 1959, Pp. 611–636.

Garner, W. R. *Uncertainty and structure as psychological concepts.* New York: Wiley, 1962.

Gilbert, E. N. Information theory after 18 years. *Science*, 1966, **152**, 320–326.

Guilford, J. P. Factorial angles to psychology. *Psychological Review*, 1961, **68**, 1–20.

Hunt, E. B. What kind of computer is man? *Cognitive Psychology*, 1971, **2**, 57–98.

Kintsch, W. *Learning, memory, and conceptual processes.* New York: Wiley, 1970.

Neisser, U. *Cognitive psychology.* New York: Appleton-Century-Crofts, 1967.

Newell, A., & Simon, H. A. *Human problem solving.* New York: Prentice-Hall, 1972.

Reitman, W. R. *Cognition and thought: An information-processing approach.* New York: Wiley, 1965.

Saltz, E. *The cognitive bases of human learning.* Homewood, Ill.: Dorsey Press, 1971.

Simon, H. A. *The sciences of the artificial.* Cambridge, Mass.: MIT Press, 1969.

12
Mathematical Learning Theory

Another theoretical innovation in psychology at mid-century was the utilization of mathematical equations as theoretical descriptions of learning processes. Though all learning researchers use mathematics in one way or another—for example, in quantifying and analyzing their data—certain researchers emphasize the value of presenting their models and theories in mathematical format rather than in verbal statements. For example, they prefer having all variables defined mathematically and the relationships stated as mathematical equations, rather than merely stating that certain factors facilitate learning. Eventually, of course, all theorists expect to reach this quantitative status; the mathematical learning theorists contend that such an approach is necessary now whereas other learning researchers feel that such quantification is still premature.

What is "mathematical learning theory"? We will find that mathematical learning theory differs in several ways from the traditional comprehensive learning theories with which we were concerned earlier in this text. Some characterize mathematical learning theory as merely providing new techniques for organizing data and for interpreting findings, whereas others contend that certain assumptions are commonly accepted by those psychology researchers who primarily rely on mathematical learning theory formulations. Thus the former group contends that mathematical learning theory is exclusively concerned with the *form* of learning theories, whereas the latter group contends that special substantive, or psychologically meaningful, descriptions of learning processes result from mathematical learning theories.

All learning theories are concerned with developing means for identifying those factors which influence learning processes, with developing a set of principles which summarize the ways in which these various factors operate singly and in combination, and with developing some model or theory which accurately describes learning processes. Most theorists contend, further, that they are interested in making accurate predictions about learning processes, although you have already seen that there are differences in the extent to which theorists have been able to predict precisely what effects will occur. Most theorists have merely focused on *qualitative* changes rather than on identifying the *quantitative* amount of the learning changes as a function of factors selected for study. The mathematical learning theorists as a group contend that they are quite interested in quantitative prediction and in casting their theory in the form of selected theoretical mathematical models.

AN EDUCATOR'S USE OF
A MATHEMATICAL MODEL

Most educators and students are familiar with the policy of some teachers who "curve" their students' grades or who try to get their classes' grades in some approximation of the normal curve. We are quite aware that there is considerable controversy as to whether such grading practices are desirable; also, we are quite familiar with the tendency in recent years either to eliminate grades in the traditional form or to set grades for an individual student in accordance with his accomplishments of delineated educational objectives. However, it will be useful for our purposes here to ignore this controversy and to focus on the use of a normal curve distribution in setting students' grades. You see, there is implied (although not always recognized by the teacher) the assumption that if measurement procedures are adequate, students' progress in a semester or year will fit certain characteristics. That is, there is the implied assumption that the population of students, of which the present class is a sample, will benefit from the educational experiences in rather predictable patterns. Most students will be "average" in their responsiveness to the educational experience. A small group of students will do very well and, at the other extreme, a similar number of students will do poorly. Without going into the details of the controversy and of the description of normal curve characteristics as they may be relevant in the measurement of various psychological processes, we can simply note here that the mathematical model dictates that 68 percent of the group will be within one standard deviation of (above or below) the mean, and that the remaining individuals will be divided equally between the top extreme group and the bottom extreme group. Some teachers approximate this distribution in their assignment of grades by selecting an average grade, for example, of 80 and setting their grade point standard deviation value as 10. Thus, most of their students (approximately 68 percent) will have grades in the 70 to 90 range, with a greater amount centered around the 80 score; an additional 16 percent of the students will have grades below 70, and another 16 percent will have grades above 90.

Of course, most teachers then go on to modify the grades in light of their observations about the students in the particular class at that given semester. However, many teachers *do* make use of the normal curve distribution at least as a frame of reference against which they can compare the students' grades in their present course. Moreover, such patterns also can be used to compare students of one class with those in other classes previously encountered by the teacher.

What we are suggesting is that teachers have sometimes used particular *mathematical models* as frames of reference for describing and for comparing both individual students and whole groups of students. As you can see, the mathematical model does not necessarily dictate what content is being learned in the class, nor even the meaningfulness nor appropriateness of the educational experience. However, there is a *formal*, or organizational, value derived from the mathematical model in aiding the teacher to interpret or otherwise describe a student's scores during that particular learning experience.

You should also recognize that there are certain assumptions implied when one decides to "curve students' grades." First of all, there is assumed that the teacher should judge an individual student's progress in an educational experience in comparison with other persons going through that experience around the same period of time. An alternative, and recently popularized approach, is to compare the student's progress in terms of his attainment of educational goals which have been delineated for that educational experience. Second, if one does accept the notion of comparing a student with the other members of the class, one need not necessarily assume that the benefits from the educational experience will actually follow the normal curve distribution. Thus, the teacher who does decide to "curve" his students' grades may have unknowingly also accepted the assumption that the students' grades will actually follow the configuration or pattern of the normal curve distribution. In fact, some teachers who do not obtain such neat, bell-shaped grade results, may "force" the students' grades to fit such a distribution. We hope that you recognize that many other types of configurations or distributions *could* be assumed as to students' grades in a particular course. (Students who are knowledgeable about test theory and about psychological research might appropriately note that many studies have shown that data obtained from general populations frequently do follow the pattern of normal curve distributions. But one need always question whether his particular group of students is sufficiently representative of such a hypothetical general population, or whether in fact one might have a group of students, for example, who are even composed of two different groups merged into the same classroom experience.)

The main point that we are trying to establish here is that teachers sometimes have used a particular mathematical model, the normal curve distribution, to set grades and to evaluate the test scores of a specific group of students. The main reason for establishing this in a chapter on mathematical learning theory is that certain learning theorists have accepted the notion that one way to develop a theory of learning is by using mathematical models to organize their findings and to evaluate data obtained from single subjects and from groups of subjects. Just as the teacher may find it a convenient frame of reference, the mathematical learning theorist selects a particular mathematical model as a frame of reference for describing his data. That is, he is particularly concerned with getting an adequate mathematical model which will summarize the data which he has obtained and which will predict future learning changes under the specified conditions. Finally, some assumptions may be associated with a given mathematical equation even though they may not be explicitly required by the user.

WHAT IS MATHEMATICAL
LEARNING THEORY?

Let's consider each of the terms in the order in which they occur. First, the researchers whom we will now consider emphasize not only that mathematical techniques should be used in the statistical analysis and quantitative descriptions of data, but also that the resulting theory should be cast in the form of mathematical equations. They are vitally concerned about the changes which occur as a function of various kinds of practice arrangements and thus are interested in "learning." However, some researchers are more interested in specific types of learning rather than in formulating a comprehensive learning theory—although there are certain assumptions and principles which typically are held by researchers active in the mathematical learning theory tradition. There is some controversy as to whether their product is most accurately described as a "theory" or as a "model" as we have used the terms in this text. Many mathematical learning theorists simply use these terms interchangeably and contend that they choose to make no distinction between theories and models.

Let's consider further the use of the term *theory* and related issues as to substantive aspects. Atkinson, Bower, and Crothers (1965) define mathematical learning theory as a particular method of theorizing which is actually quite compatible with various other learning theories, no matter whether they involve cognitive processes, stimulus-response associations, etc. They essentially contend that there are relatively few substantive assumptions which are involved whenever one tries to develop a mathematical learning theory. Bush and Mosteller similarly presented their approach as "a possible mathematical framework for analyzing data from a variety of experiments on animal and human learning" (Bush & Mosteller, 1955, p. vii). But in contrast with the above cited statements by Atkinson et al., Bush and Mosteller acknowledged that there are certain assumptions implied in the way that they use mathematical models. However, despite their personal preferences they contend that there is nothing inherent in the particular mathematical models that demand that a theorist must adopt such assumptions.

Even mathematical learning theorists themselves at times do distinguish among their approaches in terms of the assumptions and basic conceptions of learning which can be delineated. For example, Neimark and Estes (1967) refer to one of the assumptions which is basic in the Bush and Mosteller approach—the notion that behavior is essentially probabilistic (a matter which we will discuss later in this chapter). They point out a few ways in which a particular group of mathematical learning models are different from the approach advocated by Bush and Mosteller. In brief, they characterize Bush and Mosteller as working predominantly with experimental, observable data and making relatively few assumptions as to the underlying physiological mechanisms. They depict the position which they describe in their book, that of Estes' stimulus sampling theory, as being concerned both with observable data and with at least some of the details about the probable underlying psychological and physiological processes. Thus there is some range of opinion as to whether mathematical learning theory mainly provides a means for organizing and interpreting data, or whether in addition there might be certain underlying assumptions as to the actual nature of the learning process.

Part of the debate centers around the use of the terms *theory* and *model*. Some authors actually use them interchangeably, although in an earlier chapter in this text we pointed out the advantages in distinguishing between these two terms. In brief, some authors suggest that they are merely using mathematical techniques as a model of learning process or as a way of organizing and interpreting their findings, whereas others emphasize certain assumptions which they feel one needs to make about learning process if one wishes to use a specific mathematical model. Some authors essentially avoid the whole issue by primarily emphasizing the advantage of making one's formulations and predictions in quantitative rather than qualitative form. Estes (1961) suggests that the role of mathematical equations in mathematical learning theory is first to describe data and secondly to provide means for testing substantive hypotheses (p. 139).

Just as a teacher uses mathematical models for describing the students' test scores and as a means for evaluating the kind of distribution formed by the class's test scores, likewise certain learning researchers contend that there are advantages in using mathematical models to describe the data they obtained in learning research and to develop a theory which most adequately can account for such data.

Bush and Mosteller (1955) indicated that they frequently were asked whether their approach does anything other than "curve-fitting," and whether the mathematical models *really* add anything psychologically meaningful in the study of learning processes. These seem like excellent questions to keep in mind as we review the background out of which the modern mathematical learning theories have developed and as we examine a few examples of these ventures. It would also seem important that we try to identify some of the basic assumptions, if any, held by mathematical learning theorists concerning the nature of learning processes.

BACKGROUND FACTORS

Mathematical psychology was not popularly used as a descriptive term in psychology until mid-century. Mathematical learning theory is routinely identified as having started around 1950. Of course, there were various predecessors which were of varying degrees of influence on the development of mathematical learning theory.

Mathematics in Psychology before 1950

Most authors refer to the early contributions of Fechner, during the middle nineteenth century, and to the work of Ebbinghaus and Thorndike in the later nineteenth century as being examples of work by psychologists who were interested in obtaining quantitative descriptions of psychological processes and who used mathematical techniques to describe their empirical data. Coombs, Dawes, and Tversky (1970) report one mathematical model which started early in this century; this particular model was based on the assumption that initial learning proceeds at a constant rate but that amount forgotten is proportional to amount learned (p. 256). Other early researchers attempted to fit various mathematical equations to learning curves but these efforts generally involved few or no assumptions about the underlying psychological processes and essentially can be characterized as "curve-fitting" attempts. That is, they were primarily concerned with seeing whether they could find any mathematical equation which might fit the learning-curve data obtained from their subjects. This led to a whole series of mathematical equations, none of which was obviously more successful than others in describing the data. Moreover, they made no real effort to consider the psychological processes possibly being revealed by the data.

Louis L. Thurstone (1919) is generally credited with having developed the first systematic attempt to use mathematical equations in conjunction with a set of psychological assumptions about learning processes. He also is characterized as having been a pioneer in the use of a *probabilistic* approach to learning processes. That is, he suggested that it would be more meaningful to characterize learning processes as involving a range of behaviors, each of which has some lesser or greater likelihood (or probability) of occurrence. The more popular approach at that time (and even now) was to hold a "deterministic" position, implying that if we only knew all the relevant influences we could predict precisely which response the individual would make during learning. To some extent, this parallels the debate in physics concerning classical deterministic theory versus the somewhat more recent relativity (probabilistic) theory. Other psychologists also tried to extend Thurstone's use of mathematical equations for describing psychological processes but they did not receive widespread support from other researchers in experimental psychology. Some suggest that their failures may have been partly due to the fact that their ventures were not closely identified with ongoing experimental learning research. But another plausible explanation is that such mathematical efforts were associated with the test and measurement (psychometric) research in psychology at a time when this "correlational" tradition was becoming separated from experimental psychology (cf. Cronbach, 1957). Luce, Bush, and Galanter (1963) suggest that this "temporary cleavage between mathematical and experimental psychology ensued because the mathematical research focused on the scaling and multi-dimensional responses to questionnaire items and attended less to the traditional problems of experimental psychology."

But what about the early comprehensive learning theories? Didn't they try to develop quantitative laws of learning? Although they aspired to such formulations, most of the principles were presented in verbal form, and qualitative rather than quantitative changes were predicted. They stated that a given factor would have a significant effect on learning processes, but they usually were not able to state how much of a change in the independent variable would produce how much of an effect in the dependent variable.

Atkinson, Bower, and Crothers (1965) acknowledge the interest of Clark Hull in obtaining quantitative principles of learning. However, they make certain critical comments as to why they did not regard it as an essential part of the contemporary development in mathematical learning theory: His principles were frequently presented in verbal rather than quantitative form. He *stated* that he was interested in a quantitative theory of learning, but they characterize his approach as mainly involving relatively few quantitative features, with many descriptions of learning process involving qualitative rather than quantitative differences. Moreover, they note the current emphasis on stochastic (probabilistic) conceptions of learning process, and by contrast point out that Hull's theory particularly emphasized a deterministic approach.

Mid-Century Developments

Modern learning theory is generally characterized as having started about 1950. But even in the post-World War II era (1945 to 1950) there were various indications of a developing interest in characterizing behavior in mathematical terms. Some (for example, Luce, Bush, & Galanter, 1963) point to the close relationship between experimental psychologists and engineers and mathematicians during World War II as a factor of influence in psychologists' becoming more interested in mathematical formulation. Many also suggest that Wiener's cybernetics movement and Shannon's information theory conceptualization were particularly important in stimulating interest in mathematical formulations about learning process.

George Miller, to whom we have referred in the chapter on information processing models, was also a person of influence in the development of mathematical learning theory. Many authors cite his 1949 paper with Frick, "Statistical Behavioristics and Sequences of Responses," as being a significant influence in stimulating psychologists to consider utilization of mathematical equations in their theoretical formulations. However, we will not consider his many contributions in use of mathematics in psychology (cf. Miller, 1963) because he subsequently focused on mathematical analyses of language and linguistic processes rather than on the learning process with which this book is primarily concerned.

Atkinson, Bower, and Crothers (1965) identify two major sources or influences which led to the movement, in the 1945-1950 period, toward mathematical theories of learning. One is the general body of learning research findings which had been collected over a period of years by various learning theorists, leading to a fund of information which could be treated mathematically. Secondly, they indicate several ways in which information theory was of influence on learning conceptions and learning theorizing. It emphasized the probabilistic nature of events, the consideration of sequential effects, rather than the more static characterizations found typically with classical learning theories. It also emphasized Markov chain representations for learning data rather than the previous statement of principles without consideration of state changes. We will elaborate on these points when we outline some of the main characteristics of mathematical learning theory.

Falmagne suggests that there are three periods of development since 1950. He characterizes the first period as being that of enthusiasm and optimism about the possibilities of using mathematical models to describe learning processes.

The first period is an era of enthusiasm, aroused by the exciting discovery that laboratory learning situations could be formalized by stochastic models that would yield detailed, and sometimes accurate, predictions about the "fine grain" of the data. In the second period, questions appear. Everything considered, the construction of learning models that fit the data is a rather easy task. The problems lie elsewhere, for example, in choosing among several models that fit the data equally well; or, when a model is found to be reasonably successful, in deciding what the implications are for psychological theory. (Falmagne, 1969, p. 483)

Depicting this second period as one in which mathematical learning theorists expressed doubts and reservations after the initial enthusiasm, the third and current era was characterized as one of more measured enthusiasm with somewhat limited but more confident expectations again being expressed. Accepting that there must be some limitations in this particular approach (or, more correctly, approaches), advocates of mathematical learning theory now seem to be consolidating their gains and attempting to find ways in which mathematical models might be useful for research and theory about learning as well as about other psychological processes.

Operator Models and State Models

Though most authors acknowledge the influence of other psychologists in the utilization of mathematics in psychology, it appears that mathematical learning theory (at least in its early stages) developed primarily along two lines—*operator models* and *state models*. Bush and Mosteller are identified as pioneering in the development of operator models, whereas Estes and his colleagues are generally credited with starting the state-model tradition in learning theory. However, these approaches did not develop in isolation from each other. Quite to the contrary, there was considerable communication and influence among the various individuals working in mathematical learning theory. Nonetheless, we can better understand some characteristics of mathematical learning theory if we delineate the course of development of mathematical models along these two lines.

Operator models get their name from their focus on the mathematical operations or operators which characterize trial-to-trial (learning) changes in correct response probability. For example, the prelearning probability of a correct response in a two-choice situation would be .50, whereas the correct response probability would be around 1.00 after learning had fully occurred. Operator models typically involve the assumption that learning consists of a gradual, incremental process with practically an infinite number of levels between the unlearned and the learned levels. In our hypothetical situation, we might find that the probability increases .01 for each trial—that is, .50 on the first trial, .51 on the second trial, .52 on the third trial, etc., until 1.00 is reached. In this case the mathematical operator would be a constant sum added to the probability from one trial to the next. In another situation, the change might consist of a constant fraction of the difference between the probability on a given trial and 1.00. For example, the fraction might be 1/10 of the amount remaining to be learned. In this case, the initial probability would again be .50, the probability on trial number two would be .55 (.50 plus 1/10 of 1.00 minus .50), on trial three would be .595 (.55 plus 1/10 of 1.00 minus .55, or .55 plus .045), on trial four would be .595 plus .04 or .635, on trial five would be .6715, etc.

There is practically no limit to the complexity of the equation or equations which might account for trial-to-trial changes in learning as evident from the changes in probability of correct responses. Moreover, one could posit several changes occurring on each trial in complex learning processes, and the calculations would become quite complicated when many more than two responses are identifiable.

Given the practical orientation of this book, it is noteworthy that operator models were first used for practical clinical problems. In the late 1940s Bush and Mosteller (cf. 1955) had been attempting to analyze data on the ways that hospital patients respond to certain drugs. They wanted some systematic, quantitative means for characterizing these changes, and they realized that there may be relatively irreversible changes—both from the drugs and from general learning processes in their measurement procedures—so that they wanted to observe changes within each of the patients studied. Moreover, they suspected that the amount a patient could change would depend at least in part on how much "room" for further change remained. Although they modified their original model many times, it was quite early in their work that they became attracted to mathematical models in general and to operator models in particular. It should also be noted that they had a definite preference for generating conceptions of the trial-to-trial changes from the data collected, with comparatively minimal assumptions about the learning process.

State models get their name from the fact that their proponents typically assume that there are only two states (an "unlearned" and a "learned" state), or some finite number of states involved in learning. State model proponents, frequently deriving some of their fundamental ideas from Guthrie's theory, typically contend that learning in its most basic form is an all-or-none process. Many state model enthusiasts also focus on the process by which an organism changes from one state to another, typically conceptualizing the organism as "sampling" stimuli and responses. One rather widely used type of mathematical model or group of models is called a "Markov model." Not only do Markov mathematical models focus on changes from one state to another, they also involve the assumption that the change from one state to the next can be simply characterized by indicating what that "first" state is without any additional information as to the "paths" by which the organism arrived at that particular "starting" state. At some risk of oversimplification, one can say that in the basic Markov models the organism only has a "memory" for what state of learning it is in at a given point with no recollection of the learning changes previous to that "starting" state. In addition, Markov models have an assumption that an organism cannot return to a previous state once a change in states has occurred. Finally, as should be evident from our above comments, there is no "improvement" in learning as measured by correct response probability *until* the state change occurs. As a result, there typically is some variability in response probability around a theoretical or actual mean for *each* state, but there is *no* gradual increase in correct response probability from one state to the next.

Thus the state-model correct response probabilities from trial to trial would be quite different from those of our hypothetical example for the operator model above. As you will recall, the operator models have correct response probabilities gradually increasing from one trial to the next, with the mathematical equation for such increments constituting the basis for naming that particular operator model. In contrast, state model probabilities for the first ten trials—in a hypothetical example where the state change occurs at the sixth trial—might follow a pattern such as .50, .55, .45, .59, .51, .90, .85, .95, .90, .89.

We have restricted our comments here to the simplest forms of operator and state models. The mathematical model literature reveals a very large number of models, some of which are quite complex and which attempt to depict more complicated learning processes. Although our brief comments here do not indicate details of the more complex models, the reader should be aware of the fact that a number of mathematical probability models have been used to conceptualize the "fine" features of learning changes. The operator and state models illustrate some of the more fundamental characteristics embodied in the more complex mathematical learning models.

It is noteworthy that the work on state models was begun around the same period of time but independent of Bush and Mosteller's work on operator models. William K. Estes at Indiana University had extensive training and experience on operant research. Around 1948 he began searching for better ways for describing the acquisition of bar pressing in animal operant conditioning studies. One major early paper (Estes, 1950), "Toward a Statistical Theory of Learning," indicates some of his objectives and reports some initial research. Somehow in the process of trying different models Estes became more intrigued with the possibilities of using some of Guthrie's conceptions of learning as a stimulus and response sampling process. Partly as a result of the Guthrie influence, many of the state models later were included under a more general learning theory called "Stimulus Sampling Theory" (cf. Neimark & Estes, 1967). Simply described, stimulus-sampling theorists contend that there are numerous stimuli in any situation which *may* influence an organism but only a portion of which actually have been detected or sampled by that organism to the extent that its behavior is influenced. They also recognize that organized patterns as well as isolated stimuli may be treated as potentially influential units. Similarly, it is assumed that there is some variability in stimulus-response connections rather than that they are fixed and invariably determined. In part this sampling of responses is indirectly produced by the organism's sampling of isolated stimulus elements and more organized stimulus patterns, and by the probabilistically described connections between stimuli and responses.

Increasing Interest in Mathematical Theories

An important series of conferences were held in the early 1950s. For example, during the summer of 1951 and the summer of 1952, George Miller, William Estes, Robert Bush, Frederick Mosteller, and other early workers in mathematical learning theory had extensive opportunities to exchange their points of view and to develop further their ideas concerning mathematical learning theory. Atkinson, Bower, and Crothers (1965) report that the number of contributors to mathematical psychology began increasing at a substantial rate at least as early as 1955. From that point on a great number of mathematical models were developed and explored. To some extent this variety of models reflected the various kinds of experimental situations from which data had been obtained, but some development in models also seemed to reflect an advance in the uses of mathematics in psychology.

A three-volume *Handbook of Mathematical Psychology* (Luce, Bush, & Galanter, 1963*a* and 1965*a*) was published; these handbooks plus the two volumes of *Readings in Mathematical Psychology* (Luce, Bush, & Galanter, 1963*b* and 1965*b*) provide an extensive description of the development in mathematical psychology from the beginning work around 1950. The rate of growth is evident in that these authors reported that only limited work was evident in the early 1950s but that numerous models were being explored by 1965. The volume of literature became large enough that the *Journal of Mathematical Psychology* was established in 1964 and has flourished since that time.

Why Mathematical Models Were Developed

It is of interest to consider the announced intentions of these pioneers in mathematical learning theory. Some of Estes' (1950) comments are representative. Estes pointed to the long-ranging battles among proponents of the various comprehensive learning theories and observed that none really had received universal support. He took the position that some of the major controversies might be resolved if theories were presented in the form of mathematical equations rather than in verbal statements using words which frequently leave too much room for variations in interpretations. In addition, he contended that mathematical theories might have the additional advantage of forcing researchers to stay close to their data (to avoid overgeneralizing) and to keep at a minimum the number of inferences drawn about processes allegedly occurring inside the organism.

While awaiting resolution of the many apparent disparities among competing theories, it may be advantageous to systematize well-established empirical relationships at a peripheral, statistical level of analysis. The possibility of agreement on a theoretical framework, at least in certain intensively studied areas, may be maximized by defining concepts in terms of experimentally manipulable variables, and developing the consequences of assumptions by strict mathematical reasoning. (Estes, 1950, p. 8)

Estes advocated conceptualizing stimuli and responses in terms of probability (likelihood) of occurrences and trying to formulate mathematical equations which would accurately describe simple behavioral processes. From them one would have a basis for conceptualizing more complex processes. But one major advantage of mathematical learning theory is that it would diminish the number of debates which stem from disagreements about definitions of terms and it would put theorizing at a more objective level, while also stimulating more productive research activities.

He proposed that the emerging mathematical learning theories should be judged "solely" in terms of "fruitfulness in generating quantitative functions relating various phenomena of learning and discrimination" (Estes, 1950, p. 321).

SOME GENERAL CHARACTERISTICS OF MATHEMATICAL LEARNING MODELS

We have noted that literally hundreds of mathematical models have been proposed in the few decades of modern mathematical learning theory, thus at least raising the implication that they do not take a *monolithic* approach to learning processes; rather, they seriously entertain the possibility that different types of learning processes may be involved. Now let us consider some of the features which seem to be common across these various mathematical models.

We have selected five characteristics which can be found in all or most of the extant mathematical learning models: (1) use of theoretical mathematical models to describe and to interpret data; (2) probabilistic (stochastic) models rather than deterministic ones; (3) concern with sequential effects, involving some examination of trial-to-trial changes; (4) comparatively few outside assumptions, with parameters primarily derived directly from the data; and (5) some preference for linear transformations in accounting for trial-to-trial changes.

Mathematical Equations to Organize Data

Mathematical learning theorists use as their dependent variable the probability of occurrence of a specified class of responses. Although it is possible to consider a relatively unlimited number of responses within a quite complex mathematical model, we will primarily restrict ourselves in our discussions here to conditions involving a "correct" versus an "incorrect" response. Thus it is reasonably accurate to say that we will be primarily concerned with the probability that a specified correct response occurs.

Typically the "naïve" subject starts with a zero probability or a chance probability of making the correct response, and learning is evident in his increasing consistency or probability in making correct responses to the point that he is either 100 percent accurate in his responses or has reached some *asymptotic* level. Bush and Mosteller (1955), for example, indicate that they consider learning to be "complete" when some asymptote or degree of stability is obtained, so that the data indicate that no further performance increase is possible for that subject at least under those conditions.

The dominant characteristic of mathematical learning theory is the utilization of some kind of theoretical mathematical equation to describe and to interpret data obtained in the learning experiment. Whereas all agree that some mathematical model is to be used, there are many disagreements as to *which* theoretical mathematical model should be used. In brief, each mathematical learning theorist selects the theoretical mathematical model which he feels would be most appropriate for the particular kind of data of interest to him. His subsequent efforts in using the mathematical model *may* provide implications to the mathematician for further mathematical theorizing, but the major purpose is to use the mathematical model because of its anticipated potential value for making sense of the learning data.

Probabilistic (Stochastic) Models

Virtually all extant mathematical learning models subscribe to the point of view that learning processes and behavior in general can be best understood in stochastic or probabilistic terms. Thus, they avoid the classical conception of causation in science that events are *invariably determined* and hold instead that events (including behavior of subjects during the course of learning) have a certain *probability* of occurrence. Certain types of mathematical learning models are conventionally identified as "stochastic learning models" but it is important for you to recognize that virtually all mathematical learning models do accept this stochastic approach to learning processes. For example, Bush and Mosteller (1955) have taken this position: "We tend to believe that behavior is intrinsically probabilistic, although such an assumption is not a necessary part of our model. Whether behavior is statistical by its very nature or whether it appeared to be so because of uncontrolled or uncontrollable conditions does not really matter to us. In either case we would hold that a probability model is appropriate for describing a variety of experimental results presently available" (p. 3).

Other mathematical learning theorists vary as to the extent to which they contend that behavior is *intrinsically* probabilistic. But as a group they are substantially different from most traditional learning theorists in their adoption, at least for working purposes, of a probabilistic model rather than a deterministic one. Thus, despite the contention by mathematical learning theorists that they are neutral with regard to theory in psychology, it is important to recognize that their basic strategy is quite different from that of most of the theorists we have considered thus far in this book.

Sequential Effects

Virtually all mathematical learning theorists have some major concern about the *sequential* and cumulative effects of learning processes. As we noted earlier, it was particularly because of the learning processes involving essentially irreversible changes that Bush and Mosteller (1955) originally became interested in certain kinds of mathematical models. Although most of the traditional learning theorists primarily focused on general laws of behavior which were essentially static—laws which were essentially considered applicable no matter what level of learning was involved—the mathematical learning theories are particularly concerned about trial-to-trial changes and the general cumulative effects during learning processes.

Some mathematical learning theorists (state-model advocates) focus primarily on the two or more "states" which an organism reaches—an "unlearned" and a "learned" state in a two-state model. Others (operator-model advocates) particularly emphasize the kinds of changes or increments which occur during learning—summarized as mathematical operations (additions, subtractions, multiplications, divisions, etc.) which account for the changes. But practically all mathematical learning theorists are concerned with conceptualizing the sequential effects.

Emphasis on Observable Events

In contrast with most of the previous, traditional comprehensive learning theorists, mathematical learning theorists tend to formulate their theory at a level quite close to the observable events. Moreover, they primarily look to the data obtained for generating statements of trial-to-trial changes. Estes (1961) contrasted modern mathematical learning theory with the theories of Hull and Hebb, noting that the mathematical learning theorists operate almost exclusively at the level of observable events. Estes acknowledged that mathematical learning theorists subsequently may have to make inferences about processes within the subject, but whenever possible they relate the theoretical statements to stimulus and response characteristics which lend themselves to direct observation and measurement.

The facts seem to be that for every limited empirical area, taken by itself, hypothetical entities or mechanisms have trouble proving their worth and usually turn out to be clearly dispensable. Sometimes they play a useful role in suggesting the form of laws or models, but once the latter becomes operational, the hypothetical constructs can be discarded, much like the scaffolding after completion of a building. Only when we wish to bridge the gap between superficially distinct problem areas and to integrate hitherto unrelated findings do we find that interpretation in terms of hypothetical, "molecular" events turn out to be of critical importance. (p. 113)

Stated simply, the mathematical learning theorist is interested in trial-to-trial changes as the subject shows evidence of learning. The mathematical learning theorist attempts to delineate those "parameters" which accurately and efficiently summarize the changes.

Let's consider a very simple illustration which may serve to indicate what mathematical learning theorists do in much more complex mathematical learning models. Let's assume that we have a subject whose task is to make a right or a left response. To keep our example simple here we'll ignore any initial tendency or preference for making one of these two responses. Then the probability of his making a right response is approximately .5; that is, there is a 50-50 chance that a right response will be made when only two responses are possible. When "learning" has taken place in our illustration, the subject would have an almost perfect likelihood, or a probability of 1.00, of making a right response. Simply stated, the mathematical learning theorist is interested in understanding the course of changes from one trial to another by which a subject initially has only a .5 probability of making a right response but subsequently has almost certain likelihood of making a right response. Moreover, since it is likely that greater changes in probability will occur while there is room for substantial improvement, most mathematical models consider the particular trial-to-trial changes in contrast with the amount of learning which still *can occur.*

Although some characteristics are indicated by the particular mathematical equation, others ("free parameters") are not stated in the mathematical equation itself. These free parameters are based on observations of the particular subject's behavior. For example, the theory may include a value for the subject's rate of responding. The experimenter would have to measure the subject's rate of responding during the appropriate points in the experiment in order to compute predictions about the subject's subsequent learning in that situation. With some exceptions, it is generally considered desirable to have only one or a few free parameters in a mathematical learning theory equation.

Of course, it is practically impossible to estimate response probability from data from only *one subject* on *one trial.* Therefore, in some cases blocks of trials for single subjects are used; more frequently, data from many subjects are analyzed as they move from trial one at the beginning of the experiment to the last trial in the study.

Atkinson, Bower, and Crothers (1965) delineated three levels of predictions which are of interest to mathematical learning theorists. At the lowest level of prediction, particular numbers are computed from data at the beginning of an experiment, and the numbers are then used to predict what the subject will do subsequently during the course of that same experiment. A higher level of prediction, and one which is somewhat more demanding as well as more valuable, involves "overdeterminism" of the particular parameters. In a given situation, if you can estimate a parameter and get the same value several different ways or from several different parts of the available data, that parameter would be considered to be overdetermined. The third level involves predictability not only within that particular experimental session but also within other kinds of sessions, with similar learning types, and/or within learning situations more generally. At this last level the experimenter is concerned with "parameter invariants" across different kinds of learning tasks and types; to some extent this deals with the fundamental issue as to whether there is (are) one or more types of learning processes.

Assumption of Linear Changes

The point to be made here is quite simple and should be almost self-explanatory. We are all familiar with the fact that, in any given series of numbers, the change from any number to the next in the series may be linear (involving a constant to be added, multiplied, etc.) or may be so complicated as to require an extensive equation to describe or summarize the differences across the numbers in that series. With few exceptions, most mathematical learning models assume that transformations (changes) from trial to trial are linear rather than that they follow some more complicated form. In part this reflects the belief that learning changes probably are linear, but it also involves an assumption which constitutes practical convenience: A less complicated mathematical model is required if one assumes linear changes. Most theorists who accept the linear change assumption also acknowledge that the models would have to be changed substantially if it is found that other than linear transformations actually occur.

In addition to this general assumption of linearity by most mathematical learning theorists, many authors also use the term *linear model* to refer to an even more restrictive case. Certain mathematical models place such great emphasis on the constant characteristics of the trial-to-trial changes that they are called *linear models* or *linear operator models*. Thus many authors use the term to refer to the simpler forms of certain operator models, but you should understand that most other mathematical learning models (such as state models) also involve an assumption that state-to-state changes are linear.

The general point here is that most mathematical models used for learning processes have involved assumptions that the sequential changes are linear. It should be recognized that this was at least partly for reasons of simplicity and convenience and that future models may be more complex in their mathematical structure. But following the general principle of parsimony, the simpler possible equation is chosen as long as experience shows that such a model is adequate to account for data obtained and interpretations generated.

THEORETICAL CONTRIBUTIONS
FROM MATHEMATICAL MODELS

Earlier we reviewed some of the reasons presented by mathematical learning theorists as to why their particular approaches might provide contributions to psychology learning research and theory. One major idea presented was that mathematical learning theories would diminish some of the controversies by providing sharper testing of competitive hypotheses about learning. It was contended, for example, that more precise quantitative formulations of learning principles would diminish the controversy and general disagreement as to adequacy of various learning principles; thus, it was suggested that mathematical learning models could foster or stimulate more constructive development of psychological learning theory.

Apparently skeptics were more accurate in their expectations about the fruitfulness of the approach than were the early proponents. Thus far, mathematical learning theory seems to have contributed little to reducing disagreements about some of the major principles in psychological learning theory. Part of the reason is the relative isolation of the body of workers who pursue the mathematical theory approach. But even more important is the fact that most of the effort of the mathematical model builders has been in the direction of identifying various kinds of mathematical models, rather than in using widely accepted models as the basis for clarifying theoretical issues. As a result, the *Journal of Mathematical Psychology* (and other journals and books in which such papers are published) has spent most of its efforts on comparisons of alternative mathematical models rather than in the utilization of such models for building a learning theory.

Of course, one should not diminish the importance of the theoretical contributions of the mathematical models. They have demonstrated adequately that one can deal with the fine details of learning data as well as with the cruder, less precise statements about learning processes. That is, it has been adequately demonstrated that theoretical models derived in the form of mathematical equations can describe satisfactorily data about sequential changes in quite fine detail. Moreover, they have fostered an interest in the changes over time in learning process to the extent that is not true of the more traditional learning approaches, with the possible exception of the operant approach. As you will recall, its concern with changes over time is not so much a product of the findings of the mathematical models as it is merely a reflection of the basic assumptions as to how the mathematical theorists felt they should formulate their learning theory. That is, the concern with sequential changes over time does not result from any *breakthrough* in findings about learning processes; rather, it merely represents a basic assumption of the mathematical learning theorist as to how one can best formulate theories about learning process. Of course one should not underestimate the importance of this emphasis on sequential rather than static formulation. Indeed, it probably can be indicated as a telling criticism of the traditional learning theories that they did not adequately handle dynamic, ongoing changes but rather focused almost exclusively on static conceptions of learning.

Similarly, there is an important contribution from learning theory developed by the mathematical model builders concerning the *probabilistic* nature of behavior and learning processes. Again, we have an example of a contribution which stems from the assumptions of the theorist rather than from the data which were obtained from the mathematical model per se.

Finally, a major theoretical contribution which arose in some undefined manner in conjunction with mathematical models is a conception of learning processes as information processing rather than as stimulus-response associations. One can readily obtain evidence of this emphasis by casual perusal of the current issues of the *Journal of Mathematical Psychology* and various journals and books which publish papers and data from mathematical models; most of these papers conceptualize learning processes as involving information processing. This theoretical preference is easily discernible despite protestations by the proponents of mathematical models who have regularly insisted that utilization of mathematical models is necessarily neutral with regard to such issues. It is quite obvious that with the developments in mathematical models there has emerged acceptance of the conception of man as a processor of information, and a formulation of learning processes which more and more is similar to the cognitive or neocognitive orientation than to the traditional S-R approaches.

In conclusion, we have a curious state of affairs whereby the basic assumptions rather than empirical data must be credited with some of the theoretical contributions associated with mathematical learning theory. It is quite feasible to identify a number of patterns in theorizing with the mathematical theory approach, but one would be hard pressed to explain how these characteristics are *necessarily* dictated by the *data* obtained by these researchers. Thus, just as with the other theorists we have considered in this text, we find that some of the major "contributions" from the mathematical learning theorists may stem not so much from the data they obtained but rather from the assumptions embodied in their approach as it was initiated and changed over time.

PRACTICAL APPLICATIONS IN EDUCATION

We have already pointed out the orientation of the mathematical learning theorists toward rather narrowly defined theoretical areas and the distinct tendency to develop rather precise mathematical formulations for organizing learning data. Moreover, we have pointed out that "applicability" to the mathematical model builder frequently means that he is attempting to apply a way of organizing data (some specific mathematical equation or other model) which was shown useful with one set of data as he evaluates its *applicability* to another set of data. Somewhat similarly, he takes this strategy or means of organizing data as a major guiding orientation when he attempts to solve practical problems. There is less emphasis on the substantive principles which he derives from his mathematical model approach than on the procedures and methods in going about the task. When educators raise the question of applicability in educational situations, he tends to point out the virtues of his strategy and general organization for managing attempted solutions to the educational problem.

Thus the reader should not be surprised to find that where mathematical model builders have become involved in various kinds of practical educational problems they have tended to deemphasize any *substantive* theoretical contributions which they could derive from their basic science model and instead have pointed to their particular mathematical models and general ways for organizing their data as having implications for coping with educational problems. However, it is important to add that they do draw from contemporary learning theory more generally in deriving substantive principles.

Estes' (1970) *Learning Theory and Mental Development* constitutes one of the few available examples in which there is a concerted attempt to utilize mathematical learning theory with a practical problem area. Even though the discussion of learning theory tends to be quite abstract and theoretical and never really reaches the specificity of educational *methods*, it would be useful to review briefly Estes' conception of the role that learning theory should play in practical situations. Note the general approach that he takes to his topic, and the recommendations he makes to the practitioner.

Estes contends that learning theory can primarily be of value in the diagnosis and management of individual cases. He criticizes the long-established expectation that one might derive a basis for instructional methods from the results of learning theory research. In brief, he asserts that learning theory is primarily concerned with a detailed and somewhat microscopic analysis of the factors which influence learning rates. In contrast, he contends that the student's learning *ability* and, by implication, the student's responsiveness to particular instructional methods will depend upon a variety of other factors. Most importantly, it would depend on the respective learning histories which individuals bring to a situation, including the kinds of skills, concepts, and general learning strategies which they have developed over a period of time. "Therefore there is no reason to expect that learning theory, as it evolves towards a higher level of scientific adequacy and rigor, should be increasingly able to dictate methods which will produce major changes in rate or limit of learning when applied across the board to groups of individuals with differing learning histories" (Estes, 1970, p. 87).

Thus he seemed to be suggesting two major reasons why learning theory should not be expected to have direct implications for educational practice or instructional methods: (1) learning theorists typically are concerned with factors which have relatively small influence on learning process; and (2) the student's individual past history is of far greater importance than the characteristics of an immediate situation in determining how he will respond to the particular instructional methods. Throughout the book he makes suggestions as to how, for example, earlier stimulus sampling theory and more recent studies on discrimination learning will enable the practitioner to diagnose or to describe more precisely the progress and the problems evidenced in the individual learner's performance. Secondly, somewhat in contradiction to his earlier comments, he does suggest that learning theory may provide implications for the design of equipment, materials, and procedures in instructional technology. Moreover, in his discussion of instructional technology, he primarily refers to the work of various operant researchers and especially the teaching machine type of programmed instruction movement. He does make some reference to "autotelic environment" influences. He does not specifically describe ways in which *mathematical learning theory principles* can be applied in instructional design. The closest that he comes to this use of mathematical learning theory is his reference to the importance of short-term memory research for computer-assisted instruction.

In fairness to Estes, one should keep in mind that his major thesis was "a critical analysis of research on mental retardation in relation to theories of learning" (Estes, 1970, p. ix). Thus it is not surprising to find that he primarily focused on *diagnostic* considerations rather than on methods of instruction and remediation in exploring relationships between mental retardation and learning theory.

One of his major conclusions drawn from his review of mental retardation research in the context of contemporary learning theory is the "impossibility of sharply dissociating learning abilities from the results of learning. In every type of learning situation which has been subjected to considerable experimental study one finds that, when an individual of a given age is exposed to a learning task, both what he learns and how he learns it depend in major ways upon the results of past learning in other situations" (Estes, 1970, p. 183). He suggests that future research should proceed along two lines—identification and study of (genetically) structurally determined characteristics as they emerge in the maturing organism, and identification and study of those learning experiences whose product may play a major role in determining future learning.

Thus, it would appear that he sees little inherently derived from mathematical learning theory which has implications for application in terms of instructional methods, at least at this point in time.

Some mathematical learning theorists have helped in resolving educational problems and in designing educational experiences. But one does not find any concerted attempt to "apply" mathematical learning theory as has been the case with some of the more traditional comprehensive learning theories. Actually, it is almost as if by coincidence that some mathematical learning theorists who have been engrossed in resolution of educational problems also have training and experience as mathematical model builders. Thus, for example, Suppes has written a number of papers on his computer-assisted instruction projects at Stanford. But despite his identification with mathematical learning theory one finds him making relatively few comments about applicability of any particularly unique *learning principles* derived from mathematical learning theory. For example, in a sample of papers written by Suppes and colleagues in recent years (Suppes & Jerman, 1969, *Educational Television International*; Suppes & Morningstar, 1969, *Science*; Suppes & Jerman, 1970, *National Association of Secondary School Principals Bulletin*; Suppes & Searle, 1971, *Scholastic Review*) only relatively few comments are made about the underlying psychological learning theory for the design of the computer-assisted instructional sequences. In one paper (Suppes & Searle, 1971, p. 223) he observes almost in passing: "The underlying model of student learning and performance is drawn from contemporary work in learning theory." No real details are provided, nor is there any explicit reference to the rationale for the design of the educational experiences as having come from one or more substantive areas or any particular mathematical learning model. However, there is a consistent tendency either implied or explicit in each of the papers to have some *systematic basis for making decisions* about designing educational experiences.

Restle (1964) provides some clarification on this point. He acknowledges that mathematical models of learning are almost exclusively concerned with the fine detail of learning process rather than with either the educational philosophy or the design of the curricular structure. Thus, by *omission* he implies that there are relatively few direct implications to be derived from mathematical learning theory at least at this point in time for the design of educational experiences as far as the basic conception of learning process is concerned. However, he does indicate ways in which the utilization of mathematical models for basic science data on learning processes might have implications for utilization of similar mathematical models in planning for decisions in the *management* of instruction. Whereas there are few or no *substantive* contributions directly available from mathematical learning theory to educational practice, the formal ways of organizing basic science learning data might have utility in the *organization and making of decisions* about the management of learning and instruction in a practical situation.

By now the alert reader should recognize the relevance of some of our early comments about mathematical models being *formal* rather than *substantive* contributions in the study of learning more generally. The way that mathematical model builders *seem* to have reacted to such practical concern is consistent with the way in which they have gone about development of basic science learning theory.

Restle's (1964) remarks illustrate the point: "An educator may ask why certain parts of a course are difficult and how the difficulty can be overcome. He may ask how much it would help to increase teacher-time for the teaching of an item which has been difficult to learn. He wonders how fast an accelerated course could be pushed without losing the children. He may ask whether expensive teaching devices will be worth their cost to his students" (p. 111). Restle then goes on to suggest that, just as in engineering and the physical sciences, one might first develop some *model* of the tentative, ideal practical educational design rather than go directly from the basic science theory into the classroom to try to bring about the desired educational changes. He suggests that the process of planning educational experiences is quite complex and that one can best proceed by identifying the specific decisions which have to be made in planning such experiences while drawing from whatever basic science theory one has available. "Each decision is about a detail; each decision requires a gross oversimplification of the remainder of the problem; each decision requires specific information and measurement; each is calculated from knowledge of the detail; each is subject to error if an important variable is not taken into account; and each, anyway, is subject to the skepticism reflected in the safety factor" (Restle, 1964, p. 112).

Restle then draws from stimulus sampling theory, summarizing his general learning approach as: "The theory is that learning of a single, unitary item is an all-or-nothing event. Before learning occurs, no partial progress is made; after learning has occurred, performance on the problem stabilizes. This theory has been found to fit some simple paired-associate learning and other verbal-learning tasks in the laboratory, and also to fit discrimination-learning and conception-formation experiments" (Restle, 1964, p. 113). Moreover, he reveals that his theory, at least at that stage in its development, makes an assumption that all learners are alike and that learning occurs only at the point of the specific trials rather than in between such trials. Restle indicates that some of these assumptions reflect the state of the mathematical learning models, rather than inherently demand that one must accept such assumptions. Presumably, further development in the theory would enable more appropriate assumptions in terms of crucial practical considerations. He then goes on to use the theory to identify optimal class size as a function of teacher cost and student cost, and optimal speed of teaching a cumulative course. By cumulative course he is referring to a type of educational experience in which subsequent learning segments depend critically upon satisfactory mastery of the preceding segment. Mathematics courses would represent an example of such a real-life learning experience. Restle concludes his discussion by acknowledging that his approach is somewhat unrealistic and rather impoverished, but presents these illustrations as examples of contributions which one can derive from mathematical learning theory in making plans for the management of learning or for the design of ideal instructional procedures. Note that his comments about the substantive aspects of the theory are rather guarded in comparison with the traditional comprehensive learning theory proponents. The latter group, of course, was primarily concerned with substantive implications from their particular theory, sometimes even basing such proposals on only one or a few learning principles. In contrast, Restle—as an example of a mathematical learning model builder—emphasizes the formal characteristics of mathematical learning theory rather than the substantive principles in outlining implications for education.

Writing several years later about educational problems, Smallwood (1971) also focused on the formal rather than the substantive implications of mathematical learning models. Making assumptions about the underlying learning processes which are quite compatible with those proposed by Restle, Smallwood likewise delineated some systematic procedures for determining when one should maintain instructional experiences, based both on the cost of the instruction and on the extent to which some students still were in an "unconditioned" or unlearned state—that is, that they were short of the delineated learning objective for that experience. He presented an algorithm—a method for calculating the optimum policy to be followed—basing his suggestions primarily on the way that subjects handle individual items in the list to be learned.

In planning the day-to-day operations of an educational system, we should like to allocate the system's limited resources so as to maximize the effectiveness of the instruction. To examine the trade-offs that inevitably occur between commitment of educational resources and industrial effect, it is imperative that we have available rational tools for attacking the problem. This paper is an attempt to contribute to the development of such a set of tools. A classical instructional situation is defined as an economic formulation of the instructional decision process is presented. A method for solving the economic optimization of the instructional strategy is developed and applied to several examples. (Smallwood, 1971, p. 285)

Interested readers may wish to examine in detail the kind of algorithm which Smallwood developed. For our purposes, it is primarily of importance to note that he focused on the formal rather than the substantive contributions which mathematical learning theory can make to resolution of educational problems.

Smallwood presented a study in which students' performance on paired-associate items was presented as being analogous to the way that students might actually learn meaningful educational material on foreign-language vocabulary, spelling drills, arithmetic tables, or other simple mathematical concepts. He characterized such situations as involving learning that when a particular stimulus item is presented one is to make a specific response to it. Smallwood adopted the usual stimulus sampling theory assumption that learning consists of two states—unlearned and learned. He presented schematic diagrams showing how a subject's performance with each of the items would provide a basis for stating what his understanding or learning of the material was to any given point during the educational sequence. He made the assumption that once the student has learned the appropriate association so that he could give the correct answer for each stimulus, thereafter he would give the correct answer whenever that stimulus was presented. Secondly, he contended that one could characterize the subject's performance in the unlearned state as having a definable probability of guessing the correct answer. Learning progress within this framework would then constitute an increase in the probability of giving correct responses, based on an analysis of estimated probability of giving correct responses for the "unlearned" items at some probability level, with 100 percent probability of giving the correct answer on each of the items which had been taken to the learned state. Although using a very simple analogy in this paper, Smallwood contended that similar strategies could be extended to more complex types of meaningful human learning. He suggested, for example, that such procedures might help educators to schedule learning experiences or to decide at what point one should stop "instructing" or "teaching" unlearned items. At some point there is an optimal balance where most students have learned the material and there are no adverse consequences resulting from the fact that some students have not attained all the educational objectives. He proposed that mathematical models might be useful in facilitating objective decision making for group-paced instructional situations or for parallel decisions in individualized learning situations.

EDUCATIONAL R&D IMPLICATIONS

As the title of this chapter suggests, mathematical learning theorists are particularly concerned with defining their variables quantitatively and with formulating their theoretical principles as mathematical equations. This comparatively small but enthusiastic group of researchers tends to be somewhat isolated from other learning researchers, apparently because of the mathematical terminology and techniques they use, although there are numerous instances of researchers who can be identified with mathematical psychology as well as with one of the other theoretical positions. For example, one can find Pavlovian, Hullian, and Skinnerian theory proponents who are also advocates of mathematical theory construction. As a result, mathematical psychology can be identified both as a theoretical orientation in its own right and as a methodological and conceptual resource for other theories. In this context it is not too surprising that practical educational problems have not constituted a matter of high priority among mathematical psychologists. But perhaps the key to deriving educational R&D implications from mathematical learning theory may lie in recognizing this dual identity of mathematical psychology noted above.

It is likely that the most direct implications will consist of formal means for organizing and interpreting data. In the previous section we described ways in which some mathematical learning theorists have proposed techniques for making decisions about the planning of instruction. Somewhat similarly, such techniques could also be useful in trying to identify optimal combinations of conditions whereby instructional methods can be matched with students' individual learning styles and preferences. Despite the current interest in individualization of instruction, and the common-sense support of the belief that tailoring methods to individual students' needs *should* improve learning, empirical evidence thus far has not indicated that such matching markedly facilitates educational progress. Thus the mathematical models might serve as means by which various combinations of learning conditions could be evaluated with students identified in terms of their preferred sensory modalities for receiving information (for example, reading, hearing, manipulating), the range of abstractness-concreteness with which they can best understand concepts, etc.

Another potential implication involves both the methods and the substantive assumptions of mathematical learning theory. There is considerable current interest in finding ways by which students' progress can be evaluated with regard to delineated objectives or criteria (referred to as *criterion-referenced* measures). Previous evaluations typically have compared one student with other students' responsiveness to the same learning experiences, using the other students' data as norms (referred to as *normative-referenced* measures). One of the problems is that though we have units of measurement by which we can compare a student's standing with other students—for example, standard deviations for group scores—we do not have any standardized measurement units by which we can compare how well a student is learning at one point versus his learning at a later point. With their concern about cumulative effects over time and their recognition of the possibility that students' progress may differ, depending upon how much more it will be possible for them to learn, mathematical learning theorists have explored numerous mathematical models which may be useful in evaluating such sequential changes. It may be that some of these models could also be useful in monitoring individual students' progress in educational situations while one develops and refines instructional methods as well as later when the instructional methods are being used under usual classroom conditions.

In brief, the mathematical learning literature can provide information about mathematical models which have been used to answer theoretical questions and which may lend themselves to organizing data to solve practical problems. Though some papers require substantial background in mathematics, there is a growing group of papers and books which have been written to help readers to use mathematical models with practical as well as with theoretical questions.

SUGGESTED READINGS

Atkinson, R. C., Bowen, G. H., & Crothers, C. J. *An introduction to mathematical learning theory.* New York: Wiley, 1965.

Bush, R. R., & Mosteller, F. *Stochastic models for learning.* New York: Wiley, 1955.

Coombs, C. H., Dawes, R. M., & Tversky, A. *Mathematical psychology: An elementary introduction.* New York: Prentice-Hall, 1970.

Estes, W. K. *Learning theory and mental development.* New York: Academic Press, 1970.

Greeno, J. G., & Bjork, R. A. Mathematical learning theory and the new "mental forestry." *Annual Review of Psychology,* 1973, 81–116.

Hanna, J. F. A new approach to the formulation and testing of learning models. *Synthese,* 1966, 16, 344–380.

Levine, G., & Burke, C. J. *Mathematical model techniques for learning theories.* New York: Academic Press, 1972.

Neimark, E. D., & Estes, W. K. *Stimulus sampling theory.* Cambridge: Holden-Day, 1967.

Snyder, H. I. *Contemporary educational psychology: Some models applied to the school setting.* New York: Wiley, 1968.

Part

III

Focus

Part Three contains five chapters which describe different approaches to formulating instructional theories based on or in reaction to psychological learning research and theory. The behavior modification chapter and the cognitive construct instructional theory chapter (Chapters 13 and 14) each draw from certain learning theories (respectively, Skinner's operant conditioning and the information processing theories). Chapters 15 and 16 describe alternative approaches to formulating instructional theories which draw eclectically from different theories. Chapter 17 describes the humanistic psychology conceptions of instruction which are partly drawn in reaction against psychological learning theory, but which also have interesting similarities to learning theory–derived ideas.

Each chapter contains introductory remarks and descriptions of background information concerning origins and the general nature of the instructional theory. Then the essentials of the theory are described and information is provided concerning illustrative practical applications. The final section in each chapter uses the ASCD criteria for instructional theories (described in Chapter 5) as a framework against which each theory can be evaluated. The main purpose in these brief concluding sections is to provide some evaluative comments and general suggestions about questions one may wish to raise about possible uses of the theory. As in Part Two, these comments partly refer to descriptions provided in the chapter and partly result in questions which the reader may wish to pursue through suggested readings at the end of each chapter. These readings can provide additional information about the empirical support of the theory as well as about steps to follow if one wishes to use that instructional theory.

13
Behavior Modification and Instructional Technology

Behavior modification refers to utilization of modern learning princi-ples in the design and improvement of educational and clinical practice. *Programmed instruction* is an example of an educational application; *behavior therapy* is the term commonly used to refer to applications in clinical psychology and psychiatry. Although the term behavior modifica-tion is sometimes used in a loose sense to mean changing behavior as the goal of all educational practice (for example, Christopoles and Vallentutti, 1969), in this chapter we use the term only with reference to those procedures which were developed from certain learning theories. Because of space limitations we will primarily focus on derivatives of Skinnerian operant principles, although you should be aware that some behavior modifiers also draw from such traditional learning theorists as Hull, Guthrie, and Pavlov, as well as from some more contemporary theorists such as Bandura and Rotter. The operant-based behavior modification approach was selected because it illustrates the general behavior modifica-tion orientation and because Skinner and his colleagues have played major roles in the emergence of behavior modification and instructional technol-ogy.

In this chapter we will consider the origin and general characteristics of instructional theory and technology as developed within the behavior modification orientation. We will examine four facets of this approach and will consider ways in which it is related to Skinner's operant condi-tioning principles and research procedures. After describing an example of one educational application, we will evaluate behavior modification as an approach to instruction and as to its contributions to the development of instructional theory.

OPERANT CONDITIONING
AND BEHAVIOR MODIFICATION

Although various authors identify several different antecedents of the behavior modification movement, and despite the fact that many varia-tions have evolved over the years, it is commonly acknowledged that the prime moving force in behavior modification was B. F. Skinner and his colleagues in their various projects at Harvard University starting in the middle 1950s.

Since the middle 1930s, Skinner has maintained prominence among experimental psychologists for his experimental learning research pri-marily conducted with infrahuman subjects. In the middle 1950s, he became quite concerned about the status of educational practice and felt that his operant learning procedures and principles could be utilized in the improvement of educational practice.

There is a fundamental reason why we have included behavior modifi-cation as one of our instructional theories: it constitutes a venture which in many respects is related to operant conditioning but which in addition has developed an identity of its own.

There are two major ways in which operant conditioning is related to behavior modification in addition to the fact that many behavior modifiers also conduct operant conditioning research. First, operant reinforcement learning principles are extensively used as a basis for instructional procedures although some behavior modifiers are more eclectic in their use of other psychological principles. Secondly, behavior modifiers share with operant conditioners the emphasis on inductive theory construction and a major commitment to using research results for evolving their principles. There is a distinct preference for *direct* analyses of the behaviors which are most pertinent to the problem under study. Wolpe's (1969*b*) comments about the importance of research in the formulation and refinement of behavior therapy principles are relevant also to the behavior modification instructional principles: "(B)ehavior therapy is not a school homologous with the schools of psychoanalysis. Neither its principles nor practices are sacrosanct. Both are ever vulnerable to the findings of research" (p. 159). It will help the reader to understand many of the facets of behavior modification if it is recognized that some behavior modifiers tend to emphasize the utilization of operant reinforcement principles, whereas others place greater emphasis on the research procedures per se.

FOUR FACETS OF OPERANT BEHAVIOR MODIFICATION

There are at least four facets which can be discerned in the development of behavior modification instructional principles and procedures. We can refer to the first as a "teaching machine" phase, the second an emphasis on "programmed instruction," the third a focus on "token economies" and "contingency management," and the fourth phase involving wider concern about educational problems and typically referred to as "behavioral engineering." These facets will be discussed roughly in the order that they emerged historically but the reader should realize that all four can be found today in the activities of behavior modifiers.

Teaching Machine Revolution

Skinner (for example, 1968) theorizes that instruction involves arranging contingencies of reinforcement under which students learn. He acknowledges that students can learn without any special assistance in the natural environment, but he contends that learning can best be assured and expedited if teachers make appropriate provisions so that gradual changes in behavior in desired directions are systematically reinforced. He suggested that various means can be used for systematically providing reinforcement for appropriate behaviors, and he introduced the notion of a *teaching machine* in this context. It is probably a commentary on our country's fascination with gadgets that this first identifiable phase of behavior modification came to be known as a "teaching machine revolution." Consideration of Skinner's rationale for his instructional procedures will help us to see how he expected to use machines and how others subsequently recognized the importance of programming instruction.

In one of Skinner's early papers (1954), "The Science of Learning and the Art of Teaching," he pointed out that by taking Thorndike's law of effect quite seriously he had been able to arrange conditions which seem optimal for producing learning in animals. In this and other papers he proposed that similar applications would be valuable with humans in formal educational situations.

He critically characterized formal education as primarily using aversive control, thus resulting in reinforcement of various kinds of avoidance behavior. Listing many undesirable consequences which may occur for the student in conventional classrooms if he does not learn satisfactorily—the teacher's expressions of displeasure, ridicule by classmates, censure by the principal, low grades, punishment by the parents, etc.—Skinner contended that learning and getting *right* answers becomes an *insignificant* event in education. In contrast with these many kinds of aversive control, he contended that the real focus in education should be on consistent, immediate, positive reinforcement for appropriate behaviors and for the attainment of delineated educational objectives. Moreover, he concluded that experimental evidence indicates that the novice student will be more likely to respond correctly if he is provided with a gradual progression of learning experiences which starts with tasks which are relatively easy and familiar and which advances quite gradually through new material and more demanding tasks.

But such analyses and prescriptions require highly reliable presentations of educational experiences and consistent provisions of reinforcements each time appropriate responses are made. In this context he recommended that programmed materials and some kind of "teaching machine" would enable educators to maintain these optimal conditions of instruction. The term "program" subsequently was used to refer to specially arranged educational materials; "teaching machine" was defined as any device which presents the educational materials and which provides feedback (reinforcement) to the learner as to his progress.

Somehow this new approach to instruction became known as a "teaching machine revolution." Skinner had presented many talks and publications in which he prominently used the term *teaching machine* but he consistently tried to point out that the really important aspects were the arrangements of the educational materials so that the student could make correct responses and the provision of reinforcements when correct responses were made. Even the name of his project group at Harvard University's Graduate School of Education, the Committee on Programmed Instruction, bears witness to his ordering of priorities. Nonetheless, the term "teaching machine" was routinely used to refer to this innovation in instruction throughout the 1950s.

Many educators took issue with the notion, which some felt was implied, that such machines would "revolutionize" education and *replace teachers*; they even raised questions whether teaching machines could make *any* contributions to instruction. Various histories of programmed instruction and behavior modification provide details on the debates which ensued about this issue.

Many felt that the term "teaching machine" was a poor choice since some had misconstrued the notion that the learning process is necessarily mechanical, that it was characterized as overly simplistic, and that the whole movement could be depicted as being generally antiprofessional and superficial. Nonetheless, for some time alternative descriptions such as "self-instructional devices" and "auto-instructional devices" were considered but discarded in favor of retention of "teaching machines" to designate this approach to instruction. It was probably the gradual recognition of the importance of the "program," the educational content in a particular form, which subsequently led to the second facet of this movement, that of *programmed instruction.*

Programmed Instruction

By the early 1960s it was recognized that it was the *program* rather than the *teaching machine* which was the more important aspect of the behavior modification approach to instruction. It was pointed out that the success of the approach was based on the specially sequenced educational materials and the arrangements of contingencies of reinforcement so that students were being reinforced as they made progress in reaching delineated educational objectives. In this context, "programmed instruction" rather than "teaching machines" emerged as the preferred term.

It would be helpful to understand some of the contemporary trends in behavior modification if we consider some of the steps that were involved in developing programs in the programmed instruction movement. As we noted above, the "program" is the name for the educational materials after they have been arranged in the *best possible* sequence *for students.* Certain procedures are typically followed in programmed instruction: (1) A program is typically made up of small, relatively easy-to-take steps, beginning with tasks which the student initially can handle and gradually leading up to those which were either too difficult or unfamiliar prior to the instructional sequence. (2) It is generally expected that most efficient and effective learning will occur when the student has an active role in the educational process. In some approaches to programmed instruction, it is emphasized that the student, for example, should construct responses rather than merely choosing from a set of multiple choices available to him. (3) Extrapolated findings from operant research (discussed earlier in this book) led to the contention that positive reinforcement should be *immediate* and should follow *each* correct response. Typically, "reinforcement" in this context refers to knowledge of results and, particularly, to knowledge that the student is in fact learning the materials presented. In certain instances some "extrinsic" reinforcer is used, such as candies, teachers' praise, or other supplementary rewards. (4) It is also emphasized that programs should provide for individualization of instruction at least in that students should be able to work at their own pace. Therefore, instead of holding constant the amount of time (such as one academic semester) which would be available for a student to work on a block of educational experiences, it is contended that the attainment of the educational objectives should be held constant and that students should be permitted to take as much time as they need in order to complete those educational objectives. In some programs the content and sequencing are also based on the individual student's needs as assessed in pretests. (5) A final and very important principle is that of student testing or validation of the educational materials. In programmed instruction it usually is possible to determine how students perform or learn on each section of the educational materials, thus providing a record as to whether such materials produce learning effectively and efficiently. A basic assumption is that programs would be developed initially as best could be arranged by the programmers, but that all subsequent modifications leading up to the final program would be based on results from representative students going through the program. Thus changes are to be made until it is shown that students would have a high probability of making correct responses to items presented and that their progress through the program has enabled them to attain the delineated educational objectives.

Some myths and misconceptions should be clarified about *the* Skinnerian approach to programmed instruction. Susan Meyer Markle (1964) retrospectively published some notes she had made during planning discussions for the Harvard University projects which were conducted in the 1950s. In addition to Dr. Markle this staff, headed by Dr. Skinner, included such persons as Lloyd Homme, Douglas Porter, Irving Saltzman, Wells Hively, and Matthew Israel. Markle's (1964) retrospective analysis of the notes revealed that there was considerable emphasis on the needs for *exploratory* applied research to determine what best procedures could be identified for facilitating learning. This flexibility is particularly noteworthy in that many authors have presented stereotyped versions of "*the* Skinnerian program." It has frequently been misconstrued as being one in which subjects *must* construct their responses rather than choose from a multiple-choice type arrangement, one where *all* students should go through the same linear sequence, and one where the *only* educational objectives could be those involving simple, factual learning. Markle's notes (1964) indicate that much greater flexibility and openness to alternative approaches to instruction were embodied in their initial plans despite critics' comments to the contrary.

But whatever the contributions and limitations of programmed instruction, additional changes were to be made in behavior modification conceptions of instruction. Some led to the use of computers as more flexible teaching machines. Others explored the use of specially designed workbooks which provided opportunity for immediate knowledge of results without the use of a teaching machine. Typically this involved using a mask to hide correct answers or involved having students check different pages in the book depending on which answer they chose. But others felt that it would be desirable to expand beyond printed materials to maximize behavior modification contributions.

Contingency Management and Token Economies

A third facet can be described as "contingency management" or "token economies." In this application of operant learning principles, the focus is on a somewhat wider range of activities than was typically true of the teaching machine and programmed instruction phases. Some psychologists felt that the Skinnerian operant approach could have considerable implications for dealing with a broad range of practical educational problems, but they felt unduly constrained by the teaching machine and programmed instruction approach. More specifically, they felt that, despite other aspirations held by Skinner initially, there had been too great a tendency to restrict operant applications to verbal behavior (reading, talking, writing, etc.) and that other more important aspects had been ignored. The contingency management-token economy phase was especially stimulated by the work of several investigators in psychiatric hospital situations and in special education classrooms.

Theodore Ayllon, a psychologist with some operant training, was working as a clinical psychologist in a Saskatchewan psychiatric hospital when he observed that patients received more attention from ward personnel when they were acting psychotic than when they were acting more appropriately. For example, a patient who would refuse to eat would receive tremendous interest from staff members lest he starve or otherwise suffer from malnutrition. Ayllon became principal investigator of an experimental clinical program on a psychiatric ward in which he and other psychologists tried to apply reinforcement principles. For example, they pointed out to ward personnel that a considerable amount of effort was being devoted to patients who were acting inappropriately and that comparatively little attention was being paid to those patients who were acting in a manner which could be considered "more normal" in our society. They further pointed out that the very attentiveness of the staff personnel could be at least partly responsible for maintaining such inappropriate behavior, if one accepts the reasonable hypothesis that the psychiatric patients were quite desirous of having attention and concern expressed by the hospital staff. Therefore, they suggested that the hospital personnel continue to give the same amount of attention to their patients but that they now offer it *only* when patients acted more appropriately rather than inappropriately. In a sense, it could be said that the staff members were instructed to reinforce *acting appropriately* rather than *acting inappropriately*. When this system showed initial success it was then extended to the total activities within a special ward situation. Because watching TV, having special grounds or town visiting privileges, and having other special "luxuries" in the hospital situation were made *contingent* upon "payment" by "tokens" which the patient could "earn" by acting appropriately, the term *token economy* has come into use to refer to this application of operant principles. Alternatively, because the general organization of the token economy primarily stemmed from the relationships between appropriate behavior and the "reward" of the token, many have come to designate this as "reinforcement contingency management" or simply "contingency management."

The first educational applications of the contingency management approach primarily occurred in special education situations. For example, it was recognized that some characteristics of behavior of children with learning disabilities were most likely determined by their physiological condition, but it was felt that some "inappropriate behavior" might also be maintained by the students' contact with other people. Thus, it was posited that perhaps one reason that the students displayed inappropriate behavior at times might be due in part to the "rewards" which were being provided for such behavior—although not intentionally so—by the students' teachers and peers. Projects were set up in which teachers ignored inappropriate responses but gave attention when students were acting in a socially appropriate way and/or were demonstrating educational progress.

Subsequent applications of contingency management principles have been made with general educational populations on academic content areas as well as with management of classroom behavior problems. In each application, appropriate and inappropriate behaviors are delineated, existing effective reinforcers are identified in the situation (such as teacher's attention and praise to the student), and rules are implemented whereby the rewards are made available to each student as he demonstrates progress toward educational objectives.

As psychologists continued to develop their behavior modification procedures, they usually found the reinforcement principles of considerable value in solving educational problems and in designing instruction. But they also encountered many problems for which no obvious solutions were forthcoming from existing basic operant research. In some instances they found that applications to real-world problems were either not consistent with laboratory-based predictions or even resulted in outright contradictions of the theory. Some psychologists (e.g., Baer, 1971) began arguing for the judicious use of punishment even though this is quite contradictory to Skinner's theoretical formulations. This and numerous other puzzling practical problems caused some to become more eclectic theoretically and to identify themselves as behavioral engineers.

Behavioral Engineering

We noted earlier that there are two general ways in which operant procedures have influenced behavior modification. First, Skinner's laboratory operant learning research resulted in refinement and extension of principles drawn from Thorndike's law of effect. Second, operant researchers emphasize direct experimental analysis of an individual subject's behavior, with response rate or probability of response as a major dependent variable. Both emphases have been prominent in each of the three aspects of behavior modification we have considered thus far. *Behavioral engineering*, the fourth and more eclectic facet of behavior modification, primarily emphasizes the research-measurement aspect; there is considerable variation in the extent to which behavioral engineers ascribe importance to reinforcement principles.

Homme's Contingency Contracting Lloyd Homme, one of Skinner's early collaborators on programmed instruction, and Homme's colleagues (Homme et al., 1968) provide interesting comments about the nature of behavioral engineering. They first concur with another behavior modifier, Roger Ulrich, in characterizing behavioral engineering as "arranging the environment so that one gets the behavior one wants" (p. 425). Then they point out that both Lloyd Homme and Ogden Lindsley—whose work we will review shortly—had been operant conditioners previously but that both had "quit" and become more eclectic behavioral engineers instead.

Homme depicts behavioral engineering as the combination of two technologies: the technology of contingency management and the technology of stimulus control. Contingency management is very closely related to the operant reinforcement principles. He defines stimulus control as involving the extent that the presence or absence of a stimulus controls the probability of a response. Stimulus control technology also, according to Homme, depends primarily on reinforcer control and contingency management; however, there are many instances in which Homme has found it necessary to go beyond operant principles in practical situations, frequently drawing from Guthrie's nonreinforcement conditioning by contiguity principles. Thus there are some contradictions across Homme's various papers and books as to the extent to which he relies on reinforcement principles. Whereas he does show a distinct preference for reinforcement theory formulations, he does not hesitate in drawing from other learning theories when such is indicated by requirements of the practical situation.

Homme and his colleagues (Homme, Csanyi, Gonzales, & Rechs, 1970) have devised ten rules for using contingency contracting in the classroom. In brief, they recommend using immediate reinforcement for behaviors which gradually approximate the desired educational goals. Small amounts of reward are to be given regularly for small increments of improvement, with the rewards consistently following rather than preceding the desired acts. They emphasize that a "contract" should be orally made between teacher and student, and that this contract should be clearly described, fair, and honest (actually followed) and that it should emphasize positive features of the student's activities. Finally, they stress that the success of the approach depends greatly on how systematically and consistently the contingency contracting procedures are followed. Homme identifies himself as a behavioral engineer in designing the program, and he characterizes the teacher as a manager of contingencies. Systematic and frequent evaluations are conducted both as a means for motivating the student by informing him of his favorable progress and as a basis for identifying any aspects of his instructional program which may need modification.

Lindsley's Precision Teaching   Precision teaching is another of the behavioral engineering positions which was developed for use in educational situations. Precision teaching is defined as an approach to education in which instructional procedures are planned, implemented, and modified in light of the student's progress toward selected educational goals. Ogden R. Lindsley originally developed the idea of precision teaching to meet the needs of exceptional children, that is, for use in special education, but the procedures are now being used widely in other general educational situations. It is of some interest for the reader to know that Lindsley was one of the first persons to use *laboratory* operant procedures with human subjects. In the middle 1950s, after having learned operant techniques while studying animal subjects, he developed a laboratory for use of modified techniques with schizophrenic and other psychiatric patients in Massachusetts' Metropolitan State Hospital as part of a Harvard Medical School research project. Lindsley is quite knowledgeable about the operant learning principles as well as the research procedures. Thus it is noteworthy that he apparently has concluded that it is the research methodology rather than the substantive learning principles (that is, the modifications of the law of effect principles) which constitute operant conditioning learning theory's more important contribution to education.

Precision teaching is a system for monitoring the progress of an individual student toward selected educational goals. In many cases both the teacher and the student participate in selecting these specific goals. Precision teaching is centered around a "Standard Daily Behavior Chart." One of the novel features is that the child or student is the person who is responsible for maintaining the chart, rather than the teacher or some other adult in the room. In fact there's even available an eighteen-minute colored slide presentation on precision teaching which was written and narrated by a five-year-old kindergarten pupil (Bates & Bates, 1971). In brief, the procedures include identifying a particular educational goal, setting up a chart which will enable either the student or the teacher to compare the frequency at which the desired behaviors occur over a period of time, and proceeding to count and record the actual frequency of those behaviors on each of the days. Thus precision teaching consists of daily recording frequencies of different classroom behaviors on regular chart sheets. Both the pupil and the teacher, as well as any other appropriate person, have access to information as to the child's progress towards the delineated educational objectives. The goals involve statements of frequency of selected behaviors, and the charts are used to show the extent to which there is an increase or decrease in frequency of that behavior over time.

The techniques were developed primarily with special educational situations, but advocates of precision teaching contend that it has considerable potential for all aspects of general educational situations as well. Proponents of the approach contend that the procedures are highly motivating for students, in that students who previously had difficulty in subjects typically show not only a substantial improvement in their performance but also a more positive attitude towards the subject matter which previously had given them trouble. Of course, critics can raise questions as to whether it is the charting per se, or whether merely calling attention to a specific goal may actually account for the facilitative effect. Despite the denials by Lindsley and his colleagues, other "reinforcement" or "contingency management" behavior modifiers most likely would contend that the charts provide "knowledge of results" and that precision teaching is really another example of behavior modification applications of reinforcement principles.

Lindsley *disclaims* any interest in utilizing contingency management procedures *exclusively* as a means for designing instruction. Rather, he contends that the major contribution from the operant approach is that of a measurement procedure by which one can evaluate and so improve whatever method of instruction one selects. He has even suggested that such diverse positions as those of Piaget, Summerhill, and the British Infant School could benefit from utilization of precision teaching methods. He suggests that the precision teaching techniques can be utilized to monitor the extent to which truly individualized learning progress has been accomplished and to derive implications for modifying one's educational procedures when a reasonable degree of progress is not evident. Moreover, Lindsley and his colleagues contend that one can use whatever style of teaching has been found to be satisfactory by students and teachers, and that precision teaching can serve as a tool for improving those methods. "Precision Teaching simply adds a more precise measurement instrument to present teaching, make teaching more economical, more effective, more enjoyable, and more loving" (Duncan, 1971, p. 119).

For our purposes, it is noteworthy that this "brand" of behavior modification or derivative of operant procedures has taken on a far more eclectic character than is true of some of the rather narrowly conceived early applications in the programmed instruction and teaching machine stages. Moreover, in contrast with Homme's approach, Lindsley's conception of behavioral engineering puts greater emphasis on the research-measurement aspects of the operant tradition and relies at least as much on educational theory as it does on operant reinforcement or other learning principles.

BEHAVIOR MODIFICATION AND INSTRUCTIONAL PRINCIPLES

Behavior modifiers as a group are more apt to talk about instructional technology than about instructional theory or instructional principles. They primarily endorse a set of procedures for designing and improving instruction and they tend to be flexible in adapting such procedures for whatever instructional problem may be presented to them. Nonetheless they are interested in evolving principles which have been proven to be effective as a result of empirical tests and they assume that their inductive approach to theory construction will eventually lead to a more formal instructional theory. In the meantime, certain features and procedures can be identified for behavior modification, although there is considerable variation across various behavior modifiers' approaches, as we have tried to indicate in our earlier discussion of the four representative facets of behavior modification.

Certain features are common to almost all behavior modifiers. First, there is considerable reliance on observable behaviors or objectively measurable characteristics, with comparatively minimal concern with internal experiences of the student. It is true that contemporary behavior modification researchers have become increasingly interested in complex cognitive processes. However, wherever there is a choice they prefer to deal with more directly observable behaviors than with inferences as to one's internal experiences, thinking, feeling, etc. Second, in addition to drawing extensively from basic experimental learning research there is a universal rule that the behavior modifier must include evaluative procedures for the initial development and the subsequent improvement of his instructional procedures. As a result most behavior modifiers contend that they have self-correcting procedures built into their instructional programs.

Third, closely linked to this all-pervasive emphasis on evaluation is the requirement that one provide explicit descriptions of one's objectives and procedures. This involves specifying educational objectives in some objectively measurable form, identifying the entering characteristics of the individual students, describing the instructional procedures which are to be implemented, and outlining what evaluative procedures are to be used in assessing students' progress and in planning modifications to the instructional procedures. Fourth, there is a distinct preference for basing initial plans for instruction on operant reinforcement principles. Behavior modifiers differ in the extent to which they draw from other psychological and educational principles.

Skinner (1968) has described other principles which are considered useful in maximizing the likelihood that students will make appropriate responses and thus be reinforced. They lie in the area which Homme et al. call stimulus control technology. Skinner points out that a critical but difficult task is to identify the educational objectives in such a way that one can assess the student's progress. Once having delineated the goals, it is the educator's responsibility to find some means for strengthening those acts which indicate that the educational goals are gradually being attained. But how can you get the student started? Skinner dismisses as inefficient merely waiting until appropriate behavior is spontaneously emitted. He also places little stock in physically assisting the student to act or in using stimuli which elicit the desired responses. Instead, he looks to stimuli which "prime" the student to make correct responses (for example, by having the student imitate the teacher who serves as a model, or by showing the student at least partly completed products of appropriate behavior which he can copy). But it is very important that one uses priming stimuli which either will be available in the transfer situation or can be faded out in such a way that other characteristics of the transfer situation can prompt the appropriate behavior. Throughout his discussion Skinner distinguishes between those cues which quickly prompt the student to respond—and thus which may fool the teacher into thinking that learning is occurring more satisfactorily than is actually the case—and those cues which will also be available and effective in the real-life transfer situation.

Skinner also emphasizes the importance of sequencing educational experiences in such a way that he can integrate the various aspects of the particular learning topic. He notes that sequencing is important both so that learning experiences will be presented at a size or rate that the student can handle and so that prerequisite skills will have been mastered before more complex tasks are attempted. He distinguishes between the orders which one may find inherent in the subject matter and the sequences which may be most manageable for the student. Cautioning *against blind reliance* on sequencing by difficulty level, order of complexity, or logical structure of the subject matter, he ackowledges their usefulness but notes that the key matter is to determine the readiness of the student for whatever is to be presented next.

These are some of the rather loosely organized instructional procedures and principles which are utilized by behavior modifiers. In the next section we will examine illustrations of behavior modification educational applications.

BEHAVIOR MODIFICATION APPLICATIONS

Behavior modification instructional principles have been used with preschool children, in elementary schools and high schools, in universities and professional schools, and in military and industrial training programs. They have been used with children's emotional problems in the classroom and in the management of problem students as well as with numerous academic subject areas.

The range of problems with which these procedures have been used is illustrated by the following sampling of topics drawn from journals which report behavior modification applications: increase of fourth graders' spelling accuracy; changes in relevant speech productivity of an aphasic through verbal conditioning; effects of teacher attention on study behavior; reduction of test anxiety; production and elimination of disruptive classroom behavior by systematically varying teacher's behavior; influencing classroom study behavior of preschool children; developing correspondence between nonverbal and verbal behavior of preschool children; reduction of stuttering and stammering; establishing use of descriptive adjectives in the speech of disadvantaged preschool children; behavior modification of children with learning disabilities using grades or tokens and allowances as back-up reinforcers; use of learning principles in reading acquisition; basic interpersonal relations; improving communication—a self-study program for two persons; application of programmed instruction principles to classroom instruction; programmed materials for mathematics courses; improving executives' administrative procedures; clinical neuroanatomy by programmed instruction.

AN EXAMPLE: KELLER'S
CONCEPTION OF COURSE PROCEDURES

Fred S. Keller (1967; 1968) a psychologist who has been knowledgeable about operant basic research procedures for several decades, was about to retire from university teaching in 1962 when he was asked by the Brazilian government to play a key role in designing a psychology course for their newly established University of Brasilia. Keller devised a behavior modification approach for an undergraduate course in general psychology. He tried it out in a short-term laboratory course at Columbia University in 1963, and then established the program at the University of Brasilia the following year. Though internal university problems resulted in abrupt termination of the Brasilia course, sufficiently successful results were obtained that his procedures have been adopted for courses in psychology and other academic areas in universities in several countries. They can be used, with some modifications, in high school classes and elementary schools as well.

His program incorporates most of the behavior modification instructional procedures outlined above. It emphasizes individualization in pacing, delineation of educational objectives, frequent assessments to determine each student's progress toward the objectives, modification of instructional procedures based on these assessments, and systematic use of positive reinforcement to stimulate and maintain favorable progress. In addition, instructors can use small-group discussions and large-group presentations at selected points throughout the course.

All students are given detailed information about the course at their first meeting. They are told that they will work at their own pace throughout the course. It is possible for some to complete the course in less than a semester, while others may require more than a semester. Grades for the course are based on the number of units they complete (about 60 to 75 percent of their course grade) and their performance on a comprehensive final examination (25 to 40 percent of their course grade). There is a combination of independent reading assignments and laboratory projects, regular sessions with the student's proctor (a specially trained student who has previously successfully completed the course and demonstrated skills in helping fellow students), contact with graduate student laboratory assistants, small group discussions, and selected special lectures and demonstrations.

Keller's course for one semester is broken down into thirty units of content consisting of homework assignments and laboratory exercises. Students are required to pass a mastery test on each unit before they are permitted to start the next unit. Failure to pass the test is not held against them, even if several attempts are required; instead, they are given advice in taking remedial work on that unit. The special lectures and demonstrations are made available when a number of the students have passed the unit which prepares them to understand the particular lecture or demonstration. They are not compulsory, but rather are used to motivate students and to permit exploration of areas previously found to be of interest to students.

It was noted above that tests are used quite frequently, with one mastery test taken whenever the student feels that he has adequately covered a given unit. It should also be emphasized that immediate feedback is given for test results, and that this information is used for diagnosing any difficulties or for otherwise advising the student. But perhaps the most important point is that the tests at the end of each of the thirty units are used to determine whether the student has *mastered* the contents of that unit. Keller (1968) describes one example in which students either would be expected to have a near-perfect score on a ten-item mastery test or would have to defend their answers in conferences with the proctor. Typically, if the student has missed only a few questions, he is directed to specific remedial work. But if four or more items are missed, he is advised to repeat the whole unit. Under these circumstances, the proctor also makes certain that the student now has a better understanding of the educational objectives for that particular unit.

Keller points out that the role of the teacher in his program is quite different from that found in traditional classrooms. He characterizes conventional teachers as frequently serving as "classroom entertainer, expositor, critic, and debator" (p. 88). In contrast, Keller contends that his teachers primarily serve as educational engineers and as contingency managers for all of their students, rather than as successful learning facilitators for the typically small number of students who do well on proficiency tests in conventional classrooms.

The results obtained by Keller and others using his approach have been quite striking. In several instances where the procedures have been used, students have been given the same examination as that administered to a group of students in a traditional college lecture course. Unlike the traditional lecture course, where a normal distribution of scores was obtained, the Keller procedures have resulted in a very high proportion of "A" and "B" grades. But, more importantly, Keller's students also have been consistently successful in attaining the delineated educational objectives. Moreover, he contends that students like their educational experiences and that they feel they have gained a more thorough understanding of the content than is characteristic of other classroom experiences.

Keller contends that students can do substantially better in their classes than is commonly believed to be the case if we carefully delineate our educational objectives and if we systematically use tests to provide feedback to students as to their gradual progress toward their course goals. It is noteworthy that he entitled one of his most widely read papers on his procedures "Good-bye, teacher . . ." (Keller, 1968). Though there are multiple meanings for the title, he mainly seems to be pleading the case that students really are interested, willing, and able to learn if only we can find instructional procedures which work with them. Keller suggests that the key lies in providing the right contingencies of reinforcement. He expresses some concern and urgency when he concludes: "But if we don't provide them, and provide them soon, he (the student) too may be inspired to say, 'Good-bye!' to formal education" (Keller, 1968, p. 88).

CRITIQUE: CURRENT STATUS
AND FUTURE PROSPECTS

Several comments can be made about behavior modification as an approach to designing instruction and to evolving instructional principles, as well as about its general contributions to instructional theory. In terms of the ASCD criteria, it is evident that this group has not provided a complete theory at the present time though substantial efforts have been exerted to conduct empirical tests for using those instructional principles which have been developed. Given their inductive theory construction orientation, this is not an unexpected state of affairs: instead of a neat theory with interrelated principles, one finds mainly an orientation and a set of working procedures.

Proponents consider the approach to be sufficiently broad and flexible that it can be utilized with all instructional problems. Thus they indicate no explicit limitations as to educational objectives, clientele, or type of educational situation. Critics point to the emphasis on measurable objectives and contend that this approach is only useful where educational objectives can be readily stated in some measurable form. Some critics would limit this approach to factual learning; they especially would exclude complex cognitive objectives and practically all forms of affective objectives. Critics also object to the extent of control which is assigned to the educator and they question whether such an orientation is compatible with contemporary views that students should actively participate in selecting educational goals and in making decisions about instructional experiences. But here again proponents contend that there is no such limitation inherent in the approach, although they acknowledge that such criticisms may be applicable to specific examples.

Those principles and procedures which have been outlined have met most of the other ASCD criteria in that they lend themselves readily to empirical test and to making predictions about students' probable behavior. However, like most budding instructional theories, their predictions are more frequently qualitative than quantitative.

Perusal of contents of an extensive variety of educational and psychological journals will review countless papers reporting successful applications of behavior modification instructional principles to a wide range of learning situations with virtually all types of students. Of course, one can always reserve judgment about the enthusiasm of proponents or adopters of any new innovations. But even research literature reviewers (for example, Hanley, 1970; Lipe & Jung, 1971) conclude that behavior modifiers have been quite successful in attaining their *delineated* educational objectives. But therein one finds debates on some rather complicated issues.

It is with regard to criterion number 4, concerning the instructional theory's compatibility with empirical data, that extensive comments could be made. There are few instances in which the principles can be described as inconsistent with empirical data. Though there are numerous gaps where empirical data have not yet been collected for some aspects of the principles (especially those concerning sequencing of educational principles), few instructional theorists have as much of a commitment to continuing research and evaluation as do the behavior modifiers. But in this stress on measurement and evaluation are both strengths and the bases for numerous criticisms.

Through the emphasis on operational definitions and *behavioral* change as main indices of learning, some critics contend that the approach is overly simplistic at best and grossly in error at worst. It has been suggested that it is all too easy to restrict one's objectives to those which are more easily presented in measurable form, such as those involving factual rote memorization and psychomotor responses, and to ignore complex but meaningful human learning (Krutch, 1970).

Proponents point to the merits of delineating what one is trying to accomplish, that is, specifying educational objectives in measurable terms, and then evaluating how successful the selected procedures have been. Engler (1970) has taken the position, as has the author, that selection of educational objectives is a curricular matter and remains a separate decision from that of choosing instructional methods. In many respects, instructional theories, including behavior modification, are neutral with regard to such issues as rote learning versus complex human learning and effective objectives; they must be capable of providing procedures for attaining whatever educational objectives are selected *unless* there are statements to the effect that the theory is not applicable with certain objectives. Behavior modifiers advocate that one should identify both the changes which are desired and the techniques which are to be used. Then with provisions for systematic evaluation, one can begin to identify the extent to which the respective instructional procedures are facilitating the student's attainment of the selected educational objectives. In this context they argue that even instructional failures may be helpful since one can more precisely identify the sources of the problem.

Many object to the emphasis on the behavior of the student and the general ignoring of the student's feelings and internal experiences. They object to this "empty organism" approach and question whether one can achieve significant educational changes without taking into account the student's mental experiences of the situation. The potential disadvantages—ignoring the dignity of the student, overlooking some useful or critical personal experience—seem obvious; the merits of such an approach may not be as clear.

The behavior modifier is actually quite concerned about the individual characteristics and the rights and welfare of the student. However, in order to achieve desirable educational objectives, the behavior modifier takes the position that he should use all the reliable information which is available but that unvalidated information or procedures should be ignored. He holds that one can only know how someone else is "feeling" or "thinking" by observing his verbal and functioning behavior. Hence his preference for working with the reliable information that is available—the delineated educational objectives, the specified instructional procedures, and the actual behavior of the student as he responds and is reinforced while approaching the educational objectives.

Considering the focus of the present book on relationships between learning theory and instructional theory, some of the most serious criticisms have been leveled at one of the basic features of behavior modification—the assertion that the instructional procedures are based on modern operant reinforcement principles derived from laboratory experimental research. These critics justifiably note that the central reinforcement principles are closely related to Thorndike's law of effect and thus are quite old, and they protest that some of the more specific principles may now be obsolete in light of contemporary information processing research and other recent findings. Moreover, they point out that the "operant laboratory studies" have been conducted mainly with rats, pigeons, monkeys, and other animals, that comparatively few principles come from studies with human subjects. Furthermore, they question whether the basic research (with humans or with animals) has involved laboratory analogues which are appropriate for the practical problems dealt with in the educational setting.

Quite complex issues are raised by these criticisms. Since it is usual to have a lapse of some time, even several decades, between delineation of a finding and subsequent practical use of that principle, it does not seem surprising nor critical that some instructional procedures are based on theory formulated earlier this century. More serious is the charge that behavior modifiers have not exercised adequate caution in applying findings derived from infrahuman subjects and that researchers have used inappropriate laboratory analogues. Kantor (1970), a proponent of Skinnerian-type research and behavior modification applications, acknowledges that comparatively few studies have focused on complex human learning processes. He suggests that instead of relying on simple experimental models too long it would be appropriate now to do some of these long-needed studies. His comments are especially relevant to behavior modification applications. Instead of direct application of principles derived from animal research to classroom behavioral management methods as sometimes seems to be suggested, it is very important that the instructional procedures be evaluated primarily in terms of their applicability with human subjects and their utility in the practical situation. Fortunately, such precautions are frequently an essential part of the behavior modifier's approach to instruction.

There are many questions which cannot be resolved now as to relationships between basic learning research and behavior modification instructional principles. We have delineated four facets of this approach and we have pointed out that there are differences of opinion as to how closely the instructional principles should be related to operant reinforcement principles. Some contend that reinforcement principles have been and will continue to be the main basis from which instructional principles can be drawn. Other behavior modifiers hold that they should practically ignore basic research generally and should expend their research efforts on evaluations of their instructional procedures without being concerned about relationships with any academic psychology theory. It is the author's conjecture that a majority may follow the lead of those behavior modifiers (such as Davison, Goldfried, & Krasner, 1970) who use reinforcement principles but who also openly endorse the use of any psychological theory which can be useful in the practical situation.

Finally, we'll venture an observation about the probable impact of the behavior modification approach on the emergence of instructional theory more generally. It has been suggested that early behavioral psychology's main effect on academic psychology took the form of stimulating more rigorous research methodology. Somewhat similarly, it may well be that behavior modification's major influences on instructional theory may be better delineation of educational objectives and instructional methods and more routine inclusion of evaluative research procedures as bases for modifications in instructional design.

SUGGESTED READINGS

Bandura, A. *Principles of behavior modification.* New York: Holt, Rinehart, & Winston, 1969.

Bijou, S. W. What psychology has to offer education now. In P. B. Dews (Ed.), *Festschrift for B. F. Skinner.* New York: Appleton-Century-Crofts, 1970. Pp. 401–407.

Fargo, G. A., Behrns, C., & Nolen, P. *Behavior modification in the classroom.* Belmont, Calif.: Wadsworth Publishing Co., Inc., 1970.

Hanley, E. M. Review of research involving applied behavior in the classroom. *Review of Educational Research*, 1970, **40**, 597–625.

Homme, L., Csanyi, A. P., Gonzales, M. A., & Rechs, J. R. *How to use contingency contracting in the classroom*. Champaign, Ill.: Research Press, 1970.

Kanfer, F. C., & Phillips, J. S. *Learning foundations of behavior therapy*. New York: Wiley, 1970.

Krasner, L., & Ullman, L. (Eds.) *Research in behavior modification*. New York: Holt, Rinehart, & Winston, 1965.

Krasner, L. The operant approach in behavior therapy. In A. E. Bergin & S. L. Garfield (Eds.), *Handbook of psychotherapy and behavior change: An empirical analysis*. New York: Wiley, 1971.

London, P. The end of ideology in behavior modification. *American Psychologist*, 1972, **27**, 913–920.

Neuringer, C., & Michael, J. L. *Behavior modification in clinical psychology*. New York: Appleton-Century-Crofts, 1970.

O'Leary, K. D., & Drabman, R. Token reinforcement programs in the classroom: A review. *Psychological Bulletin*, 1971, **75**, 379–398.

Snelbecker, G. E. Behavior modification in education and in the clinic: Facets, origins and probable future. *Clinical Pediatrics*, 1970, **9**, 617–621.

Ullmann, L. P., & Krasner, L. *Case studies in behavior modification*. New York: Holt, Rinehart, & Winston, 1965.

Wenrich, W. W. *A primer of behavior modification*. Belmont, Calif.: Brooks-Cole Pub. Co., 1970.

14
Cognitive Construct
Instructional Theories

Certain psychologists and educators have proposed that instructional theories can best be derived from the learning research and theory which have focused on thinking, problem solving, concept formation, and other comparatively complex cognitive processes. In opposition to the behavior modifiers' concern with overt, observable behavior, they have emphasized the student's internal representations or *cognitive constructs* as the really important concern in education. Thus we have characterized their approach to instruction as an attempt to formulate a *cognitive construct instructional theory*.

The main instructional position which we will consider in this tradition is that of Jerome Bruner. Bruner has been one of the more vocal advocates of instructional theory and has devoted considerable efforts to the development and use of his own approach to instruction. Although by training and earlier experience a perception and social psychologist, by the 1950s he displayed substantial interest in the nature and development of cognitive processes and in their potential implications for educational practice. We have selected his position to illustrate some of the characteristics which have emerged in the instructional theories which predominantly rely on cognitive learning research and theory. As a more specific emphasis in Bruner's approach, we have identified *inquiry training* or the *discovery learning method*; but readers should recognize that Bruner contends that this is only one of several methods by which his instructional theory can be implemented. We have selected the discovery learning method primarily because many contemporary educators and psychologists consider it to be almost synonymous with Bruner's conception of instructional theory.

We will also briefly consider some alternative formulations which likewise have been based on cognitive learning research, namely the positions presented by Ojemann and by Ausubel. Again we feel that it is important to stress that these are not exhaustive comprehensive statements but are illustrations of instructional theory positions which have primarily been derived from research and theory on cognitive learning processes. After describing a representative educational application, we will evaluate the cognitive construct approach in terms of its discovery learning and inquiry training methods, as well as its contributions to the development of instructional theory.

JEROME BRUNER AND COGNITIVE CONSTRUCT INSTRUCTIONAL THEORY

As we noted in our discussions of learning theories, some psychologists have emphasized more complex cognitive processes such as thinking, language, problem solving, concept formation, and information processing. Such ventures in learning research and theory usually have not been given as much status among psychologists as the more behaviorally oriented theories—at least until recent times. The cognitive theory proponents have been legitimately criticized for having more in common in what they are *against* (namely, principles which emphasize behavioral processes rather than internal cognitive processes) than what they are *for*, in that they have been far from clear in articulating an alternative theory.

But there are certain features which have been emerging in these cognitively oriented learning theories. Typically they have attributed a greater degree of autonomy and initiative to the learner and they have tried to conceptualize learning processes as experienced by the learner. As is illustrated by the gestalt approach, some have emphasized the perceptual processes involved in learning. Others, such as the contemporary information processing theorists, have characterized stimuli as potential information inputs, and they have been concerned with the ways that the learner receives, reorganizes, retains, and subsequently uses this information.

Unlike the behavior modification approach, which was stimulated by Skinner and was modeled after his operant principles, the cognitive construct instructional theories are rather loosely organized and have had several persons influential on their formulations. These include Ausubel, Bruner, Newell, Ojemann, Piaget, Simon, Torrance, Woodruff, and many others. The best-known spokesman is Jerome Bruner of Harvard University. He was an early advocate of development of instructional theories in general, and he has been particularly active in promoting his theory which emphasizes cognitive processes.

A Perception-Social-Cognitive
Psychologist's Involvement with Education

It should be useful in understanding Bruner's approach, as a representative of the cognitive instructional theories, to note some of the professional background and interests which led to his involvement with educational matters. Now depicted as a "Harvard University elder statesman in psychology," Jerome Bruner (1915–   ) showed minimal interest in psychology as a profession until he enrolled as a graduate student in psychology at Duke University in the late 1930s. Shortly thereafter he transferred to Harvard University where he completed a Ph.D. under the well-known experimental psychologist Karl S. Lashley. Both during his graduate work and during his pre-World War II years he maintained a major interest in the psychology of perceptual processes, studying animals and humans. But during World War II he spent a great deal of time in social psychology research, particularly the propaganda techniques used by Nazi Germany.

It was in the several years immediately following World War II that Bruner really became involved in the study of cognitive processes. Combining different aspects of his earlier work, he had a major role in the development of a "new look" in perception research. It had long been recognized that the physical characteristics of an object (for example, actual size, shape) and the conditions in the viewing situation (such as amount of light in the room, distance from the observer to the object) are very important determinants of our perceptions of physical objects. What was "new" was the notion that the observer personally "contributes" emphases and distortions in his perception of the object's physical characteristics. For example, it was theorized by Bruner and other researchers that the way one perceives the size of a coin will be directly influenced by his feelings about money and indirectly determined by his socioeconomic background and personality characteristics.

When research results supported these predictions, Bruner became more intrigued with the notion that much of our behavior may be dependent on how we structure our knowledge about ourselves and the world around us. Some would go so far as to say that Bruner was a major influence in bringing cognitive processes to the attention of American psychology at mid-century and in fostering a more systematic and empirical examination of these processes. Of particular relevance for our current concern with Bruner's instructional theory is the fact that it was the study of cognitive processes that initially caused him to be interested in developmental psychology and, subsequently, educational psychology and education.

Apparently it was mainly in reaction to the Russian launching of Sputnik in 1957 that Bruner and many other noneducator professional persons became very concerned about the status and progress of education in the United States. In subsequent years Bruner participated in a series of study groups and workshops along with other eminent scientists and mathematicians who made various attempts to improve the quality of educational curriculum and methodology. Considering the nature of our present discussion of instructional theories and their relationship to learning theory and research, one of Bruner's comments is of interest: "The essays are, in effect, the efforts of a student of the cognitive processes trying to come to grips with the problems of education" (Bruner, 1966, p. vii). This quotation, taken from Bruner's *Toward a Theory of Instruction*, suggests both the approach he takes to education and the particular area of psychology on which he most typically relies for generating suggestions and hypotheses about the instructional process.

Although Bruner has expressed a preference for describing himself as "a psychologist" without any qualifying adjectives, many contemporaries consider him to be primarily aligned with cognitive studies and developmental theory, especially the developmental cognitive theory of Jean Piaget. He prefers conceptualizing thinking and other cognitive processes as information processing whereby organisms receive, transform, retain, and subsequently use information about the world and about themselves.

Titles from some of the books which he wrote around the late 1950s into the middle 1960s give some indication of his orientation: *A Study of Thinking* (Bruner, Goodnow, & Austin, 1956), *The Process of Education* (Bruner, 1960), *Studies in Cognitive Growth* (Bruner, Olver, & Greenfield, et al., 1966), *Toward a Theory of Instruction* (Bruner, 1966), and *Learning about Learning: A Conference Report* (Bruner, 1966) are representative titles.

Some Views about Education

Bruner has studied both "primitive" human cultures and animal social groups to help understand how our society has developed its formal educational institutions. As a result of his studies he has depicted education in its broadest meaning to include the ways by which we pass on our culture from one generation to another. But he is careful in noting that the strategies by which we add to our fund of knowledge are at least as important as the facts which have been attained. Thus he views schools as transmitting our cultural heritage in the form of the fund of knowledge, how we can add to it, and how we can use it.

Bruner's conceptions of education and our formal educational institutions in society have undergone some interesting changes during the past decade (Bruner, 1971). In his earlier involvement with educational matters, Bruner seemed to accept the school as an established institution within our society, and he apparently considered the means for improvement to be primarily through curriculum modifications within the constraints of such an existing institution. Of course, he did not consider all learning to take place within any formal educational institution, for he was quite aware of the extensive learning experiences which occur in the home and family situation during preschool years. He obviously was very much aware of the extracurricular learning experiences which occur throughout adolescence. However, in the early 1970s we see Bruner expressing a great deal of concern about reevaluating our whole conception of schools and their status as educational institutions in our society.

He had always considered schools to have a function of enabling students to cope more effectively with their environment and in fact to improve upon the social and physical environment in which they live. Moreover, he was quite careful to emphasize that educational objectives should not be restricted to the very abstract descriptions of our world and the mere transmittal of "factual information" and the "bodies of knowledge" which had been accumulated by a given student's predecessors. He was quite concerned with the personalized way in which each individual develops his conception of himself and his world and he considers a learner to have a very active role in the educational process and in dealing with life more generally. However, in his earlier writing on the design and improvement of education, including his various positions concerning the development of theories of instruction, he apparently expected that the major changes would come within the educational institutions through improvements of curriculum and general educational methods.

But by the early 1970s, Bruner was raising questions as to whether such an approach would be adequate to meet the changing needs of society. Without detracting from the considerable attempts to improve educational curricula and methodology, he began to raise serious questions as to whether it may be necessary to change the whole concept of schools and other educational institutions in our society. Some educators were apparently even shocked to hear that he considered such changes to be sufficiently important that he was willing to diminish the role which he had placed on "the structure of knowledge" in his earlier formulations.

I would be quite satisfied with de-emphasis on the *structure* of knowledge, and deal with it in the context of the problems that face us. We might put vocation and intention back into the process of education. . . . If I had my choice now, in terms of a curriculum project for the "70s," it would be to find a means whereby we could bring society back to its sense of values and priorities in life. *I believe I would be quite satisfied to declare, if not a moratorium, then something of a de-emphasis on matters that had to do with the structure of history, the structure of physics, the nature of mathematical consistency, and deal with it rather in the context of the problems that face us.* (Bruner, 1971, pp. 20–21)

By the early 1970s Bruner was contending that we need to rethink our whole conception of the characteristics and roles of schools in our society, and that we need to examine carefully the extent to which such educational institutions are truly meeting the needs they had been designed to satisfy. His earlier concern with enabling students to cope with their environment began to play a more dominant role in his writings about the process of education.

But since most of the principles of instruction reflecting this more recently developed interest are only being formulated at the time of this writing, we will primarily focus on those aspects of Bruner's instructional principles which were articulated in the late 1950s to middle 1960s and which continue to be featured in more recent papers. More specifically, we will examine Bruner's instructional theory in light of his concern with transmitting a fund of knowledge; developing a favorable attitude toward learning; developing an attitude and skill to enable the learner to discover and to continue his learning experiences beyond his formal education; and developing a learner's unique talent so as to cope more effectively with his physical and social environment and to grow intellectually in general.

We will find in most of the writings by Bruner, and by other instructional theorists who are particularly influenced by cognitive theory, an emphasis on thinking processes and inquiry skills as more important educational objectives than the accumulation of factual details. Of course they recognize that one cannot think and cannot solve problems without facts, but they contend that it is the basic fundamental principles and these inquiry skills which are more important than facts. For example, Bruner has described such efforts: "The prevailing notion was that if you understood the structure of knowledge, that understanding would then permit you to go ahead on your own; you did not need to encounter everything in nature in order to know nature, but by understanding some deep principles you could extrapolate to the particulars as needed. Knowing with a canny strategy whereby you could know a great deal about a lot of things while keeping very little in mind" (Bruner, 1971, p. 18).

To understand Bruner's conception of instruction, it is important to recognize that he characterizes school learning as *intellectual growth*, especially as an increase in one's ability to integrate and to use new information. He cautions the educator to consider certain "benchmarks about the nature of intellectual growth against which to measure one's efforts at explanation" (Bruner, 1966, p. 5): (1) Intellectual growth involves increasing independence from the direct eliciting influence of stimuli through the development of cognitive mediating processes which enable one to deal with stimuli on a symbolic level. (2) Thus growth involves development and refinement of one's internal system for representing objects and events. (3) It also involves increasing ability to use words and symbols to logically analyze what we have done and can do in the future. (4) This intellectual growth is fostered by systematic and exploratory tutor-tutee relationships with various significant persons serving as tutor. (5) Language constitutes a tool and instrument which enables the learner to comprehend order in his environment as well as constitutes a means which facilitates learning. (6) With intellectual growth we become capable of engaging in more than one transaction at a time and to allocate our intellectual resources wisely in coping with different stresses from our environment.

In 1959 Bruner participated in a conference in which thirty-five scientists, scholars, and educators were attempting to find ways for bringing science education up to date and improving its presentation in primary and secondary schools. As editor for the conference proceedings (Bruner, 1960), he delineated four themes about education. Although these themes were based on general contributions during this conference, Bruner acknowledges that they especially reflect his own views about education. This report has been widely acclaimed as having had a profound impact on contemporary views about curriculum and instruction. The themes are especially relevant to our present discussion because they are evident in Bruner's subsequent formulations of his theory of instruction.

Bruner's first theme noted the importance of how knowledge is organized or *structured*. He depicted psychology as having influenced educators to move from an emphasis on general understanding, around the turn of the century, to a concern in subsequent decades with more specific skills. Contending that this resulted in excessive stress on factual details, Bruner proposed that the school curricula should be changed to emphasize the *structure* of knowledge. This is necessary, he argued, to help the student to see how seemingly unrelated new facts are related to each other and to the information he already possesses. In order to accomplish this change in teaching, we need to identify methods for teaching fundamental structure and procedures for arranging learning conditions which foster it.

His second theme, concerned with *readiness* for learning, dealt with the intellectual development of students and its implications for both curriculum and instruction. He questioned popular notions that certain educational material may be "too difficult" to be taught in early grades and proposed instead that it may be possible to teach practically all subjects even to young children. One of his most quoted statements was: "We begin with the hypothesis that any subject can be taught effectively in some intellectually honest form to any child at any stage of development" (Bruner, 1960, p. 33). Referring to research on cognitive development, he contended that each person, even a child, has a characteristic way of "viewing the world and explaining it to himself" (p. 33). He contended that if the teacher understands how the student conceptualizes his world, it is possible to teach the fundamental foundations of any topic; of course he recognized that a more sophisticated understanding of the topic areas would be attainable at later stages of the educational programs. This prompted him to suggest the use of a "spiral" approach to curriculum.

A key to his approach is the notion that one can start with the fundamental notions about a topic and expand into more details and more abstract descriptions. "(A)n essential point often overlooked in the planning of curricula . . . is that the basic ideas that lie at the heart of all science and mathematics and the basic themes that give form to life and literature are as simple as they are powerful" (Bruner, 1960, pp. 12–13). Ideally, according to Bruner, education proceeds by identifying these fundamental ideas and then elaborating and expanding on them. Moreover, if these fundamentals are presented in the more concrete, personalized way by which we all approach new information, both children and adults will grasp the new information and integrate it with their previous knowledge. "A curriculum as it develops should revisit these basic ideas repeatedly, building upon them until the student has grasped the full formal apparatus that goes with them" (Bruner, 1960, p. 13).

One other aspect was considered within this theme about readiness to learn. Bruner characterizes the act of learning as involving three almost simultaneous processes, and he acknowledges that different learning situations may involve different relative emphases or different combinations of these aspects. First, there is *acquisition* of new information which either supplants or refines the student's previous knowledge. Although some "revolutionary" changes may occur, Bruner depicts learning as typically involving a gradual process. Secondly, learning involves *transformation* of this knowledge so that it will be useful to the student. He suggests that through transformation we change the information in various ways so that we are able to go beyond the facts as they are originally given. Thus he is critical of passive, rote memorization, taking the position that some transformation of knowledge is necessary in order for it to be useful in new situations. The third aspect, *evaluation*, refers to the extent to which such "new" information has been transformed so that it is adequate for selected tasks. He presumes that such evaluations are conducted primarily by the learner and that the teacher's function may often be crucial in helping the student to develop skills in evaluating his own progress.

The third theme emphasized the value of *intuition* in the educational process. By intuition, he meant "the intellectual techniques of arriving at plausible but tentative formulations without going through the analytical steps by which such formulations would be found to be valid or invalid conclusions" (Bruner, 1960, p. 13). Here Bruner is talking about the "educated guess" which is used frequently by scientists, artists, and other creative persons. Conceding that one can make better intuitive guesses if one is knowledgeable about a topic, he cautioned against stifling students' creative thinking and against promoting the notion that every question has *one correct* answer. He proposed that research and theorizing be devoted to identifying means for developing intuitive thinking and that we reexamine the appropriateness of those existing procedures—for example, some grading practices—which may stifle it.

In each of these first three themes, Bruner was primarily concerned with trying to get students to think about any given substantive area very much the same way as do scholars at more advanced stages of understanding of that area. He contended that it was a matter of differences in degrees, not in kinds, of the thinking or cognitive processes involved. Therefore, he went on to emphasize the importance of teaching these cognitive processes to students even when they are first introduced to the substantive areas. "The school boy learning physics *is* a physicist, and it is easier for him to learn physics behaving like a physicist than doing something else" (Bruner, 1960, p. 14).

The fourth and final theme involves *motivation* or the desire to learn and the means available to instructors to stimulate such motivation. Obviously, the ideal situation is one in which the student is primarily deriving satisfaction from learning per se. Although Bruner acknowledged the fact that such inherent interest in learning frequently may have to be supplemented by various kinds of extrinsic factors, he felt that much more effort should be devoted to trying to get students more interested in learning. In various papers he has contended that the educational experiences which stimulate motivation are those in which the learner actively participates and personally experiences competence in dealing with his world. According to Bruner, this type of learning experience is best exemplified by some intuitive discovery learning experience. We'll consider the implications of this assumption for his instructional theory in a later section.

Guidelines for Developing an Instructional Theory

Bruner has been one of the earliest and most vocal advocates for the development of instructional theories. However, several problems arise when one tries to understand Bruner's notions about instructional theories generally and his own theory in particular. First, as noted in Chapter 6, educators have not been especially precise in their definitions of "instructional theory" versus "curriculum theory." We have acknowledged the overlapping concerns of these two areas, but we have attempted to delineate the two by ascribing to the former a focus on methods to attain educational objectives, and to the latter concern with the substance of intended learnings. At times Bruner endorses similar distinctions, but at other times he incorporates so many curricular emphases in his conceptions about instruction that some (for example, Lawrence, 1969) contend that Bruner has a curriculum theory rather than an instructional theory. Moreover, a review of educational developments during the past few decades reveals that his "instructional theory" admonitions have had about as much influence on curriculum reform as they have had on instructional innovations.

Secondly, Bruner's influence from developmental theory is so great that he frequently depicts learning as intellectual growth and development, thereby obliterating conventional psychological distinctions between the two terms, learning and development. However, as noted at the beginning of this book, this distinction will probably cause fewer problems for educators than for psychologists, since many educators use these terms almost synonymously.

Third, Bruner's enthusiasm for his own position and for the general development of instructional theories sometimes makes it difficult to discern which are mere hopes for the future and which are empirically tested accomplishments. Bruner has obviously recognized such a problem and he occasionally apologetically notes that his gropings to develop an instructional theory are "marred by the fault of too little data, too little systematic observation, too sparse an arsenal of analytic tools" (Bruner, 1966, p. 171).

But Bruner's antidote should also be noted: Take seriously the task of building a scientific theory of instruction and the pragmatism of today will be replaced eventually by a more systematically developed and tested instructional theory. In the meantime, it will be helpful to keep in mind these three problems as we consider some of Bruner's notions about instructional theories.

He identifies instruction as an effort to facilitate intellectual growth, development, or learning by diverse means. Although he sometimes departs from his own definitions, he identifies instructional theories as being "concerned with how what one wishes to teach can best be learned, with improving rather than describing learning" (Bruner, 1966, p. 41). He further notes that an instructional theory focuses on the means for attaining selected educational goals rather than on the actual selection of such goals.

In contrast with learning theories and developmental theories which merely *describe* processes, an instructional theory should *prescribe* the optimal arrangements of conditions which will facilitate meaningful school learning. An instructional theory should be developed alongside learning and development theories, and its principles should be congruent with psychological theories. It should be a normative theory in the sense that it should provide general principles of instruction rather than detailed methods. He anticipates, for example, that an instructional theory will outline procedures and techniques for teaching mathematics from which a teacher can derive instructional plans for teaching a particular section of ninth-grade algebra.

Four major features outline the scope of a theory of instruction. First, the theory should specify experiences which most effectively foster a favorable predisposition toward learning generally and toward the particular educational topic at hand.

Secondly, it should indicate how to structure the body of knowledge so that the student can readily learn and use it. This should take into account the structure which may be inherent in the body of knowledge as well as the learner's internal organization of information about his world. The theory should show how to present the new knowledge so that the learner can incorporate it within his existing personal knowledge. In this regard he contends that the real test of such structure lies in its "power for *simplifying information*, for *generating new propositions* and for *increasing the manipulability of a body of knowledge*" (Bruner, 1966, p. 41).

Third, an instructional theory should specify optimal sequences in which to present learning experiences. Here the theory should identify relevant factors of influence, such as difficulty level and degree of concreteness/abstractness, and should indicate what learning effects are produced by the various possible sequences.

Fourth, the theory should specify the nature of rewards and punishments so as to facilitate meaningful school learning. Two aspects are enumerated—intrinsic versus extrinsic rewards, and optimal timing in the presentation of the rewards.

Bruner's Instructional Theory and Discovery Learning

As we have seen, Bruner's views about education are wide-ranging and extensive. When we search for a formulized theory of instruction, we can find four general principles, corresponding to those four features which we outlined in the previous section, and a preference for using "discovery learning," or "inquiry training," educational methods because they seem to embody most of the favorable features outlined in the four principles. These four principles and the discovery learning method are quite compatible with and predictable from Bruner's general views about school learning and education which are reviewed above. Moreover, though the discovery learning techniques were described over a decade ago (Bruner, 1961) and the four principles several years ago (Bruner, 1966), they seem to maintain their importance in his more recent views about instruction. Thus we will use these 1961 and 1966 sources as our main guides to Bruner's instructional theory.

Predisposition to Learning The first principle outlines conditions which predispose the student to be willing and able to learn when he enters the classroom. "It has been customary, in discussing predispositions to learn, to focus upon cultural, motivational and personal factors affecting the desire to learn and to undertake problem solving" (Bruner, 1966, p. 42). But after having identified these different personal and social processes as being of "enormous importance," he focuses on three cognitive aspects, apparently because he feels that the teacher can more readily exert some influence via them. Of primary importance is the predisposition to explore alternative solutions to problems. The three cognitive aspects are activation, maintenance, and direction—"exploration of alternatives requires something to get it started, something to keep it going, and something to keep it from being random" (p. 43).

Generally, the way one initiates systematic research behaviors is by creating some degree of uncertainty for the learner. But this is more simply stated than accomplished. A task which is "cut and dried" provokes little or no exploration, but too much uncertainty may create confusion and anxiety without producing exploration. The problem is to find a satisfactory extent of uncertainty and ways to arrange for it in the task.

Maintaining exploratory activities likewise presents problems. He provides a rule of thumb that "the benefits from exploring alternatives (should) exceed the risks incurred" (p. 44). But here again some optimal balance must be found: An instructor, or the conditions in the learning situation, must provide some structure without overguiding the learner in his search patterns.

To provide for productive searching, and to avoid sheer random activities, the learner needs to evolve some means for ascertaining whether he is making progress in solving the problem. This requires, at a minimum, some sense of the goal which is involved and at least a few tests for evaluating progress. "Put in briefest form, direction depends upon knowledge of the results of one's tests, and instruction should have an edge over 'spontaneous' learning in providing more of such knowledge" (p. 44). Assuming that correct responses and errors will be made, instruction must maximize the information derivable from both correct and incorrect responses. The latter must result in information which leads to their correction; the former must cause the student to be aware of his progress.

Structure and the Form of Knowledge   The second principle outlines the need for structural features. The body of material to be learned should be organized in some optimal form so that the content can be managed and grasped by the learner, whatever his developmental stage or ability level may be. Bruner enumerates three ways by which one can characterize the structure of a body of knowledge—its mode of representation, its economy, and its effective power. An instructor should take into account the characteristics of the student in selecting the appropriate mode, economy, and power of the information to be learned.

Mode of representation refers to the conceptual means whereby the information is presented. It can consist of a set of actions, or of concrete representations. It can involve summary images, most likely visual or auditory, which graphically present the concept. Or it can be represented by symbolic or logical propositions, such as can be done with words or numbers.

Bruner cites developmental research which indicates that children first are capable of comprehending concrete operations, later graphic representations, and finally abstract verbal and numerical symbolic presentations. Similarly, he suggests that even adolescents and adults can initially more readily comprehend information, when it is unfamiliar or if they are anxious in the situation, if it is presented in the order: concrete, graphic, symbolic. The instructor should consider the learner's current developmental level, degree of familiarity with the material, and general emotional comfort in selecting the appropriate mode of representation.

Economy refers to the amount of information which the learner must keep in mind and must process in order to solve a problem. The more information one must "juggle," the more successive processing steps one must take and the lower the economy in processing. Economy varies with the mode of representation in that it is easier to handle symbols than concrete actions. It also varies with the sequence and manner in which the material is presented; generally, the more readily applicable to problem solution is the information presented, the fewer information processing operations (hence, more economical) will be required.

As an example of different degrees of economy resulting from information presentation, Bruner provides a list of hypothetical line routes among several cities and poses the problem of a traveler who may wish to make travel plans based on this information. Following is the original list:

Boston to Concord
Danbury to Concord
Albany to Boston
Concord to Elmira
Albany to Elmira
Concord to Danbury
Boston to Albany
Concord to Albany   (Bruner, 1966, p. 46)

He describes several ways of reorganizing or representing this information. One could memorize the list as originally presented, or reorganize it in alphabetical order according to the first and second cities for each pair. Or, one could prepare diagrams denoting available plane routes.

Finally, one could generate several rules about the routes, such as the fact that Elmira is a "trap," that there is only one way to Danbury from Albany, etc. He suggests that the harried traveler and the more casual reader would both find greater economy in the latter graphic or rule presentations of information than in the former ones. As with mode of representation, the teacher should select a degree of economy in presenting information which is compatible with the learner's capabilities, the learning situation, and the kind of educational objectives involved.

The *effective power* of information structure refers to the extent to which the particular structure enables the learner to go beyond the facts presented in generating new propositions and in using the information in solving problems. He acknowledges that the effective power rating is not completely independent of economy nor of mode of representation, and that it is somewhat difficult to measure quantitatively. Nonetheless, Bruner feels that one of the major tests of the structure of information, and thus a major consideration for the instructor to keep in mind, is the extent to which it enables the learner to generate new propositions and to recognize connections between matters which otherwise might seem to be quite separate.

Sequencing A theory of instruction should, according to Bruner, specify optimal sequences for presenting educational experiences. "Instruction consists of leading the learner through a sequence of statements and restatements of a problem or body of knowledge that increase the learn-er's ability to grasp, transform, and transfer what he is learning" (p. 49). Acknowledging that a number of sequences may be equivalent and that there is no sequence which is necessarily best for all learners or for all educational objectives, he suggests that some general rules can be enumer-ated for planning instruction. Generally, sequencing must take into account the limited capabilities of students to process information. Usually an instructor should arrange for more economical organizations for new information so that the student can more readily comprehend and process it. Bruner suggests that these more economically organized materi-als may also serve as a model for subsequent more complex information.

He refers to the general developmental progression from concrete behaviors and the corresponding "enactive" representation, through graphic relationships and "iconic" representation, to the verbal or numeri-cal statements in symbolic representation as bases for planning instruc-tional sequences. He suggests that one follow such a progression of learning experiences with young children or with presentations of new information to adolescents and adults. Thus, one might present a concrete example to high school students before presenting graphic descriptions or before explaining the abstract principle or concept which it illustrates.

Secondly, he suggests that one should consider the appropriateness of encouraging the learner to search widely versus evaluating the alternatives which he has already identified when one selects sequences of instruction. Third, the instructor should provide a sequence of experiences which will maintain interest by the learner for the particular educational topic at hand.

Sequencing cannot be determined independently of the specific learn-ing conditions or of the learner's progress. Rather, in selecting sequences, one must consider previous errors, degree of creativity being encouraged, probable ability to transfer what has already been learned, general speed or economy in learning, and many other factors in arriving at optimal sequences.

Form and Pacing of Reinforcement   "Learning depends upon knowledge of results at a time when and at a place where the knowledge can be used for correction. Instruction increases the appropriate timing and placing of corrective knowledge" (p. 50). Thus Bruner, although recognizing the rewards and punishments which are of such central concern to behavior modifiers, prefers an informational rather than a drive reduction interpre-tation of their value in facilitating learning. In this regard he is closer to Tolman than to Hull, but he probably draws this instructional principle concerning reinforcement from various researchers on problem solving. While not specifying one particular theory or researcher, he refers to authors who contend that learning and problem solving involve a cycle of "the formulation of a testing procedure or trial, the operation of this testing procedure, and the comparison of the results of the test with some criterion" (pp. 50-51). In this context, he contends that reinforcement in the form of knowledge of results should come when the learner is comparing the results of his tryout procedure with the learning criterion which he is trying to achieve. Rather than merely indicating whether one's answer is correct or incorrect, this information should indicate whether the learner is making progress toward the desired educational goal. He contends that this feedback about progress must take such a form that the learner can relate it to his attempts at solving that problem or achieving those educational goals.

Bruner comments about types of feedback which may not be useful to the learner. The student may not be influenced by the feedback because he is so anxious, so highly motivated, or so intent in pursuing certain activities that he cannot change to alternative activities. Feedback about what one should *not* do is not as effective as information as to what *is* appropriate. There is a limit on the amount of information which we can handle; if the feedback exceeds such limitations, it cannot be used. The feedback must be in a presentational mode and at a degree of economy which will translate readily to the problem-solving activities of the learner, or else it cannot be used.

Bruner also expresses a strong preference for using intrinsic reinforcement rather than extrinsic, and he advocates designing instruction so that the learner will most quickly be able to evaluate his own progress and gain reinforcement from learning per se. It is not an overstatement to interpret practically all the above comments about the instructor's interventions as generally being judged in terms of the extent to which they make the learner self-sufficient.

Discovery Learning Certain methods of instruction have been identified as encompassing so many of Bruner's views of education and so many of the aspects outlined in his instructional principles that many educators and psychologists have come to equate these methods as synonymous with Bruner's instructional theory. On some occasions Bruner has denied that these "discovery learning" or "inquiry training" methods, as they are called, constitute implementation of his principles, and he has then suggested that other instructional procedures should be used along with discovery learning. However, he has closely identified himself with these methods and he has not provided further information as to alternative methods. Thus we will examine discovery learning procedures as exemplary applications of Bruner's instructional principles.

Bruner (1961) has distinguished between two types of teaching modes, the *expository* and the *hypothetical* (or discovery learning) modes, and he has conjectured that four benefits *might* accrue for students who are exposed to the discovery (hypothetical) mode. He depicted the expository mode as one in which the teacher makes practically all the decisions and the student is essentially in a passive, receptive role. The teacher, who is acknowledged as being more knowledgeable about the subject matter, typically lectures to the student and presents an analysis of the information which is to be learned. Bruner seemed to feel that such procedures are found in typical classrooms from elementary school through university undergraduate and graduate programs and that they are especially emphasized in the behavior modification approach to instruction. The hypothetical or discovery learning mode requires that the student participate in making many of the decisions about what, how, and when something is to be learned and even may play a major role in making such decisions. Instead of being "told" the content by the teacher, it is expected that the student will have to explore examples and from them "discover" the principles or concepts which are to be learned. Many contend that the discovery learning versus expository mode debate continues a timeless debate as to how much a teacher should help a student and how much the student should help himself. Similar controversies had ensued, for example, between proponents of Thorndike's connectionism and proponents of gestalt principles.

In Bruner's conjectures about possible benefits from use of discovery learning procedures one finds a curious mix of instructional methods and educational objectives. Bruner suggested that there would be four benefits of the discovery method. (1) *Increase in intellectual potency*. The learner will be more likely to develop problem-solving search patterns, to learn how to transform information and to organize it so that he can get the most out of that information, and to develop an expectancy that there usually is some orderliness in nature whether or not a "correct" answer is quickly forthcoming. "Practice in discovering for oneself teaches one to acquire information in a way that makes that information more readily viable in problem solving" (p. 26). (2) *Shift from extrinsic to intrinsic rewards*. Bruner conjectured that learning a concept or principle by discovering relationships among examples, in contrast with being given analytical statements about that concept or principle, would stimulate the student to gain greater satisfaction from the learning process itself and thus would foster an attitude that learning provides intrinsic rewards. The main gratification would come from stimulated curiosity and through realization that the learner had gained mastery over something, that he had experienced an increase in his competence. (3) *Learning the heuristics or working strategies for making future discoveries*. One can best learn *how* to discover new information if one has had practice with effective discovery procedures. "I have never seen anybody improve in the art and technique of inquiry by any means other than engaging in inquiry" (p. 31). (4) *Aid to retention and retrieval of information*. Basing his recommendation on many psychological studies, he theorized that organization of new information which decreases complexity by embedding it in the learner's personal cognitive structure will facilitate retention and will make it more accessible for retrieval. Information organized around one's interests and existing personal cognitive structure will make the information more useful and more readily transferred to new situations. "In sum the very attitudes and activities that characterize 'figuring out' or 'discovering' things for oneself also seem to have the effect of making material more readily accessible in memory" (p. 32).

"Discovery learning" thus has come to refer both to a method of instruction and to an educational objective. As an educational *method*, discovery learning consists of providing a learner with a situation without articulating what the teacher already knows about that situation. The assumption is that, with minimal help from the teacher, the student will learn more if he "discovers" the lesson that is to be learned there. By contrast, the "expository method" (or some other similar type designation) involves either more directed activity by a teacher or a more highly structured learning situation. As an educational *objective*, discovery learning constitutes those attitudes, strategies, and skills which enable the person to identify and to solve problems, thus making him more capable of coping with life's demands.

OTHER CONCEPTIONS OF
INSTRUCTION WITHIN THIS TRADITION

Many educators and psychologists reacted enthusiastically and favorably to Bruner's views about instruction. Changes in educational practice were evident throughout the 1960s and early 1970s in the form of curriculum changes and innovations which supposedly implemented his recommendations for use of discovery learning procedures. A comment by Reavis and Whittacre (1969), who adapted some of his recommendations in their design of a teacher education program, is illustrative of the generally uncritical reception of Bruner's ideas. Referring to Bruner's emphasis on the central importance of structure, his hypothesis that a subject can be taught in an intellectually honest form to students of any age, and his endorsement of the spiral curriculum, they proclaimed: "His three principles have received such wide acceptance that they scarcely need defense" (p. 259).

But others were more selective in their acceptance of Bruner's views. Though they acknowledged that his ideas may sound plausible, they began to search for the evidence in support of them. In some cases, finding either controversial findings or no empirical evidence, they expressed reservations as to how widely Bruner's recommendations should be implemented.

Especially of concern to some was his apparently general application of discovery learning principles. Even those colleagues who endorsed the cognitive approach to learning and instruction had reservations as to the extent to which such methods would be either feasible or sufficiently effective with different students and diverse subject matter.

Some colleagues had long been working on their own formulations of instructional models within the cognitive construct tradition. It is to the work of David Ausubel, Paul Torrance, and Ralph Ojemann which we will now turn so as to sample briefly more conceptions of instruction which draw from cognitive learning research and theory.

Ausubel's Subsumption Principles and Advance Organizers

David P. Ausubel is another example of a psychologist who advocates utilization of cognitive learning research and theory in the formulation of instructional principles. He is an active researcher and a very prolific author who has written several books and many papers in which he has conceptualized educational psychology as that aspect of psychology which is primarily concerned with the nature, conditions, outcomes, and evaluation of school learning and retention. Strongly criticizing the frequent use of behavioral psychology principles, he advocates primary reliance on principles drawn from studies of meaningful verbal learning.

He agrees with Bruner as to the central importance of cognitive processes in the planning of instruction. He has developed a rather elaborate theory as to how one forms cognitive structures which are useful in solving real-life problems, and he has identified a number of implications for educational practice.

For many years he has expressed concern about the problems which may result if educators use discovery learning procedures too extensively. He has advised that discovery learning simply may be too inefficient in many situations, and he has even raised serious questions as to whether there is empirical support for all of the alleged advantages of using discovery procedures—even when it is feasible to use them. While recognizing that there probably is a time and place for discovery procedures, he also recommends quite extensive use of expository and other instructional procedures. He even suggests that expository learning is a more mature and economical means for learning new information.

He agrees with Bruner's emphasis on the centrality of cognitive processes for meaningful human learning, and he additionally provides a theoretical description of the manner in which we integrate and subsequently use new information. He presents his *principle of subsumption* as a key explanation as to how one increases and reorganizes one's fund of knowledge. New ideas and information are grasped and retained by the learner "only to the extent that more inclusive and appropriately relevant concepts are already available in cognitive structure to serve a subsuming role or to provide ideational anchorage" (Ausubel, 1967, p. 222). Thus we accumulate more and more information only to the extent that we are able to subsume it under the categories and within the cognitive framework we already possess, or through some simultaneous reorganization of this framework so that it can accommodate the new information and our existing knowledge. Moreover, these reorganizational processes may or may not follow principles which seem "logical" to the observer, because the real determinant is whether they are compatible with the organization which that learner has *personally* developed.

Ausubel outlines a number of ways for measuring these ongoing cognitive changes, and he identifies many factors which seem to facilitate effective information processing and retention. In many instances his resulting recommendations for educators are similar to those suggested by Bruner. However, there is one type of educational intervention which is unique to Ausubel's theory and which seems to be very important for the design of instruction, namely that of *advance organizers*.

He identifies attainment of a clear, stable, organized body of knowledge as both an important educational objective and a means for enhancing the learner's capacity to learn new information. "This knowledge (cognitive structure), once acquired, is *also* in its own right the most significant *independent* variable influencing the learner's capacity for acquiring more new knowledge in the same field" (Ausubel, 1968, p. 130). Thus it is important for the educator to find ways for helping the student to attain this clear, stable organization of the information which is to be learned. Ausubel contends that this can be accomplished by providing "advance organizers," which are special introductory statements which are sufficiently fundamental, abstract, and inclusive that they can subsume and serve as anchoring ideas for the information to be learned.

These advance organizers facilitate learning and retention of meaningfully learned information in three ways. First, if properly designed, they call attention to and build on those relevant anchoring ideas which the learner already has in his cognitive structure. For example, the advance organizer would refer to fundamental concepts and principles learned in previous lessons and would relate them to the material which is to be learned. Second, they provide a kind of scaffolding for the new material by encompassing the areas to be covered and by delineating the fundamental ideas under which the rest of the information can be subsumed. Thus, having first identified previously learned fundamental notions relevant to the new material, the instructor then relates them to anchoring ideas contained in the new material. Third, this kind of stable and clear organization essentially renders unnecessary having the student learn the material by rote memorization. Ausubel contends that avoidance of rote learning procedures will have a positive motivating influence on the student and will actually make the newly learned information far more useful in subsequent real-life situations.

As we noted above, Ausubel has expressed great reservations about uses of discovery learning techniques, despite his obvious commitment to the notion that cognitive processes are of central importance in designing instruction. He has frequently characterized proponents of discovery learning as creating a mystique and an emotional basis for use of these procedures, and he has questioned both the logical and empirical evidence in support of almost exclusive reliance on such methods. He suggests that there will be variations in the amount of guidance which an educator should provide for students and that some extent of structure will be desirable for most situations.

But other cognitive construct theorists have made "guided discovery" a central concern in their formulation of instructional principles. Thus it is to the work of Paul Torrance, Ralph Ojemann, and others that we turn next.

Guided Learning

We noted earlier that discovery learning procedures have frequently been depicted as implementing many of Bruner's suggestions about the design of instruction. Bruner vacillated in the extent of his endorsement of such procedures, sometimes seemingly recommending their universal use and at other times characterizing them as only one of several preferred methods. For example, in *The Process of Education* (Bruner, 1960), he called attention to the fact that various curriculum study groups had encouraged use of discovery methods in mathematics and science courses. The Arithmetic Project of the University of Illinois recommended that it may be more effective for a student to discover the generalization that lies behind a particular mathematical operation, than for the teacher to first state the generalization and simply ask the students to proceed through the proof. Moreover, he reported that the Illinois group had considered discovery procedures to be too time-consuming for all mathematics teaching, with the implications that some form of expository methods would also be needed. But Bruner then went on to make the recommendation that they "need not be limited to such highly formulized subjects as mathematics and physics" (p. 21). Moreover, in a more recent book (Bruner, 1971) written a decade after *The Process of Education*, Bruner continued to feature discovery teaching in his recommendations for designing instruction. Given these continuing comments, it is not surprising that many educators have ignored the comments about selective use and have proclaimed that discovery learning procedures should be *widely* adopted.

At issue, in simple terms, is whether one gets better educational results if one requires that the student discover at least some of what the teacher already knows about the particular learning experience. Throughout the history of formal education there always have been debates on this matter. In part, this was the basis of some controversies during the first few decades of this century between proponents of Thorndike's connectionistic proposals and the less structured recommendations of the gestalt advocates. One can trace positions back to the traditional drill-and-practice, rote learning methods which were popular before this century, and one can relate them to the laissez-faire suggestions frequently identified with the progressive education movement.

Periodically conferences have been held on the topic, at which time theoretical rationales and empirical evidence are examined and various interpretations are debated. For example, interest in discovery learning had become sufficiently great by the middle 1960s that the Social Science Research Council's committee on learning and the educational process conducted a conference on "Learning by Discovery" in 1965. Proceedings of that conference (Shulman & Keislar, 1966) highlight some of the issues and positions.

Keislar and Shulman (1966), in their retrospective analysis of that conference, depicted the controversy as involving several levels of discourse, three of which are of concern to our present discussion. First, with regard to classroom instruction, should the teacher first give a rule and then provide examples, or should a wide variety of examples be presented from which the student is expected to infer the rule? Contending that there is no single best way, Keislar and Shulman concluded that decisions should be made for specific contexts, taking into account the type of subject matter as well as the maturity and prior learning experiences of the students. Acknowledging ambiguity in defining "discovery learning," they contended that much more research is required before scientifically based answers can be provided. Second, with regard to curriculum sequences, who should decide what subject matter is to be covered next, the teacher or the student? Here again they cited ambiguities in definitions of terms and confounding of educational objectives with educational methods. They identified a curriculum as "the organization and sequence of a subject matter in which statements about that subject, methods of teaching, and the activities of the learner are intricately interrelated to form a single entity" (p. 190). They concluded that this aspect of the controversy about discovery learning could not be resolved nor even assessed "until we can obtain a broad evaluative base to assess the effectiveness of the curriculum" (p. 190).

Third, what transfer effects really result from use of the discovery learning procedures? In essence they concluded that the matter is most frequently decided on rational or emotional grounds rather than on empirical evidence. Because the concept of discovery learning is so ambiguously defined, it is not surprising that controversial results have frequently been obtained. Moreover, they pointed out that much of the "research" on discovery learning has been devoted to determining whether students have been engaged in discovery strategies rather than to evaluating the long-range effects of such involvement. They called for more explicit descriptions of what teachers and students do, rather than simply labeling certain procedures as discovery learning. There was sharp conflict between those who favored measurable specification of educational objectives and those who contended that specifying objectives leads to constricting of instruction. The former group typically had greater reservations or limitations about discovery learning procedures, whereas the latter group was more enthusiastic in their support and tended to advocate more widespread use of discovery procedures.

More recent research literature reviews (for example, Craig, 1969) and the author's perusal of the literature lead to the conclusion that the status of the controversy is very much the same now as it was at the time of the 1965 conference. However, there have been certain individuals who have long advocated that one need not make an "either-or" choice. Instead, they contend that it would be more appropriate to characterize all learning as involving some degree of "guidance," and that different degrees of guidance will be appropriate for respective instructional situations.

Torrance (1966, p. 40) has contrasted "guided learning" with a more extreme, laissez-faire conception of discovery learning. He criticized some advocates of discovery learning as overestimating the ability of the student to benefit from his experiences *without any* guidance. He cautioned that if a learner is not given any guidance or direction, "there is danger of emotional disturbance, of giving up, of failing to keep going. Man has to have some anchors in reality; he has to have some guides to behavior in order to behave effectively" (Torrance, 1966, p. 40).

Torrance cited some of the relatively recent work of Ojemann and colleagues as exemplary of attempts to design instructional methods with some form of guidance and direction. Tracing the controversy back to ancient Greece, Torrance characterized such moderate positions as typically being caught between two powerful extremes, " 'coerced' learning (i.e., learning by authority, overdirection, force, reproduction, or imitation of a compulsive type)" versus " 'unguided' or 'laissez-faire' learning with its lack of discipline, direction, and anchors or guides to behavior" (p. 6).

He attacked both extremes as untenable positions and he advocated that some moderate position is necessary for realistic design of instruction. He identified proponents of guided learning as taking such a moderate position, and he enumerated seven characteristics of instruction endorsed by those who advocate guided learning:

1   The human learner is self-acting and creative, requiring guidance and direction but not dictation and coercion.

2   It is natural and healthy for learning to be a continuous process, and it becomes such with appropriate guidance.

3   Human intelligence is not a single function but consists of a union of all of the little functions of discrimination, observation, retention, reasoning, analysis, synthesis, divergent thinking, judgment, and the like.

4   All of these abilities are susceptible to development through learning experiences, function differentially in different learning tasks and in different ways of learning the same task, and may develop at different rates and to different levels.

5   All learners require that learning tasks have some degree of structure, but the degree of structure varies greatly among the individual learners.

6   Learning is accomplished most effectively when learning tasks are arranged in some sequence appropriate to the stage of development of the learner, his strategies or skills in learning, and the like.

7   Guidance of learning may be accomplished through a variety of both verbal and non-verbal means, other than through the structure and sequence of the tasks to be learned. (Torrance, 1966, pp. 8-9)

TYPICAL CHARACTERISTICS OF COGNITIVE CONSTRUCT APPROACHES TO INSTRUCTION

As you can see from the foregoing comments, there is considerable variation in opinion as to how one can use cognitive learning research and theory in the formulation of instructional principles. But some characteristic emphases can be discerned. First, they are almost unanimous in disclaiming that one can derive implications from the more behaviorally oriented learning theories. Second, they propose instead that the student should be conceptualized as a processor of information who actively selects and interprets certain stimuli from all those which impinge on him in the learning situation. Third, the major task of the instructor is to provide whatever guidance seems necessary to help him to organize new information in a meaningful way. Opinions vary as to how much the student should be expected to "discover" things for himself and how much guidance should be provided by the teacher or through the materials. But there is a distinct preference for featuring situations which stimulate inquiry search patterns, and for avoiding those situations which make the student a passive recipient of facts to be memorized by rote practice. Fourth, it is expected that guides will be given as to how he might structure the information either through advance organizers or through other features provided by the teacher or the educational materials. Fifth, in designing their instructional procedures, cognitive theorists draw as extensively from psychology's developmental theory as they do from learning theory, though the emphasis is more on age-group patterns than on individual differences. However, they seem to be as aware as any other instructional theorists about the need for considering individual differences in planning instruction.

Sixth, they seem to divide their concerns for improving educational practice equally between curriculum reforms and instructional method innovations, so that it is sometimes difficult to determine which is of greater concern in a given instructional principle. They emphasize that the structure must be meaningful for the learner, no matter whether it is meaningful for professional educators; it is also held that more active, exploratory, discovery learning procedures will assist the student in organizing new information and integrating it with his existing knowledge. Seventh, in the instructional materials or in the directions provided by the teacher, there should be some means whereby the *student* can develop skills in evaluating *his own progress*. It is recognized that this is easier to do in courses such as mathematics where right and wrong solutions can be identified, and that it is quite difficult where one is attempting to encourage divergent thinking.

DISCOVERY LEARNING AND OTHER EDUCATIONAL APPLICATIONS

Principles like those enumerated in this chapter have been utilized from preschool programs through elementary and high school courses, as well as in undergraduate and graduate programs. Although some of the programs were planned in the early 1960s by special study groups focusing on mathematics and sciences (including biology, physics, and chemistry), perusal of the educational and psychological literature will reveal similar applications in more recent years in practically every subject matter area imaginable. Obviously, there have been wide differences among these applications. However, brief descriptions of one program, in whose development Bruner was an active participant, will illustrate some of the main features.

An Example—Man: A Course of Study

"Man: A Course of Study" is an upper elementary (fifth grade) social science course. It was developed mainly from 1963 to 1965 with many instructional procedures based on Bruner's ideas. In addition to Bruner's personal involvement, it represents the combined efforts of anthropologists, psychologists, zoologists, theoretical engineers, teachers, children (representative of those who would later take the course), artists, designers, camera crews, and other scholars and technicians, supported by grants from the National Science Foundation and the Ford Foundation, in conjunction with the Education Development Center.

The basic intent was to produce a course about man as a species wherein man is seen as constantly coping with changing demands of his environment, using his cultural and physical heritage both to survive and to maintain his uniquely human qualities. Three questions recur throughout each topic covered: "What is human about human beings? How did they get that way? How can they be made more so?" (Bruner, 1971, p. 57). The intent not only was to provide students with substantive learning but also, more importantly, to stimulate them to consider the characteristics of man as a species, to see the influences of different cultures, and to recognize the potential for man's further physical and psychological evolution. Five major topics covered are tool making, language, social organization, management of man's prolonged childhood, and man's urge to explain.

Bruner (1971) has identified five goals which they hoped to achieve with this course:

1   To give our pupils respect for and confidence in the powers of their own minds.

2   To give them respect, moreover, for the powers of thought concerning the human condition, man's plight, and his social life.

3   To provide them with a set of workable models that make it simpler to analyze the nature of the social world in which they live and the condition in which man finds himself.

4   To impart a sense of respect for the capacities and plight of man as a species, for his origins, for his potential, for his humanity.

5   To leave the student with a sense of the unfinished business of man's evolution. (p. 58)

There are several aspects of this course which reflect Bruner's views about instruction. Although there are aspects which involve expository teaching, wherever possible provisions have been made to encourage students to think about the information being provided; to formulate their own ideas; and to try to discover what patterns, concepts, and principles bring order to the various kinds of information presented. To stimulate making of comparisons and to help students to recognize patterns, extensive use is made of sharp contrasts between different ideas presented.

For example, our own technologically oriented society is contrasted with the more primitive hunting society of the Netsilik Eskimos of Pelly Bay. Rather than merely *telling* the students how these particular cultures are similar and different, this course involves presenting films, stories, pictures, descriptions of artifacts, and myths from the two cultures and encourages the learners to talk about them. In the course of these conversations, which may or may not be "guided" by the teacher, the students begin to form their own opinions and their own ways of organizing information about the two cultures. At this point it is possible for the teacher to provide some guidance as to different features which one might note and different ways of characterizing the societies in particular and the nature of man more generally.

Similar contrasts are made between man and child, human social patterns and those of baboons and other primates, and different cultural groups within our own society. Throughout the course dramatic and emotionally charged materials are used to involve the students in their examination and to foster their formation of subjective feelings and opinions about the content. In this context Bruner attempts to make the learning experiences very personally relevant. It is only after this that he typically tries to delineate more objective descriptions of the concepts and principles involved. Wherever possible, students are encouraged to think creatively and divergently so that they can experience different ways for viewing the topics. Although it is recognized that there are some "right" and "wrong" ways for some aspects of the topic, much weight is also given to the many real-life experiences in which judgments are made on relative rather than absolute bases.

In summary, Bruner tries to maintain two key features of his views about instruction in the way that Man: A Course of Study has been developed. He places a high premium on the role of *discovery* learning, and he emphasizes the central role that *structure* of knowledge should play in the design of instruction.

Perusal of the course materials and the various papers written about development of them suggests that Bruner and the other developers were more concerned with implementing the discovery and structure features than they were in evaluating their educational contributions. This is not necessarily a negative comment, since a certain degree of enthusiasm is probably essential for implementation of any innovative ideas. But it does raise some questions for potential educator-adopters who may have reservations about the large-scale implementation of these ideas. For those who are already convinced of such merits, this seems a good example of the implementation of Bruner's ideas.

CRITIQUE: CURRENT STATUS
AND FUTURE PROSPECTS

As you recall, one of Bruner's books was entitled *Toward a Theory of Instruction*. In many ways it appears that the title is still an apt one for the approach to instruction being developed within the cognitive construct tradition. Many principles or guidelines can be identified. Certainly, the orientation taken is in many ways quite a contrast with the approach taken by the behavior modification groups, though there are many overlapping emphases. Perhaps one can best say that, as with the behavior modification approach, there is an identifiable position but no complete instructional theory in terms of the ASCD criteria.

Guidelines are indicated but very few formal principles can be identified. As for Bruner's position, he mainly seems to be restating some of his earlier "notes for" a theory of instruction rather than presenting formalized terms and postulates. In contrast with the behavior modification approach, there are many terms (such as discovery learning, personalized structure of knowledge) which do not lend themselves readily to operational definition. But the ideas and many of the terms are much more readily accepted by educators than are some of the more behaviorally described behavior modification terms.

Proponents of the cognitive construct approach apparently see no bounds for the applicability of their ideas. With only minor adjustments here and there they expect that all subject matter and all students can benefit from their approach. Some (for example, Ausubel) have suggested that certain aspects (discovery learning) might be more appropriate for some age groups than for others (such as young children), but such delimiting statements are the exception rather than the rule.

At least at this stage there seems to be a satisfactory degree of internal consistency, but this could stem from the fact that the principles and their corollaries have not been fully drawn. Some have raised questions about Bruner's assertions that any subject can be taught to any person in an intellectually honest form, since at other times he contends that Piaget's developmental theory indicates that one's abilities are age-related. The criticism has been most frequently raised with regard to certain concepts and principles which are quite abstract and which do not permit concrete illustrations. But proponents of Bruner's position answer that the instructor simply must find a way of presenting the information in a form which the student is ready for and capable of mastering. At present it appears that we must characterize such debates as a standoff; perhaps with more explicit descriptions and more empirical evidence we may be able to determine whether inconsistencies actually exist.

As for compatibility with empirical data, the cognitive construct notions typically are related, at least by analogy, to one or more empirical cognitive learning studies. But proponents typically are so enthusiastic that there is insufficient effort to assess their worth as instructional principles. When studies are conducted, results are frequently equivocal, with proponents typically finding empirical support and critics somehow getting contradictory evidence. Whereas the behavior modifiers seem to have an edge in empirical support for learning changes *as operationally defined*, the cognitive theorists' conceptions of instruction and of educational objectives less frequently are criticized by educators.

As for the other ASCD criteria, the cognitive construct approach seems quite capable of generating hypotheses which can be submitted to empirical test and of producing instructional principles which can predict students' performance and learning under stated instructional conditions.

Judging from activities in recent years, it is likely that the use of cognitive learning theory will continue to be favorably regarded as a basis for formulating instructional principles. The major influence on instructional theory more generally will probably lie in characterizing the learner as an active processor of information and in emphasizing that learners should be able to formulate problems and search for alternative solutions, rather than in merely looking for some externally designated "correct" answer.

SUGGESTING READINGS

Ausubel, D. P. A cognitive-structure theory of school learning. In L. Siegel (Ed.), *Instruction: Some contemporary viewpoints*. San Francisco: Chandler, 1967. Pp. 207-257.

Ausubel, D. P., & Robinson, F. G. *School learning: An introduction to educational psychology*. New York: Holt, Rinehart, & Winston, 1969.

Bruner, J. S. *On knowing: Essays for the left hand*. Cambridge: The Belknap Press, 1964.

Bruner, J. S. *Toward a theory of instruction*. Cambridge: The Belknap Press, 1966a.

Bruner, J. S. (Ed.) Learning about learning: A conference report. *Cooperative Research Monograph*, 1966b, No. 15.

Bruner, J. S. Culture, politics and pedagogy. *Saturday Review*, May 1968, 69-72, 89-98.

Bruner, J. S. The process of education revisited. *Phi Delta Kappan*, 1971, 18-21.

Craig, R. C. Recent research on discovery. *Educational Leadership*, 1969, **26**, 501-505.

Dow, P. B., et al. *Man: A course of study*. Cambridge: Educational Development Center, Inc., 1968.

Hermann, G. Learning by discovery: A critical review of studies. *The Journal of Experimental Ecuation*, 1969, 38, 58-72.

Hunt, J. M. Toward a theory of guided learning in development. In R. R. Ojemann & K. Pritchett (Eds.), *Giving emphasis to guided learning*. Cleveland: Educational Research Council, 1966.

Ojemann, R. H., & Pritchett, K. (Eds.) *Giving emphasis to guided learning*. Cleveland: Education Research Council of Greater Cleveland, 1966.

Rowland, G. T., & McGuire, J. C. *The mind of man: Some views and a theory of cognitive development*. New York: Prentice-Hall, 1971.

15
Principles of Learning Instructional Theories

As has already been stated, practitioners cannot afford the luxury of relying exclusively on one learning theory if other theories can provide useful guidelines for planning instruction. In a similar vein, many books and papers reviewing learning research have been concluded with a distillation of principles which seem to be supported by empirical evidence. Typically, the educator is encouraged to consider the resulting principles for potential practical implications.

In this chapter we will consider one psychologist's efforts to go a step further—the formulation of an instructional theory based on such a collection of empirically supported learning principles. Bugelski's theory has been selected because it illustrates some of the prospects and problems in using eclectic learning principles to formulate instructional theories.

Our critique at the end of this chapter will not only evaluate Bugelski's theory but will consider its implications for other psychologists and educators who may follow Bugelski's lead and use their own collection of learning principles as a basis for formulating an instructional theory.

RATIONALE FOR USE OF AN ECLECTIC COLLECTION OF LEARNING PRINCIPLES

Throughout this book the notion has been expressed that learning theories should *somehow* lead to suggestions about the design of instruction. In previous chapters we have identified one instructional position (behavior modification) which was largely guided by Skinner's operant learning principles. Another (cognitive construct) instructional theory drew primarily from those learning theories which have conceptualized man as a processor of information and which have focused on thinking, problem solving, and other cognitive processes. But many psychologists and educators have expressed reservations about relying on only one (or a few) learning theory(ies) as a basis for formulating instructional principles.

On the one hand, they have noted many problems in using only one theory. How does one decide *which* theory should be chosen? Our review of learning research and theory does not provide a basis for identifying any one approach as clearly *the best* on either logical or empirical grounds. All learning theories have tended to focus on certain processes to the exclusion of others, a fact quite readily acknowledged by even the most enthusiastic advocates of each position. Many have doubted that such an admittedly incomplete learning theory could singly serve as a basis for formulating instructional principles. Others have pointed to the continuing controversies among learning theorists as to the best ways for studying learning and the most appropriate means for conceptualizing learning processes. Since the debates remain unresolved, many psychologists and educators have questioned whether it is reasonable to choose one position and to exclude all others. Finally, we noted in earlier chapters that many researchers in recent years have avoided involvement with any particular theory. Should their findings be ignored by educators? It simply has not seemed appropriate to some educators and psychologists that they should try to derive instructional procedures from any one particular learning theory.

On the other hand, many of these same psychologists and educators feel that it would be equally unwise totally to disregard learning research and theories. They look askance at educators who take a purely pragmatic approach to instruction and ignore underlying psychological principles. Somehow a compromise must be found.

This kind of reasoning has led some psychologists and educators to try to delineate a collection of learning principles which seem to have reasonable empirical support and which might be relevant to training and educational situations. Authors disagree somewhat as to what constitutes "reasonable empirical support." Some interpret this as meaning that practically all learning theorists must agree, or at least *not dis*agree, about the respective principles. Others point out that many principles which could be useful in education are studied by comparatively few investigators; thus they interpret "reasonable support" to be empirical evidence obtained by well-designed studies on problems which are especially relevant to the educational process. In either case, the collection is proffered to educators and other practitioners for their consideration when they plan their students' learning experiences.

The idea of identifying a collection of empirically supported learning principles has been around for at least a few decades. Many research and theory reviews have been concluded with a set of descriptive statements summarizing "what we now know about learning." They have been included in various psychology and educational psychology textbooks, and they have even been included in a book which attempted to identify general findings from behavioral sciences (Berelson, 1963). Professor B. R. Bugelski (1971) has proposed that these same collections of learning principles could serve as a sound basis for formulating theories of instruction and he has presented his own tentative instructional theory. Given the popularity of such collections of learning principles in the past, it is quite likely that others will follow Bugelski's lead. Because of their origins and eclectic character, we will refer to instructional theories evolved this way as *principles of learning instructional theories.*

BUGELSKI'S PRINCIPLES OF LEARNING INSTRUCTIONAL THEORY

Bergen Richard Bugelski is a distinguished general experimental psychologist who has conducted research on various psychological processes, including learning and cognition. After receiving his Ph.D. from Yale University in 1938, he initially worked as an academic experimental psychologist. He became closely involved in resolution of practical problems during World War II when he and other experimental psychologists were asked to use their skills in resolving training and man-machine problems in the military. He also has had extensive experience in using experimental procedures in working with practical problems in industry, including those concerning safety, work, and fatigue.

As a result of these engineering-psychology (or human-engineering) experiences, he adopts a somewhat different approach than is characteristic of most learning researchers. He is interested in basic learning research especially because of its potential relevance for solving specific practical problems. He is also somewhat different from most educational psychologists in his emphasis on the outcomes of instruction and in his attempts to find ways of improving instruction. In this regard, many of his ideas are quite compatible with the contemporary research and development movement in education. In brief, he holds that underlying psychological principles may serve as guides to identifying "a better way" for planning instruction.

It is a little difficult to trace the evolution of Bugelski's instructional theory because he currently identifies four main principles out of an earlier (Bugelski, 1964), much larger collection of suggestions and conclusions. However, the process seems to have gone something like this. The main guiding notion was that instructional principles should be based on identifiable learning research rather than on some educator's anecdotal descriptions of procedures which "seemed to work." On this basis he reviewed the learning literature and identified those findings which seemed to be relevant to training and education. From these findings he organized answers to three major questions (on characteristics of a good teacher, use of examinations, and size of classes), and he enumerated several (fifty-eight in 1964; fifty-nine in 1971) documented suggestions for teachers. He acknowledged that some might consider them to be "educated guesses" (Bugelski, 1964, p. 253), but he contended that his notions were consistent with available empirical evidence. He then tried to generate a few general integrating principles from this larger collection. Thus he presented his "Preamble to a Theory of Instruction" along with four major principles and three corollaries. He again presented his comments about the three aspects of teaching (the teacher, examinations, and class size) and his collection of documented suggestions to the teacher.

He made several interesting comments about his theory. He identified the theory as a tentative formulation, subject to revision in light of new evidence. He acknowledged a somewhat tenuous relationship between his more specific suggestions and his general principles, but he explained that such problems result when one attempts to use a few general integrated principles to summarize a large assortment of data or observations. He characterized his theory as incomplete because it has only four principles. However, he expressed a preference for identifying only these four principles until additional data justifies providing more. Moreover, he suggested that educators may have their hands full just trying to apply the first two of his principles.

Thus Bugelski seems to be advocating an inductive approach to instructional theory construction. Parsimony and well-documented principles are favored over more encompassing but loosely supported assertions. Unless otherwise indicated, the following comments about his theory are based on his 1971 presentation. (Adapted from *The Psychology of Learning Applied to Teaching* by B. R. Bugelski, copyright © 1964, 1971, by The Bobbs-Merrill Company, Inc., used by permission of the publisher.)

Preamble

Bugelski depicts learning as a *"continuous process*, inseparable from living, so long as the organism is responsive to stimulation"* (p. 279). He conceptualizes learning as "the formation of associations between neural events (consequence of stimulation)" (p. 280), without reference to response aspects. He identifies his model as a general derivative of Pavlovian conditioning; others may link it more closely with Guthrie's theory and with information processing conceptions, although he draws principles from all learning research. He designates the function of the teacher as arranging the conditions under which school learning can take place, recognizing that students may differ in their responsiveness to such conditions. Apparently the intended function of his principles and corollaries is to give the teacher guidance as to what conditions should be provided to facilitate school learning.

Principle I Attention

In order for learning to occur, at a minimum the learner must be paying attention to pertinent stimuli. This attentiveness may involve observable actions, such as looking toward the teacher or listening to what is being said; or, it may consist of activities which are not readily discernible to the observer, such as the learner thinking about what is to be learned.

Corollary 1 Anything Arousing Attention Is Learned "An organism will learn anything that arouses attention whether it wants to or not" (p. 281). If the organism is attending to something, at least some minimal amount of learning will occur. Thus the teacher should capitalize on those stimuli which most naturally get and hold the attention of the students.

Principle II All Learning Takes Time

The essence of this principle is that learning a given thing takes a certain amount of time and that there probably are optimal ranges of time beyond which (either too short or too long) the student will decrease in efficiency. If it takes an hour to learn something, it may be possible to schedule two half-hour sessions *unless* the half-hour sessions are not long enough for a meaningful portion of that learning to occur. Students differ in the amounts of time they need to learn particular things.

Corollary 1 Limit on How Much One Can Learn If the instructor attempts to teach too much within a time period, the student may actually learn less than if the lesser, optimal amount had been presented.

Corollary 2 Limit on How Many Things Can Be Learned Some people learn one thing, others learn something else; but there are limitations on the number of things that we can learn at one time. What we have learned at the end of a given time period reflects both how much time we need per task and which of many possible tasks we actually learned.

Principle III The Internal Regulator or Model

There seem to be internal "thermostat-like" devices or mechanisms which serve to maintain behavior when certain signals are received and to terminate the activity when other signals are sensed. These regulators may be physiological in origin or they may reflect internalization of psychological models, probably learned when one is still quite young. Bugelski uses this principle as a more fundamental explanation of the common ways in which eliciting stimuli, rewards, punishments, knowledge of results, and other types of cognitive feedback all seem to regulate behavior, particularly at more advanced stages of learning. It is suggested that these models probably develop during childhood and that they play increasingly important roles in learning and behavior as the learner grows older. Moreover, it is possible that different maintaining and terminating events may be of influence at different stages or under different conditions but that the basic underlying mechanism and process remains the same.

Principle IV Knowledge of Results as a Response Control

To this author, this principle seems to overlap with principle III. Students need to know what is expected of them and to understand the nature of the experiences to be learned. Consistent with principle III, Bugelski suggests in principle IV that various auditory, visual, tactile, etc., stimuli enable the learner to activate the appropriate model of activities for a given situation. Having the wrong model (a misconception of the activities appropriate there, including shifts, starts, and stops in activities) will either impair or bar learning progress. "The teacher should make every effort to insure the development of proper models by directing attention to significant features of any new experience" (p. 285). The teacher should even go so far as to anticipate any problems which students might encounter in calling up appropriate models and to take preventive steps through prerequisite learning or instructions.

Some Basic Questions about Instruction

Following his principles and corollaries, Bugelski commented on three aspects which he considers to be very important in teaching—the role of the teacher, the function of examinations, and the issue concerning optimal class sizes. Acknowledging that some of his suggestions may be idealistic, he implied that they were related to his instructional theory and, thus, that they were formulated on the basis of available empirical evidence.

Beyond competence in subject matter—an absolute prerequisite—Bugelski characterizes "good teachers" as those who "like to teach," "love their subject," and are sufficiently aware of students' needs that they can anticipate and resolve students' problems even before they develop. Moreover, good teachers can instill in their students enthusiasm about learning and about the particular subject matter. Endorsing Carl Rogers's conceptions of teaching (which we discuss in detail in a later chapter), Bugelski characterized the teacher as primarily serving in the role of a facilitator of learning rather than a taskmaster. He also related his notions to Skinner's emphasis on frequent positive reinforcement and his contention that teachers should avoid using punishment and other aversive measures.

Bugelski strongly recommends that students "be informed of the specific (detailed) objectives of every course of instruction" (p. 290) and that students be advised in advance about examinations, including the dates, coverage, and nature of scorable correct answers. Where essay-type examinations or term papers are involved, steps should be taken to insure independent, objective evaluations of them. But if at all possible, he recommends that pass-fail systems be instituted wherein students would continue working until they had met the objectives of the course.

He acknowledges that no available empirical evidence can resolve the issues about appropriate class sizes. In lieu of hard data, he suggests that logical bases be used for such decisions. In brief, although there are instances in which large audiences can benefit from special presentations, he prefers that classes be small enough so that interactions among students and with the teacher can be consistent with attainment of objectives for that class. In typical courses, he recommended "that a class must be small enough for the instructor to be able to react to each individual member as often as necessary to meet the goals in the time allotted" (p. 293).

Suggestions for Teachers

Bugelski provided a collection of fifty-nine specific suggestions to teachers which he contends are supported by empirical evidence. Some of them were already incorporated in the presentation of his instructional theory and/or in his answers to the above three basic questions about instruction. His sub-headings reveal the range of his recommendations—goals, standards, and criteria; role of the teacher; individual differences; motivation; analysis of the learning situation; reinforcement and extinction; control of the learning process; retention and transfer; insight and understanding; teaching and learning (pp. 294-299).

As noted above, these suggestions were generated as a result of his perusal of learning research and theory. The suggestions, as the titles indicate, cut across usual theoretical lines and, in some instances, could conceivably lead to incompatible prescriptions for a given practical situation. But Bugelski either doesn't expect this to happen or apparently hasn't made provisions to handle such events since he does not inform the reader as to what one should do if that does happen. Even in those many cases where several suggestions might be complementary but some priorities may need to be established, he does not provide guidelines as to which principles should receive primary consideration. Perhaps he assumes that his four instructional principles and their corollaries, along with the three basic recommendations, will provide the reader with sufficient guidelines. But, more likely, Bugelski simply may expect the educator to use these suggestions while evaluating his present educational practice so as to find a better way for instructing his students.

A few examples of his suggestions and his derivation of them will illustrate the relationships which he envisions between learning research and educational practice. Suggestion number 9 is: "Attention is a learned response. Students must be reinforced for attentive behavior" (p. 295). In a previous chapter Bugelski had reviewed some of the psychological theory and research on attention; the suggestion was followed by a reference to this earlier discussion.

Many of his comments had pointed out the great impact in getting students' attention which seems to come from the stimulus, per se, following along the lines of Pavlov's classical conditioning paradigm; an example would be Pavlov's work which showed that the orienting response can be triggered by a stimulus presented loudly or suddenly. Within this particular context, some theorists would hold that the individual is learning to attend to *certain* stimuli but that the process of orientation/attention is not being learned. Thus teachers may use bright colors, unusual sounds, and other stimuli to get the attention of students. Other theorists would argue that there are two or more levels of attentiveness and that certain factors may control attentiveness under some circumstances and other factors may be of greater influence under others. Finally, some (for example, operant researchers and behavior modifiers) would simply advocate use of reinforcement principles to build up and to maintain "attending behaviors," such as "looking at the teachers" or "looking at his book." Bugelski selected some of these theoretical issues for presentation to his reader, and then he derived a few practical suggestions from that discussion. It is quite likely that some researchers on attention would fault Bugelski for having ignored their point of view or for having placed insufficient emphasis on certain aspects of the attending process in his suggestions to teachers.

Another point of interest is that Bugelski's main, and sometimes only, justification for his suggestions is that the basic notion has been derived from relevant learning research. He does not cite evidence indicating that these suggestions "work" in practical educational situations. However, his general comments suggest that he expects the reader to take his suggestions as tentative ideas which should be evaluated when implemented by the reader. Thus he seems to look to his readers to obtain their own empirical evaluation of the respective suggestions.

Some principles may tend to cause confusion or may conflict with other suggestions. For example, suggestion number 24 is: "Any rewards, to be effective, must be immediate. The reward value might really be motivational or 'arousing' in its operation" (p. 296). Under suggestion number 49, he states: "To secure persistent behavior, develop partial reinforcement schedules" (p. 298). His referenced discussion for this latter suggestion contained the additional information that Skinner's reinforcement schedule laboratory research has indicated that it is effective to use immediate positive reinforcement of every correct response during initial acquisition but that partial reinforcement (some intermittent schedule) is more effective in maintaining such behaviors.

There are several problems with these suggestions. First, there has been some question as to the ways that the "immediacy" admonition would apply to partial or intermittent reinforcement. There has been considerable controversy in recent years as to whether these laboratory-based principles involving reinforcement of single responses are actually directly applicable to the more complex real-world situations. Actually, there is even some debate as to what constitutes "immediate" versus "continuous" or "regular" reinforcement in the laboratory situations. In addition, the reader receives no guidelines as to when one should follow suggestion number 24 and provide immediate and (presumably) 100 percent reinforcement for correct responses and when to provide the partial reinforcement arrangements called for in suggestion number 49.

Such problems are general ones rather than merely related to these two suggestions. These issues are raised to illustrate some of the problems that *anyone* encounters in trying to derive practical implications from laboratory learning research. It is quite possible that such suggestions may prove to be effective when applied in the practical situation, but that is not guaranteed from the fact that the original idea was derived from laboratory research.

We make these rather critical comments so that the reader can appreciate the problems which Bugelski and others face in trying to formulate practical suggestions and so that the suggestions will be recognized as tentative recommendations until they have been evaluated empirically in practical situations. Bugelski is apparently quite aware of these problems, but he introduced his discussion of practical implications by acknowledging that teacher-readers expect such pronouncements and that he feels an obligation to meet their requests. As we have already noted above, it is in this vein that many other authors and speakers have given their views about instruction on the basis of their knowledge and interpretations of current learning research and theory.

A curious thing typically happens when such suggestions are offered. The speaker or author usually qualifies his comments. For example, Bugelski concluded this particular chapter with a word of caution: "My suggestions, are meant to be tentative, subject to revision, omission, and addition" (p. 299). But educators frequently ignore such precautionary statements and uncritically adopt respective suggestions because they were mentioned by the speaker or author. Thus readers typically forget the *tentative* sense in which they were presented.

Practical Applications

Bugelski's recommendations for instruction are reasonably clearly outlined and his rationale and empirical basis for each suggestion and principle are rather explicitly identified. But what happens when one tries to apply the principles? How might one proceed to use his theory? The approach that he seems to recommend is quite compatible with the contemporary R&D movement in education discussed in previous chapters. However, the general engineering psychology approach he uses is more readily discernible than is the actual application of his instructional principles.

Bugelski uses a hypothetical example of reading instruction as a means for showing how to use the instructional principles he is advocating. He suggests that the application to this particular subject matter is illustrative of what one would do with other educational topics. One of the most fundamental notions is that one should recognize that the course was taught before—long before psychology existed as a discipline—and that some of the long-established practices may actually be quite good. Start with some existing set of instructional procedures and systematically try to improve on results obtained by those procedures.

These systematic attempts to improve instruction involve four major steps: identify the desired educational objectives and prepare to determine how well they are being attained by current teaching procedures; establish criteria for measuring the goals and for determining what effort and costs (time, materials, etc.) are required by different instructional methods;

conduct a careful analysis of the different tasks required by students who attain the end objectives and of the various tasks which they must go through in order to reach those educational goals; and identify the different environmental stimuli and other conditions in the educational situation which seem to influence students' learning (either helping or hindering).

In his reading instruction example, Bugelski reviewed the history of different educational methods which have been used and he identified some of the contemporary issues about reading instruction. Then he chose one of the approaches (advocated by Edmund Burke Huey in 1908) and began analyzing how he might improve on it. He characterized reading as involving two major components, identification and comprehension, but he emphasized that each can be broken down into several additional steps. Moreover, he contended that there are many different purposes for reading (detail, main idea, directions, etc.), each of which may involve different instructional programs.

He outlined several different goals which one might have for teaching reading in one or more of its many forms, and he selected one (to make sense out of written communications) for further consideration. Once having selected an educational objective, he advocated that the educator actually start with the end objective and work backwards. Thus one would start with the objective of teaching students how to understand the meaning in written messages and ask "ourselves what step is needed just prior to the goal, the step before that, then the next preceding step, and so on backward to the first" (p. 313).

Bugelski made a number of interesting comments about the fact that certain variables might influence one's learning to read for some purposes but not for others. For example, he pointed out that we actually do not read every individual letter when we derive meaning from written materials—actually there is a considerable amount of redundancy or repetitiveness of letters and combinations which do not give us *additional* meaning. Thus, though precise perception would be important in some phases of reading instruction, it would not necessarily be critically important in extracting meaning from written materials. Thus those variables which are found to be greatly influential in determining precision in perception may actually be of little importance in the present situation.

He referred to a discussion which he had presented earlier concerning some of the major factors of influence on teaching for understanding. In essence, he suggested that the collections of visual stimuli which we call alphabetical letters and words tend to elicit different meaningful emotional, sensory, and cognitive responses. When we see a word or hear it, these various associated images and experiences occur. "The argument thus far is that reading for sense is a matter of arousing feelings and images" (p. 318). It is beyond the scope of the present discussion to present more details of Bugelski's analysis of the reading-for-meaning process and its implications. However, it is appropriate to say that, once having conceptualized the process in this manner, he seemed to be using his instructional theory, principles, and suggestions in trying to improve upon the teaching of this particular topic. Acknowledging that empirical data are needed to assess the validity of his instructional assertions, he implied that this constituted an example of ways by which one might try to apply his notions about instruction to other educational topics.

CRITIQUE: CURRENT STATUS AND FUTURE PROSPECTS FOR PRINCIPLES OF LEARNING INSTRUCTIONAL THEORIES

As indicated earlier, Bugelski's theory is representative of the kinds of theories which may be developed from a collection of principles drawn from various learning theories and research. Given the predisposition of psychologists to prepare such lists of statements on "what we now know about learning processes," what prospects and problems can one anticipate if one attempts to develop instructional principles and theory in this somewhat modified inductive manner?

Answers to this question may be indicated by some general observations about his approach and by an evaluation of Bugelski's theory in terms of the ASCD criteria. But such an evaluation will vary, depending upon how much of his notions about instruction are included. We will base our comments on the contents which we have been discussing on these previous pages, including his ideas about teacher roles, examinations, class size, and his more specific suggestions to teachers.

Bugelski provides more specific details about the premises and characteristics of his instructional theory than was true of the two theories considered in previous chapters. Moreover, he makes a concerted successful effort to identify the empirical bases and learning theories from which he has derived his instructional principles. However, on the basis of the available information, thus far he has not systematically collected sufficient empirical evidence to determine the feasibility and validity of his recommendations in actual educational situations. Nonetheless the theory, even in its present form, would lend itself readily to such tests.

In terms of ASCD criterion I, Bugelski provides four major principles and a large collection of related propositions. At least implicitly, he seems to expect that his theory will be comprehensive and will not be limited to particular age groups nor to specific subject matter areas. However, the general strategy which he recommends for using the theory would require very explicit statements of this kind for the particular educational situation in which it is to be used.

One of the major concerns expressed by Bugelski is that all relevant variables and methods should be indicated in readily measurable form. As we have already noted, Bugelski apparently anticipated that his theory would be applicable to widely ranging situations and clienteles. Thus like many other theorists and contrary to views of the ASCD Commission, he does not choose to make the kinds of delimiting statements called for in criterion II.

Criterion III calls for internal consistency. This poses a curious problem. If one merely considers Bugelski's Preamble and his four principles and three corollaries, it would be appropriate to answer in the affirmative. But if one includes his widely ranging fifty-nine suggestions (as this author contends must be done), then there are many aspects of actual or potential conflict. However, it is very likely that the explicit general character of the theory will lend itself to resolution of such conflicts when tryouts in educational situations provide empirical evidence for subsequent modifications of the theory.

Criterion IV, involving congruency with empirical data, poses a number of problems. Some probably will fault Bugelski for his reading and interpretation of learning research literature and his subsequent delineation of his theory. This occurs whenever *anyone* draws conclusions and interpretations from such a large body of research and theory literature. However, he has quite conscientiously and successfully articulated the rationale and empirical bases for his recommendations. But with regard to empirical tests of their validity as *instructional* principles per se, there seems to be little or no evidence available at the time this review is being written. One should add, however, that no negative empirical findings exist either. Fortunately, or unfortunately, such seems to be all too common with most extant instructional theories. Given the systematically described relationships between the instructional principles and underlying learning principles, it *seems* likely that many of the recommendations would be supported by empirical evidence.

Bugelski's theory also seems quite good in terms of the other criteria, in that it lends itself readily to delineation of operational statements which can make predictions about students' probable learning progress and thus can be submitted to systematic empirical test and verification. In addition, Bugelski provides comparatively explicit instructions for implementation of his recommendations and for evaluation of them.

His particular theory will probably be of influence on instructional theory in two general ways. First, it may encourage others to draw from different aspects of contemporary research in formulating their instructional principles. Bugelski does tend to have some bias toward more behaviorally oriented research findings but he also seems open to at least some of the more cognitively oriented notions, and he enthusiastically endorses at least certain aspects of Rogers's humanistic psychology-oriented proposals. Second, his explicit suggestions about implementation of his theory may prompt other theorists to provide similar guidelines appropriate to their own approach.

A number of observations can be made about the potential for deriving instructional principles in this manner. First, at a minimum, Bugelski's theory does seem to constitute a viable approach. One may not agree entirely with his views or even may disagree strongly; nonetheless, it would appear that one can get at least the rudiments for an instructional theory from an eclectic collection of learning principles. Second, judging from the mixed character of his fifty-nine suggestions, it would appear that one may encounter considerable difficulties in trying to envision how these many different recommendations can fit together. Although Bugelski personally seems to handle the problem of synthesizing this information in his comments about reading instruction, very few (if any) guidelines are provided to a novice educator-reader about integrating and determining priorities among these different ideas. It seems likely that this reflects a basic problem in this approach to theory construction rather than that it reveals any special problems in Bugelski's theory.

If one chooses to evolve an instructional theory from such an eclectic collection, it would seem very important to give the reader guidelines as to priority ratings for the respective principles and suggestions. One should also provide guidelines as to how to resolve conflicts which develop when separate principles indicate different practical implications. Finally, it would appear that individual preferences even influence a theory drawn from diverse empirical sources. Perusal of Bugelski's main principles and specific suggestions reveals numerous instances of personal biases both in the selection of theoretical data and in the interpretations of the data. It seems quite evident that even though one tries to adopt ideas from different theories one still may develop an instructional theory which is different from that developed by another person reviewing the same sources. This is *not* meant to indicate that there is anything wrong with Bugelski's or any other person's distillation of principles. We merely point to the fact that one cannot be completely neutral but must exercise judgment and express preferences even in drawing from different sources of ideas.

SUGGESTED READINGS

Anderson, G. L. What the psychology of learning has to contribute to the education of the teacher. *Journal of Educational Psychology,* 1950, **41**, 362-365.

Atkin, J. M. Basing curriculum change on research and demonstration. *The Educational Forum,* 1966, **31**, 27-33.

Bayles, E. E. Theories of learning and classroom methods. *Theory Into Practice,* 1966, **5**, 71-76.

Berelson, B. *Behavioral Sciences Today.* New York: Basic Books, Inc., 1963.

Blair, G. M. How learning theory is related to curriculum organization. *Journal of Educational Psychology,* 1948, **39**, 161–166.

Breger, L., & McGaugh, L. L. A critique and reformulation of "learning theory" approaches. *Psychological Bulletin,* 1965, **63**, 338–358.

Brownell, W. A. Learning theory and educational practice. *Journal of Educational Research,* 1948, **41**, 481–497.

Bugelski, B. R. *The psychology of learning applied to teaching.* New York: Bobbs-Merrill (1st ed.) 1964, (2d ed.) 1971.

Carroll, J. B. Basic and applied research in education: Definitions, distinctions and implications. *Harvard Educational Review,* 1968, **38**, 263–276.

Chapanis, A. The relevance of laboratory studies to practical situations. *Ergonomics,* 1967, **10**, 557–577.

Crane, D. *Invisible colleges: Diffusion of knowledge in scientific communities.* Chicago: University of Chicago Press, 1972.

Gagne, R. M., & Gephart, W. J. (Eds.) *Learning research and school subjects.* Itasca, Ill.: Peacock, 1968.

Glaser, R. (Ed.) *The nature of reinforcement.* New York: Academic Press, 1971.

Glaser, R., & Resnick, L. B. Instructional psychology. In P. H. Mussen & M. R. Rosenzweig (Eds.), *Annual Review of Psychology,* 1972, **23**, 207–276.

Hilgard, E. R. (Ed.) Theories of learning and instruction. *63rd yearbook of the national society for the study of education.* Chicago: University of Chicago Press, 1964.

Hill, W. What can psychology offer education? A review of some recent opinions from psychologists. *Journal of Teacher Education,* 1963, 443–448.

Leonard, W. P. Books that practice what they preach. *AV Communication Review,* 1971, **19**(4), 454–460.

Lindgren, H. C. Learning theory and teaching practice. *Educational Leadership,* 1959, **16**, 333–336.

Mathis, C. Implications of modern learning theory for the secondary school. *High School Journal,* 1964–1965, **48**, 411–418.

Meierhenry, W. C. (Ed.) Learning theory and av learning. *AV Communication Review,* 1961, **9**, 2–88.

Meierhenry, W. C. Implications of learning theory for instructional technology. *Phi Delta Kappan,* 1964–1965, **46**, 435–438.

Norman, D. A. (Ed.) *Models of human memory.* New York: Academic Press, 1970.

Smith, K. U. *Cybernetic principles of learning and educational design.* New York: Holt, Rinehart, & Winston, 1966.

Symonds, P. M. What education has to learn from psychology. II Reward, III Punishment. *Teachers College Record,* 1955–1956, **57**, 15–25, 449–462.

A symposium: Can the laws of learning be applied in the classroom? *Harvard Educational Review,* 1959, **29**, 83–117.

16
Task Analysis
Instructional Theories

In the previous chapter we considered an approach to the formulation of instructional principles which draws eclectically from many different kinds of learning research and theory. The general strategy there was to identify those learning principles which are reasonably well supported by empirical evidence and which have implications for educational practice.

In the present chapter we will encounter an approach which, likewise, draws from many sources in learning psychology. However, the present group contends that one must first identify what *types* of learning are involved in an educational situation. This "task analysis" is prepared with reference to some inventory or "taxonomy" of learning types. Further, one can derive more specific indications not only as to *what* is to be taught but also as to *how* it is to be taught because the learning types are hierarchically arranged in the taxonomy and the conditions for facilitating each type of learning are indicated. Thus we refer to the present approach to instructional theory construction as a *task analysis instructional theory*. As examples of this approach to instruction, one could consider the work of Leslie J. Briggs, Robert M. Gagne, Robert Glaser, Arthur W. Melton, and many others.

This chapter will contain four major sections. In the first section we will review results of the attempts of a number of experimental psychologists who had training and experience in psychology learning research and who were asked to "apply learning principles" in military and industrial training situations. We will consider examples of problems which led to their disillusionment with some laboratory-based learning principles and to their eventual emphasis on the need for task analysis. We will take Gagne's task analyses and taxonomy as an illustration of an approach to instructional design within this orientation. We will consider mainly the eight types of learning which he has identified, based on previous traditional learning theories, and we will note some of his views about instructional design associated with these eight types. Then we will describe how Briggs has used Gagne's task hierarchy as a basis for designing instruction and we will enumerate some of the ways by which Briggs uses multimedia in implementing his approach. Finally, we will consider the prospects and problems for this approach to instructional theory formulation.

EMERGENCE OF TASK ANALYSES AND TAXONOMIES FOR TRAINING AND EDUCATION

The approach to instructional theory discussed in this chapter originated in military and industrial training situations in the 1940s and 1950s. The nature of these origins prompts us to consider two rather peripheral issues before we examine the importance of task analyses and taxonomies in the formulation of instructional theories. The first issue concerns relationships between military and civilian psychology developments; the second issue concerns relationships between "training" and "education."

Contributions of Military Psychology?

It has long been recognized that scientific and technological developments which were initiated because of military defense problems may also have implications for applications in civilian life. But in the past several years many have expressed concern as to whether we have been diverting too large a proportion of our nation's resources to military purposes, and they have begun to question *whether any* real benefits have been derived for resolution of our nation's social problems, including those in education. For example, papers have been published in psychology journals describing the progress and contributions of military psychology (for example, Crawford, 1970). Sometimes, these papers have been followed by letters to the editor in which complaints have been registered about having spent the money for military problems rather than for pressing social problems.

It would be beyond the scope of the present chapter to consider the merits of the arguments presented. Rather, it is simply our purpose here to report that certain events did occur in conjunction with military training programs and that resulting techniques, principles, and procedures have been found to have some use for civilian education applications. In an objective manner we will report how the ideas originated and will describe some of their implications for educational practice.

"Training" and "Education"

Throughout this century there has been some controversy as to relationships between "training" and "education" (for example, see Dewey, 1916). The term *training* is typically used in military and industrial situations where rather specific objectives can be readily identified. In contrast, *education* has usually been characterized as having broader, somewhat more global objectives of preparing a person to be a good citizen generally and to be a happy and productive person in society. Lavisky (1967, p. 443) depicts training as fitting "a person for a particular job in a particular system" while education is more concerned with "the growth and development of the individual" as a person.

But during the past few decades training personnel have recognized the importance of considering their workers as individuals rather than merely as parts of the system, and they have become concerned with education as well as training. On the other hand, educators have recognized the advantages of delineating their objectives in measurable form, wherever possible, and they have become aware of training principles which may be useful in educational situations. Though communication between training personnel and educators has not been good in the past, in recent years there have been a number of attempts to exchange ideas on topics of mutual interest. These topics have included audiovisual devices and other educational media, programmed instruction, computer-assisted instruction, and the task analysis approach to instructional theory. Without further comment about this "training versus education" issue, we will describe how certain ideas about instruction were initially formulated in training situations and subsequently were adapted for educational practice more generally.

Learning Principles versus Task Analyses and Taxonomies

It is generally recognized that psychology's major contribution to the military services during World War I was the delineation of procedures for selecting personnel for various assignments. Out of these experiences emerged a number of strategies and techniques for assessment of applicants in industrial situations and for placement and vocational guidance in education.

The main objective delineated for psychologists at the beginning of World War II was selection and classification of personnel. However, the continuing technological advances made in military equipment resulted in a need for training personnel how to operate and use the equipment. While training programs in the past were mainly pragmatic and atheoretical, during the latter part of World War II it was suggested that psychological research might be useful in improving the training procedures. Thus, during the late 1940s and the 1950s many projects were started in which attempts were made to use psychological principles to design and to improve training procedures. These projects were initiated in industrial training programs and in other government agency training programs, as well as in the military services. Moreover, a series of basic and applied research programs were instituted partly in support of these training efforts.

The general idea was that it should be possible to apply some of the learning principles which had been derived from laboratory research. Many experimental psychologists who had long conducted such studies had been called into military service during World War II or had become involved in the various training and research projects in the postwar era. It was expected that their expertise would facilitate the application of the laboratory-based learning principles to the applied military training problems. And, in a number of cases, there were quite successful results obtained. For example, Crawford (1970) describes how research was used to improve techniques for teaching electronics maintenance training personnel just as effectively and in about half the time as had previously been required.

But some very puzzling things happened when the psychologists tried to make direct, practical use of the factors which had been found to be of influence in laboratory learning studies. In a widely cited paper, Gagne (1962) has described a series of training situations in which either the predicted learning results were not obtained or the learning situation performance was not maintained when the learner was confronted with the real-life transfer situation. Gagne described several different practical learning problems—teach a gunner how to track a moving target; learn the fourteen or more steps required to put a radar set in operation; find the source of malfunctions in complex equipment. In each instance, he related how reinforcement and other laboratory-based principles were applied and how the real learners did not act in accordance with predictions from the subjects in the laboratory studies. Given the fact that it had been expected that the learning psychologists' assumptions and principles would be useful, Gagne concluded: "On the whole, it may fairly be said, I think, that the assumption was often wrong and the principles were seldom useful in bringing about training improvement" (p. 86). But Gagne hastened to add that the experimental psychologists usually *were* able to improve training results. The problem was that they had to make adjustments when they used such assumptions and principles. This prompted Gagne to raise questions as to what kinds of contributions to training might be derived from the psychology of learning.

What does the learning psychologist have to offer to training personnel and educators? Gagne did *not* conclude that there was *nothing* to offer. Rather, he held that the wrong tack had been taken. Instead of assuming that there is only one kind of learning process and that, therefore, a given principle would be applicable no matter what was being learned, Gagne proposed that we need to conduct a careful analysis of each training-education situation to determine what kinds of tasks are involved in each. Once having delineated the kinds of tasks involved in the final goal performance, as well as the many intermediary subgoals with their respective tasks, one can specify principles for that training situation. The specific principles will depend upon the particular kinds of learning processes and the conditions which produce that type of learning, as well as the kinds of processes which are required to carry over this learning to the next subtask or to the ultimate real-life transfer situation. Thus he proposed that learning psychologists could talk to training personnel and educators about different types of learning arranged in a classification or taxonomic system and about such processes and principles as *"task analysis, intratask transfer, component task achievement,* and *sequencing"* (p. 88).

Gagne was not alone in drawing such conclusions. Many others concurred with his views. Actually, many authors credit Robert B. Miller (1953) with having been one of the first to emphasize the relevance of task analyses and task taxonomies for training and education. Other spokesmen whose views are especially relevant to our present discussion include Robert Glaser, Arthur W. Melton, and Leslie J. Briggs. We will sample comments by Glaser and Melton before we examine the kind of task analyses and the taxonomy which Gagne proposed and the instructional design procedures which Briggs has related more specifically to general educational practice.

One thing about Gagne, Glaser, Melton, and Briggs should be noted: they have the unusual combination of training and experience in basic academic psychology as well as in quite applied problems in training and education. Thus they can view some of the problems of translating information from psychology to education in a manner not easily possible for an individual with experience in only one of these areas.

In various papers Glaser has long criticized the rather common assumption among psychologists and educators that one can take laboratory-based psychological principles directly into educational practice. Instead, he has contended that there is need for some kind of development process so as to "bridge the gap between the science of learning and the management of training and education" (Glaser, 1964, p. 168). As part of the process of planning instructional procedures, he contends that a basic step is to identify one's educational objectives and to identify the characteristics of the various tasks so that appropriate procedures can be identified. He has proposed that both psychology as a science and teaching as a scientifically based technology will benefit if instructional theories and methods are presented and tested empirically. In this context he has encouraged formulation of some sort of taxonomy of learning and educational objectives so that the objectives may be more precisely formulated and more specific information provided about effective instructional procedures. According to Glaser, school objectives and processes should be examined not only as to academic course subject matter but also as to the kinds of behaviors and activities which are involved. These activities should be categorized so that they can be measured and so that the appropriate learning conditions and teaching procedures can be identified and evaluated.

Melton has long recognized the need for a taxonomy both for basic research theoretical purposes and for practical use in training and education. In 1962 he headed a conference on human learning which resulted in a book entitled *Categories of Human Learning* (Melton, 1964). Several of his remarks as editor and summarizer of that conference are especially pertinent to our present discussion. He acknowledged that much of the concern for a taxonomy had been generated by the kinds of military training problems which we mentioned above. He noted that it can be quite frustrating for training personnel who are trying to find optimal plans for instruction when they find quite conflicting recommendations from studies, for example, on rote learning, motor skill learning, and problem solving—particularly if there is no means by which to determine which kinds of studies would be most relevant for the practical problem at hand.

He expressed reservations about the extent to which traditional laboratory research paradigms could serve as a basis for formulating a taxonomy, and he noted that there have been and will continue to be numerous problems to be resolved before we have a satisfactory taxonomy. The symposium and book were organized around quite traditional topical categories—classical conditioning, operant conditioning, rote verbal learning, probability learning, incidental learning, concept learning, perceptual-motor skill learning, and problem solving. Nonetheless, he acknowledged that many other psychologists might have selected a different number of categories and/or different combinations. He pointed out the extent to which current categories are operationally oriented and suggested the need for having a better theoretical basis for evolving a taxonomy.

Recognizing that the categories selected are probably not the ones which will be contained in an ultimate taxonomy, he explained: "The best that can be said for them is that each category does include a task aspect or behavior requirement which is important and is given heavy weight or emphasis in at least some of the subcategories within it" (Melton, 1964, p. 333). Some, for example, provide many of the essentials of the activities involved, and the task for the subject is merely to form appropriate associations; in others there is a response which must be "discovered" as well as associated with stimuli. In his discussions, Melton raised the possibility of justifying different numbers of types of learning and speculated that more research and theoretical integration is necessary before we can have some degree of assurance that proper categories are being selected and used. But he argued that it is long past time to get started on such a taxonomy, and he presented the fruits of this symposium for scrutiny and modification.

Instructional Design and Task Analysis—Some General Observations

The need for a taxonomy has primarily been recognized by persons in practical situations when they have attempted to use learning principles derived from laboratory research. Some basic researchers have also acknowledged such a need for practitioners, and a few have displayed some *mild* interest in the *theoretical* value. But the more that the basic researcher is concerned with some delimited aspect of learning, the less he becomes enthused about a general taxonomy. Conversely, the more interest he has in evolving some general learning theory, the greater the potential he envisions in using a taxonomy.

Out of such deliberations come two questions of relevance to our focus. First, how might a taxonomy relate to the various previous theories and studies on learning? Second, how might such a taxonomy be useful in formulating instructional theories and in designing instructional procedures and materials? Perusal of the literature provides mixed reactions on both matters.

Some would prefer to follow the lead in developing an *education* taxonomy started in the middle 1950s by Bloom and colleagues (see discussions in Bloom, Hastings, & Madaus, 1971) because it is quite closely related to educators' conceptions of their objectives. Others prefer a taxonomy which is developed by psychologists and which is more closely related to the paradigms used in laboratory studies of learning processes. Within the latter group there is a further division, with some emphasizing the traditional theories of learning and others placing much greater emphasis on the currently popular diverse miniature models especially because they emphasize *verbal* learning.

There is rather common agreement that a taxonomy should provide descriptions of relationships among its components so that matters can be resolved as to hierarchical relationships among the types, and as to the learning factors of influence on each type. This kind of information would provide guidelines for optimal sequencing of different learning types and for instructional arrangements which most likely will facilitate the respective types of learning. At a minimum, the taxonomy should be sufficiently clearly described that it can be used reliably in a practical situation, and it should provide enough information about conditions which facilitate the respective types of learning so that appropriate instructional procedures and materials can be developed. Either through a deductive or an inductive theory construction process, at least ultimately, the taxonomy should contribute to the general development of instructional theory.

Most of the proponents of task analyses and taxonomies seem to recognize that there are other aspects of the educational process which must be considered. Some of them have rather specific suggestions as to how the design of instructional procedures relates to the more general design of instruction. For example, Glaser (1966) has outlined some of the psychological bases which he envisions for instructional design. It would first be necessary to analyze the particular subject-matter content and the kinds of activities which learners are typically expected to complete. One would be concerned not only with the subject knowledge but also with the various kinds of activities and the conditions under which they would have to be completed. These activities would ideally be classified in terms of some taxonomy.

Second, it would be necessary to identify in rather specific terms all those initial or "entering" characteristics of the students themselves which might be associated with successful completion of the learning experience, including especially any prerequisite skills, previous learning, handicaps, and other features which might be pertinent to the learning tasks at hand. Third, plans would be prepared by which the student might go from his status at the beginning of the learning to successful completion of the educational objectives. This would include the instructional procedures as well as all the materials which would be required for successful completion of the learning experience. Many aspects would have to be anticipated and considered in formulating such plans, including, for example, the motivation of the learner, the fatigue and boredom which might emerge, the individual differences in students' approach to the learning situation, the ability of students to generalize from their learning situation and to transfer their learnings to the real-world situation beyond the classroom.

Fourth, it would be necessary to have provisions whereby the individual student's progress could be monitored as well as means whereby periodic evaluations can be conducted to determine the extent to which the educational practices seem to be facilitating students' learning more generally. He labeled the respective steps: "(a) analyzing the characteristics of subject-matter competence, (b) diagnosing preinstructional behavior, (c) carrying out the instructional process, and (d) measuring learning outcomes" (Glaser, 1966). Elsewhere (Glaser, 1966, p. 14) he strongly emphasized the need for analyzing the terminal objectives and program tasks as a major means for improving instruction.

To illustrate the ways in which the task analyses and taxonomies would be used in preparing instructional procedures and developing instructional theories, we will now turn to two kinds of projects. First, we will consider Gagne's taxonomy and conditions for learning which have some promise for delineating instructional principles and plans. Then we will describe the ways in which Briggs has used Gagne's ideas to formulate instructional principles and methods. Whether these systems are the best ones available is not our main concern. We use them because they illustrate attempts to delineate instructional principles and to plan instructional methods through utilization of task analysis and taxonomies.

GAGNE'S LEARNING TYPES AND
THEIR IMPLICATIONS FOR INSTRUCTION

One of the experimental psychologists with experience in learning research who became involved in training and educational problems is Robert M. Gagne (1916–). Since receiving his Ph.D. from Brown University in 1940, he has had a wide range of experiences with academic theoretical research activities as well as with applied psychology aspects, especially those concerned with military training problems and various educational research and development projects. He has written numerous papers on basic and applied psychology topics and he has authored, edited, or coauthored various books. But most of his ideas about the task analysis-taxonomy approach to instructional theory and design are contained in his book *The Conditions of Learning* (1966; 2d ed., 1970). Most of the comments which follow will be drawn from that source.

Some Views on Education and Instruction

Gagne sets for himself the task of selecting those aspects of the psychology of learning which will help in designing better education. He sees instruction as being only one aspect of education, albeit an important aspect to be considered if one wishes to improve educational practice. For example, he recognizes that many daily transactions in schools, for example, administrative matters and general interpersonal relationships, do not directly involve the process of instruction per se. But instruction is a central part of education. He roughly categorizes instruction as being "predesigned," in which procedures are planned and tested before being used in the classroom, or as being "extemporaneously designed," in which the teacher works more or less intuitively and pragmatically without following any detailed plans. While acknowledging the desirability of maintaining some air of spontaneity in the educational process and admitting that even the most elaborate plan cannot avoid some need for judgment and intuition when implemented in practice, he does favor a "predesign" approach to instruction wherever possible.

He depicts instruction as mainly involving the arrangement of those conditions which facilitate learning—hence the title of his book, *The Conditions of Learning*. He notes that some features to be considered in designing instruction exist within the learner (that is, are "internal") and that others involve conditions in the environment (that is, are "external" to the student). Thus the teacher is concerned with some combination of internal conditions (what the student has already learned, what aptitudes and limitations are pertinent to the present learning, etc.) and external conditions (how materials are sequenced, how presented to the student, what kinds of feedback, etc.) which will facilitate attainment of the desired educational objectives.

But one rather unique quality in the task analysis-taxonomy approach is the emphasis on planning instruction after one has analyzed the educational process. "The point of view of this text is that learning must be linked to the design of instruction through consideration of the different kinds of capabilities that are being learned" (Gagne, 1970, p. v). Thus he rejects an assumption which seemed prevalent among some traditional learning theorists that there is only one or only a few types of learning.

Instead, he identifies eight types of learning and indicates how the kinds of conditions which facilitate each type of learning have practical implications for appropriate instructional procedures for the respective types.

Another somewhat unique emphasis is his contention that these different types of learning are hierarchically arranged so that one must consider the relevance of subordinate types whenever one tries to prepare instruction for a higher type. This prompts him to be quite concerned with the initial characteristics of his students as well as with their eventual status following the learning experiences. "The attempt is made to show that each variety of learning described here begins with a *different state of the organism* and ends with a different capability for *performance*" (Gagne, 1970, p. 65). Thus one of the major differences among the learning types is the kind of internal state which is prerequisite to instruction.

He acknowledges that most school learning probably does involve the complex learning processes to a greater extent than it does solely involve the simpler processes. However, drawing from the hierarchical relationships, he cautions educators to be quite alert to *all* of the components in a particular educational situation, including prerequisite conditions and simpler components involved in more complex objectives.

Acknowledged Limitations of the Taxonomy and Instructional Principles

The strategy which Gagne adopted is to assume that there are several different types of learning, some of which are subordinate to and components of other, more complex types. It is further assumed that one can use these types to classify "everyday observations" about learning in the world outside the laboratory, even though the foundations for the taxonomy are drawn mainly from laboratory research paradigms. This assumption is based on the fact that many laboratory studies actually had originated with some practical problem, but it essentially ignores the many additional changes which were made in devising arrangements suitable for laboratory investigation.

Gagne has drawn eclectically from many diverse and sometimes possibly incompatible theories in his search for a comprehensive taxonomy of learning types. But he acknowledges that there may be more learning types than he has identified and that others might select different categories. He contends that he has not actually formulated a *new* theory of learning but, rather, has drawn liberally from the various theories proposed by others. Some (for example, Hilgard & Bower, 1966) suggest that he may be understating the significance of his taxonomy, and they depict his taxonomic arrangement as "the beginning of a unified theory" of learning (Hilgard & Bower, 1966, p. 569).

Of the instructional theory proponents whose work is reviewed in these five chapters, Gagne seems to be most aware of the limitations of his particular approach and of learning principles in general. For example, he explicitly acknowledges "that there are some problems of great importance to education which *cannot* be solved by applying a knowledge of the principles of learning as they are here described" (Gagne, 1970, p. 25). He enumerates some of the many aspects which are not actually covered by learning principles. These include "the personal interaction between a teacher and his students," "motivating, persuading, and the establishment of attitudes and values," and others. He explicitly indicates that such very important educational matters may be of peripherical or tangential relevance, but that they are not a central concern for his taxonomy and instructional principles. His instructional theory is "restricted to what may be termed the intellectual, or subject matter content that leads to improvement in human performances having ultimate usefulness in the pursuit of the individual's vocation or profession" (Gagne, 1970, p. 25).

Another limitation which he identifies for his theory and for learning principles has to do with instilling an interest in continuing one's education, especially culminating in complex intellectual and creative activities. "It does not seem possible at present to specify all the conditions necessary to attain the highest and most complex varieties of human performance such as those displayed in invention or esthetic creativity" (p. 25). Perhaps, he proposes, those types of learning with which his theory is concerned may be some of the key prerequisites and components of these more complex human activities.

Gagne delineates four aspects of the educational process for which educators can derive ideas and prescriptions from his approach to instruction. The taxonomy and instructional principles provide guidelines as to how one may (1) plan educational objectives and delineate pertinent prerequisite capabilities of entering students before they actually enter the learning situation; (2) manage the learning situation so that the student will be motivated and will continue involvement in learning, as well as make recommendations about content to be learned and conditions under which it will most readily be learned; (3) plan and test out instructional procedures so that those conditions which are external to the learner will be selected and arranged in optimal ways for facilitating learning; and (4) select media (oral or written materials, various audio and visual devices, teaching machines or programmed texts, computer-assisted instructional devices, etc.) which will provide the greatest utility and effectiveness in attaining the educational objectives.

Eight Types of Learning and Their Implications for Instruction

Gagne has delineated eight different kinds of learning, each of which allegedly has a particular beginning state and ends with a particular performance capability. Each type has rather specific learner's "internal conditions" or prerequisite skills, attitudes, and information which are necessary for the respective type of learning to occur. Each type also has a rather unique set of "external conditions" or conditions in the learning situation, such as ways of presenting information and giving feedback to students about their progress which facilitate that learning type. In this section we will enumerate the eight types of learning and we will provide descriptions of each type, its origin in psychology learning research, *some* of the conditions which are important in facilitating each type of learning, and an educational example of the learning type.

Obviously it will not be possible to provide as much detail here as Gagne does in his book concerning his conceptions of these eight learning types and their implications for instruction. We will only have space here to provide *samples* illustrating the use of task analyses and taxonomies in formulating instructional principles. Our later discussion of Briggs's approach will provide a *brief* illustration of ways in which Gagne's principles and taxonomy can be used in designing instruction.

Type 1: Signal Learning   Basing this type on Pavlov's classical conditioning paradigm, Gagne described it: "The individual learns to make a general diffuse response to a signal" (1970, p. 63). This is one of the most basic types of learning. Gagne is not certain whether or not it is subordinate to or parallel with type 2. Basically, there do not seem to be any special prerequisite conditions other than that the individual must be capable of sensing a range of stimuli and of making the appropriate response to at least one stimulus. As with Pavlov's paradigm, the conditioned and unconditioned stimuli must be presented in close proximity, with such paired presentations occurring until the conditioned stimulus or signal stimulus elicits the response. An educational example would be learning to associate a spoken name of an object with the printed name of the object (signal stimulus) as a result of its (printed name) having been presented repeatedly with a picture of the object (unconditioned stimulus in this case *if* the student already knows the spoken name for the picture).

Type 2: Stimulus-Response Learning   "The learner acquires a precise response to a discriminated stimulus" (Gagne, 1970, p. 63). This type of learning is primarily based on Thorndike's trial-and-error learning and Skinner's operant conditioning. As we stated above, Gagne is not certain as to relationships between type 1 and type 2, although he suspects that type 1 is subordinate to type 2. At a minimum, there must be some identifiable reinforcing stimulus or reinforcing activity which can follow the occurrence of the desired response pattern. Gagne discusses some of the phenomena of operant conditioning which we have considered in an earlier chapter. It is noteworthy that the key idea is to provide systematic reinforcement for emission of appropriate responses and that this process can be carried out without any great concern about the general internal experiences of the student. An educational example would be having the teacher provide praise and encouragement as the student of a foreign language more and more accurately approximates the correct pronunciation of words and sentences.

Type 3: Motor Chaining   A chain is a sequence of activities which consists of two or more stimulus-response units. Here Gagne drew from a variety of theories, including primarily certain concepts from Skinner and Guthrie. With this type it becomes apparent how the first two types are both prerequisite associations and components of a higher-level type. At a minimum, the learner must have learned previously some of the stimulus-response associations which are components of the chain to be learned. Moreover, these previously learned associations may serve as a model for learning additional associations which are also components of the chain. A major consideration in the learning situation is to find some ways to get the appropriate stimulus-response units to occur. Ideally, the results of one unit should naturally lead to the eliciting or emitting of the subsequent unit, all culminating in stimuli or acts which are reinforcing for the learner. One can begin with the *terminal* act and work backwards (Gilbert, 1962), a procedure which is quite compatible with Skinnerian and Hullian theory; or, one can start with the first act and try to identify stimuli which will elicit or prompt occurrence of the response, a strategy more compatible with Guthrian and Pavlovian theory. In either case, it is important to provide for frequent repetition and to insure that relevant units rather readily can occur in close proximity to others to be associated with them. Educational examples include mastering the sequences involved in writing, swinging a golf club, operating a typewriter, or playing a piano.

Type 4: Verbal Association   This is similar to type 3 except that both stimulus and response elements are verbal. However, it appears that internal conditions may be more important and more complicated than is true with type 3. The theoretical bases are largely the same as in type 3, although Gagne's instructional procedures also reflect some of the contemporary miniature-model research on verbal learning, including paired-associate learning in particular. Gagne acknowledges that the more recent studies suggest that internal mediating ideas may be more critical here than with type 3. Educational examples would include such short associations as learning French equivalents of English words and such long associations as learning a poem or a speech. Gagne also provides some words of caution to the educator by noting that Ausubel and others have expressed reservations about the extent to which the verbal association principles may be relevant to meaningful verbal learning.

Type 5: Discrimination Learning (Among Previously Learned Pairs) "The individual learns to make *n* different identifying responses to as many different stimuli, which may resemble each other in physical appearance to a greater or lesser degree" (Gagne, 1970, p. 63). Here the learning research origins are multifaceted. Gagne's bases range from stimulus-response studies of discrimination processes in which reinforcement principles are emphasized to Gibson's views and research on perceptual learning which suggest that the really significant influences lie in the stimuli and in one's perception of them rather than in stimulus-response associations. Not only stimulus-response associations seem prerequisite but many forms of chains as well. Moreover, as one examines more complex learning types, the problems of interference and retention in general become more complicated. Beyond already having learned the separate components (stimulus-response associations, chains, etc.), the learning situation should provide opportunity for practice in identifying each component in the proper sequence and for diminishing the likelihood of forgetting. Apparently a major contribution of repetition is that it diminishes interference of one component with others; thus repetition's main function is in avoiding forgetting. A major consideration is that the stimuli should be presented in such ways that it is easy to contrast the different components both in terms of their concrete characteristics as stimuli and in terms of their meanings. An educational example in biology is learning the different characteristics which distinguish one animal species from another, or one class of plants from others.

Type 6: Concept Learning This involves "making a common response to a class of stimuli that may differ from each other widely in physical appearance" (Gagne, 1970, pp. 63-64) typically through repeated exposure to concrete examples of the class or classes to be learned. This type is mainly drawn from verbal learning studies and "learning how to learn" studies with human and animal objects. Gagne suggests that each of the previous types of learning constitutes essential components of type 6, especially those that culminate in the attainment of multiple discriminations among potentially relevant stimuli. In the learning situation it is important that the learner has assistance in identifying pertinent characteristics of concrete examples of the class presented to him through receiving clearly presented verbal instructions about the task. Leading questions should be used to assist the learner in identifying and stating the common features for the concept class. Reinforcement here really acts as confirmation that the learner is identifying relevant stimulus features. Apparently repetition is not as important as assisting the learner in identifying the pertinent characteristics. Educational examples include learning what is meant by such concepts as little, many, mass, gravity, power, influence, edge, large, hexagon, etc.

Type 7: Rule Learning Whereas type 6 involved learning through exposure to concrete examples of the class, type 7 involves learning definitions and rules concerning concepts. Thus type 7 is at a higher level of abstraction than is type 6. In a sense, this can be depicted as learning *rules*, where a rule is defined as "*an inferred capability that enables the individual to respond to a class of stimulus situations with a class of performances*, the latter being predictably related to the former by a class of relations" (Gagne, 1970, p. 191). He again illustrates the hierarchical relationships by noting that a rule typically is composed of two or more concepts and a statement of relationships between them. At a minimum, the prerequisites include knowing the relevant concepts to which the rules refer. Learning conditions which facilitate rule learning are not limited to mere verbal statements of the rule; rather, the learner may benefit from stating analogies or by demonstrating applications of the rule. Gagne (1970, p. 203) provides five instructional principles which facilitate rule learning. In brief, these include giving the learner information about the nature of successful learning, assistance in identifying critical component concepts, verbal instructions and guidelines which facilitate forming chains of pertinent concepts, leading questions which encourage the learner to demonstrate the rule, and encouraging the learner to give verbal descriptions of the rule. Educational examples include learning how to find the number of square feet in a rectangle, learning what procedures are necessary to determine whether a subject and predicate agree in number, etc.

Type 8: Problem Solving Problem solving involves internal cognitive processes to a greater extent than is necessarily true of the previous seven types. In brief, problem solving involves making use of the concepts and rules which have been learned and generating new concepts or rules so as to define a problem and find its solution(s). Type 8 even involves the establishment and use of hierarchical relationships among concepts and rules so that appropriate problem-solving strategies can be developed and modified until the problem is satisfactorily defined and solved. Gagne cites Dewey's (1910) sequence of steps in problem solving—presentation of a problem (either through actual contact with a situation or through a verbal description of the problem), definition of the problem (identifying pertinent characteristics of the situation), formulation of hypotheses about possible solutions to the problem, and verification of one or more potential solutions until an effective solution is found. Building on all previous learning types. Gagne characterizes type 8 learning processes as especially being dependent on use of rules and strategies (that is, rules about using rules). For problem-solving learning, the learner must have mastered all the concepts and rules which are relevant to the problem at hand. Ideally, the instructor should provide guidelines and suggestions on using these concepts and rules but should avoid giving direct leads to the problem solution itself. In a sense, Gagne recommends giving guidance about ways to search for problem solutions but recommends against giving the learner cues as to the correct problem solution or solutions. "Problem solving as a method of learning requires the learner to *discover* the higher-order rule without specific help" (Gagne, 1970, p. 225). Thus type 8 learning is quite similar to the cognitive construct instructional theory. Gagne suggests that type 8 learning may be "of overriding importance as a goal of education. After all, should not formal instruction in the school have the aim of teaching the student 'how to think'?" (Gagne, 1970, p. 232). Educational examples involve finding how to do something that is not possible by merely following a single rule. This might occur in social studies where students are to resolve differences between two hypothetical competing countries which have both mutual interests and incompatible goals, or in mathematics courses where students are to find solutions to complicated algebra problems.

Task Analysis and Instructional Design

Gagne couches his suggestions for instruction by noting that many other aspects of the educational process are quite influential in determining how successful instruction can be. He identifies three main processes which determine whether the student is "ready" for instruction—attention, motivation, and developmental level. He depicts attention as an internal condition and suggests that it probably involves several different levels, but he leans toward reinforcement principles as major explanations as to how and why students selectively attend to certain stimuli of all of those present in any given situation. In order for instruction to be effective, the student must be attending to pertinent stimuli. Motivation is important with regard to getting the student to attend school and to take part in learning activities. In addition, a student's response to instruction will be greatly influenced by the kinds and levels of aspiration which he has for the tasks at hand. Gagne's third process which determines the student's readiness for instruction is developmental level. He points out that there are cognitive as well as physical characteristics which determine what an individual can do and is most likely to do at respective developmental stages. He refers to the work of Piaget and other contemporary developmental theorists and suggests that their work has implications for curriculum and instructional planning. "Theories enjoying widespread acceptance are based upon the idea that stages of neurophysiological growth impose certain limitations upon the kind and degree of cognitive development that can occur" (Gagne, 1970, pp. 299–300). Such implications must be considered before one can be assured that the learner is ready to benefit from instructional plans.

In using his instructional principles, Gagne identifies nine instructional events which affect the learner's responsiveness to instruction and his retention of what he learns: "Gaining and controlling attention . . . Informing the learner of expected outcomes . . . Stimulating recall of relevant prerequisite capabilities . . . Presenting the stimuli inherent to the learning task . . . Offering guidance for learning . . . Providing feedback . . . Appraising performance . . . Making provisions for transferability . . . Insuring retention" (Gagne, 1970, p. 304).

For more explicit descriptions of ways in which Gagne's taxonomy and instructional principles have been used in designing instruction, we will now turn to the work of Leslie J. Briggs.

BRIGGS'S SYSTEM FOR INSTRUCTIONAL DESIGN

Leslie J. Briggs (1919–   ) is another psychologist with a combined background of experimental and practical experience who has been closely identified with task analysis instructional theory. He received his B.S. and M.S. degrees from Ft. Hays Kansas State College by 1942, but further graduate work was postponed by a four-year tour of duty in the Army. He subsequently did receive his Ph.D. from Ohio State University in 1948.

Apparently partly as a result of his military experiences, both his graduate work and his subsequent professional contributions have been concerned with the use of psychological principles in the design of instruction, especially as they relate to the use of different kinds of educational media. He has published studies from experimental psychology learning research. But he also has extensive experience in various aspects of educational research and development, several years of which were spent with the American Institute for Research (a research and development organization with which both Glaser and Gagne are rather closely identified).

In a series of papers and monographs he has used Gagne's taxonomy and instructional principles in the systematic design of instruction. Several of his publications are especially relevant to our present discussion (Briggs, 1967a, 1968a, 1968b, 1970), although space limitations will require that we focus primarily on one (1970).

It should be of interest to readers that Briggs believes that his approach should be useful to users as well as to producers of instructional materials and procedures. A major objective, of course, is to help those who are designing or redesigning instruction. However, he contends that his guidelines should also be helpful for teachers and other educators in selecting and using materials and procedures developed by others.

Briggs's Systems Model for
Instructional Design

Briggs depicts his procedures for the design of instruction as involving a "systems" model. By a systems model, he means that he advocates specifying the educational goals in terms of the learner's terminal performance, providing for periodic assessment of the extent to which the learner is reaching the subgoals and goals, identifying alternative instructional materials and procedures which would be appropriate, and using empirical evidence as a main basis for selecting the instructional procedures and materials which are most appropriate for the students' initial entering characteristics and ultimate educational goals.

He contends that wherever possible the recommended steps are based on empirical research findings or on psychological theory, while he acknowledges that common reasoning and judgment are required for the numerous gaps in extant evidence and theory. But he consistently advocates reliance on predesigned approaches rather than on extemporaneous designs (that is, rather than on strictly intuitive, extemporaneous teaching), and he expresses preference for empirical evidence rather than for logical bases in the designing process.

Earlier (Briggs, 1968b) he had reviewed a wide range of studies concerning the relevance of taxonomies for curriculum and instructional design. As a result of that survey he concluded that there are wide differences of opinion as to what constitutes the best taxonomy and as to whether one can really identify reliable hierarchical relationships among different types of learning. With full awareness of the problems inherent in using any of the several currently available taxonomies, he has based most of his approach to instruction on Gagne's taxonomy which· we discussed in the previous section. Briggs reports: "The present model is designed to be compatible with and to extend Gagne's work" (Briggs, 1970, p. ix).

Acknowledged Limitations and Problems

Like Gagne, Briggs is quite explicit in pointing out some of the limitations and problems in using his approach to instructional theory and design. Although he strongly advocates the use of his approach because he believes that it will aid in improving educational practice, he acknowledges "that applying such advanced concepts in the technology of instructional design is often laborious, time consuming and difficult" (Briggs, 1968b, p. vii).

He points out that his particular approach "would not be acceptable nor useful to those who feel learning is limited to just one or two types" (1970, p. 185). In addition, he delimits the scope to which his instructional principles are applicable by excluding the "skills of inquiry needed for advanced types of problem solving" (1970, p. 185). Nonetheless, he proposed his system because he feels that having a more systematic basis for some of these less complex educational goals may quite likely be useful in attaining the more complex goals.

He identifies several areas in which one may encounter some difficulties in using his approach. First, there is some difficulty in classifying educational goals under Gagne's eight types. This could be due to the fact that they are more psychological than educational in origin, although Briggs points out that similar problems are encountered in using Bloom's educationally oriented taxonomy. Hopefully, additional use and research will provide better guidelines.

Second, many educators are accustomed to rather simple, global suggestions for selecting educational media. In contrast, Briggs recommends more detailed and careful analyses so that the most appropriate media will be used. He acknowledges that one must be flexible in using his guidelines for selection of media, at least at the present status of his guidelines.

Third, Briggs acknowledges that one needs much practice in using the task analysis procedures and the taxonomy in classifying educational competencies into Gagne's learning types. Briggs acknowledges that Gagne had been somewhat hesitant in linking instructional sequencing to the hierarchical relationships of learning types. However, Briggs feels that it would be best to assume that one should present the lower-level types before the more complex ones until more empirical evidence is obtained as to the extent to which one can ignore the role of the lower types as prerequisites for higher types of learning. He suggests that "the practical thing to do is to sequence the teaching of competencies in the order implied by the structural analysis, and to sequence instructional events for each competency in an order logically suggested by both experimental and pedagogical considerations" (Briggs, 1970, p. 186). He acknowledges that this requires some judgment on the part of the course designer and instructor.

But all such limitations and difficulties can be overcome through research and experimental use. Briggs presents his ideas as tentative procedures, based on the best information now available, and he proposes that they be continually submitted to evaluation and modification.

Some Illustrations of Briggs's
Use of Gagne's Taxonomy

There are five major parts in Briggs' approach to instructional design. First, he identifies the educational goals by describing the learner's expected terminal performance capabilities and he classifies them in terms of

Gagne's eight types of learning. As part of this first step, he also outlines subordinate components for each major goal, again using Gagne's eight learning types as a taxonomy. Second, he designs evaluative procedures which further clarify the nature of the major goals and their related components, and which later can serve as a means for evaluating the extent to which each student attains the desired goals. Third, the initial abilities, attitudes, and skills, or entering characteristics, of the students are identified, and provision is made for students who do not have the usual expected entering characteristics. Fourth, alternative strategies of instruction are identified and appropriate materials and procedures are selected. This fourth step involves another use of Gagne's taxonomy in that the materials and media are selected on the basis that they most closely can provide the stimulus and response conditions necessary for the respective learning types. Fifth, first-draft materials are developed and are tried out with representative students. Then begins a continuing cycle of modification and further tryouts with students until it is evident that the students are able to attain the educational goals as a result of using the instructional materials and procedures.

Two examples will be selected to illustrate Briggs's use of Gagne's taxonomy. First, we will briefly describe how the taxonomy is used to analyze instructional objectives; second, we will illustrate how it is used to select educational media.

Briggs contends that both the major objectives and the subordinate components of each major objective should be submitted to an analysis based on Gagne's taxonomy. In both cases, he holds that the results of the analysis provide suggestions as to the appropriate sequencing and structure of instruction. "In this form of structure, sequencing implies that transfer of training occurs from the bottom to the top of the hierarchy in an upward direction; i.e., the learning of units placed early in the course facilitates learning of later units" (1970, p. 73). While he acknowledges that learning may actually occur if such sequences are not followed, he asserts that, on the average, more efficient uses of instructional procedures will be made if sequences are based on the hierarchical arrangements.

Thus, similar steps are followed in organizing the separate, more major units to be covered and in identifying the component competencies for each of the major objectives. This consists of several steps, including analyzing the objectives and subordinate components in terms of the one or more learning types they represent; indicating them in terms of their relationships as to higher or lower levels of learning; delineating those components which are to be learned as distinguished from those which the learner is expected to possess when starting the educational program; and identifying the kinds of learning conditions and instructional procedures which are implied by the respective learning types.

He seems particularly concerned with the implications for sequencing the instructional experiences, suggesting that in some instances a form of "spiral sequencing" may be necessary. This involves developing the basic skills by recycling through instructional sequences, further developing each skill in the respective cycles rather than completing that learning before going on to the next skill. Throughout his current *Handbook*, Briggs generally places greater emphasis on these sequencing aspects than he does on the other conditions of learning, although he does focus on stimulus and feedback conditions particularly in his description of procedures for selecting media.

Selecting media seems to be a more central concern to Briggs than it is to most other instructional technologists and theorists. He uses Gagne's taxonomy extensively as a basis for selecting media, frequently ending up with several rather than one form of media to be used for each objective. "In the present model, media are selected for each instructional event for each competency of each objective" (Briggs, 1970, p. 113). He points out that he is trying to find the most effective combination of media for instruction, rather than either relying exclusively on one medium or trying to see how many different media can be used. "Media are deliberately and carefully chosen to comprise a certain strategy of instruction, and materials are carefully developed (programmed) for each medium chosen in order to supply the *instructional events* needed to implement the instructional strategy" (1970, p. vii).

Some of his recommendations will illustrate how Briggs uses Gagne's taxonomy in the selection of media and also will show the major role which he assigns to media selection as a means for creating appropriate instructional conditions. He suggests that the designer should think of "the *kind* of stimulus necessary to produce" (p. 98) the particular learning conditions required for the respective learning types. He suggests that these might involve statements, concrete objects, social stimuli (such as through group discussions), pictures or movies, etc. "*Then* select a medium which has the right characteristics for presenting the desired kind of stimuli" (p. 98). He implies that a great deal of judgment is necessary in taking account of all aspects of the educational situation, but he contends that the systematic analysis is made possible by Gagne's taxonomy.

As an educational example, he notes that the concepts "triangle" and "idealism" require the same general instructional conditions since they both involve type 6 concept learning. However, some judgment is required by the designer because, in fact, quite different considerations are needed as to the specific stimuli which are to be presented. Although both require presentations of different examples of the concept, the concept "triangle" most likely will require presentations of concrete objects or pictures, whereas it may be more effective to present verbal examples to illustrate the concept "idealism." As a result, the media selection would be quite different even though both involve the same type of learning.

He goes on to note that similar complications arise even when the two specific examples come from the same course or subject matter area. "In psychology, for example, two needed concepts are 'brightness' and 'reinforcement.' Different media would be used to provide the right stimuli to present a *variety of examples* of these two *concepts*" (1970, p. 100).

CRITIQUE: CURRENT STATUS AND FUTURE PROSPECTS OF TASK ANALYSIS INSTRUCTIONAL THEORIES

Task analysis instructional theorists propose that many diverse learning theories and areas of research can contribute to the development of instructional theory. They advocate the use of task analyses and taxonomies to identify the different types of learning embodied in educational objectives and programs. They contend that, once such classifications have been accomplished, the necessary learning conditions and instructional procedures will be evident from the learning types. A number of such taxonomies have been proposed, of which Gagne's is one of the best known. Briggs has taken Gagne's task analyses and taxonomy and has developed systems-based procedures for designing instruction.

Using Gagne's and Briggs's approaches, what can be said about the current status and future prospects of task analysis instructional theories, and of their contributions to instructional theory more generally? Gagne provides a rather elaborate and comprehensive system for delineating objectives and identifying necessary instructional conditions. For the most part, the recommended procedures are derived from and are rather closely related to psychological learning paradigms. Thus there seems to be a reasonably sound empirical base from which the principles have been derived. But therein lies a problem, too.

One concern to some psychologists and educators is that the taxonomy which is based on psychological processes may be overly biased toward those learning aspects which have been studied by psychologists. Some are concerned that the taxonomy, therefore, may not adequately deal with the kinds of learning changes which are of greatest concern to educators. Both Gagne and Briggs seem reasonably aware of such potential problems, and they feel that they have chosen their approach quite carefully. Quite correctly, they point out that there will be problems with practically any taxonomy one chooses, a view which Melton and others share.

One matter should be mentioned concerning the kinds of theories which they select. Most task analysis proponents seem to be partial to behavioral theories over cognitive theories whenever a choice is to be made. Gagne and Briggs similarly follow this pattern. They do show great interest in concept formation, problem solving, creativity, and other complex cognitive processes. However, the basic structure of their theory is behavioral in orientation, as is illustrated by their consistent reference to stimuli and responses when they discuss practically all types of learning. Information-processing theorists, for example, would work from a different framework even when dealing with simpler types of learning.

One of the curious and favorable things about their theory is that they cover a wide range of educational objectives and processes but they do provide quite explicit statements about those aspects with which their theory does not directly deal. Of the many instructional theories reviewed by the author (including many not even mentioned in the present text), this is one of the few instances where proponents rather carefully give explicit descriptions of the educational processes with which their theory does *not* deal.

But despite an elaborate description of psychologically based principles and procedures for instructional principles and procedures, we do not find a formal statement of an instructional theory. In a sense, it seems more accurate to call it an elaborate and rather sound framework for developing such a theory. Many of the essentials are there, and perhaps considerable detail is implied. But the present offerings seem more like sound working guidelines than they resemble a formal theory.

As for the ASCD criteria, there exists an elaborate and quite comprehensive framework and set of guidelines, but there does not now exist a formal theory as called for in criterion I. It seems that the lack lies not so much in operational statements, for the proponents stay quite close to their data and their operational definitions. Rather, the present need is for more elaboration at the general, conceptual level of the theory presentation.

Concerning criterion II, both Gagne and Briggs provide quite explicit statements about the boundaries of central concern with regard to subject matter and educational processes. By omission of qualifying statements to the contrary, they seem to imply that their approach is applicable to any age group and to any educational level. This broad coverage is further supported by their reference to the need for considering developmental processes, attention, and motivation as other psychological-educational processes which make the student "ready" for learning and instruction. Once one takes into account these and other processes, apparently it is expected that the approach can be widely used.

No particular internal inconsistencies were noted (ASCD criterion III), a somewhat surprising observation when one considers the range allegedly covered by this approach and the eight types of learning. Perhaps conflicts may become apparent if future research and theorizing indicates that some of the learning types are redundant or that they must be further subdivided. At present, internal inconsistency does not seem to be a pressing problem.

With regard to criterion IV, the instructional principles seem to be compatible with existing learning data, but there does not seem to have been a great deal of research conducted on the value of this approach as an instructional theory per se. Literature does suggest that the approach has been used in a variety of situations, especially training situations, and there does seem to be some growing interest in the approach more generally. With the exception of the behavior modification approach, few other instructional theories have as much emphasis on self-corrective evaluative procedures as an integral part of the instructional system itself. In a sense, each use of this approach involves continual assessment of its attainment of the educational goals which have been selected. What is not clear, and may not be readily determined, is whether this approach is necessarily better or worse than other instructional theories.

The task analysis instructional theory seems to provide readily testable hypotheses about instruction and should stimulate empirical tests of its general principles. Thus it seems to meet the other ASCD criteria as to verifiability and predictability, although qualitative rather than quantitative predictions must be expected for the near future term.

Whether one endorses the particular taxonomy and systems approach proposed respectively by Gagne and by Briggs, the task analysis instructional theory contribution to instructional theory more generally may lie in stimulating more systematic approaches to instructional design. Moreover, it may also encourage selection from a wide range of learning research and theory, rather than mere reliance on one specific theory or approach. Finally, it lends support to the growing notion that instructional theories should be tested empirically even though educational practice will always require some intuition and judgment by the instructor.

SUGGESTED READINGS

Bloom, B. S., Hastings, J. T., & Madaus, G. F. *Handbook on formative and summative evaluation of student learning.* New York: McGraw-Hill, 1971.

Bracht, G. H. Experimental factors related to aptitude-treatment interactions. *Review of Educational Research,* 1970, **40,** 627-645.

Briggs, L. J. Sequencing of instruction in relation to hierarchies of competence. *AIR Monograph,* 1968*b,* No. 3.

Briggs, L. J. Handbook of procedures for the design of instruction. *AIR Monograph,* 1970, No. 4.

Briggs, L. J., Campeau, P. L., Gagne, R. M., & May, M. A. *Instructional media: A procedure for the design of multi-media instruction, a critical review of research, and suggestions for future research.* Pittsburgh: American Institutes for Research, 1967.

Gagne, R. M. (Ed.) *Learning and individual differences.* A symposium of the Learning Research and Development Center, University of Pittsburgh. Columbus, Ohio: Charles E. Merrill, 1967.

Gagne, R. M. *The conditions of learning.* New York: Holt, Rinehart, & Winston, 1970.

Gagne, R. M. Some new views of learning and instruction. *Phi Delta Kappan,* 1970*b*, 51, 468–472.

Glaser, R. Individuals and learning: The new aptitudes. *Educational Researcher,* 1972, 1 (6), 5–12.

Kantor, J. R. *The aim and progress of psychology and other sciences.* Chicago: Principia Press, 1971.

Melton, A. W. *Categories of human learning.* New York: Academic Press, 1964.

Mitchell, J. V. Education's challenge to psychology: The prediction of behavior from person-environment interactions. *Review of Educational Research,* 1969, 39, 695–721.

Vale, J. R., & Vale, C. A. Individual differences and general laws in psychology: A reconciliation. *American Psychologist,* 1969, 24, 1093–1108.

17
Humanistic Psychology and Instructional Theory

One final movement within academic psychology and within education should be considered in our survey of instructional theories. This one needs to be considered not because it is derived from learning theory but because it emerged in reaction to established academic psychology learning research and theory. We are referring to a somewhat heterogeneous group of psychologists and educators who have come to be known as *humanistic psychologists.*

There was no central figure whose ideas dominated the emergence of this approach. Rather, this new movement or school in psychology emerged because of a conviction common among several groups that no extant psychological theory was adequately describing the whole, normally functioning human, and because of a general belief that each person has a capacity and a drive to develop his human potential. The theory and research of several persons have been of great influence in the development of humanistic psychology. A list of influential persons would include but not be restricted to persons such as Abraham H. Maslow, Carl R. Rogers, Charlotte Buhler, James F. T. Bugental, Arthur W. Combs, and many others. Partly as a result of these diverse sources, there is no single position which is readily identified as *the* humanistic psychology approach, although certain characteristics can be identified which are common to most proponents of this approach.

We will review the context and the manner in which humanistic psychology emerged as an influential force in academic and applied psychology, and we will identify certain characteristic features of this orientation, especially as it relates to instructional theory. Then we will examine Carl Rogers's conception of education in which the instructor attempts to arrange conditions so that students will be free to learn and to develop themselves intellectually and emotionally. Finally, we will consider the status of this approach as an instructional theory and we will identify some of the probable influences on learning theory–derived instructional theories.

EMERGENCE OF HUMANISTIC PSYCHOLOGY

Throughout this century some psychologists have felt that academic psychology and applied psychology have not dealt adequately with man's abilities to think, experience feelings, make decisions, and generally determine his fate. They have contended that academic psychology has been so overly concerned with "rigorous" research methodology, especially *experimental* research methodology, that psychologists may have been screening out the very process and substance of man qua man. The policy of basing psychological learning principles on studies of rats, monkeys, pigeons, and other animals has drawn special criticism. Psychoanalysis, which has emphasized the need for studying the "whole" person and which has favored human case-study methods rather than experimental procedures, has been criticized because some of its principles allegedly tend to characterize man in "mechanistic" terms and because its fundamental notions have been derived from studies of emotionally disturbed rather than emotionally healthy persons. Even some of the more recently emerging cognitive conceptions have been attacked because they rely too much on the computer as a model of man's thinking and thus *allegedly* connote a depersonalized conception of man. In the 1960s humanistic psychology emerged as a movement and a school which was proposed as a more *genuine science of man*. Because criticisms were focused especially on neobehavioristic learning theory and psychoanalysis, its promoters have frequently depicted it as a "third force" in psychology.

Some observations about its emergence and the sources from which its concepts were drawn will illustrate both the recency and the multifaceted character of its orientation. Charlotte Buhler (1971), in her 1970 address as first president of the International Invitational Conference on Humanistic Psychology, notes that humanistic psychology has deep roots and origins in Western *philosophical* thinking but that it really has emerged as a potent force in *psychology* only within the past few decades. For example, she cites the relevance of concepts from earlier European existential philosophy and the contributions of several psychotherapy theories.

James F. T. Bugental was elected as first president of the American Association for Humanistic Psychology when it was formed in 1962. He later published a book outlining some of the *Challenges of Humanistic Psychology* (1967). In it he identified the goal of humanistic psychology as "the preparation of a complete description of what it means to be alive as a human being" (p. 7). He went on to indicate that a truly relevant and valid psychology must deal with man's feelings and views about experiences as well as his behavior in any given situation. Such common-sense concepts as love, fear, happiness, humor, choice, beliefs, trust, values, etc., must be incorporated in psychological theory.

The basic notions of humanistic psychology have been drawn mainly from those who have focused on personality theory and clinical psychology theory (especially those concerned with psychotherapeutic techniques for aiding relatively normal persons to develop their human potential). Many cite Abraham H. Maslow as the founder of humanistic psychology at mid-century and they identify his book, *Toward a Psychology of Being* (1962), as one of the key writings. But Maslow's ideas have not dominated humanistic psychology conceptions. The works of many other authors have been greatly influential. Although Sigmund Freud's views can be said to have had some indirect influence, more directly relevant principles and concepts have been presented by such persons as Carl Rogers, Gordon W. Allport, Arthur Combs, Charlotte Buhler, James F. T. Bugental, Karen Horney, Kurt Goldstein, Rollo May, Erich Fromm, Clark Moustakas, and others.

There are certain characteristics which are dominant in the humanistic psychology tradition, although there are considerable differences of opinion among proponents of this position. They especially emphasize that psychology should deal with the *whole person* rather than with some kind of fragmented, reductionistic analysis of all the sub-aspects of man. They are concerned with describing activities from the viewpoint of the person rather than from that of an observer. The humanistic psychologists contend that most other psychologists take a "third-person" point of view in looking at man, whereas they feel that the real way for studying psychology is through the "eye" of the person himself; that is, from a "first-person" point of view. They are especially concerned about "self-actualization," "self-fulfillment," or "self-realization." There is a concern with the growth of the person in whatever direction that person chooses or values. Buhler (1971) has acknowledged that there are many different opinions within the movement but that certain common features can be identified. For example, "all humanistic psychologists see the goal of life as using your life to accomplish something you believe in, be it self-development or other values. From this they expect a fulfillment towards which people determine themselves" (p. 381). Thus, *self-understanding* to better make choices about one's own directions for growth and *creativity* as a means of *fulfillment* are central concepts in the humanistic psychology position.

There is a basic assumption that, in any situation, a person's acts depend upon how he perceives a situation from his own personal viewpoint. Humanistic psychologists are particularly concerned with the way that an individual views himself and the values which one prefers in directing and developing oneself. They do not view with favor any plans for having society determine conceptions of man's ultimate nature. Instead, they emphasize the importance of trusting man individually to have the capacity and the initiative to grow, to "become," and to fulfill himself in such a way as to contribute to society rather than to threaten societal standards. Thus there is a frankly positive expectation of the results which will occur when man is permitted and encouraged to develop his human capacities.

In an extreme and distorted description of the humanistic psychology approach—a distortion which has been popularized in recent years by many fringe groups in society—there is a tendency to extend this self-realization to a "do-your-own-thing" theme. In this latter, distorted view of humanistic psychology, there is a very great emphasis placed on self-gratification. Quite to the contrary, humanistic psychology was based on the assumption that the wholly functioning, self-actualizing individual would be a contributor rather than a parasite in society.

HUMANISTIC PSYCHOLOGY AND EDUCATIONAL IMPLICATIONS

Various humanistic psychologists have explored educational implications which can be derived from their point of view. Despite some variations, practically all endorse the notion that we act as we do because of the ways in which we perceive ourselves and the various situations in which we find ourselves. Such a psychology theory orientation is generally described as "existential," "perceptual," "interactional," "phenomenological," or by some similar term. Four basic features are commonly found:

1. Behaving and learning are products of perceiving.
2. Behavior exists in and can, therefore, be dealt with in the present.
3. All people everywhere have a basic drive toward health and actualization.
4. Much of a person's behavior is the result of his conception of himself (Combs, 1962, p. 67).

Maslow (1968) has depicted the humanistic conception of education as being so different from conventional notions that it demands a change in direction rather than a mere improvement over our present educational practices. He claims that humanistic psychology provides a new philosophy of psychology and of education which is capable of, and which requires, fundamental changes in our conception of education.

He characterizes educational practices found in the typical classroom and those newer practices derived from psychology learning theory as grossly inadequate and inappropriate for today's students and society. He contends that such practices merely bring about surface, superficial learnings for students—if, indeed, they are at all successful in influencing students—and that they do not begin to develop the "higher nature of man" which can be found in all persons.

True learning, according to many humanistic psychologists, involves and pervades the total person rather than merely providing him with facts to be memorized or motions to be executed. True learning experiences enable the learner both to discover his own unique or "idiosyncratic" qualities and to find in himself those features of loving, caring, experiencing, and thinking which make him one with all mankind. Learning in this sense is becoming, and becoming (learning how to be) fully human is the only true learning.

Acknowledging the central role that schools have in our society, the humanistic psychologists claim that educators have the major responsibility of helping students to become more fully developed persons. Useful learning is that which pervades the whole person and which is relevant to one's personal style, needs, and human development. Although they acknowledge that intense personal experiences (such as Maslow's "peak experiences") occur only infrequently for the most self-actualizing persons and rarely if at all for most people, humanistic psychologists contend that education should foster rather than stifle one's sensitivity to one's feelings and to the feelings of others. They recognize the importance of facts and current knowledge. However, they contend that it is far more important for the student to learn how to find new knowledge and to cope with a changing world than it is to merely absorb that information which we have about the world of today and yesterday.

In this context, the roles of both students and teachers are markedly different from those in traditional classrooms and quite different from each of the learning theory–related instructional theories which we considered in previous chapters, including even the cognitive construct theories. The student is seen as having a very active role throughout the educational process, including decisions about what is to be learned as well as how and when it is to be studied. The teacher is characterized as a facilitator who tries to help provide a climate in which the student can feel free to develop emotionally as well as intellectually and motorically. Downgraded are the most usual notions of the teacher as a repository of information and an authority who is to guide the student. Especially in the evaluation process are marked changes advocated, since the student is to be a major evaluator of the merits of different educational directions and of the rates of his progress. And pervasive throughout is the notion that education must involve the student as a whole person, that all forms of academic and personal reductionism should be avoided.

As you can recognize from these few brief comments, the humanistic psychologists take exception to many of the principles and procedures advocated by those preceding instructional theorists who derived their notions from academic psychology learning theory. Not only have the humanists questioned the methods of instruction, but they have also raised issues as to who should set educational goals for the student, whose values should be considered in identifying desired educational directions and in evaluating progress, and what criteria should be used to assess the personal and societal relevance of education in general.

With this framework, one's approach to education and to the design of instruction is quite different from any of the foregoing instructional theories. Here the focus is on creating the kind of emotional and intellectual climate in which the student can grow intellectually and affectively. One must communicate acceptance of the student as a person and must try to understand him as a unique individual. Questions to be answered would include:

What is his style, what are his aptitudes, what is he good for, not good for, what can we build upon, what are his good raw materials, his good potentialities? (Maslow, 1968, p. 693)

Beyond the accumulation of facts, skills, knowledge, and even learning how to cope with life's changing demands lies a higher educational objective which is on a par with man's uniquely human qualities. It is man as a creative person who knows periods of inspiration and enthusiasm as well as man as a methodical hard worker. Maslow (1968) suggests that we "think of the peak-experience, the experience of awe, mystery, wonder, or of perfect completion, as the goal and reward of learning . . . its end as well as its beginning" (p. 695).

ROGERS'S FREEDOM TO LEARN
INSTRUCTIONAL PRINCIPLES

One humanistic psychologist whose views on education have been frequently sought and rather extensively applied is Carl R. Rogers. If one keeps in mind the fact that humanistic psychology is composed of diverse views, Rogers' position is illustrative of the general orientation of humanistic psychology toward educational practice.

Personal and Professional Background

Carl R. Rogers (1902–) went through a number of changes in personal and professional plans which reflect, and even may have caused, some of his views about psychology and education. With a farm background, one of his early plans led him to enroll in an agriculture program at the University of Wisconsin. But while there, he decided to enter the ministry; thus he changed his undergraduate major to history. After graduation and marriage in 1924, he enrolled at Union Theological Seminary in New York. There he was confronted with a liberal, philosophical approach to religion which contrasted sharply with his own conservative Protestant background. After deep personal thought, he transferred to Teachers College, Columbia University, where he majored in psychology and received his Ph.D. in 1931. Having specialized in guidance and clinical psychology, he took a position as psychologist (later, as director) at the Rochester Child Guidance Center. It was in the 1930s that Rogers began to examine extant practice in clinical psychology much as he would subsequently, in the 1960s, raise questions about educational practice.

One of the key ideas in clinical psychology to which Rogers took exception was the assumption that the therapist or counselor should have the major responsibility in directing sessions with clients. It was reasoned by leaders at that time that since the therapist had extensive professional training and the client was the one with the problems, the therapist should be the one to take charge in the therapy sessions and would best be able to decide what is good for the client. Though there were variations on this basic approach, few before Rogers had questioned whether such is an appropriate arrangement for facilitating changes during psychotherapy. By the late 1930s he was convinced that some new tack was necessary, and in 1942 he published his now well-known book, *Counseling and Psychotherapy*, in which he advocated the use of "nondirective procedures." Since publication of that book there has been some controversy as to the extent to which therapists should ask probing questions, make suggestions, and in general take the initiative in directing the flow of the verbal interaction during psychotherapy. Rogers placed such stress on the avoidance of highly authoritarian psychotherapeutic procedures that adherents to his approach at that time became known as "nondirective therapists."

Conditions for Facilitating
Therapeutic Changes

Rogers later continued to explore potentially more effective ways for helping therapy clients, and he personally was highly instrumental in conducting and stimulating systematic research on the process of therapy. By 1951 he was referring to his approach as *client-centered therapy* (as in Rogers, 1951). He had also begun formulating theory- and research-based principles as to how one can create an emotional climate in which the client can begin to take initiative and to help himself not only to cope with life's demands but to become a more fully functioning person. He has regularly asserted and followed the belief that client-centered therapy practices and theory should be "noted for its growing, changing, developing, quality. It has not been a fixed or rigid school of thought" (1966, p. 183). However, the results of his research and clinical experience led him (1957) to formulate certain conditions which are necessary and sufficient to bring about therapeutic personality change. We will briefly review the conditions which he delineated because they have continued to be identified with his approach to clinical psychology and because they are germane to his instructional principles.

Three general conditions, according to Rogers, are necessary and sufficient to bring about the kind of learning in therapy which is referred to as therapeutic personality change. Rogers theorizes and cites research evidence in support of his theory that it is not the skills or training of the therapist, nor the systematic use of reinforcements, which facilitate change in clients. "Instead, I believe it is the presence of certain *attitudes* in the therapist, which are communicated to, and perceived by, his client, that effect success in psychotherapy" (1966, p. 184). Rogers and his colleagues have delineated three conditions which must be created by the therapist and be perceived by the client—therapist's congruence, unconditional positive regard, and sensitively accurate empathic understanding. Although it is recognized that these three concepts are intertwined, Rogers contends that the first one, *therapist's congruence*, is the most basic of the three.

Therapist's congruence means that the therapist presents himself as an open, consistent, genuine person to his client. "Genuineness in therapy means that the therapist is his actual self during his encounter with his client. Without facade, he openly has the feelings and attitudes that are flowing in him at the moment" (Rogers, 1966, p. 185). Basically, this means that the therapist acts as a human being in the interaction, rather than hiding behind some professional mask or role. While he need not confide in his client all his innermost feelings, he must communicate honestly and openly those feelings which do relate to the client's discussions. This requires that the therapist understand himself, be sensitive to his own feelings, and that he can comfortably acknowledge those feelings—even negative ones—which emerge and persist relevant to the client's discussions.

Unconditional positive regard involves having the therapist communicate "to his client a deep and genuine caring for him as a person with human potentialities, a caring uncontaminated by evaluations of the patient's thoughts, feelings, or behavior" (Rogers, 1966, p. 186). Although it is recognized that the therapist may not condone all acts of the client nor agree with all viewpoints, it is meant that the therapist fully and conditionally accepts the client as a worthwhile person entitled to have independence of ideas and actions.

Sensitively accurate empathic understanding requires that the therapist experience the world and self much as the client does. This means that the therapist must communicate to the client the fact that he understands how the client feels about himself, about the world around him, and about life's problems facing him. This empathic understanding is an essential component of the moment-to-moment interactions during the therapy sessions. It does *not* refer to intellectual insights which the therapist may gain later while going over his notes and reviewing the transactions of a particular session.

Rogers routinely depicts these three conditions as being at the heart of his client-centered approach to therapy. But it is important to add that there is considerable flexibility in the manner or ways by which a therapist can relate to his client during actual sessions. In a sense, the therapist tries to use himself as an influence and essential part of the relationship so that the client can feel comfortable and "free" enough to recognize bases for his present modes of living and to explore alternative ways of thinking, feeling, and acting. It should be noted that many psychotherapists have acknowledged these as *necessary* conditions but that reservations have been expressed as to whether they are *sufficient* virtually to assure personality change (Strupp & Bergin, 1969*a* and 1969*b*). Nonetheless, those who advocate Rogers's position contend that both theory and empirical data support his assertions on the importance of these conditions.

As we now examine Rogers's approach to education, we will find a similar point of view expressed about educational practices. Instead of characterizing the teacher as one who lectures and gives out information, or one who structures the learning situation for reinforcement of correct responses, or even as one who provides conditions which permit discovery and which facilitate *purely cognitive* (that is, not affective) learning experiences, Rogers emphasizes the primary importance of affective experiences and total emotional involvement in the learning process. Such involvement by the student (like the client) comes about when educators help students to experience that kind of emotional climate in the learning situation which permits them to be free to learn. Rogers envisions the procedures and the process of therapy as serving as a model for the procedures and the process of education.

Some Views about Education

Although Rogers had often been asked to present talks to educators and had published a series of papers on educational practice in various edited books and journals, it was not until 1969 that he published his own book outlining his proposals for education. Two comments about the book are noteworthy because they are so consistent with his general approach. First, he made extensive use of his own personal learning experiences in proposing educational practices. Second, he provided illustrations of applications of his views in the first several chapters before he finally (Chapter 7) provided his assumptions and principles for facilitating learning. In a sense he seemed to be providing the reader with ample opportunities to "experience" his methods vicariously before giving an abstract description of his fundamental ideas about education. We will use the contents of his book as the main basis for identifying his conceptions of instruction.

One of the fundamental ideas is that *teaching* does not seem to be an interesting or an important process to Rogers but that the student's learning is tremendously important and interesting. In a paper written in 1952 for a Harvard conference on classroom approaches to influencing behavior he had explained that he had lost his interest in teaching mainly because conventional education seems either to have *no* effects or to have *bad* effects on students. It seemed to him that the only valuable kind of learning was that which involved self-discovery, self-appropriated, self-initiated learning. This prompted him in papers written later to theorize that there are two basic kinds of learning, and to propose that only one type is really appropriate. From these foregoing comments, some readers may mistakenly have gained the impression that Rogers's views are identical with those of the cognitive construct theorists which we considered in a previous chapter. His delineation of these two types of learning will show that to some extent Rogers is almost as sharply critical of *cognitive* discovery learning as he is critical of more behavioristic principles.

The two basic types of learning which Rogers delineates and which are cast at two extremes along a continuum of *personal* meaning are "cognitive learning" (learning from the neck up) and "experiential learning" (gut level learning) (Rogers, 1967, pp. 37-38). By *cognitive learning* he refers to those kinds of associative processes which are typified in practically all traditional psychological learning theories, including some aspects of cognitive theories. This kind of learning requires that the student absorb some body of knowledge; there is some tendency to emphasize rote factual learning, but Rogers even seems to include more complex associative processes and objectives as well. In contrast, Rogers depicts experiential learning as something which is personally meaningful and emotionally as well as cognitively relevant. Experiential learning "has a quality of personal involvement . . . is self-initiated . . . is pervasive . . . is evaluated by the learner . . . (and its) essence is meaning" (1967, p. 38).

He contended that traditional educational programs almost exclusively focus on such cognitive learning and that the more important experiential learning is ignored. In contrast, he argued that the opposite would be more appropriate: humanistic psychology principles support the idea that the only true learning is that which totally involves the student as a person.

Rogers (1969, pp. 221-237) drew from his own personal experiences as well as from his psychotherapy theories to identify guidelines as to what constitutes personal involvement and kinds of experiential learning. The most fundamental idea is that one must be oneself, without apologies and defensiveness, and with sensitivity and congruence. Such learnings occur when we can keep channels of communication open both with our own internal feelings and beliefs and with those of other people whom we encounter. In a sense, one's own experience must be seen as trustworthy and as one's only valid criteria against which we assess life's experiences. What constitutes the kind of interpersonal communication which is characteristic of experiential learning? He characterizes each of the following as types of learnings. It is the sense of knowing that one can hear and understand others, and that they can hear and understand me; for either of these not to happen is frustrating. It is extremely satisfying learning to be real (congruent) in relating to others and in encountering persons who are likewise real. Unleashing freedom in others is almost as rewarding a learning experience as is the sense of personal freedom. A final, rewarding learning is that of accepting and giving love—prizing or loving others, and experiencing the same feelings from them.

Rogers sets for education—as he has for psychotherapy—the goal of enabling students to become fully functioning persons. He takes the above as examples of experiential learnings which occur as students become more fully functioning and self-actualizing. Moreover, he holds that the real challenge of education is to find what it takes to produce whole communities of learners who maintain their curiosity about life—a curiosity found universally in infants and too infrequently in adults—and who thirst for continuing education without any barbs or requirements to prod them. Education for Rogers, and for most humanistic psychologists, must be changed so as to "free curiosity; to permit individuals to go charging off in new directions dictated by their own interests; to unleash the sense of inquiry; to open everything to questioning and exploration; to recognize that everything is in process of change" (Rogers, 1969, p. 105).

Some Assumptions and Principles for
Facilitating Experiential Learning

In a number of different papers Rogers has presented two different sets of assumptions and learning principles, one of which is usually associated with the cognitive learning defined above, the other with the experiential learning which Rogers and the other humanistic psychologists favor. We should note at this point that Rogers thus does not distinguish between selection of educational objectives and selection of instructional methods. Instead, most of his papers suggest that the two are inseparable. We will consider this matter in the final section of this chapter. For now, we will accept Rogers's assumption that certain educational objectives can only be obtained by the methods he describes. We'll consider some of the assumptions he delineates, and then we'll examine instructional principles and methods derived from these assumptions.

First, he contrasts two views as to the motivating forces which lead students to want to learn. He characterizes traditional education and most learning theories as holding that students will not pursue their own learning unless they are *forced* to do so. In contrast, he assumes that all persons have a natural inclination to want to learn. Moreover, he assumes that they will continue their motivation to learn throughout their life unless conditions stifle such a desire. The main idea here is: "Human beings have a natural potentiality for learning" (Rogers, 1969, p. 157).

Second, traditional educational practice is characterized as bearing the assumption that students learn whatever teachers present to them. Thus the real task would be to find economical ways of presenting the most material possible. He argues that students may temporarily memorize such forced learnings but that they will only really learn and retain those things which are personally relevant for them.

Third, instead of focusing on the organization of the subject matter, the real concern should be with those experiences which make it possible for the student to integrate the new information and ideas as part of himself. Rogers assumes that one should avoid those experiences which call for drastic changes in one's self-perceptions and that *any* changes in self-structure can come about in an emotionally supportive climate when external threats seem to be at a minimum (1969, p. 159).

Fourth, he criticizes the allegedly common assumption that the main truths about the world are already known and that education thus consists of accumulating "brick upon brick of factual knowledge" (1967, p. 40). In place of this allegedly fallacious assumption, he assumes that the "most socially useful learning in the modern world is the learning of the process of learning, a continuing openness to experience and incorporation into oneself of the process of change" (1969, p. 163).

Fifth, he questions the assumption that learning should be a passive process, an assumption which he contends pervades both traditional lecturing and other recently emerging procedures which put the instructor in the role of dispensing information and providing reinforcements. Rogers assumes that learning optimally occurs "when the student participates responsibly in the learning process" (1967, p. 42).

Sixth, he expresses considerable alarm at traditional as well as contemporary emphases on evaluation, particularly when the evaluations are conducted by the instructor. He assumes that experiential learning will be facilitated and creative learning will result "when self-criticism and self-evaluation are primary, and evaluation by others is of secondary importance" (1967, p. 43).

Finally, throughout his writings runs the assumption that experiential learning as an educational objective can be attained only to the extent that the student is involved in the learning experience. Further, it is assumed that meaningful involvement requires that the student must participate as a major decision maker throughout the educational process.

Given these assumptions about the nature and the importance of experiential learning, Rogers contends that the teacher-role is greatly overestimated and advocates instead that emphasis be placed on the facilitation of learning. Thus his principles of instruction mainly consist of statements about how one can create an emotional and intellectual climate so as to facilitate experiential learning. Moreover, they are derived from psychotherapy theory and research rather than from extensive studies on the instructional process. However, as we will see later, these principles have been adopted in various educational situations ranging from preschool through undergraduate and graduate studies. Not too surprisingly, they contain many of the same suggestions which were earlier provided for conducting therapy sessions.

Several guidelines are provided through practical examples in several chapters. He seems to rely on these as descriptions of his "instructional theory" to a greater extent than he does on more formalized enumeration of instructional principles.

He contends that experiential learning can't really take place until the person recognizes some need for that learning. Thus instruction should be scheduled and planned in accordance with the manner in which students will quite likely confront problems in which they will need the respective learnings. Once the student is aware of a problem requiring learning, the major role of the instructor is to create a climate in which the student will feel free and be stimulated to learn.

Before describing what the teacher does to create such a climate, it is important to recognize some of the things which the teacher is *not* to do. He does not determine lesson tasks, specifically require readings, give lectures (unless requested to do so by the student), volunteer criticisms or evaluations (unless requested), give formal examinations, nor assume sole responsibility for assigning grades. In short, he should avoid doing anything which will subvert the student's assumption of responsibility or which makes him unduly dependent on the teacher.

Rogers (1969, pp. 164-166) provides ten guidelines for creating a desirable emotional and intellectual climate. First, the teacher should recognize that he is an important influence in setting the tone for the class; thus it is important that he communicate his trust in the students right from the start. Second, he should stimulate students to articulate their individual and group objectives and should help them to clarify such purposes, recognizing that there may be quite contradictory purposes among group members. Third, he should expect and depend upon individual students to have the motivation to pursue those learnings which are relevant for them. Fourth, he should serve as a resource person who makes available the widest range of learning experiences possible for the objectives selected. Fifth, he should serve as a general resource person for group members. Sixth, he should recognize and accept both the emotional and intellectual messages expressed within the group. Seventh, he should be an active participant member of the group. Eighth, he should be open in expressing his feelings with the group, using himself as a constructive instrument in furthering experiential learning. Ninth, he should attempt to maintain accurate and sensitive empathic understanding of the group members' feelings, especially when strong emotions are expressed. Finally, he must know himself well enough to recognize his limitations as well as his strengths in working with the group.

Examples of Practical Methods

Rogers has identified seven rather practical methods which, in his opinion, can facilitate experiential learning. Some of them are derived more directly from the humanistic conceptions, whereas others are procedures from various sources which can help students to learn. As we move from the basic assumptions to these practical methods, Rogers seems to become more eclectic in his views about instruction. These methods include provision for students' choices in extent of structure, use of contracts, inquiry training, simulation, basic encounter groups, special facilitator-learning groups, and programmed instruction.

Students' Choices in Extent of Structure   Rogers recognizes that students differ in their preferences and in their abilities to respond to different instructional procedures. Thus, he suggests that the instructor give students the option of participating in a "free classroom" experience or in a more traditional, more highly structured approach. In many cases, he suggests, the teacher will be able to handle such diversity because of the extent of responsibility assumed by the majority of the students.

Use of Contracts   Most readers are familiar with "contracts" which are agreed upon between teacher and students, especially those contracts for the work to be covered in one or a few days. In brief, the student and teacher discuss optional study goals and procedures, and they agree as to what is a meaningful unit of work. In some cases these contracts also are tied to academic grades contingent upon the student's completing an agreed-upon amount and quality of work. Rogers recommends this in part to reduce the anxiety of students and teachers who are not accustomed to having students take responsibility in their classes.

Inquiry Training   He recommends the use of inquiry training or discovery learning advocated by cognitive construct theorists. However, he places greater emphasis, compared with that group, on relating inquiry training to personally relevant educational goals. In addition to understanding science as an ongoing enterprise with far more to learn than we now know, he sees inquiry training as a useful way for "learning how to learn."

Simulation   One way of making classroom learning seem more personally relevant is by having some chunk of real-life experiences simulated in the classroom. Simulation techniques have been used for teaching how different political and governmental organizations operate, for showing the economic aspects of business operations, etc. He favors the approach not only because it captures the interest and enthusiasm of students but because it gives much of the responsibility for learning to the students.

Sensitivity Training   Sensitivity training groups or basic encounter groups are primarily designed to help persons learn more about themselves as humans. The learnings include how they feel about themselves and about other people. He characterizes the group as being almost autonomous and having no initially formalized structure until group members evolve their own purposes and working procedures. The object mainly is to help individuals to explore their feelings and to share them with other group members. Rogers reports that they have been used with elementary students as well as adults and that they typically result in increased ability to handle freedom and responsibility.

Facilitator-Learning Groups These essentially are relatively autonomous, student-directed study groups ranging in sizes from seven to ten members. It is a technique which is used with larger classes when it is not otherwise feasible to have extensive student participation in discussions.

Programmed Instruction Given Rogers's strong objections to externally dominated instructional experience, many readers may be surprised to find him advocating the use of programmed instruction. Nonetheless, he does; but he is careful to point out that there are many different ways in which one can use programmed instruction. In brief he envisions a role for those many instances in which the student encounters "gaps in his knowledge, tools which he lacks, information which he needs to meet the problem he is confronting. Here the flexibility of programmed instruction is invaluable" (Rogers, 1969, p. 140). Warning against indiscriminate use of programmed instruction (as a substitute for thinking, for example), he proclaims "that it is one of the most powerful tools which psychology has as yet contributed to the field" (Rogers, 1969, p. 141) when it is used to achieve flexibility in education.

EDUCATIONAL APPLICATIONS

Applications of humanistic psychology approaches to education have been attempted, since the early 1960s, at practically all levels of education on almost every conceivable topic. For example the Association for Supervision and Curriculum Development devoted a series of meetings and the focus of their 1962 yearbook to this orientation. The title of the yearbook indicates both the major characteristics of humanistic psychology and the warm reception expressed by the ASCD—*Perceiving, Behaving, Becoming: A New Focus For Education* (Combs, 1962). Some school systems have established departments or committees on affective curricula (for example, Borton, 1970; Weinstein, 1971; Weinstein & Fantini, 1970). Others have advocated integration of humanistic concerns along with other more traditional educational objectives and methods (for example, Brown, 1971*a* and 1971*b*). One could also cite the numerous "free schools" as being consistent with this approach although not all of them have specifically derived their ideas from humanistic psychology. The range of age levels is illustrated by the proposals which Rogers has made for graduate-level training (Rogers, 1969) down to the many innovations in preschool education which can be traced to humanistic psychology influences (for example, Frost, 1968; Maccoby & Zellner, 1970; Weber, 1970).

Describing specific educational applications of this approach is more difficult than describing those of other instructional theories because many features lie in the interactions among students and with their instructor. To understand an example, one really should visit the educational situation itself as well as read the numerous materials utilized. However, we will try to sketch some features which are found with humanistic psychology applications by summarizing an example which Rogers (1969) presented at the beginning of his book. Rogers contends that the essential features are virtually the same no matter what age group or subject matter is involved, since in all cases the individual needs, values, and interests of students must be taken into account.

A sixth-grade teacher decided to adopt Rogers's approach when she concluded that she wasn't getting anywhere with a particularly difficult group of students and that she'd have little to lose in trying some new approach. She characterized the problem as including discipline problems, lack of interest, and problems with some of the parents. There were thirty-six students, ranging from 82 to 135 in IQ, and they included various emotional and adjustment problems as well as children who were well adjusted.

The teacher attempted the approach on a tryout basis by telling the students that they would attempt a new approach on a one-day experimental basis. They were already familiar with expectations about their sixth-grade program, but she informed them that during this special day they could do what they thought was important. The teacher would be available if needed. Some did nothing, some tried art and other specific projects, while some worked on the projects which they would routinely have studied that day. Others were confused and somewhat distressed about the lack of structure.

At the end of that day the teacher and students discussed their experiences. It is noteworthy that some students had not accomplished anything notable during this first day but that this had also been true when the teacher had tried conventional approaches as well. Moreover, many of the students had expressed such enthusiasm about their new-found freedom to explore and learn what they felt was important that they had invested more energy and time in their work than had been characteristic previously. There was sufficient enthusiasm that they decided (both students and teacher) to try two more days before evaluating their experiences again.

At this point, the teacher instituted a contract system with each student. She gave them a listing of the usual class subjects and suggestions as to how they individually would study each. The sheets provided for them to choose what they wanted to do and for a record of projects which they had completed. A meeting was held with each child to discuss his plans, and the teacher was available for additional conferences with individuals or with small informal groups as they were needed. Time for such conferences was now available because the students were taking much of the responsibility for their own instruction and they only needed help for occasional problems. The teacher also used her time to find and to provide additional resource materials which the students could use in their studies.

The teacher subsequently extended the program for the rest of the term and expanded on the provisions for giving more responsibilities to students for planning, implementing, and evaluating their own educational progress. When it became apparent quite early that some students could not easily tolerate such new-found freedom, she instituted a teacher-led group with the provision that students could later re-enter the "free" learning experiences. The teacher continued to serve as a resource person and to do many of the things she would ordinarily have done with regard to planning different ways of studying each topic. However, instead of having the teacher decide when and how to study different units, the students now had the major responsibility for such decisions.

Here are some descriptions of typical daily activities. Note the similarities between this approach and that of Keller described earlier in the behavior modification chapter. During informal sessions, the students individually planned their work contract for that day, sometimes on an individual basis, sometimes working in small groups. Moreover, there was constant changing of the membership of the groups, so that students worked with different peers, all on a voluntary, student-initiated basis. Once the day's plans were made, the students began their work. Although the class did have to meet requirements of the state-devised curriculum time schedule, they did have choices with regard to daily and weekly uses of their time. Where appropriate, the teacher pointed out the sequential and cumulative nature of certain subjects (for example, mathematics) and made recommendations for the students to consider as to study sequences. A major part of the experience was that students had the responsibility for scheduling evaluations and for determining when they had mastered subject matter to a sufficient level.

There were days of stress as well as of ecstasy—days when the teacher wondered whether she should have started the project in the first place, and days when she wondered how she could ever have taught any other way. She acknowledged that it had been somewhat threatening for her to relinquish her control over the group and to risk having students assume responsibilities. But she suggested that this did not constitute an "either/or" proposition, that there were ways by which one could gradually adopt such "freedom to learn" principles.

It is noteworthy that discipline problems diminished sharply and that some of the more difficult students not only showed as much educational progress as previously but even became greatly involved in their studies. Overall, the results were so satisfactory that the principal and the other teachers were able to note changes in the students even outside the classroom situation. Moreover, despite the fact that this sixth-grade teacher had had reservations about the method initially, she later changed her procedures almost entirely to a student-centered, Rogerian approach and she began conducting workshops for other teachers to try out similar ideas.

CRITIQUE: CURRENT STATUS
AND FUTURE PROSPECTS

At the present time humanistic psychology seems to have provided more of a philosophical position and a general orientation than it has any formalized instructional theory. Most of the statements provided are admirable but somewhat vague when it comes to attainment of usual educational objectives. Even when one takes into account the preferences for open-ended statements and freedom for students in choosing goals, it is sometimes difficult to see how one might use scientific methods to assess the merits of this approach. Some humanistic psychologists have provided more concrete presentations of their ideas and have given more specific indications of their educational objectives and methods. Carl Rogers's position is exemplary in this group which has tried to articulate their ideas. But even with Rogers's conception of instruction, at least in its present form, many philosophically based rather than empirically tested assertions are presented (for example, see Brown & Tedeschi, 1972). It is noteworthy that as one moves from his philosophical assumptions through his "instructional principles" to his practical methods he seems to become more and more eclectic in his recommendations. Instead of a weakness, this may constitute a strength in his approach since it facilitates use by educators who may choose some of his ideas as well as those who endorse his position in toto.

As you should recognize from the foregoing comments, the humanistic psychologists have taken exception to many of the principles advocated by instructional theorists who have some direct affiliation with psychology learning research and theory, such as the representative theorists we have considered in the four previous chapters. Not only have they raised questions about the *methods* of instruction advocated by these instructional theorists, but they have also raised questions as to who should set goals for the individual and who should determine educational objectives, and have emphasized the need for examining value systems and the relevance of education for society as a whole.

With regard to ASCD criterion I, Rogers has not provided a set of postulates which are formally organized, with critical terms operationally defined. Instead, he has elaborated on the major features of the humanistic psychology approach to education, and he has provided some guidelines as well as specific methods for educators to follow. By virtue of their concern with the *whole* person, many of the basic terms do not readily lend themselves to operational definition. For example, it is difficult—but not impossible—to determine whether a student is a fully functioning person.

One matter of concern is the extent to which educational objectives are associated with specific instructional methods. You may recall that a similar situation prevailed with regard to discovery learning in the cognitive construct position. In the present approach, this seems to be a general problem. There is a tendency to make the assumption, for example, that only by feeling free in the learning situation will a student later be free and creative in the real-life transfer situation. This is a plausible thesis but it should be submitted to empirical test.

Second, proponents of this approach—like all the others—hold that their theory is unlimited in the range of students and subject matter to which it is applicable. The only qualifying comments lie in Rogers's methodology recommendations where he suggests that other techniques—such as programmed instruction—are useful. But even in this suggestion he stresses the need for permitting students to be free to learn, so that the programmed materials are used only when the student recognizes some problem and feels that certain content or skills should be learned. Thus even when he uses methods derived from other theories, Rogers maintains the integrity of his approach in his incorporation of such methods.

Third, as for the internal consistency of Rogers's approach, ASCD criterion III, his idea that students should be free to learn is pervasive in all of his writings and recommendations. It may be that inconsistencies will become evident when more formal principles are drawn, but none is clearly evident at this stage.

Fourth, there are a number of problems with regard to empirical data. Rogers has been as responsible as any other single person for stimulating research on psychotherapy methods, so it is likely that he will encourage his colleagues to conduct extensive studies on his instructional procedures as well. But at the present time there is some hesitation on the part of humanistic psychologists to collect empirical data *testing* their approach because they are so completely convinced that their methods work. Moreover, their broad-based objectives do not as readily lend themselves to scrutiny as do, for example, the more narrowly defined behavior modification goals. The methods as they are now described seem to be consistent with available empirical evidence, especially with those data drawn from psychotherapy situations. However, it would be worthwhile keeping in mind the fact that many non-Rogerian psychotherapists accept his principles as being necessary to facilitate therapy changes but they question whether the principles are *sufficient* alone to bring about such changes. A similar state is developing in education: Some feel that the points Rogers makes are appropriate but they question whether creating an appropriate emotional and intellectual climate is *sufficient* to bring about desired educational changes. Available empirical data do not permit clear answers at this time.

In particular, some are willing to accept the idea that a person may be "expert" about his own needs, feelings, beliefs, etc., with regard to psychotherapy situations. Thus they accept Rogers's contention that the client rather the therapist should have the major responsibility in the psychotherapy relationship. However, many question whether the student can similarly be "expert" about educational objectives to the extent that he can know better than professional educators what would be worthwhile for him to learn. This seems to be one center of controversy around which much more empirical evidence will be required before more than speculative answers can be provided.

With regard to the other ASCD criteria, Rogers's approach compares favorably with other instructional theories. At times the task may be difficult but his approach to instruction is capable of generating hypotheses which can be submitted to empirical tests. Moreover, the guidelines provide rather clear statements about what one should expect students to do under the conditions outlined.

It seems likely that the major contribution of Rogers's approach, and of humanistic psychology more generally, will be as corrective factors to learning theory-based instructional theories. His approach may even serve as a means for drawing eclectic principles, since he has already moved in that direction with the presentation of his practical methods. The main influence lies in the focus on interpersonal relationships and on the importance of the students' expectations and contributions to their own learning experiences. Certainly his concern with man's unique qualities may serve to broaden the conception of educational objectives even out into the realms of self-fulfillment and self-actualization—beyond mere mastery of minimum basic skills needed for mundane survival. Perhaps incorporation of his ideas along with those of the other instructional theories will enable us to have a more systematic approach for the improvement of educational practice without losing sight of man's "higher nature."

SUGGESTED READINGS

Borton, T. *Reach, touch and teach; student concerns and process education.* New York: McGraw-Hill, 1970.

Bugental, J. F. T. The challenge that is man. *Journal of Humanistic Psychology*, 1967*a*, **7**(1), 1-9.

Bugental, J. F. T. *Challenges of humanistic psychology.* New York: McGraw-Hill, 1967*b*.

Buhler, C. Humanistic psychology as an educational program. *American Psychologist*, 1969, 24(8), 736-742.

Buhler, C. Basic theoretical concepts of humanistic psychology. *American Psychologist*, 1971, **26**, 378-386.

Kahn, T. C. *An introduction to hominology: The study of the whole man.* Springfield, Ill.: Charles C Thomas, 1970.

Kahn, T. C. Hominology instead of humanistic psychology. *American Psychologist*, 1971, **26**, 1162.

Littleford, M. Some philosophical assumptions of humanistic psychology. *Educational Theory*, 1970, **20**, 229-244.

Rogers, C. R. *On becoming a person.* Boston: Houghton Mifflin Co., 1961.

Rogers, C. R. *Freedom to learn.* Columbus, Ohio: Charles E. Merrill, 1969.

Rogers, C. R. Can schools grow persons. *Educational Leadership*, 1971, **29**, 215-217.

Rogers, C. R. Forget you are a teacher. *Instructor*, 1971, **81**, 65-66.

Rogers, C. R., & Skinner, B. F. Some issues concerning the control of human behavior. *Science*, 1956, **124**, 1057-1065.

Weinstein, G., & Fantini, M. *Toward humanistic education: A curriculum of affect.* New York: Praeger Press, 1970.

References

Alpren, M. (Ed.) *The subject curriculum: Grades K-12.* Columbus, Ohio: Charles E. Merrill, 1967.

Anderson, G. L. What the psychology of learning has to contribute to the education of the teacher. *Journal of Educational Psychology,* 1950, **41**(6), 362-365.

Atkin, J. M. Basing curriculum change on research and demonstration. *Educational Forum,* 1966, **31**, 27-33.

Atkinson, R. C. Ingredients for a theory of instruction. *American Psychologist,* 1972, **27**, 921-931.

————, Bower, G. H., & Crothers, C. J. *An introduction to mathematical learning theory.* New York: Wiley, 1965.

Attneave, F. *Applications of information theory to psychology.* New York: Holt, Rinehart, & Winston, 1959.

Ausubel, D. P. A cognitive-structure theory of school learning. In L. Siegel (Ed.), *Instruction: Some contemporary viewpoints.* San Francisco: Chandler, 1967. Pp. 207-257.

————. *Educational psychology: A cognitive view.* New York: Holt, Rinehart, & Winston, 1968.

————, & Robinson, F. G. *School learning: An introduction to educational psychology.* New York: Holt, Rinehart, & Winston, 1969.

Azrin, N. H., & Holz, W. C. Punishment. In W. K. Honig (Ed.), *Operant behavior: Areas of research and application.* New York: Appleton-Century-Crofts, 1966. Pp. 380-447.

Babkin, B. P. *Pavlov: A biography.* Chicago: University of Chicago Press, 1949.

Baer, D. M. Let's take another look at punishment. *Psychology Today,* 1971, **5**(5), 32-37 and 111.

————, Wolf, M. M., & Risley, T. R. Some current dimensions of applied behavior analysis. *Journal of Applied Behavior Analysis,* 1968, **1**, 91-97.

Baker, R. L., & Schutz, R. E. (Eds.) *Instructional product development.* New York: Van Nostrand Reinhold Co., 1971.

Bandura, A. *Principles of behavior modification.* New York: Holt, Rinehart, & Winston, 1969.

Barrett, B. H., & Lindsley, O. R. Deficits in acquisition of operant discrimination and differentiation shown by institutionalized retarded children. *American Journal of Mental Deficiency,* 1962, **67**, 424-436.

Bartlett, F. C. *Remembering.* Cambridge, England: Cambridge University Press, 1932.

Bates, S., & Bates, D. F. ". . . and a child shall lead them": Stephanie's chart story. *Teaching Exceptional Children,* 1971, **3**, 111-113.

Bayles, E. E. Theories of learning and classroom methods. *Theory into Practice,* 1966, **5**, 71-76.

Beauchamp, G. A. *Curriculum theory.* Wilmette, Ill.: Kegg Press, 1961 (1st ed.), 1968 (2d ed.).

Berelson, B. *Behavioral sciences today.* New York: Basic Books, Inc., 1963.

Berlyne, D. E. Uncertainty and conflict: A point of contact between information-theory and behavior-theory concepts. *Psychological Review,* 1957, **64**, 329-339.

————. Effects of spatial order and inter-item interval on recall of temporal order. *Psychonomic Science,* 1966, **6**(8), 375-376.

Bigge, M. L. *Learning theories for teachers.* New York: Harper & Row, 1964.

Biggs, J. B. *Information and human learning.* North Melbourne, Victoria: Cassell Australia, Ltd., 1968.

Bijou, S. W. What psychology has to offer education now. In P. B. Dews (Ed.), *Festschrift for B. F. Skinner.* New York: Appleton-Century-Crofts, 1970. Pp. 401–407.

————, & Baer, D. M. *Child development.* Vol. 1. *A systematic and empirical theory.* New York: Appleton-Century-Crofts, 1961.

————, & Baer, D. M. *Child development: Readings in experimental analysis.* New York: Appleton-Century-Crofts, 1967.

Bindra, D. A unified account of classical conditioning and operant training. In A. H. Black & W. F. Prokasy (Eds.), *Classical conditioning II: Current research and theory.* New York: Appleton-Century-Crofts, 1972. Pp. 453–481.

Black, A. H., & Prokasy, W. F. (Eds.) *Classical conditioning II: Current theory and research.* New York: Appleton-Century-Crofts, 1972.

Blair, G. M. How learning theory is related to curriculum organization. *Journal of Educational Psychology*, 1948, **39**(3), 161–166.

Bloom, B. S. (Ed.) *Taxonomy of educational objectives: The classification of educational goals. Handbook 1. Cognitive domain.* New York: McKay, 1956.

————, Hastings, J. T., & Madaus, G. F. *Handbook on formative and summative evaluation of student learning.* New York: McGraw-Hill, 1971.

Bolles, R. C. *Theory of motivation.* New York: Harper & Row, 1967.

Borton, T. *Reach, touch and teach; student concerns and process education.* New York: McGraw-Hill, 1970.

Bourne, L. E., Jr., Ekstrand, B. R., & Dominowski, R. L. *The psychology of thinking.* Englewood Cliffs, New Jersey: Prentice-Hall, 1971.

Bowne, B. P. *Introduction to psychological theory.* New York: Harper & Brother, 1887.

Bracht, G. H. Experimental factors related to aptitude-treatment interactions. *Review of Educational Research*, 1970, **40**, 627–645.

Breger, L., & McGaugh, L. L. A critique and reformulation of "learning theory" approaches. *Psychological Bulletin*, 1965, **63**, 338–358.

Breland, K., & Breland, M. The misbehavior of organisms. *American Psychologist*, 1961, **16**, 681–690.

————. *Animal behavior.* New York: Macmillan, 1966.

Briggs, L. J. Instructional media. *American Institutes for Research Monograph.* 1967a, No. 2.

————. Learner variables and educational media. *Review of Educational Research*, 1968a, **38**, 160–176.

————. Sequencing of instruction in relation to hierarchies of competence. *AIR Monograph*, 1968b, No. 3.

————. Handbook of procedures for the design of instruction. *AIR Monograph*, 1970, No. 4.

————, Campeau, P. L., Gagne, R. M., & May, M. A. *Instructional media: A procedure for the design of multi-media instruction, a critical review of research, and suggestions for future research.* Pittsburgh: American Institutes for Research, 1967.

Broskowski, A. Clinical psychology: A research and development model. *Professional Psychology*, 1971, **2**, 235–242.

Brown, G. Human is as confluent does. *Theory into Practice*, 1971a, **10**, 191–195.

————. *Human teaching for human learning: An introduction to confluent education.* New York: Viking Press, 1971b.

Brown, R. C., Jr., & Tedeschi, J. T. Graduate education in psychology: A comment on Rogers' passionate statement. *Journal of Humanistic Psychology*, 1972, **12**, 1–15.

Brownell, W. A. Learning theory and educational practice. *Journal of Educational Research*, 1948, **41**, 481–497.

Bruner, J. S. *The process of education.* New York: Random House, 1960.

————. *The act of discovery. Harvard Education Review*, 1961, **31**, 21–32.

————. *On knowing: Essays for the left hand.* Cambridge, Mass.: The Belknap Press, 1964.

————. *Toward a theory of instruction.* Cambridge, Mass.: The Belknap Press, 1966a.

————. (Ed.) Learning about learning: A conference report. *Cooperative Research Monograph*, 1966b, No. 15.

————. Culture, politics and pedagogy. *Saturday Review*, May 1968, 69–72, 89–90.

————. The process of education revisited. *Phi Delta Kappan*, 1971, **53**, 18–21.

————. *The relevance of education.* New York: W. W. Norton, 1971.

————, Goodnow, J. J., & Austin, G. A. *A study of thinking.* New York: Wiley, 1956.

————, Olver, R. R., Greenfield, P. M., et al. *Studies in cognitive growth.* New York: Wiley, 1966.

Bugelski, B. R. *The psychology of learning applied to teaching.* New York: Bobbs-Merrill, 1964 (1st ed.), 1971 (2d ed.).

Bugental, J. F. T. The challenge that is man. *Journal of Humanistic Psychology*, 1967a, **7**(1), 1–9.

————. *Challenges of humanistic psychology.* New York: McGraw-Hill, 1967b.

Buhler, C. Humanistic psychology as an educational program. *American Psychologist*, 1969, **24**(8), 736–742.

————. Basic theoretical concepts of humanistic psychology. *American Psychologist*, 1971, **26**, 378–386.

Bush, R. R., & Mosteller, F. *Stochastic models for learning.* New York: Wiley, 1955.

Carroll, J. B. Basic and applied research in education: Definitions, distinctions and implications. *Harvard Educational Review*, 1968, **38**, 263–276.

Catania, A. C. Concurrent operants. In W. K. Honig (Ed.), *Operant behavior: Areas of research and application.* New York: Appleton-Century-Crofts, 1966.

Cellura, A. R. The application of psychological theory in educational settings: An overview. *American Educational Research Journal*, 1969, **6**(3), 349–382.

Chapanis, A. The relevance of laboratory studies to practical situations. *Ergonomics*, 1967, **10**, 557–577.

Chapman, J. Early childhood research and development needs, gaps, and imbalances: Overview. Mimeograph paper, 1972.

Chase, F. S. R & D in the remodeling of education. *Phi Delta Kappan*, 1970, **51**, 299–304.

Chein, I., Cook, S. W., & Harding, J. The field of action research. *American Psychologist*, 1948, **3**(2), 43–50.

Cherry, C. The communication of information. *Endeavor*, 1964, **23**(88), 13–17.

Chomsky, N. Review of B. F. Skinner, Verbal behavior and language, *Language*, 1959, **35**, 26–58.

Christoplos, F., & Vallentutti, P. Defining behavior modification. *Educational Technology*, 1969, **9**, 28–30.

Combs, A. W. (Ed.) Perceiving, behaving, becoming. *1962 ASCD yearbook.* Washington, D. C.: Association for Supervision and Curriculum Development, 1962.

Coombs, C. H., Dawes, R. M., & Tversky, A. *Mathematical psychology: An elementary introduction.* New York: Prentice-Hall, 1970.

Corso, J. F. *The experimental psychology of sensory behavior.* New York: Holt, Rinehart, & Winston, 1967.

Craig, R. C. Recent research on discovery. *Educational Leadership*, 1969, **26**, 501–505.

Crane, D. *Invisible colleges: Diffusion of knowledge in scientific communities.* Chicago: University of Chicago Press, 1972.

Crawford, M. P. Military psychology and general psychology. *American Psychologist*, 1970, **25**, 328-336.

Cronbach, L. J. The two disciplines of scientific psychology. *American Psychologist*, 1957, **12**, 671-684.

Cumming, W. W., & Berryman, R. The complex discriminated operant: Studies of matching-to-sample and related problems. In D. I. Mostofsky (Ed.), *Stimulus generalization.* Stanford: Stanford University Press, 1965.

Cuny, H. *Ivan Pavlov: A biography.* New York: Eriksson, 1965.

David, H. Behavioral sciences and the federal government. *American Psychologist*, 1969, **24**, 917-922.

Davison, G. C., Goldfried, M. R., & Krasner, L. A postdoctoral program in behavior modification: Theory and practice. *American Psychologist*, 1970, **25**, 767-772.

Day, W. F. Review of B. F. Skinner, *Beyond freedom and dignity. Contemporary Psychology*, 1972, **17**, 465-469.

Dewey, J. Psychology and social practice. *Psychological Review*, 1900, **7**, 105-124.

_____ . *How we think.* Boston: Heath, 1910.

_____ . *Democracy in education.* New York: Free Press, 1916.

_____ . *The sources of a science of education.* New York: Liveright, 1929.

Dews, P. B. (Ed.) *Festschrift for B. F. Skinner,* New York: Appleton-Century-Crofts, 1970.

DiVesta, F. J. Review of *Education and the black box. Contemporary Psychology*, 1969, **14**(9), 467-468.

Dollard, J. Twenty-five years later: Retrospective comments by members of the original Harvard commission. *American Psychologist*, 1970, **25**, 414-418.

Dow, P. B., et al. *Man: A course of study.* Cambridge, Mass.: Educational Development Center, Inc., 1968.

Drucker, P F. School around the bend. *Psychology Today*, 1972, **6**(1), 49-51, 86-89.

Duncan, A. D. Precision teaching in perspective: An interview with Ogden R. Lindsley. *Teaching Exceptional Children*, 1971, **3**, 114-119.

Eaton, T. H. *An approach to a philosophy of education.* New York: Wiley, 1938.

Engler, D. Instructional technology and the curriculum. *Phi Delta Kappan*, 1970, **51**, 379-381.

English, H. B., & English, A. C. *A comprehensive dictionary of psychological and psychoanalytical terms.* New York: Longmans, Green & Co., 1958.

Estes, W. K. Toward a statistical theory of learning. *Psychological Review*, 1950, **57**, 94-107.

_____ . Growth and function of mathematical models for learning. In R. Glaser (Ed.), *Current trends in psychological theory.* Pittsburgh: University of Pittsburgh Press, 1961. Pp. 134-151.

_____ . *Learning theory and mental development.* New York: Academic Press, 1970.

_____ . Reward in human learning: Theoretical issues and strategic choice points. In R. Glaser (Ed.), *The nature of reinforcement.* New York: Academic Press, 1971. Pp. 16-36.

Falmagne, J. C. Review of H. Rouanet, *Les modeles stochastiques d'apprentissage. Contemporary Psychology*, 1969, **14**, 483-484.

Fargo, G. A., Behrns, C., & Nolen, P. *Behavior modification in the classroom.* Belmont, Calif.: Wadsworth, 1970.

Feigenbaum, E. A. *An information processing theory of verbal learning.* Santa Monica, Calif.: Rand Corp., 1959.

_____ . The simulation of verbal learning behavior. In E. A. Feigenbaum & J.

Feldman (Eds.), *Computers and thought.* New York: McGraw-Hill, 1963, Pp. 329–346.

Ferster, C. B., & Perrott, M. C. *Behavior principles.* New York: Appleton-Century-Crofts, 1968.

———, & Skinner, B. F. *Schedules of reinforcement.* New York: Appleton-Century-Crofts, 1957.

Fitch, S. K. Examining the merits of Connectionism for typewriting. *Journal of Business Education,* 1961, **36**, 236–238; 285–286.

Frick, S. C. Information theory. In S. Koch, *Psychology: A study of a science.* Vol. 2. New York: McGraw-Hill, 1959. Pp. 611–636.

Frost, J. L. (Ed.) *Early childhood education rediscovered: Readings.* New York: Holt, Rinehart, & Winston, 1968.

Gage, N. L. Paradigms for research on teaching. In N. L. Gage (Ed.), *Handbook of research on teaching.* Chicago: Rand McNally, 1963. Pp. 94–141.

Gagne, R. M. Factors in acquiring knowledge of a mathematical task. *Psychological Monographs,* 1962, **76**, No. 7.

———. Military training and principles of learning. *American Psychologist,* 1962, **17**, 83–91.

———. (Ed.) *Learning and individual differences.* Columbus, Ohio: Charles E. Merrill, 1967.

———. *The conditions of learning.* New York: Holt, Rinehart, & Winston, 1970a.

———. Some new views of learning and instruction. *Phi Delta Kappan,* 1970b, **51**, 468–472.

———, & Gephart, W. J. (Eds.) *Learning research and school subjects.* Itasca, Ill.: Peacock, 1968.

———, & Rohwer, W. D., Jr. Instructional psychology. *Annual Review of Psychology,* 1969, **20**, 381–418.

Garner, W. R. *Uncertainty and structure as psychological concepts.* New York: Wiley, 1962.

Garry, R., & Kingsley, H. L. *The nature and conditions of learning* (3d ed.). Englewood Cliffs, New Jersey: Prentice-Hall, 1970.

Getzels, J. W. Educational psychology and teacher training. *Elementary School Journal,* 1952, **52**, 373–382.

Gibson, E. J. *Principles of perceptual learning and development.* New York: Appleton-Century-Crofts, 1969.

Gideonse, H. D. An output-oriented model of research and development and its relationship to educational improvement. In H. J. Klausmeier & G. T. O'Hearn (Eds.), *Research and development toward the improvement of education.* Madison, Wis.: Debar Educational Services, Inc., 1968. Pp. 157–163.

———. (Ed.) *Educational research and development in the United States.* Washington: USOE, HEW, 1969.

Gilbert, E. N. Information theory after 18 years. *Science,* 1966, **152**, 320–326.

Gilbert, T. F. Mathetics: The technology of education. *Journal of Mathetics,* 1962, **1**, 7–73.

Glaser, R. Implications of training research for education. In E. R. Hilgard (Ed.), Theories of learning and instruction. *63rd NSSE yearbook.* Chicago: University of Chicago Press, 1964.

———. Psychological bases for instructional design. *AV Communication Review,* 1966, **14**, 433–449.

———. Variables in discovery learning. In L. S. Shulman & E. R. Keislar (Eds.), *Learning by discovery: A critical appraisal.* Chicago: Rand-McNally, 1966.

———. (Ed.) *The nature of reinforcement.* New York: Academic Press, 1971.

———. Individuals and learning: The new aptitudes. *Educational Researcher,* 1972, **1**(6), 5–12.

———, & Resnick, L. B. Instructional psychology. In P. H. Mussen & M. R. Rosenzweig (Eds.), *Annual review of psychology,* 1972, **23**, 207–276.

Goble, F. G. *The third force: The psychology of Abraham Maslow.* New York: Grossman, 1970.

Goldstein, H., Krantz, D. L., & Rains, J. D. (Eds.) *Controversial issues in learning.* New York: Appleton-Century-Crofts, 1965.

Goodlad, J. I. Curriculum: State of the field. *Review of Educational Research,* 1969, 39(3), 367–375.

Gordon, I. J. (Ed.) *Criteria for theories of instruction.* Washington, D. C.: Association for Supervision and Curriculum Development, 1968.

————. An instructional theory approach to the analysis of selected early childhood programs. In Early childhood education, *71st NSSE yearbook,* 1972, Part 2, Chapter 10.

Green, Bert F., Jr. Introduction: Current trends in problem solving. In B. Kleinmuntz (Ed.), *Problem solving: Research, method and theory.* New York: Wiley, 1966.

Greeno, J. G., & Bjork, R. A. Mathematical learning theory and the new "mental forestry." *Annual Review of Psychology,* 1973, 81–116.

Guetzkow, H. Conversion barriers in using the social sciences. *Administrative Science Quarterly,* 1959, 4, 68–81.

Guilford, J. P. Factorial angles to psychology. *Psychological Review,* 1961, 68, 1–20.

Guthrie, E. R. *The psychology of learning.* New York: Harper & Row, 1935.

————. Conditioning: A theory of learning in terms of stimulus, response and association. In The psychology of learning, *41st NSSE yearbook,* 1942, Part 2, Chapter 1.

Hall, C. S., & Lindzey, G. *Theories of personality.* New York: Wiley, 1957.

Hanley, E. M. Review of research involving applied behavior in the classroom. *Review of Educational Research,* 1970, 40, 597–625.

Hanna, J. F. A new approach to the formulation and testing of learning models. *Synthese,* 1966, 16, 344–380.

Hebb, D. O. *Organization of behavior.* New York: Wiley, 1949.

————. Interviewed by Elizabeth Hall in *Psychology Today,* 1969, 3(6), 20–28.

Heidbreder, E. *Seven psychologies.* New York: Appleton-Century-Crofts, 1933.

Hendry, D. P. *Conditioned reinforcement.* Homewood, Ill.: Dorsey, 1969.

Hermann, G. Learning by discovery: A critical review of studies. *The Journal of Experimental Education,* 1969, 38, 58–72.

Hilgard, E. R. (Ed.) Theories of learning and instruction. *63rd NSSE yearbook.* Chicago: University of Chicago Press, 1964.

————, & Bower, G. H. *Theories of learning* (3d ed.). New York: Appleton-Century-Crofts, 1966.

Hill, W. What can psychology offer education? A review of some recent opinions from psychologists. *Journal of Teacher Education,* 1963, 443–448.

Hitt, W. D. Two models of man. *American Psychologist,* 1969, 24, 651–658.

Homme, L. E. Contiguity theory and contingency management. *Psychological Record,* 1966, 16, 233–241.

Homme, L., Csanyi, A. P., Gonzales, M. A., & Rechs, J. R. *How to use contingency contracting in the classroom.* Champaign, Ill.: Research Press, 1970.

Homme, L., C'de Baca, P., Cottingham, L., & Homme, A. What behavioral engineering is. *Psychological Record,* 1968, 18, 425–434.

Honig, W. K. (Ed.) *Operant behavior: Areas of research and application.* New York: Appleton-Century-Crofts, 1966.

Hull, C. L. Knowledge and purpose as habit mechanisms. *Psychological Review,* 1930, 37, 511–525.

————. The conflicting psychologies of learning—a way out. *Psychological Review,* 1935, 42, 491–516.

————. Conditioning: Outline of a systematic theory of learning. In The psychology of learning, *41st NSSE yearbook*, 1942, Part 2, Chapter 2.

————. *Principles of behavior.* New York: Appleton-Century-Crofts, 1943.

————. Behavior postulates and corollaries—1949. *Psychological Review*, 1950, **57**, 173-180.

————. *Essentials of behavior.* New Haven, Conn.: Yale University Press, 1951.

————. Autobiography. In H. S. Langfeld et al. (Ed.), *A history of psychology in autobiography.* Vol. 4. Worcester, Mass.: Clark University Press, 1952*a*, 143-162.

————. *A behavior system: An introduction to behavior theory concerning the individual organism.* New Haven, Conn.: Yale University Press, 1952*b*.

Hunt, E. Computer simulation: Artificial intelligence studies and their relevance to psychology. *Annual Review of Psychology*, 1968, **19**, 133-168.

Hunt, E. B. What kind of computer is man? *Cognitive Psychology*, 1971, **2**, 57-98.

Hunt, J. McV. Toward a theory of guided learning in development. In R. R. Ojemann (Ed.), *Giving emphasis to guided learning.* Cleveland: Educational Research Council, 1966.

James, W. Talks to teachers on psychology. *Atlantic Monthly*, 1899, **83**, 155-162.

————. *The principles of psychology.* New York: Holt, 1908.

Johnson, E. M. A bibliography on the use of information theory in psychology (1948-1966). *Bibliographic Supplement No. 1.* Aberdeen Proving Ground, Md.: U.S. Army Human Engineering Laboratories, 1967.

Johnston, J. M. Punishment of human behavior. *American Psychologist*, 1972, **27**, 1033-1054.

Joncich, G. M. (Ed.) *Psychology and the science of education: Selected writings of E. L. Thorndike.* New York: Columbia University, 1962.

————. *The sane positivist: A biography of Edward L. Thorndike.* Middletown, Conn.: Wesleyan University Press, 1968.

Kahn, T. C. *An introduction to hominology: The study of the whole man.* Springfield, Ill.: Charles C Thomas, 1970.

————. Hominology instead of humanistic psychology. *American Psychologist*, 1971, **26**, 1162.

Kanfer, F. C., & Phillips, J. S. *Learning foundations of behavior therapy.* New York: Wiley, 1970.

Kantor, J. R. An analysis of the experimental analysis of behavior. *Journal of the Experimental Analysis of Behavior*, 1970, **13**, 101-108.

————. *The aim and progress of psychology and other sciences.* Chicago: Principia Press, 1971.

Keislar, E. R., & Shulman, L. S. The problem of discovery: Conference in retrospect. In L. S. Shulman & E. R. Keislar (Eds.), *Learning by discovery: A critical appraisal.* Chicago: Rand McNally, 1966.

Keller, F. S. *The definition of psychology.* New York: Appleton-Century-Crofts, 1937.

————. Neglected rewards in the educational process. *Proceedings of the American Conference of Academic Deans*, Los Angeles, January 1967.

————. "Good-bye, teacher ..." *Journal of Applied Behavior Analysis*, 1968, **1**, 78-89.

————, & Schoenfeld, W. N. *Principles of psychology.* New York: Appleton-Century-Crofts, 1950.

Kendler, H. H. "What is learned?"—A theoretical blind alley. *Psychological Review*, 1952, **59**, 269-277.

————. Review of B. F. Skinner, *Contingencies of reinforcement: A theoretical analysis. Contemporary Psychology.* 1970, **15**, 529-531.

————, & Spence, J. T. *Essays in Neobehaviorism.* New York: Appleton-Century-Crofts, 1971.

Kimble, G. A. *Hilgard and Marquis' conditioning and learning* (2d ed.). New York: Appleton-Century-Crofts, 1961.

————, & Garmezy, N. *Principles of general psychology* (2d ed.). New York: Ronald Press, 1963.

Kintsch, W. *Learning, memory, and conceptual processes.* New York: Wiley, 1970.

Koch, S. Theoretical psychology, 1950: An overview. *Psychological Review,* 1951, **58,** 147–154.

————. Psychology and emerging conceptions of knowledge as unitary. In T. W. Wann (Ed.), *Behaviorism and phenomenology.* Chicago: University of Chicago Press, 1964.

Korolev, F. F. Main trends of methodological research in the field of pedagogy. *Soviet Education,* 1969, **11**(12), 7–24.

Krasner, L. The operant approach in behavior therapy. In A. E. Bergin & S. L. Garfield (Eds.), *Handbook of psychotherapy and behavior change: An empirical analysis.* New York: Wiley, 1971.

————, & Ullmann, L. (Eds.) *Research in behavior modification.* New York: Holt, Rinehart, & Winston, 1965.

Krutch, J. W. A humanist's approach. *Phi Delta Kappan,* 1970, **51,** 376.

Kumar, V. K. The structure of human memory and some educational implications. *Review of Educational Research,* 1971, **41,** 379–417.

Langhery, K. R., & Gregg, L. W. Simulation of human problem solving behavior. *Psychometrika,* 1962, **27,** 265–282.

Lanyon, R. I. Mental health technology. *American Psychologist,* 1971, **26,** 1071–1076.

————, & Broskowski, A. T. An engineering model for clinical psychology. *Clinical Psychologist,* 1969, **22,** 140–141.

Lavisky, S. Training research for the Army. *Phi Delta Kappan,* 1967, **48,** 443–445.

Lawrence, G. D. Bruner—Instructional theory or curriculum theory? *Theory into Practice,* 1969, **8,** 18–24.

Leonard, W. P. Review of books that practice what they preach. *AV Communication Review,* 1971, **19**(4), 454–460.

Levine, G., & Burke, C. J. *Mathematical model techniques for learning theories.* New York: Academic Press, 1972.

Lindgren, H. C. Learning theory and teaching practice. *Educational Leadership,* 1959, **16,** 333–336.

Lindsley, O. R. Characteristics of the behavior of chronic psychotics as revealed by free-operant conditioning methods. Diseases of the nervous system (*Monograph Supplement*), 1960, **21,** 66–78. No. 2.

Lipe, D., & Jung, S. M. Manipulating incentives to enhance school learning. *Review of Educational Research,* 1971, **41,** 249–280.

Littleford, M. Some philosophical assumptions of humanistic psychology. *Educational Theory,* 1970, **20,** 229–244.

Logan, F. A. The Hull-Spence approach. In S. Koch (Ed.), *Psychology: A study of a science.* Vol. 2. New York: McGraw-Hill, 1959. Pp. 293–358.

————. Incentive theory, reinforcement and education. In R. Glaser (Ed.), *The nature of reinforcement.* New York: Academic Press, 1971. Pp. 45–61.

————. Experimental psychology of animal learning and now. *American Psychologist,* 1972, **27,** 1055–1062.

London, P. The end of ideology in behavior modification. *American Psychologist,* 1972, **27,** 913–920.

Luce, R. D., Bush, R. R., & Galanter, E. (Eds.) *Handbook of mathematical psychology.* Vol. 1, Vol. 2. New York: Wiley, 1963; Vol. 3. New York: Wiley, 1965.

————, Bush, R. R., & Galanter, E.

(Eds.) *Readings in mathematical psychology.* New York: Wiley, 1963.

Luchins, A. S. Implications of Gestalt psychology for AV learning. *AV Communication Review*, 1961, **9**, 7–31.

Lynch, J. M. The applicability of psychological research to education. *Journal of Educational Psychology*, 1945, **43**, 289–296.

Maccoby, E. E., & Zellner, M. *Experiments in primary education: Aspects of project follow through.* New York: Harcourt Brace Jovanovich, 1970.

MacCorquodale, K. B. F. Skinner's *verbal behavior:* A retrospective appreciation. In P. B. Dews (Ed.), *Festschrift for B. F. Skinner.* New York: Appleton-Century-Crofts, 1970*a*. Pp. 340–350.

————. On Chomsky's review of Skinner's *verbal behavior. Journal of the Experimental Analysis of Behavior*, 1970*b*, **13**, 83–99.

————, & Meehl, P. E. On a distinction between hypothetical constructs and intervening variables. *Psychological Review*, 1948, **55**, 95–107.

Macdonald, J. B. Myths about instruction: The myth of learning theory. *Educational Leadership*, 1965, **22**, 573.

Mackie, R. R., & Christensen, P. R. *Translation and application of psychological research.* Goleta, Calif.: Human Factors Research, Inc., 1967.

MacRae, A. W. Channel capacity in absolute judgment tasks: An artifact of information bias? *Psychological Bulletin*, 1970, **73**, 112–121.

Markle, S. M. The Harvard teaching machine project: The first hundred days. Paper presented at the National Society for Programmed Instruction Convention, San Antonio, Texas, April 1964.

Marx, M. H. (Ed.) *Theories in contemporary psychology.* New York: Macmillan, 1963.

Maslow, A. H. *Toward a psychology of being.* Princeton, New Jersey: D. Van Nostrand, 1962.

————. Some educational implications of the humanistic psychologies. *Harvard Educational Review*, 1968, **38**(4), 685–696.

Mathis, C. Implications of modern learning theory for the secondary school. *High School Journal*, 1964–1965, **48**, 411–418.

McClelland, D. C. *Studies in motivation.* New York: Appleton-Century-Crofts, 1955.

McDonald, F. J. The influence of learning theories on education (1900–1950). In E. R. Hilgard (Ed.), Theories of learning and instruction. *63rd NSSE yearbook.* Chicago: University of Chicago Press, 1964. Pp. 1–26.

McMurrin, S. M. To improve learning. A report to the President and the Congress of the United States by the Commission on Instructional Technology. Washington: U.S. Govt. Printing Office, 1970.

Medley, D. M., & Mitzel, H. E. Measuring classroom behavior by systematic observation. In N. L. Gage (Ed.), *Handbook of research on teaching.* Chicago: Rand-McNally, 1963.

Meierhenry, W. C. (Ed.) Learning theory and AV learning. *AV Communication Review*, 1961, **9**, 2–88.

————. Implications of learning theory for instructional technology. *Phi Delta Kappan*, 1964–1965, **46**, 435–438.

Melton, A. W. The science of learning and the technology of educational methods. *Harvard Educational Review*, 1959, **29**, 96–106.

————. *Categories of human learning.* New York: Academic Press, 1964.

Millenson, J. R. *Principles of behavioral analysis.* New York: Macmillan, 1967.

Miller, G. A. The magical number seven, plus or minus two. *Psychological Review*, 1956, **63**, 81–97.

————, & Frick, S. C. Statistical behavioristics and sequences of responses. *Psychological Review*, 1949, **56**, 311–324.

————, Galenter, E., & Pribram, K. H. *Plans and the structure of behavior.* New York: Holt, Rinehart, & Winston, 1960.

Miller, J. G. Toward a general theory for the behavioral sciences. *American Psychologist*, 1955, **10**, 513–531.

————. Living systems: Basic concepts. Structure and process. Cross level hypothesis. *Behavioral Science*, 1965, **10**, 193–237, 337–379, 380–411.

Miller, R. B. *A method for man-machine task analysis.* Wright Air Development Center, Ohio: U.S. Government, 1953.

Milsum, J. H. *Biological control systems analysis.* New York: McGraw-Hill, 1966.

Mitchell, J. V. Education's challenge to psychology: The prediction of behavior from person-environment interactions. *Review of Educational Research*, 1969, **39**(5), 695–721.

Moray, N. Where is capacity limited? A survey and a model. *Acta Psychologia*, 1967, **27**, 84–92.

Mowrer, O. H. Apparatus for the study and treatment of enuresis. *American Journal of Psychology*, 1938a, **51**, 163–166.

————. Enuresis: A method for its study and treatment. *American Journal of Orthopsychiatry*, 1938b, **8**, 436–459.

————. Review of B. F. Skinner, *Beyond freedom and dignity. Contemporary Psychology*, 1972, **17**, 469–472.

National Science Foundation. Federal funds for research, development, and other scientific activities. Washington, D. C.: National Science Foundation, 1965.

Neimark, E. D., & Estes, W. K. *Stimulus sampling theory.* Cambridge, Mass.: Holden-Day, 1967.

Neisser, U. The imitation of man by machine. *Science*, 1963, **139**, 193–197.

————. *Cognitive psychology.* New York: Appleton-Century-Crofts, 1967.

Neuringer, C., & Michael, J. L. *Behavior modification in clinical psychology.* New York: Appleton-Century-Crofts, 1970.

Newell, A., Shaw, J. C., & Simon, H. A. Elements of a theory of human problem solving. *Psychological Review*, 1958, **65**, 151–166.

————, & Simon, H. A. The simulation of human thought. In W. Dennis (Ed.), *Current trends in psychological theory.* Pittsburgh: University of Pittsburgh Press, 1961. Pp. 152–179.

————, & Simon, H. A. *Human problem solving.* New York: Prentice-Hall, 1972.

Norman, D. A. *Memory and attention: An introduction to human information processing.* New York: Wiley, 1969.

————. (Ed.) *Models of human memory.* New York: Academic Press, 1970.

Ojemann, R. H., & Pritchett, K. (Ed.) *Giving emphasis to guided learning.* Cleveland: Education Research Council of Greater Cleveland, 1966.

O'Leary, K. D., & Drabman, R. Token reinforcement programs in the classroom: A review. *Psychological Bulletin*, 1971, **75**, 379–398.

Parsons, T. *The social system.* Glencoe, Ill.: Free Press, 1950.

————, & Shils, E. *Toward a general theory of action.* Cambridge, Mass.: Harvard University Press, 1952.

Paul, G. L., & Berstein, D. A. *Anxiety and clinical problems: Systematic desensitization and related techniques.* Morristown, New Jersey: General Learning Press, 1973.

Pavlov, I. P. *Conditioned reflexes.* London: Oxford University Press, 1927.

————. *Lectures on conditioned reflexes.* New York: International, 1928.

————. *Conditioned reflexes and psychiatry.* New York: International, 1941.

Pfaffman, C. The behavioral science model. *American Psychologist*, 1970, **25**, 437–441.

Pierce, J. R. *Symbols, signals and noise.* New York: Harper & Row, 1961.

Pitts, C. E. *Introduction to educational psychology: An operant conditioning approach.* New York: Crowell, 1971.

Popper, K. R. *The poverty of historicism.* Boston: The Beacon Press, 1957.

Postman, L. Short-term memory and incidental learning. In A. W. Melton (Ed.), *Categories of human learning.* New York: Academic Press, 1964. Pp. 146-201.

Premack, D. Toward empirical laws. I. Positive reinforcement. *Psychological Review*, 1959, **66**, 219-233.

Prokasy, W. F. (Ed.) *Classical conditioning: A symposium.* New York: Appleton-Century-Crofts, 1965.

Quastler, H. (Ed.) *Information theory in psychology.* Glencoe, Ill.: The Free Press, 1955.

Rachlin, H. *Introduction to modern behaviorism.* San Francisco: W. H. Freeman and Co., 1970.

Razran, G. Russian physiologist's psychology and American experimental psychology. *Psychological Bulletin,* 1965, **63**, 42-64.

————. *Mind in evolution: An east-west synthesis of learned behavior and cognition.* Boston: Houghton-Mifflin, 1971.

Reavis, C. A., & Whittacre, F. R. Professional education of teachers: A spiral approach. *Peabody Journal of Education,* 1969, **46**, 259-264.

Reese, E. P. *The analysis of human operant behavior.* Dubuque, Iowa: Wm. C. Brown Co., 1966.

Reitman, W. R. *Cognition and thought: An information-processing approach.* New York: Wiley, 1965.

Restle, F. The relevance of mathematical models for education. In E. R. Hilgard (Ed.), Theories of learning and instruction. *63rd yearbook of the NSSE,* Part 1. Chicago: University of Chicago Press, 1964. Pp. 111-132.

Reynolds, G. S. *A primer of operant conditioning.* Glenview, Ill.: Scott, Foresman & Co., 1968.

Rogers, C. R. *Counseling and psychotherapy.* Boston: Houghton-Mifflin, 1942.

————. *Client-centered therapy.* Boston: Houghton-Mifflin, 1951.

————. The necessary and sufficient conditions of therapeutic personality change. *Journal of Consulting Psychology*, 1957, **21**, 95-103.

————. *On becoming a person.* Boston: Houghton-Mifflin, 1961.

————. Client-centered therapy. In S. Arieti (Ed.), *American handbook of psychiatry.* New York: Basic Books, 1966. Pp. 183-200.

————. The facilitation of significant learning. In L. Siegel (Ed.), *Instruction: Some contemporary viewpoints.* San Francisco: Chandler, 1967. Pp. 37-54.

————. *Freedom to learn.* Columbus, Ohio: Charles E. Merrill, 1969.

————. Can schools grow persons. *Educational Leadership*, 1971, **29**, 215-217.

————. Forget you are a teacher. *Instructor*, 1971, **81**, 65-66.

————. Comment on Brown and Tedeschi's article. *Journal of Humanistic Psychology*, 1972, **12**, 16-21.

————, & Skinner, B. F. Some issues concerning the control of human behavior. *Science*, 1956, **124**, 1057-1065.

Rowland, G. T., & McGuire, J. C. *The mind of man: Some views and a theory of cognitive development.* New York: Prentice-Hall, 1971.

Royce, J. R. Toward the advancement of theoretical psychology. *Psychological Reports*, 1957, **3**, 401-410

Saettler, P. Design and selection factors. *Review of Educational Research*, 1968*a*, **38**, 115-128.

————. *A history of instructional technology.* New York: McGraw-Hill, 1968*b*.

Salter, A. *Conditioned reflex therapy.* New York: Capricorn Books, 1949 (1st ed.), 1961 (2d ed.).

Saltz, E. *The cognitive bases of human learning.* Homewood, Ill.: Dorsey Press, 1971.

Sanford, N. Whatever happened to action research? *Journal of Social Issues*, 1970, **26**(4), 3-23.

Scheerer, M. Cognitive theory. In G. Lindzey (Ed.), *Handbook of social psychology*, 1954. Pp. 91-137.

Schmidtlein, F. A. The programs of the fifteen regional educational laboratories. *Journal of Research and Development in Education*, 1970, **3**, 18-38.

Schoenfeld, W. N. (Ed.) *The theory of reinforcement schedules.* New York: Appleton-Century-Crofts, 1970.

Schroeder, H. H. A real problem for educational psychology. *Journal of Educational Psychology*, 1913, **4**, 465-470.

Schutz, R. E. The nature of educational development. *Journal of Research and Development in Education*, 1970, **3**, 39-64.

Scriven, M. Views of human nature. In T. Wann (Ed.), *Behaviorism and phenomenology: Contrasting bases for modern psychology.* Chicago: University of Chicago Press, 1964.

Seagoe, M. V. *The learning process and school practice.* Scranton, Pa.: Chandler, 1970.

Segal, E. M., & Lachman, R. Complex behavior or higher mental process: Is there a paradigm shift? *American Psychologist*, 1972, **27**, 46-55.

Shane, H. G. Looking to the future: Reassessment of educational issues of the 1970s. *Phi Delta Kappan*, **54**, 326-337.

Shannon, C. E. A mathematical theory of communication. *Bell System Technical Journal*, 1948, **27**, 379-423, 623-656. (Republished: Shannon, C. E., & Weaver, W. *The mathematical theory of communication.* Urbana: University of Illinois Press, 1949.)

Shepard, R. N. Computers and thought. *Behavioral Science*, 1964, **9**, 57-65.

Shulamn, L. S., & Keislar, E. R. (Eds.) *Learning by discovery: A critical appraisal.* Chicago: Rand-McNally, 1966.

Siegel, L. (ed.) *Instruction: Some contemporary viewpoints.* San Francisco: Chandler, 1967.

Simon, A., & Boyer, E. G. *Mirrors for behavior.* Philadelphia: Research for Better Schools, 1969.

Simon, H. A. The future of information processing technology. *Management Science*, 1968, **14**, 619-624.

————. *The sciences of the artificial.* Cambridge, Mass.: MIT Press, 1969.

————, & Newell, A. Human problem solving: The state of the theory in 1970. *American Psychologist*, 1971, **26**, 145-159.

Singer, B. F. Toward a psychology of science. *American Psychologist*, 1971, **26**, 1010-1015.

Sizer, T. Three major frustrations: Ruminations of a retiring dean. *Phi Delta Kappan*, 1972, **53**, 632-635.

Skinner, B. F. Two types of conditioned reflex: A reply to Konorski and Miller. *Journal of General Psychology*, 1937, **16**, 272-279.

————. *Walden two.* New York: Macmillan, 1948.

————. Are theories of learning necessary. *Psychological Review*, 1950, **57**, 193-216.

————. *Science and human behavior.* New York: Macmillan, 1953. Pp. 98-106.

————. The science of learning and the art of teaching. *Harvard Educational Review*, 1954, **24**, 86-97.

————. *Verbal behavior.* New York: Appleton-Century-Crofts, 1957.

————. A case history in scientific method. In S. Koch (Ed.), *Psychology: A study of a science.* Vol. 2. New York: McGraw-Hill, 1959. Pp. 359-379.

————. Teaching machines. *Scientific American*, 1961, **205**(5), 90-102.

————. Why we need teaching machines. *Harvard Educational Review*, 1961, **31**, 377-398.

————. Operant behavior. *American Psychologist*, 1963, **18**, 503-515.

————. An operant analysis of problem solving. In B. Kleinmuntz (Ed.), *Problem solving: Research, method and theory.* New York: Wiley, 1965. Pp. 225-257.

————. *The behavior of organisms: An experimental analysis.* New York: Appleton-Century-Crofts, 1966 (7th printing).

————. *The technology of teaching.* New York: Appleton-Century-Crofts, 1968

————. *Contingencies of reinforcement: A theoretical analysis.* New York: Appleton-Century-Crofts, 1969.

————. *B. F. Skinner . . . An autobiography.* In *Festschrift for B. F. Skinner.* New York: Appleton-Century-Crofts, 1970.

————. *Beyond freedom and dignity.* New York: Alfred A. Knopf, 1971.

Smallwood, R. D. The analysis of economic teaching strategies for a simple learning model. *Journal of Mathematical Psychology,* 1971, **8**, 285–301.

Smith, B. O. Critical thinking. In Recent research developments and their implications for teacher education. *13th yearbook, American association of college teachers of education.* Washington, D. C.: The Association, 1960. Pp. 84–96.

Smith, K. U. *Cybernetic principles of learning and educational design.* New York: Holt, Rinehart, & Winston, 1966.

Smith, S., & Guthrie, E. R. *General psychology in terms of behavior.* New York: Appleton-Century-Crofts, 1921.

Snelbecker, G. E. Behavior modification in education and in the clinic: Facets, origins and probable future. *Clinical Pediatrics,* 1970, **9**, 617–621.

Snyder, H. I. *Contemporary educational psychology: Some models applied to the school setting.* New York: Wiley, 1968.

Soar, R., & Soar, R. M. An empirical analysis of selected follow through programs: An example of a process approach to evaluation. In Early childhood education, *71st NSSE Yearbook,* 1972, Part 2, Chapter 11.

Spence, K. W. The nature of discrimination learning in animals. *Psychological Review,* 1936, **43**, 427–449.

————. The nature of theory construction in contemporary psychology. *Psychological Review,* 1944, **51**, 47–68.

————. Cognitive versus stimulus-response theories of learning. *Psychological Review,* 1950, **57**, 159–172.

————. *Behavior theory and conditioning.* New Haven, Connecticut: Yale University Press, 1956.

————. The relation of learning theory to the technology of education. *Harvard Educational Review,* 1959, **29**, 84–95.

————. *Behavior theory and learning.* Englewood Cliffs, New Jersey: Prentice-Hall, 1960.

————, & Spence, J. T. (Eds.) *The psychology of learning and motivation.* Vol. 1. New York: Academic Press, 1967.

Starch, D. F. *Educational psychology.* New York: Macmillan, 1919.

Strupp, H. H., & Bergin, A. E. (Eds.) Some empirical and conceptual bases for coordinated research in psychotherapy: A critical review of issues, trends, and evidence. *International Journal of Psychiatry,* 1969, **7**, 18–90, 116–168.

Suppes, P., & Jerman, M. Computer assisted instruction at Stanford. *Educational Television International,* 1969, **3**(3), 176–179

————, & Jerman, M. Computer assisted instruction. *National Association of Secondary School Principals Bulletin,* 1970, **54**, 27–40.

————, & Moringstar, M. Computer assisted instruction. *Science,* 1969, **166**, 343–350.

————, & Searle, B. The computer teaches arithmetic. *Scholastic Review,* 1971, **79**, 213–225.

Symonds, P. M. What education has to learn from psychology. II Reward, III Punishment. *Teachers College Record,* 1955–1956, **57**, 15–25, 449–462.

A symposium: Can the laws of learning be applied in the classroom? *Harvard Educational Review,* 1959, **29**, 83–117.

Terrace, H. S. Stimulus control. In W. K. Honig (Ed.), *Operant behavior: Areas of research and application.* New York: Appleton-Century-Crofts, 1966.

————. Review of B. F. Skinner, *Contingencies of reinforcement: A theoretical analysis. Contemporary Psychology,* 1970, **15**, 531–535.

Thorndike, E. L. Animal intelligence: An experimental study of the associative processes in animals. *Psychological Review, Monograph Supplement*, 1898, **2**(8).

————. Darwin's contribution to psychology. *University of California Chronicle*, 1909, **12**, 65–80.

————. The contributions of psychology to education. *Journal of Educational Psychology*, 1910, **1**, 5–12.

————. *Education: A first book.* New York: Macmillan, 1912.

————. *Educational psychology.* Vol. 1. *The original nature of man.* New York: Teachers College, Columbia University, 1913*a*.

————. *Educational psychology.* Vol. 2. *The psychology of learning.* New York: Teachers College, Columbia University, 1913*b*.

————. Educational diagnosis. *Science*, 1913, **37**(943), 133–142.

————. *Educational psychology.* Vol. 3. *Mental work and fatigue and individual differences and their causes.* New York: Teachers College, Columbia University, 1914.

————. *Human learning.* New York: The Century Co., 1931.

————. *Selected writings from a connectionist's psychology.* New York: Appleton-Century-Crofts, 1949.

————. *Educational psychology.* New York: Arno Press, 1969.

Thorne, F. C. *Integrative psychology.* Brandon, Vermont: Clinical Psychology Publishing Co., Inc., 1967.

Thurston, L. L. The learning curve equation. *Psychological Monographs*, 1919, **26**, No. 3.

Titchener, E. B. *Experimental psychology.* Vol. 1. New York: Macmillan, 1901.

Tolman, E. C. Purposive behavior in animals and men. New York: Appleton-Century-Crofts, 1932. (Republished: University of California Press, 1949.)

Torrance, E. P. History of the concept "guided learning" and its application in teaching for creative development. In

R. R. Ojemann (Ed.), *Giving emphasis to guided learning.* Cleveland: Educational Research Council of Greater Cleveland, 1966.

Travers, R. M. W. A study of the relationship of psychological research to educational practice. In R. Glaser (Ed.), *Training research and education.* Pittsburgh: University of Pittsburgh Press, 1962. Pp. 525–558.

————. Towards taking the fun out of building a theory of instruction. *Teachers College Record*, 1966, **68**, 49–59.

————. Some further reflections on the nature of a theory of instruction. In I. Westbury & A. A. Bellack (Eds.), *Research into classroom processes: Recent developments and next steps.* New York: Teachers College, Columbia University, 1971.

Tyler, F. B. Shaping of the science. *American Psychologist*, 1970, **25**, 219–226.

Tyler, R. W. *Constructing achievement tests.* Columbus, Ohio: Ohio State University, 1934.

Ullmann, L. P., & Krasner, L. *Case studies in behavior modification.* New York: Holt, Rinehart, & Winston, 1965.

Underwood, B. J. Verbal learning in the educational process. *Harvard Educational Review*, 1959, **29**, 107–117.

Vale, J. R., & Vale, C. A. Individual differences and general laws in psychology: A reconciliation. *American Psychologist*, 1969, **24**, 1093–1108.

Wann, T. W. *Behaviorism and phenomenology: Contrasting bases for modern psychology.* Chicago: University of Chicago Press, 1964.

Weber, E. *Early childhood education: Perspectives on change.* Belmont, Calif.: Wadsworth, 1970.

Weiner, H. Controlling human fixed-interval performance. *Journal of the Experimental Analysis of Behavior*, 1969, **12**, 349–373.

Weinstein, G. The trumpet: A guide to humanistic psychological curriculum.

Theory into Practice, 1971, **10**, 196-203.

———, & Fantini, M. *Toward humanistic education: A curriculum of affect.* New York: Praeger Press, 1970.

Wenrich, W. W. *A primer of behavior modification.* Belmont, Calif.: Brooks-Cole Publishing Co., 1970.

Wolman, B. B. (Ed.) *Historical roots of contemporary psychology.* New York: Harper & Row, 1968.

Wolpe, J. *Psychotherapy by reciprocal inhibition.* Stanford, Calif.: Stanford University Press, 1958.

———. *The practice of behavior therapy.* Elmsford, New York: Pergamon, 1969*a*.

Wolpe, J. Psychotherapeutic efficacy and objective research. In H. H. Strupp & A. E. Bergin (Eds.), Critical evaluation of some empirical and conceptual bases for coordinated research in psychotherapy. *International Journal of Psychiatry*, 1969*b*, **7**, 157-159.

Womer, F. B. *What is national assessment?* Ann Arbor: National Assessment of Educational Progress, 1970.

Wrigley, C. Theory construction or fact-finding in a computer age? *Behavioral Science*, 1960, **5**, 183-186.

Yoakam, G. A., & Simpson, R. G. *An introduction to teaching and learning.* New York: Macmillan, 1934.

Name Index

Subject Index